B.C.

THE CAMBRIDGE BIBLE
FOR SCHOOLS AND COLLEGES

General Editor for the Old Testament:—

A. F. KIRKPATRICK, D.D.

DEAN OF ELY

THE BOOK OF THE PROPHET

EZEKIEL

CAMBRIDGE UNIVERSITY PRESS
C. F. CLAY, Manager
London: FETTER LANE, E.C.
Edinburgh: 100, PRINCES STREET

New York: G. P. PUTNAM'S SONS
Bombay, Calcutta and Madras: MACMILLAN AND CO., Ltd.
Toronto: J. M. DENT AND SONS, Ltd.
Tokyo: THE MARUZEN-KABUSHIKI-KAISHA

THE BOOK OF THE PROPHET

EZEKIEL

In the Revised Version

With Notes and Introduction

by the late

A. B. DAVIDSON, D.D., LL.D.

revised by the late

A. W. STREANE, D.D.

Fellow of Corpus Christi College, Cambridge

Cambridge :
at the University Press

1916

First Edition 1892
Reprinted 1893, 1896, 1900, 1906
Revised Edition 1916

PREFACE

BY THE

GENERAL EDITOR FOR THE OLD TESTAMENT

THE present General Editor for the Old Testament in the Cambridge Bible for Schools and Colleges desires to say that, in accordance with the policy of his predecessor the Bishop of Worcester, he does not hold himself responsible for the particular interpretations adopted or for the opinions expressed by the editors of the several Books, nor has he endeavoured to bring them into agreement with one another. It is inevitable that there should be differences of opinion in regard to many questions of criticism and interpretation, and it seems best that these differences should find free expression in different volumes. He has endeavoured to secure, as far as possible, that the general scope and character of the series should be observed, and that views which have a reasonable claim to consideration should not be ignored, but he has felt it best that the final responsibility should, in general, rest with the individual contributors.

A. F. KIRKPATRICK.

CAMBRIDGE.

PREFATORY NOTE TO THE REVISED EDITION

IN the present edition of Dr Davidson's *Ezekiel* the R.V. has been employed as the text, and the necessary changes in detail have been introduced in the notes.

A few omissions or abbreviations have been made, but all that is characteristic of Dr Davidson's work has been retained. In certain cases where it has seemed that he gave too little consideration to a different interpretation from that which he adopted, sub-notes in square brackets have been added, calling attention to the claims of another explanation.

During the twenty-three years since the first edition was published in 1892, much study has been devoted to the Book of Ezekiel, and generally to the function of the prophets in the development of O.T. religion. The present editor has accordingly made some additions to the notes, giving what appear to him to be the most important results of this study. These additions are distinguished by square brackets.

A. W. STREANE.

August, 1915.

Dr Streane had completed his work of revision, but had only passed a few sheets for press at the time of his regretted death on September 10, 1915. It is hoped however that the accuracy of the book has not suffered seriously from the loss of his final corrections.

A. F. K.

PREFATORY NOTE TO THE FIRST EDITION

THE Book of Ezekiel is less suited than most others to be the subject of merely popular annotation. The state of the Text is such that frequent references to it as well as to the Versions are unavoidable. It was no part of the purpose of the following Notes to construct a Text; the thing aimed at has been to shew the general meaning of the Book, and, if possible, the connexion of its parts with one another; but the readings of the LXX. have generally been adduced when they presented any important deviation from the Hebrew. In the later chapters the MS. of which the Greek is a translation was in many instances more correct than that of which the present Hebrew is a copy.

Such aids as were available have been used, and obligations are acknowledged to a number of works, besides those named at the end of the Introduction. A number of passages in the Text have baffled the ingenuity of the best scholars, and appear to be incurably confused. Other parts of the book are rendered obscure by allusions not now understood. And altogether the student of the Book must take leave of his task with a certain sense of defeat.

A. B. DAVIDSON.

CONTENTS

ERRATUM

p. 62, l. 24, *for* eight miles *read* about 20 miles

INTRODUCTION

CHAPTER I

THE BOOK OF EZEKIEL

THE Book of Ezekiel is simpler and more perspicuous in its arrangement than any other of the great prophetical books. It was probably committed to writing late in the prophet's life, and, unlike the prophecies of Isaiah, which were given out piecemeal, was issued in its complete form at once. The prophecies are disposed upon the whole in chronological order, though the book may contain much that was never actually spoken, and even the prophecies that were orally delivered may have undergone considerable modification under the pen of the prophet when reproducing them. None of the prophets shews any anxiety to record his discourses in the precise form in which he delivered them. The aim of the prophets in their writings was not literary but practical, as it was in their speeches. It was their purpose to influence the minds of the people when they spoke, and this was equally their purpose when they wrote, and, if in the interval the circumstances of the people had to some extent changed, they did not hesitate to accommodate their former discourses to the new situation.

The Book of Ezekiel is occupied with two great themes: the destruction of the city and nation; and the reconstitution of the people and their eternal peace. The book thus falls into two equal divisions of 24 chapters each:—

First Division, ch. i.—xxiv., Prophecies of the destruction of the city and nation, its certainty and necessity.

Second Division, ch. xxv.—xlviii., Prophecies of the restoration of the people, their regeneration and eternal peace as the people of the Lord.

These prophecies are for the most part symbolical actions, of which the explanation is added; or allegories and riddles, the meaning of which is read to the people. Though a good many actual events are referred to, the book contains little that is historical. It is rather a book of general principles. These principles are all only deductions from the prophet's conception of Jehovah, God of Israel and God over all. In this respect Ezekiel resembles the author of Is. xl—lxvi, though he has neither the breadth of sympathy nor the glow of emotion that distinguish the Evangelist of the Old Testament.

First Division, ch. i.—xxiv. Prophecies of the destruction of the nation.

First section, ch. i.—iii. 21. The prophet's consecration to his calling, and first period of his ministry (July 592 B.C.).

(1) Ch. i. Vision of Jehovah, the God of Israel, who calls and sends him.

(2) Ch. ii. 1—iii. 9. His mission to Israel as a prophet. His inspiration, under the symbol of eating the roll of a book presented to him in the hand of Jehovah.

(3) Ch. iii. 10—21. He goes to the exiles, and when among them receives a clearer view of his mission, which is to be a watchman to warn every individual person, the wicked that he may turn from his evil, and the righteous lest he fall from his righteousness.

The theophany of ch. i. is a vision of Jehovah as He is in Himself (final note to the Chapter). The appointment of the prophet to be a watchman is not a change on his original appointment to be a prophet, it is a more precise definition of it. The prophet of this age is a watchman, a warner of individual men. For the old order has changed, the state is disappearing, and only individuals remain out of which the new and eternal kingdom of the Lord has to be reconstructed (note on iii. 16). On the general meaning of the whole section cf. note on iii. 21.

Second section, ch. iii. 22—vii. 27. Symbolical prophecies of the overthrow of the city and state. (Under foregoing date.)

(1) Ch. iii. 22—27. Change in the prophet's procedure: he is commanded to cease for a time from being a public reprover.

(2) Ch. iv. Symbols of the siege of the city, of the terrible scarcity within it, and of the people's bearing their iniquity in exile.

(3) Ch. v. Further symbols of the fate of the inhabitants: a third shall die of famine; a third fall by the sword around the city; and a third be scattered among the nations, still pursued by the sword.

(4) Ch. vi. Prophecy of destruction on the mountains, the mountain-land of Israel, where idolatries everywhere prevailed.

(5) Ch. vii. Dirge over the downfall of the city and nation.

Third section, ch. viii.—xi. More precise symbolical prophecies of the destruction of the city and people at Jehovah's own hand, because of the idolatrous pollution of His house (Aug. 591 B.C.).

(1) Ch. viii. The multiplied idolatries in the Temple: the image of jealousy in the court; the worshippers in the chambers of imagery; the women wailing for Tammuz; and the sun-worship between the Temple and the altar (cf. final note to the ch.).

(2) Ch. ix. Symbol of the slaughter of the idolatrous people. A messenger from the Lord passes through the city putting a mark on the forehead of all who bewail the evils that prevail, and he is followed by divine executioners who slay all not so sealed.

(3) Ch. x. Symbol of the destruction of the city by fire from God.

(4) Ch. xi. Symbol of the Lord's departure from His house, and abandonment of the city to the fury of her enemies.

Fourth section, ch. xii.—xix. The same theme of the certainty of the destruction of the nation, with proofs of its moral necessity. (Without date, but later than preceding.)

(1) Ch. xii. 1—20. The unbelief of the people is such that new signs must be given them. Symbolical prophecy of the attempted escape of the king, and his capture by the Chaldeans.

(2) Ch. xii. 21—28. The people's unbelief is partly due to their observation of the character of prophecy. But the popular imagination that prophecies of evil fail to come true, or refer to the distant future, shall receive a speedy and terrible refutation.

(3) Ch. xiii., xiv. These delusions of the people are fostered by the false prophets, who prophesy only of prosperity. The prophets who deceive and those who are deceived by them shall perish together.

(4) Ch. xv. But will the Lord destroy the nation of Israel, the vine of His planting?—The nation of Israel among the nations is like the vine branch among the trees. Good for little when whole, what is it good for now when half-burnt in the fire? Only to be flung again into the fire and wholly consumed.

(5) Ch. xvi. Parable of the foundling child who became the faithless wife. Let Israel's history be judged. What has it been but one persistent course of ingratitude and unfaithfulness to Jehovah? Her chastisement cannot be deferred.

(6) Ch. xvii. And must not Zedekiah's perfidy against the king of Babylon, and his breaking the oath of Jehovah be punished? He has brought ruin both on himself and on the kingdom. Yet the Lord will set up a new kingdom on the land of Israel, into which all nations shall be gathered.

(7) Ch. xviii. The principles of this kingdom: the righteous shall live in his righteousness and the sinner die in his sin. The Lord hath no pleasure in the death of him that dieth. None shall perish for the sins of another: neither does any

man lie under a ban from his own past life. Therefore let every man repent that he may live (cf. final note to the ch.).

(8) Ch. xix. Lament over Judah and her royal house.

Fifth section, ch. xx.—xxiv. Concluding prophecies demonstrating the necessity of Israel's destruction. (Ch. xx.—xxiii., Aug. 590 B.C.)

(1) Ch. xx. That which has preserved Israel from destruction at every stage of her history, and that which has given her a history, has been Jehovah's regard for His own name—lest it should be profaned among the nations.

(2) Ch. xxi. But now His threats uttered long ago must take effect. The sword of the Lord is whetted and furbished against Jerusalem.

(3) Ch. xxii. The aggravated sins of all classes of the people: the royal house, the priests, the prophets, and the people of the land.

(4) Ch. xxiii. New exposure of the life-long immoralities of the two adulterous women, Oholah and Oholibah (Samaria and Jerusalem).

After a silence of several years the military movements of Nebuchadrezzar drew from the prophet a new and final oracle against Jerusalem, Jan. 587 B.C., the time when Nebuchadrezzar began to invest the city.

(5) Ch. xxiv. Final symbol of the siege and the dispersion of the people, and of their purification from evil amidst the afflictions of the exile. A rusted caldron is set upon the fire that its contents may be seethed and pulled out indiscriminately (the siege and dispersion), and that its brass may glow and its rust and foulness may be molten and purged away.

Second Division, ch. xxv.—xlviii. Prophecies of the restoration and reconstruction of the nation (xxv.—xxxix); and vision of the final and perfect state of Israel as the people of the Lord (ch. xl. *seq.*).

First section, ch. xxv.—xxxii. Prophecies concerning the nations.

These prophecies occupy the place in the prophet's book

proper to their contents. They are an introduction to the positive prophecies of the restoration of Israel. The judgements on the nations prepare the way for the restitution of the people. The purpose and effect of them is to make Jehovah, God of Israel, and God over all, known to the nations, so that they shall no more vex or seduce His people, as they have done in the past (ch. xxviii. 23, 26); and no more lift themselves up in pride of heart against the one living God (cf. introductory note to ch. xxv.). The prophet does not pursue the destiny of the nations further, nor state how much their recognition of Jehovah implies. (But cf. final notes, ch. xvi.)

(1) Ch. xxv. Judgement on the smaller nations around Israel—Ammon, Moab, Edom, and the Philistines—and revelation to them of Jehovah.

(2) Ch. xxvi.—xxviii. 19. Judgement on Tyre for her pride of heart, and on the prince of Tyre, who said, " I am God!"

(3) Ch. xxviii. 20—26. Judgement on Zidon that it may no more be a pricking brier to the house of Israel.

(4) Ch. xxix.—xxxii. Judgements on Egypt. It shall be humbled and reduced to be a base kingdom, that it may no more be a delusive stay to the house of Israel, nor seduce them from trust in Jehovah alone.

Second section, ch. xxxiii.—xxxix. Positive prophecies of the restoration of the people, and reconstitution of the kingdom of the Lord.

(1) Ch. xxxiii. The place of the prophet in preparing for the kingdom. He is a watchman, warning every individual soul that by repentance and righteousness it may live. The conditions of entering the new kingdom and of life are altogether moral, and each man shall enter it for himself (cf. final note to the ch.).

(2) Ch. xxxiv. The Ruler. The former evil shepherds, who fed themselves and not the flock, shall be removed; Jehovah Himself will take in hand the feeding of His flock, and will set up one shepherd over them, even His servant David, to feed them for ever.

(3) Ch. xxxv., xxxvi. The Land. The land of the Lord, rescued from the grasp of Edom and the nations who have usurped it, shall be given again to Israel for ever; it shall be luxuriant in fertility and teem with people.—The principle that moves the Lord to do these things for Israel is regard to His holy name, even that He may reveal Himself, as He truly is, to mankind. His forgiveness and regeneration of the people, who shall henceforth be led by His Spirit (xxxvi. 16—38, cf. final note).

(4) Ch. xxxvii. The People. Thus the nation, now dead, shall be reawakened into life and restored. In the restitution Ephraim and Judah shall no more be divided, but shall have one king, even David, over them for ever.

Thus the restitution of the people is complete, and their holiness as the people of the Lord perfect. Jehovah sanctifies them by dwelling among them; the people know that He is their God, and the nations know that He sanctifies them (xxxvii. 28). So far that which is the purpose of all history has been attained: Jehovah has been revealed both to His people and to the nations. The nations, however, who have learned to know Jehovah, whether from His judgements lighting on themselves (xxv.—xxxii.), or from their observation of the principles on which He rules His people, are the nations who have long been on the stage of history and played their parts beside Israel. There are far-off peoples lying in the ends of the earth who have not heard Jehovah's fame nor seen His glory. One great act in the drama of history has still to be performed. He who is God alone is known to the world as the God of Israel, and it is only through Israel that He can reveal Himself to all. These distant peoples shall come up from the ends of the earth, and, like other nations, also touch on Israel, and then shall the glory of the Lord be revealed and all flesh shall see it together. History as the prophet conceives it, whether of Israel or of the nations, is Jehovah's revelation of Himself to mankind; every movement of it carries this burden, "Ye shall know that I am the LORD." The wave of history pauses on the shore when Jehovah's glory rises on the uttermost ends of the earth.

(5) Ch. xxxviii., xxxix. Invasion of Israel in the latter day by Gog and all the nations lying in the far-off corners of the earth. The Lord's defence of His people, now that they are holy and true, reveals to the nations not only His power but His nature, and the principles on which He rules His people and the world. He is known to the ends of the earth.

Third section, ch. xl.—xlviii. A vision of the final glory and peace of the redeemed people of the Lord[1].

Preceding prophecies described the redemption and restoration of the people (xxxiii.—xxxvii.); the present section gives a picture of the condition of the people thus for ever redeemed. The background of the picture is the whole preceding part of the book. The last words of ch. i.—xxxix. are, "Neither will I any more hide my face from them: for I have poured out my spirit on the house of Israel, saith the Lord GOD." The people are all righteous, led by the Spirit of the Lord, and knowing that Jehovah is their God. The passage does not describe how salvation is to be attained, for the salvation is realized and enjoyed; it describes the state and life of the people now that their redemption is come. The fact that the subject of the passage is the *final* blessedness of the people accounts for the supernatural elements in the picture. But both the natural and the supernatural features of the people's condition are to be understood literally. The Temple, the services, and the like are meant in a real sense, and no less literally meant is the supernatural presence of Jehovah in His house, the transfiguration of nature, the turning of the desert into a garden, and the sweetening of the waters of the Dead Sea (cf. introductory note to ch. xl.).

(1) ch. xl. 1—xliii. 27. Account of the Temple buildings. (*a*) ch. xl. 1—27, description of the outer gateway and outer court. (*b*) ch. xl. 28—47, the inner gateway and inner court.

---

[1] [About twelve years have elapsed.]

(c) ch. xl. 48—xli. 26, the house itself with its annexed build-ings. (d) ch. xlii., other buildings in the inner court, and dimensions of the whole. (e) ch. xliii. 1—12, entry of Jehovah into His house. (f) ch. xliii. 13—27, the altar of burnt-offering, and the rites consecrating it.

(2) ch. xliv.—xlvi. Ordinances regarding the Temple. (a) ch. xliv., those who shall minister in the house, priests and Levites. (b) ch. xlv. 1—17, revenues of priests, Levites, and prince; the duties devolving on the prince in upholding the ritual. (c) ch. xlv. 18—xlvi. 24, the special and daily services in the Temple; the special offerings of the prince.

(3) ch. xlvii., xlviii. The boundaries of the holy land, and new disposition of the tribes within it. (a) ch. xlvii., the life-giving stream issuing from the Temple; the boundaries of the holy land. (b) ch. xlviii., disposition of the tribes in the land; dimensions and gates of the holy city.

CHAPTER II

EZEKIEL'S HISTORY AND PROPHETIC WORK

EZEKIEL was the son of Buzi, of whom nothing further is known. This name has some resemblance to the word "to despise," and a Rabbinical fancy interprets it of Jeremiah, "the despised," making Ezekiel the lineal descendant of this prophet, as he is his child in thought and faith. Ezekiel is styled the priest, and in all probability he was of the family of Zadok. The priests had already in this age attained to great influence; they were the aristocracy, standing next to the royal family (xxii. 25, 26). It is not certain whether Ezekiel had actually been engaged in priestly duties before his captivity, though it is not unlikely, both from the name priest applied to him and from the minute acquaintance which he shews with the Temple, its dimensions and furniture, and with the sacerdotal rites. The passage iv. 14 is not certain evidence, as the prohibition to eat carrion was binding on all the people (Exod. xxii. 31, though some consider this verse a later insertion[1]). The age at which priests undertook their duties is not clearly stated in the Law. Ezekiel began to prophesy five years after the captivity of Jehoiachin (597 B.C.), and he states that this was in the thirtieth year. If this statement referred to his age he would have been grown up to manhood some years before his exile, but the words are obscure (notes on i. 1—3). It is doubtful if the statement of Josephus (*Ant.* x. 6, 3) that he was carried captive "when a youth" has any ground beyond the historian's own fancy. The evidence points in a different direction. In several passages the prophet's "house" is referred to (iii. 24, xii. 3 *seq.*); the "elders" occasionally assemble there (viii. 1, xiv. 1, xx. 1), and according to xxiv. 18 he was married. Reuss is hardly right in regarding his wife and her death as fictions; the language used implies that she was a real person and that her death occurred as stated, though, as usual, the prophet employed the incident for didactic purposes, and some of the details may be creations of his idealism; for it is characteristic of him that real events float before his eye in a moral atmosphere, which magnifies them and gives them an outline which is ideal only. The uncompromising attitude taken up by him towards his fellow captives is a thing hardly to be expected from a mere youth (Jer. i. 6); and even in the earliest part of his book his views appear fully formed, and his convictions regarding the impending fate of his country unalterably fixed. The weight due to the last fact, however, may not be so great, because the book was written at an advanced period of life, and even the earlier parts of it may be coloured with reflections of a later time.

[1 Not so Driver in his Commentary in this series.]

Influences affecting his youth.

The period at which the prophet's youth was passed was rich in influences that must have powerfully affected him. Though too young to take part in the reform of Josiah (621), or perhaps to remember it, he grew up in the midst of the changes which it had introduced, and probably learned to estimate previous history from the point of view which it gave him. The tragic events which followed one another closely at this epoch, such as the death of Josiah (608), and the exile of Jehoahaz to Egypt and of Jehoiachin to Babylon, made a lasting impression on his mind. The last event formed the chief landmark of his life, and that not solely because his own history was so closely connected with it; how deeply the fate of the two young princes touched him, and how well he could sympathise with the country's sorrow over it, a sorrow recorded also by Jeremiah (xxii. 10), is seen in his Elegy on the princes of Israel (ch. xix.). He has a fondness for historical study, and no history is to him without a moral; and silently the events of this time were writing principles upon his mind to which in after years he was to give forcible expression.

It was not, however, merely the silent teaching of events from which Ezekiel learned. He had a master interpreting events to him to whose influence every page of his prophecies bears witness. Jeremiah, indeed, may not have been Ezekiel's only master; there were other prophets of the time like-minded with him, such as that Uriah whom Jehoiakim dragged from his hiding-place in Egypt and slew with the sword (Jer. xxvi. 20 *seq.*), and perhaps others of whose names no record has been kept, for it is almost an accident, and only because his fate cast light on the history of Jeremiah in a moment of peril, that the name of Uriah has been preserved. There were also priests who cherished the same aspirations as these prophets, and pursued in their own province the same ends. It is not without significance that Jeremiah no less than Ezekiel was of a priestly family, and that too a rural one, for it was not .

in the capital alone that true religion had its representatives—
like Micah Uriah was a prophet of the country, being of
Kiriath-jearim (Jer. xxvi. 20). And among Ezekiel's predecessors
in the priesthood and also among his contemporaries there
were some who, if they had spoken to the world, would have
spoken in the same manner as he did, for the favourable
judgement which he passes on the Zadokite priests (xliv. 15)
is not altogether due to mere caste prejudice.

Still, the teaching and life of Jeremiah were probably the most
powerful influence under which the young priest grew up. It
would, no doubt, be a mistake to ascribe every idea in Ezekiel
which coincides with Jeremiah's teaching to the influence of that
prophet. There is a common circle of thoughts and feelings
which even the greatest minds share with those of their own
age. Striking out some new conceptions, and opening up some
lines of advancement which mark an epoch, the chief elements
of their faith and life are common to them with others of their
day and have been inherited from the past. The surprise with
which we read Jeremiah might be lessened if the means of
comparing him with others were not so narrow as the paucity
of writers in the century before the exile causes it to be. At
any rate his influence upon the language and thought of Ezekiel can readily be observed. It could hardly have been otherwise. For thirty years before Ezekiel's captivity Jeremiah had
been a prophet, speaking in the courts and chambers of the
Temple and in the streets of Jerusalem, and having such a history as made him the most prominent figure of the day. Ezekiel was familiar with his history and had listened to his words
from his infancy. Many of his prophecies had probably been
in circulation in writing for a number of years previous to the
captivity of Jehoiachin which Ezekiel shared, and the constant
intercourse between Jerusalem and the exiles kept the prophet
of the Chebar well informed regarding the course of events at
home, and the views which prominent persons there took of
them (xi. 2 *seq.*, xvii. &c.).

The prophet in exile. The character of his mission.

In the year 597 B.C. Nebuchadrezzar took Jerusalem and carried into captivity the young king Jehoiachin, the flower of the population including many priests, Ezekiel among them, as well as a multitude of other citizens, particularly craftsmen. Ezekiel with a community of other exiles was settled at Tel-Abib by the river Chebar—not to be identified with the Chabor which falls into the Euphrates near Carchemish, but some stream or canal in Babylonia proper [see note on i. 1]; and five years later he was called to occupy among them the place of a "watchman" (592 B.C.). How large the community was does not appear, nor what kind of place Tel-Abib was, for the references of the prophet to walls (xii. 7, xxxiii. 30) hardly justify the conclusion that it was a walled town. The community appears to have been left, as was usually the case, to regulate its internal affairs and govern itself according to its own mind. The prophet repeatedly mentions the "elders," and though he calls them elders of Judah (viii. 1) or Israel (xiv. 1, xx. 1), he identifies them with the captivity (xi. 25), of which they must have been the heads and representatives. The lot of the exiles might in some cases be hard, but there is no evidence that they were harshly treated by their conquerors or suffered want. When the prophet speaks of famine he refers to Canaan (xxxvi. 29, 30, xxxiv. 27, 28), and the phrase "served themselves of them" [i.e. made servants of them] (xxxiv. 27) has more a national than an individual reference, like such expressions as "prison houses" in the second part of Isaiah (xlii. 22). The exiles possessed houses (iii. 24, xxxiii. 30), and there is no allusion to persecution from their heathen neighbours. Cf. Jer. xxix. 5 *seq.*

The picture, if it can be called so, which the prophet gives of the life of the exiles and their circumstances is singularly colourless. His interests were exclusively religious, and any insight which he affords us is into the religious condition of his fellow captives, from whose mouth he occasionally quotes an expression very suggestive as to their state of mind (xii. 22, 27, xviii. 2, 25, 29, xx. 49, xxxiii. 10, 30, xxxvii. 11). His own mind was occupied with the largest conceptions, and the exiles were to his eye representatives of a larger subject. When bidden go to "them of the captivity" (iii. 11) he felt sent to the "children (house) of Israel" (ii. 3, iii. 4), and while addressing his fellow exiles he fancies before him the people in Canaan or the nation scattered abroad throughout the world. This identification of the exiles with the people as a whole, and this occupation of the prophet's mind with great national interests, make it difficult to know how far in his apparent addresses to the exiles he is touching upon their actual practices. Nothing is more likely than that the captives continued the evil courses in which they had grown up at home, so far as this was possible in a foreign land. They certainly shared in the fanaticism or optimism of those left in the country, and heard with incredulity the prophet's predictions of the speedy downfall of the city (xii. 22, 26 *seq.*). It is known from Jeremiah (xxix. 8) that there were false prophets among the exiles who confirmed them in their delusive hopes, and Ezekiel might refer to these prophets in such passages as ch. xiii., xiv. But such language as "ye have not gone up into the gaps" (xiii. 5), "I sought for a man...that should... stand in the gap before me for the land" (xxii. 30), shews that it is the circumstances of the nation as a whole and not those of the exiles that occupy the prophet's attention. The same appears from such expressions as those in xiv. 7, "every one of the house of Israel, or of the strangers that sojourn in Israel, which...taketh his idols into his heart." In one passage (xx. 32) the people are represented as resolving to adopt the religion of the nations, "We will be as the nations,...to serve wood and stone"; and such a spirit might very naturally reveal itself among the exiles surrounded by heathen neighbours. But probable as this is, the chapter is a review of the nation's history, and the language may be little more than the prophet's interpretation of the spirit shewn by the people all through its history. It is only on rare occasions that he draws any distinction between the exiles and those remaining in the land. When he does so he shares the feeling of Jeremiah (ch. xxiv., xxix. 16 *seq.*) that the flower of the people had been carried into captivity with Jehoiachin, and that the hope of the nation lay in them (xi. 14—21). But usually the exiles are regarded as the representatives of the house of Israel; the "elders" are the elders of Judah or Israel, and when addressing them the prophet desires to speak in the ears of all his countrymen; just as it is the fate of Jerusalem (iv.—xi.), the history of the nation (xvi., xx., xxiii.), and its future destinies (xxxiii.—xxxvii.), that form the theme of his discourse. The idea that the prophet's office was limited to the exiles, among whom he was a sort of pastor, with a cure of souls, is supported by nothing in the book.

His relation to his fellow exiles.

It would be a mistake, however, to press this general bearing of Ezekiel's mission, and his preoccupation with the destinies of the house of Israel as a whole, so far as to infer from it that he had no actual prophetic ministry among the exiles; that he was a writer simply, unused to the life of men—a solitary theorist, whose "stuff for removing" (xii. 4), if he had brought it forth, would have been little more than an inkhorn; and that the form of oral address which he gives his words is a mere literary artifice. It may not be allowable to assume that his operations among the exiles were literally altogether such as he describes them, but, apart from his own representations, several things afford evidence indirectly that he did exercise a ministry of some kind and of some duration. In ch. xx. 49 (Heb. xxi. 5), when commanded to prophesy of the great conflagration which the Lord would kindle in the forest of the South, he exclaims, "Ah Lord GOD! they say of me, Is he not a speaker of parables?" And in xxxiii. 30 he is represented as being the subject of conversation among the people: "The children of thy people talk of thee by the walls and in the doors of the houses...saying, Come,...and hear what is the word that cometh forth from the LORD." These incidental allusions imply that the prophet had a manner which the people had learned to recognise, and that they were in the habit of meeting to consult him. The frequent assembling of the elders before him implies the same thing. It is true that these elders are very subordinate figures ; they are mentioned, and then the discourse passes on to the "house of Israel" or even the strangers that sojourn in Israel, but they cannot be wholly fictitious, or (to speak with Reuss) mere "dummies." Again, though it may be true that the prophet's book was written as it now is at a late period, and though its present form suggests careful planning, all passages relating to the destruction of Jerusalem and the principles of Jehovah's government and the attributes of His nature illustrated by it being embraced in the first part, and the second part being devoted to the Restoration and the illustrations of Jehovah's purposes which it affords, the fact that in the first part there are many promises of restitution is evidence of actual oral communication (xi. 14—20, xvi. 52—63, xvii. 22—24, xx. 39—44). These consolatory passages naturally arise, as in other prophets, out of the preceding threatenings, if these were actually spoken, while in an orderly dogmatic treatise they would have been postponed to the second part of the book. The passage xxix. 17—20 possibly implies that the prophet felt that his predictions against Tyre had received a less literal fulfilment than was expected from them. If so, his retention of the predictions without change affords ground for believing that upon the whole he has reproduced his discourses with fidelity. The severe, even harsh, tone pervading the early part of the book is evidence to the same effect. It is scarcely conceivable that the prophet should have adopted such a tone after the fall of the city unless he had been reproducing in the main what he had spoken before it. And in like manner the people's mind, buoyant and impatient of the prophet's anticipations of disaster in the first half of the book, appears prostrated and plunged into despair in the second (xxxiii. 10). It is beyond belief that so many circumstances, all harmonious if real, should be nothing but elaborate fictions.

Idealization of events.

It cannot be assumed that the prophet's exercise of his office was just literally such as it is represented. Circumstances of actual occurrence are idealized by him and made the expressions of general conceptions and principles, and it is not always possible to distinguish between events which were actual but are idealized, and things which are purely creations of the symbolizing imagination (note on xi. 13). The prophet appears to have entered on his mission with his convictions in regard to the fate of his country fixed. He clearly foresaw the downfall of the state. But like all the prophets he was assured of the reconstitution of the kingdom of God on a securer basis. It is for this chiefly that he is appointed to labour (ch. xxxiii.); and this position suggests to him from the beginning the nature of his prophetic calling, which is to be a "watchman" to warn every individual man (note iii. 16—21). It is probable that the first section of the book (ch. i.—iii. 21) covers the earliest period of his ministry. After this a change of procedure, occasioned by the incredulity of the people, appears to have been adopted by him; he ceased to be a public reprover, confining himself to the instruction of those who visited him in his house (iii. 22—27, note, p. 26). The meaning of this so-called "silence" is obscure; it was only comparative, though it is represented as lasting till tidings arrived of the fall of the city (xxiv. 27, xxxiii. 22), when, his anticipations being verified, his mouth was again opened. Little is said of the prophet after this beyond mention of occasional visits from the elders. But, though the book may contain a good deal that was never publicly spoken, and though, being edited after the events foretold had occurred, the predictions in it may even have received in some parts a certain colour from the fulfilment, it may be assumed that the main contents of the oral addresses are faithfully reproduced in it; and the passage xx. 49 is warrant for supposing that the more striking peculiarities of the prophet's manner are truly reflected.

His style.

The prophet's style, though stately and polished, is less elevated and more prosaic than that of the earlier prophets, though he occasionally rises into wild and irregular poetry (ch. vii., xxi.), and in particular affects the *Ḳinah* or Lament (ch. xix., xxvi. 17, xxxii. 17)[1]. His language begins to shew incorrectness, though some of the faults may be due to the very depraved state of the text; and his diction has a certain luxuriance, which must sometimes be called redundancy, unless we may infer from the more sober text of the LXX. that many of the cumulative phrases are glosses with which the Heb. text has been overgrown (note, vi. 6). The frequent recurrence of the same phrases produces a feeling of monotony, though the repetition appears due to mannerism and the ascendancy of certain ideas in the prophet's mind quite as much as to defective literary skill. The expression "son of man" (ii. 1) occurs nearly a hundred times, and others very frequently, such as "idols" (block-gods, vi. 4); "the mountains of Israel" (vi. 2, &c.), a phrase found in no other writer (cf. Is. xiv. 25); "satisfy my fury" (v. 13, &c.); "stumblingblock of iniquity" (vii. 19); "rebellious house" (ii. 5, and often in ch. i.—xxiv. cf. xliv. 6); "a desolation in the midst of the countries that are desolate" (xxix. 12, xxx. 7); "the time of the iniquity of the end" (xxi. 25, &c.); "the Lord Jehovah" [E.VV. the Lord GOD] (ii. 4[2], and extremely often, though much seldomer in LXX.); "I Jehovah have spoken" (v. 13, &c.); and the characteristic "ye (they) shall know that I am Jehovah" (vi. 7, &c.), language by which Ezekiel expresses his conception of the purpose and issue of all history, whether it be the dispersion and restoration of his own people or the commotions and changes that take place among the nations.

---

[1] [See introductory note to ch. xix.]
[2] [Where see note.]

Symbolic figures, symbolic actions, and visions.

There are three things in particular which are characteristic of the Book: symbolical figures, symbolical actions, and visions. The three seem all due to the same cast of mind, and are related to one another, being all more or less the creations of an imagination or phantasy always grandiose and often beautiful.

(1) One of the finest of the ideal symbols appears in the Elegy on the princes of Israel (ch. xix.), in which the nation is represented as a mother lioness rearing her whelps, one after another of which, when they had learned to catch the prey, was taken by the nations in their pit and caged in captivity. There is a touch of pathos, rare in the prophet, when in reference to the captive prince he speaks of the young lion's voice being no more heard on the mountains of Israel. Of singular beauty also is the representation of the merchant city Tyre, rising out of the waters on her island rock, under the symbol of a gallant ship moored in the seas (ch. xxvii.). Her mast is a cedar of Lebanon, her sail fine byssus of Egypt, her decks of sherbin wood inlaid with ivory[1]. All the ships of Tarshish attend on her and pour into her the richest products of the nations to form her cargo. But she is broken by the east wind and founders in the heart of the seas, to the dismay and inconsolable grief of all seafaring men. If the author of the Apocalypse be a purer poet than Ezekiel, the prophet has given him his inspiration and furnished him with materials for his most splendid creations. Again, though marked by a breadth which offends against modern taste, the allegory of the foundling child which became the faithless wife is powerful, and, when the details are forgotten and only the general idea kept in mind, even beautiful as well as true. An outcast infant, exposed in the open field and weltering in her blood, was seen by the pitying eye of a passer by. Rescued and nourished she grew up to the fairest womanhood and became the wife of her benefactor, who heaped on her every gift that could please or elevate.

[1] [See note on *v*. 6.]

But the ways into which he led her were too lofty to be understood, and the atmosphere around too pure for her to breathe; the old inborn nature (her father was the Amorite and her mother a Hittite) was still there beneath all the refinements for which it had no taste, and at last it asserted itself in shameless depravity and insatiable lewdness. Other figures are the familiar one of Israel as a vine (ch. xv.), to which a pathetic turn is given by a studious silence regarding its fruit; that of Egypt as the crocodile, a semi-mythical monster, fouling his waters in his restless energy, but dragged out by the hook of Jehovah and flung upon the land, his carcase filling the valleys and his blood the water-courses; and that of Nebuchadrezzar as a great speckled eagle with long pinions, hovering over Lebanon and cropping its highest branches. It is the prophet's manner to develop his symbols into a multitude of details, which sometimes has the effect of obscuring the brilliancy of the central conception.

Though scarcely, with Ewald, to be called "learned," Ezekiel has a knowledge of designing and architecture (ch. xl. *seq.*), and his acquaintance with foreign lands and their natural and industrial products is wide. In this respect he comes nearest to the author of Job, though the latter delights rather to dwell on the phenomena of nature, the luxuriant vegetation of the Nile valley, the wild creatures of the desert, and the monstrous creations of the waters, while Ezekiel is more attracted by the precious stones and metals for which various lands are famed, and by the rich fabrics produced by human skill (ch. xxvii.). Naturally his imagination luxuriates in mythological tradition, especially of a weird kind, such as tales of the "mighty" which were of old (ch. xxxii.), legends of paradise, the garden of God (xxviii.), and impressions of the popular mind regarding Sheol the abode of the dead.

(2) The prophet's symbolical actions have been variously understood. It is beyond doubt that actions of this kind were occasionally performed by prophets. Zedekiah made him "horns of iron" wherewith to push (1 Kgs xxii. 11). Jeremiah put a

yoke upon his own neck, which Hananiah broke from off him
(Jer. xxvii. 2, xxviii. 10). The symbolical act, Jer. li. 59—64,
may also have been literally executed, as well as that in xix. 10.
Whether his act in hiding his girdle (ch. xiii.) was real or not
may be doubtful, and the same doubt exists in regard to Isaiah's
walking naked and barefoot (ch. xx.); the fact that the sign was
continued for three years rather tells against a literal performance.
of it; and it may be held certain that Jeremiah did not send
yokes to the kings of Edom and Moab (Jer. xxvii. 3)[1]. It is
possible that Ezekiel may in some cases have had recourse to
this forcible way of impressing his teaching. Some of the actions
described might well have been performed, such as joining two
sticks together into one to represent the future union of Judah
and Israel under one king (xxxvii. 15 *seq.*). He might also have
refrained from all outward mourning on the death of his wife, as
a sign of the silent grief under which the people would pine
away when tidings reached them of the destruction of the city
and the death of all dear to them (xxiv. 15 *seq.*). But on the
other hand how could the prophet "eat his bread with quaking
and drink his water with trembling" as a sign to the house
of Israel? (xii. 18). And can it be seriously supposed that he
actually took a sharp sword as a razor and shaved off the hair
of his head and beard, burning a third of it in the city (what
city?), smiting a third of it with the sword about the walls, and
scattering the remaining third to the winds (v. 1 *seq.*)? Such
actions, and others like them, could not have been performed,
and this fact casts doubt on the literality even of those which
were possible. Even if 190 days be the true reading in iv. 5, it is
most improbable that the prophet should have lain on his side
immoveable for half a year, and it appears impossible when
other actions had to be done simultaneously. The hypothesis
of Klostermann[2] hardly deserves mention. This writer supposes that the prophet lay on his side because he was a cataleptic
and temporarily paralysed, that he prophesied against Jerusalem

---

[1] [See note in C.B.]   [2] *Stud. u. Krit.*, 1877.

with outstretched arm because his arm could not be withdrawn, being convulsively rigid, and that he was "dumb" because struck with morbid *alalia*. It is surprising that some reputable scholars should seem half inclined to accept this explanation[1]. They perhaps have the feeling that such an interpretation is more reverential to Scripture. But we need to remind ourselves, as Job reminded his friends, that superstition is not religion (Job xiii. 7—12, xxi. 22). The book itself appears to teach us how to interpret most of the symbolical actions. In xxiv. 3 the symbol of setting the caldron on the fire is called uttering a parable (cf. xx. 49). The act of graving a hand at the parting of the ways (xxi. 19) must certainly be interpreted in the same way, and, though there may be room for hesitation in regard to some of them, probably the actions as a whole were imagined merely. They passed through the prophet's mind. He lived in this ideal sphere; he went through the actions in his phantasy, and they appeared to him to carry the same effects as if they had been performed[2].

(3) The vision is a mental operation of the same kind, though higher. The simplest and most beautiful of them all is the vision of the dry bones and their resurrection (ch. xxxvii.). Three elements are observable in it: first, certain truths and ideas in the prophet's mind, truths not new but often expressed elsewhere, at least partially, such as the idea of the people's restoration. Secondly, the operation on these truths of the prophet's mental genius, giving them a unity, throwing them into a physical form, and making them stand out before the eye

---

[1] Orelli, *Kurzgef. Kommentar* ; Valeton, *Viertal Voorlezingen* ; Gautier, *La Mission du Prophète Ezéchiel.* See on the other side Kuenen, *Onderzoek*, ii. p. 268.

[2] In regard to ch. iv. 1—3 Calvin remarks, Hoc fuit puerile spectaculum, nisi a Deo jussus fuisset Propheta sic agere. But that which would be puerile unless commanded by God remains puerile in itself, and the sound sense of men will conclude that God did not command it. [The opposite view, however, viz. the actions were not merely imagined, but were actually performed, seems to deserve more consideration than Davidson admits. See sub-note to the note introductory to ch. iv. 1—v. 4.]

of his phantasy as if presented to him from without. And thirdly, there may be a certain literary embellishment. This last element is most conspicuous in the visions of the Cherubim (ch. i.) and of the new Temple (ch. xl. *seq.*)[1]. But it must be maintained that the second element, the constructive operation of the phantasy, was always present, and that the visions are not mere literary invention. Occasionally, however, the prophet does use the vision, like other things, in an ideal way, bringing considerable stretches of his own prophetic work under the outline of a single vision, as in ch. i.—iii. 21 and ch. viii.—xi. (cf. note, iii. 21). Ezekiel felt such visions as that in ch. xxxvii. to be a revelation of God. And from whence else could his assurance of the people's restoration have come? There was nothing in the state of the world and the nations to suggest it, and everything in the past history of the people and their present condition to make it seem impossible (xxxiii. 10). The singular struggle between hope and fear revealed in Lam. iii. 21 *seq.* is typical of the state of mind even of those in whose hearts hope was not dead ; and the very energy of the utterance in Is. l. 4—8 is evidence of the obstacles which faith had to overcome.

Break in the Chronology of the Book.

Between the latest date in ch. i.—xxxix. [with the exception of ch. xxix. 17—21, where see notes] and the date of ch. xl. *seq.* there is an interval of eleven or twelve years. Ch. i.—xxxix. may be considered to have been composed a considerable time before ch. xl. *seq.* The latter chapters are quite unique in a prophetic book, while the contents of the earlier part do not

---

[1] The difference between Isaiah's knowledge of God and that of Ezekiel, and consequently the greater detail of the latter in ch. i. compared with Is. vi., is very prettily expressed by Abarbanel, who says that Ezekiel was a villager who saw the Divine Majesty but rarely and therefore minutely described it, while Isaiah dwelt in the capital and was familiar with the great King. [The comparison is placed in the mouth of the Jewish teacher, Rabba †A.D. 353) in the treatise *Chagigah* (Tal. Bab.), fol. 13*b*.]

differ from those of other prophetic writings. The difference of the two parts may have suggested to Josephus (*Ant.* x. 5, 1) the idea that Ezekiel wrote *two* books, unless, indeed, the words he uses should apply rather to Jeremiah. Although ch. i.—xxxix. form the background to ch. xl.—xlviii., a certain change in the prophet's view seems to have taken place in the interval, particularly in regard to the *rôle* of the Prince. The passage xxix. 17—21 is a later insertion dated two years after ch. xl. After this date (570 B.C.) nothing is known of the prophet. Tradition asserts that he met his death in Babylonia at the hands of a prince of his people whom he had upbraided for his idolatrous practices[1].

Date and Canonicity.

The contention of some scholars that the book is later than the exile and pseudepigraphic has not met with any wide acceptance. Zunz[2] would place it in the Persian period (*c.* 440—400 B.C.). The view of Geiger[3] is similar; while Seinecke[4], who identifies Gog with Antiochus Epiphanes, brings the book as low as the Maccabean age.

Ezekiel was received into the Canon along with the other prophetical books. The date of the canonising of the Prophets is uncertain, though it must have been prior to 200 B.C. (Ecclus. Prol. and ch. xlix. 8, Dan. ix. 2). The differences between the ritual details in ch. xl. *seq.* and the Law naturally created difficulties, which, however, do not seem to have been widely felt, as no scholar's name or school is mentioned in connexion with them. Hananiah ben Hezekiah, of blessed memory (a contemporary of Gamaliel the master of St Paul), resolutely grappled with them; he had 300 measures of lamp-oil brought him, and betaking

---

[1] For this and other traditions cf. Knobel, *Prophetismus*, p. 301.

[2] *Gottesdienst. Vorträge*, p. 157, and *Zeit. Deut. Morg. Ges.*, vol. xxvii. p. 676.

[3] *Urschrift*, p. 23.

[4] *Gesch. d. V. Is.*, i. 138, quoted in Kuenen, *Onderz.*, ii. 316.

himself to an upper room he sat and reconciled the differences, of which no more was heard[1].

CHAPTER III

JEHOVAH, GOD OF ISRAEL

EZEKIEL'S general doctrine of God does not differ materially from that of other prophets of the same age, such as Jeremiah and Isaiah xl. *seq.*, though the character of his mind causes him to bring some Divine attributes into more prominence than others, and his education as a priest leads him to a way of thinking or at least to the use of a kind of phraseology not observed in other prophets.

His conception of Jehovah's personality and universal sovereignty.

His conception of Jehovah appears in the "visions of God" which he describes (chs. i., viii., x., xliii.). These visions were all alike, and they reveal his general impression of that which Jehovah is. The fourfold nature of the cherubim, of their faces and wings and of the wheels, all forming a chariot moving in every direction alike, and with the velocity suggested by the wings and wheels, symbolizes the omnipresence of Jehovah, while the eyes of which the whole was full are a token of His omniscience. The throne above the firmament on which He sat indicates that He is King in heaven, God over all, omnipotent. The Divine Being Himself appeared as of human form, while His nature was light, of such brightness that fire fitly represented Him only from the loins downwards, from the loins upwards the effulgence was something purer and

---

[1] See Buhl, *Kanon und Text*, p. 30 (Trans., p. 24, 30). Wildeboer, *Het Ontstaan van den Kanon*, p. 59. Bleek, *Einleitung*, 4 Ed., p. 551 [note]. [See for examples of these difficulties the present reviser's translation of *Chagigah*, p. 71, note.]

more dazzling, and He was surrounded by a brightness like that of the rainbow in the day of rain. This "glory," which contains Himself within it (x. 4, 18, xliii. 5, 6), is that which is manifested to men (final note, ch. i.).

The name by which the prophet calls the God of Israel is Jehovah, or the Lord Jehovah [E.VV. the Lord GOD]. Whether the name Lord expresses something judicial or no may be uncertain, it expresses at least something sovereign (Is. vi. 1); but the other name Jehovah now in Ezekiel's age expresses the idea of God absolutely. Jehovah has all power: the nations as well as Israel are in His hand. He brought Israel out of Egypt, and gave them the good land of Canaan, and He will disperse them among the nations, delivering them over to the king of Babylon; but yet again He will recover them out of the hand of those who have served themselves of them, and save them with an everlasting salvation. With the same omnipotence He rules among the nations. His judgements fall upon the peoples around Israel, Ammon, Moab, and Edom, whose name He causes to perish among the nations; but they light also on Tyre and even upon Egypt, which He gives into the hand of Nebuchadrezzar. He breaks the arm of Pharaoh and strikes the sword out of his hand, putting His own sword into the hand of Nebuchadrezzar. He brandishes His sword in the eyes of all the nations, while creation shudders and the waters of the great deep stand motionless. He puts His hook in the jaws of Gog and brings him up from the ends of the earth, revealing Himself to the most distant lands and the far-off islands of the sea. He reverses the past, bringing again the captivity of Sodom and her daughters. He sends forth His life-giving Spirit, and the nation that was dead and its bones scattered feels the breath of life and rises to its feet a great army. His rule of the nations is the judgement of the nations; and His verdict upon a nation is seen in the last act which it plays upon the stage of history and is eternal (xxxii. 17 *seq.*).

At the sight of His glory the prophet fell upon his face, but it is not Jehovah's will that His servants should be overborne

by His majesty (Job ix. 32—35, xiii. 21), and He says to the
prophet "stand upon thy feet, and I will speak with thee"
(ii. 1). Though profoundly devout and but a "son of man"
in the presence of Jehovah, the prophet is far from regarding
God as a mere transcendent majesty and abstract omnipotence.
He is the living God. He has "a likeness as the appearance
of a man" (i. 26). He has "a mighty hand and a stretched
out arm" (xx. 33), a "face" (vii. 22, xiv. 8, xv. 7, xxxix. 23, 24),
a "mouth" (iii. 17, cf. xxii. 21), "eyes" and "ears" (viii. 18),
His fury comes up into His "nostrils" (xxxviii. 18), and the
sanctuary is the place of the "soles of his feet" (xliii. 7; cf.
Is. lx. 13). These representations in Ezekiel mean neither
more nor less than they do in other prophets, such as Is. xl.
—lxvi.; they are not to be dwelt upon individually but taken
together, and when thus combined they express the idea of
a living personality possessing all the powers of personal being.
Even when the prophet represents Jehovah's judgements as
executed by the mediation of Divine messengers (ch. ix.), or
when he interposes a "man" between God and himself (xl. 3
sq.), this is due to his tendency to personify rather than to
any feeling of the distance of God from men or the world,
as appears from xliii. 5—7.

Jehovah's moral attributes.

Again, Jehovah appears in the prophet endowed with all
the attributes and emotions of moral being. He expresses His
own consciousness of that which He is by using His own name,
as when He says, "Ye shall know that I am Jehovah"; and His
sense of Himself when injured, as it is when His people worship
other gods or when the nations touch that which is His, op-
pressing His people or usurping His land, reacts and manifests
itself as "jealousy." He pities the outcast infant weltering in
its blood and bids it live (xvi. 6), and the little children passed
through the fire to Molech, whom He calls "my children"
(xvi. 21). He has compassion on "his sheep," broken or lost

and scattered on the mountains through the selfishness of
hirelings who feed themselves and not the flock, and He binds
up that of them which was broken, and strengthens that which
was sick (xxxiv. 16). His "soul" is "alienated" from His people
(xxiii. 18). His "anger" is kindled by their ways, He pours out
His "fury" upon them and "satisfies" it in their punishment.
Yet He has no pleasure in the death of the wicked; His will is
that men should live (xviii. 23, xxxiii. 11). He is conscious of
being God alone, and directs all history, whether of His people
or the nations, towards one goal, the revealing of Himself as
that which He is to the eyes of mankind. If He sends afflictions
on His people it is that He may break their whorish heart and
eyes (vi. 9 marg.), and when His chastisements fail He forgives
for His name's sake (xxxvi. 22; cf. Is. xlviii. 9), brings Himself
near and dwells by His spirit in men's hearts (xxxvi. 27), even
tabernacling in a visible form among them for ever, so that
the name of the new Jerusalem to all generations is, JEHOVAH-
SHAMMAH, *The* LORD *is there* (xlviii. 35).

His relation to His people and to other nations.

His relation to His people or the prophet is not that of one
distant or unapproachable. Being King in Israel,—and He
expresses His resolution to be King over them yet in truth
(xx. 33),—He gives them statutes and judgements. Yet these are
"good," they are "statutes of life" (xxxiii. 15), which if a man
do he shall live by them (xx. 11). In like manner He com-
municates His word to the prophet, commanding him to receive
it and not be rebellious like the rebellious house (ii. 8). The
prophet represents his inspiration under the symbol of eating
the roll of a book, but why this symbol should imply a more
"mechanical" idea of inspiration than the language of Jer.,
"Behold, I have put my *words* in thy mouth" (i. 9), does not
appear. Though the roll was written on the front and on the
back with lamentation and woe, it was in the prophet's mouth
"as honey for sweetness" (iii. 3). The same joy in Jehovah's

service even amidst persecutions was felt by Jeremiah: "Thy words were found, and I did eat them; thy words were a joy and the rejoicing of mine heart; for I am called by thy name" (xv. 16). Sympathy with Jehovah in His alienation from the people because of their evil is expressed by both prophets, "I sat alone because of thy hand, for thou hast filled me with indignation" (Jer. xv. 17, and in a more violent form vi. 11; cf. Ezek. iii. 14). Both prophets have such fellowship with Jehovah that they can venture to intercede for the people, though they are repulsed with the answer that the time for intercession has gone by, "Though Moses and Samuel stood before me, yet my mind could not be toward this people: cast them out of my sight" (Jer. xv. 1; Ezek. ix. 8, xi. 13).

Jehovah is God over all, and the self-exaltation of peoples or their rulers in any place of the world, as when the prince of Tyre says, "I am God," or when the Pharaoh says, "My river is mine, I have made it," is an offence against the majesty of Him who is alone exalted. What might be called moral forces are no less subservient to His will and ruled by Him than those that are physical. The prophet, indeed, represents Jehovah as the Author of all that occurs, whether on the stage of history or in the minds of men. Even the evil that men do is in many instances ascribed to Him, without men, however, being thereby relieved of responsibility for it. In one aspect men's deeds are their own, in another they are occasioned by God. Jerusalem sets her bloodshed on a bare rock, without covering it; but from another point of view it is the Lord Himself who sets it on a bare rock "that it might cause fury to come up to take vengeance" (xxiv. 8). A prophet allows himself to be enticed, and entering into the purposes of the people—whitewashing the wall which they build—speaks such a prophetic word as fosters their delusive hopes. It is the Lord that deceives this prophet that both he and those whom he deludes may perish together (xiv. 10). The laws given to the people were "good," statutes of life. But the people neglected and disobeyed them, they perverted their meaning, extending the law of the offering of the firstborn, even to children whom they burnt in the fire. This perversion was caused by God Himself; He gave them laws that were not good, that He might destroy them (xx. 25, 26). Evil things come into the mind of Gog, he devises an evil device, saying, "I will go to them that are at quiet,...to take the spoil, and to take the prey." It is Jehovah that puts hooks in his jaws and brings him forth; "I will bring thee against my land, that the nations may know me, when I shall be sanctified in thee" (xxxviii. 4, 11, 16).

His attitude towards sin.

These representations in Ezekiel are similar to others in Scripture, and, no doubt, raise difficult questions. Perhaps two things may be said in general: first, Jehovah is nowhere represented as causing nations or men to do evil acts, which they are not also represented as doing of their own accord and with evil intent; and secondly, Jehovah is nowhere represented as the author of sin in such a sense that He causes an innocent mind to sin. He adds to the sin of one already sinful for wider purposes which He has in view. The instances of Pharaoh, the Amorites (Deut. ii. 30; Josh. xi. 20; cf. Gen. xv. 16; Lev. xviii. 24, 25), Saul (1 Sam. xxvi. 19), Ahab (1 Kgs xxii. 20), Israel (Is. vi. 9, xxix. 10, lxiii. 17, cf. lxiv. 5, 6; Ezek. xx. 25, 26), the false prophets (Ezek. xiv. 9), Gog (Ezek. xxxviii.) are all of this kind. They are so clearly of this kind that none of them needs discussion except the case of Saul's persecution of David. The words of David are, "If it be the Lord that hath stirred thee up against me, let him smell an offering." David's view appears to be that Saul's persecution of him is due to an aberration with which the king has been struck by Jehovah. This aberration is a punishment for some previous unwitting offence, and he advises an atoning offering that the offence may be forgiven and the aberration removed. The aphorism *quem deus vult perdere prius dementat* may have its application in Scripture, but there at least the previous question needs to be carefully raised.

Whom does God will to destroy? It is always assumed that they are evil men, either in themselves or as the adversaries of Jehovah or of His people. On broader grounds the propriety or justice of this assumption may in some cases appear to need investigation. But, the assumption being made, God appears as the author of sin only in a secondary and very modified sense. He uses sin already existing, punishes it with delusion and worse sin, laying a stumblingblock before the sinner, over which he falls and perishes (Jer. vi. 21; Ezek. iii. 20)[1].

Jehovah's justice as exhibited to Israel and to the nations.

The view has been suggested that to the prophet's mind the prevailing characteristic of Jehovah is His justice—Jehovah is "the rigidly just one"; and that this conception of Jehovah's justice is but the reflection of the prophet's own "scrupulous and precise character." Jehovah's punctilious righteousness appears in His way of dealing with different classes of men, ch. xiv. 12—20, xviii., xxxiii. 10—20; and the prophet's own scrupulous and somewhat pedantic nature in the way he feels the responsibilities of his office as watchman, ch. iii. 16—21, xxxiii. 1—9[2]. This representation appears to invert the true order, putting that first which is last. The prophet's conception of his office is a reflection, if there be reflection in the case, of his idea of the Divine method of dealing with men. It is because God will deal with each man individually that the prophet feels he must warn each separately. The reality of his office and of his sense of responsibility in the discharge of it being admitted, his statements about himself are in the main an indirect way of impressing upon men the true nature of their relations to God and of the method in which He will treat them (initial note to xxxiii.). And the point of view from which

---

[1] The Essay of Dr J. C. Matthes, "Oorsprong der Zonde," *Theol. Tijds.*, 1890, p. 225, appears to overlook the previous assumption referred to.

[2] Kuenen, *Modern Review*, Oct. 1884, pp. 630 f.

passages like ch. xviii. and xxxiii. are to be looked at is scarcely that of the Divine rectitude merely (final notes to xviii.).

There are several expressions used by Ezekiel of interest in connexion with his conceptions of God. They are the words frequently spoken by the Lord, (1) "Ye (they) shall know that I am Jehovah"; (2) "I will be sanctified (shew myself holy) in you (them)"; and (3), "I wrought for my name's sake, that it should not be profaned in the sight of the nations." From the occasional combination of these phrases together it appears that they differ little from one another in meaning; thus: "I will magnify myself and sanctify myself, and I will make myself known in the eyes of many nations; and they shall know that I am Jehovah" (xxxviii. 23). "And my holy name will I make known in the midst of my people Israel;...and the nations shall know that I am Jehovah, the Holy One in Israel" (xxxix. 7). "I will be jealous for my holy name" (xxxix. 25). "That the nations may know me, when I shall be sanctified in thee, O Gog, before their eyes" (xxxviii. 16). "And the nations shall know that I am Jehovah, when I shall be sanctified in you (Israel) before their eyes" (xxxvi. 23).

In the words spoken by the Lord, "Ye shall know that I am Jehovah," the term "Jehovah" expresses the Speaker's own consciousness of that which He is. The language is frequently used towards the nations: His judgements on them reveal to them that He is Jehovah, or they learn the same truth from observation of His restoration and protection of Israel (the former, xxv. 5, 7, 11, 17, xxvi. 6, xxviii. 22, 23, xxix. 9, xxx. 19, xxxv. 9, 15, xxxviii. 16, 23, xxxix. 6, 7; and the latter, xxxvi. 23, 36). The phrase is also addressed to Israel, both in connexion with judgements and in connexion with blessings such as restoration and final peace (the former, vi. 7, 10, 14, vii. 4, 27, xi. 10, 12, xii. 15, 16, 20, xiii. 9, 23, xv. 7. xx. 38, xxiv. 24; and the other, xx. 42, 44, xxviii. 26, xxxiv. 27, 30, xxxvi. 11, 38, xxxvii. 13). The words mean more than that those addressed shall learn that it is "Jehovah" who inflicts the judgement or confers the blessing upon them; they mean that they shall learn to know the nature of Him who is dealing with them, or at least His nature on some side of His being. This appears from an occasional variation in the expression: "Ye shall know that I am the Lord Jehovah" (xiii. 9, xxiii. 49, xxiv. 24, xxix. 16). The term "Jehovah," however, is not a mere synonym for "God"; it appears always to carry a historical element in it. When addressed to the nations it connotes "the God of Israel"; and when addressed to Israel it carries a reminder of that which they have been told of Him by His servants the prophets, or that which they have learned of Him from His presence in their history. How much is suggested by the name "Jehovah" must perhaps be learned from each particular passage. When spoken to the nations in general it may suggest His power, and that He will not leave injuries done to His people unrequited; in some cases it may imply that He is God over all, as when the words are spoken in regard to the Pharaoh (xxix. 9). At any rate, to Ezekiel certainly "Jehovah," the God of Israel, is He who is God alone, and who, in right-eousness and power and all other attributes, is that which one who is God alone is—although in each several passage where the word is used some special Divine attribute may be more particularly suggested.

Jehovah's holiness, its significance.

The expression "I will be sanctified," or, "sanctify myself," or, "shew myself holy" (or, get me sanctifying), does not differ materially from the phrase just discussed. In modern usage the term "holy" has drifted away from its proper sense and lost its original comprehensive meaning. The word is an adj. derived from a neut. verb which probably expressed some physical idea, though the idea is not now recoverable. What-ever the idea was, the term "holy" was very early felt to be an appropriate epithet for deity, not as expressing any particular attribute but rather the general notion of Godhead. Jehovah swears by His "holiness" or by "Himself" without difference of meaning (Am. iv. 2, vi. 8). The term was so much appropriated to the Divine that when coupled with the word "god" or "gods" it became a mere otiose epithet, "the holy gods" meaning nothing more than "the gods" (Dan. iv. 8, 9, 18, v. 11, cf. v. 14; Inscription of Eshmunazar). In Israel the epithet is transferred to Jehovah, who is the Holy One of Israel, or, *in* Israel (xxxix. 7), or the Holy One, or even Holy One, almost as a proper name (Heb. in Prov. xxx. 3; Is. xl. 25; cf. Josh. xxiv. 19).

It appears to be a secondary use, though also very early, when the term was applied to that which belongs to the sphere of deity, which lies near God's presence or has come into it (Exod. iii. 5; Numb. xvi. 37, 38), or which belongs to Him, whether as part of Himself or as His property. Hence His arm, His Spirit are "holy"; and so His house, city, hill, people, land, and the like; His sabbath, His offerings, and His ministers. Hence the angels, belonging to the sphere of deity, are the "holy ones" (Job v. 1). The word in this sense is applied both to things and men, and expresses primarily not a quality but a relation. But naturally, just as the idea of godhead would always carry some attribute or perhaps several with it, so that which was considered the possession of God or near Him, whether things or men, would also be considered to have certain characteristics. These characteristics would be regulated by that which God was thought to be. Things repulsive to His nature could not be His nor come near Him, and could not be "holy"; neither could men unlike Him in character, or in any physical condition repugnant to His nature. But things and men that were His shared His "holiness" and could be "profaned," such as His sabbaths or His holy princes (Ezek. vii. 22, 24, xx. 16; Is. xliii. 28).

The term "holy" applied to Jehovah is very elastic, and may embrace much or little, one thing or another. To call Jehovah "holy" tells nothing in regard to Him further than that He is God, with the attributes of God. The idea has to be distinguished from the details brought at different times under it. There might be included under the idea the sole godhead of Jehovah; such natural attributes of deity as power, manifested in the rule of nature (Exod. xv. 1, 11), or in judgements on the enemies of His people (Ezek. xxviii. 22, xxxviii. 16, 23, xxxix. 7); moral attributes, as punitive righteousness (Is. v. 16), or ethical purity (Lev. xix. 2); and finally physical or what might be called æsthetic purity (Lev. xi. 44 *seq.*, xx. 25, 26; Ezek. xliii. 7, 9, cf. initial note to xl.—xlviii., last par.). When Jehovah reveals Himself as that which He is, or in any of His attributes and aspects of that which He is, He "sanctifies" Himself. Hence to "magnify" or "glorify" Himself or set His glory among the nations are particulars coming under the more general "sanctify" (xxxviii. 23, xxxix. 21). In like manner men "sanctify" Jehovah when they recognise that which He is or ascribe to Him His true nature (xxxvi. 23; Is. viii. 13). On the other hand when the iniquities of His people constrain Him to act in such a way as to disguise any of His great attributes, such as His power, in the eyes of the nations, so that they misinterpret His being, His holy name is "profaned," as on the contrary He is "sanctified" in the eyes of the nations by the restoration of His people and their defence when restored and righteous (xxxvi. 23, xxxviii. 16).

His revelation of Himself through Israel to the nations.

The phrase, "I wrought for my name's sake, that it should not be profaned in the sight of the nations," has a meaning but little different. The expression is chiefly used in reference to Israel and its destinies. It contains the prophet's philosophy of history. History, particularly that of Israel in the face of the nations, is Jehovah operating for His name's sake. It is His regard for His name that explains Israel's history, that, indeed, has given her a history, for otherwise she would many a time have been cut off for her iniquities. The "name" of God here is not the mere word "Jehovah," neither is it what might be called His "reputation," though both are included in it. The idea of the prophet is suggested by the fact that He who is God alone and over all is known to the world as Jehovah, God of Israel. He whom the peoples of mankind know as the God of Israel has the consciousness of being true God, and wills to reveal Himself to all mankind (Is. xlii. 8, xliii. 10, xliv. 8, xlv. 21—24). Within Israel He can reveal Himself as He is in Himself; to the nations He must reveal Himself as that which the God of Israel is. He who knows Himself as God alone (Is. xliv. 8) has become historically God of Israel, has begun His revelation of Himself to the world thus, and will thus carry it to an end till He is known to all the earth. Therefore He cannot destroy Israel, for this would undo the first steps of His great purpose already taken, and efface from the minds of the nations the knowledge of Him which they have received by His redemption of His people in their sight (xx. 9, 14, 22; cf. Deut. ix. 28, 29, xxxii. 26, 27; Num. xiv. 15, 16; Exod. xxxii. 11, 12). Henceforth His "name," the name of Him who knows Himself to be God alone, is inseparably linked with the destinies of Israel. Within Israel His revelation of Himself as He is went on, though thwarted by the rebelliousness of the people. Eventually their want of receptiveness was so great that they had to be rejected for a time and cast out of Jehovah's land. In the world of the nations without this was a retrograde movement. Unable to conceive of a moral rule of His people by Jehovah, the nations concluded that He was without power to protect them (xxxvi. 20). Thus His name was profaned; the knowledge which the nations had of Him was obscured. It was perhaps not among the nations only that Jehovah's name had suffered an eclipse: the feet of many in Israel also well-nigh slipped. It took time for them to accommodate themselves to what had happened. It was only when they were enabled to read their past history in a new light, the light shed on it by the prophets, that their minds came to rest. But this new reading both gave them a profounder knowledge of Jehovah and awakened a new enthusiasm for the future. And Jehovah's recovery of His people from all lands not only restored the prestige of His power among the nations, but taught them the deeper moral principles of His rule (xxxix. 23), as it sealed to Israel the ancient truths which they had heard concerning Him (xx. 42—44, xxxvi. 11, 37, xxxix. 28, 29).

The prophet's idea is a large one, and might comprehend more than he fills into it. It is that God's revelation of Himself is historical; that He becomes the God of one people with whose destinies His name is linked; that His rule of this people in their history, its progress and final issues, the way He leads them and that into which at the last He fashions them, is His revelation of Himself to the eyes of mankind.

This conception how reached by the prophet.

The conception that Jehovah acts only for His own name's sake, to sanctify His great name, is capable of being set in a repellent light. It seems to make the Divine Being egoistic and His own sense of Himself the source of all His operations. The way too in which He brings the nations to know that He is Jehovah, through judgements mainly, invests the idea with additional harshness. The conception is not found in the earlier prophets, but is familiar in the age of Ezekiel. Perhaps two things, if considered, would help to explain the prophet's idea. One is his lofty conception of Jehovah, God alone and over all, and his profound reverence before Him. The "son of man" cannot conceive the motive of Jehovah's operations to be found anywhere but in Himself. But that name for whose sake He works is a "great name" (xxxvi. 23), and a "holy name" (xxxix. 25), it is that of Him who is God. The prophet thinks of Jehovah as one of his predecessors did: "For Jehovah your God, he is God of gods, and Lord of lords, the great God, the mighty, and the terrible, which regardeth not persons, nor taketh reward" (Deut. x. 17). And other prophets of his age, very unlike him, move among similar thoughts: "my glory will I not give to another" (Is. xlii. 8, xlv. 23); "for mine own sake, will I do it; for how should my name be profaned" (Is. xlviii. 11).

And the second thing is this: the conception arose out of the conflicts of the time. There were antagonisms within Israel, and more powerful antagonisms without, between Israel and the nations. These conflicts on the stage of history were but the visible forms taken by a conflict of principles, of religions, of Jehovah God with the idolatries of which the nations of the earth were the embodiments. The prophet could not help drawing up this antagonism into his conception of God; and not unnaturally he reflected his own feeling upon the mind of God, and conceived Him thinking of Himself as he thought of Him. If it was but half a truth, it was perhaps the half needful for the age. When the fulness of time was come the centre of Divine motive was shifted, "God so loved the world." Coming from the bosom of the Father and knowing him, the Son's mind was altogether absorbed in the positive truth, the stream of which was so broad and deep that all antagonisms were buried beneath it.

CHAPTER IV

ISRAEL, THE PEOPLE OF THE LORD

THE tone of the prophet towards the people in the early part of his book is severe and threatening, though the threats are here and there relieved with consoling promises and a brighter outlook (xi. 16 *seq.*, xvi. 53 *seq.*, xvii. 22 *seq.*, xxi. 27). In the second half he adopts a kindlier tone. In both parts his teaching agrees in many things with that of his predecessors, particularly Jeremiah.

1. It is surprising how much the two prophets have in common. Both enter upon their office with opinions already formed of the people to whom they are sent, and with the expectation of opposition from them (Jer. i. 19); those around Ezekiel are briers and thorns and he dwells among scorpions (ii. 6); they are impudent and stiffhearted (ii. 4). Both receive assurance of Divine assistance in their contention with them: "I have made thy face hard against their faces...harder than flint have I made thy forehead" (iii. 8, 9; Jer. i. 8, 17, 18, xv. 20; Is. l. 7).

Both sympathise with the anger of Jehovah in His controversy with His people and share it (iii. 14; Jer. vi. 11, xv. 17), and keep aloof from the people, refusing to enter into their sorrow or joy, for a doom from heaven hangs over them (iii. 26, cf. xxiv. 15—27; Jer. xvi. 5 *seq.*). Israel is a "rebellious house," and their rebellion has been continuous throughout their history, "they and their fathers have transgressed against me, unto this very day" (ii. 3, 5, chs. xvi., xx.); "since the day that your fathers came forth out of the land of Egypt unto this day, I have sent unto you all my servants the prophets;...yet they hearkened not unto me... they did worse than their fathers" (Jer. vii. 25). Both assert that Jerusalem has outbidden Samaria in wickedness (xvi. 47, 51, xxiii. 11; Jer. iii. 11, xvi. 12), and that both peoples have been more perverse than the heathen (v. 6, xvi. 48; Jer. ii. 11). The degeneracy has infected all classes and persons, it is vain to look for a "man" in the streets of Jerusalem: "I sought for a man among them that should stand in the gap before me for the land,...but I found none" (xxii. 30; Jer. v. 1).

2. In one respect Ezekiel appears to exceed his predecessors in the condemnation of his people: he recognises no good time in Israel's history[1]. To older prophets a halo surrounded Israel's earliest time, though it soon faded away: "I found Israel like grapes in the wilderness;...but they came to Baal-Peor and consecrated themselves unto the shameful thing; and became abominable like that which they loved" (Hos. ix. 10); "I remember for thee the kindness of thy youth...how thou wentest after me in the wilderness" (Jer. ii. 2). And Isaiah even speaks of Jerusalem as at one time "the faithful city," though in his own day she had become an harlot (i. 21). Jeremiah appears to date the declension from the settlement in Canaan (ii. 5—7, 21, cf. Is. v. 2; Mic. vi. 3), and Ezekiel agrees with him that at that time the people sank into deeper degeneracy, seizing the occasion presented by the Canaanite shrines to add to their

---

[1] ["Die Stadt, die nach Jesaia (i. 21 ff.) treu war und voll von Recht und Gerechtigkeit, ist nach Hezekiel immer eine Hure gewesen." Duhm, *Die Theologie der Propheten*, p. 255.]

provocation and blasphemy (xvi. 15 *seq*., xx. 28; Deut. xii. 2).
But he goes further, pushing the people's idolatries back as far
as the wilderness (xx. 24), and even into an earlier time: "Son of
man, there were two women...and they committed whoredoms
in Egypt" (xxiii. 2). Jerusalem came of tainted blood: her
father was the Amorite, and her mother an Hittite (xvi. 3).
The history of Israel in Egypt is told so briefly in the Pent.
that no corroboration of the prophet's idea is found, which,
however, has everything in its favour (see on xx. 7, 8); and for
the wilderness the oldest part of the Pent. supports him (Ex.
xxxii., cf. Deut. ix. 6, and often). The revelation of Jehovah
was not first made to Israel in Egypt, Jacob was his "servant"
(xxviii. 25, xxxvii. 25), as well as Abraham (xxxiii. 24); and the
prophet supposes the state of the people in Egypt to be very
much their state in his own day: they knew Jehovah, but they had
abandoned Him for the idols which they refused to forsake
(xx. 5 *seq*.). It is possible that Ezekiel may judge the past
history of his people from the point of view of his own attainment in religious knowledge; he may regard the worship at
the high places, though meant by the people for service of
Jehovah, as nothing better than Canaanitish heathenism; and
looking at the darker side of the people's history, and regarding
the nation as a moral personality (xx. 30—44), he may not
advert to much that deserved to be excepted from his sweeping
charge of apostasy. The nature of the prophetic discourse
has always to be taken into account. Its object was to shew
to Jacob his transgressions (Mic. iii. 8; Is. lviii. 1). The judgement of the prophets on the people in every age was not
a comparative but an absolute one. They condemn the people
because they fall short of the ideal which they themselves
perceive to be true. They also represent this shortcoming as
a declension and forsaking of a position formerly attained.
The latter part of the prophetic judgement has been thought by
many to be scarcely historical: their own ideal which they contrast with the popular religion is always true, but their verdict
on the people, it is thought, would have been fairer if, instead

of charging them with declension, they had blamed them for backwardness and slowness of attainment. The written history of Israel is so greatly occupied with external events that it affords little insight into the religious condition of the people before the prophetic age, but the unanimous feeling of the prophets as to the past must have a historical ground. Ezekiel's judgement on Jerusalem (ch. xvi.) finds a parallel in a singular passage in Jer. xxxii. 31 *seq.*: "For this city hath been to me a provocation of mine anger and of my fury from the day that they built it even unto this day."

3. Further, the two prophets are in agreement on much else, the details of the people's sin and the issue of it. Both name the chief sin of Israel "whoredom," as had been common since Hosea, though Isaiah uses the metaphor only once (i. 21); and the figures by which Ezekiel describes it, realistic and repulsive enough though they be, in nothing exceed those used by Jeremiah (xvi. 25, 34, xxiii. 8, 17, 20, 40; Jer. ii. 23, 24, iii. 2, v. 7, 8, xiii. 27). Apart from figure, this whoredom or infidelity to Jehovah includes two things, idolatry and alliances with foreign states, those "lovers" on whom Israel and Judah doted (xxiii. 5, 16; Jer. iv. 30). The idolatry was partly real, a worship of "other gods" (Jer. xvi. 11), the Baals or shame (Jer. xi. 13), the host of heaven (Jer. xix. 13; Ezek. viii. 16), and the queen of heaven (Jer. vii. 18, xliv. 17 *seq.*, cf. Ezek. viii. 14). It is not certain to what deities the small shrines were erected which were to be found in every street and at the head of every way (xvi. 24, 25). Jer. xi. 13 appears to call them altars to the shame or Baal, though it might be inferred from Ezek. xvi. 23 that they were dedicated to deities not native to Canaan. Besides this, however, both prophets stigmatise with the same odious name the whole service at the rural altars, on the high hills and under the evergreen trees, with its accessories of images, sun-pillars, and *asherim* (vi. 6; Jer. ii. 20, iii. 2, 6). It is not the mere localities nor the number of the altars that arouses their aversion; it is the nature of the worship and its evil memories (Hos. iv. 13, 14; Am. ii. 7), for Ezekiel regards the rural shrines as a survival of

Canaanitish paganism (xx. 27, 28). The images or block-gods (vi. 4) standing in these shrines were probably in many instances figures of Jehovah, for since the verdict of Hosea on the calf-image (viii. 6), "The workman made it and it is no God," little if any distinction was drawn between the images which did, and did not, represent the God of Israel (Is. ii. 8, xvii. 8, xxx. 22). Both prophets name these objects of worship "abominations," and represent them as being placed in the house of the Lord to defile it (Jer. vii. 30, xix. 4; Ezek. viii. 3 *seq.*), and as polluting the land (Jer. xvi. 18). Since Hosea foreign alliances had been stigmatised as "hiring lovers" (Hos. viii. 9, 10), and both the later prophets adopt the phraseology (xvi. 37, xxiii. 9, 22; Jer. xxx. 14; cf. Lam. i. 19). From the earliest times the prophets regard these alliances as due to a false conception of the nature of the kingdom of the Lord, and as evidence of mistrust in Jehovah (Is. vii. 9, x. 20, 21, xxx. 15, xxxi. 1); and, naturally, they were opposed to them for another reason, because the customs and idolatries of the foreign nations followed in their train (Is. ii. 6, cf. on xvi. 23 *seq.*; initial note to xxiii., and final note to xvi.).

4. In other details the two prophets are in harmony: they both reprobate the "bloodshed" of which Jerusalem is guilty. This "blood" was partly judicial murders (ix. 9, xxii. 6; Jer. vii. 6, xxii. 3), partly that shed in partizan conflicts within the city (xi. 7), but especially the child sacrifices of later days (xvi. 20, 36, xx. 26; Jer. vii. 31, xxxii. 35, cf. notes on xvi. 20, xx. 25). Jerusalem is "the bloody city" (xxiv. 6, cf. xxii. 3, 4, &c.); she has shamelessly set her blood upon the bare rock instead of pouring it upon the ground and covering it with dust; and it cries for vengeance (xxiv. 7; Job xvi. 18). But both prophets enter into greater details regarding the sins of the people than earlier prophets were wont to do, though Jeremiah adheres more to the ancient custom of denouncing civil wrongs (vii. 5 *seq.*, xxii. 1—5), while Ezekiel descends lower and exposes the social abominations of his day (ch. xviii., xxii., xxiii., cf. Jer. ix. 2—9). In these descriptions (e.g. xxii. 1—13) he shews affinities with

some parts of the Law, particularly with the code of laws preserved in Lev. xvii.—xxvi.[1], and reveals how deeply the taint of
Canaanitish impurity had infected the moral life of Israel, though
it may not be easy to say whether what he describes be a recent
outbreak of immorality due to the decaying vigour of the national
life and the moral paralysis rapidly advancing to its heart, or
whether the conscience of the teachers of Israel was only now
awakening to the enormity of vices that had long been prevalent.   On the prophet's moral ideal compared with others cf.
on xviii. 9.

5.   The sin of Israel is universal, infecting all classes, the
royal house, the priests, the prophets, and the people of the land
(xxii. 23—31).   The time for intercession has gone by ; the sword
of the Lord is whetted for the slaughter (xxi.) ; Jerusalem, the
rusted caldron, must be set upon the fire that its contents may
be seethed, and that its brass may glow and its rust be molten
away (xxiv.).   When the catastrophe came, verifying the prophet's
anticipations, his mouth was opened.   The people perceived
that the view taken of their history by their prophetic teachers,
from Amos downwards, was just, and that they were true interpreters of the mind of their God.   So the old era was closed.
The prophet had now to inaugurate the new.

6.   Like all other prophets Ezekiel, though he sees the destruction of the state to be necessary, believes in its restitution.
And this restitution will be the operation of Jehovah.   A complete section of his prophecies (xxxiii.—xxxvii.) is devoted to
this future, in which all its details are set forth ; but even in
the earlier part of his book many allusions to it occur.   As
early as ch. xi. the exiles are consoled with the promise: "I
will gather you from the peoples...and I will give you the land
of Israel....And I will put a new spirit within you,...and they
shall be my people, and I will be their God" (xi. 17—20).   And
in xvi. 60 a new and everlasting covenant is promised to

---

[1] [Frequently called "The Law of Holiness."   See Chapman's
Comm. on *Leviticus* in this series, pp. 179 *seq.*]

Jerusalem, under which she shall not only be restored herself, but receive her sisters Samaria and Sodom for daughters.

7. As in other prophets these prophecies of restitution assume a Messianic form, a universal kingdom being promised to the house of David: "I will also take of the lofty top of the cedar...in the mountain of the height of Israel will I plant it; and under it shall dwell all fowl of every wing" (xvii. 22—24). In xxi. 27 the Messiah is alluded to in the words "until he come whose right it is" (the ref. in xxix. 21 is more general, to the restoration of Israel). The passages xxxiv. 23 *seq.*, and xxxvii. 24 *seq.* are even more explicit. In the restitution the two kingdoms shall be reunited, with one shepherd over the two peoples, even the Lord's servant David (Am. ix. 11; Hos. iii. 5; Jer. xxxiii. 15). David shall be their prince for ever (xxxvii. 24, 25; Is. ix. 7). In these passages "prince" and "king," are used without distinction, and as the Messianic king is called "David" it is probable (Jer. xxiii. 5—8) that there is allusion to the Davidic house, though "David" might mean one in the spirit and power of David (cf. on xxxiv. 23, xxxvii. 25). In all these passages Ezekiel's representations are quite parallel to those of other prophets. In ch. xl. *seq.* the "prince" seems to play a more subordinate *rôle*, though there his functions in the worship of the restored community are specially referred to. Chs. xxxiii.—xxxvii. describe the reconstitution of the kingdom on all its sides: the culmination of the monarchy in the Messiah (xxxiv.); the recovery of the land and its transfiguration (xxxv., xxxvi.); the regeneration of the people, with the redemptive principles which it illustrates, such as will leave eternal impressions on the people's mind (xxxvi.); and the re-awakening of the dead nation into life and the union of all the disjointed members of the north and of the south into one living subject again, as seen in the grandiose vision of the dry bones (xxxvii.).

8. The conditions on man's part of entering this new kingdom appear to be stated in such passages as xviii. and xxxiii. The object of the prophet here is scarcely to vindicate the strict retributive righteousness of God or to shew how this

righteousness operates at all times.   The passages refer more to
the future than to the present, more to how God is about to deal
with men than to how He has dealt with them; and there is
a certain ideal element in the delineation, as there is in all
prophetic references to the coming kingdom of the Lord.   Of
course the general principle is sometimes stated that the
righteous will be spared and the wicked perish (ix.), though
in other places the judgement is represented as sweeping away
all indiscriminately (xx. 45 *seq.*); and ch. xiv. 12 *seq.* depends
on Jer. xv. 1 *seq.*, and is meant to shew that the wicked will
no longer be spared for the sake of the righteous rather than
to exemplify the strict retributive righteousness of God.

9.   That the reference in these chapters is to the future, a
future somewhat indefinite and ideal, is probable both from the
parallel passage in Jeremiah and from the prophet's own
language.   It is in the ideal times of Israel restored that the
proverb, "The fathers have eaten sour grapes, and the children's
teeth are set on edge," shall no more have currency (Jer. xxxi.
27 *seq.*); and Ezekiel's language is similar, "As I live, saith the
Lord GOD, it shall no longer be permitted to you to use this
proverb in Israel" (xviii. 3).   The prophet stands before a new
age, and it is its principles that he reveals.   His purpose is practical, to meet the conditions of the people's mind, and to awaken
them to a new moral activity, in preparation for the sifting
and crisis that shall try every individual mind (xxxiii. 1—6).
His principles do but form the background to his exhortation to
repentance.   He attaches them to two expressions which he
had heard from the mouths of the people: "The fathers have
eaten sour grapes, and the children's teeth are set on edge"
(xviii. 2), and, "our iniquities are upon us, and we pine away in
them; how then should we live?" (xxxiii. 10).   To the one, which
means that men are inexorably involved in the sins of their
people or forefathers, he opposes the principle that every individual mind stands in immediate relation to God, and none shall
perish for the sins of another, the soul that sinneth shall die;
and to the other, which means that the evil past of life is

irremediable, he opposes the principle that God has no pleasure in the death of the sinner, there is place for repentance. The last principle is developed with a certain theoretical completeness, which means no more, however, than that man has moral freedom to do good or evil, that he who is righteous may become a sinner, and that the sinner may turn from his evil, and that men will be judged not according to that which they have been but according to that which they are. The real point upon which the prophet's mind is operating is the spiritual relation of the individual mind to God : but like others he may not be able to keep this distinct from the external condition of the person, or as he calls it "life" or "death." At the same time the future and ideal time to which he applies his principles exonerates him from the charge of teaching a doctrine false to everyday experience (cf. notes on xviii. and xxxiii.).

10. This emancipation of the individual soul, whether from a doom inherited from a former generation or from one entailed on it by its own evil past, was perhaps the greatest contribution made by Ezekiel to the religious life and thought of the time[1]. He probably reached his individualism by reflection on such events as the downfall of the state, leaving now no place for religion except in the individual mind, and on the sentiments which he heard expressed by men around him. His contemporary Jeremiah reached the same truth from another direction, from his own experience of the *inwardness* of the relation of God to men. The very nature of this relation required that the religious subject should be the individual mind[2].

[1] ["The doctrine of individual responsibility had been taught by Jeremiah (Jer. xxxi. 29, 30), but Ezekiel repeats it with an emphasis which is peculiarly his own" (Kirkpatrick, *Doctrine of the Prophets*, p. 345). Nevertheless, the national, as opposed to the individual attitude of his countrymen towards God, retained its prominence in his teaching. It is the nation which is arraigned for its idolatries (chs. vi., xxiii.). It is the nation which is the subject of chs. xl.—xlviii.]

[2] ["Jeremia ist Gefühlsmensch, Hezekiel Verstandesmensch," Duhm, *Die Theologie der Propheten*, p. 252.]

11. Yet, as in the case of other prophets, Ezekiel no sooner states the conditions on man's part of entering the new kingdom than he seems to desert them. Jeremiah, after demanding of the people a radical reformation (iv. 3), pauses to ask himself, Can the Ethiopian change his skin? (xiii. 23) and his hope at last is in a Divine operation: "I will put my law in their inward parts ...and their sin will I remember no more" (xxxi. 31—34). The transition in Ezekiel from ch. xxxiii. to ch. xxxvi. is similar. It was the hope of the prophets that the fires of the exile would purify the people, and that they would come out as silver tried in the furnace. They are constrained to confess that this hope has been disappointed: Israel will be saved, but only by Jehovah working for His name's sake (Is. xliii. 25, xlviii. 10, 11). Ezekiel perhaps hardly saw so much of the exile as to reason in this way, but his conclusion in xxxvi. 24—29 is the same. This remarkable passage has no parallel in the Old Testament, and reads like a fragment of a Pauline epistle (final note on xxxvi.). The doctrine of the spirit of God receives fuller development in it than anywhere else in the Old Testament. Only one thing is wanting to complete this doctrine on its practical side, a statement of the means which the Spirit shall use in His operations (John xvi. 14). Of singular beauty are the prophet's references to the eternal impressions which God's goodness in their history will leave on the mind of His people (xxxvi. 31, 32, xvi. 61, 63, xx. 42—44, xxxix. 26 *seq*.). Like that of Hosea and others Ezekiel's eschatology occupies itself chiefly with the destinies of Israel; the place of the nations in the regenerated world is not dwelt upon. How much is implied in the oft-repeated words, "They shall know that I am Jehovah," is not clear. Profounder conceptions of the relations of Jehovah to the nations are at least touched upon in ch. xvi. (see final notes); and in one passage it is foretold that the nations will seek refuge under the rule of the Messiah (ch. xvii. 23).

12. The final section (xl. *seq*.) is an ideal picture of the perfection and eternal peace of Israel restored. It has been remarked that in these chapters Ezekiel supplies a programme for

the subsequent development of Judaism. It is possible that a subsequent generation imposed his ideal of Israel's final state upon the historical restoration that took place under Zerubbabel and under Ezra. But such a thing was not the prophet's idea, and never came into his mind. In his view Israel's development reaches its culmination in the restoration itself, and the regeneration of the people accompanying it (cf. Is. lx.). The ritual observances which he enjoins are not the "statutes of life" elsewhere spoken of. These statutes are the moral requirements of the decalogue, practically carried out so as to exclude idolatry and the impurities often referred to (ch. xxii.); and the fulfilment of these statutes is ensured by the moral regeneration wrought by God upon the people (xi. 18—20, xvi. 60—63, xxxvi. 25 *seq*.: cf. initial note to xl. *seq*.).

13. The points of contact between Ezekiel and the ritual Law have raised many interesting though complicated questions of criticism, upon which this is not the place to enter. The questions mainly relate to the age of the Law in its present written form as this has to be determined by the antiquity of some of the practices contained in it, e.g. the Day of Atonement (Lev. xvi., cf. Ezek. xlv. 18—20), the distinction of Priests and Levites within the tribe of Levi (Ezek. xliv., cf. Deut. xviii. 1, 6—8; 2 Kgs xxiii. 8, 9), and the High-priesthood (see on xliv. 22). Inferences from comparison of Ezekiel with the Law have to be drawn with caution, for it is evident that the prophet handles with freedom institutions certainly older than his own time. The feast of Weeks (Exod. xxiii. 16, xxxiv. 22) forms no element in his calendar; the law of the offering of the firstlings of the flock is dispensed with by him; there is no gilding in his Temple, and no wine in his sacrificial libations. His reconstruction of the courts of the Temple is altogether new: and so is his provision in the "oblation" of land for the maintenance of priests, Levites, and prince. On any hypothesis of priority the differences in details between him and the Law may be easiest explained by supposing that, while the sacrifices in general and the ideas which they expressed were fixed and current, the

particulars, such as the kind of victims and the number of them, the precise quantity of meal, oil, and the like, were held non-essential and alterable when a change would better express the idea. The prince is left to regulate some of these things at his own discretion (xlvi. 7, 11). The affinities of Ezekiel with the small code, Lev. xvii.—xxvi., are remarkable both in subject and in some parts in phraseology (Lev. xxvi.). The differences, however, are too important to admit the view that he is the author of this code; and the question whether he had some parts of it at least before him in a written form is a very complicated one[1].

14. Of more interest than the question, What amount of the Law was known to Ezekiel in writing? is the other, How much of it was familiar to him in practice? It is evident that the ritual as it appears in his book had long been a matter of consuetudinary law. He is familiar not only with burnt, peace, and meal offerings, but with sin and trespass[2] offerings. All these are spoken of as things customary and well understood (xlii. 13, xliv. 29—31); even the praxis of the trespass offering is so much a thing familiar that no rules are laid down in regard to it (xlvi. 20). The sin and trespass offerings are little if at all alluded to in the ancient extra-ritual literature, but the argument from silence is a precarious one, for Ezekiel himself, when not precise, uses the comprehensive phraseology "burnt offerings and peace offerings" (xliii. 27). The people's dues to the priests are also so much customary that no rules are needful to regulate them (xliv. 30). Ezekiel is no more a "legislator" than he is the founder of the Temple.

15. The affinities in language between Ezekiel and the ritual law are scarcely literary; they arise from the fact that the writers move among the same class of conceptions, and, in Ezekiel's case at least, from the fact that these conceptions had long ago

---

[1] [For a comparison of the "small code" ("Law of Holiness") with Ezekiel see Chapman's *Intr. to Pent.* in this series, pp. 240—255, and for the question of priority, his Comm. on *Leviticus*, Appendix III.]

[2] *i.e.* guilt-offerings.

created for themselves a distinct phraseology. The question of interest is, how ancient the conceptions are. In the literature outside the Law little light is cast on the history of the priesthood or ritual or on the class of conceptions prevailing in priestly circles. The prophets, while furnishing abundant evidence of the existence of a sumptuous ritual, shew little sympathy for it, and reveal more the popular perversion of priestly conceptions than their legitimate meaning. Sparse as historical allusions are, they suffice to shew the antiquity of the conceptions, e.g. the sacredness of blood (1 Sam. xiv. 33), the distinctions of clean and unclean (1 Sam. xxi. 4), and the atoning virtue of sacrifice (1 Sam. iii. 14, xxvi. 19). It is evident that two streams of thought, the prophetic and the priestly, both issuing from a fountain as high up as the very origin of the nation, ran side by side down the whole history of the people. In the one Jehovah is a moral ruler, a righteous king and judge, who punishes iniquity judicially or forgives sins freely of His mercy. In the other He is a Person dwelling among His people in a house, a holy Being or nature, sensitive to every uncleanness in all that is near Him, and requiring its removal by lustrations and atonement. Those cherishing the latter circle of conceptions might be as zealous for the LORD of hosts as the prophets. And the developments of the national history would extend their conceptions and lead to the amplification of practices embodying them just as they extended the conceptions of the prophets. A growth of priestly ideas is quite as probable as a growth of prophetic ideas. That the streams ran apart is no evidence that they were not equally ancient and always contemporaneous, for we see Jeremiah and Ezekiel both flourishing in one age. At one point in the history the prophetic stream was swelled by an inflow from the priestly, as is seen in Deuteronomy, and from the Restoration downwards both streams appear to coalesce.

CHAPTER V

BIBLIOGRAPHY, ETC.

AMONG the older Commentaries referred to in the original edition of this work (1892) are Hävernick, 1843; Hitzig, 1847; Fairbairn, 1851; Henderson, 1855; Hengstenberg, 1867; Ewald 1868 (Eng. Tr., Vol. IV. 1880), C. G. Keil, 1868 (Eng. Tr. 1876) and 1882; Reuss, 1876; Currey, *Sp. Comm.*, Vol. VI. 1876; Smend, 1880; also Boettcher, *Proben Alttest. Schrifterklärung*, 1833, and *Aehrenlese*, Vol. II. 1864. These, however, have been to a large extent superseded by later works.

Besides the valuable discussions in Driver, *Introduction to the Literature of the Old Testament* (9th ed. 1913), and in Kuenen, *Onderzoek*, II. (1889), the following are contributions to the exposition of Ezekiel:—Duhm, *Die Theologie der Propheten*, 1875; H. Klostermann, *Studien u. Kritiken*, 1877; Cornill, *Der Prophet Ezechiel*, 1882, and *Das Buch des Propheten Ezechiel*, 1886, the latter containing a (somewhat arbitrary) reconstruction of the text on the basis of the Septuagint (his work has recently been carried further by O. Jahn); Kühn, *Ezechiel's Gesicht vom Tempel*, 1882; Plumptre, "Ezekiel: an Ideal Biography," *Expositor*, 1884; Valeton, *Viertal Voorlezingen* (third lecture), 1886; Arndt, *Die Stellung Ezechiel's*, 1886; Meulenbelt, *De Prediking van den Profeet Ezechiel*, 1888; Gautier, *La Mission du Prophète Ezéchiel*, 1891. To these we may add Horst, *Leviticus xvii.—xxvi. und Hezekiel*, 1881 (critical); Kuenen in *Modern Review*, Oct. 1884, pp. 617—640.

Later commentaries are: C. von Orelli in Strack and Zöckler's *Kgf. Kommentar*, 2nd ed. 1896; A. Bertholet, *Das Buch Hesekiel*, in Marti's *Kurzer Hand-Commentar zum A. T.*, 1897[1]; C. H. Toy's Commentary, with important notes on points of archaeology, and good illustrations, 1899; the same writer's

---

[1] See also his *Hesekiel's Verfassungsentwurf*, or *Ezekiel's Sketch of Israel's Theocratic Constitution* (chs. xl.—xlviii.), 1896.

careful but freely emended edition of the Hebrew text in Haupt's *Polychrome Old Testament*, in the same year; R. Kraetzschmar, in Nowack's *Hand-kommentar zum A. T.*, 1900; H. A. Redpath, in the *Westminster Commentaries Series*, 1907; W. R. Lofthouse, *Century Bible Series*, 1909.

Articles by Skinner in Hastings' *Dictionary of the Bible*, by Toy in the *Encyclopædia Biblica*, and by Black in *Encyclopædia Britannica*, 9th ed., form important contributions in the shape of "Introduction."

Other useful works dealing with the subject are Schrader, *Die Keilinschriften und das Alte Testament*[1] (1883) (tr. by White-house); Kirkpatrick, *Doctrine of the Prophets*, 3rd ed., 1902; Buchanan Blake, *How to read the Prophets*, Part IV. (Ezekiel), 1894: Kent, *The Sermons, Epistles, and Apocalypses of Israel's Prophets*, 1910; D. H. Müller, *Ezechiel-Studien*, 1894; A. B. Davidson, *Theology of the O.T.*, 1904; F. H. Woods and F. E. Powell, *Hebrew Prophets for English Readers* (containing the R.V. with short notes), 1909–12.

---

[1] The 3rd ed. entirely rearranged by Zimmern and Winckler (1903) is referred to as KAT.[3]

Abbreviations used in this Volume

O.T.　Old Testament.

N.T.　New Testament.

Heb. or M.T.　The original Hebrew text as edited by the Massoretes or Jewish scholars from about the 6th to the 10th century A.D.

LXX. or Sept.　The translation of the Old Testament into Greek ; traditionally said to have been made by seventy persons, but really made gradually, wholly or mostly during the 3rd and 2nd centuries B.C.

Vulg.　The Latin translation of the Bible made by St Jerome (latter part of the 4th and beginning of the 5th century A.D.).

Syr.　The Syriac translation known as the Peshiṭṭo.

A.V.　The Authorised Version (A.D. 1611).

R.V.　The Revised Version (O.T., A.D. 1885 ; N.T., 1881).

E.VV.　The Authorised and Revised Versions

SBOT.　(Haupt's) *Sacred Books of the Old Testament*.

C.B.　Cambridge Bible for Schools and Colleges.

Ber.　Bertholet ⎫
Cor.　Cornill　｜
Dill.　Dillmann　｜
Ew.　Ewald　｝ *Commentaries.*
Kr.　Kraetzschmar　｜
Lofth.　Lofthouse　｜
Redp.　Redpath ⎭

LOT.　Driver, *Introduction to the Literature of the Old Testament* (9th ed., 1913).

Oxf. Lex.　*Hebrew and English Lexicon of the Old Testament*, by Brown, Driver, and Briggs.　Oxford, 1906.

HDB.　Hastings' *Dictionary of the Bible.*

Encycl. Bibl.　*Encyclopædia Biblica.*

J. Th. S.　*Journal of Theological Studies.*

c.　(*circa*) *about.*

Chronological Table.

THE BOOK OF THE PROPHET
EZEKIEL

NOW it came to pass in the thirtieth year, in the fourth **1**
month, in the fifth *day* of the month, as I was among

First Division, Ch. I.—XXIV., Prophecies of the
Destruction of the Kingdom.

First Section.   Ch. I.—III. 21.

THE section consists of two divisions : First, Ch. I. inaugural vision of
Jehovah ; second, Ch. II.—III. 21, the various steps by which Jehovah,
thus seen, initiated the prophet into his work.

The inaugural vision Ch. i. has two parts ; (1) *vv.* 1—3, definition of
the time and place of the appearance of the vision of God ; and (2) *vv.* 4
—28, description of the vision itself, with its influence upon the prophet.
1—3.   The manifestation of Jehovah was made to the prophet in the
thirtieth year, in the fourth month, on the fifth day of the month, and
in the midst of the captives by the river Chebar (*v.* 1) ; or, it was on
the fifth day of the month, in the fifth year of the captivity of king
Jehoiachin, in the land of the Chaldeans, by the river Chebar (*vv.* 2, 3).

Vv. 1—3 appear to contain two superscriptions, one in *v.* 1, in which
the prophet speaks in the first person, and which is syntactically connected with *v.* 4 *seq.*; and one in *vv.* 2, 3, in which the prophet is
spoken of, his name and descent and priestly rank are stated, and the
thirtieth year of *v.* 1 is identified with the fifth year of the captivity of
Jehoiachin, [which coincides with the year B.C. 592, the first siege
of Jerusalem and the deportation of that king being dated B.C. 597.]
The language in *v.* 1 is precisely similar to almost all the other specifica-
tions of time in the Book, e.g. viii. 1, xx. 1, xxiv. 1, xxvi. 1, xxix. 1,
17, xxx. 20, xxxi. 1, xxxii. 1, 17, xxxiii. 21, xl. 1.   In two cases the
phrase " and it came to pass " is not used (xxix. 1, xl. 1).   If the verse
stood alone the natural inference from the other dates would be that
the year was the thirtieth of Jehoiachin's captivity, as in other cases, or
as it is put in two instances " our captivity " (xxxiii. 21, xl. 1).   The
latest date mentioned in the Book is the 27th year of the captivity (xxx. 17),

the ¹captives by the river Chebar, that. the heavens were

¹ Heb. *captivity.*

and it has been conjectured that *v.* 1 refers to another prophecy or vision three years later, and that *vv.* 2, 3, form the real heading. Against this, however, is (1) that the specification of circumstances and place in *v.* 1 is natural in an introductory statement, but not to be expected in any other. In point of fact it nowhere occurs after the introductory visions by which the prophet received his commission, except in references to these visions (x. 15, 20, 22, xliii. 3). And (2) the words "which was the fifth year" *v.* 2 evidently refer to some year already mentioned, which is now said to coincide with the fifth of Jehoiachin's captivity. The two parts of the superscription are awkwardly connected. [It is probable that *vv.* 2, 3 are a gloss added by an editor to elucidate *v.* 1, or an alternative title taken from another recension of the Book.]

What, however, is the meaning of "the thirtieth year" in *v.* 1? It might refer to some event or era from which Ezekiel reckoned. (1) As such an event the discovery of the Book of the Law and Josiah's consequent reformation of worship (621 B.C.) already occurred to the author of the Targum. Between this date and 592, the fifth year of Jehoiachin's captivity, there is a period of 29 years. There is, however, no other instance of such a kind of reckoning, nor any evidence that the discovery in Josiah's eighteenth year was ever regarded as an era. (2) That the prophet should refer to a Babylonian era is quite possible, seeing he lived in Babylonia. But no such era has been discovered. The beginning of the reign of Nabopolassar, when Babylon became independent of Assyria, is usually dated in 625 ; and the fifth year of Jehoiachin's captivity would be the thirty-third year of such an era. [(3) According to Kr., following Duhm, "the thirtieth year" is the attempt of an editor to reconcile Jeremiah's "seventy years" of exile (xxv. 11) with Ezekiel's "forty" (iv. 6) by making the latter's prophecies commence in the thirtieth year of the longer period.] (4) It is possible that the prophet might refer to the year of his own age¹. There is not much probability in the suggestion (Klostermann, *Stud. u. Krit.* 1877) that *v.* 1 is a fragment of a longer passage in which the prophet's history before his call was narrated. In such a case reference to the thirtieth year of his age would certainly lose its strangeness, but such a history would be without example, as a prophet's life always opens with his call. [No certain explanation of the expression is forthcoming, but perhaps the conjecture numbered (4), although unsupported by any parallel, is the best.]

1. *the river Chebar*] Not to be identified with the Habor (2 Kgs xvii. 6) which falls into the Euphrates at Circesium. [The river here meant must have been much further to the S., as being "in the land of the Chaldeans" (*v.* 3). The name seems to denote *the Great River*, or "the Grand Canal." The word *Kabaru* occurs twice, apparently not as a

[¹ Cf. Num. iv. 3 as to the Levites.]

opened, and I saw visions of God.   In the fifth *day* of the 2
month, which was the fifth year of king Jehoiachin's captivity,
the word of the LORD came expressly unto Ezekiel the 3
priest, the son of Buzi, in the land of the Chaldeans by
the river Chebar; and the hand of the LORD was there
upon him.   And I looked, and, behold, a stormy wind 4

proper name, but as an adjective, meaning great, in inscriptions found at
the ancient Nippur, S. of Babylon, and bearing a date corresponding to
B.C. 424.   We are perhaps to identify the river with the present *Shat
en-Nil*, the large navigable canal (about 120 feet wide) which divides
the mounds of Nippur into two approximately even halves" (Haupt,
SBOT. ad loc.; see also Kr. *ad loc.*).]

heavens were opened]   In his trance the prophet saw the heavens
opened (*v.* 3).

visions of God] perhaps mean visions given by God, or visions in
which God was seen.   The expression is probably to be taken somewhat generally, as meaning heavenly or divine visions (viii. 3).

2. *fifth year...captivity*]   Jehoiachin, son of Jehoiakim and grand-
son of Josiah, reigned only three months and ten days.   He is also
styled Jeconiah or Coniah, Jer. xxii. 24 *seq.*, xxiv. 1, xxvii. 20; 1 Chr.
iii. 16.   His captivity dates B.C. 597, and Ezekiel's call 592, six years
before the fall of Jerusalem.

3. *came expressly*]   Omit *expressly*.   The name Ezekiel [arising from
the Latinized form (*Ezechiel*) of the Greek Ἰεζεκιήλ,] probably means
"God is strong."   The Hebrew is יְחֶזְקֵאל (*Yĕhezk'ēl*).   Nothing
further is known of Ezekiel or of his father Buzi.   The designation
"priest" appears to apply to Ezekiel, not to his father.   As the prophet
excludes all Levites from priestly office except the "sons (seed) of Zadok"
(xl. 46, xliii. 19, xliv. 15, 16), it may be inferred that he belonged himself to this family.   It appears from Jer. xxix. 1 *seq.* that among the
captives carried away with Jehoiachin were both priests and prophets.

hand of the LORD, &c.]   i.e. the Divine power laid hold of him and
threw him into a state of prophetic ecstasy or something akin to it.
[The expression is frequent in this Book (iii. 14, 22, viii. 1, xxxiii. 22,
xxxvii. 1, xl. 1).]

I. **4—28.** THE THEOPHANY, OR, VISION OF GOD.

This is described first generally, as a stormy wind and great cloud
coming from the North, with a luminous splendour around it, due to a
fire sending out continuous flashes within it (*v.* 4).

Secondly, more particularly that is described which appeared within
the storm-cloud (*vv.* 5—28).   This was the chariot of God, in which He
rode, descending to the earth and moving from one place to another
(cf. ch. x.).   This chariot is represented as foursided.   On each of the
four sides was a living creature of human shape, with outstretched
wings.   Also on each of the four sides, beside each of the living

came out of the north, a great cloud, with a fire ¹infolding

¹ Or, *flashing continually*

creatures, there was a wheel.   The living creatures are not represented as having any platform or basement under them on which they stand ; the wheels are usually said to be " beside " them, in ch. x. 2 " under " them. The wheels are to be conceived as at right angles to each of the four sides of the chariot, presenting their rims to the four points of the compass.

Above the heads of the four living creatures, or over their wings when horizontally expanded, was a firmament of crystal.   Above the firmament was the appearance of a throne, and upon the throne was the appearance of one like fire, encircled with a glory which was like the rainbow in the day of rain.

4.   God appears in cloud and storm: clouds and darkness are round about Him, Exod. ix. 24 ; 1 Kgs xix. 11 ; Job xxxviii. 1 ; Ps. l. 3.

out of the north]   In Ps. xxix. the theophany also comes from the north, and passes southward to the desert.   The idea of the prophet can hardly be that the "place" or abode of God, from which He now comes, is situated in the northern part of the earth, for he saw "the heavens opened" (*v.* 1).   In other places he refers to Eden, the garden of God (xxviii. 13, xxxi. 8, 9), for which he appears also to use the name "mount of God" (xxviii. 14, 16), though without indicating any locality for it, but it would be very precarious to bring these passages into any connexion with the present one.   When Jehovah leaves the city (ch. xi. 23) His glory passes out by the East gate and stands over the "mountain which is on the East side of the city," the mount of Olives ; and when He returns to the new temple He enters by the same East gate, which therefore is to remain for ever shut (xliii. 2, xliv. 2).   In Is. xiv. 13 the King of Babylon resolves to seat himself in the mount of assembly, in the recesses of the north, above the stars of God ; but whatever this passage means, it has no reference to the God of Israel.   On the other hand the idea that the theophany appears to come from the north because the north was the region from which the enemies of Israel, the instruments of God's vengeance, were to advance, is altogether to be rejected.   The theophany here is not a manifestation of God specially in the character of an avenger or judge ; He does not appear to the prophet as inflamed with anger.   The theophany no doubt expresses the prophet's conception of God, but it is his conception of God as He is in Himself and in His nature, not as He is in preparation for any signal act of judgement.   This is conclusively shewn by the fact that the three theophanies, viz. here, and in chs. viii.—xi., and in ch. xliii., are all identical, according to the statement of the prophet : "and it was according to the appearance of the vision which I saw...when I (read *he*) came to destroy the city ; and the visions were like the vision I saw by the river Chebar " (xliii. 3).

a fire infolding itself]   better, as marg. *flashing continually*.   The expression is suggested by the zigzag, chain-like flash of the lightning.

itself, and a brightness round about it, and out of the midst
thereof ¹as the colour of ²amber, out of the midst of the fire.
And out of the midst thereof came the likeness of four 5
living creatures.   And this was their appearance ; they had

¹ Or, *as amber to look upon*   ² Or, *electrum*

colour of amber] Or, as marg. *as amber to look upon*.   The word
rendered "amber" is of uncertain meaning.   [The Heb. is *ḥashmal*,
corresponding to the Assyr. *esmaru*, the name of a costly glittering sub-
stance.   R. Jehudah (†c. A.D. 210) fancifully interpreted the four
consonants of which the name is composed as standing for three Heb.
words, which mean "living creatures who speak."]   The LXX. render
elektron, which probably was some very brilliant metal, usually supposed to be an amalgam of gold and silver.

out of the midst of the fire].   Probably the words are a marginal gloss
referring the expression "out of the midst thereof" to the fire, while in
fact it refers to the whole whirlwind and cloud.

I. 5—14. THE FOUR LIVING CREATURES.

When the prophet looked more narrowly the general splendour
resolved itself into definite forms.   These are described as having in
general the human form ; they were erect, and had apparently two feet
(*vv*. 5, 7) ; they had four faces, one looking each way ; the faces of a
man, a lion, an ox, and an eagle (*v*. 10).   The man's face was the front
face of each, and met the eye of the beholder who looked at the chariot
on any of its four sides, and thus when the chariot moved in any
direction the creature on that side had the appearance of an advancing
man.   The living creatures had each four wings, one pair being used in
flight, and the other pair covering the body (*vv*. 6, 11).   The two pairs
of wings were probably at right angles to one another, one pair belonging
to the front and back sides and the other pair to the two lateral sides,
for it is said that they had human hands under their wings on their four
sides (*v*. 8).   They had thus four hands or arms like those of men.
Their feet, that is, their limbs, were straight like those of men, but their
feet proper were round like those of a calf (*v*. 7).   When in motion each
creature expanded one pair of wings, that is the wings on the right and
left of the front face ; the expanded wings of the four thus formed a
square, the tips of the wings of each creature touching those of two of
its fellows on the right and on the left (*v*. 11).   When the living
creatures stood still their wings dropped (*v*. 24).   [The connexion of
the "living creatures" with the shapes evolved in Assyrian mythology
is at the most but slight.   Lofthouse (*Cent. Bible*) points out that Dante
in his *Purgatorio* XXXI. makes some use of Ezekiel's description.]

5.   *out of the midst thereof*]   Most naturally, out of the midst of the
whole phenomenon of the tempestuous fiery cloud, though it might be
out of that splendour which was like electrum.   Four "living creatures,"
as Rev. iv. 6 *seq*.

6 the likeness of a man.　And every one had four faces, and
7 every one of them had four wings.　And their feet were
straight feet; and the sole of their feet was like the sole of
a calf's foot: and they sparkled like the colour of burnished
8 brass.　And they had the hands of a man under their wings
on their four sides: and they four had their faces and their
9 wings *thus*; their wings were joined one to another; they
turned not when they went; they went every one straight
10 forward.　As for the likeness of their faces, they had the
face of a man; and they four had the face of a lion on the
right side; and they four had the face of an ox on the left
11 side; they four had also the face of an eagle. [1] And their faces

[1] Or, *And* thus were *their faces; and their wings were &c.*

6.　*had four faces*]　These were a man's in front of each, an eagle's
opposite to this at the back of each; a lion's on the right hand of each,
and the face of an ox on the left of each.　Thus four different faces
were presented in each direction, so that in whatever direction the whole
moved, while a man's face was presented first, those of a lion, an ox, and
an eagle were also encountered.　In this view the four living creatures
made up one creature, and each of the four was in small that which the
four were when combined.

7.　*straight feet*]　"Feet" here means limbs.　These appear to have
been two in number, though this is not expressly stated [1].　The foot
itself was round, or as much so as that of a calf.　The word "straight"
means without protuberance or knot such as a knee-joint would be.　The
living creature did not need to turn.

8.　Each living creature appears to have had four hands or arms, cf.
ch. x. 21.　The last words of *v.* 8 must be joined with *v.* 9.　The
meaning is that as each creature with his outstretched wings formed one
side of the square his wings touched or were joined to those of two
other creatures, one on his right and another on his left.　The words
"they turned not" refer to the faces.　For "and they four...when
they went" (*vv.* 8, 9) the LXX. has simply "and the faces of them four
turned not when they went."

10.　*the right side*]　viz. of the living creature, not of the beholder.
["The human face takes the lead; next to it stand the symbols of bodily
vigour and power, which are completed by the form of the eagle of far-
reaching vision and buoyant strength."　D. H. Müller, *Ezechiel-Studien*,
p. 13.]

11.　*And their faces and their wings were separate above*]　The rendering
of the A.V. Thus were *their faces* is retained in the mg.　But the
words are to be omitted (with LXX.); and "inwards" (*pĕnīmah*)

[1 Kr., however, holds that the conception of the chariot, as constructed to move
uniformly in all directions, requires that each living creature should have but one
foot, while this is also indicated by the sing. ("foot") in the Heb.]

and their wings were separate above; two *wings* of every one were joined one to another, and two covered their bodies. And they went every one straight forward: whither 12 the spirit was to go, they went; they turned not when they went. [1]As for the likeness of the living creatures, their 13 appearance was like burning coals of fire, like the appearance of torches; it went up and down among the living creatures: and the fire was bright, and out of the fire went forth

[1] The Sept. has, *And in the midst of the living creatures was an appearance &c.*

is to be read for "their faces" (*pĕnēhem*) with Wellh. and attached to *v.* 10—*the face of an eagle inwards*, i.e. towards the centre of the chariot. The same change is required ch. xl. 22, 26.

their wings were separate above] This was their appearance when in flight; each creature stretched out one pair of wings above, while the other pair covered its body. The wings being expanded horizontally would be nearly on a level with the head of the living creature, hence the "firmament" is said to be over the heads of the living creatures or over their expanded wings (*vv.* 22, 23). The next clause reads literally: *everyone* (of the living creatures) *had two wings joining everyone* (of the living creatures to the others). If the text be correct it states somewhat elliptically what is said with more precision in *v.* 23 (cf. *v.* 9), viz. that the tips of the expanded wings of one creature touched the tips of the wings of two other creatures, on his right and on his left. [That each had four wings accords with Ezekiel's conception of the chariot and all belonging to it as square; so in the case of the restored temple and its courts.]

12. *went...straight forward*] i.e. in the direction to which the living creature's face was turned. The chariot had four sides facing the four quarters of the heavens; on each side of the chariot was a living creature whose principal face, the human, looked in the same direction as the side of the chariot on which it stood. Thus the whole, the chariot and living creatures, presented exactly the same front to each of the four directions, and there was no need to "turn." See what is said of the wheels, *v.* 15 *seq.*

whither the spirit was to go] The "spirit" is the active Divine principle or impulse acting as guide. It did not belong to the individual living creatures but to the whole manifestation composed of living creatures, wheels, and the like. [For Ezekiel's conception of "spirit" cf. iii. 12, 24, viii. 3, &c.]

13. There appears to be a good deal of corruption of the text. We should read with the LXX., as marg., **And in the midst of the living creatures was an appearance like**, &c. The whole phenomenon represents not only a chariot on which Jehovah rides, but also a throne on which He sits and a place where He abides. Hence as in Is. vi. there is an

14 lightning. And the living creatures ran and returned as the
15 appearance of a flash of lightning. Now as I beheld the
living creatures, behold one wheel upon the earth beside

altar with fire. With the idea of Isaiah, however, the prophet has
combined the other that coals of fire accompany the manifestation of
Jehovah (Ps. xviii. 13), and the altar fire gives out flashes like the
lightning. This again has suggested the combinations in Rev. vi. 9,
viii. 3—5[1].

14. The verse both in regard to terminology and construction is
untranslateable [and is evidently an insertion, arising from the mistaken
conception that the motion of the living creatures and of the fire in the
midst of them was not uniform, but irregular, like lightning flashes].
The word rendered "ran" has no existence, and that translated "flash
of lightning" is equally unknown. Attempts have been made to amend
the verse by substituting for "ran" a real word, "went out" (*yāzo* for
rāzo), and the ordinary word for "lightning" (*bārāk*) for the unknown
term so rendered (*bāzāk*).

I. 15—21. THE FOUR WHEELS.

The prophet saw four wheels beside the four living creatures, one
wheel beside each creature. The wheels touched the ground, and were
all alike, having the appearance of tarshish-stone. The construction
of each appeared as if a wheel were within a wheel, that is, each of the
four wheels looked like two wheels, cutting each other at right angles.
In this way each of the four wheels had a rim or circumference facing
each of the four directions, just as the living creature had a face looking
in each direction, so that toward whatever quarter the chariot moved
four wheels seemed to be running in that direction. Their felloes were
full of eyes. The movements of the wheels corresponded entirely with
those of the living creatures, they went, rose, or stood still according as
the living creatures did. The wheels were not inanimate, but part of
the living chariot of God; the "spirit" of the living creature was also
in the wheels.

15. *beheld the living creatures*] lit. *and I saw the living creatures
and behold*. LXX. reads, *and I saw and behold*—precisely as ch. viii. 2,
x. 1, 9.

[The "one wheel" is identified in later Jewish thought with Sandalphon, who in the Liturgy for the Feast of Tabernacles (see Hershon,

[1 "Like the appearance of torches" is very possibly a marginal gloss on "like
burning coals of fire," while "it went...living creatures" may also be a gloss (a view
to which the LXX. lends some support) intended to refer to the "burning coals of
fire," but subsequently inserted from the margin at a wrong place in the text. The
excision of the words "it went up and down among the living creatures" would
remove grammatical irregularity from the M.T. as it now stands, and further would
suit the description in x. 2, which assumes that the brightness in the midst of the
living creatures is not itself (as opposed to the flashes proceeding from it) in motion,
but stationary. Thus Kr. If we make these omissions, the *v.* will read "and in
the midst of the living creatures was an appearance like burning coals of fire, and
the fire was bright," &c.]

the living creatures, for each of the four faces thereof. The 16
appearance of the wheels and their work was like unto the
colour of a beryl: and they four had one likeness: and their
appearance and their work was as it were a wheel [1]within
a wheel. When they went, they went upon their four sides: 17
they turned not when they went. As for their [2]rings, they 18
were high and dreadful; and they four had their rings full
of eyes round about. And when the living creatures went, 19
the wheels went beside them: and when the living creatures
were lifted up from the earth, the wheels were lifted up.

[1] Heb. *in the midst of.*   [2] Or, *felloes*

A Talmudic Miscellany, p. 150, and cf. Longfellow, *Sandalphon*) is
spoken of as gathering in his hands the prayers of Israel, and then,
forming a wreath of them, he adjures it to ascend as an orb for the head
of the Supreme King of kings.]

for each of the four faces thereof] The general sense appears to be
that for each face of each living creature there was a wheel. The
appearance would be so if the wheel really seemed two wheels cutting
one another transversely. The position of the living creature was above
the wheel.

16. *the colour of a beryl*] Heb. *tarshish-stone*, apparently as obtained
from Tarshish, i.e. Tartessus in Spain [perhaps the yellow jasper (so
Petrie). See Driver (*C.B.*) on Exod. xxviii. 20]. "Colour" is lit.
gleam, sparkle. The words "and their work" in first clause, and "and
their appearance" in second clause are wanting in LXX.

wheel within a wheel] [See introd. note to the section, which agrees
with the general view of commentators[1].]

17. *upon*] Rather **toward.**

they turned not when they went] See *v.* 12.

18. *high and dreadful*] lit. *as for their rings* [mg. *felloes*], *there was
height to them and there was fear to them.* The word "fear," however,
nowhere means terribleness but always terror. The statement also that
the rings or felloes were high has little meaning. The text has probably
suffered some corruption. [We should (with LXX.) omit "as for their
rings" (which in the Heb. is suspiciously like the word, "height"), and
read, by a slight change in the original for "and dreadful," *and I saw
them.*]

full of eyes] The eye is the expression of life and intelligence (ch. x.
12 [cf. 2 Chr. xvi. 9; Zech. iv. 10; Rev. iv. 6). There was nothing
capricious or blind about their motion hither and thither (Gautier,
p. 109)].

19—21. The movement of the wheels corresponded with that of
the living creatures. They were animated by the same spirit as the

[1 Kr., however, holds that the four wheels were in contact with each other in
such a way as to enclose a rectangular space containing the burning coals.]

20 Whithersoever the spirit was to go, they went; thither was
the spirit to go: and the wheels were lifted up [1]beside them;
21 for the spirit [2]of the living creature was in the wheels. When
those went, these went; and when those stood, these stood;
and when those were lifted up from the earth, the wheels
were lifted up beside them: for the spirit of the living
22 creature was in the wheels. And over the head of the living
creature there was the likeness of a firmament, like the
colour of the terrible [3]crystal, stretched forth over their
23 heads above. And under the firmament were their wings

----

[1] Or, *over against*   [2] Or, *of life*   [3] Or, *ice*

creatures, and were part of the whole living phenomenon. In the Book
of Enoch [chs. lxi. 10, lxx. 7] "wheels" (Ophannim) are a class of
angels, named along with Seraphim and Cherubim. [The three verses
seem to have undergone expansion.]

20. *thither was the spirit to go*] i.e. the general spirit moving the
whole manifestation. The words are wanting in LXX., and are possibly
an accidental repetition of those in the beginning of the verse[1].

spirit of the living creature] The "living creature" is hardly the
complex being formed by the four living creatures; the four were exactly
alike, and the term is used generically (v. 22, ch. x. 20) to express the
kind of creature.

I. 22—25. The firmament, and throne, and glory of God.

Over the heads and outstretched wings of the four living creatures
there appeared a firmament like crystal (vv. 22—25); and above the
firmament an appearance as of a throne, like a sapphire stone; and
upon the throne the appearance of a man (v. 26). From his loins
upwards he had the appearance of glancing amber (electrum), and from
his loins downwards of fire; and there was a splendour around him
like that of the rainbow in the day of rain (vv. 25—28).

22. *the likeness of a firmament*] The term "firmament" has come
from the LXX. (στερέωμα) through the Vulgate (*firmamentum*). The
verb is used of the creation of the earth, Is. xlii. 5, xliv. 24; Ps. cxxxvi.
6, and once, Job xxxvii. 18, of the creation of the heavens; and the noun
is always used of the heavens. In the above passages LXX. render the
verb "make strong." The word "firmament" occurs only in Gen. i.;
Ezek. i., x.; Ps. xix. 1 [Heb. 2]; Dan. xii. 3.

the terrible crystal] Cf. Exod. xxiv. 10, "and they saw the God of
Israel; and there was under his feet as it were a paved work of sapphire
stone, and as it were the very heaven for clearness." In Rev. iv., which
is largely indebted to Ezek. i., the crystal firmament here becomes "a

----

[1] Toy (Haupt's *SBOT*.) considers "and the wheels were lifted up beside them"
to be a gloss in this verse.]

straight, the one toward the other: every one had two which covered ¹on this side, and every one had two which covered ¹on that side, their bodies. And when they went, 24 I heard the noise of their wings like the noise of great waters, like the voice of the Almighty, a noise of tumult like the noise of an host: when they stood, they let down their wings. And there was a voice above the firmament 25

¹ Or, *for them*

glassy sea like unto crystal" (*v.* 6). The word "terrible" is wanting in LXX., which read also "*as* a firmament" in the first clause¹.

23. *were their wings straight*] "straight" is even, level, and the reference appears to be to the upper side of the wings stretched out horizontally under the firmament. It is not meant that the firmament *rested* on the wings or heads of the living creatures, it was over them.

the one toward the other] See *vv.* 9, 11.

on this side...on that side] These words are obscure, and the Heb. (see marg.) admits of our rendering *every one had two covering them*, *and every one had two covering them*, even *their bodies*—the words "their bodies" giving a more exact definition of "covering them." Cf. for the construction the Heb. of Is. xi. 9. The statement is repeated in order to distribute it over each of the creatures, although the *and* before the repetition is less usual (ch. iv. 6, xlvi. 21). LXX. reads simply: "each one had two, covering their bodies."

24. The sound of the wings of the living creatures when in flight was as the noise of many waters, as thunder, or, as the roar of a host.

the voice of the Almighty] that is, thunder, Ps. xxix. 3; Job xxxvii. 4. The comparison to waters occurs again, ch. xliii. 2, and that to the voice of the Almighty, ch. x. 5 (God Almighty). The name Almighty (Heb. *shaddai*, of uncertain derivation) occurs alone chiefly in poetical pieces, e.g. about thirty times in Job, a few times in prophecy (Is. xiii. 6=Joel i. 15; and here) and in the idyl of Ruth (i. 20, 21); but in prose has the word "God" (El) prefixed to it (Gen. xvii. 1). [See Driver (*C. B.*) on Exod. vi. 3.]

a noise of tumult] Cf. Jer. xi. 16, where the word occurs again in the sense of a storm. The A.V.'s rendering "speech" assumes a different vocalisation of the Heb. As to noise of a "host" cf. Is. xvii. 12; Joel ii. 5. The LXX. omits (not so Theodotion) all that stands between "waters" and "when they stood."

25. *above the firmament*] The voice may be that of Him who sat above the firmament². The verse repeats the last words of the preceding

[¹ Delitzsch and apparently Lofthouse incline to the marginal rendering "ice," the former on the analogy of an Assyrian word, the latter pointing out that ice may be called terrible, as suggesting the storms and desolation of the north. He compares Job xxxvii. 22. Probably, however, we should somewhat modify the Heb. so as to read (with LXX.) for "terrible crystal" *ice* (or *crystal*) *which appeared*.]

[² But this is rather the crowning feature of the vision (*v.* 28). Accordingly Kr. explains it of the noise made by the attendant host of heaven (cf. *v.* 24).]

that was over their heads: when they stood, they let down
26 their wings.   And above the firmament that was over their
heads was the likeness of a throne, as the appearance of a
sapphire stone: and upon the likeness of the throne was
27 a likeness as the appearance of a man upon it above.   And
I saw as the colour of [1]amber, as the appearance of fire
within it round about, from the appearance of his loins and
upward; and from the appearance of his loins and downward I saw as it were the appearance of fire, and there was
28 brightness round about [2]him.   As the appearance of the bow
that is in the cloud in the day of rain, so was the appearance
of the brightness round about.   This was the appearance of
the likeness of the glory of the LORD.   And when I saw

---

[1] See v. 4.   [2] Or, *it*

verse and otherwise is almost identical in words with the following one,
and possibly it may not be original.

they let down their wings] We might render: *their wings dropped*;
so *v.* 24.

I. 26—28.   THE THRONE AND THE GLORY OF HIM WHO SAT ON IT.

Above the firmament was the appearance of a throne, like a sapphire
stone; and on the throne the appearance of One sitting, from His loins
upwards like amber, and from His loins downwards like fire. And
round about Him was a glory like the rainbow in the day of rain.

26. A throne of sapphire-blue emerges from the dark cloud. That
the throne itself and not a pavement on which it rested is of "sapphire"
seems clear. [See Driver on Exod. xxiv. 10, who also points out (*ib.*
xxviii. 18) that the "opaque blue lapis lazuli" is the stone here thought
of.] Cf. Ezek. x. 1.

the likeness, &c.] The prophet is careful to avoid anything like crude
anthropomorphism. Cf. *v.* 28.

27. *the colour*] See *v.* 4.

as the appearance of fire within it round about] [i.e. a brightness, as of
fire, within the amber. The upper part of the figure seems intended
to be more sharply defined than the lower.] The clause is wanting
in LXX.

there was brightness round about him] viz. Him who sat on the throne
(*v.* 28). [Marg. less well refers the pronoun to the "appearance of
fire."]

28. [Kr. refers to his *Bundesvorstellung im A. T.*, pp. 195 f. as
shewing that at a period long anterior to that in which Gen. ix. 12 ff.
was written, the rainbow was a symbol to early Semitic peoples of a
friendly attitude of the Deity towards mankind. Thus it here introduces
the element of reconciliation following upon wrath.]

the glory of the LORD] probably refers to the particular glory of the

it, I fell upon my face, and I heard a voice of one that
spake.

appearance sitting on the throne and the rainbow colours around Him,
not to the whole manifestation embracing the cherubim and wheels.
The glory of God is described as leaving the cherubim and standing
elsewhere, e.g. ch. ix. 3, x. 4. At the sight of this glory the prophet
fell upon his face.

Note on Ezekiel's Vision.

That which ch. i. presents is a theophany, a manifestation of God to
the prophet. It is not a vision of the cherubim nor of anything else,
but of God. The cherubim, wheels, firmament, and throne are all subordinate; they have no meaning in themselves, they merely help to
suggest what God is who thus manifests Himself.

[The "Chariot" vision, as taken to contain the mysteries belonging
to the government of the world, was a favourite subject for Kabbalistic
investigation. Abarbanel (*Pref.* to his *Comm. on Ezekiel*) gives the
chief explanations of "the Chariot" which have commended themselves
to Jewish teachers. See also summary in J. H. Hottinger, *De Incestu*,
&c., pp. 41 ff. The subject was to be approached with caution and not
to be discussed except under close restrictions. Jews under thirty years
of age were forbidden to read the section. The following quotation
from the treatise *Chagigah* (Tal. Bab.), fol. 13*a*, will shew the attitude
of the Rabbis. "Our Rabbis have taught, There is a story of a certain
child who was reading in his teacher's house in the Book of Ezekiel, and
he was pondering over Chashmal[1], and there came out fire from Chashmal
and burnt him."]

The vision is a composite one, made up of a number of elements
drawn from several sources. There is first the idea that God moves
and descends to the earth upon the cherubim (Ps. xviii. 10, civ. 3);
He is borne upon them. It is possible that the storm-cloud on which
Jehovah rode and in which His presence was enshrouded became personified into a being, which bore Him on its wings. Cf. Is. xix. 1. But
if this was the origin of the idea of the cherub, the conception of
the cherubim as "living creatures" had become established long
before the time of this prophet, as appears from Gen. iii. 24. [J.] The
cherubim being thus the means of Jehovah's manifesting Himself, that
on which He was borne and moved, wherever they were seen Jehovah
was known to be present. They were the means and the tokens of His
manifestation. Hence two great cherubim were placed by Solomon in
the *Děbîr*, or innermost shrine of the temple. On these Jehovah was
enthroned: He dwelt or sat enthroned upon the cherubim (Ps. lxxx. 1,
xcix. 1).

Again in Isaiah's vision of "the King, the LORD of hosts" (ch. vi.)

[1 The Chashmal (amber) was that part of the passage relating to the Chariot which
was called by this name as being a prominent word in it.]

there is naturally a palace and a throne. The palace, though the heavenly one, is the counterpart of the earthly one or temple, and has a hearth or altar fire. Both the fire and the throne reappear in Ezekiel's vision in an amplified form. The fire is no more a mere hearth from which a hot coal might be taken; it shoots forth flames and thunderbolts. This is a combination of the phenomena of the theophany in the thunder-storm with the representation of Isaiah. Similarly Isaiah's idea of Jehovah's throne being in the heavenly temple has been amplified by Ezekiel with various details. There was seen by him the appearance of a firmament like crystal, and above the firmament the appearance of a throne like a sapphire stone. Jehovah in His manifestation carries heaven, the place of His abode, with Him. Further His throne is surrounded by the glories of the rainbow, another element borrowed from the theophany in nature. In this way there is in the vision a com-bination of the theophany in nature with Jehovah's self-manifestation to men among His people in redemption.

And finally according to his manner the prophet has descended to elaborate details in describing the various elements of the manifestation, the cherubim, the wheels, and the like. In all the prophet's symbols throughout his Book the idea is first and the symbol but the expression of it. In the present case, however, the whole phenomenon is a vision of God, and the ideas which the symbols express are ideas in regard to God. This is evident so far as the wheels, the firmament, the throne, and the like are concerned. But the same is true of the cherubim. These are hardly yet independent beings, with a significance belonging to themselves. They are still half in the region of symbol, and what meaning they have has to be transferred to God, whose movements they mediate, just as much as that of the wheels or the flashing fire. [For the "wheels" at a later time see on *vv.* 19—21 *supra.*]

It may be assumed that in the prophet's mind each detail of the symbolism expressed some idea, though it may not be possible now to interpret the details with certainty. The firmament and throne repre-sent Jehovah as God of heaven, God alone over all, the omnipotent. The fourfold character of the living creatures, their wings, and the wheels which moved in all directions, and presented the same face to every quarter, suggest the power of Jehovah to be everywhere present. The wheels, called whirl or whirling things (ch. x. 13), may have been suggested by the sweeping whirlwind and tempest in which Jehovah moves. The conception of velocity which they express does not differ greatly from that of ubiquity expressed by their number. The eyes of which they and the living creature were full are symbols of life and intelligence. That the faces of each creature are four is but part of the larger general conception that the creatures are four in number. The four faces, those of a man, a lion, an ox, and an eagle or vulture, are the highest types of animal life. It is possible that to the prophet's mind these types represented four different attributes. Probably the cherubim in the temple had the human face, though this is not expressly stated. The prophet represents those carved on the walls of the new temple as having two faces, those of a man and a young lion (ch. xli. 19). Jehovah

And he said unto me, Son of man, stand upon thy feet, 2

is frequently compared to a lion[1]. He is also called by a name which may be an epithet of the ox[2]. The symbol of the ox was a familiar one, 1 Kgs vii. 25. Ezekiel may have been familiar with the mixed animal forms seen in the Assyrian temples, though it is scarcely necessary to suppose him influenced by these. The multiplication of details in his symbols is so characteristic of him that he may be credited with the creation of the four faces himself, just as of the four hands and four wings of the cherub. Cf. Is. vi. 2. The derivation and meaning of the word cherub are uncertain. It has been supposed that the word has been found in Assyrian, but this also is not quite certain. See Schrader *KAT.* on Gen. iii. 24. Cf. the Arts. in *HDB.* and *Encyc. Brit.* (Cheyne); Riehm in his *Bible Dictionary*, and *Stud. u. Krit.*, 1871, also his paper, "De Natura &c. Cheruborum," 1864. Also *Die Lehre des A. Test. über die Cherubim*, von J. Nikel, Bres. 1890, [Gautier, *La Mission du Prophète Ezéchiel*, esp. p. 111.]

II. 1—III. 21. THE STEPS OF THE PROPHET'S INITIATION INTO HIS MISSION BY JEHOVAH WHO HAD THUS APPEARED TO HIM.

The points touched upon are the character of those to whom he is sent, and the position he is to take in regard to them; and his dependence upon Jehovah for all that he is to speak and in all that he is to do. The passage has these divisions :

(1) Ch. ii. **1—7.** The character of those to whom the prophet is sent. They are the rebellious house of Israel, who have rebelled against Jehovah, they and their fathers, unto this day. The prophet is not to fear them but to speak Jehovah's words unto them.

(2) Ch. ii. **8—iii. 3.** Symbolical representation of the communication of Jehovah's words to the prophet. He is commanded to eat the roll of a book presented to him in Jehovah's hand.

(3) Ch. iii. **4—9.** Thus furnished with the words of the LORD, the prophet is commissioned to go to the house of Israel, not to foreign nations, which would not understand him. Israel will understand but will not listen.

(4) Ch. iii. **10—15.** Particularly he is sent to them of the captivity of Tel-Abib.

(5) Ch. iii. **16—21.** Now among the exiles there is brought home to his mind the precise nature of the office he is to fill ; he is to be a "watchman," warning everyone—the sinner that he may turn from his sin, and the righteous lest he fall from his righteousness.

II. 1—7. THE REBELLIOUS PEOPLE TO WHOM THE PROPHET IS SENT.

1. *Son of man*] Better, **child of man.** The phrase is used over ninety times [always by Jehovah addressing the prophet (elsewhere

[1 E.g. Job x. 16 ; Is. xxxi. 4, xxxviii. 13.]
[2 "*strong* bulls" (of Bashan, Ps. xxii. 12) is an expression closely akin in the Hebrew to an old name for God, e.g. in Gen. xlix. 24, "the *Mighty* One (of Jacob).]

2 and I will speak with thee.   And the spirit entered into me
when he spake unto me, and set me upon my feet; and
3 I heard him that spake unto me.   And he said unto me,
Son of man, I send thee to the children of Israel, to nations
that are rebellious, which have rebelled against me: they
and their fathers have transgressed against me, even unto
4 this very day.   And the children are impudent and stiffhearted; ¹I do send thee unto them: and thou shalt say

---

¹ Or, *unto whom I send thee*

---

similarly only in Dan. viii. 17)].   It expresses the contrast between
the prophet, as one of mankind, and the majesty of God, whose glory
he had just seen.

stand upon thy feet] At the sight of the great glory of God the prophet had fallen to the ground (ch. i. 28).   He is bidden stand on his
feet.   Not paralysis before Him is desired by God, but reasonable
service.   The prophet's falling down was natural, yet a condition unfit
for God's purposes, and not desired by Him to continue.   Those whom
He calls to His service are His fellow-workers, who may look upon His
face.   It is man erect, man in his manhood, with whom God will have
fellowship and with whom He will speak—stand upon thy feet "that I
may speak with thee."

2.   *And the spirit*] Perhaps, **and spirit**.   It is not said directly to be
the spirit of God, though in a sense this is meant.   Spirit is strength,
or, rather the source of strength and life; a power or energy entered into
the prophet and set him on his feet.   But this power was external to
him and came from God.   While God desires man to stand erect before
him and be man, it is only spirit from God that enables man to take
this right place.   [Spirit denotes "the vital energy of the Divine
nature," "the well-spring of inspiration" in the Hebrew prophets
(Swete, Art. Holy Spirit, *HDB*.   It serves here to revive Ezekiel's
powers, shaken by the vision.]

3.   *to nations that are rebellious*] [If the plural stands it must refer
to the two (Northern and Southern) kingdoms, as in xxxv. 10, xxxvii. 22.
The LXX. omit the clause, but it is needed for rhythmical reasons.
The epithet "rebellious" is a favourite one with the prophet (about
15 occurrences).]

4.   *And the children...stiffhearted*] [LXX. om., and the words
have the air of an inserted gloss.]   The "children" are the present
generation, who are like their fathers.   Outwardly they are "impudent," lit. *hard in face*, resolute, whose eyes do not quail before one
that opposes them; and within they are *strong of heart*, unyielding and
stubborn in will and feeling.   The word here used of the face is said of
the heart, ch. iii. 7, and the term applied to the heart is said of the face
and forehead, ch. iii. 8.   More often the term used of the face is
applied to the neck, "stiffnecked" (Exod. xxxiii. 3).   For the idea

unto them, Thus saith the Lord GOD.   And they, whether 5
they will hear, or whether they will forbear, (for they are
a rebellious house,) yet shall know that there hath been a
prophet among them.   And thou, son of man, be not afraid 6
of them, neither be afraid of their words, though briers and
thorns be with thee, and thou dost dwell among scorpions :
be not afraid of their words, nor be dismayed at their looks,
though they be a rebellious house.   And thou shalt speak 7
my words unto them, whether they will hear, or whether
they will forbear : for they are most rebellious.   But thou, 8

comp. Is. xlviii. 4, " I knew that thou art obstinate, and thy neck is
an iron sinew, and thy brow brass."

I do send thee unto them]   Rather, as marg.

Thus saith the Lord GOD] lit. the Lord Jehovah.   The word "Jehovah" was pronounced *Adonai*, "Lord," and when Adonai, Lord, was
combined with it in the text, Jehovah was pronounced God, *Elohim*.
In E.VV. "God" is then printed in small capitals to shew that it
represents the sacred name, Jehovah.   This is what the prophet shall
say on his part : "Thus saith the Lord Jehovah"; he shall announce
himself a prophet from Jehovah, bearing His word.   And the people
shall eventually know that a prophet has been among them (*v*. 5).
By various omissions LXX. reads *vv*. 3, 4 in a shorter form : "Son
of man, I send thee to the house of Israel, who provoke me; who
have provoked me, they and their fathers, unto this day, and thou shalt
say unto them, &c."   This reading certainly reflects a more natural
Hebrew sentence than our present text.

5.   *for they are a rebellious house*]   Whether they hear or whether
they refuse to hear—and they will refuse to hear, for they are a rebellious house—yet shall they know that a prophet has been among them.
The future shall bring this home to them.   They shall see the prophet's
words come to pass, and shall know that a true messenger from the
Lord spoke to them (Deut. xviii. 21 f.).   The true prophet, the
man who has anything to announce from God, may assure himself
that, however he be received when he speaks, in the long run he shall
receive his due and be recognized for what he was.

6.   *be not afraid of them*]   Cf. Jer. i. 8, 17.

briers...thorns...scorpions]   Things that pierce and wound, and that
strike and sting, are figures for intractable and injurious men.   The
prophet must understand their character and not fear them.   [For the
figure cf. xxviii. 24.]

though they be]   Rather : **for they are.**   Stubborn opposition and
injurious words may be expected of them ; such conduct has always
characterized them.   Be not dismayed before them, as if they were in
the right and not thou; thou art in the right, and thou shalt speak my
words to them (*v*. 7).

EZEKIEL   2

son of man, hear what I say unto thee; be not thou rebellious like that rebellious house: open thy mouth, and

II. 8.—III. 3.   THE PROPHET'S INSPIRATION.

Being commanded to speak God's words to the people, the prophet
is next assured by a symbol, a book given him to eat, that God's words
shall be given him.

8. *be not thou rebellious*] In addition to the positive command,
"hear what I say unto thee," the prophet is warned not to refuse and
be rebellious like the house of Israel. There was need for this double
peremptoriness of the command. The instinctive act of men before any
great undertaking of the kind set before the prophet is to shrink from it.
Jonah fled that he might escape from the task laid on him; Moses and
Jeremiah both entreated that they might be relieved of it. The work
was both arduous and painful: painful because it was against his own
people that the prophet had to speak; and arduous because leading to
opposition and persecution. There is no easy situation in God's service.
Had the prophet refused the great commission he would have rebelled
like Israel. And no doubt Israel's rebellion was also from an arduous
and painful commission, whether we regard its task to have been to
walk before God as His people, or to be the prophet of Jehovah to the
nations, being entrusted as Ezekiel was with His word. In both Israel
may be said to all appearance to have failed. Yet not wholly: the
Servant of the Lord, the true Israel of God, existing throughout the
history of the outward Israel, could say, "the Lord GOD hath opened
mine ear, and I was not rebellious, neither turned away backward"
(Is. l. 5).

The command to hear and not be rebellious is hardly to be confined
to the act of eating the Book, but refers rather to the whole ministry of
the prophet, although, considering that the Book was a symbol of all
God's words to him, and his eating it a symbol of his receiving them,
the sense in either case is the same (cf. *v.* 10).

The passage suggests: (1) the Divine source of that which the prophet
was to say and has said—"eat that I give thee" (*v.* 8), "an hand
was put forth unto me; and, lo, a roll of a book" (*v.* 9), "this roll
that I give thee" (iii. 2); (2) the definiteness of it: it was a roll of a
book (ii. 9), although its contents were large, the roll being written
both in front of the page and on the back, a thing unusual, rolls being
generally written only on one side (cf. Rev. v. 1); (3) the nature of
the contents—"lamentations, and mourning, and woe" (ii. 10), the
prophet being made well aware of the nature of the contents as well as
of their extent, "he spread the roll before me" (ii. 10); (4) the acceptance by the prophet of the Book as his own; he "did eat it," and
after eating it, it was in his mouth "as honey for sweetness" (iii. 3).
The sweetness was not due to this, that, though the Book contained
bitter things at the first, at the end it was filled with promises which
were sweet, for there was written therein lamentations and woe; it was

eat that I give thee.   And when I looked, behold, an hand 9
was put forth unto me; and, lo, a roll of a book was
therein; and he spread it before me; and it was written 10
within and without: and there was written therein lamentations, and mourning, and woe.   And he said unto me, 3
Son of man, eat that thou findest; eat this roll, and go,
speak unto the house of Israel.   So I opened my mouth, 2
and he caused me to eat the roll.   And he said unto me, 3
Son of man, cause thy belly to eat, and fill thy bowels with
this roll that I give thee.   Then did I eat it; and it was in
my mouth as honey for sweetness.

due rather to this that the things written were from God, whose bitter
word is sweet.   "Thy words were found, and I did eat them; and thy
words were unto me a joy and the rejoicing of mine heart: for I am
called by thy name (am thine and thy servant), O LORD God of hosts,"
Jer. xv. 16.   Cf. Ps. xix. 10; Rev. x. 8—11.

The prophet's idea of what we call his inspiration is perhaps more
precise and stringent than that of Isaiah.   In the inaugural vision of the
latter prophet (ch. vi. 6, 7), "Then flew one of the seraphim unto me,
having a live coal in his hand,...and he touched my mouth with it, and
said, Lo, this hath touched thy lips; and thine iniquity is taken away."
Immediately on this an impulse seized the prophet to enter upon the
service of God: "I said, Here am I; send me."   The forgiveness of
sin and moral purity, carrying with it sympathy with the great King
and the ministering spirits around Him, and elevating the man into that
exalted sphere of life, seemed enough to Isaiah to constitute him a
prophet.   There was in him a strength and power of character which
needed only the removal of the moral hindrance to set them free.   But
both Jeremiah and Ezekiel were weaker men.   Ezekiel as is usual with
him makes Jeremiah his model, and he can hardly be said to go beyond
that prophet: "The LORD said unto me,...whatsoever I shall command
thee thou shalt speak....Then the LORD put forth his hand, and touched
my mouth; and the LORD said unto me, Behold, I have put my words
in thy mouth": Jer. i. 7—9.   Both the later prophets represent themselves as receiving not merely the "word" but the "words" of Jehovah.

[9.   Ezekiel, unlike Jer. (i. 9), hesitates to say whose hand. Cf. his
circuitous language, induced by reverence, in i. 28.]

10.   *lamentations, and mourning, and woe*]   Ezekiel's later message
was one of consolation and hope.   Here, on the other hand, in the
opening of his prophetic life, only the dark side was shewn him.

iii. 1.   *eat that thou findest*]   The last word is peculiar in this connexion.   The clause is not in LXX. and may be a gloss suggested by
Jer. xv. 16.

3.   *as honey for sweetness*]   apparently owing to its character as a
charge coming from the Lord; cf. Rev. x. 9 f.

4   And he said unto me, Son of man, go, get thee unto the
5 house of Israel, and speak with my words unto them.   For
thou art not sent to a people ¹ of a strange speech and of
6 an hard language, but to the house of Israel; not to many
peoples of a strange speech and of an hard language, whose
words thou canst not understand.   Surely, if I sent thee
7 to them, they would hearken unto thee.   But the house of
Israel will not hearken unto thee; for they will not hearken
unto me : for all the house of Israel are of an hard forehead
8 and of a stiff heart.   Behold, I have made thy face hard
against their faces, and thy forehead hard against their fore-
9 heads.   As an adamant harder than flint have I made thy

¹ Heb. *deep of lip and heavy of tongue.*

III. **4—9.** The prophet shall be strengthened to perform
his hard task.

[Kr. would reject this section as a "doublet" or parallel recension of
ii. 3—7.   This view, however, is without any very weighty arguments
in its favour, and has no support from the LXX.   While we find in
part repeated here the thoughts of the earlier passage, that contained
in *vv.* 5, 6 is quite new.]

Having taken in the "words" of the Lord (*v.* 4) there opens up before
the prophet a general view of the mission upon which he is sent.   It is an
arduous one.   The difficulties are not of a superficial kind.   He is not
sent to foreign nations, who would not understand his words, but to
Israel.   They can well understand, but they will not listen.   Their
refusal to listen unto him is but an example of their life-long refusal to
listen unto God.   They are resolute and obstinate in their disobedience,
but the prophet shall be made more resolute than they.

5.   *a strange speech...language*] lit. *deep of lip* (or speech) *and heavy
of tongue.*   The former expression perhaps refers to the inarticulateness
with which, to one unacquainted with their language, foreigners appear
to speak ; and the other to the thickness of their utterance.   The first
half of the expression occurs again Is. xxxiii. 19, "a people of a deep
speech that thou canst not perceive," and the second half is said of
Moses, Exod. iv. 10.

6.   *many peoples*] i.e. different foreign nations.

Surely, if I sent thee, &c] There is some difficulty about the construction, but the sense is sufficiently clear.   The heathen have a greater
susceptibility for the truth than Israel, which has acted more wickedly
than the nations (ch. v. 6, 7, xvi. 48, 51.   Cf. Jer. ii. 10, 11; Matt. xi.
28 ff., xii. 41).

7.   *hard forehead...stiff heart*] See on ch. ii. 4.

9.   *harder than flint*] Cf. Jer. v. 3, "they have made their faces
harder than a rock; they have refused to return."

forehead: fear them not, neither be dismayed at their looks, though they be a rebellious house. Moreover he said unto 10 me, Son of man, all my words that I shall speak unto thee receive in thine heart, and hear with thine ears. And go, 11 get thee to them of the captivity, unto the children of thy people, and speak unto them, and tell them, Thus saith the Lord GOD; whether they will hear, or whether they will forbear.

Then the spirit lifted me up, and I heard behind me the 12

though they be] Rather: **for they are.** See ch. ii. 6. What gave the prophet invincible courage in the face of the opposition of the people was in the main the assurance that he was sent of God, that God was with him, and that His word was given him to speak. Comp. Is. l. 7, "For the Lord GOD will help me; therefore have I not been confounded: therefore have I set my face like a flint, and I know that I shall not be ashamed."

III. 10—15. THE PROPHET'S PARTICULAR MISSION TO THE EXILES AT TEL-ABIB.

Though Ezekiel's mission, like that of all the prophets, was to the house of Israel as a whole (*v.* 5), yet his immediate work lay among the captives in the midst of whom he lived. It is remarkable, however, how little reference is made in his prophecies to the particular circumstances of the exiles. The attention of the prophet, as well as of those around him in captivity, seems to have been engrossed by the events occurring in Palestine, and especially in the capital. And the truths spoken by him, though uttered in the ears of the exiles, bear reference to all Israel. Though he occasionally draws a distinction between those left in the land and the exiles carried away with Jehoiachin, of whom he was one (ch. xi. 15), in general he regards the latter as representatives of Israel, and feels when addressing them that he is speaking to the whole house of Israel. In the gradual defining of his task more clearly these exiles now come into view. He is bidden go "to them of the captivity" (*v.* 11), and he came to them at Tel-Abib. And now that he is entering upon his ministry there comes to him: (1) the command anew to hear and receive into his heart the words that God shall speak to him (*v.* 10); (2) next the command to announce himself as a prophet of the Lord: "thus saith the Lord GOD" (*v.* 11); and (3) with this command the sense of the Divine impulse carrying him forward to His service: "then the spirit lifted me up...and I came to them of the captivity" (*vv.* 12, 14, 15).

12. *the spirit lifted me up*] See on ii. 2. This "lifting up" by the spirit must be interpreted according to ch. viii. 1—3. It was part of the trance. The great theophany or vision of God in ch. i. was not an external phenomenon which the prophet beheld with his actual eyes, it was

voice of a great rushing, *saying*, Blessed be the glory of the
13 LORD from his place.   And *I heard* the noise of the wings

a vision which he saw, being in a trance. The same is true of all the
words heard by him, and all the actions done in ch. ii., iii. ; they took
place in the spirit, not outwardly. See after *v.* 21.

I heard behind me] The prophet had been in the presence of the
theophany (ch. i.) during all that has hitherto been narrated (ch. ii. 1—
iii. 12), and thus when he was lifted up and carried away it seemed to
him that he left the theophany *behind* him.

a great rushing] The word is used of an earthquake, and of the roar
of battle (Is. ix. 5 [Heb. 4], tumult) ; also of the rattling of chariots (Jer.
xlvii. 3 ; Nah. iii. 2). In ch. xxxvii. 7 it is said of the sound of the
coming together of the dry bones, but it appears nowhere else to be
employed of the noise caused by voices speaking.

Blessed be the glory of the LORD] According to the present text these
words were uttered with a sound like "a great rushing," though no
intimation is given who they were who uttered the words and the word
"saying" is not in the Heb. text.   But (1) the phrase "blessed be the
glory of the LORD" has no parallel ; and it is hardly admissible to take
the "glory of the LORD" as equivalent to "the LORD" or "the name
of the LORD" or even His "glorious name" (Ps. lxxii. 19).   Even the
fact that the "glory" is distinct from the Divine chariot, which it may
leave (ch. ix. 3), and that a voice may come from where it is (xliii. 6), is
hardly sufficient to justify such an expression.   (2) It is natural to take
the "great rushing" of this verse to be the same as that in *v.* 13, where
it is the roar of the wings of the living creatures and the wheels when
the chariot is in motion.   (3) With the present text the exclamation
"Blessed," &c., might come from the cherubim.   There is no other
passage in the prophet where the cherubim are represented as praising
God, although the seraphim do so in Is. vi., and the living creatures in
Rev. iv., and this might possibly be the meaning, particularly as the
reading "Blessed," &c., is the only one known to the versions.   Luzzatto,
and independently of him Hitzig, proposed to read: *when* the glory of
the LORD *rose up* from its place ; cf. ch. x. 5, 19, xi. 22, 23.   The reading
implies a change of only one letter (*bᵉrûm* for *bᵉrûch*).   Still the M.T.'s
reading is as old as the LXX.   [If we accept this probable emendation,
the M.T.'s reading may have arisen from a fear of irreverent (anthropo-
morphic) representation of the Godhead.   In *Chagigah*, 13 *b* (see on
i. 15) it is quoted as militating against the Kabbalistic statement that
Sandalphon stands behind the "chariot," and binds crowns for his
Maker.   The point of this objection is that the vagueness of the expression in the text implies that God's "place" is unknown and
unapproachable even by so mighty an angel.   The reply follows, viz.
His place it is impossible to know, but he (Sandalphon) utters the
Name over the wreath, and thereupon it goes and rests by His head.]

13.   *And* I heard *the noise*] lit. **and the noise.** The words seem to
state the cause of the great rushing sound in *v.* 12: it came from the

of the living creatures as they touched one another, and the
noise of the wheels [1]beside them, even the noise of a great
rushing. So the spirit lifted me up, and took me away: 14
and I went in bitterness, in the heat of my spirit, and the
hand of the LORD was strong upon me. Then I came to 15
them of the captivity at Tel-abib, that [2]dwelt by the river
Chebar, [3]and to where they [2]dwelt; and I sat there astonied
among them seven days.

[1] Or, *over against*   [2] Or, *sat*   [3] Another reading is, *and I
sat where they sat.*

wings of the living creatures touching one another when they flew, and
from the wheels. Cf. ch. i. 9, 11, 23.

14. *in bitterness*] i.e. indignation, or anger, Jud. xviii. 25 (angry
fellows), 2 Sam. xvii. 8. Similarly "heat of spirit" is fury or wrath.
The prophet was lifted up into sympathy with God and shared His
righteous indignation against Israel. Again Jeremiah is his model:
"Therefore I am full of the fury of the LORD; I am weary with holding
in: pour it out upon the children in the street, and upon the assembly
of young men together." Jer. vi. 11. LXX. omit "bitterness."

heat] excitement.

and the hand] [Perhaps we should render *for* instead of "and."]
See on ch. i. 3. [The prophet realises God's firm, compelling grasp.]
Cf. Jer. xv. 17, "I sat not in the assembly of them that make merry,
nor rejoiced: I sat alone because of thy hand; for thou hast filled me
with indignation."

15. The name Tel-Abib means possibly, Hill of corn-ears, or shortly,
Cornhill; but see against this Frd. Delitzsch *Heb. Lang.* p. 16. Names
compounded with the word Tel, mound, hill, are very common. The
place is not otherwise known[1].

and to where they dwelt] The Heb. mg. (Ḳri) is, *and I sat where
they sat.* [This only involves a change of one consonant.] The passage
is almost certainly corrupt. Most probably the words: "that dwelt by
the river Chebar, and" should be omitted: "then I came to them of the
captivity **to Tel-Abib where they dwelt**; and I sat there astonied among
them seven days."

astonied among them] i.e. dumb and motionless. Ezr. ix. 3, 4, "And
when I heard this I rent my garment and my mantle,...and sat down
astonied, cf. Dan. viii. 27. There was enough in the prophet's circumstances to produce a conflict of feelings in his mind—the sin of Israel,
who were yet his own people; the task before which he stood, and his
close and awful communications with heaven. The simple feeling of

[1] [The original name is much more probably *til-abūbi* (Assyrian), a mound or heap
produced by the action of storms. Sandhills of this kind were numerous in Babylonia, and formed barren spots where the conqueror might very well place his
captives. The Heb. ear then detected in the sound the more attractive meaning
which it suggested in their own tongue, and modified the word accordingly. So Kr.]

16   And it came to pass at the end of seven days, that the
17 word of the LORD came unto me, saying, Son of man, I
have made thee a watchman unto the house of Israel:
therefore hear the word at my mouth, and give them

bitterness and indignation which filled his mind when he newly left the
presence of God became broken into a tumult of feelings when he
saw the face of men. Zeal for God becomes tempered and humanized
in actual service. Ezekiel felt himself a prophet a moment ago, now he
feels himself a watchman (v. 17 seq.). Comp. the pathetic story of
Samuel and Saul, 1 Sam. xv. 25—31.

seven days] Job's friends "sat down with him upon the ground seven
days and seven nights; and none spake a word unto him: for they saw
that his grief was very great." The week was the first large division of
time, and the long period of motionless silence expresses the strength of
the prophet's emotions. [Ezra sat in stupor only until the evening.
"Seven days" would have a special significance for Ezekiel as a priest,
as being a period prescribed in connexion with rites of purification (Lev.
viii. 33, xiv. 8. Cf. Ezek. xliii. 25, 26).]

III. **16—21.** MORE PRECISE DEFINITION OF THE PROPHET'S
APPOINTMENT: HE IS SET TO BE A WATCHMAN.

So soon as the prophet is face to face with the exiles, and is able to
see the sphere and materials of his work, he receives a more precise
account of his position—he is appointed a watchman or sentinel. The
watchman stands on his watch-tower to observe, and his office therefore
is to *warn*, should danger be seen approaching. Is. xxi. 6, "Thus
hath the LORD said unto me, Go, set a watchman; let him declare
what he seeth." Jer. vi. 17, "And I set watchmen over you, *saying*,
Hearken to the sound of the trumpet; but they said, We will not
hearken"; Hab. ii. 1; comp. 2 Kgs ix. 17—20. The appointment
of Ezekiel as watchman was not a change upon his original appointment
as "prophet" (ch. ii. 5), it is only a more precise definition of it. The
term, which had already been used by Jer. (vi. 17), expresses the duties
of a prophet of this age. Ezekiel entered on his prophetic career with
his ideas as to the course of events to come fixed and matured. The fall
of Jerusalem was a certainty. And his true place was in the midst of a
people whom this great calamity had overtaken. The destruction of the
state was not the end of Israel or of the kingdom of God. Israel would
be gathered again, and the kingdom of God reconstituted. But it would
be on new principles. God would no more deal with men in the lump
and as a state; He would deal separately with each individual soul
(ch. xviii.). The destruction of the former state, however, was not the
final judgement. Before the new kingdom of God arose men would
have to pass through a new crisis, and to pass through it as individual
persons, and the issue of this crisis would be "life" or "death" to
them. It is in this full sense that Ezekiel speaks of the wicked dying
and the righteous living. To "live" is to be preserved and enter the

warning from me. When I say unto the wicked, Thou 18
shalt surely die; and thou givest him not warning, nor
speakest to warn the wicked from his wicked way, to save
his life; the same wicked man shall die in his iniquity; but
his blood will I require at thine hand. Yet if thou warn 19
the wicked, and he turn not from his wickedness, nor from
his wicked way, he shall die in his iniquity; but thou hast
delivered thy soul. Again, when a righteous man doth turn 20
from his righteousness, and commit iniquity, and I lay a
stumblingblock before him, he shall die: because thou hast
not given him warning, he shall die in his sin, and his
righteous deeds which he hath done shall not be remembered;
but his blood will I require at thine hand. Nevertheless 21

new kingdom of God, to "die" is to perish in the crisis and be excluded
from it. The idea of a "watchman" implies danger imminent (ch. xxxiii.
1—6), and the coming crisis is the ideal danger before the prophet's
mind. Hence the part of the watchman is to warn men in regard to
this coming sifting of individual souls, and to prepare them for it. The
idea is part of the prophet's individualism, his teaching regarding the
freedom and responsibility to God of the individual mind (ch. xviii.,
xxxiii.). Hence the watchman warns all classes of men, the wicked
that he may turn from his evil lest he "die," and the righteous that he
may be confirmed in his righteousness and "live."

18. *When I say unto the wicked*] The watchman spies danger approaching, so the prophet receives intimation from the LORD (*v.* 17).
This intimation given to the prophet is represented as a threat spoken
directly to the wicked. If the prophet as a watchman perceive this
danger of death to the wicked and fail to warn him, the wicked shall
die for his own sin indeed, but his blood will be upon the watchman.
He that fails to save life kills; and blood will be required of him, of
every man's hand the blood of his brother. Prov. xxiv. 11, 12, "Deliver them that are carried away unto death...If thou sayest, Behold,
we knew not this: Doth not he that weigheth the hearts consider it?"

in his iniquity] Perhaps: *through* his iniquity. It is of the nature
of sin that it is made the instrument of its own punishment, Job viii. 4.
"Warning" will naturally be of many kinds, suitable to those warned:
some may be deterred and others allured from their evil.

20. *I lay a stumblingblock*] i.e. something over which he shall fall
and perish; Lev. xix. 14, "Nor put a stumblingblock before the blind."
When God prepares such a stumblingblock for the righteous who has
sinned, unless he is warned he will fall and be broken, and his blood
will be on the prophet. [On the difficulty of temptation being attributed
to God, see Driver, Exod. (*C. B.*), pp. 53 f.]

21. The case of the righteous is even more complex and perilous for

if thou warn the righteous man, that the righteous sin not, and he doth not sin, he shall surely live, because he took warning; and thou hast delivered thy soul.

the watchman than that of the wicked, though it might not be thought so. The wicked has to be warned to turn from his evil, and so has the righteous if he sins. But the righteous has also to be warned, in ways that are suitable, lest he fall into evil. Only when the righteous is seen maintaining his righteousness unto the end can the watchman feel that he has delivered his own soul in regard to him. Like a ship laden with a precious freight he has to be anxiously piloted into the haven.

Note on the nature and circumstances of the prophet's call.

This passage, ch. i. 1—iii. 21, is not quite easy to estimate. There are two questions suggested by it, viz., first, how does the prophet represent the occurrences? and secondly, how is his representation to be interpreted? In answer to the first question, it is evident that all narrated from ch. i. 1 to iii. 12 or iii. 15 belongs to the prophet's trance. The vision of God in ch. i. and his inspiration under the symbol of eating a book, as also his commission generally, all belong to the sphere of ecstatic experience. This is manifest so far as the great Theophany of ch. i. is concerned; but all that follows, ch. ii. 1—iii. 12, was transacted in the presence of this Theophany, and like it must be regarded as part of the trance or ecstasy. In iii. 12, however, it is said that the vision of God went up from him, and if this were to be interpreted as ch. xi. 24, 25, where the same vision of God departed from him and he reported all he had seen during it to them of the captivity, we might suppose that the ecstasy was over. In ch. iii. 15, it is said that he came to them of the captivity. It is added, however, that the spirit took him up and carried him there, that he sat among the captives dumb seven days, and that the hand of the LORD was strong upon him. All these expressions are usual to describe prophetic ecstasy, e.g. viii. 3, xxxvii. 1, xl. 2. In the passage ch. xxxiii. 22, "the hand of the LORD" might describe something less than the full ecstasy, though this is not certain. After the prophet's statement that he came to them of the captivity to Tel-Abib, we might have expected some account of his ministry among them, but nothing of this is given; what follows is a more precise definition of his office, which is to be that of a watchman. The representation appears to be that the place by the river Chebar where the vision of God was seen by him was at some distance from Tel-Abib, and that when the vision went up from him he "came" to the captives at that place. This "coming," however, is described as being taken up and carried by the spirit, terms usual to describe prophetic ecstasy, and it almost seems that the prophet does not strictly distinguish between what he did in the spirit, in vision, and what he did bodily and in reality.

If the last remark be true, it may suggest how the prophet's representation is to be interpreted. On the one hand the extent and variety of the incidents represented as occurring in the trance, the things seen and heard, the prophet's emotions and the like, hardly form any argument against the literal reality of the account. The rapidity of the mind's operation in such conditions is well known. Naturally the thoughts of God and of the people and of himself and all the general ideas described as presenting themselves in the vision are not to be regarded as absolutely new to the prophet's mind. They had many times before occurred to him, at least separately and in fragments. But now in a more exalted frame of mind than usual they are reproduced in connexion with one another and with a power to influence the mind to action which they had not before possessed. This is how the inaugural visions of all the prophets, Isaiah (vi.) and Jeremiah (i.) as well as Ezekiel, are to be understood. It is probable that the prophet was subject to trances, for the vision is but a higher form of the mental condition which clothes its thoughts in symbols, and this symbolism is characteristic of the whole Book.

On the other hand the presumption is that the various incidents described did not occur precisely as represented. It is probable that these three chapters cover the earliest part of the prophet's ministry, extending over a considerable period. But in the first place he has condensed the events and experiences of this period, the thoughts and feelings which he had in his intercourse with the exiles and the reception he met with at their hands, into the present brief statement. And secondly, he has thrown the experiences of this period into a symbolical form; the thought of God, of the Divine majesty and greatness, which filled his mind at first and constantly, is presented under the form of the Theophany (ch. i.) always present with him. The feeling that he was a true prophet of God, commissioned to declare His will, and that the Divine presence was always with him, is symbolized in the other actions which follow (ii., iii.). At a later time looking back over this early period, recalling his vivid sense of God, of His presence with him directing all he did and inspiring all his words, he has presented the religious meaning of the period under the symbol of a trance in which he was in the immediate presence of God (cf. viii.—ix.).

SECOND SECTION. CH. III. 22—VII. 27.

The second section of the Book contains these parts :

(1) Ch. iii. 22—27. A preface in which the prophet is commanded to confine himself to his own house, and abandon for a time his public ministry.

(2) Ch. iv. 1—v. 4. A series of symbols representing the siege of Jerusalem, the scarcity of food at that time, the pollution of the people in exile among the nations, and the terrible fate of the inhabitants on the capture of the city.

(3) Ch. v. 5—17. Exposition of these symbols.

(4) Ch. vi. Prophecy against the mountains of Israel, the seats of Idolatry.

(5) Ch. vii. Dirge over the downfall of the state.

22   And the hand of the LORD was there upon me; and he

III. 22—27.   THE PROPHET ABANDONS PUBLIC EXERCISE OF HIS MINISTRY.

[We should rather have expected Ezekiel at once to commence his duties as "watchman," and it has in fact been supposed, but unnecessarily, that *vv.* 22 ff. are the continuation of an omitted passage. For the delay Lofthouse compares St Paul's three years in Arabia (Gal. i. 17) and our Lord's 40 days in the desert after His Baptism.]

The verses from the preface to ch. iv.—xxiv., all the prophecies that bear upon the fate of Jerusalem and its inhabitants, up to its fall. The prophet under the "hand" of God goes out into the "valley," and the same Theophany appears to him as at the first by the river Chebar. He is in communication with the same great God, and all his actions are determined by His commands. According to the interpretation put upon ch. i. 1—iii. 21 above, he had exercised his office of watchman among the people, speaking to them publicly in the name of the LORD, for some time. Possibly the time was not very long, for this passage comes in under the same general date as all that preceded it. His ministry had met with resistance, the people would not hear, as he had anticipated. A public ministry among them was fruitless; the burden of his preaching to them was distasteful. He warned them against their idolatries, from which they would not turn; and foretold the downfall of their city and country, a thing which they heard with an incredulous ear and would have none of. Therefore the prophet feels instructed of God to cease to be a public "reprover" (*v.* 26) for a time. The people refuse to believe his words when he speaks of the downfall of their beloved city, but they will be constrained to believe events when they happen; and then the prophet, his word being confirmed, will speak with boldness, his mouth will be opened, and he will be able to impress upon more ready listeners the lessons of God's righteous providence. His silence meantime is not an absolute one, it is only a change of method; but this so-called silence continues till the actual destruction of the city. In ch. xxiv. 27, it is said, "in that day (when tidings come of the city's fall) shall thy mouth be opened...and thou shalt speak, and be no more dumb,...and they shall know that I am the LORD"; and in ch. xxxiii. 21 *seq.*, when those who escaped came bringing tidings, saying, the city is fallen, it is said: "my mouth was opened, and I was no more dumb." No motive is assigned for the change in his prophetic method, beyond the unwillingness of the people to listen, "for they are a rebellious house" (*v.* 26). At the same time as a prophet of the restoration with its new principles (ch. xviii., xxxiii.), a watchman appointed to speak no more to the state but to individual men, his ministry proper could not commence till the state had fallen. See note on *v.* 17.

22.   *the hand of the LORD*] A trance or ecstasy from the LORD. The prophet felt impelled to remove himself from the presence of men to some lonely retreat, and there the glory of the LORD, [meaning

said unto me, Arise, go forth into the ¹plain, and I will there
talk with thee.   Then I arose, and went forth into the 23
¹plain : and, behold, the glory of the LORD stood there, as
the glory which I saw by the river Chebar : and I fell on
my face.   Then the spirit entered into me, and set me 24
upon my feet ; and he spake with me, and said unto me,
Go, shut thyself within thine house.   But thou, son of man, 25
behold, they shall lay bands upon thee, and shall bind thee
with them, and thou shalt not go out among them : and 26
I will make thy tongue cleave to the roof of thy mouth, that
thou shalt be dumb, and shalt not be to them a reprover :
for they are a rebellious house.   But when I speak with 27
thee, I will open thy mouth, and thou shalt say unto them,

¹ Or, *valley*

apparently the "Chariot,"] seemed again to stand before him (cf. ch. viii.
1—3).

into the plain]   marg. *the valley*.   The term is scarcely a general
one, meaning the plain country in opposition to Tel-Abib, where the
exiles dwelt ;   some particular place in the neighbourhood called the
"valley" is meant.   According to *v*. 23 the place was not identical
with the other by the river Chebar, where the Vision of God first appeared to the prophet.   Cf. ch. xxxvii. 1 *seq*.

24.   *shut thyself within thine house*]   The words are not to be
pressed to mean more than abstention from the exercise of his ministry
in public.   Cf. ch. viii. 1, xi. 25, xiv. 1 &c.

25.   *they shall lay bands upon thee*]   that is, the exiles, as the words
"thou shalt not go out among them" imply.   The expression can hardly
be merely equivalent to the *passive*, "cords shall be put upon thee"
(Sept., Vulg.).   The language is a figure for the restraint of opposition.
Cf. ch. iv. 8, although the "binding" there refers to a much briefer
period.

26.   *I will make thy tongue cleave*]   The restraint imposed by the
opposition of the people is acquiesced in by God, it is part of His
purpose.   His providence will meantime be the best teacher of the
people.   The prophet's "dumbness," however, is compatible with much
speaking at least by signs to those who will hear.   He is "dumb" in
the sense of the Psalmist, "I was dumb, I opened not my mouth ;
because thou didst it" (Ps. xxxix. 9 ; Is. liii. 7 ; cf. Ezek. xxiv. 27,
xxxiii. 22).

27.   Eventually the prophet's mouth will be opened, his word will be
confirmed, and he will no more have to speak to incredulous ears.
(Cf. ch. xix. 21.)   During the existence of the kingdom all the prophets
from Amos downward had stood in opposition to the mass of the people.
Their teaching whether on religion or on policy ran counter to the

Thus saith the Lord GOD: He that heareth, let him hear; and he that forbeareth, let him forbear: for they are a rebellious house.

inclinations of the multitude. The fall of the state, however, which they had so unanimously predicted, gave them consideration in the eyes of the people, and led even the unthinking masses to feel that they were true interpreters of the mind of God and of His government. Passages like ch. xxxiii. 10, "Our transgressions and our sins are upon us, and we pine away in them; how then should we live?" shew the change taking place in the people's thoughts, and how they were coming round to take that view of their history which this prophet, as well as his predecessors, had so persistently inculcated. It is not easy to form any clear conception of the prophet's ministry during the years preceding the fall of the state, but such passages as the above suggest the kind of thoughts which he expresses under the symbols of "dumbness" and "opening of the mouth." It is scarcely necessary to say that the "binding" of the prophet here (v. 25), which continues till the fall of Jerusalem, is quite different from the binding in ch. iv. 8, which lasts only for a period of days, and is a symbol of Israel bearing its iniquity in exile.

IV. 1—V. 4.   SYMBOLICAL ACTIONS REPRESENTING THE SIEGE AND CAPTURE OF JERUSALEM, AND THE FATE OF THE INHABIT-ANTS—THEIR SLAUGHTER AROUND THE CITY AND DISPERSION AMONG THE NATIONS.

(1) Ch. iv. 1—3. Symbol of the siege of Jerusalem.

(2) Ch. iv. 4—8. Symbol of the people's bearing their iniquity in the siege and exile.

(3) Ch. iv. 9—17. Symbol of scarcity during the siege, and pollu-tion among the nations.

(4) Ch. v. 1—4. Symbol of the slaughter of the inhabitants around the city on its capture, and their dispersion over the world.

The following symbols seem as much designed for the prophet him-self as for the people. He is commanded of God to perform them. They represent the thoughts which under the inspiration of God filled his mind at this time, regarding the fate of the city and the state. His thoughts as well as those of the captives around him are occupied with Jerusalem, for Jerusalem is almost Israel. Being far from it and from its inhabitants his imagination is fertile in devising means to bring it before him. Sometimes he pourtrays a picture of it on a brick, and sometimes he is carried by a lock of his head through the air and set down in the midst of it, in order to behold its iniquities (ch. viii. 1). Though some of the symbols here might have been actually represented, others could not, such as lying on his side immoveable for many days (iv. 4—8), and probably none of them were actually performed. The prophet no more drew a sketch of Jerusalem upon a brick than he was

Thou also, son of man, take thee a tile, and lay it before 4
thee, and pourtray upon it a city, even Jerusalem: and lay 2
siege against it, and build forts against it, and cast up a

carried by the hair of his head from the Chebar to Palestine[1]. At the
same time there is more than mere literary artifice. The symbols stood
actually before his imagination, and the narration of them to the people
would convey the same instruction as the actual representation of them
(v. 3, cf. ch. xi. 25). The three symbolical actions (ch. iv.) must go on
simultaneously, viz. the siege, the lying on his side or bearing iniquity,
and eating bread by measure and in pollution. For the three are the
same thing under different aspects; first the actual siege, then the meaning of this, God's judgement for sin, and finally some of the ways in
which this judgement is felt, straitness of food and water, and dispersion
and defilement among the nations.

IV. 1—3. SYMBOLICAL SIEGE OF JERUSALEM.

The prophet is commanded to take a brick (it is to be supposed still
soft) and pourtray on it a city, even Jerusalem. Around the city he is
to draw representations of siege operations, towers, a mound, camps,
and battering-rams. Between him and the city he is to set an iron
plate to represent an iron wall. The determination of the besiegers is
shewn by his attitude, he sets his face against the city. All this is
symbol of a hard siege, carried on with great determination and apparatus against a lofty city.

1. *take thee a tile*] or, brick. The brick would be such as those
found in the ruins of the cities of Mesopotamia, covered with figures and
inscriptions, engraved on them when still moist. Libraries of such
bricks have been found by explorers in this region, and deciphered.

2. *forts against it*] The word is always used in the sing., though
sometimes rightly rendered *forts* (2 Kgs xxv. 1), as the term is the
name of a *class* of offensive siege works. The work was probably a
species of tower, of which a number might be erected "round about"
the walls (2 Kgs xxv. 1), and was used as a station for archers, or to
discharge projectiles from (cf. LXX. ch. xvii. 17). Towers of this kind,
manned by archers, are seen on the Assyrian bas-reliefs. Layard, *Nin.
and Bab.* p. 149.

cast up a mount] The "mount" or mound was an embankment raised
till the besiegers standing on it were on a level with the top of the wall
and able to command the streets of the city, cf. Lam. iv. 18. See Is.
xxxvii. 33; Jer. vi. 6, xxxii. 24.

[1 But as Kr. points out, Ezekiel would have all materials at hand (tile, griddle,
etc.) for symbolic action, as here described. We must also remember the love of
the Oriental mind for dramatic action. Moreover, actions which might seem to us
ludicrous or even revolting need not have had this aspect in their eyes. See also on
v. 4. Cf. ascetics in India at the present day, and see also Is. xx. 3, Jer. xiii. 1 ff.;
Acts xxi. 11.]

mount against it; set camps also against it, and plant
3 battering rams against it round about. And take thou unto
thee an iron ¹pan, and set it for a wall of iron between thee
and the city: and set thy face toward it, and it shall be
besieged, and thou shalt lay siege against it. This shall be
a sign to the house of Israel.

¹ Or, *flat plate*

set camps] detachments of soldiery.

battering rams] These were beams of wood with a head of iron,
suspended by chains or ropes from a cross plank, and swung with great
force by a number of men against the walls to batter them down. [The
original word, though identical in form with the Heb. for *lamb*, is
probably derived from the Assyrian root, *karâru*, to pull down, destroy. The term "round about" indicates that they were applied
to different parts of the wall, perhaps where it might be thought
weakest. It is not probable that the siege works were also engraved
upon the brick. The latter rather by its elevation above the ground
represented the city, and the siege works would be upon the ground, if
we are to suppose them anywhere. But as the whole is a creation of
the imagination it may be doubtful if the prophet was so precise or
consistent as to put to himself the question where the siege works were
placed¹.

3. *an iron pan*] as marg. *flat plate*, i.e. griddle on which cakes were
fried (Lev. ii. 5). This common article the prophet is to set up between
him and the city to represent an iron wall. As the plate is said to be
an iron wall between him and the city, it is most natural to interpret it
of the powerful fortifications of Jerusalem (Ew.). It might, however,
be a symbol of the implacable and iron severity of the siege, which
itself but shews the inexorable grasp which the judgement of God has
taken of the city. The word *it* in the end of the verse refers to the
city; and the prophet plays the rôle of besieger.

All this is a sign to the house of Israel of what shall come to pass.
Cf. ch. xii. 11.

IV. 4—8. SYMBOL OF THE PEOPLE'S BEARING THEIR INIQUITY.

In the former symbol the prophet carried on the siege, representing
the besiegers; here he changes his part and represents the besieged.
This symbol is shewn contemporaneously with the former, of which it
is but the inner side. He is commanded to lie first on his left side for
a great number of days; thus he bears the iniquity of the Northern
Kingdom. To bear the iniquity means to endure the punishment due to
it. [When the prophet is said to bear the iniquity of Israel, the meaning is that in his action he is a sign or symbol of the house of Israel
bearing its iniquity.] Lying on his side, held down as with cords (*v.* 8)
and unable to turn, he represents Israel pressed down and held in the

¹ But see note on p. 31.

Moreover lie thou upon thy left side, and lay the iniquity 4
of the house of Israel upon it: *according to* the number of
the days that thou shalt lie upon it, thou shalt bear their
iniquity. For I have appointed the years of their iniquity 5
to be unto thee a number of days, even three hundred and
ninety days : so shalt thou bear the iniquity of the house of
Israel.   And again, when thou hast accomplished these, 6

grasp of the punishment of its iniquity.   The left side represents the
Kingdom of Israel, which lay to the left or north.   The number of
days during which the prophet lies on his side corresponds to the number of years during which Israel shall be bound under the weight of its
iniquity (*v.* 5).   Secondly, having finished the days for the Northern
Kingdom the prophet has to lie on his right side forty days to represent
Judah, which lay on the south or right, bearing its iniquity for forty
years.   The prophet being unable to lie on both sides at once has to
lie first on one and then on the other.   It is obvious, however, that the
symbolism here cannot be quite exact.   Israel and Judah bear the
penalty of their iniquity for part of the time simultaneously.   The period
of bearing iniquity ends for both at the same moment, when both are
restored together as the prophet hopes.   Consequently Judah's forty
years are concurrent with the last forty years of Israel's chastisement.
The whole period is not 390 + 40 = 430, but 390 in all for Israel and the
last 40 of that period for Judah.   See on *v.* 6.

4.   *lay the iniquity...upon it*]   The meaning seems to be that as
when one lies on his side it bears his weight, so this laying of the
prophet's weight upon his side is a symbol of the weight of punishment
which shall be laid on Israel for its iniquity.   Others propose to alter
the Heb. slightly and read : *and I will lay* the iniquity of the house of
Israel *upon thee.*   The alteration is unnecessary.

according to *the number of the days*]   [The difficulty which has
been felt in accepting this action to have been literally carried out
is materially lessened if we hold with Gautier (*La Mission du prophète
Ézéchiel*, p. 93) that the symbolic posture was confined to the times
when there were lookers on.   There would have been little point in its
adoption when he was alone.   Others, less satisfactorily, have explained by a species of catalepsy or hypnotism.]

thou shalt bear their iniquity]   To "bear iniquity" is a standing expression meaning to bear the punishment of iniquity.   Possibly the
word actually means "punishment of iniquity" in such phrases[1].   The
prophet does not bear the iniquity of Israel *instead* of Israel, as the
servant of the Lord in Is. liii.: his act is entirely symbolical, representing
how Israel shall bear its iniquity.

6.   In *v.* 5 the number of days for Israel is stated to be 390, and in

[1 For the attitude of the Heb. mind, which led to this ambiguity, see Kennett,
Conceptions of Righteousness and Sin, p. 8, and cf. Lev. v. 6 (*C.B.*) for another
example.]

thou shalt lie on thy right side, and shalt bear the iniquity
of the house of Judah : forty days, each day for a year,

v. 6 the number for Judah 40. The number 390 creates a difficulty.
Several things have to be borne in mind. (1) To bear iniquity means to
bear the penalty of it. The period of bearing iniquity, therefore, does
not refer to the time of sinning but to the time of being punished for
sin. Consequently any allusion to the period of the *duration* of the
Northern Kingdom is excluded. (2) The representation in this prophet,
as in all the prophets, is that the overthrow of the state is due to the
sin of the people, and this overthrow with the continued state of the
Exile and its hardships is the punishment of the people's sin. To be
subdued by the heathen and driven into exile is for the people to have
to bear their iniquity. Hence restoration is impossible until the iniquity
of the people is paid off, or atoned for, in suffering (Is. xl. 2). Israel's
bearing of iniquity comes to an end with the Restoration : "Cry unto
her, that her warfare is accomplished, that her iniquity is pardoned."
(3) It is the view of all the prophets, Ezekiel included, that the Restoration will embrace all the existing captives both of the North and
South, every one called by Jehovah's name (Is. xliii. 6, 7 ; cf. Is. xi.
12 *seq.*; Jer. iii. 12, 18 ; Ezek. xxxvii. 16 *seq.* &c.). And this restoration is final. (4) It follows from all this that the periods during which
Israel and Judah bear their iniquity terminate simultaneously. Israel
bears iniquity longer than Judah because it began to bear earlier. It is
evident (cf. *v.* 9) that the whole period of bearing iniquity in exile is
390 years, not 390 + 40 or 430, but 350 + 40, the 40 years of Judah
running parallel to the last 40 of Israel. The period of 40 years for
Judah's exile is confirmed by ch. xxix. 11—14, where it is said that
Egypt shall be carried into captivity 40 years by Nebuchadrezzar, and
at the end of that period restored, though not to its former greatness.
Forty years is the period of Chaldean supremacy ; at the end of that
period Babylon shall fall, a new world arise, and the captive nations
shall be restored. Now the prophet cannot possibly have supposed
that Israel went into exile 350 years before Judah. From the fall of
Samaria (722) to the destruction of Jerusalem (586) is only 136 years.
In *v.* 5 LXX. reads 190 (so *v.* 9) ; in *v.* 4 the reading is 150, which
probably is an addition (see Field's *Hex.*). The number 190 is probably
the original one. It is not quite certain from what point the prophet
computed, whether from the fall of Samaria (722), which is most
natural, or from the deportation of the Northern tribes by Tiglath
Pileser twelve years earlier ; as he spoke also before the fall of Jerusalem
even this point may be somewhat indefinite. Most probably he used
general and round numbers, computing the time which Israel had
already passed in captivity at 150 years, to which, if the 40 years still
to be undergone in common with Judah be added, the whole period is
190 years. [The additional 200 may be accounted for as computed
from the secession of the Northern kingdom, and so expressing approximately the interval between that event (*c.* B.C. 937) and its overthrow.]

have I appointed it unto thee.   And thou shalt set thy face 7
toward the siege of Jerusalem, with thine arm uncovered;
and thou shalt prophesy against it.   And, behold, I lay 8
bands upon thee, and thou shalt not turn thee from one
side to another, till thou hast accomplished the days of thy
siege.   Take thou also unto thee wheat, and barley, and 9

Verses 7, 8 recapitulate *vv.* 1—6: *v.* 7, *vv.* 1—3, and *v.* 8, *vv.* 4—6.
Verses 1—6 form one passage describing first the siege (*vv.* 1—3), and
secondly the rigours of the siege, which are prolonged into exile
(*vv.* 4—6).   While enduring these hardships in siege and exile the
people are bearing their iniquity.   The apparent incongruity of the
prophet's playing two rôles, that of besieger (*vv.* 1—3), and that of
being besieged (*vv.* 4—6), could hardly be avoided if both things were
to be represented.

7. *And thou shalt set*, &c.] In this verse the prophet resumes *vv.* 1—3,
representing the besiegers; he sets his face towards the siege, presses
it steadily and with determination; his arm is bare—the instrument
with which he works unentangled and effective (Is. lii. 10); and he
prophesies against the city, for all that is done to Jerusalem is but the
carrying into effect of the Lord's irresistible word.

8. *from one side to another*] lit. *from thy side to thy side*.   Here the
prophet represents those pressed by the rigours of the siege, as in
vv. 4—6.   The "days of thy siege" most naturally mean the days of
thy suffering a siege (ch. v. 2)[1].

IV. 9—17.   SYMBOL OF SCARCITY DURING THE SIEGE AND POL-
LUTION IN THE DISPERSION FROM HAVING TO EAT UNCLEAN
THINGS AMONG THE GENTILES.

The passage continues *v.* 8.   The prophet is commanded (while
lying immoveably on his side in siege) to take of all kinds of grain,
coarse as well as fine, of everything that will satisfy hunger, and cast them
into one vessel.   These are to be baked into cakes and fired with hot
ashes of men's dung, though on the prophet's entreaty a relaxation of
this repulsive condition is granted and he is allowed to substitute the dung
of cows.   These cakes are to be eaten sparingly in small quantity from
time to time, and water drunk with them sparingly.   And this use of the
cakes so prepared is to continue all the time that the prophet lies on his
side.   These actions symbolize first, great scarcity and straitness during
the siege (*vv.* 16, 17); and secondly, pollution from eating unclean
things in the exile among the nations (*v.* 13).

9.   Bread was usually made of wheat: the addition of the other

[1 Kr., however, considers that the slight difference in vocalisation of the Heb.
substantive here indicates that, while perhaps a play on the word "siege" in *vv.* 2,
3, is also intended, it here primarily denotes the prophet's *binding, confinement*.
Cf. on v. 2.]

beans, and lentils, and millet, and spelt, and put them in
one vessel, and make thee bread thereof; *according to* the
number of the days that thou shalt lie upon thy side, even
10 three hundred and ninety days, shalt thou eat thereof.   And
thy meat which thou shalt eat shall be by weight, twenty
11 shekels a day: from time to time shalt thou eat it.   And
thou shalt drink water by measure, the sixth part of an hin:
12 from time to time shalt thou drink.   And thou shalt eat it
as barley cakes, and thou shalt bake it in their sight with
13 dung that cometh out of man.   And the LORD said, Even
thus shall the children of Israel eat their bread unclean,

coarser materials and their mixture indicate the straits to which men
will be reduced in the siege and perhaps after the fall of the city;
cf. Lam. v. 6, 10, "We gave the hand to the Egyptians and to the
Assyrians to be satisfied with bread....Our skin was black like an oven
because of the terrible famine." It is not [absolutely] certain [but
highly probable] that a mixture of various kinds of grain was regarded
as a thing unclean, just as the Law forbade sowing the field with divers
sorts of seed, Lev. xix. 19; cf. Deut. xxii. 9.

three hundred and ninety] Probably 190 should be read as in *v.* 5.
The language here shews that the 190 (or, 390) was the whole number,
and that the 40 for Judah were not additional but included.

[**10—12.** There seems to be some confusion in the order. *Vv.* 10,
11 would more naturally follow *v.* 12. Cor. and Kr. consider that
the whole passage consists of a mixture of two recensions, the one
dealing with the conditions of the siege, the other with those of the
exile.]

10. *twenty shekels a day*] Twenty shekels might be eight or nine
ounces. In this country two pounds of bread is held an ordinary
allowance.

11. *sixth part of an hin*] The hin was rather less than a gallon,
and the sixth part under a pint and a half. Both the bread and water
were to be consumed from time to time, always in unsatisfying quan-
tities.

12. It was customary in the East to use the dung of animals when
completely dried as fuel. The hot ashes remaining from it are perfectly
clean, and retaining their glow for a considerable time were used in the
preparation of cakes. See Wetzstein in Delitzsch, *Job*, p. 261 (Trans.
i. p. 377). Whether the Hebrews would have considered such fuel unclean is not certain (cf. Lev. v. 3, vii. 21; Deut. xxiii. 13); the material
for firing which the prophet is commanded to use would certainly be
unclean (Deut. xxiii. 13) as well as loathsome. The command is explained in *v.* 13.

13. *eat their bread unclean*] [This is the meaning of the symbol:
the food which the people shall eat among the nations will be unclean.

among the nations whither I will drive them.   Then said 14
I, Ah Lord GOD ! behold, my soul hath not been polluted :
for from my youth up even till now have I not eaten of that
which dieth of itself, or is torn of beasts; neither came
there abominable flesh into my mouth.   Then he said unto 15
me, See, I have given thee cow's dung for man's dung, and
thou shalt prepare thy bread thereon.   Moreover he said 16
unto me, Son of man, behold, I will break the staff of bread
in Jerusalem : and they shall eat bread by weight, and with
carefulness ; and they shall drink water by measure, and

Cf. Hos. ix. 3, 4 with marg.]   A foreign land was in itself unclean (Am.
vii. 17), no presence of Jehovah sanctified it; all food eaten in it was also
common, for it was not hallowed by part of it being brought into the house
of the LORD and offered to Him.   Food eaten among the heathen was
as the bread of mourners in Israel, all who partook of it were polluted.
But, as the words of the prophet suggest (v. 14), in addition to this
general uncleanness the people were forced in their straits or induced
to eat many things actually prohibited by the Law, such as that which
died of itself or was torn by wild beasts (ch. xliv. 31 ; Lev. xvii. 15 ;
Deut. xiv. 21.   Cf. Is. lxv. 4).   And it is natural that in the sore
famine during the siege such unclean food was eaten, as indeed more
terrible practices prevailed (ch. v. 10).   Verse 13 appears in a shorter
form in LXX., but there is no reason to regard the whole verse as a
gloss.

14.   *abominable flesh*]   This word "abomination" is applied to the
sacrificial flesh kept over till the third day (Lev. vii. 18, xix. 7), and
in Is. lxv. 4 broth of "abominations" is coupled with swine's flesh.
The meaning seems to be "carrion."   The word occurs only these four
times.

15.   *thou shalt prepare thy bread thereon*]   [This is still a practice of
the Fellahin in Palestine (Lofth., *ad loc.*).]

16, 17.   Explanation of the symbol of eating bread by measure (*vv.*
10, 11).

16.   *the staff of bread*] i.e. the staff which bread is ; a common figure,
ch. v. 16 ; Lev. xxvi. 26 ; Is. iii. 1 ; Ps. cv. 16.

carefulness] [anxiety; cf. xii. 18].

It is scarcely necessary to say that the symbolical actions of this
chapter were not actually performed[1].   They naturally passed through
the mind of the prophet as described, but so far as others were concerned they were merely narrated.   The truth expressed by the symbolical action was as plain when the action was merely described as it
would have been had the action been performed and seen.   It is evident
that the actions referred to here could not have been performed because

[1] But see note on p. 31.

17 with astonishment: that they may want bread and water,
and be astonied one with another, and pine away in their
iniquity.

they are represented as being done simultaneously. It is while he
presses the siege with arm uncovered that the prophet also lies on his
side held down by bands, bearing the sin of the people (vv. 5, 7, 8), and
it is while lying immoveable in this condition that he prepares cakes
upon the coals and eats them (vv. 8, 9). The prophet's symbols merely
express an idea; it is only when supposed to be actually performed that
inconsistencies appear.

The siege and the hardships of it prolonged into the exile—the
people's bearing their sin—are the two chief ideas of the chapter. These
are of course contemporaneous with one another so far, but they are
spoken of separately in vv. 1—6, the siege in vv. 1—3, and the hardships
of it and the exile in vv. 4—6. But from v. 7 onwards they are somewhat mixed together. Wellh. (Hist. p. 273, note) considers that in v. 9,
390 is the right reading (though erroneously transferred also to v. 5 for
190), and that the reference is exclusively to the siege, which the prophet
calculated would last so long. Further, the prophet's lying on his side
and being bound with bands, v. 8, is a different thing from his lying on
his side, v. 5. In v. 5 he represented the bondage of the exile, in v. 8
seq. the straitness of the siege. This view requires that v. 13, which
interprets v. 8 seq. of eating unclean food in the dispersion, should be
struck out as a gloss. The verse certainly appears in a shorter form in
LXX., though there seems no ground for considering it wholly inter-
polated. And it is more natural that the repulsive symbol of v. 12
should refer to the fact that all food eaten in exile was unclean rather
than to uncleanness due to scarcity of fuel during the siege. The introduction too of a literal number of 390 days among other numbers of
days which are symbolical is scarcely probable.

V. 1—4. SYMBOL SHEWING THE FATE OF THE POPULATION DURING
      THE SIEGE AND AFTER IT, AND THEIR DISPERSION AMONG
      THE NATIONS.

The prophet is commanded to take a sharp sword and use it as a
barber's razor. With this he is to shave off the hair of his head and
beard. He is then to take balances in order accurately to weigh the
hair into three parts. One third is to be burned in the fire within the
city; a second third to be cut to pieces with the sword round about the
city; and the last third is to be strewn to all the winds, and pursued by
the sword. Of these last a few were to be taken and bound in the skirts
of the prophet's garment; though of these again some were to be thrown
into the fire and consumed. The sense of the symbol is clear; a third
part of the population shall be consumed by pestilence and famine
within the city (v. 12); a third shall fall by the sword round about the
city, on its capture; and a third shall be scattered among all nations,

And thou, son of man, take thee a sharp sword, *as* a 5
barber's razor shalt thou take it unto thee, and shalt cause
it to pass upon thine head and upon thy beard: then take
thee balances to weigh, and ¹divide the hair.   A third part 2
shalt thou burn in the fire in the midst of the city, when the
days of the siege are fulfilled; and thou shalt take a third
part, and smite with the sword round about it; and a third
part thou shalt scatter to the wind, and I will draw out a
sword after them.   And thou shalt take ²thereof a few in 3
number, and bind them in thy skirts.   And of these again 4
shalt thou take, and cast them into the midst of the fire, and

---

¹ Heb. *divide them.*   ² Heb. *thence.*

pursued by the sword.   Of these a few shall meantime escape, but shall
be subjected anew to consuming judgements.

1. *a sharp sword*] The term may suggest the devouring divine
sword, ch. xxi. 8 *seq.*

as *a barber's razor shalt thou take it unto thee*] The sword is to be
used as a razor. [Cutting off the hair was closely connected with
mourning. Cf. Jer. xvi. 6, xli. 5, xlviii. 37.] Isaiah (ch. vii. 20)
had already said : "In that day shall the Lord shave with a razor that
is hired,...*even* with the king of Assyria, the head and the hair of the
feet."   The land is likened to a man ; the enemy sweeps off the population as clean as the razor does the hair of the body.

balances to weigh] The divine justice is accurate, assigning to each
part its destined chastisement ; Jer. xv. 2, "Such as are for death to
death ; and such as are for the sword to the sword ; and such as are for
the famine to the famine ; and such as are for captivity to captivity."

2. *in the midst of the city*] If we could suppose that the prophet
were strict in his symbolism the "city" here would be that graven
upon the brick (ch. iv. 1).   There is no reason to suppose that he has
this in his mind.

[*of the siege*] But Kr. renders "of (the prophet's) binding" or confinement.   See on iv. 8.]

smite with the sword round about it] i.e. around the city (*v.* 12).
This is the fate of many of those who seek to escape before and after
the capture of the city.

draw out a sword] Comp. Jer. ix. 16, "I will scatter them also
among the nations...and I will send the sword after them." Lam. i. 3,
"Judah...dwelleth among the heathen, she findeth no rest : all her
persecutors overtook her within the straits."   The phrase occurs again
Lev. xxvi. 33.

3. *few in number*] Or, "by number,"—accurately numbering them.
(Is. xl. 26.)   Of those dispersed a few shall meantime be preserved.

4. Yet of those preserved some shall be cast into the fire and consumed.

burn them in the fire; therefrom shall a fire come forth into all the house of Israel.

5   Thus saith the Lord GOD: This is Jerusalem: I have set her in the midst of the nations, and countries are round 6 about her.   And she hath ¹rebelled against my judgements

¹ Or, *changed my judgements into wickedness*

therefrom shall a fire] i.e. from that remnant which is subjected to new consumption in the fire. The "fire" that goes out from this remnant must be destructive, not purifying, as in xix. 14 (cf. Jud. ix. 15; Ezek. xv. 5, xxx. 9, xxxix. 6), but the meaning is not quite clear. It is the prophet's belief that those left in the city after the captivity of Jehoiachin were more debased and wicked than those already carried away (ch. ix. 9, xi. 15). When the city is destroyed and its inhabitants come as captives among the former exiles, these when they see their wickedness will be comforted over the fall of Jerusalem, acknowledging that it was inevitable (ch. xiv. 22). Further Jehovah expresses His determination that He *will* yet subdue Israel unto Him and rule over them, though this implies purging out from among them the rebels, as of old in the wilderness of the Exodus (ch. xx. 33—38). And the prophet feels himself a watchman (ch. iii. 17); an approaching judgement looms before him, which all the people, each one for himself, will have to pass through. And the idea may be that the judgement, beginning with the inhabitants of Jerusalem, shall spread from them over the whole house of Israel. [Kr. avoids the difficulty by reading 'from Me' (Jehovah). *SBOT.*, Ber. and Cor. consider the clause a gloss, the last attributing its origin to a scribe's recollection of the (quite irrelevant) words in xix. 14.]

V. 5—17. EXPLANATION OF THE FOUR PRECEDING SYMBOLS.

Jerusalem, set in the midst of the nations and favoured of God above them all, has even exceeded them in wickedness (*vv.* 5, 6). Therefore God's judgements upon her shall be unparalleled in severity, first in the horrors of the siege, and secondly in the terrible miseries of pestilence, famine, and bloodshed, that shall follow it (*vv.* 7—17).

5. *This is Jerusalem*] Or, *This Jerusalem*—I set it! (Ex. xxxii. 1; Ezek. xl. 45). Jerusalem is placed emphatically at the head of the sentence; the thoughts which the name suggests are then developed in the succeeding clauses.

and countries are round about her] The geographical position of Jerusalem in the midst of the nations, distinct from them all, was but the external side of the exclusive favours bestowed on her by God. She should have been distinguished above the nations in righteousness, but her corruption was become deeper than theirs. Comp. on the idea of the central position of Jerusalem and Canaan, ch. xxxviii. 12—"the navel of the earth." [So the Greek poet Pindar (*Pyth.* IV. 131) assigns this distinction to Delphi.]

in doing wickedness more than the nations, and against my
statutes more than the countries that are round about her:
for they have rejected my judgements, and as for my
statutes, they have not walked in them.   Therefore thus 7
saith the Lord GOD: Because ye are turbulent more than
the nations that are round about you, and have not walked
in my statutes, neither have kept my judgements, neither
have done after the ¹ordinances of the nations that are
round about you; therefore thus saith the Lord GOD: Be- 8
hold, I, even I, am against thee; and I will execute
judgements in the midst of thee in the sight of the nations.
And I will do in thee that which I have not done, and 9

¹ Heb. *judgements*.

they have rejected my judgements] My ordinances. "They," i.e. the
people, who compose Jerusalem.

7—17. Because she has surpassed the nations in evil, her chastisements shall be without example in severity.

7. *ye are turbulent*] The A.V. "ye multiplied" cannot be justified.
The form in the M.T. *hămonkhem*, however, is anomalous, and it is best,
with most modern commentators, to read *hamrothkem, ye rebelled*, as
v. 6 is then resumed. The sense of R.V. is got by a very slight change
(*hămothkhem*), cf. xxii. 5, last words; Am. iii. 9¹.

neither...after the ordinances] the practices of the nations [a recognition, even though a somewhat obscure one, that God was not
without witness in the heart of the heathen; cf. Rom. ii. 15]. Others
with Syr. would omit the neg.: *but have done according to....* The
charge of the prophet, however, is that Israel had exceeded the nations
in wickedness; cf. xvi. 47, 48; Jer. ii. 11, "Hath a nation changed
their gods, which yet are no gods?"

8. *am against thee*] [A favourite expression with this prophet
(xiii. 8, 20, xxi. 3 [Heb. 8], xxvi. 3 &c.), but once (xxxvi. 9) *towards* in
a favourable sense. See *LOT.*⁹ p. 297.]

in the sight of the nations] The nations saw Israel's wickedness,
and they shall also see her judgements, and they shall know that Jehovah
is God alone.

9. *that which I have not done*] This is no mere rhetorical threat.
It is possible that the miseries of the siege and exile were no greater
than those endured by other nations in those days, but the same miseries
may be felt more acutely. Israel was a nation fervidly patriotic, and
patriotism was inspired by the glow of religion; it was also for that
time a nation highly cultured; and moreover its calamities were felt to
come from the hand of its own God. The feelings of the godly Israelite
after the fall of the city corresponded to the prophet's words here before

¹ [The Oxf. Lex., however, recognises the sense of "turbulent" as that of the
root which appears in the Heb. text.]

whereunto I will not do any more the like, because of all
10 thine abominations.   Therefore the fathers shall eat the
sons in the midst of thee, and the sons shall eat their
fathers; and I will execute judgements in thee, and the
whole remnant of thee will I scatter unto all the winds.
11 Wherefore, as I live, saith the Lord God, surely, because
thou hast defiled my sanctuary with all thy detestable
things, and with all thine abominations, therefore will I
also ¹diminish *thee*; neither shall mine eye spare, and I also
12 will have no pity.   A third part of thee shall die with the
pestilence, and with famine shall they be consumed in the
midst of thee; and a third part shall fall by the sword
round about thee; and a third part I will scatter unto all

¹ Or, *withdraw mine eye that it shall not spare*   Another reading is,
hew thee *down.*

its fall: "Behold, and see if there be any sorrow like unto my sorrow
which is done unto me, wherewith the Lord hath afflicted me in the
day of his fierce anger" (Lam. i. 12).   "See, O Lord, and behold, to
whom thou hast done thus!" (Lam. ii. 20).   "For the punishment of
the iniquity (see marg.) of the daughter of my people is greater than the
punishment of the sin (see marg.) of Sodom, that was overthrown as in
a moment, and no hands were laid upon her" (Lam. iv. 6).

    10.   *the fathers shall eat the sons*]   Neither is this, as it might be,
a generality merely to suggest severe straitness.   Lam. iv. 10, "The
hands of the pitiful women have sodden their own children; they were
their meat in the destruction of the daughter of my people."   See the
story 2 Kgs vi. 24—29; cf. Lev. xxvi. 29; Deut. xxviii. 53; Jer. xix.
9; Lam. ii. 20.

    11.   *defiled my sanctuary*]   The commentary on this is supplied by
ch. viii.

    will I also diminish thee]   The word is so rendered ch. xvi. 27,
where, however, an object follows the verb.   The balance of clauses
here: I also will—and mine eye shall not spare: I also will not pity,
appears to shew that the word expresses one idea along with the
words "mine eye shall not spare."   This can hardly be expressed
otherwise than: I also will withdraw mine eye and it shall not spare;
I also will have no pity.   For the phrase "withdraw the eye" cf.
Job xxxvi. 7.   In ch. xxiv. 14 a similar word occurs, but there with
the negative.   Targ. Vulg. render "hew down," but this kind of
reading (*d* for *r*, the two letters being very similar in Hebrew) is too
familiar to be of any value.   Perhaps the reading might be: I also am
against thee and mine eye shall not spare (form of "against thee" as
xxi. 8, cf. here *v.* 8).   Cf. ch. viii. 18.

    12.   Explanation of the symbol *vv.* 1—4.

the winds, and will draw out a sword after them. Thus 13
shall mine anger be accomplished, and I will ¹satisfy my
fury ²upon them, and I will be comforted: and they shall
know that I the LORD have spoken in my zeal, when I
have accomplished my fury upon them. Moreover I will 14
make thee a desolation and a reproach, among the nations
that are round about thee, in the sight of all that pass by.
So it shall be a reproach and a taunt, an instruction and an 15
astonishment, unto the nations that are round about thee,
when I shall execute judgements in thee in anger and in
fury, and in furious rebukes: I the LORD have spoken it:
when I shall send upon them the evil arrows of famine, that 16
are for destruction, which I will send to destroy you; and I
will increase the famine upon you, and will break your staff
of bread; and I will send upon you famine and evil beasts, 17

¹ Heb. *bring to rest.*   ² Or, *toward*

13. *I will satisfy my fury upon them*] i.e. as marg., *will bring to
rest*, by its being fully expended. Cf. Zech. vi. 8, "they have quieted
my spirit in the north country." The phrase occurs again, ch. xvi. 42,
xxi. 17, xxiv. 13.

I will be comforted] i.e. appeased by the vengeance taken on the
people's sins, cf. Is. i. 24.

I the LORD have spoken] [A frequent closing asseveration in Ezekiel,
and peculiar to him. See *v.* 15, xv. 17, xvii. 21, xxi. 17, 32 (Heb. 22,
37), etc.]

in my zeal] The word, usually rendered "jealousy," expresses the
heat of any passion, here resentment, ch. xvi. 38, 42, xxiii. 25, xxxvi.
5, 6, xxxviii. 19. Cf. ch. ii. 5, vi. 10, xxiv. 22.

14. *reproach, among the nations*] Lam. ii. 15, 16, "All that pass
by clap their hands at thee; they hiss and wag their head at the
daughter of Jerusalem, *saying*, Is this the city that men called The
perfection of beauty?"

15. *So it shall be*] Rather, as LXX., *and thou shalt be.*

an instruction] i.e. a lesson of warning, cf. ch. xxiii. 48, "that all
women may be taught (take warning) not to do after your lewdness."
Cf. Deut. xxix. 23 *seq.*

16. *arrows of famine*] Cf. Deut. xxxii. 23, 24.

I will increase] lit. *add*, i.e. send famine after famine upon you. On
"staff of bread" cf. ch. iv. 14.

17. *evil beasts*] The three great plagues often specified are, famine,
pestilence, and sword (ch. xiv. 13, 17, 19), to which a fourth is sometimes added, evil beasts (ch. xiv. 15, 21, xxxiii. 27, xxxiv. 25; Lev.
xxvi. 22; Deut. xxxii. 24).

In the above verses the cumulative expressions are often wanting

and they shall bereave thee; and pestilence and blood shall pass through thee; and I will bring the sword upon thee: I the LORD have spoken it.

6 And the word of the LORD came unto me, saying, Son
2 of man, set thy face toward the mountains of Israel, and
3 prophesy ¹unto them, and say, Ye mountains of Israel, hear the word of the Lord GOD: Thus saith the Lord GOD to the mountains and to the hills, to the ²watercourses and to the valleys: Behold, I, even I, will bring a sword upon

---

¹ Or, *against*   ² Or, *ravines*

in LXX. e.g. *v.* 11 the words "and with all thine abominations." Differences of this kind do not affect the sense, and it is unnecessary to notice them in detail.

VI.   PROPHECY AGAINST THE MOUNTAINS OF ISRAEL, THE SEATS OF HER IDOLATRY.

Ch. iv. v. were directed chiefly against Jerusalem, because she had rebelled against the statutes of the LORD (ch. v. 6) and because she had polluted His sanctuary with her abominations (ch. v. 11). Therefore the arrows of Jehovah's judgements shall come upon her, famine, pestilence, and sword. For the same reason His judgements must overtake the land, especially the mountains, on which the high places were situated, where the idolatries and false worship were practised.

(i) *vv.* 1—7. The high places, altars, and sun-images shall be utterly destroyed; the carcases of the worshippers shall fall before the idols, and their bones be scattered about them.

(2) *vv.* 8—10. A remnant shall escape and shall remember the LORD among the nations whither they are scattered, and shall loathe themselves for all the evils which they have done; and they shall know that He who spake to them was Jehovah, God alone.

(3) *vv.* 11—14. Renewal of the threat of destruction with every expression of scorn and hatred on the prophet's part for the people's doings. They shall know when their slain fall down and lie around their altars that Jehovah has done it.

2. *Son of man*] See on ch. ii. 1.

mountains of Israel] i.e. the mountain-land of Israel, but with special reference to the mountains as the seats of idolatrous worship. [The expression is also significant in the prophet's mouth, as pointing to the contrast with the wide-reaching Babylonian plains.]

3. *watercourses*] marg. *ravines*; the gorges where there were streams and thick trees, and where idolatrous worship was practised (ch. xxxv. 8, xxxvi. 4, 6), cf. Is. lvii. 5, "that slay the children in the valleys (a different word), under the clefts of the rocks. Among the smooth *stones* of the valley is thy portion; they, they are thy lot: even to them hast thou poured a drink offering, thou hast offered an oblation." (Cf. Jer. ii. 23.)

you, and I will destroy your high places.   And your altars 4
shall become desolate, and your sun-images shall be broken:
and I will cast down your slain men before your idols.   And 5
I will lay the carcases of the children of Israel before their
idols; and I will scatter your bones round about your altars.
In all your dwelling places the cities shall be laid waste, and 6
the high places shall be desolate; that your altars may be
laid waste and ¹made desolate, and your idols may be
broken and cease, and your sun-images may be hewn down,
and your works may be ²abolished.   And the slain shall fall 7

---

¹ Or, *bear their guilt*   ² Heb. *blotted out.*

---

your high places] The word properly means a height or hill (ch.
xxxvi. 2), then a sanctuary situated on such a height (1 Sam. ix. 13), and
finally any sanctuary (Is. xvi. 12, and so in Moabitish. See Moabite
stone, l. 3), particularly in Israel the rural sanctuaries.   These
sanctuaries had probably been mainly Canaanitish (Deut. xii. 2; Lev.
xxvi. 30), but had been adopted by Israel and devoted to the service
of Jehovah (ch. xx. 28).   Along with the sanctuaries themselves no
doubt much of the native religious practice was also adopted.   After
a long struggle these rural high places were abolished by Josiah, and
public service of Jehovah confined to the temple at Jerusalem, but
they grew up again under Manasseh.   Even the worship of Jehovah
at such sanctuaries would be very corrupt, and in the last years of the
kingdom the worship of other deities was no doubt also practised.
This prophet condemns all worship at the high places as "abominations" (v. 11).   This does not appear to be with him a question of
mere locality or number of sanctuaries; he considers the high places
to be Canaanitish and the service at them no worship of Jehovah.

4.   *sun-images*] i.e. symbols of the sun-god, probably in the shape
of a pyramid or obelisk.   They stood beside the altars.   So again *v.* 6.

your idols] The term used is an opprobrious or contemptuous
epithet, applied to idols, though its precise meaning is doubtful.   Most
probably it means *block*-gods [primarily something rolled, then a long
sacred stone, then a stone image, and lastly an idol in general, with
allusion to its helplessness], though others connect it with the word
dung (ch. iv. 12) and render dung-gods, which is less probable.   The
term occurs in Ezek. nearly 40 times, also in Lev. xxvi. 30; Deut.
xxix. 17; 1 Kgs xv. 12, xxi. 26; 2 Kgs xvii. 12, xxi. 11, 21, xxiii. 24;
Jer. l. 2.   Most of these idols were probably meant to represent Jehovah.
The same had already been threatened by Jer. viii. 1, 2.

5.   The same had already been threatened by Jer. viii. 1, 2.

6.   *your works*] the works of your hands, the idols.   [Cf. Is. xvii.
8.]   All the cumulative phrases in the verse are wanting in LXX.
viz. "and made desolate," "and cease," "and your works may be
abolished."   The term "abolished" is lit. "blotted out."   The rendering "made desolate" is probably right, though as spelled the word

in the midst of you, and ye shall know that I am the Lord.
8 Yet will I leave a remnant, in that ye shall have some that
    escape the sword among the nations, when ye shall be
9 scattered through the countries.　And they that escape of
    you shall remember me among the nations whither they
    shall be carried captives, how that ¹I have been broken with

---

¹ Or, according to most of the ancient versions, *I have broken their &c.*

might mean "suffer" or "be punished," R.V. marg. "bear their guilt."
The apparatus of worship in the prophet's time comprehended (1) the
high place, the general name for the sanctuary, which might be a
building of various degrees of simplicity or splendour, or perhaps a
mere tent; (2) the altar, an essential of course of every high place;
(3) the obelisk or sun-pillar; and (4) the idol, with which probably
most of the rural high places were provided, as Is. ii. 8 says, "Their
land also is full of idols; they worship the work of their own hands."
Cf. Jer. ii. 27, 28, who complains that their gods (which he describes
as "stocks" and "stones") were as numerous as their cities.　With
this religious inventory may be compared that given by Hosea iii. 5.
Ezekiel does not mention the Asherah, except in the form of the "evergreen tree" (ch. vi. 13).

　　7.　*I am the Lord*]　The term Jehovah is used in the later prophets
to mean the true and only God.　In this prophet the purpose and the
effect of all the judgements on Israel is that they may know that He
who inflicts them is Jehovah—God alone.　The same is the purpose
and effect of His judgements on the heathen—*these* learn also the same
truth.　But further, the redemption of Israel reveals this truth to the
heathen fully.　When the idols were cut down to the ground and the
bones of their worshippers lay scattered around them, the futility of
serving them could not but be perceived; Jer. ii. 28, "where are thy
gods that thou hast made thee? let them arise, if they can save thee in
the time of thy trouble."　Cf. Hos. ii. 7; Is. lvii. 12, 13.

VI. **8—10.**　A remnant shall be preserved, and shall remember the Lord among the nations whither they are
scattered.

　　8.　*in that ye shall have some that escape*]　The original reads very
awkwardly, and in LXX. the words: "yet will I leave a remnant"
are wanting.　It seems best to take *v.* 9 as the apodosis, "And if I
leave a remnant...then shall they that escape of you remember, &c."

　　9.　*how that I have been broken with*]　Such a sense as "have been
broken with" is altogether impossible [and the marg. must be accepted as
the best conjectural emendation of a probably corrupt text].　The natural
sense is: they shall remember (think of) me...*when I have broken*.
Their idolatrous heart shall be broken with their calamities, and then
shall they return unto the Lord: Hos. ii. 7, "I will return unto my
first husband, for then was it better with me than now."　The present

their whorish heart, which hath departed from me, and with
their eyes, which go a whoring after their idols: and they
shall loathe themselves in their own sight for the evils which
they have committed in all their abominations.   And they 10
shall know that I am the LORD: I have not said in vain
that I would do this evil unto them.

Thus saith the Lord GOD: Smite with thine hand, and 11
stamp with thy foot, and say, Alas! because of all the evil
abominations of the house of Israel: for they shall fall by
the sword, by the famine, and by the pestilence.   He that 12
is far off shall die of the pestilence; and he that is near
shall fall by the sword; and he that remaineth and is ¹be-
sieged shall die by the famine: thus will I accomplish

¹ Or, *preserved*

reading has probably arisen from the similar word "carried captive"
being in the copyist's mind.

and with their eyes] Render **...and their eyes**, in accordance with
preceding note. The harshness of the zeugma, "and their eyes," is
relieved by the distance from "break" and the metaphorical nature
of the expression. Cf. the phrase "lifted up his eyes to the idols,"
ch. xviii. 6, 12, 15, xxxiii. 25.

loathe themselves] lit. *their faces*; a use of "face" for self, not
uncommon in the later language, ch. xx. 43, xxxvi. 31; Job xxiii. 17.

VI. 11—14. RENEWAL OF THE THREAT OF DESTRUCTION BECAUSE OF IDOLATRY.

11. *Smite with thine hand*] i.e. Clap thine hands. Cf. xxv. 6,
"Because thou (Ammon) hast clapped thine hands, and stamped with
the feet, and rejoiced with all the despite of thy soul against the land of
Israel." The gestures are those of scorn and ill-will, and of rejoicing
over another's misfortune; ch. xxii. 13; Job xxvii. 23. In ch. xxi. 17
the same gesture is attributed to Jehovah.

Alas! because of all] Rather: **Ha**! *because of*, &c. The interjection
seems a shorter form of that used elsewhere, as ch. xxv. 3, "Because
thou (Ammon) saidst, Aha! for my sanctuary, when it was profaned,
and against the land of Israel, when it was made desolate." The prophet
hates and scorns the evil practices of Israel so deeply that he rejoices
at the vengeance about to overtake them [but contrast his attitude in
xi. 13]. The grammatical anomaly in "evil abominations of" is
obviated in LXX. by omission of "evil."

12. *and he that remaineth and is besieged*] In LXX. "he that
remaineth" is wanting. With this omission "he that is besieged"
might stand, cf. ch. vii. 15, "he that is in the city, famine...shall devour
him." Otherwise the sense seems rather as in R.V. marg. *preserved*, as
in Is. xlix. 6.

13 my fury upon them. And ye shall know that I am the
LORD, when their slain men shall be among their idols
round about their altars, upon every high hill, in all the
tops of the mountains, and under every green tree, and
under every thick ¹oak, the place where they did offer
14 sweet savour to all their idols. And I will stretch out my
hand upon them, and make the land desolate and waste,
²from the wilderness toward Diblah, throughout all their
habitations: and they shall know that I am the LORD.

7 Moreover the word of the LORD came unto me, saying,

¹ Or, *terebinth*   ² Or, *more than*

13. Comp. *v.* 7 on the effect of these judgements on the minds of the
people. On "idols," cf. *v.* 4. The cumulative phrases "in all the
tops of the mountains," and "under every thick oak" (better as marg.
terebinth), are wanting in LXX.

sweet savour] said of the smoke or steam of the sacrificial fat burnt
upon the altar, ch. xvi. 19, xx. 28, 41, and often in the ritual laws of the
Pentateuch [, e.g. Exod. xxix. 18; Lev. i. 9, 13, 17; Numb. xv. 3, 7].

14. *desolate and waste*] Cf. ch. xxxiii. 28, 29, xxxv. 3.

from the wilderness toward Diblah] The marg. *more than* may
safely be rejected. But a wilderness of Diblah is unknown; Diblathaim
besides being in Moab could not be called desert. The construction
is difficult, but probably the reading should be: *from the wilderness
to Riblah*, i.e. from south to north. Riblah was situated on the
northern border of the country (Numb. xxxiv. 11). [It lay on the high
road from Palestine to Babylon between the mountain ranges of
Lebanon and Hermon.] It is spoken of as "in the land of Hamath,"
Jer. lii. 9, 27 (where by the substitution of *d* for *r*, LXX. read
Diblah). A few MSS. read Riblah. It must be acknowledged that
this way of designating the whole extent of the land from S. to N.
is nowhere else employed, the northern limit being usually expressed
by "the entering in of Hamath."

VII. DIRGE OVER THE DOWNFALL OF THE KINGDOM OF JUDAH.

The passage is probably in some confusion; *vv.* 8, 9 are virtually a
repetition of *vv.* 3, 4. In LXX. *vv.* 3, 4 stand immediately after *vv.* 8,
9, and have the appearance of being a duplicate. [This divergence of
LXX. from M.T. was noticed by St Jerome. See Swete, *Intr. to
O.T. in Greek*, p. 242.] In other respects the text is very difficult,
and in several places no longer presents the original reading. The
chapter appears to have two divisions:—

First, *vv.* 1—13, announcement that the end of the state is come, in
a series of interjectional sentences, and

And thou, son of man, thus saith the Lord GOD unto the 2
land of Israel, An end: the end is come upon the four
corners of the land.   Now is the end upon thee, and I will 3
send mine anger upon thee, and will judge thee according
to thy ways; and I will bring upon thee all thine abominations.   And mine eye shall not spare thee, neither will 4
I have pity: but I will bring thy ways upon thee, and thine
abominations shall be in the midst of thee: and ye shall
know that I am the LORD.

Thus saith the Lord GOD: An evil, an only evil; behold, 5
it cometh.   An end is come, the end is come, it awaketh 6

Secondly, vv. 14—27, a picture of its dissolution, in language somewhat calmer and more connected.

First, announcement of the end, in three short strophes:
(1)   vv. 1—4.   The end is come upon the four corners of the land.
(2)   vv. 5—9.   The end is come upon the inhabitants of the land.
(3)   vv. 10—13.   The ruin is common and universal.   Persons and
possessions alike perish.

VII. 1—4.   THE END IS COME UPON THE WHOLE LAND, UNSPARING DESTRUCTION FROM THE LORD.

This destruction is the fruit of the abominations of the people, their
idolatries and crimes (v. 23).   They shall know when it overtakes them
that He who inflicts it is Jehovah, God alone.

2.   v. 2 might read: "Thus saith the Lord GOD, Unto the land of
Israel an end! the end is come upon, &c."   Cf. Am. viii. 2.

3.   send mine anger] an unusual form of expression.   [The Divine
anger is personified.   Cf. Ps. xliii. 3.]

will bring] or put.   Chastisement is but sin assuming another form,
a form which it inevitably takes.

4.   mine eye shall not spare] So v. 9, ch. v. 11, viii. 18, ix. 10.
From their calamities the people shall learn not only that He that
inflicts them is their God, whom they called Jehovah (a thing which
they were slow to learn, Am. iii. 2, v. 18), but also what the nature of
that God is—that He is Jehovah, the true and righteous God (a thing
which they were even slower to learn), cf. v. 27, ch. vi. 7, xii. 20, &c.

VII. 5—9.   THE DIRGE TAKES A FRESH TURN, ANNOUNCING IN NEARLY THE SAME WORDS THAT THE END IS COME UPON THE INHABITANTS OF THE LAND.

5.   an only evil] lit. one evil, scarcely a "unique" evil, to which
there is nothing like, but an evil which is "one" and final, 1 Sam.
xxvi. 8; Hag. ii. 6, "Yet once, it is a little while, and I will shake
the heavens and the earth" (see Heb. xii. 26).

6.   it awaketh against thee] The word forms an alliteration with

7 against thee ; behold, it cometh. ¹Thy doom is come unto
  thee, O inhabitant of the land : the time is come, the day
  is near ; *a day of* tumult, and not *of* joyful shouting, ²upon
8 the mountains.   Now will I shortly pour out my fury upon
  thee, and accomplish mine anger against thee, and will
  judge thee according to thy ways; and I will bring upon
9 thee all thine abominations.   And mine eye shall not spare,
  neither will I have pity : I will bring upon thee according
  to thy ways, and thine abominations shall be in the midst
  of thee ; and ye shall know that I the LORD do smite.
10 Behold, the day, behold, it cometh : thy doom is gone

---

¹ Or, *The turn*   Or, *The crowning time*   ² Or, *from*

"the end" (*hakkez, hēkîz*), and suggests that the vengeance slumbering
long is now ready to fall on them. A similar paronomasia in Am. viii.
2, between "end" (*kēz*) and "summer fruit" (*kayîz*), and in Jer. i. 11,
between "almond tree" (*shākēd*) and "watching" (*shōkēd*).

7. *Thy doom is come*] The term occurs in Is. xxviii. 5 in the sense
of diadem, probably from the idea of encircling, going a round or
circuit (Jud. vii. 3, R.V. marg.); hence the conjecture that the word
may have the sense of "turn" (vicem), naturally with the meaning
"calamitous turn," misfortune or fate (as *da'irah* in Arab.), "doom."
So Abulwalid followed by most moderns. [Kr. derives from a root
meaning to purify.] Dukes quotes an Aramaic proverb of Sirach in
which another form of the word has the sense of *times* (a hundred times,
Blumenlese, p. 80). LXX. does not recognise the word either here or
in *v.* 10.

joyful shouting] This rendering assumes that the word translated
"joyful shouting" is another form of the term rendered "vintage shout,"
Is. xvi. 10 ; cf. Jer. xlviii. 33—"the shouting shall be no shouting"
but tumult of invasion.

8, 9. Verses 8, 9 are virtually *vv.* 3, 4 repeated, except that *v.* 9
ends with the words "that I the LORD do smite." The order of
vv. 1—9 in LXX. differs from the Heb. thus : *vv.* 1, 2, 6, 7, 8, 9, 3, 4.
This order is certainly not original, because *vv.* 3, 4, being virtually
the same as 8, 9, cannot have followed these verses immediately (see
introd. note). On the other hand they might be regarded as a kind of
refrain, first to the judgement on the land (*vv.* 3, 4) and then to the
judgement on the inhabitants (*vv.* 8, 9); if so the pronouns in 8, 9 should
possibly be read in the *masculine*.

VII. 10—13. THE RUIN IS UNIVERSAL, OVERTAKING ALL CLASSES.

10. *thy doom is gone forth*] Rather : **is come forth,**—the figure of a
plant springing up ; Job xiv. 2, man "cometh forth like a flower." On
"doom" see *v.* 7.

forth; the rod hath blossomed, pride hath budded. Vio- 11
lence is risen up into a rod of wickedness; ¹none of them
shall remain, nor of their multitude, nor of their wealth:
neither shall there be ²eminency among them. The time 12
is come, the day draweth near: let not the buyer rejoice,
nor the seller mourn: for wrath is upon all the multitude
thereof. For the seller shall not return to that which is 13

¹ Or, *not from them, nor from their multitude, nor from their wealth*
² Or, *wailing for them*

the rod hath blossomed] i.e. sprouted and grown so as to become a
rod. The general scope of the passage seems to imply that the "rod"
here is that by which Israel shall be chastised. In Jer. l. 31 Babylon is
named "pride" (R.V. marg.), and the words "pride has budded"
may serve to explain "the rod has blossomed." If the pride were
that which the rod was to humble, the words would better be attached
to the next verse.

11. "Violence" must be that in Israel, not that of the enemy. This
violence has risen up so as to be, or to bring down, a rod of wickedness,
i.e. a rod due to wickedness or in chastisement of it (*v.* 23). All this,
however, is language very unnatural.

The rest of *v.* 11 is very obscure, and the text certainly corrupt.
The general sense conveyed when the words *shall remain* (A.V.) are
inserted is that Israel and her multitude and her possessions shall be
wholly swept away.

neither shall there be eminency] (marg. *wailing*). The words rendered
"wealth" and "eminency" are both entirely unknown; the former is
probably no word at all, but a false repetition of the previous expression
"none of them"; if it be a word, the natural rendering is that of Ew.,
moaning or sighing (*v.* 16 of doves), or unquietness. For the word
"eminency" recourse is had to the Arab., generally a precarious proceeding. LXX. renders no account of either of the words. Cor.
in his reconstruction of the text follows LXX. generally to the end of
v. 9; *vv.* 10, 11 he emends thus: "Behold the crown (as Is. xxviii. 5)
is come forth, the sceptre blossoms; but the crown shall wither, 11 and
the sceptre fade; what are they, and what their multitude?" The
crown and sceptre are those of Israel. The emendation may be left
to itself.

12. The inhabitants shall be overwhelmed in a common ruin, in
which all social relations shall be forgotten—the buyer shall not rejoice
nor the seller sorrow. A universal "wrath" shall be on all classes,
involving them in a common destruction. Cf. Is. xxiv. 2, "it shall be...
as with the buyer, so with the seller; as with the lender, so with the
borrower," &c.

13. *return to that which is sold*] Sales, particularly of real property,
were usually temporary, the subjects sold being redeemable. When
they were redeemed the seller would "return to that which was sold."

sold, [1]although they be yet alive : for the vision is touching
the whole multitude thereof, [2]none shall return ; neither
shall any strengthen himself [3]in the iniquity of his life.
14 They have blown the trumpet, and have made all ready ;
but none goeth to the battle : for my wrath is upon all the
15 multitude thereof. The sword is without, and the pestilence
and the famine within : he that is in the field shall die with
the sword ; and he that is in the city, famine and pestilence

---

[1] Heb. *though their life be yet among the living.*   [2] Or, *it shall
not turn back*   [3] Or, *whose life is in his iniquity*

By the Law real property returned to the original owner at the year of
freedom. [Lev. xxv. 10, 13.] This hope is vain: the coming calamity
shall obliterate all titles. Others conjecture that the prophet has before
his mind the case of the captives carried away with Jehoiachin, who
were compelled to make forced sales of their property before going into
exile, and who longed to return to claim what was theirs.

although they be yet alive] Or, *while they are* : i.e. never, so long
as they live.

for the vision] Instead of "vision" (by a change of one Heb.
letter) *wrath* should be read: **for wrath is upon all the multitude
thereof,**" as *vv.* 12, 14. Probably the clause : "for the vision (wrath)
...return " should be omitted as accidental repetition of previous words.

strengthen himself...his life] Perhaps: *neither shall any one keep
hold of his life* (maintain his life) *in his iniquity* [but better as marg.
(strengthen himself) *whose life is in his iniquity*]. Those driven out
shall not return, and those remaining shall die in their sins. Or if
there be no reference to those two classes the statements are general :
none shall return to his possessions, and none shall live in his iniquity.

VII. 14—27. PICTURE OF THE DISSOLUTION OF THE STATE.

(1) *vv.* 14—18. The trumpet shall sound the alarm, but none shall
prepare himself for the battle. The sword shall devour without and
famine consume within. A paralysing terror shall seize upon all.

(2) *vv.* 19—22. They shall cast their gold and silver into the streets,
for it cannot buy wherewith to appease their hunger. Their wealth
which was their pride and which they used to further their abominations
shall become the prey of the invader.

(3) *vv.* 23—27. The city is full of violence; therefore it shall be given
over to the worst of the heathen. Perplexity and stupefaction shall
seize king and people, priest and prophet alike. They shall know
Jehovah when His judgements overtake them.

14. Defence is fruitless. Preparations are made but there is no
courage to face the enemy, for the wrath of God upon them prede-
termines their defeat.

15. Cf. Lam. i. 20.

shall devour him. But they that escape of them shall 16
escape, and shall be on the mountains like doves of the
valleys, all of them mourning, every one in his iniquity.
All hands shall be feeble, and all knees shall be weak as 17
water. They shall also gird themselves with sackcloth, and 18
horror shall cover them ; and shame shall be upon all faces,
and baldness upon all their heads. They shall cast their 19
silver in the streets, and their gold shall be as an unclean
thing; their silver and their gold shall not be able to deliver
them in the day of the wrath of the LORD ; they shall not

16. Read: **and when** (if) **they that escape of them shall escape,
they shall be upon the mountains.**

mourning] This refers to the doves: the fugitives shall be on the
mountains (seeking refuge) like doves of the valleys (but LXX. omit
the comparison), all of which mourn. Is. lix. 11, "We roar all like
bears, and mourn sore like doves"; xxxviii. 14, "Like a swallow...
so did I chatter; I did mourn as a dove." The Arabic poets often
refer to the mourning of the dove or ring-dove (*Ḳumrī*) as being
like their own. See the citations of Ahlwardt, Chalef el Ahmar,
p. 102 *seq.* Similarly in the Babylonian Penitential Psalms (Zimmern), Ps. i. 10, "Like doves do I mourn; on sighs I feed myself";
so in vi. 4, vii. 10.

in his iniquity] in the consciousness of it and its consequences.

17. The description returns from the condition of the fugitives to
that of the besieged. Prostration and despair seize them. The figures
of the hands "hanging down," and the knees becoming "water" are
expressive of complete paralysis of strength. LXX. and Hitz. interpret
the latter phrase literally. Cf. ch. xxi. 7 ; Is. xiii. 7; Jer. vi. 24.

18. *horror shall cover them*] Or, **trembling**, terror, Job xxi. 6. It
shall take such hold of them that it shall be all over them, like a garment covering them. Cf. Is. lix. 17, "was clad with zeal as a cloke";
Ps. lv. 6.

baldness] A sign of mourning: Is. xv. 2, "on all their heads is baldness"; Mic. i. 16, "enlarge thy baldness as the vulture." This tonsure
in token of mourning, common among many nations of antiquity, was
confined among the Hebrews to shaving the front part of the head
(Deut. xiv. 1), and was forbidden by the Law in the case of priests (Lev.
xxi. 5, cf. Ezek. xliv. 20), and of the whole people (Deut. xiv. 1);
cf. Lev. xix. 27 ; Jer. xvi. 6; Am. viii. 10.

19. Amidst the famine they cast their silver and gold away in the
streets ; these cannot procure them food. On the horrors of famine during
the siege of Jerusalem, comp. Lam. iv. 4, 8—10, ii. 11, 12, 19, 20, i. 11.

gold shall be as an unclean thing] lit. *uncleanness*. It is the strongest
expression for "object of abhorrence"; cf. ch. xxxvi. 17, of the people's
idolatries.

satisfy their souls, neither fill their bowels: because it hath
20 been the stumblingblock of their iniquity.   As for the
beauty of his ornament, [1]he set it in majesty: but they made
the images of their abominations *and* their detestable things
[2]therein: therefore have I made it unto them as an unclean
21 thing.   And I will give it into the hands of the strangers
for a prey, and to the wicked of the earth for a spoil; and
22 they shall profane it.   My face will I turn also from them,
and they shall profane my [3]secret *place*: and robbers shall
23 enter into it, and profane it.   Make the chain: for the land

---

[1] Or, *they turned it to pride; and they &c.*   [2] Or, *thereof*
[3] Or, *secret* treasure

hath been the stumblingblock] Their gold and silver have been to them
something on which they have stumbled and fallen, i.e. a cause of their
sinning; cf. ch. xiv. 3, xliv. 12.

20.   *he set it in majesty: but they*]   Rather (as marg.) **they turned
it to pride; and they**, &c.

therein]   Rather (as marg.) **thereof.**   The thing spoken of is still
their silver and gold; this they not only turned into pride, but made
also images of it.   Hos. ii. 8, I "multiplied unto her silver and gold,
which they used for Baal"; viii. 4, "Of their silver and their gold
have they made them idols, that they may be cut off."   Cf. ch. xvi. 11;
2 Sam. i. 24; Jer. iv. 30.

21.   Because of this abuse of their silver and gold in making it into
idols it shall become the prey of the Chaldeans, who shall profane it,
turning it from a sacred to a common use.   In a certain sense all
that was in Israel was sacred, and the mere fact of the heathen taking
possession of it profaned it.   Hos. x. 6, "It (the calf) also shall be carried
unto Assyria for a present to king Jareb"; cf. Is. xlvi. 1, 2; Mic. i. 7.

22.   The enemy shall penetrate into the temple and profane it.

turn...from them]   This most naturally refers to Israel, from whom
the LORD will turn His face in anger, cf. *v.* 11.   It might refer to the
invader, whom the LORD will not behold but permit to work His will,
cf. Lam. ii. 3.

secret place]   probably the temple (Lam. ii. 1); less naturally the city.
The word "secret," however, is not to be referred to the *arcanum*
of the Most Holy place; the meaning is "my precious thing."

and robbers]   the Chaldean pillagers.

23.   *Make the chain*]   The chain could only be for binding the
captives to carry them into exile.   In Is. xl. 19 a similar word is used
for the silver chains with which the idols were fastened to the wall lest
they should totter or fall; and in Nah. iii. 10 the verb is rendered
"were bound" in chains (Jer. xl. 1 has another word).   If the
reading be correct the sense is not doubtful.   It must be confessed,
however, that nothing in the text suggests any reference to chains.

is full of ¹bloody crimes, and the city is full of violence. Wherefore I will bring the worst of the heathen, and they 24 shall possess their houses: I will also make the pride of the strong to cease; and ²their holy places shall be profaned. ³Destruction cometh; and they shall seek peace, and there 25 shall be none.   Mischief shall come upon mischief, and 26 rumour shall be upon rumour; and they shall seek a vision of the prophet; but the law shall perish from the priest, and counsel from the ancients.   The king shall mourn, 27 and the prince shall be clothed with desolation, and the hands of the people of the land shall be troubled: I will do unto them after their way, and according to their deserts will I judge them; and they shall know that I am the LORD.

¹ Heb. *judgement of blood.*   ² Or, *they that sanctify them*   ³ Or, *Distress*

LXX. connects with the preceding (so Syr.) and reads: and they shall work disorder (defilement).   Cor. suggests two inf. abs. (after xxiii. 46) viz. raze and empty out! (cf. Ps. cxxxvii. 7; Is. xxiv. 1). Curiously neither of the words is used by Ezekiel.   The present reading is scarcely original.

24.   *worst of the heathen*] Cf. xxviii. 7, xxx. 11, "the terrible of the nations."   Jer. vi. 23; Hab. i. 7.

the pride of the strong] In xxiv. 21 "the pride of your power." Cf. xxxiii. 28; Lev. xxvi. 19.   The spelling of the Heb. for "holy places" is an Aramaism.

25.   *Destruction*] Or, **Anguish.**

26.   *Mischief...upon mischief*] i.e. calamity upon calamity; and "rumour" of misfortune upon rumour.   Jer. iv. 20; Is. xxviii. 19.

but the law] **and** the law.   It is implied in seeking a vision from the prophet that no vision is granted; and the law, i.e. decision or judgement, sought from the priest, ceases; neither can the elders give any counsel.   The same three classes of advisers, viz. prophets, priests, and elders or wise men are spoken of in Jer. xviii. 18.   All sources of revelation are dumb.   Cf. Lam. ii. 9, "Yea, her prophets also find no vision from the LORD."   Ps. lxxiv. 9; Mic. iii. 6.

27.   *The king shall mourn*] 2 Sam. xix. 1.   The "prince" is Ezekiel's usual term for the chief civil ruler, and princes for those of the royal house.   The clause "the king shall mourn" is wanting in LXX.   On "clothed with desolation," i.e. utterly appalled, cf. *v.* 18, xxvi. 16.

according to their deserts] lit. *judgements*, i.e. practices and deeds, as ch. v. 7, xi. 12 (manners).   All that should defend and save the state, from the king to the people of the land, shall be paralysed and helpless. The LORD will judge them according to their doings and they shall know that He is Jehovah.

THIRD SECTION. CH. VIII.—XI. NEW VISIONS OF JEHOVAH'S
WITHDRAWAL FROM HIS HOUSE, AND THE APPROACHING DE-
STRUCTION OF JERUSALEM.

On the fifth day of the sixth month of the sixth year of the Captivity of Jehoiachin (B.C. 591) the prophet sat in his house and the
elders of the exile sat before him. Moved by their words or by their
presence he fell into a trance and was transported by the spirit to
Jerusalem, where a series of events passed before his view.

First, ch. viii., a vision of the idolatries practised by all classes in
the house of the LORD.

Secondly, ch. ix., a vision of the messengers of divine vengeance,
and the slaughter of the inhabitants of the city.

Thirdly, ch. x., a vision of the destruction of the city itself by fire
from God, with a new description of the cherubim.

Fourthly, ch. xi., a vision of the internal condition of the city, the
counsels and thoughts of the leaders. Then the departure of Jehovah
from the city, and renewal of the threat of destruction, but with a
promise of restoration to those already in exile.

Finally, awaking out of his trance, the prophet narrates the preceding
revelations to the exiles (ch. xi. 25).

CH. VIII. THE MANIFOLD IDOLATRIES OF ISRAEL, WHEREBY
THEY PROFANE THE HOUSE OF THE LORD, CAUSING HIM TO
WITHDRAW FROM IT.

Four idolatrous scenes pass before the prophet's view.

(1) *vv.* 1—6. He is shewn an image, called the image of jealousy,
situated apparently in the outer court, but near the gateway leading
to the inner court.

(2) *vv.* 7—12, the secret idolatries practised by the elders in the
chambers of the gateway.

(3) *vv.* 13, 14, the lamentation for Tammuz or Adonis engaged in
by the women.

(4) *vv.* 15—18, sun-worship practised in front of the temple in the
inner court.

1—3. The trance in presence of the elders. The prophet, abiding
in his house (ch. iii. 25), was visited by the elders of the captivity among
whom he dwelt. They probably came to consult with him regarding the
affairs at home and the prospects of the city. Thrown into a state of
excitement by their words or by their presence he fell into a trance. The
vision of the God of Israel again appeared to him, for this thought of
Jehovah chiefly occupied his mind and led to all his other thoughts, and
he was carried away in the spirit to Jerusalem; and there the manifold
idolatries of the people were shewn him. Two chief thoughts appear
expressed by the symbolism; first, by making the "glory" of Jehovah
appear in Jerusalem the prophet points the contrast between the glorious
God whom the people had abandoned and the debased forms of worship
to which they had addicted themselves, and also implies that this

And it came to pass in the sixth year, in the sixth *month*, 8
in the fifth *day* of the month, as I sat in mine house, and
the elders of Judah sat before me, that the hand of the Lord
God fell there upon me.   Then I beheld, and, lo, a like- 2
ness as the appearance of fire ; from the appearance of his
loins and downward, fire : and from his loins and upward,
as the appearance of brightness, [1] as the colour of amber.
And he put forth the form of an hand, and took me by 3
a lock of mine head ; and the spirit lifted me up between

---

[1] Or, *as amber to look upon*

worship was done in the face of Jehovah, "to provoke the eyes of his
glory" (Is. iii. 8) ; and secondly, when Jehovah Himself shews the
idolatrous practices of the people, we see, what is characteristic of the
prophet, the effort to throw himself into the consciousness, so to speak,
of Jehovah, and look at things from *His* mind, He being who He is.
It would be a mistake to regard the details here given as due entirely to
literary artifice ; there is no doubt a foundation of reality under them,
though when in after years the prophet reflected on the facts and recorded them he gave them great expansion and embellishment.

1.   *the sixth* month]   The first vision of the prophet was in the fifth
year of Jehoiachin's captivity and in the fourth month (i. 1) ; the present
one a year and two months later.   LXX. reads *fifth* month, and many
modern scholars accept this reading, arguing that the Heb. date is due
to some copyist or reader who wished to leave room for the number of
days during which the prophet had to lie on his side (ch. iv. 5, 9).   The
copyist must have been an indifferent arithmetician, for 7 (iii. 15) + 390
+ 40 (ch. iv. 5, 6) = 437, while a lunar year and two months, 354 + 59
= 413 days.   The discrepancies between the Heb. and LXX. dates are
not easy to explain.

elders of Judah]   Cf. ch. xiv. 1, "certain of the elders of Israel."   The
meaning appears from ch. xi. 25, "Then I spake unto them of the captivity all the things that the Lord had shewed me."   The community
at Tel-Abib were probably permitted to have a certain internal government of their own.   In the "elders" before him the prophet sees represented not so much the captivity as the whole "house of Israel."   On
"hand of the Lord," cf. ch. i. 3.

2.   *as the appearance of fire*]   more naturally [by a very slight
modification of the Hebrew], the appearance **of a man**, as LXX.,
cf. ch. i. 26, 27, "the appearance of a man" (a different word, however), where the description is the same, viz. fire from the loins
downwards and amber from the loins upwards.   The prophet speaks
with reverential vagueness of God—"a likeness as the appearance of a
man," and "he put forth the form of a hand."

3.   He does not even say that it was the Divine hand that carried him ;
spirit carried him, the form of the Divine hand was merely symbolical.

the earth and the heaven, and brought me in the visions of
God to Jerusalem, to the door of the gate of the inner *court*
that looketh toward the north; where was the seat of the
4 image of jealousy, which provoketh to jealousy.   And,

the visions of God] i.e. shewn him by God, ch. i. 1.
the door of the gate of the inner court *that looketh* &c.] i.e. the northern
gate of the inner court. The word "inner" is wanting in LXX. The
general opinion has been that the prophet was set down in the inner
court, at the *inner* door of the northern gateway into that court. The
term "door," however, seems in usage to mean the outside entrance;
and if the prophet had stood in the inner court he would have had to
look northward through the gateway in order to see the image of jealousy,
which was certainly not in the inner court. It is more natural to suppose
him set down in the outer court, in front of the gateway leading into the
inner court. In front of this gateway, in the outer court, stood the image
of jealousy, near the entrance. Having seen this the prophet is next
brought *into* the gateway (*v.* 7), where he enters the chamber of imagery,
some one of the cells in the gateway building. From there he is carried
outside the sacred enclosure altogether to the north door of the outer
court (*v.* 14), where he finds the women bewailing Tammuz. And
finally he is transported into the inner court where he beholds the
sun-worship practised in front of the temple itself. Previous to this
he had not been in the inner court, for when being shewn the idolatries
he is always taken to the precise place where they are practised.
image of jealousy] not an image of "jealousy" itself, considered as
a deity, but an image which provoked to jealousy. The "jealousy" of
God is a violent emotion or resentment arising from the feeling of being
injured (Deut. xxxii. 21). It is uncertain what this image was. The
word occurs again, Deut. iv. 16, in the sense of similitude or "figure,"
and in Phœnician with the meaning of "statue," e.g. in an inscription
from Idalion (*Corp. Inscr. Sem.*, vol. i. 88, 3, 7, &c.). According to
2 Kgs xxi. 7 Manasseh put a graven image of Asherah "in the house"
of the LORD, which Josiah brought out and burnt (2 Kgs xxiii. 6;
2 Chr. xxxiii. 7, 15). In earlier times the Asherah (A.V. wrongly
grove) was a tree or pole planted beside an altar. It is not quite certain
whether the pole or stock was a substitute for the evergreen tree, when
this could not be had, or whether like the sun-image it was the symbol
of a goddess [Asherah or Ashrat]. In later times the term seems used
as the name of a goddess. The expression "in the house" is hardly to
be pressed so far as to imply that Manasseh placed the Asherah in the
temple proper; "house" is used of the whole temple buildings, including the courts. The image here may be this Asherah, whether we are
to suppose it replaced after Josiah had burnt it, or whether the prophet
be here taking a comprehensive view of the idolatries of Israel, including
the time of Manasseh. In 2 Kgs xxiii. 11 reference is made to the
horses of the sun placed "at the entering in of the house of the LORD,"
but these would scarcely be called an "image."

behold, the glory of the God of Israel was there, according
to the ¹appearance that I saw in the plain.   Then said he 5
unto me, Son of man, lift up thine eyes now the way toward
the north.   So I lifted up mine eyes the way toward the
north, and behold northward of the gate of the altar this
image of jealousy in the entry.   And he said unto me, Son 6
of man, seest thou what they do? even the great abominations that the house of Israel do commit here, ²that I should
go far off from my sanctuary? but ³thou shalt again see yet
other great abominations.   And he brought me to the door 7
of the court; and when I looked, behold a hole in the wall.

¹ Or, *vision*   ² Or, *to get them far off*   ³ Or, *turn thee yet
again, and thou shalt see greater abominations*   So also in vv. 13, 15.

4.   "The glory" was that seen by the prophet at the Chebar (ch. i.).
This glory expressed the prophet's conception of Jehovah.   And thus
that conception is placed in striking contrast with the deities worshipped
by the people, and beholding their worship.

5.   *gate of the altar*]   probably the northern inner gate.   The northern
entrance was the most frequented, partly because the royal palace and
buildings lay to the south and east, and the west was closed by the
buildings of the temple itself.   In Lev. i. 11 the sacrificial victims are
commanded to be slaughtered on the north side of the altar.   [Kr. holds
that, as all gates of the inner court were presumably equally distant from
the altar, we should by a slight change in the Heb., read *north*ward of
the gate (viz. that of *v.* 3) *was the altar of the image* &c.]

in the entry]   The image was situated on the north of the altar gate,
and the words "in (or at) the entry" are to be taken somewhat generally.
The words are wanting in LXX.

6.   *I should go far off*]   i.e. withdraw.   These abominations defiled
Jehovah's sanctuary, the place of His abode, causing Him to abandon
it.   His withdrawal is symbolized ch. xi. 1, 22, 23.

VIII. 7—12.   THE SECRET IDOLATRY OF THE ELDERS.

7.   *the door of the court*]   i.e. the outside entrance of the gateway
into the inner court.   Placed at first near the entrance the prophet
is now brought to the gateway itself, either to some chamber within
it or to some building attached to it, cf. xl. 44.   In the wall of this
building he observed a hole, through which he dug and entered a
chamber, on the walls of which were pourtrayed all manner of creatures,
and in the chamber were seventy elders offering incense to the imagery
on the walls.

behold a hole]   The symbolism is not very clear.   The "hole" is
meant to suggest that entrance into the chamber was obtained secretly
by those who practised their rites there.   The words are wanting in
LXX.

8 Then said he unto me, Son of man, dig now in the wall:
9 and when I had digged in the wall, behold a door.   And
   he said unto me, Go in,˙and see the wicked abominations
10 that they do here.   So I went in and saw; and behold
   every form of creeping things, and abominable beasts, and
   all the idols of the house of Israel, pourtrayed upon the

8.   The words "in the wall" are wanting both times in LXX.

9.   The word "wicked" is wanting in LXX.

10.   The construction is difficult: lit. "and behold every likeness (*v.* 3;
Deut. iv. 17, 18) of. creeping things and beasts (cattle), abomination,
and all," &c., the term "abomination" being descriptive both of creeping
things and beasts.   The term "beasts" is employed of the larger
domestic animals, though also of the beasts of prey; it seems nowhere
used of the smaller vermin.   On the other hand the word "abomination" is chiefly used in regard to the smaller creatures that swarm,
whether in the waters or on the land, in the latter case winged and
creeping things being included (Lev. xi.), but it is nowhere employed of
the animals called "beasts."   LXX. omits "every form of creeping
things" and "beasts," and it is possible that these words are a marginal
gloss explanatory of "abomination."   It has usually been supposed that
the reference is to the debased forms of Egyptian superstition.   This is
possible, for the other practices mentioned, the lamentation for Tammuz
and the sun-worship, came from abroad.   Israel appears to have fallen
into the idolatries of the nations about her when she came under their
influence, particularly when they became paramount over her, and
their gods were thought to be stronger than her own God.   The
Egyptian influence had been powerful from the days of Isaiah downwards, and even after the battle of Carchemish (B.C. 605) the hope
of Egyptian support induced Jehoiakim in his last years and Zedekiah
toward the close of his reign to renounce their allegiance to Babylon[1].
On the other hand the practices here mentioned may be rather a
revival of ancient superstitions which, during the prosperity of the
kingdom and amidst the vigour of the national religion, had fallen
into disuse or maintained themselves only as a secret cult, but which,
amidst the disasters of the time, when Jehovah appeared to have
forsaken the land and men looked to every quarter for aid, again
became prevalent (see W. R. Smith, *Religion of the Semites*, ed. 1907,
p. 357).   If the LXX. reading be followed the passage may have less
significance than has been attributed to it.

and all the idols] the block-gods, see ch. vi. 4.   The fact that the
"idols," which, according to ch. vi. (*vv.* 4, 6, 9, 13) are to be found
over all the mountains of Israel, are represented as pourtrayed upon

[1]   [Kr. points out that there is a strong case for a Babylonian origin, as Zedekiah
was at this time a vassal of that kingdom, and the practices referred to were specially
connected with the upper classes at Jerusalem (*v.* 11).   Moreover, the use of incense
(*v.* 11) suggests Babylonian rather than Egyptian ritual.]

wall round about.   And there stood before them seventy 11
men of the elders of the house of Israel, and in the midst
of them stood Jaazaniah the son of Shaphan, with every
man his censer in his hand ; and the odour of the cloud of
incense went up.   Then said he unto me, Son of man, hast 12
thou seen what the elders of the house of Israel do in the
dark, every man in his chambers of imagery? for they say,
The LORD seeth us not ; the LORD hath forsaken the ¹earth.
He said also unto me, Thou shalt again see yet other great 13
abominations which they do.   Then he brought me to the 14
door of the gate of the LORD's house which was toward the

¹ Or, *land*

the wall is peculiar, and suggests that the whole is symbolical.   In
ch. xxiii. 14 Jerusalem sees images of the Chaldeans pourtrayed upon
the wall and falls in love with them, but such portraits can hardly have
been a reality.

11. *seventy men of the elders*]   The seventy were not any court such
as the later Sanhedrim, but merely seventy men representing the elders
of Israel (Exod. xxiv. 1 ; Numb. xi. 16, 24, 25).   The elders were the
leaders of the people, and probably here represent them.   Prominent
among these elders was Jaazaniah the son of Shaphan.   There is no
reason to suppose the name fictitious.   Shaphan the scribe was the
person who read the Book of the Law found in the temple to king
Josiah (2 Kgs xxii. 10).   A son of his son Ahikam acted along with
him and was a protector of Jeremiah (Jer. xxxix. 14), and another son
is mentioned (Jer. xxxvi. 10) as having a chamber in the upper court
where Baruch read Jeremiah's roll in the ears of the people.   If
Jaazaniah was a son of this Shaphan he pursued a different course
from his father and brothers.

12. *his chambers of imagery*]   The language implies that there were
many chambers of imagery, and again suggests that the scene was symbolical.   On "imagery" see Lev. xxvi. 1 ; Numb. xxxiii. 52.

forsaken the earth] rather, as marg., the **land**.   The multiplied
calamities of later years suggested that Jehovah no more protected
the country (ch. ix. 9).   This was possibly the feeling of the elders and
people in some moods, but in other moods they spoke differently.   In
ch. xi. 15 they say to those already in exile, "Get you far from the
LORD : unto us is this land given for a possession."

VIII. 13, 14.   THE WOMEN BEWAILING TAMMUZ.

14. *gate of the LORD's house*] i.e. outside the whole temple buildings
to the north gate of the outer court ; cf. ch. x. 19, xi. 1.   The term
"house" embraces all the temple buildings (Jer. xxxv. 4).   The
women may have been seen sitting outside the gate, or they may have
been in some of the chambers of the outer gateway.   Of course the

north; and behold, there sat the women weeping for Tam-
15 muz. Then said he unto me, Hast thou seen *this*, O son
of man? thou shalt again see yet greater abominations than
16 these. And he brought me into the inner court of the
LORD's house, and behold, at the door of the temple of
the LORD, between the porch and the altar, were about five

temple building in Ezekiel's time did not quite correspond to his ideal
sketch in ch. xl. *seq.*, but there were no doubt chambers at that
time connected with both gateways (Jer. xxxv. 2, 4, xxxvi. 10, 12, 20,
21, cf. xxvi. 10; 2 Kgs xxiii. 11). Tammuz is identical with Adonis.
The latter name, *Adon*, "Lord," is not a proper name, being applicable
to any great god, but when the myth found its way to Greece, the
word became a proper name. The name Tammuz is Babylonian
Dumu-zi, Dûzi, said to signify "son of life," and to indicate the eternal
youth of the sun-god (cf. Fried. Delitzsch in Baer's *Ezek.*; Schrader,
KAT. on Ezek. viii. 14; Sayce, *Hibbert Lect.* IV.). The story of the
death of Tammuz is said to be a solar myth, having reference to the
death of the sun-god. The explanations given by Assyrian scholars
are not very clear. Sometimes the death is said to be that which he
undergoes each night, sometimes that which he undergoes when he
expires before the touch of winter, and sometimes the death is that of
the lusty, life-giving vernal god, who perishes along with all life on
earth amidst the summer fires which he himself has kindled. The town
of Gebal or Byblos, eight miles north of Beirut, was the great seat of
the Adonis worship in Phœnicia. It is possible that the cult passed
westward from Babylonia, but it may be that in Syria the rites had
an independent origin and a different meaning, and that it was not
till later that they were interpreted in the sense of the Babylonian
myth (W. R. Smith, *Religion of the Semites*, index under Adonis). It
was probably from Phœnicia that the worship entered Judæa. Milton's
interpretation of the rites may not quite exhaust their meaning:

> the love tale
> Infected Zion's daughters with like heat;
> Whose wanton passions in the sacred porch
> Ezekiel saw.

Such myths may originally be only beautiful nature poetry, but
we are so allied to nature that we see our feelings reflected in her,
as on the other hand her moods repeat themselves in us. Particularly
in times of decay and loss the sadder aspects of nature intensify our
own feeling by presenting to our minds a universal decay in which
we and all things are involved. It is only the sorrowful side of the
Tammuz rite that the prophet refers to.

VIII. **15, 16.** THE SUN-WORSHIPPERS IN THE INNER COURT.

16. *about five and twenty*] LXX., *about twenty*. These men were

and twenty men, with their backs toward the temple of the
LORD, and their faces toward the east; and they worshipped
the sun toward the east.   Then he said unto me, Hast thou 17
seen *this*, O son of man?   Is it a light thing to the house
of Judah that they commit the abominations which they
commit here? for they have filled the land with violence,
and have turned again to provoke me to anger: and, lo, they
put the branch to their nose.   Therefore will I also deal in 18
fury: mine eye shall not spare, neither will I have pity: and

seen adoring the sun with their faces to the east, and their backs to
the temple.   Their position between the temple and the altar seems
to imply that they were priests (Joel ii. 17), and it is not decisive
against this view that they are called "elders" in ch. ix. 6 (R.V.
marg.), for 2 Kgs xix. 2 and Jer. xix. 1 refer to "the elders of the
priests."   They may be supposed to be representatives of the priesthood.

worshipped the sun]   The worship of the sun, the queen of heaven
[probably not the moon but the planet Venus], and the host of heaven,
was adopted by Israel from their eastern conquerors: cf. 2 Kgs xxiii.
5, 11; Jer. xliv. 17; Job xxxi. 26; Deut. iv. 19.   (The Heb. is to be
read *mishtaḥavim*.)

VIII. 17, 18.   FURTHER ABOMINATIONS.

17.   *Is it a light thing*]   Probably: Is it too light a thing for the
house of Judah to commit...that they have filled: cf. Is. xlix. 6; ch.
ix. 9.

they put the branch to their nose]   This is supposed to be part of
the ceremonies of their sun-worship[1].   It is said that the Persian sun-
worshippers held before them a branch or bunch of date, pomegranate, or
tamarisk tree, or according to some of the Homa tree, probably that
their breath might not contaminate the glory of the rising deity.   The
word "nose" might mean face (Gen. iii. 19), but why, if the reference
is to the practice, does not Ezekiel say "mouth"?   And this distinctly
Persian rite is hardly probable at so early a date in Israel.   Also
the reference to idolatry seems to be ended, for it is asked whether
these idolatries were not enough, that they had also filled the land
with blood.

18.   These abominations will assuredly bring down the unsparing
chastisements of heaven.   The phrase "shall not spare nor pity" is
common in the prophet, ch. v. 11, vii. 4, 9, ix. 5, 10.

[1] [There is a Rabbinic tradition (*Tikkun Sopherim*; see C. D. Ginsburg, *Introd.
to Heb. Bible*, 1897, p. 357) that "*their* nose" is a euphemistic substitution for "*my*
nose" or "face," i.e. "they thrust their branch" (some idolatrous emblem) "into my
very face," or, again, it may be an expression intended as equivalent to "they provoke
me defiantly beyond all endurance."   Cf. the LXX. "behold them as it were mocking."   This sense accords well with "Therefore &c." of *v.* 18.]

though they cry in mine ears with a loud voice, yet will
I not hear them.

cry...with a loud voice] Cf. ch. xi. 13, and for the general idea of
vain appeal to heaven, Is. i. 15; Jer. xi. 11; Prov. i. 28.

This passage contains much that is difficult to estimate. The fact
that the things described were seen in the "visions of God" (*v.* 3), the
symbolical form in which Jehovah appeared, and the analogy of chs. ix, x,
lead to the conclusion that there is at least an ideal and symbolical
element in the representation of the idolatries practised in the temple.
The view of Hitz., and Kuen. (*Onderz.* II. 278) that the idolatrous
practices are to be taken literally but referred to the time of Manasseh
is not natural. The prophet would hardly be shewn things once but no
longer in existence, though of course he might take a continuous view
of Israel's practice, as he often does. It is not easy to say how far the
representation that the idolatrous usages were practised *in* the temple is
to be taken literally. Such practices are not referred to by Jeremiah or
other prophets of the time. It is possible that the chambers and cells
about the gateways, which appear in some cases to have belonged to
private persons, may have been used for illegitimate purposes, but that
sun-worship was actually practised between the temple and the altar has
little probability. And the scene in the chamber of imagery is obviously
ideal. The prophet certainly desires to shew that idolatry both public
and private was practised by all classes, the elders representing the
nation, the women, and perhaps also the priests; and that these idolatries
were not only the old native ones of Israel, but new imports at this
period from all the nations around. The representation, however, that
such things were done *in* the temple may rather be ideal. The temple
was the dwelling-place of Jehovah, and every impurity done not only
there but in the land and in the houses of the people was felt in the
place of His abode, which it defiled, causing Him to withdraw from it
(*v.* 6, cf. Lev. xv. 31, xx. 3; Num. xix. 13, 20; and note the elaborate
precautions to guard against defilement adopted in chs. xl.—xlviii.). On
the other hand those privileged to dwell in the land or have access to
the temple are spoken of as dwelling *in* the house, Ps. xxiii. 6, xxvii. 4,
lxxxiv. 5 &c. See preliminary remarks to the chapter.

IX. First act of the divine judgement, slaughter of the inhabitants of the city.

Ch. viii. presented a picture of the enormities practised by the inhabitants of the land and of the city, their religious debasement in contrast
with the glory of Jehovah. The description was meant to lead up to
the conclusion expressed in the end of the chapter, "Therefore will I
also deal in fury: mine eye shall not spare, neither will I have pity"
(ch. viii. 18). Now is shewn the first act in the execution of this threat.

(1) *vv.* 1—3. A loud cry proceeds from the glory of the LORD,
Bring hither the executioners of the city! and forthwith are seen

Then he cried in mine ears with a loud voice, saying, 9
¹Cause ye them that have charge over the city to draw near,
every man with his destroying weapon in his hand. And 2
behold, six men came from the way of the upper gate,

¹ Or, *Draw ye near that &c.*

approaching from the northern gate of the temple six men, each with
his weapon of destruction in his hand, and a seventh, clad in linen garments, with a writer's inkhorn at his girdle. The seven take up their
position between the house and the brazen altar.

(2) *vv.* 4—7. Ere this the glory of the Lord which was over the
cherubim had risen, or now rose, and stood over the threshold of the
temple. From there a cry came to the man clothed in linen to go
forth into the city and put a mark upon the foreheads of those who
mourned over the evils done in the midst of it, and to the six others to
follow him and slay indiscriminately all not so sealed, and to begin at
the house of the Lord.

(3) *vv.* 8—10. Immediately the work of slaughter commences,
beginning with the elders before the house (ch. viii. 16). From there
the destroying angels move outwards, polluting the courts with dead,
and pass into the city. The prophet is left alone, conscious only of the
work going on without. This work fills his mind with such a conception of the wrath of God that it seems to him the whole remnant of
Israel must perish before it. He falls on his face and intercedes for them,
but is answered that the sin is great, and must be unsparingly chastised.

(4) *v.* 11. While his intercession is repelled, the man clad in linen
garments returns, announcing the fulfilment of the commands given to
him and his fellows.

1. *that have charge over the city*] lit. either the "oversights"
(overseers), or the "visitations" (visitants) of the city. The latter is
most natural, "visitations" being said for "those who visit," that is, the
executioners. (In Jer. lii. 11 "prisons" is lit. house of visitations.)
Cf. Is. lx. 17 (officers). The verb may be rendered as text or marg.
(for the latter cf. ch. xxxvi. 8; Job xxxi. 37). To take the verb as
perf., "the executioners are at hand," is less suitable to the loud cry,
and the immediate appearance of the seven men seems in response to
the summons.

2. *six men*] The symbolism represents the judgement of God as executed by supernatural agents, immediately under His command. These
agents are called "men," having the human form to the eyes of the prophet (cf. ch. xl. 3, xliii. 6). Six of the men had instruments of destruction
in their hands, and the seventh was clothed in linen garments with an
inkhorn at his girdle. The inkhorn consisted of a case for holding the
reed pens, with an inkholder attached near the mouth of the case.
Such inkhorns are carried in the girdle at the present day¹, and those
worn by high officials are often of silver, richly chased and ornamented.

¹ [See the illustration in *HDB* 1. 626.]

which lieth toward the north, every man with his ¹slaughter
weapon in his hand; and one man in the midst of them
clothed in linen, with a writer's inkhorn ²by his side.   And
3 they went in, and stood beside the brasen altar.   And the

---

¹ Or, *battle axe*   ² Heb. *upon his loins*.

The purpose of the inkhorn appears in *v.* 4.   The linen garments mark
the man's divine sanctity and eminence, not priestly rank (Ew.); the
high angel, Dan. x. 5, xii. 6, was so clothed, as were the seven angels
having the vials of wrath, the last plagues of judgement upon the world,
Rev. xv. 6.   The seven men entering the inner court proceeded until
they stood beside the brasen altar, in front of the house, whither the
glory of the Lord had moved from the cherubim (*v.* 3).

the upper gate]   What this gate was is not quite clear.   It is usually
held to be the gate of the inner court already mentioned, ch. viii.
3, 5.   In Ezekiel's new temple the inner court is higher than the
outer, and a flight of steps leads to the gate from the level of the outer
court, but probably in the old temple the courts were much on a level.
In 2 Kgs xv. 35, Jotham is said to have built the "upper gate" of
the house of the Lord.   This gate seems identical with the "upper
gate" of Benjamin, Jer. xx. 2, probably also with the "new gate,"
Jer. xxvi. 10, xxxvi. 10.   In the last passage this new gate is said to be
in the "upper court," which can hardly be the inner court, but rather
a small court which lay at the northern extremity of the outer court,
and was elevated some feet above the latter.   (See plan in *Encycl.
Brit.*, Art. Temple.)   At all events the "men" came from the north
side of the house into the inner court.   The abominations of the people
are represented as practised on the north side (ch. viii.), and the
instruments of God's vengeance approach from the same quarter.

slaughter weapon]   [lit. weapon of shattering, a more general expression than the marg. *battle axe*.]

the brasen altar]   This is again obscure.   It is said in 1 Kgs viii.
64 that the brazen altar was too small to receive the burnt-offerings and
the fat of Solomon's holocausts, and that the king consecrated the
middle of the court, and there burnt his offerings.   Ahaz caused his
priest Uriah to build an altar after the pattern of the altar which he
saw in Damascus, 2 Kgs xvi. 10, 11.   This new altar must have been
of stone, terminating at the top in a platform or hearth for burning
the fat and sacrifices; and somewhat after this model the altar in
Ezekiel's new temple is to be constructed (ch. xliii. 13—17).   The altar
of Ahaz appears to have been placed in the middle of the court, further
from the house than the original position of the brazen altar; and it is
added that Ahaz removed the brazen altar from its former place, and
set it on the north side of his new altar (2 Kgs xvi. 14).   This sense
is given both by the Heb. and LXX., though the texts differ in some
points.   The Heb. reading is not quite natural, and as construed by
some it says nothing of a removal of the brazen altar from its former

glory of the God of Israel was gone up from the cherub, whereupon it was, to the threshold of the house: and he called to the man clothed in linen, which had the writer's inkhorn [1] by his side.   And the LORD said unto him, Go 4 through the midst of the city, through the midst of Jerusalem, and set a mark upon the foreheads of the men that sigh and that cry for all the abominations that be done in the midst thereof.   And to the others he said in mine 5 hearing, Go ye through the city after him, and smite: let not your eye spare, neither have ye pity: slay [2] utterly the 6 old man, the young man and the maiden, and little children and women: but come not near any man upon whom is the mark; and begin at my sanctuary.   Then they began at the [3] ancient men which were before the house.   And he 7 said unto them, Defile the house, and fill the courts with

[1] Heb. *upon his loins*.   [2] Heb. *to destruction*.   [3] Or, *elders*

place.   (See W. R. Smith, *Rel. of Sem.* (ed. 1907), p. 486 *seq.*)   The seven men took up their position either in the middle of the court in the vicinity of the altar, or considerably nearer the house than the altar of burnt-offering.

3. *from the cherub*][1]   For the cherubim see at the end of ch. x.

IX. **4—7.**   COMMAND TO SEAL THOSE TO BE SPARED, AND TO SLAY WITHOUT DISTINCTION ALL OTHERS.

4. *set a mark*]   The word is *Tav*, the last letter of the alphabet, the old form of which was a cross.   The term is used here as in Job xxxi. 35, of a mark in general, though perhaps the Tav or cross was the simplest form the mark could take.   The passage is imitated, Rev. vii. 3 f., though the mark there is the name of God.   All who mourned over the abominations done in Jerusalem were to be thus sealed and spared.

5.   The other executioners were to follow the footsteps of the seventh man, and slay without discrimination all not marked by him.

6. *begin at my sanctuary*]   Judgement begins at the house of God. The Lord had returned for a moment to the place of His abode in the temple, and from there the judgement went forth; Am. i. 2, "The LORD shall roar from Zion, and utter his voice from Jerusalem."   There He was most present, there most fully known, there if possible most forgotten and provoked, and there His holiness and Godhead will assert themselves with most terribleness against the sins of men.

the ancient men]   *the elders* mentioned ch. viii. 16.

7. *Defile the house*]   The "house" embraces the temple and

[1] [The word is used collectively, just as "wheel" in Heb. of xxiii. 24, xxvi. 10. See Oxf. Lex. *s.v.*]

5—2

the slain : go ye forth.   And they went forth, and smote
8 in the city.   And it came to pass, while they were smiting,
and I was left, that I fell upon my face, and cried, and
said, Ah Lord God ! wilt thou destroy all the residue of
Israel in thy pouring out of thy fury upon Jerusalem ?
9 Then said he unto me, The iniquity of the house of Israel
and Judah is exceeding great, and the land is full of blood,
and the city full of ¹wresting *of judgement*: for they say,
The Lord hath forsaken the ²earth, and the Lord seeth not.
10 And as for me also, mine eye shall not spare, neither will

---

¹ Or, *perverseness*   ² Or, *land*

---

its precincts, including the courts.   The presence of dead in the courts
defiled the whole.

IX. 8—10.   Intercession of the Prophet.

8.   *and I was left*]   The executioners passed out of the inner court,
leaving only dead behind them, and the prophet was left alone (Is. xlix.
21.   The form of the Heb. verb is anomalous.)   The terrible outbreak
of the Divine wrath seemed to forbode the extinction of all the remnant
of Israel, and the prophet fell on his face, appealing to the Lord on
their behalf.   The "residue" suggests the many calamities that had
already befallen the people, wearing them down to only a few men
(Is. xli. 14, comp. the prophet's own figure of the half-burnt brand, ch.
xv. 4 ff.), and the threat of a fire going out upon all the house of Israel
seemed about to be realized (ch. v. 4).   The prophet passes from one
state of feeling to another.   Sometimes he is in sympathy with the
Divine resentment, and is himself full of fury against the sinful people
(ch. iii. 14), and of a scorn that rejoices at their coming chastisements
(vi. 11), but when the judgements of God are abroad before his eyes he
is appalled at their severity, and his pity for men overcomes his religious
zeal (xi. 13).

9.   *wresting* of judgement]   not as marg. and A.V. *perverseness*.   Cf.
Am. ii. 7.   The Divine answer is inexorable.   Two evils are stated,
and the deeper cause of them : violence unto bloodshed, and the perversion of justice, the cause of both being the feeling that Jehovah had
forsaken the land.   This belief shews the strange length to which the
hard fate of Israel had brought men.   Possibly these persons concluded
that He had retired, being overcome by deities stronger than Himself ;
even the godly were driven to conclude that He had ceased to interest
Himself in His people (Is. xl. 27, xlix. 14).   And with the departure
of Jehovah, the righteous God, all moral restraints were relaxed.   The
persons who here speak had probably been obstinate opponents of the
prophets, but the passage shews that the prophetic preaching of
Jehovah's righteousness, even when to appearance unheeded, had lodged
itself in the consciences of men.

I have pity, but I will bring their way upon their head. And behold, the man clothed in linen, which had the ink- 11 horn by his side, reported the matter, saying, I have done as thou hast commanded me.

Then I looked, and behold, in the firmament that was **10** over the head of the cherubim, there appeared above them as it were a sapphire stone, as the appearance of the likeness of a throne.   And he spake unto the man clothed in 2 linen, and said, Go in between the whirling *wheels*, even

10.   Cf. ch. v. 11, vii. 4, viii. 18.
11.   The man clad in linen returns, announcing the execution of Jehovah's commands.

X.   Second act of the divine judgement, the scattering of fire from God upon the city.

The connexion between this chapter and the last is not quite close, otherwise ch. x. 2 would have stood at the beginning.   Unobserved by the prophet or at least unmentioned by him the glory had returned from the threshold of the house (ch. ix. 3), and the Lord again sat upon the throne above the cherubim (ch. i. 26).

(1) *vv.* 1—3.   From His place above the cherubim the Lord commanded the man clothed with linen garments to approach the fire within the wheelwork and take coals from it to scatter over the city—a symbol of the Divine judgement on Jerusalem, on which fire from God would fall as on Sodom.   The man advanced towards the cherubim.

(2) *vv.* 4—8.   Meanwhile the glory of the Lord again left the cherubim, and stood over the threshold of the house, the cloud filling the temple and the brilliancy lighting up the inner court.   The chief angel had approached the chariot, and the cherub took coals from between the wheelwork, putting them into the hands of the angel, who went forth. The actual strewing of the fire upon the city, though assumed, is not described.

(3) *vv.* 9—17.   Renewed description of the cherubim.

(4) *vv.* 18—22.   Return of the Divine glory from the threshold of the house to the cherubim, and movement of the whole manifestation from the inner court to the outside of the eastern gate of the outer court (*vv.* 18—19).   Finally the prophet lays stress upon the identity of the cherubim seen here with those which he saw by the river Chebar (*vv.* 20—22).

1.   *in the firmament*] rather **upon** or **above**. [So LXX., followed by Cor.   See beginning of introd. note on this ch.]   On the firmament and throne, cf. ch. i. 26 *seq.*

2.   *between the whirling* wheels] The word is singular and occurs again *v.* 13, being used as a collective to describe the whole wheelwork.   There were four wheels (a different word) which are called here

under the cherub, and fill both thine hands with coals of
fire from between the cherubim, and [1]scatter them over the
3 city. And he went in in my sight. Now the cherubim
stood on the right side of the house, when the man went
4 in; and the cloud filled the inner court. And the glory of
the LORD mounted up from the cherub, *and stood* over the
threshold of the house; and the house was filled with the
cloud, and the court was full of the brightness of the LORD's
5 glory. And the sound of the wings of the cherubim was
heard even to the outer court, as the voice of [2]God Almighty
6 when he speaketh. And it came to pass, when he commanded the man clothed in linen, saying, Take fire from
between the whirling *wheels*, from between the cherubim,

---

[1] Or, *sprinkle*   [2] Heb. *El Shaddai.*

collectively wheelwork, lit. whirling. The word is used of the whirlwind or tempest (Ps. lxxvii. 18 [Heb. 19]), but also of chariot wheels
(Is. v. 28; Ezek. xxiii. 24, xxvi. 10).

the cherub] [Cf. the singular also in *vv.* 4, 7. Perhaps, as Lofth.
suggests, the creature nearest to the prophet is meant. One would
always be more prominent to the onlooker than the rest.]

3. *the right side of the house*] i.e. on the south of the temple proper.
It is difficult to see any significance in the position of the cherubim,
except that the south side of the house was more in the direction of the
city than either the north or east side, and the west side was closed by
buildings.

4. *And the glory of the LORD mounted up*] This can hardly be
rendered, *And...had gone up*; consequently the implication in *v.* 1
that the glory had returned to the cherubim from the threshold is
confirmed.

from the cherub] [i.e. the cherub of the Chariot, not, as in ix. 3, the
cherub over the altar.]

5. *sound of the wings of the cherubim*] It is to be supposed that
some movement of the living creatures' wings accompanied the rising of
the Divine glory from above them, as it is said that when they stood their
wings dropped (i. 24). The language of *v.* 18 (cf. ix. 3) excludes the
supposition that the cherubim as well as the glory moved towards the
threshold (Ew.). Jehovah's "speaking" is the thunder (ch. i. 24), but
the statement that the sound was heard in the outer court is strange, as
the distance was not great. In Ezekiel's day, however, the outer court
had not the symmetry which he gives it in his final vision but extended
to a considerable distance from the house, and may have been regarded
as including the royal buildings (see the plans *Encycl. Brit.*, and
Stade's *Hist.*, vol. 1.).

6. On the fire between the cherubim, cf. i. 13.

that he went in, and stood beside a wheel.   And the cherub 7
stretched forth his hand from between the cherubim unto
the fire that was between the cherubim, and took *thereof*,
and put it into the hands of him that was clothed in linen,
who took it and went out.   And there appeared in the 8
cherubim the form of a man's hand under their wings.
And I looked, and behold, four wheels beside the cherubim, 9
one wheel beside one cherub, and another wheel beside
another cherub : and the appearance of the wheels was as
the colour of a ¹beryl stone.   And as for their appearance, 10
they four had one likeness, as if a wheel had been ²within
a wheel.   When they went, they went ³upon their four sides: 11
they turned not as they went, but to the place whither the
head looked they followed it; they turned not as they went.
And their whole body, and their backs, and their hands, 12
and their wings, and the wheels, were full of eyes round
about, *even* the wheels that they four had.   As for the 13
wheels, they were called in my hearing, the whirling *wheels*.
And every one had four faces : the first face was the face of 14

¹ Or, *stone of Tarshish*   ² Heb. *in the midst of.*   ³ Or, *towards*

7.   *And the cherub*] the one on the side approached by the man.
The cherubim interposed to hand the fire to the man in linen garments,
who received it and went forth (Job i. 12, ii. 7).   The symbolism is
suggested by Is. vi. 6.
8.   On the "hands" of the cherubim, cf. ch. i. 8.
Instead of depicting the conflagration of the city, which would have
been impossible, the prophet's attention is anew drawn to the cherubim,
and a fresh description of the living creatures and of the Divine chariot
follows.
9.   *four wheels*] The description is somewhat more exact than that
given ch. i. 15.   For "beryl stone" see on i. 16.
10.   Cf. ch. i. 16.
11.   Cf. i. 17.
the head looked] i.e. the front of the chariot.   The word is hardly to
be rendered the principal, or foremost, referring to the wheels.   Cf. ch.
i. 12, 17.
12.   *their whole body*] lit. *flesh*, a strange term to be used of the
living creatures.   LXX. omits.   The word "backs" is used of the
felloes of the wheels in ch. i. 18, and in this verse the living creatures
and the wheels are confused together.
wheels that they four had] more naturally : *even their four wheels*,
lit. "even they four, their wheels," where "they" anticipates "wheels."
14.   The verse, which LXX. omits, is difficult.   The words rendered

the cherub, and the second face was the face of a man, and
the third the face of a lion, and the fourth the face of an

"first face" might possibly have this sense or that of "one face," but
mean naturally "face of the first"; and those rendered "the second
face" can hardly mean anything but "the face of the second," for it is
precarious to extend constructions like Jer. xlvi. 2 (lit. "the year of the
fourth" (year) = the fourth year), to other words than "year." The
easiest course would be to omit the word "face" before "first" and
"second," as in fact it does not stand before "third" and "fourth"; or
perhaps it might be enough to omit it before "second" and assume that
the anomalous constr. "one face" (Lev. xxiv. 22; 2 Kgs xii. 10) had
led to the insertion of "face" before "the second."

face of the cherub] As the other faces were those of a man, a lion,
and an eagle, this face must be that of the ox (ch. i. 10). Why should
this be called the face of the cherub?[1] It is said that the winged bulls
at the portals of Assyrian temples are called cherubs in Assyrian (Frd.
Delitzsch, *Paradies*, p. 153, Lenormant, *Les origines de l'histoire*, p. 118),
but these winged bulls have not the face of an ox but that of a man,
and there is no probability that in Israel the cherubs in the temple were
ox-faced.

It seems possible to explain the verse only by making some suppo-
sitions which may appear rather artificial, viz. first that the prophet
looking at the phenomenon of the chariot and the four creatures as a
whole saw four faces presented to him, one (and a different one) by
each of the creatures, and that he named the faces which were thus
presented to him. We should then translate "the face of the first,"
"the face of the second," &c., though this seems opposed to the meaning of the first words of the verse. And secondly, that he assumes the
side of the chariot presented to him not to be the front, and regards the
side looking in another direction as the front or head. His view of
the chariot is taken when it rose and proceeded eastward (v. 19); and
he regards the side of the chariot turned to the east as the front, and
he calls the cherub which led the movement to the east *the* cherub.
Further at this moment the chariot and cherubim were standing on the
south side of the house (v. 3), and the prophet's position was probably
near the house and thus to the north or left of the phenomenon. Now
the ox-face of all the cherubs was on their left (ch. i. 10), that is, in
the case of a cherub leading the movement eastward, towards the north
where the prophet presumably was standing. Thus he would see the
ox-face of the first cherub (whose human face was eastward, leading
the whole chariot). He would also see the man's face of the cherub on
the side of the chariot facing himself, the lion's face of the cherub who
stood on the west side of the chariot, and the eagle's face of the cherub
on the south side of the chariot, for all the eagle-faces looked inward
to the centre of the chariot. This is the order followed in the verse.

[1] [A question which is raised but by no means satisfactorily answered in the
treatise *Chagigah* (*Tal. Bab.*) fol. 13 *b*.]

eagle.   And the cherubim mounted up: this is the living 15
creature that I saw by the river Chebar.   And when the 16
cherubim went, the wheels went beside them: and when
the cherubim lifted up their wings to mount up from the
earth, the wheels also turned not from beside them.   When 17
they stood, these stood; and when they mounted up, these
mounted up with them: for the spirit [1]of the living creature
was in them.   And the glory of the Lord went forth from 18
over the threshold of the house, and stood over the cherubim.   And the cherubim lifted up their wings, and mounted 19
up from the earth in my sight when they went forth, and
the wheels [2]beside them: and they stood at the door of the
east gate of the Lord's house; and the glory of the God of
Israel was over them above.   This is the living creature 20
that I saw under the God of Israel by the river Chebar;
and I knew that they were cherubim.   Every one had four 21

[1] Or, *of life*   See ch. i. 21.   [2] Or, *over against*

15.   *mounted up*]   The prophet identifies the manifestation with
that seen at the Chebar when he perceives its movement.   The verse is
resumed in *v.* 19.

16, 17.   Cf. ch. i. 19.   [Ezekiel "specially emphasizes the fact that
the quadrilateral arrangement of wheels obviated any necessity of
turning.   The significance of this can only be that Yahweh's purposes
cannot change, but must go straight forward."   Lofthouse, *ad loc.*]

18.   The glory of the Lord returns from the threshold of the house
to the cherubim, and these mount up and remove outside the precincts
of the temple altogether, and stand within the city at the eastern gateway of the outward court.   Jehovah withdraws His protection.

19.   *they stood*] lit. *it*, viz. the whole manifestation.

the east gate]   [Gautier (*Ezéchiel*, p. 113) suggests that there may be a
significance in the departure of the 'Chariot' in the eastward direction,
as that where the exiles were to be found.]

20.   *were cherubim*]   The remark that he knew that the living
creatures were cherubim is of very great difficulty.   It would scarcely
be the prophet's meaning to say that he learned that the living creatures
were cherubim from hearing them so called by the Divine Speaker
(*vv.* 2, 6) because previous to this he himself has so called them (ch. ix.
3).   The sense is rather that this third vision of them (ch. i. and ch. iii.
23) with its details and movements revealed to him that the creatures
were cherubim.   But admitting that the prophet had visions, we can
hardly escape the conclusion that the details of the phenomenon of the
cherubim repose upon reflection.   This reflection may have preceded
the visions and been reproduced in them, but where did he find the

faces apiece, and every one four wings; and the likeness of
22 the hands of a man was under their wings. And as for the
likeness of their faces, they were the faces which I saw by
the river Chebar, their appearances and themselves; they
went every one straight forward.

elements that entered into his combination? Were they not derived
from the temple largely, though also from the storm-cloud? Could he
be unaware of the source whence he derived them? It is possible that
in the excitation of the vision he did not recall the processes of his own
reflection. Or may it be that we are straining the word "knew" when
we understand it in the sense of *learned*, came to know? This is the
natural sense to put upon it in this Book, and up to this time the
prophet has not used the name cherubim.

The derivation of the word cherub is obscure. If Assyrian scholars
are right the name is Babylonian, and is found given to the colossal
winged bulls (called at other times shidu, Heb. *shēd*) which guard the
portals of palaces and temples in Babylonia. The word (*Kirubu*) is
said to have the sense of "great" (Schrader, *KAT.* on Gen. iii. 24, Del.
Paradies, p. 150 *seq.*). But though the name be common to Babylonian and Hebrew, and though originally the idea expressed by the
name may have been the same in both, the usage as known from Babylonian literature marks the end of a long development, and that in
Hebrew marks the end of another long and independent development,
and any attempt to control or explain the one by the other must be
made with caution.

The narrative and essential part of ch. x. lies in *vv.* 2, 3, 4, 6, 7, 18,
19; the rest is annotation suggested by points in the narrative, in
which ch. i. is repeated without anything essential being added to it.
[The name cherub (cherubim), the whirling of the wheels, and the
cloud (*v.* 3) are the chief new details.] A second description of the
cherubim after ch. i. looks unnecessary, and Cornill would excise
vv. 8—17 entirely. There may be occasional glosses in these verses,
but no reason exists for cutting them out which does not equally apply
to *vv.* 20—22. The whole description of the Divine chariot has an
appearance of artificiality to us now, but in Ezekiel we have a peculiar
mind, and it is safer to content ourselves with saying that we do not
altogether understand the importance which he attaches to the phenomenon of the chariot and the living creatures.

XI. THREAT OF DESTRUCTION AGAINST THE PEOPLE, ESPECIALLY
THE WAR PARTY IN JERUSALEM, WITH PROMISE OF RESTORATION
TO THE EXILES.

Though the symbolism in ch. ix. x., shewing the slaughter of the
inhabitants and the burning of the city, might have seemed exhaustive,
there were thoughts in men's minds which had to be met, and issues
to which reference had to be made. The city was thought impregnably

Moreover the spirit lifted me up, and brought me unto **11** the east gate of the LORD'S house, which looketh eastward: and behold, at the door of the gate five and twenty men; and I saw in the midst of them Jaazaniah the son of Azzur, and Pelatiah the son of Benaiah, princes of the

strong, and Jehovah's presence would protect it. The prophet symbolizes the departure of Jehovah from it, and warns those who trust to its strength that their trust is vain. Yet the fall of the city is not the last act in Israel's history; the "house of Israel" is wider than the population of Jerusalem, and towards the larger Israel Jehovah has purposes of mercy. He will restore them to their ancient heritage, where they shall serve Him in a land purified from all its uncleanness.

In ch. x. 18 it was stated that the glory of the Lord left the threshold of the house and returned to the cherubim, and in ch. x. 19 that the whole manifestation removed from the inner court and stood at the eastern entrance to the outer court of the temple. The prophet also is transported to the same place (ch. xi. 1). At the entrance to the gateway he sees twenty-five men, among them two who are named, princes of the people. The twenty-five represent the rulers of the city and the leaders of the inhabitants.

(1) *vv.* 2—12. These men are represented as plotting evil enterprizes, that is, rebellion against the king of Babylon. They are not unaware of the danger they incur, but are confident in the protection which the well fortified city will afford them—it is the pot and they are the flesh, which the fire cannot reach. The prophet receives command to prophesy against them, and declare that their confidence is vain. The city shall not protect them; they shall be dragged out of it and slain on the borders of the land, far away from it.

(2) *vv.* 13—21. While the prophet was delivering this threat one of the two princes named died. Filled with terror at the certainty with which the word of God takes effect, the prophet fell down to intercede that the remnant of Israel might not be destroyed. He is reminded that, though Jerusalem fall, his fellow exiles remain and all the house of Israel. These exiles were despised by the people of Jerusalem and denied any share in the inheritance of the land; but though the Lord had scattered them He would yet bring them to their ancient home, giving them a new heart to serve Him.

(3) *vv.* 22—25. Finally the Divine manifestation rose from the city and stood over the Mount of Olives. The prophet was carried back to Chaldæa; the hand of the Lord was lifted from him, and he awoke out of his vision, the contents of which he narrated to them of the captivity.

XI. 1—12. THE MEN THAT PLOT EVIL.

1. The gate referred to is the outer eastern gate; the position taken up by the cherubim and glory was outside the temple precincts wholly. Jaazaniah and Pelatiah are named "princes of the people." Possibly

2 people.   And he said unto me, Son of man, these are the
   men that devise iniquity, and that give wicked counsel in
3 this city : which say, ¹ *The time* is not near to build houses :
4 this *city* is the caldron, and we be the flesh.   Therefore

¹ Or, *Is not* the time *near &c.?*

they were more prominent members of the ruling party. It is the
manner of the prophet to introduce elements of reality into his symbolical pictures (cf. ch. xxiv. 16 *seq.*), and it is unnecessary to regard
these two personages as fictitious or seek for some symbolical meaning
in their names. [Azzur is possibly identical with the father of the
Hananiah of Jer. xxviii. 1. See on *v.* 13.] A different Jaazaniah was
mentioned in ch. viii. 11. The twenty-five men here are not to be
identified with those in ch. viii. 16; they are rulers and leaders of the
people (*v.* 2).

  2. *give wicked counsel*] lit. *counsel evil counsel.* The evil counsel
probably refers to the revolutionary enterprizes of these men against
the authority of Babylon, which the prophet severely condemns (ch.
xvii.).   The city was divided into factions, one part holding with
Babylon and another with Egypt, while some were for peace on any
terms. The consequence of these divisions was much bloodshed within
the city (*v.* 6). It is probable that the schemes of these plotters were
only being hatched (*v.* 5); it was not till some time later that the
steps now meditated were actually taken.

  3. The time *is not near to build houses*] The phrase "to build
houses" is to be taken as in ch. xxviii. 26, "And they shall dwell
securely therein; yea, they shall build houses, and plant vineyards, and
shall dwell securely." To build houses is a sign and a consequence of
a time of peace and security (Is. lxv. 21; Jer. xxix. 5, 28). These
agitators desire to turn men's minds away from peaceful occupations,
and make them contemplate other measures, assuring them that when
war comes the strong city will be their salvation—it is the pot which
will protect the flesh from the fire around it. Others, e.g. Ew., take
the phrase interrogatively: "Is not the building of houses near?" This,
however, hardly corresponds to the situation, which is not one of war
which it is hoped will speedily pass over, but one of contemplated
rebellion. LXX. renders: "Have not the houses been recently built? it
is the pot &c."; so Cor. This gives a closer connexion to the two halves
of the verse, but "houses" could hardly have the sense of fortifications,
nor does the phrase naturally express the meaning that the damage done
to the city when last captured (under Jehoiachin) had been fully repaired.

  this city *is the caldron*] lit. it is the caldron or pot. The phrase
implies two things, the danger of fire around, and that the strong
city will prove a protection to those within it. These revolutionary
spirits are aware of the risks they run, but with a certain grimness
of humour they make light of them. The figure here is somewhat
different from that of the boiling pot for war common in the Arabic poets.

prophesy against them, prophesy, O son of man. And the 5
spirit of the LORD fell upon me, and he said unto me,
Speak, Thus saith the LORD : Thus have ye said, O house
of Israel ; for I know the things that come into your mind.
Ye have multiplied your slain in this city, and ye have filled 6
the streets thereof with the slain. Therefore thus saith the 7
Lord GOD : Your slain whom ye have laid in the midst of
it, they are the flesh, and this *city* is the caldron : but ¹ye
shall be brought forth out of the midst of it. Ye have 8
feared the sword ; and I will bring the sword upon you,
saith the Lord GOD. And I will bring you forth out of the 9
midst thereof, and deliver you into the hands of strangers,
and will execute judgements among you.· Ye shall fall by 10
the sword ; I will judge you in the border of Israel ; and
ye shall know that I am the LORD. This *city* shall not be 11
your caldron, neither shall ye be the flesh in the midst
thereof ; I will judge you in the border of Israel ; and ye 12
shall know that I am the LORD : for ye have not walked in
my statutes, neither have ye executed my judgements, but
have done after the ²ordinances of the nations that are
round about you. And it came to pass, when I prophesied, 13

---

¹ Another reading is, *I will bring you.*   ² Heb. *judgements.*

4. The prophet felt called to prophesy against these men—and all
this is part of the vision. See on ch. iii. 21.

5. *the things that come into your mind*] i.e. your projects. Apparently
as yet the rebellion was no more than a plan which was being hatched.

6. Cf. ch. xxii. 25, vii. 23. Those opposed to the schemes of the
ruling party, or suspected of opposition, were openly or on various
pretexts cut off.

7. Those slain in the midst of Jerusalem will be the only "flesh"
that will remain in the pot. The living conspirators who think they
shall be safe shall be dragged forth and judged far away from the pro-
tecting city, on the borders of Israel. The figure of the pot and flesh is
used differently in ch. xxiv. (The Heb. is probably to be read so as
to give the meaning " I will bring you forth.")

8. *have feared*] **fear.** The language of the ruling class, in spite
of its recklessness (*v.* 3), betrays the consciousness of the risks they
incur ; and their fears shall be more than verified.

9. *strangers*] i.e. foreign conquerors, the Babylonians.

10. *in the border of Israel*] far away from the city, which they hoped
would protect them, viz. in Riblah. Cf. Jer. lii. 26 ; 2 Kgs xxv. 18 *seq.*

11, 12. These *vv.* are wanting in LXX.

that Pelatiah the son of Benaiah died.   Then fell I down
upon my face, and cried with a loud voice, and said, Ah Lord
GOD! wilt thou make a full end of the remnant of Israel?

14
15   And the word of the LORD came unto me, saying, Son
of man, thy brethren, even thy brethren, the men of thy
¹kindred, and all the house of Israel, all of them, *are they*

¹ Heb. *redemption*.   See Lev. xxv. 25, &c.

XI. 13—21.   INCIDENT OF PELATIAH.

13.   While Ezekiel was uttering this prophecy Pelatiah fell down
dead, and the prophet seemed to see in the event the coming destruction
of all the remnant of Israel before the wrath of God, and fell on his face
to intercede for them.   This incident is exceedingly difficult to
estimate.   The prophet tells us that all the occurrences in ch. viii.—xi.
were done in vision.   This does not justify us in assuming that the
death of Pelatiah was a mere symbolical death, and no reality.   For
the "vision" is in great measure a mere *schema* under which the prophet
groups much that had reality, such as his own thoughts, his discourses
to the people, and probably actual events happening in Jerusalem.   But
in grouping the events under the *schema* of the vision he idealises them,
making them expressive of general conceptions and principles, and it is
impossible to distinguish between things which were actual but are
idealised, and things which are purely creations of the symbolizing
imagination.   It is possible that Ezekiel prophesied against these
princes in Jerusalem (ch. xi. 4), as Jeremiah did against the false prophets in Babylon, whom a horrible fate overtook (Jer. xxix. 21), and
against Hananiah (Jer. xxviii. 15 *seq.*), and it is possible that soon
afterwards Pelatiah suddenly died, and that these real occurrences have
been drawn by the prophet under his *schema* of the vision.   On the
other hand the death of Pelatiah may be merely symbolical to shew
with what certainty the word of God takes effect, the symbol being
modelled on Jeremiah's prophecy against Hananiah.

    a full end]   See on ch. ix. 8.
14 *seq.*   The answer of the Lord to the prophet's intercession.   The
destruction of the inhabitants of Jerusalem is not the end of Israel.   The
Israel in exile is the Israel whom the Lord regards and will yet restore.
15.   *the men of thy kindred*]   lit. as marg. *the men of thy redemption*,
which, in accordance with Lev. xxv. 25 ff., is supposed to mean *thy
kinsmen*.   But it could only mean, the men to be redeemed, or delivered,
by thy intercession—the men for whom thou shouldst pray.   Such a
sense is difficult to draw from the words.   In usage the term has not the
meaning of "kindred."   Probably the word should be so read as to mean
"exile"—*the men of thy exile*, i.e. thy fellow captives, so LXX.   [But
the expression in this sense quite lacks support.]

    are they unto whom]   It is better to regard the first words in the
verse down to "wholly" as exclamations: "thy brethren, thy brethren,

unto whom the inhabitants of Jerusalem have said, Get you far from the LORD; unto us is this land given for a possession: therefore say, Thus saith the Lord GOD: Whereas I 16 have removed them far off among the nations, and whereas I have scattered them among the countries, [1]yet will I be to them a sanctuary for a little while in the countries where they are come. Therefore say, Thus saith the Lord GOD: 17

[1] Or, *yet have I been*   Or, *and have been*

thy fellow exiles, and all the house of Israel, all of it! they unto whom..." The sentence is not strictly grammatical, but the exclamations give an answer to the prophet's anxious question, "wilt thou make a full end of the remnant of Israel?" (*v.* 13). The destruction of those of Jerusalem is no full end; the fellow exiles of the prophet and all the house of Israel scattered abroad (ch. iv. 4, xxxvi. 16) remain. The second half of the verse is loosely attached to the first—*they to whom*, &c.

Get you far from the LORD] A slight alteration in a point would give the sense: of whom...have said (say), *They are far* from the Lord. The change is hardly necessary. Those left were in possession of the temple, the abode of Jehovah, and had the assurance of His presence, in which those gone forth had no part, for to go into a foreign land was to come under the dominion of other gods, according to the words of David (1 Sam. xxvi. 19; cf. Deut. iv. 28, xxviii. 36, 64; Jer. xvi. 13; Hos. ix. 3). See ch. viii. 12, ix. 9, for the expression of a different mood of feeling.

is this land given] is **the** land. Comp. the expression of similar pretensions, xxxiii. 24.

16—21. Answer of Jehovah. It is true He has scattered the exiles among the nations; but He will again gather them.

16. *yet will I be to them*] Rather: and **have been to them for a sanctuary but little** in the countries where they are come. [The apodosis to the *v.* will be virtually *v.* 17, so that there should be a comma at the end of 16.] The expression "for a sanctuary but little" refers to the taunt of the dwellers in Jerusalem that the exiles were far from the sanctuary and had no part in Jehovah. It is true that He had not been to the exiles in great measure that which a "sanctuary" is, viz. a presence of Jehovah, a sanctification, and a religious joy[1]. It is doubtful if "sanctuary" has anywhere (even Is. viii. 14) the meaning of asylum, protection; the sanctuary is the abode of Jehovah, and His presence there sanctifies those in the midst of whom He dwells. The exiles longed to be near the sanctuary and mourned their distance from it (Ps. lxxxiv., cxxxvii.); while those left in the land boasted of the possession of it and looked on the exiles as outcasts.

17—20. But this time of privation for the exiles shall come to an

[1] [But Hävernick and others render the Heb. adv. (with R.V.) as temporal, "a little while," although it is true that Ezek., unlike Isaiah (xlvi. 13, li. 5, lvi. 1), does not elsewhere speak of the period of exile as a short one.]

I will gather you from the peoples, and assemble you out
of the countries where ye have been scattered, and I will
18 give you the land of Israel.   And they shall come thither,
and they shall take away all the detestable things thereof
19 and all the abominations thereof from thence.   And I will
give them one heart, and I will put a new spirit within you;
and I will take the stony heart out of their flesh, and will
20 give them an heart of flesh: that they may walk in my
statutes, and keep mine ordinances, and do them: and they
21 shall be my people, and I will be their God.   But as for
them whose heart walketh after the heart of their detestable
things and their abominations, I will bring their way upon

end.   They shall be gathered out of the countries, and the land of
Israel given to them; from which they shall remove all its abominations.
They shall receive a new heart to walk in the Lord's commandments;
and He shall be their God and they His people.

give you the land of Israel] Those left in the country said: "The land
is given unto us."   They shall be cast out and the land again given to
those now in exile.   The flower of the nation had been carried away in
the captivity of Jehoiachin.   Both Jeremiah and Ezekiel regard the
exiles as the hope of the nation and speak bitterly against the population remaining at home; comp. the former's parable of the very bad
figs (ch. xxiv.), and the latter's scornful questions, ch. xxxiii. 24—26.
Cf. ch. xxviii. 25, xxxiv. 13, xxxvi. 24.

18.   *shall take away*] i.e. remove.   Cf. ch. xxxvii. 22, 23.   The "detestable things" are the false gods (1 Kgs xi. 5, 7; 2 Kgs xxiii. 13), and
all the accompaniments of the debased worship (cf. ch. xxxiii. 25, 26).

19.   *give them one heart*] Cf. Jer. xxxii. 38, "And they shall be my
people, and I will be their God: and I will give them one heart and
one way, that they may fear me for ever."   LXX. "another" heart.
Some MSS., Targ., and Syr. read *new*, which is the prophet's own
term, ch. xxxvi. 26.   Both "another" and "new" form a better antithesis to "stony heart" than "one" does.   The old stony heart, unimpressible and obstinate, shall be taken away, and a heart of "flesh,"
sensitive and responsive to the touch of Jehovah, shall be given them.

20.   *shall be my people*] Then shall the covenant between the Lord
and Israel be fully realized, for this is the idea of the covenant, that He
should be their God and they His people, ch. xxxvi. 28, xxxvii. 27;
Jer. xxxi. 33.

21.   But those who cleave to their abominations shall receive the
recompence of their ways—"there is no peace, saith the LORD, unto
the wicked" (Is. xlviii. 22).

The expression "whose heart walketh *after the heart of* their detestable
things" is without parallel or meaning; elsewhere it is: "their heart

their own heads, saith the Lord GOD. Then did the 22
cherubim lift up their wings, and the wheels were ¹beside
them; and the glory of the God of Israel was over them
above. And the glory of the LORD went up from the midst 23
of the city, and stood upon the mountain which is on the
east side of the city. And the spirit lifted me up, and 24
brought me in the vision by the spirit of God into Chaldea,
to them of the captivity. So the vision that I had seen
went up from me. Then I spake unto them of the captivity 25
all the things that the LORD had shewed me.

The word of the LORD also came unto me, saying, Son of 12
                                                        2

¹ Or, *over against*

went after their idols" (ch. xx.; cf. xxxiii. 31)¹. A different class of
persons is referred to from those spoken of in *vv.* 17—20, either the
population in Jerusalem or more naturally those in general who follow
idols. The text requires some amendment: "but as for those whose
heart goeth after their detestable things...their way will I recompense."

XI. 22—25.   VISION OF JEHOVAH'S WITHDRAWAL.

vv. 22—25. The manifestation of Jehovah rises from over the city
and moves eastward to the Mount of Olives. The city is abandoned
by Jehovah (Hos. v. 15). The prophet does not pursue the movement
further. The glory passes out by the eastern gate, by which also it
returns into the new temple (ch. xliii. 1—4). The prophet is carried
back by the spirit to the captivity; to whom he narrates all he had seen.

FOURTH SECTION, CH. XII.—XIX. THE NECESSITY OF ISRAEL'S
DESTRUCTION.

The preceding symbols and visions, such as those in ch. iv.—v. and
ch. viii.—xi., had foreshewn the certainty of the nation's fall; a new
series of discourses demonstrate the necessity of it. Many thoughts and
considerations occurred to men's minds which invalidated the force of
the prophet's threats and disinclined them to receive them, or at least left
them in hesitation. They had been for long familiar with threats of
judgement, but the threatened storm had passed over. There were
also men who saw into the future as well as Ezekiel, who, however,
discerned no signs of approaching calamity, but foretold peace and
security. And further, was not Israel the people of Jehovah, whom
He could not cast away? In a new series of discourses the prophet
disposes of such considerations, adding also positive reasons which
demonstrate the moral necessity of the nation's removal. The section
has these divisions—

(1) ch. xii. 1—20. Symbol of the king's secret flight and capture.

¹ [Kr. suggests that we should slightly alter the M.T. so as to read, "But, as for
them, because their heart walketh after their detestable things...I will bring &c."]

man, thou dwellest in the midst of the rebellious house, which have eyes to see, and see not, which have ears to hear, and hear not ; for they are a rebellious house.

(2) ch. xii. 21—28.   The popular delusion that prophecies of evil failed to come true, or referred to the distant future, shall receive a speedy and terrible refutation.

(3) ch. xiii., xiv.   The prophets who foster such delusions and preach peace, prophesy out of their own heart and lie.   The deceivers and those deceived by them shall perish together.

(4) ch. xv.   Will the Lord destroy the nation of Israel, His own people?—Israel among the nations is like the vine branch among the trees: what was it ever good for?   Particularly, what is it good for now when half-burnt in the fire?   Only to be flung again into the fire and wholly consumed.

(5) ch. xvi.   Let the history of Jerusalem be judged and estimated ! Has it not been a persistent course of ingratitude and unfaithfulness ? Can the issue of it be anything but destruction ?

(6) ch. xvii.   And the perfidy of Zedekiah against the king of Babylon, must it not be chastised ?

(7) ch. xviii.   The principles of the Divine government.

(8) ch. xix.   Dirge over Judah and her royal house.

XII.   SYMBOL OF THE FLIGHT AND CAPTURE OF THE KING.

The passage is without date, but the signs were subsequent to those already described.   The first part, *vv.* 1—20, is rather of the nature of a preface, repeating the certainty of the downfall of the city and nation, while all that follows up to ch. xix. supports this certainty by shewing the moral necessity of Israel's destruction.

(1) *vv.* 1—2.   An introduction characterizing the house of Israel as blind and unable to discern the signs of the times, and therefore in need of new proofs to convince them.

(2) *vv.* 3—7.   A symbolical action, prefiguring the fate of the king and people on the capture of the city.

(3) *vv.* 8—16.   Exposition of the symbol: the failure of Zedekiah's attempt at resistance, his flight and capture, exile and death in Babylon, with the dispersion of the people into all lands.

(4) *vv.* 17—20.   A new symbol of the life of anguish and terror which the people shall lead under the foreign invaders.

(5) *vv.* 21—25.   Warning against a proverb current in Israel to the effect that "visions," that is, prophecies of evil, did not come true.

(6) *vv.* 26—28.   Warning against a less blameable form of unbelief, the idea that prophecies, such as those now given, referred to a distant time, and that it would be long ere they were fulfilled.

2.   The people of Israel among whom the prophet dwells are a rebellious house (ch. ii. 3, 6, 7, 8, iii. 26, 27).   His former signs meet with no belief from them.   They have eyes but see not: they behold events and history with their bodily eyes, but fail to discern the moral

Therefore, thou son of man, prepare thee stuff for ¹re- 3
moving, and remove by day in their sight; and thou shalt
remove from thy place to another place in their sight: it
may be they will ²consider, though they be a rebellious house.
And thou shalt bring forth thy stuff by day in their sight, as 4
stuff for ¹removing: and thou shalt go forth thyself at even

---

¹ Or, *exile*   ² Or, *perceive that they are*

---

meaning in them. Events are just events to them, the nature of the
God who animates the events remains undiscovered by them (Is. vi. 9,
xlii. 20; Jer. v. 21; Mark viii. 18). And the signs and words of the
prophet make no impression on them; they say, "Is he not a speaker of
parables?" (ch. xx. 49). Therefore new signs must be given them (*v.* 4).

XII. 3—7. SYMBOLICAL ACTION, PREFIGURING THE ESCAPE AND CAPTURE OF THE FUGITIVES.

The details of the symbol seem to be as follows: First, the prophet
prepares "stuff for removing"—such articles as one meaning to escape
from a besieged city would carry with him. These things being prepared,
he brings them out. It is not said where he deposits them; it would be
in some place convenient to make his escape from, in the vicinity of the
wall of the city. These things he does before the eyes of the people during
daylight. His action represents the conduct of persons in a besieged
city, whose movements are free within the city; hence this part of the
action is done openly (*vv.* 3, 4). Secondly, these preparations having
been made by day, the prophet himself goes out in the evening, in the
darkness, and digs through the wall, making his escape at the opening,
and carrying on his shoulder the articles which he had prepared to
take with him in his flight. Besides doing this in the darkness he
covers his face. In doing all this he is a "sign" to the house of
Israel: in this way shall the king and those with him seek to escape
into exile from the enemy when the city is about to fall into their
hands (*vv.* 4—7).

3. *stuff for removing*] marg. *exile*, i.e. such articles as one carries
with him when going as a fugitive into exile.

and remove by day] lit. remove as into exile. The word is wanting
in LXX., which reads: "prepare for thyself articles of exile by day in
their sight." This is more natural.

remove from thy place] The words seem to describe generally the
whole symbolical action which the prophet is to perform.

consider, though they be] Rather, as marg., *perceive that they are*.

4. *And thou shalt*] The prophet is to bring forth the articles which
he had prepared, depositing them in some convenient place in readiness
to carry with him when he escapes.

and thou shalt go forth thyself] The second half of *v.* 4 is to be connected with *v.* 5, describing the prophet's action so far as it symbolizes
what refers to the *persons* of the fugitives.

5 in their sight, as when men go forth into exile. Dig thou
6 through the wall in their sight, and carry out thereby. In
their sight shalt thou bear it upon thy shoulder, and carry
it forth in the dark; thou shalt cover thy face, that thou
see not the ground: for I have set thee for a sign unto the
7 house of Israel. And I did so as I was commanded:
I brought forth my stuff by day, as stuff for removing, and
in the even I digged through the wall with mine hand;
I brought it forth in the dark, and bare it upon my shoul-
8 der in their sight. And in the morning came the word of

5. *Dig thou through the wall*] Naturally the "wall" is not the wall
of his house, but the city wall. He brought out his articles of flight by
day, making them ready for the night-time when he was to escape
through the wall. It is absurd to suppose, as is usually done, that he
carried his things back into the house, and digged through the wall of
his house in the evening. This would mar the action and be ridiculous.
The "wall" is the city wall. The question whether Tel-Abib was a
walled place is of no importance, because the actions were probably not
actually performed[1].

6. The verse refers to the prophet's going out through the city wall,
bearing on his shoulder the bundle of articles he carried with him in
his flight.

in the dark] The word occurs again only in Gen. xv. 17.

cover thy face] This might be to disguise himself, but the next words
"thou shalt not see the land" (ground) seem to require a different sense
[viz. that they hint at the blinding of Zedekiah after his flight, so that
he was unable to see the land (note marg.) which he was leaving].
Cf. *vv.* 12, 13.

a sign unto...Israel] A typical sign, as explained *v.* 11, "like as I
have done, so shall it be done unto them." Cf. ch. xxiv. 24, 27; Is. viii.
18, xx. 3; Zech. iii. 8.

7. *with mine hand*] lit. *with hand*, i.e. by force, Is. xxviii. 2. LXX.
omits.

XII. 8—16. Exposition of the Symbol.

The action of the prophet is a representation of what shall happen in
the last days of the siege. The king and those about him shall prepare
for flight; they shall go out secretly through the walls, but shall be
captured and brought to Babylon.

8. *in the morning*] This circumstance might seem to imply that the
prophet really performed the actions described. But though in this

[1] [As against Davidson's view that this and other symbols were not actually performed see sub-note on p. 31. In this case the whole meaning of the symbol seems
to depend upon its being carried out, while the apparent absurdity would have the
effect of directing attention to it.]

the LORD unto me, saying, Son of man, hath not the house 9
of Israel, the rebellious house, said unto thee, What doest
thou? Say thou unto them, Thus saith the Lord GOD: 10
This [1]burden *concerneth* the prince in Jerusalem, and all the
house of Israel [2]among whom they are. Say, I am your 11
sign: like as I have done, so shall it be done unto them:

[1] Or, *oracle*   [2] Or, *that are among them*

case performance of the action was not an impossibility it was probably
only narrated (see on ch. iv. [but see also sub-notes in square brackets
there]). The natural sequel of the action (supposing it done), the
curiosity of the people, is described, just as the action itself is related, as
if it had literally been shewn.

10, 11. The general meaning of these verses is clear enough—the
prophet's action is a representation of what shall happen in Jerusalem
in the case of prince and people, but *v.* 10 is very obscure, and probably
not in its original form.

10. *This burden* concerneth *the prince*] lit. *the prince* (is) *this burden*
in Jerusalem. The term "burden" has also the sense of "oracle" (see
marg.), but Ezek. does not use it in this sense and there is no reason to
find any play upon the word as Jer. xxiii. 33[1]. The allusion can only
be to the last words of *v.* 7—I "*bare it* upon my shoulder": and the
meaning would be: this bearing or loading has reference to the prince
(*v.* 12). With this sense the following words must run: "and all the
house of Israel which are in the midst of it" (Jerusalem—with a change
of one letter). It is objected that "all the house of Israel" could
hardly be used of the inhabitants of Jerusalem, the phrase usually
refers to the larger Israel, existing in all places; but notwithstanding
this objection the easiest course is to read: *in the midst of it* (Jerusalem) as above. Cor. omits the verse as a gloss[2].

11. *I am your sign*] i.e. a sign to you—the exiles, to whom he is
speaking; while done "unto them" refers to the inhabitants of Jerusalem. Cf. *v.* 6.

[1] [But see Oxf. Lex., and Redpath (*Westm. Comm.*), *ad loc.*, who points out that "as
the root from which the word is derived meant to lift up a burden as well as to lift up the
voice, and as the utterances to which the word is applied in prophecy (e.g. constantly
in Isaiah) generally conveyed the idea of punishment or affliction, the use of the word
'burden' can readily be understood."]
[2] [Perhaps the best way of treating the difficulty is either (with Lofth.) simply
to omit "the prince," as suggested to a copyist by *v.* 12, or to consider it as
arising from an accidental duplication of the word "the burden," which immediately
follows it in the M.T., the two Heb. words having almost the same consonants
(although the LXX. apparently read both words in some form), or (with Ber.) to read,
instead of *hannāsī*, "the prince," *nissā*, this oracle *is uttered*, or (with Kr.) *prophesy*
this oracle. Each sense can be attained by a slight change in M.T. According to
Kr. "them" instead of the sing. *it* (Jerusalem) has also arisen from the influence of
the pl. pronoun in *v.* 12.]

12 they shall go into exile, into captivity. And the prince that is among them shall bear upon his shoulder in the dark, and shall go forth : they shall dig through the wall to carry out thereby : he shall cover his face, because he shall not 13 see the ¹ground with his eyes. My net also will I spread upon him, and he shall be taken in my snare : and I will bring him to Babylon to the land of the Chaldeans ; yet 14 shall he not see it, though he shall die there. And I will scatter toward every wind all that are round about him to help him, and all his bands ; and I will draw out the sword 15 after them. And they shall know that I am the LORD, when I shall disperse them among the nations, and scatter 16 them through the countries. But I will leave a few men of them from the sword, from the famine, and from the

¹ Or, *land*

12. *shall bear upon his shoulder in the dark, and shall*] The balance of clauses requires : "shall bear upon his shoulder ; in the darkness shall he go forth" (or, carry forth, as in *v.* 5,—a slight change of reading, which gets rid of the unnatural *and*).

because he shall not see the ground] Rather as marg., **the land.**

with his eyes] lit. *by eyesight himself.* The language is unnatural. LXX. "that he may not be seen by eye, and he himself shall not see the land." Whether original or not this rendering combines the two ideas expressed by "covering the face," viz. that of disguise (Job xxiv. 15), and inability to see (Job ix. 24). The prophet clearly foresaw the fall of the city and the captivity of the king, and he may have threatened the king with a chastisement for his rebellion which, though barbarous, was not unusual in that age. If he did so it is still probable that afterwards when composing his Book he made the references to the putting out of the king's eyes more distinct (*v.* 13).

13. The king's flight shall be unavailing ; he shall be captured and brought blinded to Babylon, where he shall die. As the Lord fought against Jerusalem in the siege, so it is He that ensures the capture of the king. It is in His net that he is ensnared and taken ; Hos. vii. 12, "When they shall go, I will spread my net upon them ; I will bring them down as the fowls of the heaven." Cf. Ezek. xvii. 20, xxxii. 3.

yet shall he not see it] The eyes of Zedekiah were put out by Nebuchadrezzar at Riblah. 2 Kgs xxv. 5 *seq.* ; Jer. lii. 8, 11.

14—16. All the armies and aids of the king shall be dispersed and pursued with the sword. They shall be scattered among the nations, and their history shall bring to their knowledge what Jehovah, their God, truly is. A remnant of them shall be spared among the nations that they make known to them their abominations, and these also shall learn what the God of Israel is. Jerusalem and Israel are set in pestilence; that they may declare all their abominations among the nations whither they come; and they shall know that I am the LORD.

Moreover the word of the LORD came to me, saying, 17 Son of man, eat thy bread with quaking, and drink thy 18 water with trembling and with carefulness; and say unto 19 the people of the land, Thus saith the Lord GOD concerning the inhabitants of Jerusalem, and the land of Israel: They shall eat their bread with carefulness, and drink their water with astonishment, that her land may be desolate from ¹all that is therein, because of the violence of all them that dwell therein. And the cities that are inhabited shall 20 be laid waste, and the land shall be a desolation; and ye shall know that I am the LORD.

And the word of the LORD came unto me, saying, 21

¹ Heb. *the fulness thereof*.

the midst of the nations round about (ch. v. 5), their history is a drama enacted before the eyes of mankind, and the drama when finished will reveal Jehovah in His fulness, not only to Israel but to the nations of the world. Cf. ch. xiv. 22, 23, xvii. 24, xx. 9, xxxviii. 23, xxxix. 23; Is. v. 16; Jer. xxii. 8.

16. *that they may declare*, &c.] [Kr. points out that the purpose here mentioned has no reference to any conversion of the heathen, such as we have glimpses of elsewhere as resulting from Israel's exile, e.g. Is. xlix. 6 f., lv. 3. Here it is only the vindication before the nations of Jehovah's judicial dealings with His people, which is contemplated.]

17—20. A new symbol of the terror and violence and desolation about to come upon the land.

18. It is obvious that this symbol could not have been actually performed. [But see above, p. 31.] For "carefulness" cf. ch. iv. 16.

19. *Jerusalem, and the land*] Rather: Jerusalem in (lit. upon) the land.

because of the violence] The punishment of violence is violence. The internal wrong and oppression shall be avenged by a crushing violence and destruction from without. Am. iii. 9—11. The phrase "desolate from all that is therein," marg. *the fulness thereof*, means desolate and emptied of its fulness.

XII. 21—28. WARNING AGAINST DESPISING OF PROPHECY.

The prophet felt that such threats as those just uttered (*vv.* 1—20) were neglected and little thought of. People disposed of such prophecies by saying that they did not come true; or, if they did not go so far, by saying that they referred to the distant future. Ezekiel warns

22 Son of man, what is this proverb that ye have in the land
   of Israel, saying, The days are prolonged, and every vision
23 faileth? Tell them therefore, Thus saith the Lord GOD:
   I will make this proverb to cease, and they shall no more
   use it as a proverb in Israel; but say unto them, The days
24 are at hand, and the ¹effect of every vision. For there shall

¹ Heb. *word*.

them that Jehovah's threatenings bear upon the present time, and that
they shall be fulfilled.

22. *The days are prolonged*] i.e. time passes and becomes long.
The words are a generalization upon the fact that prophecies of judgement are not fulfilled; time goes on and "every vision faileth," i.e.
remains a dead threat.　LXX. omits "every," giving even a more
comprehensive sense.　The reference is specially to prophecies of
judgement, and there was room for misapprehension in regard to these,
because being drawn forth by moral evils existing when they were
uttered, they were of the nature of threats, the object of which was to
bring the people to repentance, and thus prevent their own fulfilment.
For the same reason they were often of a general character, and thus
when their fulfilment was postponed or when they were not literally
fulfilled, men judged that they were merely uttered in the air.　The
moral purpose and consequently the contingent character of prophecy is
expressly taught in Jer. xviii., and was well understood by intelligent
persons in Israel, as appears from the reasoning of the princes in regard
to the prophecy of Micah, Jer. xxvi. 17—19.

23.　Judgement had been so often threatened and so often deferred
that the failure of prophecy to realize itself became a proverb.　Too
superficial to apprehend the meaning of its postponement these scoffers
made light of the threatened judgement (2 Pet. iii. 3, 9).　Now they shall
be undeceived.　For similar popular sentiments, cf. Jer. v. 13, 14, xvii. 15.

the effect of every vision] lit. *the word*—the contents, of every vision.

24.　Another thing which robbed the word of the true prophets,
who threatened judgement, of its force was the fact that there were
other prophets who spoke in a contrary sense, preaching peace and
security.　Prophets, though alike speaking in the name of Jehovah,
contradicted one another, and the people, even if anxious to know the
truth, had no criterion whereby to judge between them.　The scene
between Jeremiah and Hananiah (Jer. xxviii.) is very instructive as to
the condition in which the people were left.　There was nothing in
Jeremiah to shew him to be a true prophet, and nothing in Hananiah
to prove him false.　Truth and falsehood could be distinguished in those
days in no other way than now: he who has to distinguish must find
the criterion in himself—he "that is of the truth heareth my voice"
(John xviii. 37).　The people believed that Jehovah spoke by prophets,
but by which prophets, whether Jeremiah or his opponents, they had to
decide out of their own hearts, and not unnaturally (Mic. ii. 11) they

be no more any vain vision nor flattering divination within
the house of Israel. For I am the LORD; I will speak, and 25
the word that I shall speak shall be performed; it shall be
no more deferred: for in your days, O rebellious house, will
I speak the word, and will perform it, saith the Lord GOD.

Again the word of the LORD came to me, saying, Son 26 27
of man, behold, they of the house of Israel say, The vision
that he seeth is for many days to come, and he prophesieth
of times that are far off. Therefore say unto them, Thus 28
saith the Lord GOD: There shall none of my words be
deferred any more, but the word which I shall speak shall
be performed, saith the Lord GOD.

despised Jeremiah as a false prophet and held to his opponents (Jer.
xviii. 18).

no more...flattering divination] These false prophecies of peace
shall cease, for the same judgement which confirms the true prophecy
shall annihilate the false. The term "divination" was employed of
the methods of reaching the mind of the deity used by the native populations of Canaan (Deut. xviii. 10; 1 Sam. vi. 2). They were such
appliances as lots, arrows, and other methods of augury (Ezek. xxi.
21). Possibly these methods had in some degree passed into use in
Israel, and were employed by a low prophecy. In true prophecy these
mechanical arts were discarded: Jehovah spoke to the prophet in his
mind. Here, however, the word "divination" is used of the oracles
of the prophets who were false, even though not employing any external
arts of augury. Their prophecy is called "flattering," lit. *smooth*, because it promised immunity from trouble and disaster. Cf. Jer. xiv. 14.

25. *For I am the LORD*] Rather: **for I the Lord will speak;** lit.
"for I the Lord will speak what word I shall speak, and it shall come
to pass." The word which the Lord speaks to this generation shall be
fulfilled before it pass away.

26—28. If others did not go so far as to disregard prophecy altogether, they concluded that the prophecies bore reference to the
future, and that the judgements threatened would not come in their
day (Is. xxxix. 8). This also was an inference not unnatural. The
prophecies of the true prophets were moral and designed, even when
threatening, to turn men away from their sins, and thus in a manner
to frustrate their own fulfilment. They were not absolute predictions,
but conditional threats, which might be averted on repentance and
amendment (Jonah; Jer. xviii.; Joel ii. 14). And in point of fact the
most terrible threatenings of judgement were connected with the "day
of the Lord," which might be supposed not very near (Is. v. 18, 19).
Cf. on *v.* 22; Hab. ii. 3.

28. *the word which I shall speak*] Cf. for construction, Jer. xiv. 1,
xlvi. 1; Am. v. 1.

13   And the word of the LORD came unto me, saying,
2 Son of man, prophesy against the prophets of Israel that
prophesy, and say thou unto them that prophesy out of their
3 own heart, Hear ye the word of the LORD; Thus saith the
Lord GOD: Woe unto the foolish prophets, that follow

XIII. AGAINST THE FALSE PROPHETS AND PROPHETESSES.

The passage is an expansion of ch. xii. 24, and has three main parts: first, *vv.* 1—9 denunciation of the prophets as persons who help forward the downfall of the state, as foxes among the ruins only undermine that which is still standing. Secondly, *vv.* 10—16 denunciation of them under another graphic figure—they are persons who whitewash the tottering wall which the people build. Thirdly, *vv.* 17—23 denunciation of the prophetesses who ensnare souls.

XIII. 1—9. THE LYING PROPHETS ARE LIKE FOXES AMONG THE RUINS.

(1) *vv.* 1—3. The inspiration of these prophets is not from the spirit of God but from their own heart.

(2) *vv.* 4, 5. Consequently so far as the state was concerned they were like foxes among the ruins; they burrowed among these and only helped to bring down what might still be standing.

(3) *vv.* 6, 7. They deceived the people, and were self-deceived. They prophesied lies, and looked that God would establish their lies.

(4) *vv.* 8, 9. Therefore destruction shall overtake them. The people of the Lord, when the day of chastisement has passed, shall be again a people in their own land, but the names of these prophets shall not be found among them.

2. *the prophets of Israel that prophesy*] There seems a kind of sarcasm on "prophets of Israel,"—those whom Israel accepts and delights to regard as prophets (Mic. ii. 11); and a similar sarcasm in "that prophesy." They prophesied and that without limit: their mouths were always full of "The LORD saith" (*v.* 6). Jer. xviii. 18 shews how the people regarded their prophets; they had faith in them and believed that Jehovah spoke by them, while such men as Jeremiah they judged to be false prophets: "Come, and let us devise devices against Jeremiah; for the law shall not perish from the priest, nor counsel from the wise, *nor the word from the prophet*." Cf. Jer. xliii. 2.

their own heart] The inspiration of these prophets came from their own hearts or minds—their own thoughts and hopes, and judgement upon the situation in which they were placed. They had nothing higher than human wisdom, while the inspiration of the true prophet came from the spirit of God.

3. *foolish prophets*] The word, not used again by Ezekiel, is a moral term, meaning destitute of that wisdom the beginning of which is the fear of the Lord (Prov. i. 7). Jeremiah charges the prophets of his day with shameful vices, "They...have committed adultery with their neighbours' wives" (Jer. xxix. 23; cf. xxiii. 14, and *passim*); but, without supposing that all the "false" prophets were so bad, it characterized them in general that they were superficial men in a moral sense. Their notions of religion and life were not high or strict, and hence they saw nothing in the condition of the people or the state calling for the judgement of God, and prophesied "peace." This was what distinguished them from Jeremiah and other prophets whom we call "true." Micah says in opposition to them : "I truly am full of power by the spirit of the LORD...to declare unto Jacob his transgression and to Israel his sin" (ch. iii. 8) ; and Jeremiah goes so far as to declare it to be the mark of a true prophet that he threatens judgement upon the nation (Jer. xxvii. 8, 9). A true prophet is one by whom the Lord speaks, and a "false" prophet (the expression is not used in the Old Testament[1], though the prophets are said to speak "falsely") is one by whom He does not speak. This is true : but the converse has also its truth—the Lord did not speak by these prophets because they were "false" (1 Kings xxii. 6 *seq.*). There is a spirit of false prophecy as well as a spirit of true prophecy. The spirit of true prophecy is the spirit of the theocracy and of the religion of Jehovah, the spirit that comprehends its principles, sympathises with its lofty morality, understands its aims, and therefore can perceive the true means to be used for fulfilling them. The spirit of false prophecy is the untheocratic spirit, which, even when speaking in the name of Jehovah, has not entered with any profoundness into the nature and aims of His kingdom, and consequently misapprehends the means needful to further it. In his encounters with the prophets of his day Jeremiah opposes them in three spheres : that of policy ; that of morals ; and that of personal experience. In policy the genuine prophets had some fixed principles, all arising out of the idea that the kingdom of the Lord was not a kingdom of this world. Hence they opposed military preparation (Ps. xx. 7), riding on horses and building of fenced cities (Hos. xiv. 3 ; Mic. v. 10, 11 ; Is. xxxi. 1), and counselled trust in Jehovah (Is. vii. 9, x. 20, 21, xvii. 7, xxx. 15). These prophets were moving forward (often unconsciously) towards that conception of the kingdom of God which has been realized in the "Church" ; and external providence was shaping the history of the nation on lines parallel to this conception, which eventually received form by the destruction of the state and the reduction of the people to be a mere religious community. The false prophets, on the other hand, desired their country to be a military power among the powers around, they advocated alliances with the Eastern empires and with Egypt, and relied on their national strength (Am. vi. 13). Again, the true prophets had a stringent personal and state morality (see above). In their view the true cause of the destruction of the state was its immoralities. But the false prophets had no such deep moral convictions, and seeing nothing unwonted or alarming in the condition of things, prophesied of "peace." They were not necessarily irreligious men, but their religion had no truer insight into the nature

[i.e. in the Hebrew, but the LXX. has the expression, e.g. Jer. vi. 13, and so frequently the New Testament, e.g. Matt. vii. 15, xxiv. 11.]

4 their own spirit, ¹and have seen nothing! O Israel, thy
5 prophets have been like foxes in the waste places. Ye
have not gone up into the ²gaps, neither made up the fence

¹ Or, *and* things which *they have not seen*   ² Or, *breaches*

of the God of Israel than that of the common people (Am. v. 18);
hence they pointed to the Temple as the house of the Lord, which He
must protect; while Jeremiah told them that they had made it "a den
of robbers," in which they thought themselves safe after committing
their crimes, and threatened it with the fate of Shiloh (Jer. vii., xxvi.).
And finally Jeremiah expresses his conviction that the prophets whom
he opposed did not stand in the same relation to the Lord as he did;
they had not his experiences of the word of the Lord, into whose counsel
(Am. iii. 7) they had not been admitted, and they were without that
fellowship of mind with the mind of Jehovah which was the true source
of prophecy (Jer. xxiii. *pass.*). Hence he satirizes their pretended
supernatural "dreams," and charges them from conscious want of any
true prophetic word with "stealing" words (Jer. xxiii. 30) from one
another. Cf. *vv.* 6, 7 and ch. xiv.

their own spirit] The term is used in opposition to the "spirit" of
the Lord which inspired the true prophet, who is called "the man that
has the spirit" (Hos. ix. 7). As distinct from heart "spirit" is rather
the force or power moving the prophet. In early times the prophets
were the subjects of considerable excitation; and looking on them thus
powerfully affected men recognised the influence of the spirit of God
upon them.

and have seen nothing] Rather: and (go after) **that which they have
not seen.** They did not see, though no doubt they thought they saw.
They were self-deceived.

4. *foxes in the waste places*] i.e. ruins. The prophets are like foxes
[rather, *jackals*. Cf. Lam. v. 18]; ruins are congenial to them; a
condition of decay is their proper sphere; there they can burrow as
their instincts prompt them. The main idea, however, is that their
operations only increase the devastation and undermine and bring down
anything that may yet be standing. In a declining and disastrous time
the minds of men are excited and feed on the wildest schemes, and
feeling themselves helpless they readily turn to those who pretend to
speak to them in God's name. And it only adds to their ruin when
those to whom they turn have no higher wisdom than themselves.

5. *gone up into the gaps*] marg. *breaches*. Ezekiel turning to the
prophets themselves uses "ye"—a frequent change of person in
animated speech. [*Vv.* 5, 7 are addressed to the prophets, *vv.* 4, 6
to the people. It gives a smoother text to consider the order to be
4, 6, 5, 7.]

made up the fence] If they had been true prophets they would have
done two things: stood in the breach, and made a wall of defence for
Israel. Without figure: these prophets knew neither what measures
to adopt to stop the way of the invading dangers, nor what protective

for the house of Israel, to stand in the battle in the day of
the LORD.   They have seen vanity and lying divination, 6
that say, The LORD saith; and the LORD hath not sent
them: and they ¹have made men to hope that the word
should be confirmed.   Have ye not seen a vain vision, 7
and have ye not spoken a lying divination, whereas ye say,
The LORD saith; albeit I have not spoken?

Therefore thus saith the Lord GOD: Because ye have 8

¹ Or, *have hoped*

methods to recommend that the state might be successfully defended.
They are hardly charged with want of personal courage when it is said
they go not up into the breach; rather they wanted wisdom and insight,
they had no measures to suggest which would repair or protect the
fortunes of the people.   Another prophet with more pathos describes
the incompetence of Israel's leaders in the day of her distress: "There
is none to guide her among all the sons whom she hath brought forth;
neither is there any that taketh her by the hand of all the sons that she
hath brought up" (Is. li. 18).   No doubt the one measure to adopt was
repentance and trust in the Lord; Am. v. 14, "Seek good, and not
evil...and so the LORD, the God of hosts, shall be with you, as ye
say."

the day of the LORD] [Generally, the day on which the Lord
vindicates His righteousness by judgements either on His own people
(e.g. Is. ii. 12) or other nations (e.g. Midian, in Is. ix. 4). See on
Am. v. 18 in this series. Kr. points out that, while for the prophets
generally the expression has a future reference, in Ezek. it relates to
the past overthrow of Jerusalem. See further in Davidson's Art.
Eschatology in *HDB* i. 735 ff.]

6. *have made men to hope*] Rather: **have hoped**, as marg. The
usual sense of the verb is to "hope"; only in a single passage
(Ps. cxix. 49) does it appear to mean to "cause to hope." The false
prophets looked for the confirmation (in fulfilment) of their prophecies
and visions—they were self-deceived, not consciously false. Prophecy
being an inward thing, a speaking by the spirit in the mind and to
the mind, there was no external criterion, and while the true prophet
had the witness in himself that he was true, the false prophet might not
be aware that he was false (Jer. xxiii. 21, 31). It is an interesting
question what kind of mental experience the true prophet had, which
verified to him his own genuineness.

vv. 8, 9. Chastisement from Jehovah upon these prophets.
Because these prophets speak falsely Jehovah is against them, for He
is the living and the true (*v.* 8); but that which God is against must
speedily feel the effects of His opposition—His hand will be upon them
(*v.* 9). There is no inert, inoperative opposition on God's part. The
sweep of His operation is so vast that its movement may be unperceived,

spoken vanity, and seen lies, therefore, behold, I am against
9 you, saith the Lord God.   And mine hand shall be against
the prophets that see vanity, and that divine lies: they
shall not be in the ¹council of my people, neither shall
they be written in the ²writing of the house of Israel,
neither shall they enter into the land of Israel; and ye
10 shall know that I am the Lord God.   Because, even
because they have seduced my people, saying, Peace;
and there is no peace; and when one buildeth up ³a wall,

---

¹ Or, *secret*   ² Or, *register*   ³ Or, *a slight wall*

---

as the earth appears to stand still, though moving with inconceivable
rapidity, but its effect will become apparent.

9. The punishment is described in three steps, which form a climax.
At present these prophets possess influence, they are counsellors and
leaders; when Israel is a nation again upon her own land they shall
have no place in the council of the people.   Now they occupy a high
place in the roll of citizens, and have distinguished names; then their
names shall not be written in the writing (i.e. the book or register-roll) of
the house of Israel¹; cf. Ezr. ii. 62; Is. iv. 3.   And finally, they shall
not have a place in the land at all—Israel shall return, while they shall
perish.   Jeremiah had already used the same language in regard to
Shemaiah, a prophet who misled the exiles, Jer. xxix. 32.

council]   [hence coming to mean confidential communication whether
with God (Ps. xxv. 14) or with man (Prov. iii. 32).   So marg. *secret*.]

XIII. 10—16.   The prophets whitewash the tottering wall
which the people build.

10. *Because, even because*]   A solemn and emphatic introduction of
the offence of the prophets; ch. xxxvi. 3; Lev. xxvi. 43.

seduced]   Or, **led astray**.

Peace; and there is no peace]   "Peace" includes security and prosperity; cf. Mic. iii. 5; Jer. vi. 14, viii. 11, xxiii. 17.

and when one buildeth up a wall]   Rather: **and it** (the people)
buildeth up a wall, and behold they (the prophets) **daub it with
whitewash**, or plaster.   The word for "wall" (occurring only here) is
not the usual one, though similar to the one common in Arab.; in usage
it may have meant "a slight wall," as marg., or a partition.   The figure
incisively describes the futile projects of the people, and the feeble
flattery and approval of the prophets². When a weak man cannot

---

¹ [Of genuine Jewish citizens.   Redp. compares Phil. iv. 8, and Rev. iii. 5 with
Swete's note.   Cf. the sentence on Shelemiah, Jer. xxix. 30—32.]
² [Thus, while the "wall" represents the schemes and ideals of the people, the
attitude of the prophets is likened to the whitewash or plaster which seems to
ornament, while it really conceals, jerry building.]

behold, they daub it with untempered *mortar* : say unto 11
them which daub it with untempered *mortar*, that it shall
fall : there shall be an overflowing shower ; and ye, O great
hailstones, shall fall ; and a stormy wind shall rend it. Lo, 12
when the wall is fallen, shall it not be said unto you, Where
is the daubing wherewith ye have daubed it ? Therefore 13
thus saith the Lord GOD ; I will even rend it with a stormy
wind in my fury ; and there shall be an overflowing shower
in mine anger, and great hailstones in fury to consume it.
So will I break down the wall that ye have daubed with 14
untempered *mortar*, and bring it down to the ground, so
that the foundation thereof shall be discovered :. and it shall
fall, and ye shall be consumed in the midst thereof ; and ye
shall know that I am the LORD. Thus will I accomplish 15
my fury upon the wall, and upon them that have daubed it
with untempered *mortar* ; and I will say unto you, The

originate anything himself, he acquires a certain credit (at least in his
own eyes) by strong approval of the schemes of others, saying, "Right !
I give it my cordial approval, and indeed would have suggested it."
What made the prophets whitewash the wall which the people built
was partly the feeling that from the place they occupied they must do
something, and maintain their credit as leaders even when being led ;
and partly perhaps that having no higher wisdom than the mass they
quite honestly approved their policy. Being sharers with them in the
spirit of the time they readily acquiesced in their enterprises.

11—16. Threat of destruction under the figure of a hailstorm,
which shall sweep away the wall and those who daub it with whited
plaster.

11. *and ye, O great hailstones*] The apostrophe to the hailstones is
rather unnatural. A different pointing gives the sense, *and I will cause
great hailstones to fall* [Kr. reads " and great hailstones shall fall [1]"].

wind shall rend it] Or, a strong wind **shall break forth.** [So LXX.,
followed by Kr. It implies a different punctuation from that adopted
by M.T.]

12. Confusion of the false prophets.

13. *rend it with a stormy wind*] Rather : **cause a** stormy wind **to
break forth.**

14. *shall be discovered*] i.e. uncovered, laid bare. The prophets
shall be destroyed in the ruins of the wall (Am. ix. 1). The figure
tends in these words to be replaced by the reality, namely, Jerusalem
and its downfall.

[1] [But the simplest rendering of the Heb. as it stands is, " And I will send great
hailstones ; they shall fall."]

16 wall is no more, neither they that daubed it; *to wit*, the
prophets of Israel which prophesy concerning Jerusalem,
and which see visions of peace for her, and there is no
peace, saith the Lord GOD.

17   And thou, son of man, set thy face against the daughters
of thy people, which prophesy out of their own heart; and

18 prophesy thou against them, and say, Thus saith the Lord
GOD : Woe to the women that sew pillows upon all ¹elbows,
and make kerchiefs for the head of *persons of* every stature

¹ Heb. *joints of the hands.*

16.   to wit, *the prophets*]   This construction puts "the prophets" in
apposition with the last words of *v.* 15 "they that daubed it."   The
words may be taken as an address : " Ye prophets of Israel &c."

XIII. 17—23.   DENUNCIATION OF THE FALSE PROPHETESSES.

Female prophets were not unknown in Israel whether in earlier or
later times, as Deborah (Judg. iv. 4) and Huldah (2 Kings xxii. 14).
The prophetesses referred to here were like the prophets, prophesying
out of their own heart (*v.* 17).   Their prophesying was by some species
of divination, which they used in order to obtain oracles.   The methods of divination practised are somewhat obscure : they bound fillets
upon the joints and threw cloths or veils over the heads of those who
consulted them.   By these means they "hunted" souls; they saved
souls alive that should not live and slew souls that should not die
(*v.* 19), or as expressed otherwise, they made the heart of the righteous
sad and strengthened the hands of the wicked (*v.* 22).   In other words,
like the false prophets they misled the people, promising life to the
ungodly and prophesying disaster to those who were righteous.

18.   *pillows upon all elbows*]   Probably : **fillets** or bands **to all
joints of the hand**; see marg.   Heb. appears to read "my hands,"
which is no doubt an error of transcription ; none of the ancient versions reproduces the reading.   The term rendered "kerchiefs" probably
means veils or coverings to the head, which fell down over the whole
body, and were adapted in size to the person to be covered, whether
young or old.   The language is to be understood literally [the object
probably being to conceal the operations of the prophetess], and not as
a metaphor with the meaning to lull into ease and security.   Ephrem
Syrus already considered the reference to be to amulets worn on the
arms, from which responses were brought forth, and the translation
cited in the Hexapla as the "Hebrew" renders "phylacteries¹."
Fried. Del. (Baer's *Ezech.*, pp. xii, xiii) quotes a Babylonian formula of
incantation in which reference is made to such fillets and cloths.

¹ [The word seems to be akin to the Assyrian *kasû*, to bind.   See W. R. Smith in
Journal of Philology, XIII. 286.]

to hunt souls! ¹Will ye hunt the souls of my people, and
save souls alive ²for yourselves? And ye have profaned me 19
among my people for handfuls of barley and for pieces of
bread, to slay the souls that should not die, and to save the
souls alive that should not live, by your lying to my people
that hearken unto lies.   Wherefore thus saith the Lord 20
GOD: Behold, I am against your pillows, ³wherewith ye
there hunt the souls ⁴to make *them* fly, and I will tear them

---

¹ Or, *Ye hunt...and ye save &c.* ² Or, *that are yours*
³ Or, *where ye hunt* ⁴ Or, *as birds*

---

and save souls alive for yourselves] i.e. to your advantage or profit.
R.V. marg., souls *that are yours*, may represent a sense not unusually
put upon the words; *your own souls*¹—by the earnings of false prophecy.

19. *ye have profaned*] To "profane" the Lord is to bring Him
down from the high sphere of purity or truth or power, where men's
thoughts should place Him, into the region of the impure, the false or
unworthy—the sphere of the common (ch. xx. 39). To "profane" is
the opposite of to "sanctify."

for handfuls of barley] may signify, for mean and trifling hire.
Others think that the offerings may be described which were presented
in order to obtain the oracular response. In this case the rendering
would be: *with* handfuls of barley (see W. R. Smith, *Journal of Philology*, vol. XIII. [pp. 284 f.]). But comp. 1 Sam. ii. 36; 2 Kgs xxiii. 9
with 1 Sam. ix. 8; 1 Kgs xiv. 3; 2 Kgs iv. 42; Mic. iii. 5. In Jer. xliv.
19 the women are represented as baking cakes to be offered to the
queen of heaven.

the souls that should not die] The righteous; cf. *v.* 22, "ye have
grieved the heart of the righteous." The meaning appears to be that
the tendency and direction of their prophecies, like those of the false
prophets, was in support of the wicked and adverse to those like-
minded with the true prophets. They "slay" by their prophetic word
(Hos. vi. 5; Jer. i. 10, "I have...set thee...to pluck up &c.") when they
threaten evil; and so they make the heart sad (faint and despondent)
of those whom the Lord hath not made sad.

vv. 20—23. Chastisement of the prophetesses.

20. *wherewith ye there hunt*] Or, as marg., *where* (or, *wherein*) *ye
hunt*. A slight change of reading gives, *wherewith ye hunt* (Targ.
Syr.).

to make them *fly*] Rather, with marg., *as birds* (Ew.). [The sor-
ceresses did not desire to drive away, but to retain their dupes.]
LXX. omits.

For "pillows" read as above *fillets*. The expression "from your
arms" is not to be forced so as to imply that the bands or fillets were
bound upon the arms of the prophetesses themselves (cf. *v.* 18).

¹ [i.e. save your lives, in the sense of *secure a livelihood*.]

from your arms; and I will let the souls go, even the souls
21 that ye hunt ¹to make *them* fly. Your kerchiefs also will
I tear, and deliver my people out of your hand, and they
shall be no more in your hand to be hunted; and ye shall
22 know that I am the LORD. Because with lies ye have
grieved the heart of the righteous, whom I have not made
sad; and strengthened the hands of the wicked, that he
should not return from his wicked way, ²and be saved alive:
23 therefore ye shall no more see vanity, nor divine divinations:
and I will deliver my people out of your hand; and ye shall
know that I am the LORD.

¹ Or, *as birds*   ² Or, *by promising him life*

even the souls that ye hunt] The reading here is no doubt corrupt.
The easiest change is to read: "I will let the souls go, whose life (*naph-shām*) ye hunt as birds"; cf. Prov. vi. 26 "the adulteress hunteth for the
precious life." Cornill makes the excellent suggestion: "I will let the
souls go *free* [reading *'othān hophshim*] that ye hunt."

22. *have grieved the heart of the righteous*] Or, discouraged the
heart of the righteous—opposed to "strengthened the hands" of the
wicked.

and be saved alive] So LXX.; marg. less well, as A.V., *by promising
him life.*

23. The judgement of God is at hand which shall make an end of
all false prophecy and divination. Cf. ch. xii. 24; Mic. iii. 6, 7; Am.
viii. 11. The issue of these judgements shall be that Jehovah will be
known in truth.

XIV. ANSWER TO IDOLATERS WHO INQUIRE OF THE LORD.

In ch. xiii. Ezekiel had denounced the false prophets who led the
people astray, and had threatened them with extirpation from the
community of the Lord. But the question of false prophecy is not
yet exhausted. It has another side. It is true that false prophets
mislead the people, but it is equally true that it is to a wrong-minded
people that the existence of false prophets is due. The strong current
of perverse inclination in the people sweeps the prophet away before
it; he is enticed, and entering into the mind of the people, gives such
prophecies as coincide with their desires. The evil of false prophecy
is due to a deeper and more pervasive evil than itself; it is indeed
a judgement from God upon the fundamental sin of the people, their
idolatry (*v.* 9). Therefore the true prophet has only one answer to
give to the people who consult him—Put away your idolatries. The
chapter has two parts:

First, *vv.* 1—11. There shall no answer be given by the prophet

Then came certain of the elders of Israel unto me, and 14 sat before me. And the word of the LORD came unto me, 2 saying, Son of man, these men have [1]taken their idols into 3 their heart, and put the stumblingblock of their iniquity before their face: should I be inquired of at all by them?

[1] Heb. *caused to come up.*

to idolaters who inquire through him but the answer, "Put away your idolatries or look for the judgement of God." If a prophet lets himself be enticed to answer the people after their mind, he and they shall perish together.

Secondly, *vv.* 12—13. The principle of the Divine judgement. The presence of righteous men among a sinful people shall not save the sinners; the righteous shall deliver only their own souls.

XIV. 1—8. ANSWER TO IDOLATERS WHO INQUIRE OF THE LORD.

1. *elders of Israel*] That is, in point of fact, elders of the exiles [see on viii. 1]; but in them the prophet sees representatives of the house of Israel both at home and abroad (*vv.* 4, 7), and when addressing them he feels himself speaking to his people in all places. Cf. ch. viii. 1, xx. 1. These elders came and sat before him. It is scarcely probable that their presence was due to the prophet's words in ch. xiii., denouncing their false prophets. It might no doubt be supposed that they were perplexed by these denunciations, and, not knowing whom to believe, waited on the prophet for some further enlightenment. It is more likely that their thoughts were occupied about Jerusalem and the future of their country, and that they hoped to hear something more from Ezekiel on these subjects.

sat before me] [Cf. 2 Kgs vi. 1, where, as the note in this series points out, the expression refers to the house or porch where the prophet sat to receive those who came to him. So here.]

3. *have taken their idols into*, &c.] which appears to mean, laid them on their minds, busied their thoughts and filled their affections with them.

stumblingblock of their iniquity] The reference is still to the idols. Stumblingblock of iniquity is that over which one falls and commits iniquity; see on ch. vii. 19.

before their face] i.e. have placed them in their view, or, so as to follow them; cf. *v.* 6 "turn away your faces from all your abominations"; Ps. xvi. 8, ci. 3. The language is figurative, and does not imply literal setting-up of idols[1].

should I be inquired of] Or, shall I let myself be inquired of? that is, shall I give an answer (through the prophet)? cf. Is. lxv. 1, where "inquired of" is parallel to "am found."

[1] [In view, however, of Ezekiel's strong denunciation, this does not seem quite certain.]

7—2

4 Therefore speak unto them, and say unto them, Thus saith
  the Lord GOD: Every man of the house of Israel that
  taketh his idols into his heart, and putteth the stumblingblock of his iniquity before his face, and cometh to the
  prophet; I the LORD will answer him [1]therein according
5 to the multitude of his idols; that I may take the house
  of Israel in their own heart, because they are all estranged
6 from me through their idols.   Therefore say unto the house
  of Israel, Thus saith the Lord GOD: Return ye, and turn
  yourselves from your idols; and turn away your faces from

[1] Or, *according thereto*   Another reading is, *he is come in the multitude &c.*

4.   The Lord will answer such men directly through Himself, by
involving them in the consequences of their own idolatries and destroying them.

taketh his idols into]   Cf. *v.* 3.

will answer him therein]   If the marginal reading ($K'r\bar{\imath}$) be adopted,
the rendering must be, "I the LORD will answer him; he cometh in
the multitude of his idols"—a meaning which has no probability.   The
text ($K'th\bar{\imath}b$) reads, "I will answer him according to it" (i.e. the iniquity, or the stumblingblock) (even) "according to the multitude, &c."[1]
In *v.* 7, where the same expression occurs, the reading is, "I will answer
him *by myself*"; and the present passage had better be assimilated to
v. 7.   What is meant by the Lord's answering through Himself is
stated *v.* 8, "I will. set my face against that man."   The answer will
be given in acts of judgement.

according to the multitude]   The divine chastisement will be heavy,
proportionate to the gross idolatry.

5.   *take...in their own heart*]   The sinner's sin is like a snare in
which he is captured and destroyed; sin carries its own retribution in
itself (Job viii. 4)[2].   The phrase "take...in their own heart" is explained by the words that follow, "because they are all estranged from
me through their idols."   Their "heart" is the idolatrous direction of
their thoughts and affections; in this they shall be taken (*vv.* 3, 4, 7)[3].

6.   The *prophet* is not permitted to give an answer to any inquiries
of such men.   Jehovah will answer them through Himself (*v.* 7); the
message which the prophet has to deliver is, repentance or destruction !

[1] [Rather "*in it...in* the multitude, &c." Kr. explains, in spite of.]
[2] ["What we should set down as an inevitable consequence of their sin Ezekiel
exhibits, characteristically, as the direct purpose of Yahveh." Lofth.]
[3] [It seems somewhat like forcing the word "heart" to make it thus virtually
equivalent to *sin*.   Ezekiel's expression is, however, obscure.   Kr. interprets it as
meaning the awakening to conversion by means of alarm and fear, as contrasted with
mild exhortation.]

all your abominations. For every one of the house of 7
Israel, or of the strangers that sojourn in Israel, which
separateth himself from me, and taketh his idols into his
heart, and putteth the stumblingblock of his iniquity before
his face, and cometh to the prophet to inquire ¹for himself
of me; I the LORD will answer him by myself: and I will 8
set my face against that man, and will make him an
astonishment, for a sign and a proverb, and I will cut him
off from the midst of my people; and ye shall know that
I am the LORD. And if the prophet be ²deceived and 9
speaketh a word, I the LORD have deceived that prophet,
and I will stretch out my hand upon him, and will destroy

¹ Or, *of him concerning me*   ² Or, *enticed*

7.   *every one...that sojourn in Israel*] Comp. Lev. xvii. 8, 10, 13,
xx. 2, and remark on *v.* 1 above. On "setteth up" cf. *v.* 3.

answer him by myself] Or, through Myself, directly in deeds.

8.   Jehovah's answer to the idolatrous inquirer: He will make him
a sign and a proverb, and cut him off from his people.

make him an astonishment, for a sign] This rendering follows the
M.T., while the A.V. represents a reading differing only by a diacritic
point in the Heb., but having some traditional authority, though not to
be preferred. On "sign" &c. cf. Numb. xxvi. 10; Deut. xxviii. 37.

XIV. **9—11.** FATE OF THE PROPHET WHO GIVES AN ANSWER TO
    IDOLATROUS INQUIRERS: HE AND THEY SHALL PERISH TO-
    GETHER.

9.   *be deceived* [marg. *enticed*] *and speaketh a word*] i.e. a prophetic
word, ch. xii. 25 *seq.* The meaning appears to be: if the prophet,
entering into the "heart" of the idolaters, the circle and direction of
their thoughts, and the general spirit which animates them, gives them
a prophetic oracle which coincides with the line of their thoughts, and
thus helps to foster their delusions, that prophet himself has been
seduced or enticed; and it is the Lord who has enticed him. The
passage has a resemblance to 1 Kgs xxii. 20 *seq.* There a lying spirit
came forth from the Lord and entered into the prophets of Ahab and
deceived them, so that they supported the designs of the wicked king
and gave an answer favourable to him. Here it is the Lord Himself
who entices the prophet. In both cases this enticement or deception
was in punishment for previous sin. Ezekiel does not appear to reflect
upon the point whether the prophet before being deceived was true or
false. The "prophet" became false when deceived, when he entered
into the spirit and purposes of the idolaters, and spoke a word to them
in the line of their sinful conduct and hopes. And this word merely
hardened them in their mind and was a step towards taking them in
the snare of their own heart (*v.* 5).

10 him from the midst of my people Israel. And they shall bear ¹their iniquity: the iniquity of the prophet shall be 11 even as the iniquity of him that seeketh *unto him*; that the house of Israel may go no more astray from me, neither defile themselves any more with all their transgressions; but that they may be my people, and I may be their God, saith the Lord GOD.

12 And the word of the LORD came unto me, saying, Son
13

¹ Or, *the punishment of their iniquity*

10. Both the people and prophet shall perish together; the punishment of the one shall be as that of the other. So already Jer. xiv. 15, 16, xxvii. 15.

The passage rests on such general assumptions as these: 1. That the principles of the constitution of Israel are known, and the fundamental one is, "Thou shalt have no other gods before Me." Probably Ezekiel interpreted this first principle as Hosea did, including among "other gods" not only gods different from Jehovah, but images or representations of Jehovah Himself (Hos. viii. 6). Men's first duty was to be true to this principle; cf. the summary proceeding advocated in Deut. xiii. 5. To those who sin against this fundamental article of religion all other religious offices and ordinances, so far from being beneficial, are made by God a means of destruction. The preaching of the true prophets only hardens (Is. vi.); or prophecy may be turned into false prophecy. The man who wittingly commits sin had better keep clear of religious ordinances and performances. And the "prophet" (even the modern one) had better keep clear of wicked men, lest he should be used as the instrument of their punishment and perish with them. See on iii. 20.

11. Yet all these judgements of God have a far-off merciful end in view. They are a blast of fire and of judgement to consume the sin of the people (Is. iv. 4), and when the tempest is overpast the sky rises clear behind—"that the house of Israel may go no more astray...but that they may be My people and I may be their God" [a frequent expression in Jeremiah (xxiv. 7, xxx. 22, xxxi. 1, 33, xxxii. 38)].

XIV. 12—23. THE PRESENCE OF RIGHTEOUS MEN AMONG A SINFUL PEOPLE WILL NOT SAVE THE SINNERS.

The passage may be in answer to thoughts which the prophet felt might rise in the minds of those to whom he spoke. He threatened destruction to people and prophets alike, a destruction indiscriminate and universal. Were not these threats exaggerations? Were they in harmony with God's former ways of dealing with His people? Would He slay the righteous with the wicked? would He not rather spare the wicked on the intercession of the righteous and for their sake, as often in former times? (Gen. xviii. 23; Num. xiv. 15.) To this the prophet

of man, when a land sinneth against me by committing a
trespass, and I stretch out mine hand upon it, and break
the staff of the bread thereof, and send famine upon it, and
cut off from it man and beast; though these three men, 14
Noah, Daniel, and Job, were in it, they should deliver but
their own souls by their righteousness, saith the Lord GOD.
If I cause noisome beasts to pass through the land, and 15
they ¹spoil it, so that it be desolate, that no man may pass
through because of the beasts; though these three men 16

¹ Or, *bereave*

replies after Jer. xv. that righteous men among the people shall not
avert God's judgement, they shall only save their own souls.

(1) *vv.* 12—20. A supposition is put that God brings any one of His
four great judgements, famine, evil beasts, sword, or pestilence, upon a
land to destroy it. Though these three men, Noah, Daniel, and Job,
were in that land, they should by their righteousness save neither sons
nor daughters, only their own souls.

(2) *vv.* 21—23. Application to Jerusalem. Much less shall the
righteous save the wicked when the Lord shall bring all His four sore
judgements together upon Jerusalem. And if a remnant be spared and
carried into all lands, this apparent exception will only confirm and
impress the principle by shewing to all how inevitable the utter destruction of Jerusalem was on account of its wickedness, and that God in His
righteousness could deal in no other way with it. And thus the exiles
when they see the ways and doings of those that escape from Jerusalem
will be comforted for its fall, and their minds will be lifted up into a
higher sympathy with God in His acts of righteousness.

On the prophet's own sympathy, cf. ch. iii. 14.

vv. 12—14. Famine.

13. *when a land*] The whole of *v.* 13 is supposition : when a land
sinneth...and I stretch...and break...and send...and cut off.

a trespass] [lit. an act of treachery. Cf. xvi. 8.]

14. *these three men*] By Jeremiah the Lord had already said :
"though Moses and Samuel stood before me, yet my mind could not be
toward this people" (Jer. xv. 1). The history of Noah had been written,
and was well known long before the time of Ezekiel. He is referred to
by other prophets, e.g. Is. liv. 9, "This is *as* the waters of Noah unto
me." It is scarcely probable, however, that the prophet owed his
knowledge of Daniel and Job to the books which now exist under their
names. They are more likely great traditional names, familiar to the
prophet and his people, which the authors of our present Books appropriated and used for their own purposes of edification¹. It is scarcely
natural that the prophet should name Daniel if he was a contemporary

¹ [For the support of this hypothesis of an otherwise unknown Daniel of antiquity
cf. *HDB* I. 557 and Driver's *Daniel* (in this series), p. xvii.]

were in it, as I live, saith the Lord GOD, they shall deliver
neither sons nor daughters; they only shall be delivered,
17 but the land shall be desolate. Or if I bring a sword upon
that land, and say, ¹Sword, go through the land; so that
18 I cut off from it man and beast; though these three men
were in it, as I live, saith the Lord GOD, they shall deliver
neither sons nor daughters, but they only shall be delivered
19 themselves. Or if I send a pestilence into that land, and
pour out my fury upon it in blood, to cut off from it man
20 and beast: though Noah, Daniel, and Job, were in it, as I

¹ Or, *Let the sword go*

of his own living at the court of Babylon. He refers here to his piety,
and in ch. xxviii. 3 to his wisdom. These references are quite suitable
to the Daniel known to us from the Book of that name, but of course
the picture of Daniel drawn in the Book may contain traits taken from
tradition, or even from Ezekiel. In all probability the Book of Job is
posterior to the time of Ezekiel. On "the staff of the bread" (*v.* 13),
cf. ch. iv. 16, v. 16; Lev. xxvi. 26.

vv. 15, 16. Noisome, i.e. hurtful, beasts. See Lev. xxvi. 22¹.

16. *neither sons nor daughters*] There is no support in the words
for the idea of Hävernick that the three names, Noah, Daniel, and Job
form a climax, inasmuch as Noah saved his children, Daniel only his
three fellow-exiles, while Job could deliver neither son nor daughter,
though every week he interceded and made atonement for them. This
idea is false to the sense of the Book of Job, for Job's children are
nowhere represented by the author of the Book as having been cut off
for their sins, though naturally Job's "friends" put this construction
upon their death (ch. viii. 4). The prophet does not appear to have
in view any historical details in the lives of these three men; he refers
to the men themselves as great saints famous in the traditions of his
people.

vv. 17, 18. Sword and war. Lev. xxvi. 25.

17. *Sword, go through*] This rendering assumes a grammatical
anomaly. Rather, **The sword shall go through**.

vv. 19, 20. The pestilence.

19. *my fury upon it in blood*] [Pestilence and blood are already
connected in ch. v. 17.] The term "blood" is almost a synonym for
"death"; cf. Ps. xxx. 9, "What profit is there in my blood, when I
go down to the pit?" On the Babylonian idea of "four" plagues, cf.
Delitzsch, *Wo lag das Paradies*, p. 146.

¹ [For the word in this sense, now become obsolete, cf.
              "I will go root away
      The noisome weeds, which without profit suck
      The soil's fertility from wholesome flowers."
                              Rich. II. III. iv. 38.]

live, saith the Lord GOD, they shall deliver neither son nor
daughter; they shall but deliver their own souls by their
righteousness.   For thus saith the Lord GOD: How much 21
more when I send my four sore judgements upon Jerusalem, the sword, and the famine, and the noisome beasts,
and the pestilence, to cut off from it man and beast?   Yet, 22
behold, therein shall be left ¹a remnant that shall be carried
forth, both sons and daughters: behold, they shall come
forth unto you, and ye shall see their way and their doings:
and ye shall be comforted concerning the evil that I have

¹ Heb. *they that escape.*

vv. 21—23.   Application to Jerusalem.

21.   *How much more*]   If when a single judgement is sent upon a
land the wicked shall not be spared for the sake of the righteous, how
much more shall this not happen when the wickedness of the land is
so great that God's four sore judgements together fall upon it, as they
shall fall upon Jerusalem?   Ch. v. 17, xxxiii. 22 *seq.*   Yet the history
of Jerusalem may seem an exception.   It is an exception for a wider
purpose.

22.   *Yet, behold, therein shall be left*]   Rather: **And behold, should
there be left** therein a remnant.   After "behold" the verb is hypothetical, as often, e.g. ch. xiii. 12, xv. 4.   See next note.

that shall be carried forth]   The ancient versions read the active
(hiph.) participle here: *that shall bring forth* sons and daughters out
of the captured city.   In *vv.* 18, 20 it is said that the three great
saints named should save neither sons nor daughters; and here some
would be spoken of who brought out sons and daughters.   It is very
doubtful if this pointed antithesis was in the mind of the prophet.
His point is that if some in Jerusalem, men and women, escape,
notwithstanding the principle that the righteous shall not save the
wicked, it is for a special purpose, viz. to shew to the earlier exiles
the great wickedness of Jerusalem, and thus comfort them over its
fall.   Both Jeremiah and Ezekiel regard the exiles carried away
under Jehoiachin as the flower of the nation (Jer. xxiv.), and those left
behind as the dregs of the people.   Of course it was the persons of rank
and influence that were carried captive, while those left behind were
the meanest, least educated, and probably most idolatrous (Jer. xxiv.
8—10, xxix. 16—20).

their way and their doings]   Their evil "way" of life, and their
gross idolatries.

comforted concerning the evil]   The exiles of the days of Jehoiachin
and those of earlier times, whose thoughts were keenly occupied with
Jerusalem and its fate (ch. xxiv. 25), shall be consoled for its destruction when they see the way and doings of the new exiles.   So corrupt
and gross in their iniquities shall these appear to them that they will

brought upon Jerusalem, even concerning all that I have
23 brought upon it.   And they shall comfort you, when ye see
their way and their doings: and ye shall know that I have
not done ¹without cause all that I have done in it, saith
the Lord GOD.

15   And the word of the LORD came unto me, saying,

¹ Or, *in vain*

feel that no other fate than that which has befallen Jerusalem was
possible for it; and that "not without cause" has Jehovah overthrown
it (*v.* 23). Cf. on "comforted" ch. xxxii. 31.

In the passage *vv.* 12—23 questions are not raised what "land" it is
upon which Jehovah will bring His plagues of famine, sword, and the
like, nor when He will bring them. The cases supposed are merely
illustrations of the principle that the righteous shall not save the wicked.
But the application to Jerusalem is what the prophet has in view. See
on ch. xviii.

XV.   The Vine Tree among the other Trees of the Forest.

This chapter pursues the same general line of thought as ch. xiv.
12—23, and ch. xvi. In ch. xiv. 12—23 the prophet had replied to a
feeling that might arise in men's minds that Jehovah would spare the
sinners of the people for the sake of the righteous. Here he replies to
another thought—were these predictions of wholesale destruction upon
Israel, the people of the Lord, and Jerusalem where He had placed
His name, probable? Other nations might perish, but Israel was the
Lord's heritage, the vine of His planting. The prophet accepts the
idea of the vine and replies to it.

Like Isaiah's song of the vineyard (Is. v.) the passage has two parts,
first, the similitude of the vine, *vv.* 1—5; and secondly, the application
to Israel, *vv.* 6—8.

Founding on old similitudes the prophet assumes that Israel is the
vine, and compares it as a tree or as wood with the other trees of the
forest. It is as wood that it is put in comparison with the trees. He
is studiously silent in regard to the fruit of the vine. This, which gave
the vine its preeminence (Judg. ix. 13), cannot be touched upon, for it
does not exist. It is the wood of the vine only that can be compared
with the other trees of the forest, the feeble, creeping plant with the
lofty trees around it. Judah never had any pretensions to be a powerful state, or to enter into competition in wealth or military resources
with the kingdoms round about. As a tree among the trees, a state
among the states, what was it good for? And especially now what is
it good for, when it has already been in the fire, its ends consumed and
its heart charred? What is it fit for, or need it expect, but to be flung
again into the fire and wholly consumed?

Son of man, what is the vine tree more than any tree, the 2
vine branch which ¹is among the trees of the forest? Shall 3
wood be taken thereof to make any work? or will men take a
pin of it to hang any vessel thereon? Behold, it is cast into 4
the fire for fuel: the fire hath devoured both the ends of
it, and the midst of it is burned; is it profitable for any
work? Behold, when it was whole, it was ²meet for no 5
work: how much less, when the fire hath devoured it, and
it is burned, shall it yet be ²meet for any work? Therefore 6
thus saith the Lord GOD: As the vine tree among the trees
of the forest, which I have given to the fire for fuel, so ³will

¹ Or, *was*   ² Heb. *made into*.   ³ Or, *have I given*

2.   *the vine branch which is*] the words taking up "the vine tree"
of previous clause. The usage of the verb suggests the sense: *what
shall be* made of *the wood of the vine among all wood, even the vine branch*
that is among the trees of the forest? Cf. *v.* 3. With the comparative
sense the accents should be disregarded: *what is the wood of the vine
more than any wood of the branch which is* &c. On Israel as the vine
cf. Gen. xlix. 22; Is. v. 1; Deut. xxxii. 32; Jer. ii. 21; Ezek. xvii.
5, xix. 10; Ps. lxxx. 14—16; Hos. x. 1.

which is] [marg. *was* is less likely, if the past tense is to imply that
the destruction of Jerusalem had actually taken place. A similar
remark will apply to "have I given" (*v.* 6 marg.). The word
"burned" in *v.* 4 may well imply charred rather than wholly consumed.]

3.   Uselessness of the wood of the vine.

to make any work] i.e. to use for any work or purpose. The words
may mean, to make it into any work or article of workmanship. It has
too little firmness even to be made into a peg to hang any article upon.

4.   A hypothetical sentence: "Behold, when it hath been cast into the
fire for fuel, when the fire hath devoured both the ends of it, and the
midst of it is charred, will it be profitable for any work?" This part of
the similitude is borrowed from the actual instance of Israel. As it is
Jerusalem, including Judah, that is compared to the vine, the burning
of the ends and scorching of the middle probably refer to the calamities sustained by that kingdom, such as the captivity under Jehoiachin
and other severe reverses.

5.   *meet for no work*] more lit., as marg. *made into*, used for no
work; how much less, when the fire hath devoured it and it is
charred.

XV. 6—8. APPLICATION OF THE FIGURE TO JERUSALEM.

6.   *which I have given*] The reference is to the supposition in *v.* 4.
It is nowhere said in the passage that the vinewood is fit only for fuel,

7 I give the inhabitants of Jerusalem. And I will set my
face against them ; they ¹shall go forth from the fire, but the
fire shall devour them ; and ye shall know that I am the
8 LORD, when I set my face against them. And I will make
the land desolate, because they have committed a trespass,
saith the Lord GOD.

16   Again the word of the LORD came unto me, saying,

¹ Or, *have gone forth*

nor that it has been appointed (when created by God) to be burnt ;
v. 4 is a supposition that in a particular case it has been flung into the
fire for fuel, and its ends burnt, and the inference is drawn that, good
for little as it is when whole, much less will it be good for anything in
that condition. The use of the first person "I have given" is peculiar.
Cor. suggests "it has been given," considering "will I give" which
follows immediately to have been the source of the error.

so will I give] lit., *so have I given* [but see on *v.* 2]. The comparison
is not between Jerusalem and a vine when whole, but between Jerusalem and a vine with its two ends burnt. Naturally the supposition is
made that the vinewood flung into the fire has been plucked out after
having been burnt and charred, and the question is asked, Is it good for
anything now? This is the condition of Jerusalem : it has been cast
into the fire for fuel, plucked out of it, as it were, half-burnt ; is it good
for anything?

7. *they shall go forth from the fire*] Rather as marg. : **they have
gone forth.** They are in the condition of a brand that has been plucked
for a moment from the fire (*vv.* 4, 5), but they shall be plunged again
into it to be burnt. Only scathed and charred as yet, they shall be wholly
consumed.

I am the LORD] The object of these chastisements is that they may
know that He who inflicts them is Jehovah, and learn what Jehovah is ;
and this shall be the result of them.

8. The figure of "burning" in the fire is expressed in literal language : the land shall be made a desolation. Like his predecessor
Jeremiah, the prophet sets little store by the existence of Israel as a
state or kingdom among other states. Israel's mission is religious, not
political. See on ch. xiii. 3.

a trespass] [lit. a treacherous act, viz. idolatry. Cf. xiv. 13.]

XVI. THE FOUNDLING CHILD WHO BECAME THE FAITHLESS
WIFE.

The prophet continues to pursue his demonstration of the inevitable-
ness of Jerusalem's destruction. In ch. xiii. xiv. he swept away the
delusive hopes with which the prophets of Israel filled her imagination ;
and in ch. xv. he shewed how little the fact that Israel was the people of
the Lord was fitted to inspire confidence, as other prophets had shewed

Son of man, cause Jerusalem to know her abominations, 2
and say, Thus saith the Lord GOD unto Jerusalem: ¹Thy 3
birth and thy nativity is of the land of the Canaanite; the

¹ Or, *Thine origin*

before him (Am. iii. 2). In the present passage it is the positive proof
of the necessity of Israel's destruction that he exhibits—her persistent
unfaithfulness to Jehovah through all her history, and her forgetfulness
of His goodness. He has to shew to Jerusalem all "her abominations"
(*v.* 2). This is done in the allegory of the foundling child who became
the faithless wife of her benefactor. Though marked by a breadth with
which modern taste is unfamiliar the allegory is powerful. And when
the details are forgotten and only the general conception remains in the
mind, the prophet's creation is felt to be artistically beautiful as well as
true. An outcast infant exposed in the open field and weltering in its
blood was seen by the pitying eye of a passer by. Rescued and
nourished she grew up to the fairest womanhood, and became the wife
of her benefactor, who lavished on her all that could delight and elevate. But the ways into which he led her were too lofty to be understood, and the atmosphere around her too pure for her to breathe;
the old inborn nature (her father was the Amorite and her mother a
Hittite) was still there beneath all the refinements for which it had no
taste, and at last it asserted itself in shameless depravity and insatiable
lewdness.

This moral history of Israel has these divisions:

(1) *vv.* 1—7. The exposed infant adopted and reared to womanhood.
(2) *vv.* 8—14. The foundling, now grown up to be a fair woman,
taken in marriage by her benefactor.
(3) *vv.* 15—34. Her numerous infidelities.
(4) *vv.* 35—59. Punishment of the adulterous wife.
(5) *vv.* 60—63. Her receiving again.

1—7. THE EXPOSED CHILD RESCUED AND ADOPTED BY JEHOVAH—
HIS TAKING TO HIMSELF THE FAMILY OF ISRAEL IN THE EARLY
PATRIARCHAL TIMES.

2. *cause Jerusalem to know*] The object of the chapter is to impress
on Israel the necessity of the Divine judgement because of her persistent
idolatry through all her history (ch. xx. 4, xxii. 2, xxiii. 36). Jerusalem,
which is spoken to throughout, represents the kingdom of Judah, and
even the whole family of Israel in its early history.

3. *Thy birth*] lit. "place of digging out," and so *origin* (ch.
xxi. 30 [Heb. 35], xxix. 14), the figure being taken from a mine or a
quarry, cf. Is. li. 1, "Look unto the rock whence ye were hewn, and to
the hole of the pit whence ye were digged." When Jerusalem's origin is
said to be from the land of the Canaanite several references seem to be
combined, e.g. the fact that Jerusalem was a Canaanite city; that Israel
first became a family in Canaan (*v.* 4); and that having originated there

Amorite was thy father, and thy mother was an Hittite.
4 And as for thy nativity, in the day thou wast born thy
navel was not cut, neither wast thou washed in water to
cleanse thee ; thou wast not salted at all, nor swaddled at
5 all.   None eye pitied thee, to do any of these unto thee,
to have compassion upon thee ; but thou wast cast out in
the open field, for that thy person was abhorred, in the day
6 that thou wast born.   And when I passed by thee, and saw

its moral character corresponded to its Canaanite origin and had cleaved
to it all through its history.

the Amorite[1]]   The Amorites and Hittites are named as the two
chief Canaanitish peoples, the whole population being sometimes called
the Amorites (Gen. xv. 16 ; Am. ii. 9), and at other times the Hittites
(Josh. i. 4).   Jerusalem has the one for father, and the other for
mother (*v.* 45)[2].

4. *as for thy nativity*]   The circumstances of thy birth were
as follows.   The family of Israel, represented by Jerusalem, is compared to an exposed infant, for whom the things absolutely necessary to
preserve its life were not done.   The reference is to the history of the
family in Canaan, and in its descent to Egypt, when it was feeble,
unprotected, and in danger of perishing.

to cleanse thee]   The Heb. is otherwise unknown.   Targ. "for purification," probably a guess, but some such sense is required.   [Aq.
Theod. and Vulg. "for safety," a conjecture suggested by the form of
the Heb. noun.   LXX. om.]   Frd. Delitzsch refers to an Assyrian
root signifying *to wash*.

wast not salted at all]   An ancient custom was to rub the newborn
infant with salt—"tenera infantium corpora...solent ab obstetricibus sale
contingi ut sicciora sint et restringantur," Jerome.   The ceremony was
probably partly religious as well as healthful.   ["Among the Kissil
Bashi the newborn infant is solemnly salted over before the 'Father-
priest' in front of the sacred tree."   *Quarterly Statement, Pal. Explor.
Fund,* Jan. 1905, p. 7[3].]

5.   None of the offices necessary to preserve the life of the child were
performed ; no pitying eye looked on it, no affectionate hand did aught
for it ; it was even thrown out in the open field.   It was too common
a custom among ancient nations to expose children ; among the Arabs
female children were buried alive (*Koran* 81. 8).

6.   *And when I passed*]   more pathetic in the Heb. order : *and I
passed by thee and saw thee.*

---

[1] [The Amorites, according to Gen. x. 16, were descended from Canaan.]
[2] [According to Prof. Sayce (*Expos. Times,* March, 1904, p. 280, quoted by Redp.
ad loc.), it seems established that while most of the Hittites belonged to N. Palestine,
a smaller body were among the inhabitants of Southern Canaan.]
[3] [The use of salt in Baptism (see *Dict. of Christian Antiquities,* ii. p. 1838) may
possibly be a survival of this custom.]

thee weltering in thy blood, I said unto thee, *Though thou art* in thy blood, live; yea, I said unto thee, *Though thou art* in thy blood, live. I ¹caused thee to multiply as the 7 bud of the field, and thou didst increase and wax great, and thou attainedst to ²excellent ornament; thy breasts were fashioned, and thine hair was grown; yet thou wast naked

---

¹ Heb. *made thee a myriad.*   ² Heb. *ornament of ornaments.*

---

weltering] wallowing or struggling [lit. *kicking out* hither and thither, as with the blind movements of infants' limbs].

Though thou art in thy blood] i.e. although unclean and loathsome, live! Jehovah's pitying eye looked through that which might repel, and saved. [But Kr. and Ber. connect "in thy blood" immediately with "I said unto thee."] The repetition (which LXX., however, omits) may emphasise the great act of Jehovah's pity.

7. *caused...multiply*] lit. as marg. *made thee a myriad.* This idea of multiplication in *number* deserts the figure, introducing the notion of the numerical increase of the people (Exod. i. 7; Deut. x. 22, xxxiii. 17). The rest of the verse, however, continues the figure of the child growing up to womanhood, and for "myriad" probably some word signifying "growth" should be read, "I gave thee growth like the herb of the field; and thou didst grow and wax great."

excellent ornament] lit. *ornament of ornaments.* The connexion requires that "ornament" should mean graces and beauties of the person. The word has nowhere else this sense, being always employed of such ornaments as jewelry which are worn (*v.* 11). The rendering "beauty of cheeks" (Hitz.) rests upon a sense attributed to the word in Ps. xxxii. 9¹, ciii. 5².

were fashioned] The passage is an allegorical description of the early history of the family of Israel, their struggles for existence in Canaan, their descent into Egypt, the oppressions suffered there, and the Lord's care and protection of them (Exod. iii. 7, 9; Ps. cv. 12 *seq.*). The unattractive character of the early patriarchal history as written in Genesis is plain enough (Gen. xxix.—xxxi., xxxviii.). This unattractive character is set forth in the blood and pollution of the newborn infant, and the Lord's care of them in their dependent and defenceless condition is described under the figure of His pity and adoption of the outcast child. The truth conveyed in the allegory is more delicately expressed by another writer: "The LORD did not set his love upon you, nor choose you, because ye were more in number than any people; for ye were the fewest of all peoples: but because the LORD loveth you" (Deut. vii. 7, 8).

---

¹ [Where, however, R.V. has "trappings."]
² [R.V. has "mouth" with various marginal alternatives.]

8 and bare. Now when I passed by thee, and looked upon
    thee, behold, thy time was the time of love; and I spread
    my skirt over thee, and covered thy nakedness: yea, I
    sware unto thee, and entered into a covenant with thee,
9 saith the Lord GOD, and thou becamest mine. Then
    washed I thee with water; yea, I throughly washed away
10 thy blood from thee, and I anointed thee with oil. I
    clothed thee also with broidered work, and shod thee with
    ¹sealskin, and I ²girded thee about with fine linen, and

---

¹ Or, *porpoise-skin*   ² Or, *bound thee with* a tire of *fine linen*

XVI. 8—14. THE CHILD, NOW AN ADULT VIRGIN, TAKEN TO HIM-
    SELF IN MARRIAGE BY JEHOVAH :—THE REDEMPTION OF THE
    PEOPLE FROM EGYPT, AND COVENANT WITH THEM AT SINAI
    TO BE THEIR GOD.

8.   *Now when I passed*]   Better in continuance of the historical
narrative, **And I passed by thee, and saw thee**, as *v.* 6.
   the time of love]   The outcast child was now a marriageable woman.
   spread my skirt]   Cf. Ruth iii. 9—a figure for marriage.
   a covenant with thee]   The marriage relation is a covenant, Prov. ii.
17; Mal. ii. 14.   On the "oath," cf. Deut. xxix. 12, 14.
   thou becamest mine]   She became his wife, Ruth iv. 13; Hos. iii. 3.
   9.   Whether "blood" be used somewhat generally to indicate the
uncleanness of her infancy still cleaving to her, or in a more specific
sense, may be uncertain.   For purifications before marriage see Ruth
iii. 3; Esth. ii. 12.
   10.   The costly clothing.
   broidered work]   Ps. xlv. 14; Jud. v. 30.   The word might mean
work of various colours (Exod. xxvi. 36).   So *vv.* 13, 18.
   sealskin]   [The word is used for the material of the cover of the
tabernacle, Numb. iv., v.; Exod. xxv., &c.   It is uncertain whether it
denotes the skin of some sea-animal, or, as Kr., is simply an Egyptian
word denoting leather.   According to most, it was the skin of the
sea-cow or manati, an animal allied to the dolphin, and found in the
Red Sea.   The name is found in Assyrian; the Assyrian kings crossed
the Euphrates in ships made of the skin of this animal, and Shalmaneser
pursued his foes on lake Van in such ships.   These facts suggest that
the skins were readily procured not only in Mesopotamia but even in
Armenia, and that some land-animal must have furnished them.   See
further Frd. Delitzsch (Baer's *Ezechiel*, pp. xvi, f.); also Dillm. and
Driver in *C. B.* on Exod. xxv. 5.
   fine linen]   i.e. byssus.   It is not certain whether the byssus was
cotton or linen, or both.   It was worn by the priests (Exod. xxxix. 27),
and by persons of rank (Gen. xli. 42).   The "girding" or binding here

covered thee with silk. I decked thee also with ornaments, 11
and I put bracelets upon thy hands, and a chain on thy
neck. And I put a ring upon thy nose, and earrings in 12
thine ears, and a beautiful crown upon thine head. Thus 13
wast thou decked with gold and silver; and thy raiment
was of fine linen, and silk, and broidered work; thou didst
eat fine flour, and honey, and oil: and thou wast exceeding
beautiful, and thou didst prosper unto royal estate. And 14
thy renown went forth among the nations for thy beauty;

can hardly refer to the headdress (Exod. xxix. 9), because in *v.* 13 the
"clothing" is said to be of fine linen (cf. *v.* 12 for headdress).

covered thee with silk] The word occurs again only in *v.* 13. It may
be doubtful if silk was worn as early as the time of the prophet. The
LXX. and ancients thought of some very thin and delicate material.
The kind of garment was probably some large wrapper or veil covering
the whole person.

vv. 11, 12. Her bridal ornaments.

11. On bracelets, cf. Gen. xxiv. 22, 47. On chain or necklace,
Gen. xli. 42; Prov. i. 9, iii. 3.

12. *a ring upon thy nose*] Cf. Is. iii. 21. The nose-ring was a jewel
placed on the outside of the nostril. Cf. Jud. viii. 24 (marg.), Gen.
xxiv. 47, and for earrings, Numb. xxxi. 50.

a beautiful crown] so ch. xxiii. 42; in Is. lxii. 3 rendered "a crown
of beauty." The word does not suggest royalty (xxiii. 42).

13. Her delicate fare and beauty.

fine flour] This was used in offerings at the altar (*v.* 19), and was
probably the food of persons of refinement and rank. Cf. Ps. lxxxi.
16, "He should feed them also with the finest of the wheat, and with
honey out of the rock should I satisfy thee"; Ps. cxlvii. 14; Deut.
xxxii. 13, 14.

exceeding beautiful] The beauty is less that of the mere city (Ps.
xlviii. 2) than of the personified state or people (*v.* 14).

prosper unto royal estate] The reference is not to the mere historical
fact that a monarchy arose in Israel under Saul or more permanently
under David. It was Israel herself, personified as a woman, that
attained to royalty, that is, to be an independent state among the
states around, a queen among other queens. The words are wanting
in LXX.

14. Her renown spread among the nations because of her beauty.
In this is included partly the prosperity and success of the state, not
without reference perhaps to the beauty of the city (Lam. ii. 15, "the
perfection of beauty, the joy of the whole earth," Ps. l. 2), and of the
land, which is often celebrated (ch. xx. 6, 15, "the glory of all lands,"
cf. Dan. viii. 9, xi. 16, 41; Zech. vii. 14); and partly also the glory
of a higher kind conferred on her by Jehovah and His presence, in the
sense of Deut. iv. 6—8.

for it was perfect, through my majesty which I had put upon
thee, saith the Lord GOD.

15 But thou didst trust in thy beauty, and playedst the
harlot because of thy renown, and pouredst out thy whore-
16 doms on every one that passed by; his it was.   And thou

my majesty] or, **my adornment**; that given by me (*vv.* 10—13);
hardly in the sense of Is. lx. 1, that Jerusalem's beauty was only a
reflection of the glory of Jehovah, who was in the midst of her.

These verses allegorically set forth the second period of Israel's
history: her redemption by Jehovah from Egypt, His covenant with
her to be her God, His leading her into the promised land, and making
her the paramount power there, and loading her with all the riches of
that good land.   Other prophets with more simplicity have celebrated
this early time, "I remember for thee the kindness of thy youth, the
love of thine espousals; how thou wentest after me in the wilderness,
in a land that was not sown" (Jer. ii. 2); "I found Israel like grapes
in the wilderness; I saw your fathers as the firstripe in the fig tree at her
first season" (Hos. ix. 10; cf. Deut. xxxii. 10).

XVI. 15—34.   THE WIFE'S INFIDELITIES—ISRAEL'S IDOLATRIES
AND IDOLATROUS ALLIANCES WITH FOREIGN NATIONS.

The idolatries of Israel are represented figuratively as a wife's
infidelities against her husband, as had been common in the prophets
since Hosea, particularly in Jeremiah (in Isaiah only the single passage
ch. i. 21).   These idolatries seem presented in two stages: *vv.* 13—22,
her addicting herself to the worship and religious customs of the
Canaanites among whom she dwelt; and *vv.* 23—34, her alliances
with foreign peoples and adoption of their religions.

15—22.   All the gifts of Jehovah to her she took and bestowed
on idols: her raiment (*vv.* 16, 18), her gold and silver (*v.* 17), and
her delicate fare (*v.* 19).   And as if this were a small matter, she
sacrificed also the children which were Jehovah's to her idols (*vv.*
20, 21).

15.   *because of thy renown*] in the consciousness of it.   The consciousness of her beauty and renown removed from her mind the sense
of dependence and responsibility, and she became vain in her own
imaginations.   Another prophet has expressed the same idea in regard
to Babylon: "Thou saidst, I shall be a lady for ever: so that thou
didst not lay these things to thy heart, neither didst remember the latter
end thereof...thou hast said, None seeth me" (Is. xlvii. 7, 10).
Hävern. quotes Ovid, *Fasti*, I. 419, *Fastus inest pulchris, sequiturque
superbia formam.*

every one that passed by]   A figure taken from the habit of harlots
sitting by the wayside, Gen. xxxviii. 14; Jer. iii. 2, "By the ways hast
thou sat for them, as an Arabian in the wilderness."

his it was]   The prostitution was indiscriminate, Jer. iii. 2; cf.

didst take of thy garments, and madest for thee high places
decked with divers colours, and playedst the harlot upon
them : *the like things* shall not come, neither shall it be *so.*
Thou didst also take thy ¹fair jewels of my gold and of my 17
silver, which I had given thee, and madest for thee ²images
of men, and didst play the harlot with them ; and thou 18
tookest thy broidered garments, and coveredst them, and
didst set mine oil and mine incense before them.   My 19

---

¹ Or, *beautiful vessels*   ² Or, *male images*

Ezek. xxiii. 40. The idea expressed is the ineradicable tendency of the
people to adopt the religious customs of the nations with which age
after age they came into connexion (*v.* 23 *seq.*).   The phrase is peculiar
and wanting in LXX.¹

16. She took of her "garments," the flax and the wool which
Jehovah had given her to cover herself withal (Hos. ii. 9), and made
tents upon the high places for the idols which she there worshipped.
For "high places" cf. ch. vi. 3.   The "high places decked with
divers colours" might be tents, or the reference might be to hangings
or carpets [which were gaily coloured, lit. spotted, variegated].   In
2 Kgs xxiii. 7 reference is made to women "who wove tents (marg.)
for the Asherah"; cf. 1 Kgs xiii. 32; 2 Kgs xvii. 29.

the like things shall not come] Or, *should not come*.   An exclamation
of dislike and abhorrence of the shameful practices just referred to.
The rendering given can hardly be extracted from the words, which are
probably corrupt in some way, though already read by LXX. (with a
different vocalization).   Comp. perhaps ch. xx. 29.

17. Cf. Hos. ii. 8, "I...multiplied unto her silver and gold, which
they used for Baal."

images of men] Jerusalem being an unfaithful wife the idols are
"men."   The images were of gods; and this prophet probably saw
little distinction between an image of Jehovah and that of any other
deity.   It is likely that, apart from the calf-images, the symbols of
Jehovah as well as of the other gods were of the human form; cf. as
to the Teraphim, 1 Sam. xix. 13.

broidered...coveredst them] Cf. *vv.* 10, 13.   The practice of clothing
the idols is illustrated by Jer. x. 9, "There is silver beaten into plates
...blue and purple for their clothing ; they are all the work of cunning
men."

didst set mine oil] The ref. is to the offerings made to the idols.   The
Lord calls it "mine" because due to Him, or rather because given by
Him to Israel, Hos. ii. 8, 9, "she did not know that I gave her the

---

¹ [If the words stand, they should be taken as spoken by the woman, "let it be."
But it is more likely that they are a textual corruption arising out of the expressions
at the end of *v.* 16 and of *v.* 19, and should be read "and thus it was."]

bread also which I gave thee, fine flour, and oil, and honey,
wherewith I fed thee, thou didst even set it before them for
a sweet savour, and *thus* it was; saith the Lord GOD.
20 Moreover thou hast taken thy sons and thy daughters,
whom thou hast borne unto me, and these hast thou sacrificed unto them to be devoured.   Were thy whoredoms
21 a small matter, that thou hast slain my children, and

corn, and the wine, and the oil...therefore will I take back my corn in
the time thereof."

honey] [This is forbidden as an offering made by fire in Lev. ii. 11.
Apparently as in common with leaven producing fermentation, it was
symbolical of evil.   For its not improbable use in Canaanitish sacrifices
see on Am. iv. 5 in this series.]

19. *a sweet savour*] See on ch. vi. 13.   The words "*and* thus *it
was*" emphasize what was done, with a tone of reprobation.   [But the
expression is very possibly corrupt.]

20—22. The sacrifice of children. Jehovah is the husband of the
idealized community, and the individual members are His children.
Human sacrifices, though rare, were not altogether unknown in early
Israel, as the instance of Jephthah proves (Jud. xi.).   They were
probably more common among the Canaanites and neighbouring
peoples[1], though perhaps even among them resorted to only on
occasions of great trial, in the hope of appeasing the anger or securing the favour of the deity (cf. the tragic story of the king of Moab,
2 Kgs iii. 27).   Instances (other than that above) of human sacrifices
do not occur in the early history of Israel, for neither the slaughter
of Agag (1 Sam. xv. 33) nor the hanging of seven descendants of
Saul (2 Sam. xxi. 9) comes strictly under the idea of a sacrifice; but
Ahaz king of Judah is said to have passed his son through the fire
(2 Kgs xvi. 3), and the practice introduced by him was followed by
Manasseh (2 Kgs xxi. 6), and must have spread among the people
(Jer. vii. 31, xix. 5, xxxii. 35, cf. Mic. vi. 7).   The phrase "to
pass through the fire" might be taken to mean merely a lustration or
purification by fire, not implying the death of the child.   This cannot,
however, have been the case, for Ezekiel uses the words sacrifice
(*v.* 20) and slaughter (*v.* 21), and Jeremiah says the people built high
places "to burn their sons in the fire for burnt offerings unto Baal"
(ch. xix. 5).   The child, of course, was not burnt alive, but slain like
other sacrifices, and offered as a burnt offering.   The practice was a
widespread one in the East, 2 Kgs xvii. 31.   See further on ch. xx.
25 ff.

20. *to be devoured*] Namely, in the fire.

[1] [The bones of infants deposited in jars which have been found at Gezer and
elsewhere in recent excavations are generally supposed to be those of sacrificed
infants, probably firstborn.   See Driver's *Schweich Lectures*, p. 68.]

delivered them up, in ¹causing them to pass through *the fire* unto them? And in all thine abominations and thy 22 whoredoms thou hast not remembered the days of thy youth, when thou wast naked and bare, and wast weltering in thy blood. And it is come to pass after all thy wicked- 23 ness, (woe, woe unto thee! saith the Lord GOD,) that thou 24 hast built unto thee ²an eminent place, and hast made thee a lofty place in every street. Thou hast built thy lofty 25

¹ Or, *setting them apart* Heb. *making them pass over.*   ² Or, *a vaulted chamber*

21. *delivered them up*] The child passed into the possession of the deity when consumed in the fire.

22. So absorbed was Jerusalem in her infidelities that she remembered nothing of her early history, "the days of her youth," nor the compassion shewed by Jehovah¹. On "weltering" cf. *v.* 6.

23—34. Her infidelities with strangers from abroad, i.e. her alliances with idolatrous nations and adoption of their religious rites : Egypt (*vv.* 23—27), Assyria (*v.* 28), and Chaldea (*vv.* 29 *seq.*). Hosea already stigmatized foreign alliances as whoredoms ; it is not, however, so much the political aspect of these alliances as their religious consequences that Ezekiel reprobates. Such alliances were followed by the introduction of the fashions and worship of the nations with which they were formed (Is. ii. 6 *seq.*). Naturally also when Israel became subject to the great eastern empires, the overwhelming influence of these states, with their customs and religions, was widely felt. The gods which had given them universal empire were introduced and worshipped. There appears to have been a great invasion of foreign idolatry in Judah in the declining years of the state, and the kingdom sank to a level in this respect to which the North had never fallen.

23. *after all thy wickedness*] The wickedness described in the preceding verses as idolatries of Canaan ; after this followed foreign idolatry. LXX. omits the words "woe, woe unto thee !"

24. *an eminent place*] The term is used of the "back," the "boss" of a buckler, and the like, and means something elevated to some extent and probably arched ; cf. marg. *a vaulted chamber*. It appears to be the same thing which is called a "lofty place" or rather, *height*, or elevated place, in this verse and *v.* 25 (a different word from that usually rendered "high place"). Small shrines must be meant, as they were put in every street, and at every head of the way. If the places were arches or vaults there is no reason to suppose that they were used for literal prostitution, as A.V. marg., following LXX. and Vulg., suggests. The language is figurative for idolatry, Jer. ii. 20, iii. 2.

25. *thy lofty place*] See *v.* 24.

¹ ["But it is to Israel's helplessness, not to her early piety (like Hosea and Jeremiah), that Ezekiel appeals." Lofth.]

place at every head of the way, and hast made thy beauty
an abomination, and hast opened thy feet to every one that
26 passed by, and multiplied thy whoredom.   Thou hast also
committed fornication with the Egyptians, thy neighbours,
great of flesh ; and hast multiplied thy whoredom, to pro-
27 voke me to anger.   Behold therefore, I have stretched out
my hand over thee, and have diminished thine ¹ordinary
food, and delivered thee unto the will of them that hate
thee, the daughters of the Philistines, which are ashamed
28 of thy lewd way.   Thou hast played the harlot also with

<hr>

¹ Or, *allowance*

made...an abomination]   This sense is doubtful ; the verb means to
abominate, hence dishonour or disregard, or as we might say "prostitute
thy beauty."

26.   Egyptian idolatry.

hast also committed] **and thou didst commit.**   The narrative tense
should be used throughout.

great of flesh]   In an obscene sense.   Cf. ch. xxiii. 20.   The expression is chosen probably to represent the brutality of the Egyptian
idolatries, which in some ways were baser than those of any people.

to provoke, &c.] [referring, not to the purpose, but to the result of
their wickedness.]

27.   *I have stretched*] **I stretched**...and **diminished**...of them that
hated...were ashamed.   The reference appears to be to the distant
times of the Philistine supremacy in the last days of the Judges.

thine ordinary food]   better, as marg. *allowance*, allotted portion,
Exod. xxi. 10.   The measure is one to which an offended husband
might have recourse.   Hos. ii. 9, "therefore will I take back my corn
in the time thereof, and my wine in the season thereof."

daughters of the Philistines] i.e. the cities or small Philistine lordships.
The clause might explain the phrase "diminished thine ordinary *food*"
—her territory was seized by her enemies.

which are ashamed] **were** ashamed.   Cf. Am. iii. 9, "Publish ye in
the palaces at Ashdod...and say, Assemble yourselves upon the
mountains of Samaria, and behold what great tumults are therein."
Whether the prophet speaks of Egyptian idolatry in the early times
of Israel's life from historical sources may be uncertain.   Such idolatry
at this period seems nowhere else spoken of ; comp. the list Jud. x. 6.
Possibly as he charges the people with idolatry in Egypt (chs. xx. 7,
xxiii. 3, 8, 19, 21) they may not have shaken themselves clear of it
even in the period of the Judges.   The connexion of the country
with Egypt was at all times very close.

28.   Infidelity with Assyria.

The historical tense **didst play** is better.   Already Am. v. 26

the Assyrians, because thou wast unsatiable; yea, thou hast
played the harlot with them, and yet thou wast not satisfied.
Thou hast moreover multiplied thy whoredom [1] in the land 29
of Canaan, unto Chaldea; and yet thou wast not satisfied
herewith.   How weak is thine heart, saith the Lord GOD, 30
seeing thou doest all these things, the work of an imperious
whorish woman; in that thou buildest thine eminent place 31
in the head of every way, and makest thy lofty place in
every street; and hast not been as an harlot, [2] in that thou
scornest hire.   A wife that committeth adultery! that taketh 32

---

[1] Or, *unto the land of traffic*   [2] Or, *that scoffeth at* her *hire*

appears to mention the names of Assyrian gods, for the passage can
hardly refer to any time but his own. Cf. Jer. ii. 18, 36.

29. Infidelities with the Chaldeans.   Past tense is better: **didst**
multiply.

in the land of Canaan] Rather as marg. *unto the land of traffic*. So
ch. xvii. 4, "a land of traffic." With similar contempt Hosea (xii. 7)
uses the term of Israel. Cf. Prov. xxxi. 24; Is. xlvii. 15. [Important
MSS. of the LXX., however, omit the words.]

30. *How weak is thine heart*] i.e. how passion-sick, consumed by
desire. The fem. form of the word for "heart" occurs nowhere else
in the sing. LXX. renders: "how shall I deal with thy daughter."
Our present text lay before the translator: "with thy daughter" is
"thy heart" with different points; and "weak" was probably read
as part of verb "to fill" (spelled as Job viii. 21) and rendered freely.
The text, however, may be faulty.

imperious...woman] not positive: domineering; but negative: sub-
ject to no control, unbridled. [But this distinction seems illusory.
Moreover the Oxf. Lex. supports the sense "domineering," and so Ber.,
Kr. The LXX. omits the word.]

31.   Recapitulation of the acts done in her unbridled licentiousness,
with the addition of a trait shewing that her dissoluteness was without
parallel—other harlots take hire, she gives it.

in that thou scornest hire] Rather, **that scoffeth at** her **hire** (R.V.
marg.), lit. in scoffing at hire [i.e. complaining that it is too little].
The words describe a characteristic of harlots, not one of Jerusalem in
which she is unlike them.   On "scoff" or mock at, cf. ch. xxii. 5;
2 Kgs ii. 23; Hab. i. 10; Ps. xliv. 14; Jer. xx. 8, &c.   The harlot
mocks at her hire in order to augment it; Jerusalem does not desire
hire, she rather offers it (*v.* 33).

32.   Seems to break the connexion and has been regarded as a gloss.
The words "instead of her husband" should be "under her husband,"
though she belongs to her husband (cf xxiii. 5, when she was mine;
Numb. v. 19).   The clauses are probably exclamatory: A wife that
committeth adultery! though her husband's (though married) she taketh

33 strangers instead of her husband! They give gifts to all
harlots: but thou givest thy gifts to all thy lovers, and
bribest them, that they may come unto thee on every side
34 for thy whoredoms. And the contrary is in thee from
other women in thy whoredoms, in that none followeth
thee to commit whoredom: and whereas thou givest hire,
and no hire is given unto thee, therefore thou art contrary.

35 36 Wherefore, O harlot, hear the word of the LORD: Thus
saith the Lord GOD, Because thy [1]filthiness was poured out,
and thy nakedness discovered through thy whoredoms with
thy lovers; and because of all the idols of thy abominations, and for the blood of thy children, which thou didst
37 give unto them; therefore behold, I will gather all thy
lovers, with whom thou hast taken pleasure, and all them

[1] Heb. *brass.*

strangers! It is also possible to take the language as an apostrophe:
O adulterous wife, &c. LXX. read differently, and the verse is not
without suspicion.

34. Point thus: "And the contrary is in thee from other women: in
that thou committest whoredom, and none goeth a whoring after thee;
and in that thou givest hire, and no hire is given unto thee; therefore
thou art contrary." Hos. viii. 9, "Ephraim hath hired lovers"; Jer.
ii. 23—25, iii. 1, 2. [By the "hire" or "gifts" is meant tribute paid
to Assyria or Babylon, e.g. out of the Temple treasures by Ahaz, 2 Kgs
xvi. 8, 5.]

XVI. 35—59. PUNISHMENT OF THE ADULTEROUS WIFE AND
CHILD-MURDERER.

This punishment is described in somewhat mixed figures: first,
vv. 36—39, in a figure which tends to pass into a literal account of
the destruction of Jerusalem; and secondly, *vv.* 40—43, in a figure
suggested by the punishment of the ordinary adulteress.

36. *thy filthiness*] The parallelism "nakedness" requires some such
sense; and so the Jewish tradition. The Heb. is the ordinary word
for copper or bronze, but any reference to "hire" or money here is
out of the question. Cf. Dukes, *Spr. d. Mischnah*, p. 37. Geiger,
Urschrift, p. 392. Somewhat differently Frd. Delitzsch in Baer, *Ezech.*,
p. xiv.

37. *all thy lovers*] the heathen nations whose alliance she sought,
Hos. ii. 10.

taken pleasure] lit. to whom thou hast been pleasing or sweet—with
a sensual reference.

that thou hast loved, with all them that thou hast hated;
I will even gather them against thee on every side, and will
discover thy nakedness unto them, that they may see all thy
nakedness.   And I will judge thee, as women that break 38
wedlock and shed blood are judged; and I will bring upon
thee the blood of fury and jealousy.   I will also give thee 39
into their hand, and they shall throw down thine eminent
place, and break down thy lofty places; and they shall strip
thee of thy clothes, and take thy fair jewels : and they shall
leave thee naked and bare.   They shall also bring up an 40
assembly against thee, and they shall stone thee with stones,
and thrust thee through with their swords.   And they shall 41
burn thine houses with fire, and execute judgements upon
thee in the sight of many women; and I will cause thee
to cease from playing the harlot, and thou shalt also give

that thou hast hated] the nations with whom no alliances were formed[1],
such as the Philistines.

38.   *shed blood*] a reference to child murder, *vv.* 20, 36. Cf. ch. xxiii.
45; and for "that break wedlock," Lev. xx. 10; Deut. xxii. 22.

bring upon thee the blood of fury and jealousy] i.e. bring on thee the
bloody death which fury and jealousy execute. For construction of
the Heb. cf. ch. xxvi. 21, xxxv. 6.

39.   On "eminent place" and "lofty places," see *v.* 24.

strip thee of thy clothes] Reference is probably to a barbarous
practice of publicly exposing the adulteress, *v.* 37. Cf. xxiii. 26;
Hos. ii. 10.

40.   *an assembly against thee*] A congregation or public assembly
of the people, at which the adulteress shall be tried and then executed;
Lev. xx. 2; Deut. xxii. 21 (cf. 1 Kgs xxi. 9—15), Prov. v. 8—14. The
death of the adulteress was by stoning; Lev. xx. 10; Deut. xxii. 22;
John viii. 5.

thrust thee through] [Cf. xxiii. 47. It was the form of punishment
solemnly invoked in the ceremony of taking an oath, in case the person
so binding himself should prove false to it.]

41.   *thine houses with fire*] A summary method of punishment often
adopted, as by the Philistines on Samson's father-in-law (Jud. xv. 6);
threatened by Ephraim against Jephthah (Jud. xii. 1). Comp. also the
summary act of Absalom against Joab for his inattention to the prince's
messages (2 Sam. xiv. 30), cf. Josh. vii. 25.

sight of many women] The neighbouring states. There may be
reference to a custom of making women witness the fate of the adulteress,
that they might take warning.

1 [Rather, as Kr., those of whom she had grown weary.]

42 no hire any more.   So will I ¹satisfy my fury ²upon thee, and my jealousy shall depart from thee, and I will be
43 quiet, and will be no more angry.   Because thou hast not remembered the days of thy youth, but hast fretted me in all these things; therefore behold, I also will bring thy way upon thine head, saith the Lord GOD: and ³thou shalt not commit *this* lewdness above all thine abominations.
44   Behold, every one that useth proverbs shall use *this* proverb against thee, saying, As is the mother, so is her
45 daughter.   Thou art thy mother's daughter, that loatheth her husband and her children; and thou art the sister of

---

¹ Heb. *bring to rest.*   ² Or, *toward*   ³ Or, *hast thou not committed &c.?*

---

42.   *satisfy my fury*] i.e. appease it.   Cf. ch. v. 13.
43.   The verse concludes the whole passage *vv.* 35—43, summing up its meaning compendiously, cf. *v.* 22.
   fretted] [a stronger word is needed, *provoked.*]
   thou shalt not commit] The tense is *perf.,* which can hardly be taken as fut. perf., though the prophet does use the perf. in an uncommon way (ch. xiii. 11, xxiv. 5).   The sentence can hardly be read interrogatively as marg., without altering the text.   LXX. read *and thus* for "and not": *and thus hast thou committed lewdness.*   The term "lewdness" is used by Ezekiel of sexual enormity, applied figuratively to idolatry (*v.* 27).   "Lewdness" and "abominations" would not differ, except that the former was the quality characterizing the acts called abominations.   In this case the clause must read: "and thus hast thou committed lewdness *in* (amidst) all thine abominations"; and the words would be a final summary of the preceding verses. "Lewdness," however, is used literally (ch. xxii. 9), and *v.* 45 seems to speak of literal unchastity.   The clause might thus be attached to *v.* 44, and "lewdness" being distinguished from "abominations" we might read: "lewdness *in addition to* all thine abominations."   The distinction, however, is not natural.   [Kr. by a slight change in MT., renders, "O that thou hadst not, &c."]
44.   A taunting proverb in regard to Jerusalem, the adulteress and child-murderer: she is the true daughter of her mother the Canaanite. The proverb or saying is probably to be restricted to the words: "As is her mother, so is her daughter."   In *v.* 45 *seq.* the prophet speaks and addresses Jerusalem.
45.   *that loatheth her husband*] In the sense of the allegory "loathing her husband" should mean changing her god for another; and in the case of Jerusalem and Samaria the charge is intelligible, Jehovah being the husband (ch. xxiii.).   But such a charge could hardly be made

thy sisters, which loathed their husbands and their children: your mother was an Hittite, and your father an Amorite. And thine elder sister is Samaria, that dwelleth at thy left 46 hand, she and her daughters: and thy younger sister, that dwelleth at thy right hand, is Sodom and her daughters. Yet hast thou not walked in their ways, nor done after their 47 abominations; but, as *if that were* a very little *thing*, thou wast more corrupt than they in all thy ways. As I live, 48 saith the Lord GOD, Sodom thy sister hath not done, she nor her daughters, as thou hast done, thou and thy daughters. Behold, this was the iniquity of thy sister 49

against the Canaanites, the Hittite mother and Sodom (Jer. ii. 11[1]). The prophet appears to desert the allegory, introducing real features into his description, and referring to actual adultery and unfaithfulness, and child-sacrifice, which were characteristic of the Canaanite nations. Another interpretation, as old as Theodoret, considers Jehovah to be the "husband" even of the Hittite mother, heathen idolatries being infidelity to the true God. Such a reflexion is not natural to a prophet of this age, though a similar idea occurred to St Paul (Rom. i. 21). At the same time this prophet predicts the reunion of Sodom with Israel. Cor. strikes out the words as a gloss impossible to interpret.

sister of thy sisters] The sisters of Jerusalem were Samaria and Sodom, and she had a genuine family likeness to them[2].

your mother]   *Your* (plur.) refers to the three sisters.

46. *elder sister*] "elder" is lit. greater, and the reference is to the greater political importance and wider territory of Samaria; as on the other hand Sodom was smaller than Judah. In estimating the quarters of the heavens the beholder faced the east, having the north on his left, &c.

her daughters] i.e. subordinate towns   Cf. *v.* 27.

47—51. The depravity of Jerusalem exceeded that of either of her sisters: Sodom (*vv.* 48—50), Samaria (*v.* 51).

47. *as if that were a very little* thing] Or temporally: *but a little while, and then*, i.e. *speedily thou wast corrupted;* though there seems no reference to any actual period of righteousness, such as the times of David. (The strange word *ḳāṭ* is utterly unknown; any connexion with Ar. ḳaṭ *only*, or with an Assyr. word "a little" (so Frd. Delitzsch in Baer's *Ézechiel*, p. xvi) is little probable. If the word be anything but an echo of preceding sounds it may be a fragment of the word "little," cf. Is. xvi. 14, xxix. 17.)   Cf. ch. v. 6, 7[3].

48. Cf. Matt. x. 15, xi. 24.

---

[1] [Where it is pointed out that other nations are loyal to their gods.]
[2] [For the relationship between Samaria and Jerusalem, cf. xxiii. 4, 33.]
[3] [Kr. modifies the MT. so as to render "but thou hast turned aside."]

Sodom; pride, fulness of bread, and prosperous ease was
in her and in her daughters; neither did she strengthen
50 the hand of the poor and needy.   And they were haughty,
and committed abomination before me: therefore I took
51 them away [1]as I saw *good*.   Neither hath Samaria committed
half of thy sins; but thou hast multiplied thine abominations more than they, and hast justified thy sisters by all
52 thine abominations which thou hast done.   Thou also, bear
thine own shame, in that thou hast given judgement for thy
[2]sisters; through thy sins that thou hast committed more
abominable than they, they are more righteous than thou:
yea, be thou also confounded, and bear thy shame, in that

[1] Or, *when I saw* it   [2] Or, *sister*

49.   *prosperous ease*] lit. "prosperity of quiet."   Sodom lived in
security and suffered no calamities, as Jer. xlviii. 11 says of Moab,
"Moab hath been at ease from his youth, and he hath settled on
his lees, and hath not been emptied from vessel to vessel, neither
hath he gone into captivity."   On "fulness of bread" and consequent
pride and forgetfulness of God cf. Deut. xxxii. 15; Hos. xiii. 6; Prov.
xxx. 7.

strengthen the hand]   Or, **take hold of** the hand, i.e. to help or
rescue.   Prosperity led to pride and inhumanity and then to abominations (*v.* 50).

50.   *as I saw* good]   Better, as marg. **when I saw** it.   Gen. xviii. 21,
I "will go down now, and see whether they have done altogether
according to the cry of it, which is come unto me."

51.   *hast justified*]   The abominations of Judah set Samaria and
Sodom in a comparatively righteous light.   Jer. iii. 11, "Backsliding
Israel hath shewn herself more righteous than treacherous Judah."

52.   Jerusalem has "given judgement" or interposed (1 Sam. ii. 25)
in behalf of her sisters in being more wicked than they—she has made
them comparatively righteous.   The phrase "bear thine own shame"
might mean "suffer in destruction the consequences of thy wickedness"; *vv.* 54, 61, 63, however, shew that the ref. is to the feeling of
shame due to the fact that by the grossness of her abominations she
has shewn her sisters to be more righteous than she (cf. xxxix. 26).
The prophet assumes the exile and looks forward to the time of
restoration.   Sodom also and Samaria shall be restored as well as
Jerusalem, and it is this that shall bring shame to her, for she shall
feel that they whom she did not deign to mention because of their evil
fame (*v.* 56) were not worse but better than herself.

53.   Sodom and Samaria shall be restored, and Jerusalem along with
them.

thou hast justified thy sisters. And I will ¹turn again their 53
captivity, the captivity of Sodom and her daughters, and
the captivity of Samaria and her daughters, and the captivity of thy captives in the midst of them: that thou mayest 54
bear thine own shame, and mayest be ashamed because of
all that thou hast done, in that thou art a comfort unto
them. And thy sisters, Sodom and her daughters, shall 55
return to their former estate, and Samaria and her daughters shall return to their former estate, and thou and thy
daughters shall return to your former estate. For thy sister 56
Sodom was not mentioned by thy mouth in the day of thy
pride; before thy wickedness was discovered, as at the time 57
of the reproach of the daughters of Syria, and of all that

¹ Or, *return to*

And I will turn again] The phrase "turn the captivity" probably
means : turn the fortunes (lit. the turning) of one.

captivity of thy captives] Most moderns by a slight change of
reading after LXX. render: "and I will bring again thy captivity in
the midst of them." Cf. Is. xix. 24, "In that day shall Israel be the
third with Egypt and with Assyria, a blessing in the midst of the
earth."

54. Read : "that thou mayest bear thy shame, and be ashamed
because of all that thou hast done in comforting them." Jerusalem
"comforted" Samaria and Sodom by surpassing them in wickedness,
and causing them to feel less their own guilt, as also in causing their
restoration. [For "comfort" see on xiv. 23, and cf. xxxi. 16,
xxxii. 31.]

55. *And thy sisters*] In this idea of the restoration of Israel's
heathen neighbours to their own land after being plucked up out of
it Ezekiel as usual follows Jeremiah; cf. in general, Jer. xii. 14—17;
Moab, ch. xlviii. 47, Ammon, xlix. 6, and Elam, xlix. 39.

56. Jerusalem did not deign to refer to Sodom on account of the
wickedness and evil repute of the latter. [So Cor., Ber.] Others [e.g.
Orelli, Kr.] interrogatively: "Was not Sodom a report (a moral byword)
in thy mouth?" But the interrogative form is precarious.

57. *was discovered*] i.e. manifested. According to modes of thinking
then prevalent calamity was the accepted proof of wickedness. Jerusalem's wickedness was laid bare when her great calamities fell upon
her, Lam. i. 8, 9.

the time of the reproach of the daughters of Syria] viz. that which they
cast upon Jerusalem, not conversely as A.V. The "time" must be
the present, not any previous time, and the language expresses this
awkwardly. LXX. read : "as now thou art the reproach" ("now" for
"time" and either finding or inserting the pron. "thou"). [So Kr.

are round about her, the daughters of the Philistines, which
58 do despite unto thee round about. Thou hast borne thy
59 lewdness and thine abominations, saith the LORD. For
thus saith the Lord GOD: I will even deal with thee as
thou hast done, which hast despised the oath in breaking
60 the covenant. Nevertheless I will remember my covenant
with thee in the days of thy youth, and I will establish
61 unto thee an everlasting covenant. Then shalt thou remember thy ways, and be ashamed, when thou shalt receive
thy sisters, thine elder *sisters* and thy younger: and I will

"Thou art like her (Sodom) now," adapting the M.T. in the direction
of LXX.] The rendering: "before thy wickedness was discovered *as*
(it is) *now*, a reproach &c." (Hitz. Cor.), is scarcely a Heb. construction. It would be easiest to change "time" ('*ēth*) into "thou" ('*at*)
(cf. the opposite change of "whereby" ('*ăsher*) into "ten" (*cāsār*), required in ch. xl. 49): "as *thou art* the reproach."

Syria, and...round about her] The mention of Syria (Heb. Aram)
is strange when the reference is to the downfall of Jerusalem. For
Aram Syriac gives *Edom* (*d* for *r*, cf. ch. xxvii. 16) which is more
natural (cf. ch. xxxv. 12 *seq.*, xxv. 5, 12, 15). Vulg. reads, "round
about *thee*," while the whole phrase is wanting in the Syr. The ref. is
to Jerusalem in any case. Ezekiel nowhere else brings Syria into connexion with Israel[1].

58. This and the preceding verses assume the destruction of Jerusalem, of which the prophet was fully assured.

59. The fall of Jerusalem, prophetically assumed in *v.* 58, is now
directly threatened. On the "oath" cf. Deut. xxix. 12, 14.

XVI. 60—63. HER RECONCILIATION.

60. The Lord will substitute for the old covenant which was broken
an "everlasting" covenant, cf. ch. xxxvii. 26; Is. liv. 9, 10, lv. 3;
Jer. xxxi. 35, 36, xxxii. 40, xxxiii. 20—22. The covenant will be
everlasting because He will forgive their sins (Jer. xxxi. 34), and write
His law (*v.* 33), and put His fear (xxxii. 40) in their hearts; giving them
a new heart and putting His spirit within them, Ezek. xxxvi. 26. On
the "days of thy youth" cf. Jer. ii. 2, and Is. liv. 6.

61. Sodom and Samaria, the sisters of Jerusalem, shall be restored
also with her and given her for daughters. This restoration of her sinful sisters and her receiving them for daughters shall bring the sense of
her own sin home to Jerusalem, and she shall be ashamed of all she has
done.

[1] [If the prophet does so here, Redp. (*ad loc.*) points out that the reference may
well be to the false worship rampant in the time of Ahaz, closely connected in history
(2 Kgs xvi. 4—6; Is. vii. 1, 2) with the combined attack of Syria under Rezin and
Pekah of Israel upon Jerusalem.]

give them unto thee for daughters, but not by thy covenant.
And I will establish my covenant with thee; and thou shalt 62
know that I am the LORD: that thou mayest remember, 63
and be confounded, and never open thy mouth any more,
because of thy shame; when I have forgiven thee all that
thou hast done, saith the Lord GOD.

not by thy covenant] This glory of receiving Samaria and Sodom and
her other sister cities and nationalities for daughters shall not accrue to
Jerusalem as the result of her former covenant with Jehovah, for that
covenant of His she broke. It shall be like the new covenant itself,
something altogether additional, an act of God's goodness in no way
depending on former relations (*v.* 62). [Cf. Rom. ii. 3.]

62. *I will establish*] "*I*" is emphatic, in opposition to "not by thy
covenant." The new covenant will shew that Jehovah is better than
all His chastisements.

63. *when I have forgiven thee*] The word is the technical sacrificial word for "atone" or make atonement for. It probably means
to "cover[1]," though it is no more used in the physical sense but
only in reference to sins or guilt. Hence when God is the agent this
covering of sin is pardon, Jer. xviii. 23; Deut. xxi. 8 (be merciful to);
2 Chr. xxx. 18. The important point is to retain the active sense of
the word. An act of God is described, not an effect produced upon His
mind.

The great grace of Jehovah in restoring Jerusalem will humble and
shame her, when she remembers her past evil. What all chastisements could accomplish but indifferently, goodness will accomplish fully.
Jerusalem will no more "open her mouth," but sit in abashed though
glad silence before God. His goodness and her own sin will so fill her
mind that the thoughts will be too deep for words. Formerly she ac-
cused God's providence, thinking she suffered for the iniquities of generations before her; formerly she boasted of her place before Jehovah,
and her sister Sodom was too base to be mentioned (cf. *v.* 56 with note).
Now her mind will muse on other things.

Though the language and conceptions of Ezekiel are less familiar
and natural to western minds than those of some of the other writers of
Scripture, his thoughts are very elevated.

(1) The figure of the adulterous wife expresses the conviction, felt
by him very strongly, that all through her history Israel had sinned
against Jehovah, especially in the matter of His service. While former
prophets like Amos and Hosea condemn the ritual and the manner of
the worship because this implies a false conception of Jehovah, a conception so false as to correspond in no sense to Jehovah as He really is,
Ezekiel condemns the worship at the high places as in itself false. He

---

[1] [But the Heb. verb is now held to be connected with the Assyrian *kapparu*,
which apparently means *to remove*, and *kupparu*, *to remove ritual impurity*, hence
to purge away sin. See further on Exod. xxxii. 10 in this series.]

regards the high places as Canaanite shrines, and the service there as no
service of Jehovah.   And when he says that Jerusalem was unfaithful
with Egypt, Assyria, and Babylon, besides expressing his belief that the
kingdom of Jehovah is not as one among the other kingdoms, he assails
the strange infatuation which the people displayed in adopting the gods
and rites of the nations with which in successive ages they entered into
relation.   What took place in regard to the worship of the Canaanites
when Israel entered upon possession of that land, took place all down
the history as they successively came under the influence of the great
states around.

(2)   When the prophet charges Jerusalem with outbidding Samaria
and Sodom in wickedness, his judgement agrees with that of Jeremiah,
and is founded partly on the fact that Jerusalem had fuller knowledge
of Jehovah from her more extended history, and consequently her sin
was greater than that of Samaria.   The judgement, however, may also
be partly based on objective grounds.   So far as appears from the prophets
Amos and Hosea idolatry in the strict sense was not greatly prevalent
in the North.   What prevailed was mainly a sensuous worship of Jehovah, due to false conceptions of His nature, which probably had arisen
from a long syncretism with the idea and service of the Baals.   But in
the later history of Judah idolatry in the sense of the worship of gods
different from Jehovah greatly prevailed.   Neither does the cruel rite of
child-sacrifice appear to have invaded the Northern Kingdom.

(3)   It is, however, when the prophet brings the sin of Jerusalem
into connexion with that of Samaria and Sodom, which it exceeded, and
lifts that strange fact up into the region of Divine thoughts and provi-
dential operations, that his ideas become most profound.   The sin of
Jerusalem, so great amidst all God's love and favour, reveals to himself
the nature of sin and its power over men, and he remembers with compassion those heathen peoples, like Sodom, on whom his former judgements had so unsparingly fallen.   His own people's fall causes him to
take to his heart the Gentile world.   The Apostle Paul touches the
same or a kindred idea when he says : " By their fall salvation is come
unto the Gentiles...if their fall is the riches of the world" (Rom.
xi. 11, 12).

Again when the prophet says that Jerusalem "shall bear her shame in
that she has justified her sisters," the thought is similar to that expressed
by St Paul, "Salvation is come unto the Gentiles, for to provoke them
(Israel) to jealousy" (Rom. xi. 11).   Cf. Deut. xxxii. 21.   The sight of
other peoples received by her God awakens Israel to the meaning of
her own past, and to recollections of her former relations to God.
Finally the receiving again of Israel and the incoming of the Gentile
peoples like Sodom illustrate the manner of salvation, shewing it to
be of grace, a grace that is stronger to overcome sin and awaken sorrow
for it than all judgements—He hath shut up all into disobedience that
He might have mercy upon all.   Neither the prophet nor the apostle
moves in the region of second causes ; they lift up the whole movement
of salvation into the region of the Divine thoughts and compassions.

(4)   The prophet predicts the restoration of Jerusalem, Samaria, and

And the word of the LORD came unto me, saying, Son **17**
of man, put forth a riddle, and speak a parable unto the **2**

Sodom, and that Jerusalem, though like a sister to them in wickedness,
shall receive all these greater and smaller sisters as daughters.   There
shall then in the new kingdom of Jehovah be only one mother city, all
other cities or peoples shall be her children.   To the prophet's mind
the identity of Samaria and Sodom remains even when they are destroyed, and they shall remember and turn to the Lord.   There is in
such passages, what is not unusual in Ezekiel, a struggle between the
spiritual conception or fact and the external form in which he still feels
it must be embodied.   It is the spiritual conception of the conversion to
Jehovah even of peoples like Sodom that fills his mind; but he is
unable to give this expression in any other way than by saying that
Sodom shall return to her former estate.

XVII.   THE TREACHEROUS VINEPLANT—KING ZEDEKIAH'S
DISLOYALTY TO THE KING OF BABYLON.

The chapter is without date.   Nebuchadrezzar appeared in Palestine
in the ninth year of Zedekiah to punish his disloyalty and his intrigues
with Egypt.   The present passage assumes this disloyalty and may be
dated a year or two earlier (c. 590).

The chapter contains these divisions :

First, *vv.* 1—10.   The riddle of the great eagle.
Secondly, *vv.* 11—21.   Explanation of the riddle.
Thirdly, *vv.* 22—24.   Promise that Jehovah will set up in Israel a
kingdom that shall be universal.

1—10.   THE RIDDLE OF THE GREAT EAGLE.

(1) *vv.* 1—4 introduction.   The great, broadwinged, speckled eagle
came to Lebanon, and broke off the top of the cedar, carrying it to the
merchant-land, Babylon—the captivity of Jehoiachin by Nebuchadrezzar.

(2) *vv.* 5, 6.   He took also of the seed of the land and planted it
beside the waters that it might be a spreading vine, and might turn its
branches towards him who had planted it—the elevation to the throne
by Nebuchadrezzar of Zedekiah as a feudatory monarch.

(3) *vv.* 7, 8.   There was another great eagle, and the vine bent its
roots and sent out its branches towards him—Zedekiah sought the
alliance and protection of the king of Egypt.

(4) *vv.* 9, 10.   Denunciation of the vine for its treachery.   The east
wind shall blow on it and it shall wither.

2. *a riddle*]   As requiring interpretation; the passage is also called a
"parable," as containing a similitude or comparison.   The eagle is
Nebuchadrezzar, king of Babylon.   Conquerors are often compared to
the eagle, Deut. xxviii. 49; Is. xlvi. 11; Jer. iv. 13, xlviii. 40; Lam.
iv. 19; Hos. viii. 1.

3 house of Israel; and say, Thus saith the Lord GOD: A great eagle with great wings and long pinions, full of feathers, which had divers colours, came unto Lebanon,
4 and took the top of the cedar: he cropped off the topmost of the young twigs thereof, and carried it into ¹a land of
5 traffic; he set it in a city of merchants. He took also of the seed of the land, and planted it in ²a fruitful soil; he placed it beside ³many waters; he set it as a willow tree.
6 And it grew, and became a spreading vine of low stature, whose branches turned toward him, and the roots thereof were under him: so it became a vine, and brought forth
7 branches, and shot forth sprigs. There was also another

¹ Or, *the land of Canaan*   ² Heb. *a field of seed*.   ³ Or, *great*

3. *had divers colours*] or was speckled, with reference possibly to the very diverse nationalities included in the Babylonian empire.

came unto Lebanon] The figure of the eagle coming to Lebanon and cropping off the highest branch and top of the young twigs (*v.* 4) represents the carrying off of those highest in the land of Israel. The cedar, the tree of Lebanon, appears to represent the royal Davidic house (*vv.* 12, 22), and its highest branches king Jehoiachin and the princes who were carried away to Babylon (*v.* 12). On "land of traffic" (*v.* 4), cf. ch. xvi. 29.

5. Nebuchadrezzar then took Mattaniah, son of Josiah, and made him king under the name of Zedekiah. The "seed of the land" is the native royal house.

he placed it] The unknown form so rendered might be a verb, cf. Hos. xi. 3. LXX. omits [so Kr.]; Ew. conjectures *slip* or *cutting*. The comparison to the willow (the sense is not certain, the word not occurring again)¹ is suggested by the place where it was planted, beside great waters. "Water" is the requisite of every tree in the East, and "many [marg. great] waters" are the favourable conditions granted to Zedekiah. They "that drink water" is an expression for trees, ch. xxxi. 16.

6. *of low stature*] This refers to the dependent nature of Zedekiah's kingdom, as tributary to the lord superior. Cf. Is. xvi. 8; Hos. x. 1.

whose branches turned] Or, **that its branches might turn**...and the roots thereof **be**.

7. The other great eagle, which however is not described with such imposing epithets as the former, is the king of Egypt. The vine bent its roots towards him—sought to draw nourishment from him.

¹ [As a vine cannot *become* any other tree, such as "a willow," Kr. would omit the clause, or alter the MT. so as to read "he set *its produce*, stock, or cutting." Although, however, the MT. has probably suffered corruption, the Heb., as it stands, may be taken to mean, "he set it willowwise." See for the construction Ges.-Kautzsch, *Heb. Grammar*, 118. 5 (*c*).]

great eagle with great wings and many feathers: and, behold, this vine did bend its roots toward him, and shot forth its branches toward him, from the beds of its plantation, that he might water it. It was planted in a good 8 ¹soil by ²many waters, that it might bring forth branches, and that it might bear fruit, that it might be a goodly vine. Say thou, Thus saith the Lord GOD: Shall it prosper? 9 shall he not pull up the roots thereof, and cut off the fruit thereof, that it may wither; that all its fresh springing leaves may wither; even without great power or much ³people to pluck it up by the roots thereof? Yea, behold, being 10 planted, shall it prosper? shall it not utterly wither, when the east wind toucheth it? it shall wither in the beds where it grew.

Moreover the word of the LORD came unto me, saying, 11 Say now to the rebellious house, Know ye not what these 12 things mean? tell them, Behold, the king of Babylon came to Jerusalem, and took the king thereof, and the princes thereof, and brought them to him to Babylon; and he took 13

¹ Heb. *field*.   ² Or, *great*   ³ Or, *people, plucking &c.*

from the beds of its plantation] i.e. where it was planted.

8. The happy condition of Zedekiah's monarchy under the king of Babylon, had he been content with his subordinate role as a feudatory prince.

9. Threat of punishment because of his treachery. The vine shall be pulled up and utterly withered—Zedekiah's monarchy shall be taken away before the king of Babylon.

shall he not pull up] The subject is most naturally the king of Babylon, who planted it; but the words might be used in the sense of the *passive*: shall it not be pulled up?

even without great power] It will be a light thing for the king of Babylon to pluck up this vine by the roots. Both the words and construction are peculiar; cf. *v.* 17.

10. Destruction under another figure, that of the east wind, before which vegetation crumbles into dust. Cf. ch. xix. 12; Hos. xiii. 15; Is. xxvii. 8, xl. 7; Job xxvii. 21.

XVII. 11—21. INTERPRETATION OF THE RIDDLE.

12. *the rebellious house*] i.e. Israel, ch. ii. 5.

king of Babylon came] On the captivity of Jehoiachin, cf. 2 Kgs xxiv. 11 *seq*.; Jer. xxiv. 1, xxix. 1.

of the seed royal, and made a covenant with him; he also
brought him under an oath, and took away the mighty of
14 the land: that the kingdom might be [1] base, that it might
not lift itself up, but that by keeping of his covenant it
15 might stand. But he rebelled against him in sending his
ambassadors into Egypt, that they might give him horses
and much people. Shall he prosper? shall he escape that
doeth such things? shall he break the covenant, and yet
16 escape? As I live, saith the Lord GOD, surely in the place
where the king dwelleth that made him king, whose oath
he despised, and whose covenant he brake, even with him
17 in the midst of Babylon he shall die. Neither shall Pharaoh

[1] Heb. *low*.

13. *the seed royal*] lit. seed of the kingdom, i.e. Zedekiah. See
on *v.* 5; cf. 2 Kgs xxiv. 17; Jer. xxxvii. 1.
brought him under an oath] Cf. 2 Chr. xxxvi. 13.
mighty of the land] cf *v.* 12. Probably the more influential classes
are included, those who if left might be uneasy under the yoke and
likely to stir up revolt; cf. 2 Kgs xxiv. 14, 15; Jer. xxix. 1, 2.
14. *might be base*] i.e. as marg. *low*, humble, and without preten-
sion; cf. ch. xxix. 14. It was with this purpose that Nebuchadrezzar
carried away the mighty of the land. He also hoped that the kingdom
would "stand"; it was no doubt his policy to have a dependent,
friendly state on the frontier of Egypt. The word "stand," however, may refer to the covenant: "but might keep my covenant, that
it might stand."
15. Cf. 2 Kgs xxiv. 20. The king of Egypt referred to was
Pharaoh Hophra [B.C. 588—569] Jer. xliv. 30, xxxvii. 5 *seq*. The
indignation against Zedekiah on the part of Ezekiel arises greatly from
his regarding the subjection of Jerusalem to Babylon as a thing determined by Jehovah. Hence the covenant broken by Zedekiah is not
merely the covenant of the king of Babylon but that of Jehovah (*v.* 19).
The prophet follows Jeremiah. He had possibly read the words of the
latter spoken in the beginning of the reign of Zedekiah, ch. xxvii. 17,
"serve the king of Babylon and live"; and probably he had heard
his words to the same effect spoken in the fourth year of Jehoiakim,
ch. xxv. His advice to the exiles also (ch. xxix. 4) was no doubt
known to him.
16. Zedekiah, being carried to Babylon, shall die there.
17. The aid of Pharaoh shall be in vain; cf. Jer. xxxvii. 5, and the
pathetic references to the hopes and disappointments of the besieged
during the last days of Jerusalem in Lam. iv. 17[1].

[1] [Kr. considers "Pharaoh" to be a gloss, suggested by *v.* 15. Thus he makes
the reference to be to the king of Babylon (as *v.* 16), and so the thought of the *v.* to

with his mighty army and great company make for him in the war, when they cast up mounts and build forts, to cut off many persons. For he hath despised the oath by 18 breaking the covenant; and behold, he had given his hand, and yet hath done all these things; he shall not escape. Therefore thus saith the Lord GOD: As I live, surely mine 19 oath that he hath despised, and my covenant that he hath broken, I will even bring it upon his own head. And 20 I will spread my net upon him, and he shall be taken in my snare, and I will bring him to Babylon, and will plead with him there for his trespass that he hath trespassed against me. And all his fugitives in all his bands shall fall 21 by the sword, and they that remain shall be scattered toward every wind: and ye shall know that I the LORD have spoken it.

On "mounts," &c., cf. ch. iv. 2.

19. *mine oath*] [even an oath taken to a non-Israelite was held by Jehovah as taken to Him.]

20. *spread my net*] Cf. ch. xii. 13; Hos. vii. 12.

plead with him] i.e. there subject him to the consequences of his treachery, bringing it thereby to his knowledge that he is suffering the penalty of it, cf. xx. 35, 36, xxxviii. 22; Jer. ii. 35.

21. *all his fugitives*] This form of the Heb. noun does not otherwise occur, but it has been so understood by some ancient versions. Others as Targ., Syr., and some Heb. MSS. assume a transposition of two letters and render: *his choice men*; and so many moderns (cf. ch. xxiii. 7; Dan. xi. 15). For the *v.* itself cf. ch. v. 2, 12, vi. 10, 13, xii. 12 *seq.*

XVII. 22—24. PROMISE OF A NEW AND UNIVERSAL MESSIANIC KINGDOM IN ISRAEL.

The attempt of the king of Babylon to set up a kingdom in Israel miscarried. He who set up the kingdom took it away. The shoot planted by Nebuchadrezzar was smitten by the east wind and withered. But Jehovah Himself will plant a shoot of the high cedar, the Davidic house, on a high mountain that all nations may see it (Is. ii. 2, xi. 10), even on the height of the mountain land of Israel, and it shall become a great cedar, so that all the fowls of heaven shall lodge in the branches of it. This kingdom shall be imposing and universal, and all peoples

be parallel to that of *v.* 9. The meaning will then be, "And without a great army and a numerous company will he (Nebuchadrezzar) deal with him (Zedekiah)." "Pharaoh," however, is found in the LXX. and makes good sense. Zedekiah depends on Egypt, but he will be taken prisoner to Babylon, and Pharaoh will not send a great army to help him when Jerusalem is besieged.]

22   Thus saith the Lord GOD : I will also take of the lofty
top of the cedar, and will set it ; I will crop off from the
topmost of his young twigs a tender one, and I will plant
23 it upon an high mountain and eminent : in the mountain
of the height of Israel will I plant it : and it shall bring
forth boughs, and bear fruit, and be a goodly cedar : and
under it shall dwell all fowl of every wing ; in the shadow
24 of the branches thereof shall they dwell.   And all the trees
of the field shall know that I the LORD have brought down
the high tree, have exalted the low tree, have dried up the
green tree, and have made the dry tree to flourish : I the
LORD have spoken and have done it.

18   The word of the LORD came unto me again, saying,

shall find protection under it.   And then shall it be known that
Jehovah is king among the nations, that kingdoms are in His hand, to
set one up and pull another down ; that He can make the green tree
wither and the dry tree blossom and bear fruit[1].

22.   *I will also take*]   **I will take**—"I" emphatic.   The figure refers
to the house of David, cf *vv*. 2, 3 ; Is. liii. 2.

high mountain]   This belongs partly to the figure of the cedar, but
indicates also the conspicuousness to the eyes of the nations of this
great cedar ; Is. ii. 2.

23.   *mountain of the height*]   Cf. ch. xx. 40, xl. 2.

fruit]   [Cor., Ber., Kr., favour a slight change in the Heb., so as to
render *branches*, as the cedar is not a fruit-bearing tree.   This introduces
tautology ("boughs," "branches") to which, however, *v*. 6 ("branches,"
"sprigs") lends some support.]

all fowl of every wing]   As fowls flock to a great tree, so all peoples
will put their trust in the shadow of this great monarchy in the land
of Israel ; ch. xxxi. 6 ; Dan iv. 12 ; Matt. xiii. 32.

24.   As this kingdom is compared to a cedar, other kingdoms are
likewise called trees ; cf. ch. xxxi. 5, 8, 14, 16, 18.   Kings and kingdoms are hardly distinguished, the kingdom is but the expression of the
king.   Then all shall know that this great result is the work of Jehovah,
who worketh contrary to men's expectations ; who overturneth till he
come whose right it is to rule.   Cf. 1 Sam. ii. 4—8 ; Luke i. 51—53.

XVIII.   THE MORAL FREEDOM AND RESPONSIBILITY OF THE
INDIVIDUAL MAN BEFORE GOD.

This great idea is expressed in two parts :

First, *vv*. 1—20.   The individual man is not involved in the sins and
fate of his people or of his forefathers.

[1] [Here Ezekiel gives his first hint of a Messianic character, making the coming
Ruler to belong to the Davidic house.   Cf. xxi. 32, xxxiv. 24, xxxvii. 24.]

Secondly, *vv.* 21—32. Neither does he lie under the ban of his own previous life. His moral freedom raises him above both.

The prophet as usual attaches himself to the ideas of Jeremiah, who had prophesied that in the ideal days to come, those of the New Covenant, the perfect future that was about to dawn upon men, they should no more say, "The fathers have eaten sour grapes, and the children's teeth are set on edge," but every one should die for his own iniquity (ch. xxxi. 29, 30). The outlook of Ezekiel is also in some measure ideal, and the principles which he enunciates must be judged in this light (ch. xxxiii.). His purpose is in the main practical. He desires to lay a basis for his exhortation "Turn yourselves from all your transgressions" (*v.* 30). His exhortations are addressed to the individuals of the people, for he contemplates the end of the state and only individuals remain, and he has to face and settle questions that from the circumstances of the time had begun to exercise and perplex men's minds. The strokes that had fallen one after another upon the state might be deserved, when the state was considered as a moral person who had sinned all through her history (ch. xvi.) ; but the calamities that were deserved by the general mass fell with a crushing weight on many who had not been partakers in the sins that brought them down. The captives carried away under Jehoiachin were more righteous than those still left to inherit the mountains of Israel ; and compared with the dark days of Manasseh even the generation subject to Zedekiah might think themselves better men. Such reflections made the people feel themselves involved as by a kind of fate in the deeds of their forefathers, a feeling which found expression in the proverb, "The fathers have eaten sour grapes, and the children's teeth are set on edge." This proverb might express various feelings as it came from different mouths. It might be uttered by some in self-exculpation, and in a satisfied, self-righteous tone ; or it might be the expression of a perplexed condition of mind, which found God's providence dark, and went so far as well nigh to arraign the divine rectitude ; or finally it might express the feeling of lying under a hopeless fate inherited from the past—a feeling which crushed out individual life and paralysed all personal effort after righteousness, and delivered over the mind to an inactivity of despair (ch. xxxiii. 10). These difficulties could not fail themselves to suggest their own solution. They were partly due to the consciousness, which circumstances were everywhere creating, of the worth of the individual soul ; and their solution lay in pursuing this idea further and giving it clearer expression.

The prophet meets the state of the people's mind with two great principles from the mouth of the Lord : (1) "All souls are mine ; as the soul of the father, so also the soul of the son is mine." Each soul is the Lord's, His relation to each is direct and immediate (*v.* 4). And (2) "I have no pleasure in the death of him that dieth, saith the Lord GOD" (*v.* 32).

And two conclusions follow from these principles : (1) Each soul being immediately related to God, its destiny depends on this relation—

2 What mean ye, that ye use this proverb [1]concerning the land of Israel, saying, The fathers have eaten sour grapes, 3 and the children's teeth are set on edge? As I live, saith the Lord GOD, ye shall not have *occasion* any more to use 4 this proverb in Israel. Behold, all souls are mine; as the

[1] Or, *in*

"the soul that sinneth, it shall die"; and (2) "wherefore turn yourselves, and live" (*v.* 32). The emancipation of the individual soul is complete.

First, *vv.* 1—20. The individual soul shall not be involved in the sins and fate of its people or forefathers.

(1) *vv.* 1—4. Introduction. The current proverb signifying that the children suffer the consequences of the sins of their fathers (*vv.* 1, 2). Answer of Jehovah: All souls are mine. None shall answer for the sins of another—the soul that sinneth shall die (*vv.* 3, 4).

(2) *vv.* 5—20. Development of this principle in three instances: first, a man who is upright, doing truth and righteousness—this man shall live (*vv.* 5—9). Secondly, if this righteous man beget a wicked son who doeth evil, this wicked son of a righteous father shall die (*vv.* 10—13). Thirdly, if, however, this wicked son of a righteous father himself beget a son who, seeing the evil of his father, avoids it and acts righteously, this righteous son of an evil father shall live (*vv.* 14—18). To restate the principle: the righteous shall live in his righteousness, and the wicked shall die in his own evil (*vv.* 19, 20).

2. *concerning the land*] rather, as marg., **in**, lit. upon: cf. *v.* 3 "in Israel."

The fathers have eaten] Or, *Fathers eat*; the proverb being thrown into a general form. The proverb, already noticed by Jeremiah (ch. xxxi. 29, 30), means that the children suffer the consequences of the sins of their fathers. Sour or unripe grapes are occasionally eaten[1], and naturally the effect upon the eater's teeth is immediate—his teeth are set on edge, lit. blunted, the edge of them turned. Here, however, the effect is first felt by the children. Such feelings could not but arise in the troubled times of the fall of the state, when the righteous suffered with the wicked, and the most righteous were carried into exile, and just because they still clave to their own faith in the midst of heathenism endured severer sufferings than others who accommodated themselves to their circumstances. Soon after the fall of Jerusalem we hear the same complaint in literal terms: "Our fathers have sinned, and are not; and we have borne their iniquities." (Lam. v. 7.)

3. *ye shall not have* occasion] Or, **it shall not be permitted you.**

4. *all souls are mine*] i.e. every individual soul stands in immediate relation to God; Numb. xvi. 22, "O God, the God of the spirits of all

---

[1] [Kr. quotes Delitzsch on Job xv. 33 as to their consumption in this way in Syria at the present day.]

soul of the father, so also the soul of the son is mine: the
soul that sinneth, it shall die. But if a man be just, and 5
do ¹that which is lawful and right, and hath not eaten upon 6
the mountains, neither hath lifted up his eyes to the idols of

¹ Heb. *judgement and righteousness.*

flesh, shall one man sin, and wilt thou be wroth with all the congregation?" All souls alike belong to God, and this "alike" guarantees
the treatment of each by itself, the soul of the son no less than the
soul of the father. According to former modes of thought the son had
no personal independence, he belonged to the father, and was involved
in the destiny of the father¹.

that sinneth, it shall die] *It* and not another because of its sin. "Live"
and "die" are used by the prophet of literal life and death, continuance
in the world and removal from it. They have, however, a pregnant
meaning arising from the other conceptions of the prophet. He feels
himself and the people standing immediately before that perfect kingdom of the Lord which is about to come (chs. xxxiii., xxxvii.), and
"live" implies entering into the glory of this kingdom, while "die"
implies deprivation of its blessedness; for of course, like all the Old
Testament writers, Ezekiel considers the kingdom, even in its perfect
condition, an earthly one.

Ezekiel proceeds (*vv.* 5—20) to develop the principle in three
instances, chosen so as to exhibit it in its most paradoxical form.

XVIII. 5—9. First link in the chain. The man that is
righteous shall live.

First, righteousness is defined generally as doing judgement or right
and justice, *v.* 5. Then it is analysed into: (1) religious duties, *v.* 6;
(2) duties relating to marriage and the relations of men and women,
v. 6; (3) duties to one's neighbour, *vv.* 7, 8; and (4) finally all these
duties are brought under the conception of obedience to the commands
of God, *v.* 9.

6. *eaten upon the mountains*] that is, sacrificed on the high places
and partaken of the sacrificial meal following, token of fellowship
as a guest with the idols there worshipped. The phrase occurs again
vv. 11, 15, xxii. 9. In xxxiii. 25 the reading is, eaten *with the blood;*
cf. Lev. xvii. 10 ff., xix. 26; 1 Sam. xiv. 33. Sept. renders Lev. xix. 26,
eaten *upon the mountains*, and it is possible that the same error of
reading occurs here, and that xviii. 6, 11, 15, xxii. 9, should be assimilated to xxxiii. 25 (W. R. Smith, *Kinship,* p. 312)².

lifted up his eyes] in prayer to the idols, or trust in them, or perhaps

¹ [Soul here means that which constitutes the personal existence. See for this
sense A. B. Davidson's *Theology of the O. T.* p. 199.]

² [Ber. is inclined to this view, but Kr. maintains the correctness of M.T., supporting his view by the implication contained in such verses as vi. 13, xvi. 16. He
therefore assimilates xxxiii. 25 to the other passages.]

the house of Israel, neither hath defiled his neighbour's wife,
7 neither hath come near to a woman in her separation; and
hath not wronged any, but hath restored to the debtor his
pledge, hath spoiled none by violence, hath given his bread
to the hungry, and hath covered the naked with a garment;
8 he that hath not given forth upon usury, neither hath
taken any increase, that hath withdrawn his hand from
iniquity, hath executed true judgement between man and
9 man, hath walked in my statutes, and hath kept my judgements, to deal truly; he is just, he shall surely live, saith

generally, in acknowledgment of them. Ps. cxxi. 1, cxxiii. 1; Job
xxxi. 26.

his neighbour's wife] Adultery is not seldom charged against the
people by the prophets, especially Jeremiah, e.g. Jer. v. 8, ix. 2, xxix.
23; cf. Lev. xx. 10; Deut. xxii. 22. Note Job's claims for himself, ch.
xxxi. 9. On the other impurity forbidden cf. Lev. xv. 24, xviii. 19.

7, 8. Duties to one's neighbour.

7. *hath not wronged*] In *v.* 12 the opposite course reads: "hath
wronged the poor and needy." Occasion of wronging would arise when
the poor was in debt (Am. ii. 6, 7); or being unprotected he might
be defrauded of his hire, Mal. iii. 5; Jam. v. 4. Cf. the claim made
by Job, xxxi. 13.

to the debtor his pledge] This refers to the duty of returning to the
debtor any pledge which was an article necessary to his existence or
comfort, as a garment which was his cover by night. Exod. xxii. 26;
Deut. xxiv. 6; cf. Job xxii. 6; Am. ii. 8. On the positive duties of
feeding the hungry and clothing the naked cf. again the claims of Job,
xxxi. 17—20.

8. On usury cf. the humane law, Lev. xxv. 35—37. The case
supposed is that of lending to the poor, Exod. xxii. 25; Deut. xxiii. 20[1].

executed true judgement] When acting as judge, or as umpire between
man and man.

9. The man who acts thus (*vv.* 5—8) hath walked in God's statutes
and he shall live. For "to deal truly," LXX. reads: *to do them*, by
transposition of two letters, which is more natural.

With the ideal of a righteous man here given may be compared these
others: Job's, ch. xxxi., perhaps the most inward in the Old Testament,
Ps. xv.; Is. lviii. 5—7. Such ideals differ from ours principally in that
they seem to consist of conduct exclusively external, while we express

---

[1] [According to Deut. interest may be exacted from a foreigner. In the Law of
Hammurabi it is recognised without limitation. See Johns, *The Oldest Code of Laws*,
§ 49 ff. "Usury" was interest paid in money, "increase" was on food stuffs, and paid
in kind (Johns, *Bab. and Assyr. Laws*, ch. xxiii. p. 253). "The Hebrew legislators,
like the framers of the Mediaeval Canon Law (cf. Ashley, *Economic History*, Bk. I.
iii.), were chiefly thinking of the advantages taken by the rich of the poor in their need,
when interest becomes usury." Lofth., *ad loc.*]

the Lord GOD. If he beget a son that is a robber, a 10
shedder of blood, and ¹that doeth any one of these things,

> ¹ Or, *that doeth to a brother any of these*

our ideal in terms of the thought and feelings. But first, when these
external actions are enumerated it is always assumed that they proceed
from a right condition of mind, of which they are the natural fruit.
Hence the prophet says, "Make you a new heart and a new spirit"
(*v.* 31). The same assumption is made when God is spoken of as
making men righteous by forgiveness, or by bestowing on them prosperity, the sign of righteousness. The mental state corresponding to
this right relation to God is always regarded as present. And in point
of fact the righteousness of God Himself consists in righteous acts, just
as the righteousness of man. The ancient mind fastened on the outward
acts as revealing the inward state, while the modern mind goes directly
to the internal condition. And secondly, moral conduct was never
thought of as the result of a happy or pure disposition, or as the fruit of
prevalent social custom, or obedience to laws called moral or natural ;
it was always regarded as obedience to Divine commandment. Morals
were part of religion. Every moral law was fulfilled in obedience to
God ; hence Jehovah says of this moral man, he "hath walked in my
statutes...he shall surely live" (*v.* 9).

XVIII. **10—13.** SECOND LINK IN THE CHAIN: THIS RIGHTEOUS
MAN IS THE FATHER OF A VIOLENT SON WHO SHEDS BLOOD AND
DOES EVIL ; THE WICKED SON SHALL NOT LIVE BECAUSE OF THE
RIGHTEOUSNESS OF HIS FATHER, HE SHALL DIE IN HIS OWN SIN.

10. *a robber*]   a **man of violence.**

and that doeth any one of these things]   The text is difficult. [The
marg. implies a Heb. construction which is without support.] LXX.
reads : *shedding blood, and committing sins,* 11 *who hath not walked in
the way of his righteous father, but has eaten,* &c. This text gives
the general meaning of the Heb., of which it looks like a paraphrase.
It is difficult to decide whether the last clause of *v.* 10 refers to the
father or the son. The words in the place where they stand should
refer to the wicked son, and so E.VV., but if so they cannot be
reconciled with *v.* 11. The words rendered "these *things*" (*v.* 10)
and "those *duties*" (*v.* 11) are the same, viz. the things *vv.* 6—9, and
cannot be regarded as things forbidden (*v.* 10) and things commanded
(*v.* 11) at once. The word *aḥ, brother* occurring here (cf. *v.* 18, xxi. 20)
is supposed to be the same as "only" (*akh*). but is probably a fragment of the word "one" due to an error of the copyist, and should be
neglected¹.

> ¹ [The last clause of *v.* 10 cannot refer to the father. "These" and "those" are,
> it is true, identified in the Heb., but there is no real difficulty in thus rendering them
> here. Cf. the use of the expression in the original of Is. xlix. 12 ; Ps. xx. 7 ; Heb. 8.
> The word *aḥ*, brother, if genuine here, may mean, as in text of A.V., "the like to
> (*any* one of these *things*)."]

11 and that doeth not any of those *duties*, but even hath eaten
12 upon the mountains, and defiled his neighbour's wife, hath
    wronged the poor and needy, hath spoiled by violence,
    hath not restored the pledge, and hath lifted up his eyes
13 to the idols, hath committed abomination, hath given forth
    upon usury, and hath taken increase: shall he then live?
    he shall not live: he hath done all these abominations: he
14 shall surely ¹die; his blood shall be upon him. Now, lo,
    if he beget a son, that seeth all his father's sins, which he
15 hath done, and ²feareth, and doeth not such like, that hath
    not eaten upon the mountains, neither hath lifted up his
    eyes to the idols of the house of Israel, hath not defiled
16 his neighbour's wife, neither hath wronged any, hath not
    taken aught to pledge, neither hath spoiled by violence,
    but hath given his bread to the hungry, and hath covered
17 the naked with a garment, that hath withdrawn his hand

¹ Heb. *be put to death.*   ² Another reading is, *seeth*, or,
considereth.

11. *and that doeth not*] lit. *and he hath not done any of these
things, but even hath eaten,* &c. The things which he hath not done
are those in *vv.* 6—9 regarded as positive commandments. The words
naturally refer to the wicked son. They are incompatible with those in
the end of *v.* 10, if these be said of the son. Syr., feeling the incompa-
tibility, omits. It is easier, however, to omit the words in *v.* 10, as a
gloss from Lev. iv. 2, because the words "but even hath eaten" require
a negative clause before them. [But see preceding subnote, which
renders omission needless.]

13. *shall surely die*] The formula common in the law, "shall surely
be put to death (as marg.)," Lev. xx. 11; Exod. xxi. 15, xxii. 18.

his blood...upon him] He shall suffer the death due to his own deeds,
ch. xxxiii. 4; Lev. xx. 9; 2 Sam. i. 16.

XVIII. **14—20.** THIRD LINK IN THE CHAIN OF ILLUSTRATION: THIS
UNRIGHTEOUS MAN ON THE OTHER HAND BEGETS A SON WHO,
SEEING HIS FATHER'S INIQUITIES, IS DETERRED BY THEM AND
LIVES RIGHTEOUSLY. THIS SON SHALL NOT DIE FOR THE SINS
OF HIS FATHER, BUT LIVE BECAUSE OF HIS OWN RIGHTEOUS-
NESS.

14. *and feareth*] [So LXX. With a different punctuation the word
would mean, as marg., "seeth, or, considereth." The latter is the
rendering in A.V. here and of both A.V. and R.V. in *v.* 28, where the
Heb. is clear.]

17. *withdrawn his hand*] so as not to injure or oppress—the poor.

from the poor, that hath not received usury nor increase, hath executed my judgements, hath walked in my statutes; he shall not die for the iniquity of his father, he shall surely live.   As for his father, because he cruelly oppressed, 18 spoiled his brother by violence, and did that which is not good among his people, behold, he shall die [1]in his iniquity. Yet say ye, Wherefore doth not the son bear the iniquity 19 of the father?   When the son hath done that which is lawful and right, and hath kept all my statutes, and hath done them, he shall surely live.   The soul that sinneth, it 20 shall die: the son shall not bear the iniquity of the father, neither shall the father bear the iniquity of the son; the righteousness of the righteous shall be upon him, and the wickedness of the wicked shall be upon him.   But if 21 the wicked turn from all his sins that he hath committed, and keep all my statutes, and do that which is lawful and right, he shall surely live, he shall not die.   None of his 22 transgressions that he hath committed shall be remembered

[1] Or, *for*

LXX. reads [probably rightly]: *from iniquity* for "from the poor," but cf. ch. xx. 22 [1].

18.   *spoiled his brother*]   LXX. [probably rightly] omits "brother"; the word is that occurring in *v.* 10.   Here "brother" might stand, though "neighbour" is the term elsewhere used (*vv.* 6, 11).   The word "violence" or robbery has a different form *vv.* 7, 12.

19.   *Yet say ye, Wherefore, &c.?*]   The prophet refers to the current view, and supposes it quoted as an objection to his principle.   So long as the idea prevailed that the son was, so to speak, part of the father, it was natural to suppose that he should be included in the father's punishment; hence the people ask, Why doth not the son bear, lit. *bear part of, share in bearing* (so *v.* 20), the iniquity of the father?   In opposition to this idea the prophet states his principle on both its sides, *vv.* 19, 20.

Secondly, *vv.* 21—32.   As men shall not be involved in the sins of their people or their fathers, so the individual soul shall not lie under the ban of its own past.

The sinner who turneth from his evil and doeth righteousness shall live in his righteousness, *vv.* 21—23.   And on the other hand, the righteous man who turneth away from his righteousness and doeth evil shall die in his evil, *v.* 24.

[1] [The LXX. reading has strong support from modern commentators (Cor., Ber., Kr. &c.).]

against him: in his righteousness that he hath done he
23 shall live.   Have I any pleasure in the death of the
wicked? saith the Lord GOD: and not rather that he should
24 return from his way, and live? But when the righteous
turneth away from his righteousness, and committeth
iniquity, and doeth according to all the abominations that
the wicked man doeth, shall he live? None of his righteous
deeds that he hath done shall be remembered: in his trespass that he hath trespassed, and in his sin that he hath
25 sinned, in them shall he die. Yet ye say, The way of the
Lord is not equal. Hear now, O house of Israel: Is not

23.   The verse meets a feeling of despair both in regard to themselves
and in regard to God which was beginning to take possession of the
minds of some, perhaps many, among the people. The despair in
regard to themselves is seen in ch. xxxiii. 10, "We pine away in them
(our sins); how then should we live?" and the despair in regard to God,
which is but another side of that in regard to themselves, is expressed
in such passages as Lam. iii. 42—44, "We have...rebelled; thou hast
not pardoned...Thou hast covered thyself with a cloud, that our prayer
should not pass through." The Lord had brought the evil on them
which He had purposed (Lam. ii. 8, 17), and it was final (Lam. ii. 9).
The same despondency, though softened in some measure by the
lapse of time, appears in another prophet, Is. xlix. 14, "Zion said,
Jehovah hath forsaken me, and the Lord hath forgotten me." So
long as the state existed the covenant might also be thought to remain, and the prophets could sustain the hearts of men by reminding
them that the Lord was their God; but when the state fell and Israel
was no more in appearance the people of Jehovah, they had to go
behind the covenant and fall back on that unchanging nature of Jehovah
which originated the covenant—that mercy which endureth for ever.
The prevailing disposition of the mind of Jehovah was towards the
salvation of men.

24.   Although it would have sufficed for the prophet's purpose to
assure the repentant sinner of God's forgiveness, he has a certain theoretical interest in the principle which he is insisting on which makes
him develop it on the other side also.

25.   *Yet ye say, The way...equal*]   **And** ye say.   The "way" of the
Lord is the principle on which He acts, or His action on it, Is. lv. 8,
cf. ch. xxxiii. 17, 20.   The objection of the people may really have been
expressed (cf. *v.* 19).   The prophet's principle of the freedom of the
individual and his independence was a novelty running counter to
cherished notions of that age, notions corroborated by much that is seen
in history and life.   The instance of Korah, whose children perished
with him for his sin, the case of Achan, whose transgression was imputed
to the whole camp, the history of Jonathan, and no doubt multitudes of

my way equal? are not your ways unequal? When the 26
righteous man turneth away from his righteousness, and
committeth iniquity, ¹and dieth ²therein; ³in his iniquity that
he hath done shall he die. Again, when the wicked man 27
turneth away from his wickedness that he hath committed,
and doeth that which is lawful and right, he shall save his
soul alive. Because he considereth, and turneth away 28
from all his transgressions that he hath committed, he shall
surely live, he shall not die. Yet saith the house of Israel, 29
The way of the Lord is not equal. O house of Israel, are
not my ways equal? are not your ways unequal? There- 30
fore I will judge you, O house of Israel, every one according
to his ways, saith the Lord GOD. Return ye, and turn
yourselves from all your transgressions; ⁴so iniquity shall
not be your ⁵ruin. Cast away from you all your trans- 31
gressions, wherein ye have transgressed; and make you a
new heart and a new spirit: for why will ye die, O house
of Israel? For I have no pleasure in the death of him 32

---

¹ Or, *he shall die*   ² Or, *because of it*   ³ Or, *for*   ⁴ Or, *so
shall they not be a stumblingblock of iniquity unto you*   ⁵ Heb.
stumblingblock.

---

other instances were familiar to the people where men were treated
collectively and the individuals shared the fate of the mass though
personally innocent. To us now the prophet's principle is self-evident.
Still even to us it is only a theoretical principle, and can be maintained
against facts only by drawing a distinction, which the people in Israel
had not yet learned to draw, between the spiritual relation of the mind
to God and the external history of the individual. See end of chapter.

30—32. Exhortation to repentance founded on the principle that
God will deal with every man according to the condition in which he is
found.

30. *iniquity shall not be your ruin*] More naturally: **that it** (your
transgressing) **be not a stumblingblock of iniquity to you.** Cf. marg.
The transgressions which they are called on to renounce are specially
their idolatries, cf. ch. xiv. 3, vii. 19, xliv. 12.

31. *a new heart*] Cf. ch. xi. 19, xxxvi. 26; Jer. iv. 4, xxiv. 7; Ps.
li. 10. The words are those of practical exhortation; to charge the
prophet with assigning to man a power greater than that which Scripture
in general allows to him is to distort his language. Cf. what he says
on the other side regarding the Divine operation on man, ch. xxxvi.
25—27, xi. 19.

32. The appeal to turn from evil sustained by reference to the

that dieth, saith the Lord GOD : wherefore turn yourselves,
and live.

prevailing nature of God. He is the God of salvation ; His will is
that men should live. The A.V. marg. "*others*" for "yourselves"
is altogether false here and in *v.* 30. The active form "turn" is either
used intransitively, or yourselves (lit. "your faces") is understood, as
expressed in ch. xiv. 6.

(1) The place of the present chapter may be explained by connecting
it with the Messianic prophecy immediately preceding (ch. xvii. 22—24);
the passage enunciates the principles and conditions of entering the
perfect kingdom. The same principles are stated in two other passages,
ch. iii. 16—21, and ch. xxxiii. 1—20. They are properly in place
in the last passage. The prophet feels himself, however, essentially
a prophet of the new age, and writing his Book after the fall of
Jerusalem he may have expanded principles less fully developed at an
earlier time. The age before which he stands is an ideal one, and
principles realized but imperfectly now shall then have full prevalence
(ch. xii. 16, xiv. 22).

(2) The principle which the prophet insists upon is not the strict
retributive righteousness of God, but the moral freedom and independence of the individual person. The individual is not involved
in the destiny of his fathers or of his people ; neither does he lie under
an irrevocable doom pronounced over him by his past life. The immediate relation of every spirit to God and its moral freedom to break
with its own past raises it above both these dooms. What Ezekiel
teaches regarding God is that He hath no pleasure that the wicked
should die. The prophet's whole purpose is practical, to strike off
from the people the shackles of a despair that was settling upon them,
whether they looked to themselves or to God. What he says of men
is that each stands in immediate relation to God and shall live or die
according as he repents or continues in his sin ; and what he teaches
of God is that in spite of the dark clouds of judgement behind which
He seems now hidden His prevailing will is that men should live.

(3) The conception of the prophet is a complex or double one,
having an internal and an external side. The inward element in the
conception is the spiritual relation of the individual person to God ;
the outward element is the form "life" and "death" in which this
internal relation is made manifest, rewarded or punished in God's
treatment of the individual person. We perceive a cleavage taking
place between these two elements. The principles enunciated by the
prophet refer to the spiritual relation of the individual to God, and
are true when limited to this. The individual shall not, in this sense,
suffer for the sins of his people, nor the child for the sins of his father ;
and even his own past life does not weave an inexorable fate around
him from which there is no escape. In all cases, consequences evil
enough may descend upon the son from the father, or upon himself

Moreover, take thou up a lamentation for the princes **19**

from his own past life, but not this particular consequence. His
moral freedom and independence raise him above these consequences,
and bring him as an independent person into direct relation with God,
over against others and even over against his former self. And this is
really all that the prophet is teaching of new truth here. It is truth
which the New Testament teaches, and which is the foundation of all
morals. To charge the prophet with cutting up the individual human
life into sections which have no moral relation to one another, or with
teaching that a man shall live or die according to the condition in which
he shall be found "for the moment" when the judgement overtakes
him, is grossly to distort his language.

It may be true that the prophet has not yet been able fully to
analyse his own complex conception and separate completely the
spiritual relation of the mind to God from the person's external conditions. No Old Testament writer probably has been able to do
this consciously and formally, although it is often done in principle
and in moments of spiritual elevation (Ps. lxxiii. 23 *seq.*, xvii. 14, 15).
But the ideal character of the age which the prophet feels to be about
to dawn, and to which he applies his principles, marks an approach
towards completing the distinction. This future and, though imminent,
ideal time, the time of the perfect kingdom of God, is that which
corresponds to our idea of heaven, or another future world, in which
external condition will perfectly correspond to spiritual state. The
prophet's ideal world, in which spiritual relation would be perfectly
embodied externally, was still the earth. "Life" and "death," in
the ordinary sense of these words, were the only means by which
inward spiritual relations could find proper outward expression[1].

XIX. DIRGE OVER THE PRINCES OF JUDAH.

The elegy represents the princes of Judah as young lions, reared
among lions by the mother lioness, but caught in pits by the nations
and carried away. The mother lioness cannot of course be the natural
mother of the princes, but rather the people, Judah itself. Two
princes are lamented, one captured and carried to Egypt, viz. Jehoahaz,
son and successor of Josiah (*vv.* 1—4); and another carried to Babylon,
who must be Jehoiachin (*vv.* 5—9). The elegy does not appear to
extend further. Verses 10—14 refer to Zedekiah, and are prophetic.
They are connected in general idea with *vv.* 1—9, but the figure for
the mother is now the vine.

---

[1] [See *Introd.* p. liii ff. We may note that the problem of the relation of the individual's moral responsibility to heredity and environment has been a subject of
discussion in various ages and not least in our own. The Greek tragedians dealt
abundantly with it. See Redp., p. 91.]

2 of Israel, and say, What was thy mother? A lioness: she couched among lions, in the midst of the young lions she 3 nourished her whelps. And she brought up one of her whelps; he became a young lion: and he learned to catch

The following table may be useful here.

Josiah falls at Megiddo, B.C. 608.
Jehoahaz his son reigned three months.
Jehoiakim (son of Josiah), 608—597.
Jehoiachin (his son) reigned 3 months.
Zedekiah (son of Josiah), 597—586.
Nebuchadrezzar besieges Jerusalem, (January) 587.
Fall of Jerusalem, 586.

The elegiac measure is maintained in *vv.* 1—8; it is somewhat disturbed in *v.* 9; while *vv.* 10—14 seem in the ordinary measure. The elegiac verse (which may be half or even a third of a full verse) is divided by the caesura into two members of unequal length, the second being shorter, and falling with a mournful cadence[1].

XIX. 1—4. CAPTIVITY OF JEHOAHAZ IN EGYPT.

2.   How was thy mother a lioness!—among the lions;
         In the midst of young lions she couched—she reared her whelps.
3.   And she brought up one of her whelps—he grew a young lion;
         And he learned to catch the prey—he devoured men.
4.   And the nations heard regarding him—he was taken in their pit;
         And they brought him with hooks—unto the land of Egypt.

1.   *princes of Israel*]   Probably with LXX. *prince*, as required by the pron. *thy* mother (*v.* 2). The "prince" is a general term for the king, applicable to one king after another [see on vii. 27]. The lamentation is for the "king" of Judah, represented by one person after another. For "lamentation" cf. Jer. vii. 29.

2.   *What was thy mother?*]   Rather to be taken as an exclamation, as rendered above. The mother is the people Israel, a lioness among other lions—kings or states with royalty[2].

3.   The first young lion is Jehoahaz, son of Josiah, carried to Egypt by Pharaoh Necho after the defeat of his father at Megiddo, 2 Kgs xxiii. 31—35. Cf. the touching reference to him Jer. xxii. 10—12. He also bore the name of Shallum. Coming to the throne at the age of 23 he reigned only 3 months, and died in Egypt. Cf. Jer. v. 26.

---

1 [For this metre, called *Kinah, lamentation*, see further on Amos v. 2 in this Series, or Driver, *Introd. to Lit. of O. T.* ed. 9, pp. 296 note, 457, or E. G. King, *Early Religious Poetry of the Hebrews*, pp. 39 ff. Other examples of this metre in Ezekiel are xxvi. 17, 18, xxviii. 18, 19 and parts of xxxii. 17—32.]

2 [But Kr. takes it literally as referring to Hamutal, mother of Jehoahaz. He points out the prominence accorded customarily to the queen mother (1 Kgs xv. 13, &c.), and in particular, to her sharing the exile from Jerusalem (2 Kgs xxiv. 15).]

the prey, he devoured men. The nations also heard of 4
him; he was taken in their pit: and they brought him with
hooks unto the land of Egypt. Now when she saw that 5
she had waited, and her hope was lost, then she took
another of her whelps, and made him a young lion. And 6
he went up and down among the lions, he became a young
lion: and he learned to catch the prey, he devoured men.

4. *heard of him*] This might be better read: *raised a cry against
him*, in the sense of Is. xxxi. 4; Jer. l. 29.
with hooks] or, rings, as ch. xxix. 4, xxxviii. 4; cf. 2 Kgs xix. 28.

XIX. 5—9.   JEHOIACHIN CARRIED CAPTIVE TO BABYLON.

The second young lion is Jehoiachin. The intermediate prince Jehoiakim could not be included in an elegy, because he died in peace[1].
It is the princes of Israel whom foreign nations captured that are
lamented. What is touched upon is more the humiliation and sorrow
of Israel, the mother lioness, in her young lions being captured, than
the fate of the two *persons*. The elegy is a national one, cf. on *v.* 1.

5. And she saw that she had waited—her hope was lost;
And she took another of her whelps—she made him a young
lion.
6. And he walked among the lions—he grew a young lion,
And he learned to catch the prey—he devoured men.
7. And he broke down their palaces—he wasted their cities;
And the land and its fulness was desolate—at the noise of his
roaring.
8. Then the nations set themselves against him—on every side from
the countries.
And they spread their net over him—he was taken in their pit.

5. *that she had waited*] [LXX. read "that he had been driven
from her."] If "she" be subject some such sense as deceived, "disappointed" (Ew.) would be suitable, though to reach this sense by
adding "in vain" to "waited" is hardly permissible. The subject might
be "her hope," and waited might mean tarried, *delayed*. There might
be reference to hope of the return of Jehoahaz, which appears to have
been cherished, as Jeremiah takes occasion altogether to cut it off (Jer.
xxii. 10—12). Cor. proposes "acted foolishly," but the word suggested
is too strong (Numb. xii. 11; Is. xix. 13; Jer. v. 4, l. 36).
6. Jehoiachin ascended the throne on the death of his father at the
age of 18. He reigned only 3 months, when Nebuchadrezzar carried
him away to Babylon, 2 Kgs xxiv. 8 *seq.*

[1] [But it is difficult to describe his end thus in the face of Jer. xxii. 19.]

7 And he knew their [1]palaces, and laid waste their cities ; and the land was desolate, and the fulness thereof, because of 8 the noise of his roaring.   Then the nations set against him on every side from the provinces : and they spread their 9 net over him ; he was taken in their pit.   And they put him in a cage with hooks, and brought him to the king of Babylon ; they brought him into strong holds, that his voice should no more be heard upon the mountains of Israel.

10   Thy mother was like a vine, [2]in thy blood, planted by the

[1] Or, *widows*   [2] See ch. xvi. 6.   Or, *in thy likeness*

7.   *knew their palaces*]   The word means usually "widows" as marg., but "palaces," Is. xiii. 22.   Neither translation gives any sense. Better : *he broke down their palaces* (change of *r* for *d*) ; or cf. Jer. ii. 15, 16 (marg. *fed on*), a passage very similar.   If "widows" be read the verb would need to be altered to "multiplied," ch. xxii. 25, an important passage (Jer. xv. 8).   Cor. (partly Hitz.): "and he lay down in his den, he wasted the forests."   This keeps up the figure, but requires serious alteration of the reading.   Jer. ii. 15 shews that "young lions" may burn cities, and feed on the crown of the head.

8.   *in their pit*]   A well-known method of capturing dangerous beasts.   The object to "set" may be voice or shout, *v.* 4, Jer. xii. 8.

9.   *with hooks*]   See *v.* 4.   The elegiac measure is not maintained in this verse.   Possibly the original form of the verse has not been preserved.   If the words "they brought him into strong holds" were omitted, an elegiac verse, though less regular, would be restored.

XIX. 10—14. THE FATE OF ZEDEKIAH AND HIS COUNTRY, ON WHICH HE HAS BROUGHT RUIN.

Israel was once a spreading vine by great waters; her branches rose into the clouds, and her rods were rulers' sceptres—a powerful race of kings rose out of her.   Now she is torn up and thrown down, carried into the wilderness, and planted in a dry and barren soil.   A fire also has gone out from one of her strong rods which has consumed her. Her last prince, Zedekiah, has finally broken the state to pieces (cf. ch. xvii.).

10.   *was like a vine*]   **was** like, in contrast to "And now she is planted in the wilderness" (*v.* 13).   The "prince" of Israel is addressed, not any individual prince, but the kingship or royalty by whomsoever represented.   The mother, as before[1], is the people or nationality of Israel.

in thy blood]   R.V. marg. refers to ch. xvi. 6, not wisely.   LXX. read "and as a flower on a pomegranate" (*brmn* for *bdmk*).   Ew.

[1] [But see note on *v.* 2.]

waters : she was fruitful and full of branches by reason of
many waters. And she had strong rods for the sceptres 11
of them that bare rule, and ¹their stature was exalted among
the ²thick boughs, and ³they were seen in ¹their height with
the multitude of ¹their branches. But she was plucked up 12
in fury, she was cast down to the ground, and the east wind
dried up her fruit : her strong rods were broken off and
withered ; the fire consumed them. And now she is 13
planted in the wilderness, in a dry and thirsty land. And 14
fire is gone out of ⁴the rods of her branches, it hath
devoured her fruit, so that there is in her no strong rod
to be a sceptre to rule. This is a lamentation, and shall
be for a lamentation.

¹ Heb. *his.*   ² Or, *clouds*   ³ Heb. *he was.*   ⁴ Or, *a rod*

suggests : "a vine of Carmel," Ges. "a vine of thy vineyard" [and
similarly Kr.]; Cor. as usual is for omitting. Others : "in thy likeness,"
"in thy thought," "in thy rest"—all without sense. More tolerable :
"in her height" (*bĕrumah*), cf. *v.* 11.

11. *sceptres...bare rule*] Or, **for rulers' sceptres,** i.e. royal sceptres.
Out of Israel this vine there rose powerful native kings.

among the thick boughs] Or, as marg. *clouds*, cf. xxxi. 3, 10, 14.
The phrase is designedly hyperbolical, to express the power of Israel in
earlier times. Jer. xi. 16, 17.

were seen in their height] conspicuously and from afar. The Heb.,
as the marg., has "he," "his" referring directly to Zedekiah.

12. Destruction of the vine, the nationality of Israel. The figures
employed are usual, ch. xvii. 9, 10, xxxi. 12; Am. ix. 15.

13. The deportation of the people from their own land into conditions where national life cannot thrive.

14. The fire that consumed the vine went out from her own rods.
The royal house brought destruction on the nation as well as on itself.
Reference is to the rebellion of Zedekiah.

gone out of the rods] The reference to Zedekiah (marg. *a rod*) is
expressed generally in terms of the royal house.

shall be for a lamentation] lit. *and is become a lamentation.* Sad
enough is the history, ch. xxxii. 16. It is not necessary, however, to
infer from this that the lamentation was written after the exile[1]. The
passage *vv.* 10—14 is prophetic, cf. Is. xlvii. ; Jer. ix. 16—21. In the
Book of Kings both Jehoahaz and Jehoiachin are said to have "done
evil." A three months' reign afforded little scope for much mischief.

[1] [But, if we accept the text as vocalised, we must render, "and *it was,*" thus
dating the words after the exile had begun, or making them to be a later insertion.
If on the other hand we point the consonants differently, we must render (not "shall
be" but) *let it be* (*become*).]

20   And it came to pass in the seventh year, in the fifth
month, the tenth *day* of the month, that certain of the
elders of Israel came to inquire of the LORD, and sat
2 before me.   And the word of the LORD came unto me,
3 saying, Son of man, speak unto the elders of Israel, and
say unto them, Thus saith the Lord GOD: Are ye come
to inquire of me?   As I live, saith the Lord GOD, I will

Ezekiel's treatment of the young lions is ideal, and in the case of
Jehoiachin the reference is rather to the evils which his attitude
brought upon the country, than to any ravages which he wrought
personally.

XX.—XXIV. FURTHER PREDICTIONS REGARDING THE FALL OF JERUSALEM.

These chapters pursue the same subject as that which occupied the
prophet in previous chapters, the destruction of the state, though they
appear to look at it from another point of view, and suggest another
motive for it—Jehovah's regard to His own name.

First, ch. xx.   Review of Israel's past history and emphasising of the
principle which has given Israel a history and saved her from destruction,
viz. Jehovah's regard to His own name.

Second, ch. xxi.   But this same principle—regard to His name—
requires Israel's dispersion now.   Therefore the sword of the Lord
is whetted against her.

Third, ch. xxii., xxiii.   New exhibition of the sins of Israel.

Fourth, ch. xxiv.   Final judgement on Jerusalem, under the figure of
a rusted caldron set upon the fire to cleanse it.

Ch. xx. has two divisions :

(1) *vv.* 1—29.   The principle that has saved Israel from destruction
and given her a history—Jehovah's respect to His own name.

(2) *vv.* 30—44.   The same principle will rule what of Israel's history
still lies in the future.

XX. 1—4. INTRODUCTORY.

Certain elders came to the prophet to inquire of the Lord, in the
seventh year of the captivity of Jehoiachin and tenth day of the fifth
month—Aug. 590 B.C., four years before Jerusalem fell. [For the
elders cf. viii. 1, xvi. 1.]

3.   *will not be inquired of*]   The proposed inquiries of the elders
probably related to something in the present; to such men no answer
will be given except to read the lesson of Israel's history to them.   For
the history concerns them.   They are one in spirit and conduct with
Israel of the past, and the principles which have ruled the former
history will rule also the history to come.

not be inquired of by you. Wilt thou judge them, son 4
of man, wilt thou judge them? cause them to know the
abominations of their fathers; and say unto them, Thus 5
saith the Lord GOD: In the day when I chose Israel, and
lifted up mine hand unto the seed of the house of Jacob,
and made myself known unto them in the land of Egypt,
when I lifted up mine hand unto them, saying, I am the
LORD your God; in that day I lifted up mine hand unto 6
them, to bring them forth out of the land of Egypt into
a land that I had espied for them, flowing with milk and
honey, which is the glory of all lands: and I said unto 7
them, Cast ye away every man the abominations of his
eyes, and defile not yourselves with the idols of Egypt;

4. *Wilt thou judge*] The interrogative seems to have the sense of an
impatient imperative, and the repetition gives stronger expression to the
imperative, cf. ch. xxii. 2, xxiii. 36. "Judge" is explained by "cause
them to know the abominations of their fathers." To rehearse the
history of the fathers is to hold the mirror up to themselves.

XX. 5—29. REVIEW OF THE HISTORY OF THE FATHERS.

The principle that has ruled this history is that all through it Jehovah
has acted for His name's sake. It is this principle that has given Israel
a history, otherwise their sins would have cut them off. For His name's
sake He spared the people in Egypt (*v.* 9), again in the wilderness (*v.* 14),
and again the second generation there (*v.* 22). The history is reviewed
in these divisions: *vv.* 5—10 Israel in Egypt; *vv.* 11—17 the people
led out into the wilderness; *vv.* 18—26 the children of those who fell in
the wilderness; and *vv.* 27—29 the people that entered Canaan.

5. *when I chose Israel*] The choice or election of Israel is referred
to only here in Ezek., and also once in Jeremiah, xxxiii. 24. The idea is
much insisted on in Is. xl.—lxvi., but appears already in Deut. vii. 6.

lifted up mine hand] i.e. sware, Exod. vi. 8; Numb. xiv. 30. The
thing sworn is stated *v.* 6.

made myself known] Cf. Exod. iii. 6 *seq.*, vi. 3. He made Himself
known as Jehovah their God, whose nature His acts revealed,
Ps. ciii. 7.

6. On "milk and honey" cf. Exod. iii. 8; and on the idea of Canaan
as the "glory" of all lands, a frequent judgement in late writings, cf.
Jer. iii. 19; Dan. viii. 9; Ps. xlvii. 2.

7. *abominations of his eyes*] Those to which his eyes and desires
were directed, the idols, cf. xviii. 6; Numb. xv. 39. The prophet
charges Israel with idolatry in Egypt (ch. xxiii. 3). Though history
as we have it says little of such a thing, it may be assumed as certain, considering the people's readiness to adopt the worship of their neighbours

8 I am the LORD your God. But they rebelled against me, and would not hearken unto me; they did not every man cast away the abominations of their eyes, neither did they forsake the idols of Egypt: then I said I would pour out my fury upon them, to accomplish my anger against them 9 in the midst of the land of Egypt. But I wrought for my name's sake, that it should not be profaned in the sight

throughout their history. The same view appears in Josh. xxiv. 14; cf. Lev. xviii 3.

The question how far Jehovah was known and worshipped in Egypt is an obscure one. The name cannot have been altogether unknown or the people could not have been rallied by Moses to His service nor induced to put themselves under His protection. That His worship, however, was mixed with impurities may be assumed. How far the people partook in the worship of Egyptian deities cannot be ascertained[1].

8. The history in Exodus narrates only the conflict of Israel with the Egyptians, being silent on internal struggles in Israel itself. The work of Moses in delivering his people must have extended over a period of time. His efforts in educating the people are entirely passed over in the history. The announcement, however, that Jehovah was the God of Israel implied casting away all other gods, and this principle, often expressed in His intercourse with the people, probably met with but slack acceptance. Ps. cvi. follows Ezek. closely throughout, cf. *v.* 7.

9. *for my name's sake*] This idea, very common in this prophet, also in Is. xl.—lxvi., does not appear in the earlier prophets, except Is. xxxvii. 35. Cf. however, Deut. ix. 28, 29; Jer. xiv. 7, 21; Is. xliii. 25, xlviii. 9, 11. Jehovah's name expresses that which He is, or has revealed Himself to be, and the phrase does not differ from "for my own sake," cf. ch. xxxvi. 22, 32.

should not be profaned] The words explain, "for my name's sake," viz. lest it should be profaned among the nations. Deut. ix. 28, 29 suggests one way in which the name of Jehovah might be profaned among the nations. To "profane" is the opposite of to "sanctify." The one is to cherish any thoughts of Jehovah or to attribute any deed to Him inconsistent with His being the one true God, or derogatory to Him who is so. To "sanctify" Him is to recognise Him in thought and in act, particularly in worship, to be the one true God; to assign to Him attributes and operations befitting His nature, and to live in such a way as those who are the people of Jehovah ought to live, for the manner of the people is reflected in the character of their God (Am. ii. 7). This is the way, at least, in which Ezek., with the conception

---

[1] [For the influence of Egyptian religion upon Jewish residents in the 5th cent. B.C. see Sayce, *Aramaic Papyri discovered at Assuan*, 1906, or Handcock, *Latest Light on Bible Lands*, pp. 188 ff.]

of the nations, among whom they were, in whose sight
I made myself known unto them, in bringing them forth
out of the land of Egypt. So I caused them to go forth out 10
of the land of Egypt, and brought them into the wilderness.
And I gave them my statutes, and ¹shewed them my judge- 11
ments, which if a man do, he shall live ²in them. Moreover 12
also I gave them my sabbaths, to be a sign between me

---

¹ Heb. *made them to know.*   ² Or, *by*

---

of Jehovah which in his age he had reached, uses the terms "profane"
and "sanctify."

in whose sight]   [Cf. *vv.* 14, 22, and Lev. xxvi. 45.]

11—17.   The people delivered from Egypt and brought into the
wilderness.   There also Jehovah wrought for His name's sake.

10.   First half of the verse is wanting in LXX.

11.   *gave them my statutes*]   Reference is to the Sinaitic legislation.
The fact of the legislation is confirmed by the prophet, but his language
"statutes" and "judgements" does not enable us to form an opinion
how extensive it was, nor what particulars it embraced besides the law
of the sabbath (*v.* 12), and of course the law that Jehovah was God
alone of Israel, because he uses the combination "statutes" and "judgements" very generally, for example of the conduct and principles of
the people in the wilderness themselves (*v.* 18).

shall live in them]   Or, as marg., *shall live by them.*   [Cf. *vv.* 13, 21,
and Lev. xviii. 5.]   Obedience to them will issue in "life," the word
being used in its natural sense, Deut. iv. 40, "thou shalt keep his
statutes...that thou mayest prolong thy days upon the land," Deut. v. 16
(fifth commandment).   The precepts of Jehovah given to the people
were such that obedience to them would ensure prosperity and life,
while disobedience would cause calamity and death, and this not only
in the mere government of them by their God, but because the statutes
were in themselves "good," cf. *v.* 25; Hos. viii. 3; Am. v. 14; Mic.
iii. 2, vi. 8.

12.   *my sabbaths*]   The plural refers to the stated recurrence of the
day; other festivals are not included.

to be a sign]   The prophet does not speak of the Sabbath as an older
institution than the Exodus, though his language does not decide the
point, as he refers merely to the connexion into which the day was
brought with Israel's redemption (as Deut. v. 15) and made a "sign"
to them of their relation to Jehovah.   The people were commanded to
"sanctify" the Sabbath, i.e. to dedicate it and keep it to the Lord.
This dedication of a part of their time or life to Jehovah had a similar
significance to the dedication of the firstfruits of the ground and the
firstlings of their cattle; it was an acknowledgment that they were the
Lord's.   It was the response on their side to the operation of Jehovah
on His side in "sanctifying" them, or making them His own possession

and them, that they might know that ¹I am the LORD that
13 sanctify them.   But the house of Israel rebelled against me
in the wilderness: they walked not in my statutes, and they
rejected my judgements, which if a man do, he shall live ²in
them; and my sabbaths they greatly profaned: then I said
I would pour out my fury upon them in the wilderness, to
14 consume them.   But I wrought for my name's sake, that
it should not be profaned in the sight of the nations, in
15 whose sight I brought them out.   Moreover also I lifted up
my hand unto them in the wilderness, that I would not
bring them into the land which I had given them, flowing
with milk and honey, which is the glory of all lands;
16 because they rejected my judgements, and walked not in
my statutes, and profaned my sabbaths: for their heart
17 went after their idols.   Nevertheless mine eye spared them
from destroying them, neither did I make a full end of
18 them in the wilderness.   And I said unto their children

---

¹ Or, *I the LORD do sanctify them*   ² Or, *by*

(end of *v.*).   Thus the Sabbath was a "sign" or visible token that He
was their God and they His people (*v.* 20); Exod. xxxi. 13, 14; Is. lvi.
2, 4.   This meaning of the Sabbath as a symbol of the religion of Jehovah
explains the importance attached to keeping it, particularly in the exile;
its observance sustained the feeling of the people among the heathen
that they were the people of Jehovah, Is. lvi. 2 *seq.*, lviii. 13; Neh. xiii.
19, cf. Jer. xvii. 21; Lev. xix. 3, xxvi. 2.

13.   Provocation of the people in the wilderness.   They rejected the
statutes of Jehovah and "profaned" His sabbaths, i.e. failed to dedicate
and keep them to Jehovah.   The profanation is to be taken in a wider
sense than the special instances of neglect, Exod. xvi. 27; Numb. xv. 32.
This profanation of the Sabbath was oblivion of the covenant, cf. Am.
viii. 5.

pour out my fury]   Cf. Exod. xxxii. 10 *seq.*; Numb. xiv. 11, 12, 29.

14, 15.   For His name's sake Jehovah did not make a clean end of
the people, nevertheless He sware that the generation that came out of
Egypt should not enter into the land of promise, Numb. xiv. 22, 23, 29;
Deut. i. 35; Ps. xcv. 11.

16.   *went after their idols*]   Exod. xxxii.; Numb. xxv.; Hos. ix. 10.
Am. v. 25 cannot be appealed to here.

17.   Another motive besides regard for His own name moved Jehovah
to spare Israel—pity for the sinners; cf. Ps. lxxviii. 38, "But he, being
full of compassion, forgave their iniquity, and destroyed them not: yea,
many a time turned he his anger away."   Numb. xiv. 20.

18—26.   The second generation in the wilderness.   These only

in the wilderness, Walk ye not in the statutes of your
fathers, neither observe their judgements, nor defile yourselves with their idols: I am the LORD your God; walk 19
in my statutes, and keep my judgements, and do them:
and hallow my sabbaths; and they shall be a sign between 20
me and you, that ye may know that I am the LORD your
God.   But the children rebelled against me; they walked 21
not in my statutes, neither kept my judgements to do them,
which if a man do, he shall live ¹in them; they profaned
my sabbaths: then I said I would pour out my fury upon
them, to accomplish my anger against them in the wilderness.   Nevertheless I withdrew mine hand, and wrought 22
for my name's sake, that it should not be profaned in the
sight of the nations, in whose sight I brought them forth.
Moreover I lifted up mine hand unto them in the wilder- 23
ness, that I would scatter them among the nations, and
disperse them through the countries; because they had not 24
executed my judgements, but had rejected my statutes, and
had profaned my sabbaths, and their eyes were after their

¹ Or, *by*

imitated the sins of their fathers, Numb. xxv. 1, 2; Deut. ix. 23, 24,
xxxi. 27.

22.   *withdrew mine hand*] lit. turned, or turned back his hand,
outstretched to smite. [The Heb. seems to imply a continuous or
repeated action.]   The words are wanting in LXX., and in the other
verses (*vv.* 9, 14) the phrase "I wrought for my name's sake" begins
the verse.

23—26.   Yet, though He wrought for His name's sake not to destroy
them, their sins could not be altogether passed by.   In two ways they
were marked: Jehovah laid upon the people a heavy threat of dispersion
among all nations, *vv.* 23, 24; and He gave them laws that were not
good, that by following them they might be destroyed, *vv.* 25, 26.

23.   *Moreover I lifted up*] lit. *And I on my part*, so *v.* 25.

scatter them among the nations]   The people entered Canaan laden with
this heavy threat for their sins in the wilderness.   Such threats were
always conditional, Jer. xviii. 8.   Cf. Jonah's denunciation of Nineveh.
This conditional character is expressed in other passages where a similar idea occurs, Lev. xxvi. 33 *seq.*   The prophet hardly means that the
exile was due to the people's sins in the wilderness, except in so far as
the moral character of the people remained the same throughout down
to the generation then living.   But cf. Exod. xxxii. 34.

25 fathers' idols. Moreover also I gave them statutes that
were not good, and judgements [1]wherein they should not
26 live; and I polluted them in their own gifts, in that they
[2]caused to pass through *the fire* all that openeth the womb,

    [1] Or, *whereby*   [2] Or, *set apart all* See Exod. xiii. 12.

25. *I gave them statutes...wherein* (better marg. *whereby*) *they
should not live*] These statutes are of a kind contrary to those given
before (*v.* 11) which were good. It seems plain (1) that the practice
referred to is that of passing the firstborn male children through the
fire as a burnt-offering to the deity. (2) The law in Israel was that
while firstlings of animals were to be offered, firstlings of men were
to be redeemed (Exod. xiii. 2, 12, 13, xxii. 29; cf. Numb. iii. 46, 47,
xviii. 15, 16). But in imitation of heathen nations the practice of
offering the firstborn of animals was extended so as to include children.
The practice was one prevailing among the peoples around Israel[1];
but in Jer. vii. 31, xix. 5 Jehovah vehemently protests that to command
it never came into His mind. Jeremiah expressly repudiates the false
idea that the sacrifice of children was commanded by Jehovah, and
it cannot be supposed that Ezekiel here contradicts him. The command to sacrifice children to Jehovah cannot be supposed to have
formed part of the Mosaic law. But what we now speak of *as permitted* by God is in the O.T. often attributed to His direct agency.
As a judicial punishment for their sins He left them to follow their
own ideas, which they came to attribute to His authority. In the
words of Ps. lxxxi. 12, "I let them go after the stubbornness of their
heart, that they might walk in their own counsels."
So here "I gave" and (*v.* 26) "I polluted" are equivalent to "I let
them have" and "I let them be polluted."
To whom the children were offered, lit. passed over (in the fire), it is
not quite easy to decide. In passages where the practice is condemned
it is represented as a sacrifice to "the Molech," Lev. xviii. 21; Deut. xii.
31, xviii. 10, or to the Baal, Jer. vii. 31, or generally, to the idols, Ezek.
xvi. 21; Ps. cvi. 38 ("idols of Canaan"). Though the spelling of the
name Molech is peculiar, the word probably means "the king" originally,
just as the Baal means "the lord," both names being descriptive of
the same deity[2]. In Is. lvii. 9 "the king" has the ordinary spelling.
Though borrowing the practice from the Canaanites it is probable that
in Israel the sacrifice was offered to Jehovah, particularly as the law
under which it was made was considered given by Him. On the other
hand Jer., though repudiating this popular inference, speaks of the
offering as being made to Baal. The name "Baal," however, from
Hosea downwards is used with some laxity, including the images of

    [1] [See as to the origin of the custom in heathendom, Driver, *Exodus* (*C. B.*) xiii. 12,
and p. 409.]
    [2] [See Barnes on 1 Kgs xi. 5 in this Series.]

that I might make them desolate, to the end that they might
know that I am the LORD.

Therefore, son of man, speak unto the house of Israel, 27
and say unto them, Thus saith the Lord GOD: In this
moreover have your fathers blasphemed me, in that they
have committed a trespass against me. For when I had 28
brought them into the land, which I lifted up mine hand

Jehovah, and all heathenish ceremonies in his service are called worship
of Baal.

Whether the people, familiar with the Baal worship, drew the
false inference from the law of the firstborn, or whether false teachers
set the idea before them, is uncertain (Jer. viii. 8 appears to refer to
written perversions of the law). The sacrifice of children was a practice
that gained ground in the disastrous times before the exile. Ezekiel
appears to regard the practice as ancient, as he connects it with the
second generation in the wilderness. The instances noted in early
history are transjordanic (Jud. xi. 31; 2 Kgs xvi. 3), and possibly,
though the practice became aggravated only at a later period, the
prophet may have considered that the people became acquainted with
it on the other side of the Jordan.

26. *might make them desolate*] Or, **destroy them**; less probably,
horrify them (ch. xxxii. 10). The train of thought is the same as that
expressed in ch. xiv. 9. The penalty of sin is further delusion and
worse sin, the end of which is death. The last clause "to the end…
LORD" is wanting in LXX.

27—29. The people on their entry and in their abode in Canaan.

27. *In this moreover*] i.e. the following act, v. 28, cf. xxiii. 38.

have…blasphemed…have committed] Past tense: **blasphemed**…*they*
committed. The blasphemy is not in words, but in high-handed disregard of the commands, Numb. xv. 30.

28. The prophet regards the worship on the high-places and under
the evergreen trees as a Canaanitish usage adopted by Israel, as Deut.
xii. 2, 30 f. At the same time Israel usually employed the altars or chapels
which they found for the service of Jehovah; but naturally many
corruptions would creep into such service, and it might become little
different from a service of Baal. In the oldest prophets, Amos and
Hosea, it is the *kind* of worship at the high-places that is condemned,
the revelry and heathenish merrymaking (Hos. ix. 1), the sensuousness
(Hos. viii. 13; Am. v. 21), and the false conception of deity implied in
it (Hos. vi. 6). The mere localities or multitude of altars do not seem
assailed, except that the more there were of them the more sin was
committed, because the whole worship was sinful (Hos. viii. 11; Am.
iv. 4). Later this impure worship was perceived to be inseparable from
the high-places and these themselves came under condemnation.
Ezekiel does not go further in his condemnation of the high hills and
green trees than his predecessor Jeremiah (Jer. ii. 20, iii. 6).

to give unto them, then they ¹saw every high hill, and every
thick tree, and they offered there their sacrifices, and there
they presented the provocation of their offering, there also
they made their sweet savour, and they poured out there
29 their drink offerings. Then I said unto them, What
meaneth the high place ²whereunto ye go? So the name
30 thereof is called ³Bamah unto this day. Wherefore say

¹ Or, *looked out for*   ² Or, *whereunto ye go, and the name*
whereof...day?   ³ That is, *High place.*

every thick tree] Evergreen and umbrageous trees appear to have
been regarded as abodes of deity.

offered...their sacrifices] Four words are employed: offerings of flesh,
particularly the peace or thank-offerings; what is called their "offering"
or oblation, a general word used of bloodless sacrifices as well as of
others, possibly firstfruits and the like; their "sweet savour," usually
said of the odour of the flesh or fat burnt upon the altar, but also of the
odour of meal-offerings (ch. xvi. 19); and finally, drink-offerings. The
clause "and there...provocation of their offering" is wanting in LXX.
The term "offering" (Korban) is found only in Lev., Numb., and again
in Ezek. xl. 43 (see there).

29. The word *bamah*, "high-place," has no certain etymology,
though often used and at an early period, e.g. in David's elegy on Saul
(2 Sam. i. 19), and in Moabite (Mesha's inscription). The prophet here
introduces a punning and contemptuous derivation of the word. Jehovah
asks "what (*mah*) meaneth the high place to which ye go (*ba*)?" and
the prophet seems to consider the word composed of these two syllables.
Some have supposed that "go" has the sense of "go in," and that the
allusion is to the immoralities practised on the high places (Am. ii. 7;
Hos. iv. 13, 14). This idea does not seem expressed in the words;
neither is there much probability in the conjecture that they are borrowed by Ezek. from some older prophet (Ew.).

The prophet's view of the generation of the Exodus differs from that
of earlier prophets, e.g. Hos. ix. 10; Jer. ii. 2. The generation in the
wilderness was probably not a homogeneous one, and the narratives
which we possess represent its conduct as various at different times.
Two views might be taken of it, and Ezek., as his manner is, takes the
severer view.

XX. 30—44. Jehovah's regard to His own name will fashion
    the history of the people to come as it has fashioned
    the past.

Having reviewed the past and shewn the elders their own picture in
the doings of their fathers, and how the thing which has fashioned the
history in the past has been Jehovah's regard for His own name, the

unto the house of Israel, Thus saith the Lord GOD: Do
ye pollute yourselves after the manner of your fathers?
and go ye a whoring after their abominations? and when 31
ye offer your gifts, when ye make your sons to pass through
the fire, do ye pollute yourselves with all your idols, unto
this day? and shall I be inquired of by you, O house of
Israel? As I live, saith the Lord GOD, I will not be
inquired of by you: and that which cometh into your 32
mind shall not be at all; in that ye say, We will be as the

prophet now comes to read to them the history of the future as the
same regard of Jehovah for His name will model it.

First, *vv.* 30—34. The Lord will not give any answer to such
inquirers who follow the ways of their fathers. But they may be assured
that their resolution to assimilate themselves to the heathen and become
like them worshippers of wood and stone shall not be permitted to have
effect. Jehovah *will* assert His sovereignty over them, and will gather
them out from among the heathen as He gathered their fathers from
among the Egyptians.

Secondly, *vv.* 35—40. He will bring them out from the nations into
the wilderness of the peoples, as He brought their fathers into the
wilderness of Egypt, and will plead with them anew as He pleaded
with their fathers in days long ago—and with the same result that the
rebels among them shall fall in the wilderness, but the remnant shall
again in the mountain height of Israel serve the Lord, who will accept
them.

Thirdly, *vv.* 41—44. And from this restoration these things shall
follow: 1. Jehovah shall be sanctified, seen to be God and acknowledged by the nations (*v.* 41). 2. Israel shall know what Jehovah is,
when He fulfils His ancient promise to the fathers to give them this land
(*v.* 42). 3. They shall then lay to heart their past doings and loathe
themselves (*v.* 43). 4. They shall see that not according to their
evil has Jehovah dealt with them all through their history and in their
restoration, but has wrought for His name's sake (*v.* 44).

30, 31. The Lord will not give Himself to be inquired of by such
men. What they desire to know about others or themselves they shall
be left in ignorance of; but *He* has something to tell them regarding
Himself.

32. The prophet regards the worship on the high-places as Canaanitish heathenism; but probably many of the exiles to whom he spoke
were drifting into complete conformity with the nations among whom
they were. Their minds were losing hold of their distinctiveness as the
people of Jehovah. This practical assimilation to the heathen the
prophet represents as a deliberate one, which in many cases it may have
been—cf. the answer of the exiles in Egypt to Jeremiah, xliv. 15—19,
also Jer. ii. 25.

nations, as the families of the countries, to serve wood and
33 stone.   As I live, saith the Lord GOD, surely with a mighty
hand, and with a stretched out arm, and with fury poured
34 out, will I be king over you: and I will bring you out
from the peoples, and will gather you out of the countries
wherein ye are scattered, with a mighty hand, and with
35 a stretched out arm, and with fury poured out: and I will
bring you into the wilderness of the peoples, and there will
36 I plead with you face to face.   Like as I pleaded with your
fathers in the wilderness of the land of Egypt, so will I
37 plead with you, saith the Lord GOD.   And I will cause

to serve wood and stone]   The service of the heathen is a service of
wood and stone, Deut. iv. 28, xxviii. 36; Is. xxxvii. 19.   The images
were often of wood, plated with some precious metal (Is. xl. 19; Jer. x.
4; Is. xxx. 22), or of stone; often, however, of baser metal overlaid
with gold or silver.   It is the dead matter in opposition to Jehovah, the
living God, that gives point to the antithesis.   On "cometh into your
mind" cf. xi. 5; Jer. vii. 31, xix. 5; Is. x. 7.

33.   This resolution of the people to sink themselves among the
heathen shall not stand; Jehovah *will* assert His sovereignty over them,
amidst terrible manifestations of His power and anger.

be king over you]   The mighty hand (Exod. xiii. 9; Deut. v. 15) and
the stretched out arm (Exod. vi. 6; Deut. iii. 19, xi. 2, &c.), were
turned at the Exodus against their enemies, here partly at least they are
directed upon the disobedient people themselves (*v.* 35).

34.   *the peoples*]   Though Israel was in captivity in the Babylonian
empire, this empire embraced many peoples, the world as it was then
known (cf. ch. xvii.).   Formerly Israel was entangled among the
Egyptians, now it is entangled among all nations; it shall now be
gathered out as it was in the former age.

35.   *of the peoples*]   This wilderness of the peoples is the Syro-
Babylonian wilderness, adjoining the peoples among whom they were
dispersed; as that into which their fathers were brought was the
wilderness of Egypt, i.e. adjoining Egypt.   Is. xl. 1—11 also represents Jehovah as marching at the head of His people, redeemed from
exile, through the wilderness from Babylon to Jerusalem.   Ezek. may
ollow Hos. ii. 14, 15, but cf. Jer. xxxi. 2 *seq.*

plead...face to face]   With no intermediaries, no heathen people on
whose fellowship they could stay themselves, absolutely cut off from men
and alone with their God (Hos. ii. 14).   Jehovah's "pleading" or litiga-
tion is sometimes in terrible deeds (ch. xvii. 20), sometimes in words of
reason (Is. i. 18; Mic. vi. 2 *seq.*).   Gathered out from the nations and
far from their seductive influences Israel will respond to the discipline
of her God as in former days (Hos. ii. 15).

you to pass under the rod, and I will bring you into the
bond of the covenant; and I will purge out from among 38
you the rebels, and them that transgress against me; I will
bring them forth out of the land where they sojourn, but
they shall not enter into the land of Israel: and ye shall
know that I am the LORD. As for you, O house of Israel, 39
thus saith the Lord GOD: Go ye, serve every one his idols,
¹and hereafter also, if ye will not hearken unto me: but my
holy name shall ye no more profane with your gifts, and
with your idols. For in mine holy mountain, in the moun- 40
tain of the height of Israel, saith the Lord GOD, there shall
all the house of Israel, all of them, serve me in the land:
there will I accept them, and there will I require your

¹ Or, *but hereafter surely ye shall hearken unto me, and &c.*

37. *to pass under the rod*] According to the usage of the language
(Lev. xxvii. 32, cf. Jer. xxxiii. 13) the rod or staff here is that of the
shepherd, which he uses in counting his flock. "The shepherds carried
a staff (Ps. xxiii. 4; Mic. vii. 14; Zech. xi. 7) and used it in counting
when they brought the beasts forth from the place where they were kept
or made them go into it. It was customary to count the beasts every
day (Jer. xxxiii. 13), usually at evening when they came home (Theocr.
VIII. 16; Verg. *Georg.* IV. 436), sometimes twice, morning and evening
(Verg. *Ecl.* III. 34)," Dillm. on Lev. xxvii. 32.

bond of the covenant] The word "bond" is otherwise unknown
[but gives a good sense]. LXX. reads: *and I will cause you to go in
by number*, i.e. probably in special or precise tale (Is. xl. 26; 1 Chr.
ix. 28; Ezr. viii. 34); not in the sense of *few*, which the expression
hardly of itself means (cf. ch. v. 3), neither is the idea of fewness
suitable here. Cf. Jer. iii. 14. This carries on the figure of passing
under the staff, and is amplified in *v.* 38. The word "covenant"
might possibly be a duplicate of the next word "purge" (*v.* 38).

38. Describes the other side of the process from *v.* 37, the separating
of the unworthy from among the people, ch. xxxiv. 17, 20.

but they shall not enter] They shall be brought out but shall fall in
the wilderness of the peoples as the rebellious generation aforetime fell
in the wilderness of Egypt.

39. The present text must read as marg.: "Go ye, serve every one
his idols, *but hereafter surely ye shall hearken unto me, and &c.*"
Cf. *v.* 26 and xxiii. 38, 39. The ironical advice or concession refers
to *vv.* 32, 33, cf. Am. iv. 4.

40. Resumes *vv.* 34—38, and carries these verses a step further—to
the restoration (*v.* 41).

your offerings] *Terûmah*, "denoting properly what is 'taken off'"

offerings, and the [1]firstfruits of your [2]oblations, with all your
41 holy things. [3]As a sweet savour will I accept you, when I bring
you out from the peoples, and gather you out of the countries
wherein ye have been scattered; and I will be sanctified in
42 you in the sight of the nations. And ye shall know that I am
the Lord, when I shall bring you into the land of Israel,
into the country which I lifted up mine hand to give unto
43 your fathers. And there shall ye remember your ways, and
all your doings, wherein ye have polluted yourselves; and
ye shall loathe yourselves in your own sight for all your
44 evils that ye have committed. And ye shall know that
I am the Lord, when I have wrought with you for my
name's sake, not according to your evil ways, nor according

---

[1] Or, *chief*   [2] Or, *tribute*   [3] Or, *With*

---

from a larger mass, and so separable from it for sacred purposes"
(Driver, *Exodus*, ch. xxv. 2), is always elsewhere in R.V. rendered
oblations in Ezek. The idea expressed by the word appears in ch. xlv.
and xlviii., where it is used of the portion of the land devoted to special
and sacred uses. "Firstfruits," marg. *chief*, i.e. the best of your
offerings.

41. *As a sweet savour*] lit. as marg. *With a sweet savour* (i.e. when I
smell it) I will accept you. The expression is used literally of the sweet
smoke of sacrifice, hardly figuratively of Jehovah's complaisance. R.V.
text is wholly improbable.

be sanctified in you] lit. *get me sanctifying in* (through) *you in the
sight of the heathen* (or, shew myself holy). On the idea of "sanctify,"
"be sanctified," i.e. be recognised as God, cf. *v.* 9. The dispersion
of Jehovah's people derogated in the eyes of the heathen from His
power (ch. xxxvi. 20); when they see His people restored the heathen
will know that it was for their iniquity that they were cast out (ch.
xxxix. 23), particularly when after restoration and purification they see
them protected against the countless hosts of Gog by Jehovah's arm.
Thus Jehovah will "through" His people, by His dealing with them
in their restoration, approve Himself as holy—that which God is—in
the sight of the heathen.

43. The goodness of Jehovah in restoring them shall fill their hearts
with abhorrence of their own past doings, cf. xvi. 61.

44. And the final issue of all shall be that the people will know that
He is Jehovah. Jew and Gentile shall alike know that the God of
Israel is God alone. Cf. Is. xl. 5, "the glory of the Lord shall be re-
vealed, and all flesh shall see it together," and Ps. cii. 15, 16, 22.

On the prophet's philosophy of history, his idea that history is
Jehovah operating for His "name's sake," cf. *Introd.* pp. xliii ff.

to your corrupt doings, O ye house of Israel, saith the
Lord GOD.

And the word of the LORD came unto me, saying, Son ⁴⁵
of man, set thy face toward the south, and drop *thy word* ⁴⁶

XX. 45—XXI. 32. THE AVENGING SWORD OF THE LORD.

The passage xx. 45—49 belongs to ch. xxi. (as in Heb.). The time
to which the chapter is to be assigned is the early period of Nebuchadrezzar's movements westwards. The prophet foresees the coming
desolation of Israel by the conqueror, which he expresses under the
figure of a devouring fire, consuming all indiscriminately. The passage
has two divisions, ch. xx. 45—xxi. 27, and xxi. 28—32.

First division. xx. 45—xxi. 27.

(1) xx. 45—49. A conflagration shall be lighted in the forest of the
south, which shall consume all, the green tree and the dry.

(2) xxi. 1—5. Explanation: the sword of the Lord shall be on
Jerusalem and her sanctuaries, and on the land of Israel. Righteous
and wicked shall perish; and men shall know that the Lord hath
drawn His sword.

(3) *vv.* 6, 7. Agitation of the prophet at the thought of the coming
desolation: so shall all men be agitated and confounded.

(4) *vv.* 8—17. Song of the sword—the sword of the Lord whetted
and furbished against Jerusalem.

(5) *vv.* 18—27. He who is the sword or wields it, the king of
Babylon. The prophet returning to the point from which he started
represents the king of Babylon hesitating whether to march against
Ammon or Jerusalem. He consults the oracle and the lot comes out
" Jerusalem."

xx. 45—49. Figure of a forest in which a great conflagration is
kindled. The fire is unquenchable (*vv.* 47, 48), it devours all alike,
the green tree and the dry (*v.* 47); all faces from north to south shall
be scorched by it (*v.* 47); and all flesh shall see that it is the hand of the
Lord which has kindled so great a flame (*v.* 48).

46. *the south*]. Though the reference is to Judah and Jerusalem
(xxi. 1—5), the term "south" hardly means the south of Palestine;
rather the whole land of Palestine from the point of view of the
prophet residing in the north. The "forest of the field" hardly
refers to Lebanon, but belongs to the figure, which, however, Lebanon
may have suggested (xvii. 3; Jer. xxii. 23). The "burning" of all
faces from north to south (*v.* 47) is also part of the figure, though
powerfully expressing the effect on all who behold the great judgements
on Israel. There may be, however, a certain mixture of figures, those
whose faces are scorched being no other than those who, regarded as
trees, are consumed—viz. all flesh from the south to the north in Israel
(xxi. 3, 4)[1].

[1] [The three words rendered "south (South)" are quite distinct in the Hebrew.
The first, *Teman*, is often equivalent to Edom; the second is *Dārôm*, seldom found

toward the south, and prophesy against the forest of the
47 field in the South; and say to the forest of the South, Hear
the word of the Lord; Thus saith the Lord God: Behold,
I will kindle a fire in thee, and it shall devour every green
tree in thee, and every dry tree: the flaming flame shall not
be quenched, and all faces from the south to the north shall
48 be burnt thereby. And all flesh shall see that I the Lord
49 have kindled it: it shall not be quenched. Then said
I, Ah Lord God! they say of me, Is he not a speaker of
parables?

21 And the word of the Lord came unto me, saying, Son
2 of man, set thy face toward Jerusalem, and drop *thy word*
toward the sanctuaries, and prophesy against the land of
3 Israel; and say to the land of Israel, Thus saith the Lord:
Behold, I am against thee, and will draw forth my sword
out of its sheath, and will cut off from thee the righteous
4 and the wicked. Seeing then that I will cut off from thee
the righteous and the wicked, therefore shall my sword go
forth out of its sheath against all flesh from the south to

forest] [Redpath (cf. Lofthouse) points out that this cannot mean
more than scrub and low-growing bushes that flourish in the desert.]

49. *a speaker of parables*] or, similitudes—with the suggested idea
that there lies no reality behind them (xii. 21—28). The prophet,
indeed, cannot utter a statement plainly, he must throw it first into
a figure; the same is true also of Isaiah, though the figures of the latter
prophet are brief and pointed, while those of Ezek. are overloaded
with details. The words shew how the people took notice of the
prophet's peculiarities, and how he himself was conscious of the impression his manner made. Cf. xxiv. 18.

XXI. 1—5. These verses, though still figurative, are plainer than
the preceding, of which they furnish the explanation. The sword of
the Lord is drawn finally from its sheath, to which it shall not return
(*v.* 5); it is drawn against Jerusalem and its sanctuaries (*v.* 2); it shall
slay indiscriminately righteous and wicked (*v.* 3, cf. xx. 47), and all
flesh shall know that it is the sword of the Lord, and that it is His
hand that wields it (*v.* 5).—Even to-day the study of Israel's history
occupies men, and its lessons are not yet exhausted.

2. *the sanctuaries*] These are not the rural sanctuaries or high
places, but the holy buildings in Jerusalem (vii. 24; Lam. ii. 6).

outside Ezekiel, but frequent with him; the third is *Negeb*, a common expression for
the hill country in the S. of Judah, to which region all three refer. The name
Daroma is said to survive there to the present day. The word "drop" in the sense
here used, viz. of prophecy, occurs (besides ch. xxi. 2) in Am. vii. 16 and Mic. ii. 6.]

the north: and all flesh shall know that I the Lord have 5
drawn forth my sword out of its sheath; it shall not return
any more.   Sigh therefore, thou son of man; with the 6
breaking of thy loins and with bitterness shalt thou sigh
before their eyes.   And it shall be, when they say unto 7
thee, Wherefore sighest thou? that thou shalt say, Because
of the tidings, for it cometh: and every heart shall melt,
and all hands shall be feeble, and every spirit shall ¹faint,
and all knees shall be weak as water: behold, it cometh, and
it shall be done, saith the Lord God.

And the word of the Lord came unto me, saying, Son 8, 9
of man, prophesy, and say, Thus saith the Lord: Say, 10
A sword, a sword, it is sharpened, and also furbished: it
is sharpened that it may make a slaughter; it is furbished
that it may be as lightning: shall we then make mirth? ²the

---

¹ Or, *be dim*   ² Or, *it contemneth the rod of my son*, as *every tree*

6, 7.   Agitation of the prophet at the tidings of the coming calamity. This agitation of his is only a symbol of the dismay and paralysis
that shall overtake all when the calamity comes.   On the figures in
v. 7 cf. vii. 17.

7.   *it cometh*] i.e. the overwhelming disaster. The words "and it
shall be done" are wanting in the Vatican MS. (B) of the LXX.
MSS. A and Q have "and it shall be."

8—17.   The destroying sword of the Lord.   The violent agitation
of the prophet at the thought of the coming destruction finds expression
in a wild and irregular ode upon the sword of the Lord.   The general
sense of the poem is discernible, but as in ch. vii. the text is in several
places very obscure (e.g. *vv.* 10, 13).   There appear to be four divisions:

vv. 9—11.   A sword is furbished that it may glitter terribly in the
eyes of men (cf. xxxii. 10); it is sharpened for the slaughter—furbished
and sharpened to give it into the hand of the slayer.

vv. 12, 13.   The prophet must cry and howl and smite in wild
excitement on his thigh, for the princes of Israel and the people are
delivered over to the sword.   His agitation is but the reflexion of the
carnage which shall be witnessed.

vv. 14, 15.   The sword is doubled and tripled; universal shall be
the carnage.

vv. 16, 17.   Wild apostrophe to the sword to execute its task in all
directions.   Sympathy of Jehovah with the terrible work.

10.   *shall we then make mirth?*] lit. *or shall we make mirth?*   These
words with the rest to the end of the verse appear to have little meaning in this connexion.   The R.V. is a literal rendering, the last words

11 rod of my son, it contemneth every tree.   And it is given
   to be furbished, that it may be handled : the sword, it is

meaning probably that the rod (the sword of Babylon) with which
Jehovah now chastises His son (the prince, or people) contemneth
(exceeds in severity) every tree, or, all wood, i.e. all rods of chastisement which are mere wood, for it is glittering steel.   Some ingenuity is
needed to extract the meaning, which, however, when extracted is
difficult to harmonise with v. 13.   The words "shall we then make
mirth?" still appear meaningless.   In the word for "or" or "then"
Frd. Delitzsch would find some cohortative particle after the Assyr.,—
"ha! let us make mirth!" the words being those of God (cf. v. 17),
and the following words "contemneth every tree" meaning that, in
comparison with the rod He now uses, all other rods of chastisement
are only despicable, and useless for their purpose (*Zeit. f. Keilschrift-
forschung*, II. 4, p. 385).   The text appears to be in disorder, and
though many emendations have been proposed none of them is satisfactory.   Gesenius, ..."glitter, against the prince of the tribe of my son
(Judah), which despiseth all wood"—reading *prince* for "should we
rejoice" (*nāsî* for *nāsîs*), the idea being that as Judah has hitherto
despised all ordinary chastisements with the rod of wood the sword
shall now be drawn against the prince.   Ew., "no weak rod of my
son, the softest of all wood"—the words "rod of my son" being a
phrase from the mouth of fathers and meaning a gentle rod.   Apart
from the unnatural constructions and the strong Aramaisms assumed,
the sense is feeble and improbable.   Smend, "woe, O prince! thou hast
despised the rod, contemned every tree (all wood)"—rod and wood
being used of chastening as before.   LXX. reads: "Be sharpened,
that thou mayest be for glittering, ready (=furbished) for paralysing
(enfeebling) ; slay, despise, set at nought every tree!"   The imperatives
are addressed to the sword.   The words "for paralysing" may be a
rendering of present Heb. read with Aramaic sense ; but "for" is read
for "or."   It is by no means certain that LXX. *found* imperatives,
because it renders v. 9 also in the imperative.   Cor., partly following
LXX., "for men who slay and plunder (lit. men of slaughter and
plundering) who despise every stronghold"—viz. the Chaldeans, into
whose hand the sword of the Lord is to be given.   (Cf. Is. xxxiii. 8 ;
Hab. i. 10.)   This really gives a meaning, though it is gained at considerable cost, for some of the words assumed do not occur, the
constructions are far from probable, and the changes of the text are
serious.   Further, in all the passage it is the sword itself that is dwelt
upon and those whom it shall slay ; those who are to wield it are only
alluded to.

Scholars almost unanimously assume that there is ref. in the clause
to former chastisement, hence "rod" and "all wood" are read in
that sense.   But such an idea seems little in place in the connexion ;
and the word rendered "rod" may mean sceptre or (almost) ruler
(xix. 11, 14), and "every tree" may be taken of other sceptres.   The

sharpened, yea, it is furbished, to give it into the hand of
the slayer.   Cry and howl, son of man: for it is upon 12
my people, it is upon all the princes of Israel: [1]they are
delivered over to the sword with my people: smite therefore upon thy thigh.   For there is a trial ; and [2]what if even 13
the rod that contemneth shall be no more? saith the Lord

[1] Or, *terrors by reason of the sword are upon my people*
[2] Or, *what if the sword contemn even the rod? it shall be no more, &c.*

assumption that "contemneth every tree" (all wood) means "exceeds
in severity of punishment every rod," or "looks down on every other
chastening rod," feeling its own superiority as an instrument of punishment, is a very far-fetched one.   It is certainly possible that the word
"prince" (princes) lurks in the strange "shall we then make mirth?"
(Ges., Sm.).   The prince and royal house are alluded to repeatedly in
the chapter, e.g. *vv.* 14, 25—27, 29[1].   The rendering: "against the
prince (princes), the sceptre of my son (that) despiseth all wood"
(i.e. other sceptres, or royal powers, xix. 11, 14), is not very natural.
The expression "my son," whether applied to the king or the people,
has something unexpected about it in Ezek., though "my people" is
used in the passage also (*v.* 12), and an undertone of pity, or at least a
deep feeling of the terribleness of the coming calamity, runs through
the passage.   The words "shall we then make mirth?" can hardly
stand in any case, even in this form: "or shall we make mirth
(saying), The sceptre of my son contemneth all wood!" i.e. defies
every other sceptre or royal power (*La Bible Annotée*).   Any reference
in the passage to Gen. xlix. 9 or 2 Sam. vii. 14 is without probability.

12.   *they* (the princes) *are delivered over to the sword*]   [This is to be
preferred to the marg., which is all but identical with A.V.]

smite...upon thy thigh]   A gesture implying despair or the sense of
a terrible and irreparable evil happening, Jer. xxxi. 19.

13.   *For there is a trial*]   So vocalised the word occurs again
Is. xxviii. 16, "a tried stone," lit. a stone of trial.   The word might be
read as a verb: *for trial has been made*.   In any case reference is not
to the "sword" nor the Babylonian conqueror who wields it, as if the
meaning were: trial has been made of what it or he can do!   Such
a sense has no probability.   The word must refer to those on whom
the calamity is to fall.

and what if...be no more]   The same difficulties recur here as in
v. 10, and the translation will follow that adopted there.   Ew., "for it

[1] [Kr.'s emendation of the text, "Woe to the princes of the tribe of my people,
that rejecteth me and serveth every (idol of) wood," has in its favour the probable
sense of the same word rendered "rod" in *v.* 13 (see note there), viz. the royal
house of Judah.   The marg. of R.V. [=A.V.] is difficult to harmonise with the
M.T.]

14 GOD. Thou therefore, son of man, prophesy, and smite thine hands together; and let the sword be doubled the third time, the sword of the deadly wounded: it is the sword of the great one that is deadly wounded, which 15 [1]entereth into their chambers. I have set the [2]point of the sword against all their gates, that their heart may melt, and

[1] Or, *compasseth them about*   [2] Or, *consternation*

has been tried—and what? is it also a soft rod?—that will not be, saith" &c.; i.e. the rod (the sword) has been tried, and it will be found no soft one. This is wholly improbable. Others (Hitz., Cor.) point the word "trial" differently, and read: "for with kindness what (should I accomplish)?" &c.—which is quite destitute of probability[1]. In spite of the grammatical harshness (cf. however *v.* 27) the construction followed in R.V. is perhaps the most probable, and we may then render, "for trial hath been made, and what if the sceptre (R.V. rod) that contemneth should be no more!"—reference being to the royal house of Judah which shall perish, cf. *vv.* 25—27, 29[2].

14. *doubled the third time*] The Heb. must mean: "let the sword be doubled, tripled!" lit. unto a third (sword), i.e. till it be three-fold. Of course there were not to be three swords or even two; what is called for is a double and triple intensity and operation of the one sword (cf. *v.* 16)[3].

of the great one that is deadly wounded] The reference is to king Zedekiah, cf. *v.* 25. A different division of letters gives: the great sword of the slain (collective)—which is less probable as "slain" is *plur.* immediately before.

entereth...chambers] Better, cf. marg., **which surroundeth them**, still descriptive of the sword.

15. *the point of the sword*] Or, the **glitter**, lit. whirl or swing. Others by changing a letter would read "slaughter," which Frd. Delitzsch (in Baer's *Ezechiel*) by comparison of Assyr. considers the word to mean as it stands[4].

[1] [Kr. (and similarly Ber.), but with considerable change in M.T., "In wrath will I reject the tribe that rejecteth me."]
[2] [The R.V. marg. [=A.V.] which, however, can hardly be accepted as probable, seems to mean, What if the power of Babylon, despising as it does that of the royal house of Judah, shall come to an end?]
[3] [It has been conjectured that the prophet illustrated his words by action, and seizing a sword, brandished it hither and thither. So Kr. "let the sword be doubled and trebled." Others (e.g. Redp.) see a reference to the threefold invasions by Nebuchadrezzar, viz. in the time of Jehoiakim (2 Kgs xxiv. 1), Jehoiachin (xxiv. 11) and Zedekiah (xxv. 1).]
[4] [*Slaughter* (with the change of letter) is now accepted as the meaning by the chief modern commentators. "Point" (R.V. and A.V.) has little, if anything, to support it. For R.V. marg. an Arabic root is quoted. The LXX, from slightly different Heb., renders "they have given themselves over as sacrifices to the sword."]

their stumblings be multiplied: ah! it is made as lightning,
it is pointed for slaughter. ¹Gather thee together, go to the 16
right; set thyself in array, go to the left; ²whithersoever thy
face is set. I will also smite mine hands together, and I will 17
³satisfy my fury: I the LORD have spoken it.

The word of the LORD came unto me again, saying, Also, 18, 19
thou son of man, appoint thee two ways, that the sword of
the king of Babylon may come; they twain shall come forth
out of one land: and mark out a ⁴place, mark it out at the
head of the way to the city. Thou shalt appoint a way, 20

---

¹ Heb. *Make thyself one.*   ² Or, *whither is thy face set?*
³ Heb. *bring to rest.*   ⁴ Heb. *hand.*

---

their stumblings be multiplied] Or, by a slight change in pointing:
those overthrown may be multiplied; Jer. xviii. 23, cf. xlvi. 16.
ah!] [The word comes in strangely (cf. xviii. 10). Kr. suggests
a confusion of similar letters, and would read *thou*, apostrophizing
"sword."]
16. The sword is addressed by the Lord and bidden concentrate its
force to smite on the right, and set itself on to slaughter on the left [but
it is perhaps best to render, as the original justifies, *make thyself sharp*,
a more natural injunction to apply to the sword. So LXX.].
thy face is set] Or, "thine edge is appointed." Cf. same word
"appointed" used of the sword, Jer. xlvii. 7, of the rod, Mic. vi. 9.
17. *smite mine hands*] The strong anthropomorphism suggests a
tumult of emotion in the Divine mind, and sympathy with the terrible
work. Cf. xxii. 13.
satisfy my fury] Appease, or, assuage it. Cf. ch. v. 13.
18—27. He who is, or who wields, the sword, the king of Babylon.
The verses furnish the interpretation of the preceding passage.
The prophet is commanded to represent a way which parts into
two ways. At the parting of the ways he is to set up two guide-
posts, the one pointing to Rabbath Ammon, the other to Jerusalem.
The king of Babylon, coming to the parting of the ways, hesitates which
he shall take. He consults the oracle, draws lots by means of the
arrows, and the arrow that he draws out in his right hand is the one
inscribed "Jerusalem."
19. *appoint thee two ways*] or, *make* thee. Naturally the action
was not performed in reality by the prophet[1].
mark out a place] **grave a hand, at the head of the way to**
the (each) city **grave** it. The "hand" is the pointer or sign-post
indicating direction. [Cf. 1 Sam. xv. 12; Is. lvi. 5.] LXX. reads
somewhat differently.

---

[1] [But this statement may be doubted. See sub-note, p. 31.]

for the sword to come to Rabbah of the children of
21 Ammon, and to Judah in Jerusalem the defenced. For
the king of Babylon stood at the parting of the way, at
the head of the two ways, to use divination : he shook the
arrows to and fro, he consulted the teraphim, he looked
22 in the liver. In his right hand was the divination *for*
Jerusalem, to set battering rams, to open the mouth ¹in the

¹ Or, *for*

20. On Rabbah cf. xxv. 5.

in Jerusalem] For "the defenced" LXX. reads: "in the midst of
it," i.e. of Judah.

21. *For the king...stood*] **standeth.** All the verbs had better be
rendered by the present, *standeth...shaketh...consulteth...looketh.*

he shook &c.] These ceremonies explain the phrase "to use divination." The process has several parts : a sacrifice was offered to the
deity or image, the liver of the animal apparently being inspected to
see what intimations it suggested. Then arrows (among the Arabs
they were pointless and unfeathered), inscribed with the names or
things between which a decision was sought from the god (here
Rabbah and Jerusalem), were cast into a vessel or bag; these were
shaken and brought before the god from whom the decision was sought ;
one was then drawn, and the inscription it bore was the answer of the
god to the alternative propounded for its settlement ; in the present
case the king's right hand drew out the arrow inscribed "Jerusalem."
This method of divination by arrows was common among the Arabs
(cf. Wellhausen, *Skizzen*, III. p. 127), and apparently also in Chaldea
(Lenormant, *La Divination chez les Chaldéens*, ch. II. IV.; Sayce, *Trans.
Soc. Bib. Archæology*, vol. III. 145 [Rob. Smith, *J. of Phil.* XIII.
pp. 227 ff.]). It is related of the poet Imiu'ulḳais that he used this
method of divination to ascertain whether he should avenge his father's
death or no, and the answer always coming out "no," he became
enraged and breaking the arrows flung them into the god's face, telling
him that if the case had been that of his own father he would not
have given such a decision, and (in Arab fashion) applying many foul
epithets to the god's mother.

The teraphim means the deity which Nebuchadrezzar carried with
him, who gave the oracle. The *plur.* does not imply the use of more
than one image.

22. *In his right hand*] In his right hand **is the lot** (or, oracle)
"Jerusalem," to set battering rams, to open the mouth **with a cry.**
Though "battering rams" occurs again in the verse the word can have
no other sense, such as "captains." The word "cry" seems required
by the parallel "shouting." It is obtained by transposition of two
letters in the original. [The double occurrence of "battering rams"
is probably due to scribal error.] On the apparatus of siege, cf.
ch. iv. 2.

slaughter, to lift up the voice with shouting, to set battering rams against the gates, to cast up mounts, to build forts. And it shall be unto them as a vain divination in their 23 sight, which have sworn oaths unto them: but he bringeth iniquity to remembrance, that they may be taken.

Therefore thus saith the Lord GOD: Because ye have made 24 your iniquity to be remembered, in that your transgressions are discovered, so that in all your doings your sins do appear; because that ye are come to remembrance, ye shall be taken with the hand. And thou, O deadly wounded 25 wicked one, the prince of Israel, whose day is come, in the time of the ¹iniquity of the end; thus saith the Lord GOD: 26

¹ Or, *punishment*

23. *which have sworn oaths unto them*] The words are obscure and wanting in LXX., and possibly are not original. Whether a gloss or no, their purpose appears to be to explain why Israel considered this divination of the king's to be false, i.e. believed that he would not besiege or at least capture Jerusalem. The natural sense is: they have those who have sworn oaths (to them), i.e. allies, viz. the Egyptians, &c., who will frustrate and falsify Nebuchadrezzar's divination. Others: inasmuch as they (Israel) have sworn oaths to them (the Chaldeans)¹. The construction is unnatural, and the sense without relevancy, because Israel had just broken its oath, a thing which Nebuchadrezzar came up to punish (ch. xvii.).

he bringeth...to remembrance] The subject is most naturally Nebuchadrezzar, whose presence is an accusation before God of the king and people because of their breaking their allegiance to him (cf. ch. xvii.)². The consequence of their guilt being thus brought to remembrance is that they shall be taken, i.e. captured, the city and people, by the foe. It is certainly possible that the clause "sworn oaths" may have been thrown in to explain this idea.

24. *so that...appear*] Or, "so that your sins do appear, even all your evil doings." Cf. xxix. 16.

25. *in the time of the iniquity of the end*] i.e. when iniquity shall receive its final chastisement—in the downfall of the state and captivity of the king. Cf. xxxv. 5.

¹ [Kr. takes it as referring to the oath which Zedekiah and the princes took (Jer. xxxiv. 8) and afterwards (v. 11) broke, the following words, according to him, denoting that the appearance of him (Zedekiah), the sin-defiled king, in the temple and his solemn oathtaking only brought iniquity to remembrance and rendered Jehovah more hostile. Perhaps the most natural meaning is that the perjured Israelites regard it as a false divination, but God brings their iniquity to remembrance and exposes it that they may be punished.]

² [But see preceding sub-note.]

¹Remove the mitre, and take off the crown: this *shall be*
²no more the same: exalt that which is low, and abase that
27 which is high.   ³I will overturn, overturn, overturn it: this
also shall be no more, until he come whose right it is; and
I will give it *him*.

28   And thou, son of man, prophesy, and say, Thus saith the

---

¹ Or, *I will remove &c.*   ² Heb. *not this.*
³ Heb. *An overthrow, overthrow, overthrow, will I make it.*

---

26. There can be no reference to the high-priest here: the passage
refers exclusively to the royal house, which shall be discrowned. [The
"mitre" however was properly a priestly ornament, Exod. xxviii. 4,
and Kr. (not so Ber.) refers it here to the high-priest, as having been
officially the principal in the ceremonies connected with the oath.]

this…the same]   The somewhat enigmatical words mean probably:
"this is not that," i.e. the present royal house and régime is not that
which shall be (i.e. the Messianic), as *v.* 27 explains.   Or, "this shall
not remain this," i.e. what it is; it shall be removed and give place
to something higher to come, *v.* 27.

exalt &c.]   **let that be exalted which is low, and that which is
high be abased.**   The words "overturn," &c., *v.* 27 explain the idea.
The present order shall disappear, the high shall be abased and at
last that which is humble shall be exalted, cf. xvii. 24.

27. *this also shall be no more*]   "This" does not refer to the
condition introduced by the overturning, but goes back and resumes
the present condition of things, which shall be overturned till he
comes who hath the right, the Messiah.   On the Heb. verb *to be* in
that sense, cf. Is. xv. 6; Job vi. 21.

and I will give it him]   Rather: *and I will give* it *him*¹.   He
whose right it is, or, he who hath the right, is the Messiah (cf. xvii. 22).
Reference is possibly to Gen. xlix. 10, where Ezek. read *shelloh* (whose),
not as M.T. now reads Shiloh.

Second division. xxi. 28—32. Threatening prophecy against Ammon.
The passage is of the nature of an appendix and is obscure, but
several things seem evident.   1. In spite of the similarities between
the language of *v.* 28 and that in *vv.* 9, 10, the sword here is that of
Ammon.   This is certain from the words, *v.* 30, " cause it to return into
its sheath."   2. It is against Israel, not against the Chaldeans, that
the Ammonites furbish and draw their sword.   This appears from the
words " concerning…Ammon, and concerning their reproach," *v.* 28².

---

¹ [But Davidson's rendering is not justified by the Hebrew.   The Heb. suffix
must refer to the direct object of the verb ("it") and therefore "him" [=to him] is
not expressed in the original.]

² [Kr. on the other hand takes it to be the sword of *Jehovah* directed against
Ammon, but alters the first clause of *v.* 30, so as to render " I will requite (it) upon
their head."]

Lord GOD concerning the children of Ammon, and concerning their reproach; and say thou, A sword, a sword is drawn, for the slaughter it is furbished, ¹to cause it to devour, that it may be as lightning: whiles they see vanity 29 unto thee, whiles they divine lies unto thee, to lay thee upon the necks of the wicked that are deadly wounded, whose day is come, in the time of the ²iniquity of the end.

¹ Or, *to the uttermost*   ² Or, *punishment*

Deceived by false prophecies they cherish purposes of conquest outside their own borders, which shall be far from being realised; on the contrary they shall be assailed in their own home and there annihilated (*v.* 25, cf. xxv. 4). History does not enable us to follow the progress of events. It is possible that simultaneously with Judah all the neighbouring peoples threw off the yoke of Babylon, so that it might be doubtful which of them Nebuchadrezzar would attack first (*vv.* 20, 21), but that in the course of events Ammon, true to its instincts, assumed an attitude hostile to Judah (cf. 2 Kgs xxiv. 2). The date of the present passage is no doubt later than that of the rest of the chapter, and may owe some of its colour to events subsequent to the fall of Jerusalem. Cf. xxv. 1—7.

28. *reproach*] jeers at Judah's misfortunes.

A sword...is drawn] Rather, with disregard of the accents: **a sword, a sword is drawn for slaughter; it is furbished to the uttermost in order that it may glitter**.

to cause it to devour] Rather as marg. **to the uttermost**, lit. as far as it can hold or receive. Cor. and Kr. amend: to flash (*hahêl* for *hakîl*).

29. *they see vanity unto thee*] i.e. Ammon's soothsayers falsely hold out the prospect to it of victory and conquest.

to lay thee upon the necks] The sense is doubtful, the phrase " bring, or, put, upon the necks" not occurring again. The " wicked...whose day is come, in the time of the iniquity of the end," can hardly be any other than the princes and people of Jerusalem, *v.* 25. 1. The clause " to lay thee," &c., might express the *contents* of the lying prophecy: they divine a lie and promise that thou shalt fall upon Israel, and conquer them. 2. The clause may express the *issue* of the lying divination, the eventual issue of it in God's hand. These lying prophecies lead the Ammonites to enterprises or to purpose enterprises the result of which in God's hand (or, His judgement because of which) will be that they shall have a common fate with the princes and people of Jerusalem, upon whose necks (bodies) they shall be flung slain. 3. Others (Hitz., Cor., Kr.) would alter the text, reading *it* (the sword) for *thee*, and connecting closely with *v.* 28: " that it may glitter " (whiles they divine a lie unto thee, &c.), " in order to bring it (the sword) upon

30 Cause it to return into its sheath. In the place where thou
    wast created, in the land of ¹thy birth, will I judge thee.
31 And I will pour out mine indignation upon thee; I will
    blow upon thee with the fire of my wrath: and I will deliver
32 thee into the hand of brutish men, skilful to destroy. Thou
    shalt be for fuel to the fire; thy blood shall be in the midst
    of the land; thou shalt be no more remembered: for I the
    LORD have spoken it.

22   Moreover the word of the LORD came unto me, saying,
 2 And thou, son of man, wilt thou judge, wilt thou judge the
    bloody city? ²then cause her to know all her abominations.
 3 And thou shalt say, Thus saith the Lord GOD: A city that
    sheddeth blood in the midst of her, that her time may come,

---

¹ Or, *thine origin*   ² Or, *and*

---

the necks," &c., i.e. assail and slay them with it. This is simpler,
though LXX. already reads *thee*.

30.   Return *it into its sheath!*] Ammon [but see sub-note 2, p. 172] is
commanded to put back his sword into its sheath; his dreams of con-
quests abroad are vain, he shall be destroyed in his own land. On
"nativity" cf. xvi. 3.

31.   *brutish men*] i.e. wild and savage men [the armies of Babylon].
So in xxv. 4 it is the "children of the east," the children of the desert,
who are to execute the judgement on Ammon.

skilful to destroy] lit. *the smiths* (or *forgers*) *of destruction*. Ewald's
"smiths of hell," i.e. demons who forge in hell, is fanciful.

32.   Cf. xxv. 10. Ammon shall perish in his own land.

XXII.   NEW INDICTMENT OF JERUSALEM.

The passage has three divisions:

First, *vv.* 1—12. The sins of Jerusalem, especially her two crying
ones, idolatry and bloodshed (*vv.* 1—5); along with the dark catalogue
of other offences (*vv.* 6—12).

Secondly, *vv.* 13—22. Necessity and certainty of her judgement,
which is stated first directly (*vv.* 13—16), and secondly under the figure
of a smelting furnace (*vv.* 17—22).

Thirdly, *vv.* 23—31. Renewal of the indictment against all classes
of the nation, from the prince to the people of the land.

2.   *wilt thou judge*] See on ch. xx. 4, cf. xxiii. 36.

3.   *A city that sheddeth*] Rather as address: **O city that sheddeth!**
cf. ch. xxiv. 6, 9¹. Her "time" is that of her chastisement, so xxx. 3,

---

¹ [But the LXX. reads "Woe to the city" &c., and Kr. agrees, thus assuming
that a word has fallen out of the original text.]

and that maketh idols against herself to defile her! Thou 4
art become guilty in thy blood that thou hast shed, and art
defiled in thine idols which thou hast made; and thou hast
caused thy days to draw near, and art come even unto thy
years: therefore have I made thee a reproach unto the
nations, and a mocking to all the countries. Those that 5
be near, and those that be far from thee, shall mock thee,
thou [1]infamous one *and* full of tumult. Behold, the princes 6
of Israel, every one according to his [2]power, have been in
thee to shed blood. In thee have they set light by father 7
and mother; in the midst of thee have they dealt by
oppression with the stranger: in thee have they wronged
the fatherless and the widow. Thou hast despised mine 8
holy things, and hast profaned my sabbaths. Slanderous 9
men have been in thee to shed blood: and in thee they

---

[1] Heb. *defiled of name.*   [2] Heb. *arm.*

"the time of the heathen," cf. Jer. xxvii. 7. So *v.* 4, "days" and
"years," i.e. full number of thy years.

against herself] Rather: **unto** herself, parallel to "in the midst
of her[1]."

4. The "blood" is not only that of her children sacrificed to the
idols, but judicial and other murders, cf. *vv.* 6, 9. Cf. xxiii. 37,
xxiv. 6, 9.

therefore have I made] prophetic perf. [the punishment is as certain
as though it had already taken place; "I will surely make," or "I
have determined to make"], cf. "shall mock," *v.* 5.

5. *full of tumult*] Am. iii. 9, and see on ch. v. 7.

XXII. **6—12.** PARTICULAR ENUMERATION OF JERUSALEM'S SINS.

6. The "princes" are those of the royal house.

according to his power...to shed] **have been high-minded in thee, to
shed.** The meaning is not that they shed blood to the utmost of their
power, but that they were arbitrary; their power, lit. *arm*, was the
only law[2].

7. "They" does not refer to the princes, but is said generally.
On "father and mother," Exod. xx. 12; Deut. v. 16, xxvii. 16. On
"stranger," ch. xviii. 18; Exod. xxii. 21. On "fatherless," Exod. xxii. 22.

8. *Thou hast despised*] Jerusalem or the community is addressed,
cf. *v.* 26, ch. xx. 13, 16, &c.

9. Informers and false witnesses, Jer. ix. 3; Exod. xxiii. 1; Lev.
xix. 16; Mic. vii. 2 ff. Cf. ch. xviii. 6, 11.

---

[1] [But R.V. is supported by Kr. and Ber. Her action is to her own ruin.]
[2] [See by way of illustration Jer. xxvi. 21, xxxviii. 4 ff.]

have eaten upon the mountains: in the midst of thee they
10 have committed lewdness.   In thee have they discovered
their fathers' nakedness: in thee have they humbled her
11 that was unclean in her separation.   And one hath committed abomination with his neighbour's wife; and another
hath lewdly defiled his daughter in law; and another in
12 thee hath humbled his sister, his father's daughter.   In thee
have they taken bribes to shed blood; thou hast taken
usury and increase, and thou hast greedily gained of thy
neighbours by oppression, and hast forgotten me, saith the
13 Lord GOD.   Behold, therefore, I have smitten mine hand
at thy dishonest gain which thou hast made, and at thy
14 blood which hath been in the midst of thee.   Can thine

have eaten upon the mountains] See on xviii. 6.

have committed lewdness] This clause should probably introduce
the vices in *v.* 10. Idolatry is metaphorically "lewdness," but
here it is not the community but individuals who are spoken of, cf.
v. 11.

10. Lev. xviii. 7, xx. 11,—defiled their father's wife, i.e. their stepmother, or some of their father's concubines; cf 2 Sam. xvi. 22[1].

unclean in her separation] Cf. ch. xviii. 6; Lev. xviii. 19, xx. 18.

11. Cf. Lev. xviii. 20, xx. 10. Lev. xviii. 15, xx. 12. Lev. xviii. 9,
xx. 17.

12. *taken bribes*] said of judges, Ex. xxiii. 8; Is. i. 23; Mic. iii. 11.
Cf. ch. xviii. 13, xxiii. 35.

by oppression] or violence, as *v.* 7. The vices here enumerated
follow one another without any strict connexion. 1. The despotic
conduct of the princes, whose power is their god (Hab. i. 11), *v.* 6.
2. Irreverence to parents, and want of compassion for the unprotected
and helpless, *v.* 7. 3. Irreligion, *vv.* 8, 9. 4. Immoralities and incest,
vv. 10, 11. Finally, greed of gain that overreaches and oppresses,
v. 12. The picture is dark enough, and is unmistakably that of a
people whose decline is incurable, and its time at hand (*v.* 3), cf. Jer.
v. 7, vi. 13, vii. 5, 6, xxii. 3; Hos. vii. 7; Mic. vi. 10.

XXII. 13—22. THE JUDGEMENT ON THESE VICES.

13. *smitten mine hand*] *clapped my hands*, cf. xxi. 14, 17, vi. 11. The
gesture is expressive of violent agitation, though the agitation may be
due to different emotions—here disdain and dislike.

14. Cf. xxi. 7, "every heart shall melt, and all hands shall be
feeble."

---

[1] [For the custom in relation to a stepmother, as existing in Syria and Arabia,
see Driver, *Deut.* p. 259, also (referred to by Lofth.) Rob. Smith, *Kinship and
Marriage in early Arabia*, pp. 89, 162.]

heart endure, or can thine hands be strong, in the days
that I shall deal with thee? I the LORD have spoken it,
and will do it. And I will scatter thee among the nations, 15
and disperse thee through the countries; and I will consume
thy filthiness out of thee. And thou shalt be profaned in 16
thyself, in the sight of the nations; and thou shalt know
that I am the LORD.

And the word of the LORD came unto me, saying, Son of ¹⁷
man, the house of Israel is become dross unto me: all of ¹⁸
them are brass and tin and iron and lead, in the midst of the
furnace; they are the dross of silver. Therefore thus saith 19
the Lord GOD: Because ye are all become dross, therefore
behold, I will gather you into the midst of Jerusalem. As 20
they gather silver and brass and iron and lead and tin into
the midst of the furnace, to blow the fire upon it, to melt

15. Cf. ch. xxiii. 27, 28, xxxvi. 25, 29.

16. *And thou shalt be profaned in* (through) *thyself*] The idea that
Jehovah "profanes" His people by casting them out of their land is
not uncommon, Is. xliii. 28, xlvii. 6, cf. Ezek. xxiv. 21 (xxviii. 16). It
is doubtful if it be anywhere said that this casting out of the people
is a profanation of them "in the sight of the nations." On the other
hand that phrase is often used when Jehovah Himself, or His name,
is spoken of as being profaned, ch. xx. 9, 14, 22. Particularly it is said
that Israel's dispersion among the nations profaned Jehovah's name,
ch. xxxvi. 20—23, and in xxxix. 7 Jehovah says "neither will I suffer
my holy name to be profaned any more" (by the humiliation of His
people). A slight change of reading gives: "*and I will be* profaned in
thee in the sight." The whole passage speaks of the chastisement of
Israel, not of the purging away their uncleanness (*v.* 15), which is
mentioned incidentally (cf. *v.* 22). This chastisement is dispersion
among the nations, by which Jehovah is profaned and by which Israel
learns to know that He who disperses them is the Lord. Cor. suggests:
"by which (uncleanness) I have been profaned in thee." Does the idea
appear in the prophet that Jehovah was profaned in the eyes of the
nations by Israel's idolatries?

17—22. Judgement on Israel under the figure of a smelting furnace.
Israel is dross and base metal, which must be flung into the furnace.

18. *dross of silver*] In construction "silver" is in apposition with
dross. For the figure cf. Is. i. 22, xlviii. 10; Jer. vi. 28—30; Mal. iii.
2, 3.

19. *midst of Jerusalem*] Cf. ch. xxiv.

20. *brass*] The Heb. word denotes either copper or bronze (an
alloy of copper and tin). Brass (an alloy of copper and zinc) was unknown to the ancients.

it; so will I gather you in mine anger and in my fury, and
21 I will lay you there, and melt you. Yea, I will gather you,
and blow upon you with the fire of my wrath, and ye shall
22 be melted in the midst thereof. As silver is melted in the
midst of the furnace, so shall ye be melted in the midst
thereof; and ye shall know that I the LORD have poured
out my fury upon you.

23
24   And the word of the LORD came unto me, saying, Son of
man, say unto her, Thou art a land that is not cleansed,
25 nor rained upon in the day of indignation. There is a
conspiracy of her prophets in the midst thereof, like a
roaring lion ravening the prey: they have devoured souls;
they take treasure and precious things; they have made her
26 widows many in the midst thereof. Her priests have done

will I gather you] into Jerusalem which is to be besieged by the
Chaldeans.

22. The figure of the furnace expresses mainly the idea of the terrible
trials approaching; it is not intimated that pure silver was obtained
from the process. In a prophet toward the end of the exile Jehovah
complains that His casting Israel into the furnace had been barren of
result, Is. xlviii. 10.

XXII. **23—31.** RENEWED INDICTMENTS.

vv. 23—31. All classes of the nation are rebuked : the royal house,
v. 25; the priests, *v.* 26; the princes, *v.* 27; the prophets, *v.* 28,
and the people of the land, *v.* 29. Among all the people not one is
found to stand in the breach, therefore His wrath must be poured out
upon them to the uttermost.

24. *a land...not cleansed*] The words "not cleansed" are parallel
to "nor rained upon." In the East, however, raining upon is not a
figure for cleansing, but for removing the curse and judgement, and
blessing with fertility (Jer. iii. 3). Hence it is better to read with the
LXX., "a land not watered by showers, and upon which there hath
been no rain." This reading most moderns accept, cf. ch. xxxiv. 26 ;
Lev. xxvi. 4; Deut. xi. 14; 1 Kgs viii. 35, 36.

25. *There is a conspiracy of her prophets*] Better with LXX., **whose
princes in the midst of her are like**... The prophets are spoken of *v.* 28.
The "princes" are those of the royal house, ch. xix. 1, xxi. 12, xxii. 6,
xlv. 8, 9; those called "princes" in *v.* 27 are the chiefs or heads of
the people.

take treasure] i.e. by violence from others, Jer. xx. 5.

her widows many] e.g. by the judicial murder of their husbands.
Cor. *their palaces*, cf. ch. xix. 7, Jer. xxii. 13—17. The change is
unnecessary, cf. Jer. xv. 8.

violence to my law, and have profaned mine holy things: they have put no difference between the holy and the common, neither have they caused men to discern between the unclean and the clean, and have hid their eyes from my sabbaths, and I am profaned among them. Her princes 27 in the midst thereof are like wolves ravening the prey; to shed blood, *and* to destroy souls, that they may get dishonest gain. And her prophets have daubed for them with 28 untempered *mortar*, seeing vanity, and divining lies unto them, saying, Thus saith the Lord GOD, when the LORD hath not spoken. The people of the land have used 29 oppression, and exercised robbery; yea, they have vexed the poor and needy, and have oppressed the stranger wrongfully. And I sought for a man among them, that 30 should make up the fence, and stand in the gap before me for the land, that I should not destroy it : but I found none.

26. The great influence possessed by the priests in this age appears from the place they occupy next the royal house. Jer. ii. 8, 26, iv. 9, viii. 1, xiii. 13, xxvi. 11.

between the holy and the common] It was the priests' part, by expounding the regulations of the Law (*Torah*), to protect the people from unwittingly contracting ceremonial uncleanness. See on *v.* 25 and ch. xliv. 23; cf. Lev. x. 10.

27. *Her princes*] For "princes" here, cf. Jer. xxvi. 10, xxxvi. 12.

get dishonest gain] Cf. Jer. vi. 13, viii. 10. The term is used pretty generally of selfish advantage.

28. *have daubed for them*] i.e. have supported their deeds. The persons called "princes" may be referred to, but not exclusively. Cf. ch. xiii. 10, and xiii. 6, 7.

29. *people of the land*] The mass of the people imitate their superiors. This phrase for the common people occurs already in Jer. xxxvii. 2, and is common in Ezek., vii. 27, xii. 19, &c. The "people of the land" is certainly the subject here, cf. *v.* 7, ch. xviii. 12; Jer. xxiii. 34, xxvi. 7.

30. All classes (*vv.* 25—29) are alike corrupt; a man to stand in the breach in behalf of the people is looked for in vain, cf. Jer. v. 1.

For *fence*, cf. on xiii. 5. A "man" here is not a man to intercede, but a man to interpose, to stem the tide of ruin and turn the fortunes of the people. The mortal energies of the nation were wholly exhausted, it could no more produce of itself a saviour to retrieve its fortunes. Cf. Is. lix. 16 (marg.), "And he saw that there was no man, and wondered that there was none to interpose"; Is. lxiii. 5.

31 Therefore have I poured out mine indignation upon them ;
I have consumed them with the fire of my wrath : their
own way have I brought upon their heads, saith the Lord
God.

23   The word of the LORD came again unto me, saying, Son
2 of man, there were two women, the daughters of one
3 mother: and they committed whoredoms in Egypt; they

31. *have I poured*] Prophetic perfect; the end is as good as come,
vv. 3, 4. The result of this moral paralysis of the people must be its
destruction. In the passages cited from Isaiah, written later and at a
different juncture, the Lord Himself interposes as Saviour, there being
none else.

XXIII. HISTORY OF THE TWO ADULTEROUS WOMEN, OHOLAH
AND OHOLIBAH—SAMARIA AND JERUSALEM.

The alliances and intrigues of Samaria and Jerusalem with foreign
nations had been represented as infidelity to Jehovah since Hosea.
These foreign alliances naturally carried foreign manners and worship
in their train (Is. ii. 6). In Judah at least a great flood of idolatry
from the East overflowed the country in the declining days of the
kingdom, and to some extent this had been true of Israel also (Am.
v. 26, 27). But apart from this since the earliest times the prophets
conceived the kingdom of the Lord as something different in kind from
the kingdoms of the nations : its essence consisted in fidelity to Jehovah, and its defence should have been left to Him. Therefore, when
the community of Jehovah sought alliances abroad for protection, the
prophets detected in this alienation of mind from Jehovah, distrust
of His power and dissatisfaction with His rule. Already the conception
was taking possession of the prophetic mind that the kingdom of God
was not a state but what we now call a church.

The chapter reviews the history of Israel and Judah from the
beginning, and has these divisions :

First, *vv.* 1—10. Infidelities of Samaria with Assyria and Egypt,
and the disastrous issue of them.

Secondly, *vv.* 11—21. Infidelities of Jerusalem with Assyria (11—13),
Babylon (14—18), and Egypt (19—21) successively.

Thirdly, *vv.* 22—35. Therefore her fate shall be like that of Samaria,
she shall drink to the dregs the cup which her sister drank.

Fourthly, *vv.* 36—49. A new description of the immoralities of
Oholah and Oholibah, with a fresh threat of punishment.

2. The two kingdoms are already called sisters in Jer. iii. 7. Cf.
Ezek. xvi. 46.

3. The two kingdoms are represented ideally as already existing
in Egypt. This is not so far from the truth. The great tribes of
Judah and Ephraim from the first stood apart, and in their attitude

committed whoredoms in their youth : there were their
breasts pressed, and there they bruised the teats of their
virginity. And the names of them were Oholah the elder, 4
and Oholibah her sister : and they became mine, and they
bare sons and daughters. And as for their names, Samaria
is ¹Oholah, and Jerusalem ²Oholibah. And Oholah played 5
the harlot when she was mine ; and she doted on her lovers,
on the Assyrians *her* neighbours, which were clothed with 6
blue, governors and ³rulers, all of them desirable young
men, horsemen riding upon horses. And she bestowed 7

---

¹ That is, *Her tent.*   ² That is, *My tent is in her.*
³ Or, *deputies* See Jer. li. 23, &c.

---

there lay already the germs of the two kingdoms, as appears in the
song of Deborah. On the idea of the prophet that idolatry was practised
in Egypt, cf. ch. xx. 8, xvi. 26.

4. The name Oholah may mean "her tent," though not so vocalised,
and Oholibah "my tent in her." Possibly the words mean "tent"
(or, tents) and "tent in her"; and the reference may be to the worship
practised on the high places in both kingdoms, cf. xvi. 16. [The Oxf.
Lex. makes the two words virtually equivalent in sense, meaning a tent
woman, i.e. a worshipper at a tent shrine. "*i*" in Oholibah at any
rate is better taken as an archaic ending and not the pron. affix *my*.] Cf.
the names Hephzi-bah, Is. lxii. 4, and Oholibamah (high-place tent),
Gen. xxxvi. 2. It was common in the East to give sisters or brothers
names almost the same, as Hasan and Husein (little Hasan), the two
sons of 'Ali, the son-in-law of Mohammed.

they became mine] my wives, cf. xvi. 8, 20. It is curious that Jehovah
is represented as the husband of two sisters, a thing which the law dis-
allows, Lev. xviii. 18.

[Perhaps it is an instance of the disregard of the literal meaning in
Hebrew symbolism, as in the case of the heavenly city of Jerusalem,
described as of cubical shape in Rev. xxi. 16.]

XXIII. **5—10.** THE INTRIGUES OF SAMARIA WITH ASSYRIA.

5. *when she was mine*] **though my wife**, lit. *under me.*

Assyrians her *neighbours*] In xvi. 26 the Egyptians are called
Israel's "neighbours," but the Assyrians could hardly be so called,
and indeed in *v.* 40 are referred to as "from far." The word as it
stands can hardly mean "warriors," but a slight emendation would
give this sense. Cor. suggests "famous," the term used in *v.* 23 ("men
of renown"). The verse should be connected with *v.* 6, as appears
from *v.* 12—*even on the Assyrians, warriors clothed with blue.*

6. *rulers*] Or, satraps, cf. Neh. iv. 14, v. 15.

her whoredoms upon them, the choicest men of Assyria all of them: and on whomsoever she doted, with all their 8 idols she defiled herself. Neither hath she left her whoredoms ¹since *the days of* Egypt; for in her youth they lay with her, and they bruised the teats of her virginity: and 9 they poured out their whoredom upon her. Wherefore I delivered her into the hand of her lovers, into the hand of 10 the Assyrians, upon whom she doted. These discovered her nakedness: they took her sons and her daughters, and her they slew with the sword: and she became a ²byword among women; for they executed judgements upon her. 11 And her sister Oholibah saw this, yet was she more corrupt in her doting than she, and in her whoredoms which were 12 more than the whoredoms of her sister. She doted upon the Assyrians, governors and rulers, *her* neighbours, clothed

---

¹ Or, brought *from Egypt*   ² Heb. *name*.

---

7. *with all their idols*] The alliance with Assyria brought in Assyrian idolatry, cf. 2 Kgs xxiii. 11, where horses and chariots of the sun are mentioned, and also the altars on the roofs, where incense was burnt to the host of heaven, *v.* 12, Jer. xix. 13.

8. Samaria intrigued with Assyria and Egypt alternately, or with different parties simultaneously. Hos. vii. 11, "Ephraim is like a silly dove, without understanding: they call unto Egypt, they go to Assyria."

since the days of *Egypt*] [Cf. *v.* 26. Lit. "from Egypt," i.e. from the time of Israel's sojourn in Egypt onwards. Cf. *v.* 27 and Hos. xii. 9. If we adopt the marg., the reference must be to idolatries practised in Egypt. Cf. xvi. 26, xx. 7.]

9. *I delivered*] The Assyrians overthrew Samaria in 722 B.C. Menahem was supported on the throne by Assyria (2 Kgs xv. 19); and Hoshea, the last king, was dethroned on account of his intrigues with Egypt (2 Kgs xvii. 4).

10. *a byword among women*] lit. *a name to women*, i.e. a notorious example to women to take warning from, *v.* 48, xxxvi. 3, xvi. 41.

XXIII. 11—21. THE INFIDELITIES OF JUDAH WITH ASSYRIA, BABYLON, AND EGYPT.

11. On the greater excesses of Judah cf. xvi. 47, 51; Jer. iii. 8, 11.

12. her *neighbours*] See on *v.* 5. The intervention of Assyria in the affairs of Judah was caused by the appeal of Ahaz for help against Syria and Ephraim, 2 Kgs xvi. 7. On the disastrous consequences of Ahaz's folly cf. Is. vii. 17—25.

most gorgeously, horsemen riding upon horses, all of them
desirable young men. And I saw that she was defiled; 13
they both took one way. And she increased her whore- 14
doms; for she saw men pourtrayed upon the wall, the
images of the Chaldeans pourtrayed with vermilion, girded 15
with girdles upon their loins, [1]exceeding in dyed attire upon
their heads, all of them princes to look upon, after the
likeness of the Babylonians [2]in Chaldea, the land of their
nativity. And [3]as soon as she saw them she doted upon 16

[1] Or, *with dyed turbans*   [2] Or, *the land of whose nativity is Chaldea*
[3] Heb. *at the sight of her eyes.*

14. *And she increased*] It was certainly the custom in Babylonia
to draw figures of men and the like upon the walls; it is not probable,
however, that such figures of Chaldean warriors had actually been seen
in Jerusalem. The prophet combines the Babylonian custom with the
reports of Chaldean military splendour current in Judah. Even when
Babylon was still a vassal state of Assyria, Hezekiah entered into intrigues
with it, Is. xxxix. In later times it was the rivalry between Babylon
and Egypt that drew Judah into the whirl of imperial politics, and left
her from the time of the battle of Carchemish and the defeat of Egypt
subject to Babylon (B.C. 605).

15. *girded with girdles*] The "girdles" were properly not belts or
sashes, but articles of clothing, tunics or waist-cloths (Is. xi. 5). "It
appears, however, from the monuments that the Assyrians used what
was originally the waist-cloth as an ornamental sash" (note from Prof.
W. R. Smith[1]).

exceeding in dyed attire] The word "exceeding in" means "re-
dundant"; it is used of the curtains that "hung over" the sides of the
tabernacle (Exod. xxvi. 12, 13), and possibly "dyed attire" may mean
[so marg., and in all probability rightly] "turbans," from being *wound*
(Frd. Delitzsch in Baer, *Ezech.* p. xii). The idea would be that the high
turbans folded back and hung down[2].

all of them princes] Or, *heroes.* The term is used of the choice
warriors in chariots, Exod. xiv. 7, xv. 4, but also more generally[3].

after the likeness of] It is doubtful if the word "likeness" can ever
be rendered (as A.V. here) "in the manner of" or "like" (Is. xiii. 4).
Here "likeness" resumes "images," *v.* 14.

16. *as soon as she saw them*] or, as Smend, according to what she
saw. Cf. Is. xi. 3, "after the sight of his eyes," i.e. by what he sees,
superficially.

[1] [See *Jewish Quarterly Review*, January, 1892, pp. 289 ff.; also *Expository
Times*, iii. (1893), pp. 243, 256.]
[2] [Or that they had their strings or fillets hanging from them, as seen on
Babylonian monuments. So Lofth.]
[3] [It seems to denote personal attendance on a king. Perhaps *knight* is the best
rendering. See on Exod. xiv. 7 in this Series.]

17 them, and sent messengers unto them into Chaldea.   And
the Babylonians came to her into the bed of love, and they
defiled her with their whoredom, and she was polluted with
18 them, and her soul was alienated from them.   So she discovered her whoredoms, and discovered her nakedness:
then my soul was alienated from her, like as my soul was
19 alienated from her sister.   Yet she multiplied her whoredoms, remembering the days of her youth, wherein she had
20 played the harlot in the land of Egypt.   And she doted
upon their paramours, whose flesh is as the flesh of asses,
21 and whose issue is like the issue of horses.   Thus thou
calledst to remembrance the lewdness of thy youth, in the
bruising of thy teats by the Egyptians for the breasts of thy
youth.

22   Therefore, O Oholibah, thus saith the Lord GOD: Behold,
I will raise up thy lovers against thee, from whom thy soul
is alienated, and I will bring them against thee on every
23 side; the Babylonians and all the Chaldeans, Pekod and

17. *alienated from them*]   The figure lies in the revulsion of sated
passion[1]; the reality in the weariness of the Babylonian alliance and
yoke, cf. ch. xvii.
18. "Discovered" means *uncovered, revealed*.
19.   Judah being situated between the two great empires of Babylon
and Egypt and coveted by both, was naturally a hotbed of intrigue by
partizans on both sides.   The influence of the Egyptian party was great
even in the Assyrian age (Is. xxx.—xxxi.), and the imposing and pretentious power of the Nile valley continued to delude the politicians of
Judah throughout the period of Chaldean supremacy (ch. xxix.—xxxii. ;
Jer. i. 18, xxxvii. 5 *seq.*; Lam. iv. 17).
21. *calledst to remembrance*] **didst recall**, i.e. renew, cf. xxxviii. 8.
for the breasts]   By a slight change of reading (*k* for *n*), **when thy
teats were bruised by them of Egypt, when the breasts of thy youth
were pressed** (*v.* 3).   [So Cor., Ber., Kr.]

XXIII. 22—35. CHASTISEMENT OF THE ADULTERESS.

22.   *thy lovers*] the nations once in alliance with her, *v.* 9; ch. xvi.
37; Jer. xxx. 14; Lam. i. 19. In Hos. ii. the "lovers" are the Baals.
23.   On these peoples cf. Delitzsch, *Parad.*, pp. 182, 236, 240.
According to this writer the names appear in the inscriptions as *Pukûdu,*

[1] [The verb rendered "alienated" here and in *v.* 18 means literally "torn away,"
"dislocated."]

Shoa and Koa, *and* all the Assyrians with them: desirable
young men, governors and rulers all of them, princes and
[1]men of renown, all of them riding upon horses. And they 24
shall come against thee with weapons, chariots, and [2]wagons,
and with an assembly of peoples; they shall set themselves
against thee with buckler and shield and helmet round
about: and I will commit the judgement unto them, and
they shall judge thee according to their judgements. And 25
I will set my jealousy against thee, and they shall deal with
thee in fury; they shall take away thy nose and thine ears;
and thy residue shall fall by the sword: they shall take thy
sons and thy daughters; and thy residue shall be devoured
by the fire. They shall also strip thee of thy clothes, and 26
take away thy fair jewels. Thus will I make thy lewdness 27
to cease from thee, and thy whoredom *brought* from the
land of Egypt: so that thou shalt not lift up thine eyes
unto them, nor remember Egypt any more. For thus saith 28
the Lord GOD: Behold, I will deliver thee into the hand of
them whom thou hatest, into the hand of them from whom
thy soul is alienated: and they shall deal with thee in 29
hatred, and shall take away all thy labour, and shall leave

---

[1] Or, *counsellors* Heb. *called.*   [2] Or, *wheels*

Sutu or *Su*, and *Kutu* or *Ku*, and are names of peoples lying east of
the Tigris and on the confines of Elam or Persia.

and men of renown] Perhaps: chiefs. The word is parallel to
"princes" Numb. i. 16, lit. as in marg., "called men," cf. Am. vi. 1.

24. *with weapons*] The term is entirely unknown; LXX. *from the
north*. Boettcher suggested that we should read, "a multitude of
chariots," and Kr. agrees (xxvi. 10).

commit the judgement] Cf. Deut. xi. 26; 1 Kgs viii. 46.

according to their judgements] lit. *with* their judgements, which are
cruel and savage, *v.* 25.

25. "Jealousy" differs little from fury, ch. xvi. 38.

take away thy nose] Reference is either to the ancient practice of
mutilating the adulteress (as in Egypt [see Diod. Sic. 1. 78, and for a
picture shewing this mutilation Toy, *Ezekiel*, p. 140]), or to the habit
of disfiguring captives, cf. xii. 13, xvi. 40.

26. Cf. xvi. 39.

27. brought *from…Egypt*] i.e. continued since the time they were
in the land of Egypt, cf. xvi. 41, xxii. 15.

29. *labour*] i.e. wealth, the fruit of labour. "Discovered" means
exposed.

thee naked and bare; and the nakedness of thy whoredoms shall be discovered, both thy lewdness and thy whoredoms.
30 These things shall be done unto thee, for that thou hast gone a whoring after the heathen, and because thou art
31 polluted with their idols.   Thou hast walked in the way of thy sister; therefore will I give her cup into thine hand.
32 Thus saith the Lord GOD: Thou shalt drink of thy sister's cup, which is deep and large: thou shalt be laughed to
33 scorn and had in derision; ¹it containeth much.   Thou shalt be filled with drunkenness and sorrow, with the cup of astonishment and desolation, with the cup of thy sister
34 Samaria.   Thou shalt even drink it and drain it out, and thou shalt gnaw the sherds thereof, and shalt tear thy
35 breasts: for I have spoken it, saith the Lord GOD.   Therefore thus saith the Lord GOD: Because thou hast forgotten me, and cast me behind thy back, therefore bear thou also thy lewdness and thy whoredoms.
36   The LORD said moreover unto me: Son of man, wilt thou

---

¹ Or, *too much to endure*

31.   *her cup*] that which she drank, Is. li. 22, 23 ; Jer. xxv. 15, 16.
32.   The words "thou shalt...derision" are parenthetical ; LXX. omits.
33.   *and sorrow*] Or, *affliction*.
34.   Cf. Ps. lxxv. 8; Is. li. 17.
"Drunkenness" expresses figuratively bewilderment or helpless-ness.   The act of plucking out her own breasts is that of one intoxicated to madness, Jer. xxv. 16.   The words are wanting in LXX.   Beating the breasts and tearing the cheeks was a sign of excessive grief (*Hamasa*, p. 373).   "The women rent the breast of their dress, went half-naked, tore their faces, and beat their skin with shoes till it was lacerated (*Aghani*, xiv. 101, 28; xv. 139, 6; *Hudh.* 139, 3)," Wellh., *Skizzen*, III. p. 160.
35.   *bear thou...lewdness*] Here "bear" means endure the punish-ment of it, *v.* 49.

XXIII. **36—49.** NEW EXPOSURE OF THE IMMORALITIES OF OHOLAH AND OHOLIBAH (*vv.* 36—44), AND THREAT OF THEIR PUNISH-MENT (*vv.* 45—49).

The passage is not a continuation of *vv.* 1—35, but an independent description, parallel to these verses.
   (1) *vv.* 36, 37.   The adulteries, that is, idolatries, and bloodshed of which the two women are guilty.

judge Oholah and Oholibah? then declare unto them their
abominations.   For they have committed adultery, and 37
blood is in their hands, and with their idols have they
committed adultery; and they have also caused their sons,
whom they bare unto me, to pass through *the fire* unto
them to be devoured.   Moreover this they have done unto 38
me: they have defiled my sanctuary in the same day, and
have profaned my sabbaths.   For when they had slain their 39
children to their idols, then they came the same day into
my sanctuary to profane it; and, lo, thus have they done
in the midst of mine house.   And furthermore ye have sent 40
for men ¹that come from far: unto whom a messenger was
sent, and, lo, they came; for whom thou didst wash thyself,

¹ Or, *to come*

(2) *vv.* 38, 39.   Their profaning the house of Jehovah, and breaking His Sabbaths—the former particularly in their entering His house
fresh from the sacrifice of their children.

(3) *vv.* 40—44.   Their alliances with idolatrous nations and receiving their gods, under the figure of a harlot receiving and entertaining
men.

(4) *vv.* 45—49.   Their punishment with the death of an adulteress
at the hands of righteous men.

The text in some passages is extremely difficult.

37.   The blood on their hands is that of their children whom they
sacrifice.   See xvi. 20, 21.

38.   *the same day*]   The phrase is more fully explained in *v.* 39.
LXX. omits in both places.

39.   The particular profanation of the Lord's house lay in this that
those who had sacrificed their children entered it.   The children were
no doubt offered to Jehovah, under whatever conception or name, and
the worshippers felt no incongruity in entering His house.   Jer. vii.
9 *seq.*

the midst of mine house]   It is not meant that children were sacrificed
in the house; their sacrifice was combined with other service in the
house.

40—44.   These verses hardly refer to political alliances merely;
v. 41 suggests idolatrous worship.   As the foreign gods came in, however, through intercourse with the nations which served them, they are
spoken of as being sent for by messengers (cf. *v.* 16).   The whole is
presented under the figure of a harlot receiving men from all quarters.
The passage has great resemblance to Is. lvii. 9 *seq.*

40.   *ye have sent*]   Better "*they* sent."   The change of person occurs
later.   The word is wanting in LXX.

wash thyself]   i.e. bathe thyself.

paintedst thine eyes, and deckedst thyself with ornaments;
41 and satest upon a stately bed, with a table prepared before
it, whereupon thou didst set mine incense and mine oil.
42 And the voice of a multitude being at ease was with her:
and with men of the common sort were brought drunkards
from the wilderness; and they put bracelets upon the hands
of them *twain*, and beautiful crowns upon their heads.

paintedst thine eyes] This refers to the practice of colouring the
edges of the eyelids with a dark powder (*stibium*), which made the eye
itself appear large and brilliant, 2 Kgs ix. 30; Jer. iv. 30. The word
kahal is Arab., and the root of the word Alcohol; the Heb. is *pūch* (Is.
liv. 11); Job's daughter bore the name Keren-hap-puch, "horn of paint."

41.   *a table prepared*] i.e. spread.

didst set mine incense] The words indicate that service of other gods
is referred to under the figure of the harlot's entertainment.

42.   *being at ease*] If the reading be correct "at ease" must
refer to careless living, a sense which the word has not elsewhere.
LXX. renders: "and a sound of music they raised"; but though the
word "multitude" may mean sound or noise when joined to songs
(xxvi. 13; Am. v. 23), it can hardly of itself mean music.   LXX. may
have read "they sang" for "at ease": "and with a loud noise (Dan.
x. 6) they sang"—a sense not suitable seeing the musicians must have
been the harlots themselves, Is. xxiii. 15, 16.   For the idea of multitude cf. Jer. v. 7 end.   If music were referred to the words would be
better attached to the previous verse.

was with her] Rather: **therein** or **therewith**.   LXX. om.

drunkards] So M.T., with marg. reading "Sabeans" (so A.V.
text), the two words resembling one another in Heb., but from
the nature of the passage, which speaks of a general practice,
reference to any particular nation is less probable.   Even for these
vulgar guests the harlots, so indiscriminate was their whoredom, put
bracelets on their hands and decked themselves.   The idea that it was
"men of the common sort" who adorned the harlots with bracelets as
their hire (A.V. &c.) has little to recommend it, cf. xvi. 31 *seq.* (the
verb "they put" is *mas.* because *fem.* is not in use, cf. Esth. i. 20).
Even in Mohammed's days the Arabs were addicted to drunkenness.
LXX. om. "drunkards," which might be a duplicate of "brought,"
and certainly the mention of *two* classes here is rather improbable.   The
common sort and those brought from the wilderness might rather be
the same, viz. the vulgar and petty peoples in contrast to the larger and
nobler such as Babylon.   The omission makes the clause difficult to
construe.   Cor. reconstructs the clause in accordance with Prov. vii.
16, making it a description of the "bed of love" (*v.* 17), but with
little probability.   If the adulterous act be anywhere referred to it is
in *v.* 43.

Then said I [1]of her that was old in adulteries, Now will 43
they commit [2]whoredoms with her, [3]and she *with them*. And 44
they went in unto her, as they go in unto an harlot: so
went they in unto Oholah and unto Oholibah, the lewd
women. And righteous men, they shall judge them with 45
the judgement of adulteresses, and with the judgement of
women that shed blood; because they are adulteresses, and
blood is in their hands. For thus saith the Lord GOD: 46
I will bring up an assembly against them, and will give
them to be tossed to and fro and spoiled. And the 47
assembly shall stone them with stones, and despatch them
with their swords; they shall slay their sons and their
daughters, and burn up their houses with fire. Thus will 48

---

[1] Or, *She that is old will commit adulteries*   [2] Heb. *her whoredoms.*
[3] Or, *even with her*

43. *her that was old in adulteries*] *Old* is worn out, e.g. of clothes,
Josh. ix. 4, 5, and the verb is used of the body, in the decay of nature
(Gen. xviii. 12, of Sarah). The construction is unusual; the words
might be read (see marg.) as an exclamation: "She that is old will
commit adulteries!" or, "With her that is aged shall they commit adulteries!" Ew., reading "old" as a noun, "To perdition with adulteries!"
None of these senses is very natural. LXX., as in some other places,
appears to assume a contraction, which it expands, "Do they not commit
adultery with these?"

The meaning put upon the rest of the verse can hardly be drawn
from the words, which are extremely obscure. The natural sense is:
"now shall her whoredom commit whoredom even itself" (Hitz.); but
the idea that what the faded harlot can no more do herself her vicious
propensity continues to do, though true in itself, is scarcely to be
expected here. LXX., which had nearly our present text before it,
disposes the letters differently: "And she too has gone a whoring after
the manner (with the doings) of a harlot." So Syr., "And according
to the doings of harlots have they committed whoredom."

44. The verse sums up all that precedes.

the lewd women] The form of the Heb. *plur.* "women" does not occur
again, though the usual one in Assyr. LXX., "*to work* lewdness."

45—49. Judgement on the adulterous women.

45. *righteous men*] The prophet carries on the figure of the
punishment of adulteresses. They are judged by righteous men. He
has not in his mind the nations, the actual executors of judgement
in the case of Israel.

46. Cf. xvi. 40.

I cause lewdness to cease out of the land, that all women
49 may be taught not to do after your lewdness. And they
shall recompense your lewdness upon you, and ye shall
bear the sins of your idols: and ye shall know that I am
the Lord GOD.

24   Again, in the ninth year, in the tenth month, in the tenth
day of the month, the word of the LORD came unto me,
2 saying, Son of man, write thee the name of the day, *even*
of this selfsame day: the king of Babylon ¹drew close unto
3 Jerusalem this selfsame day. And utter a parable unto the

---

¹ Heb. *leaned upon.*

48. *all women*] i.e. the nations around.

be taught] **take warning** [more literally, *be disciplined*], the form
nithpaʻel, cf. Deut. xxi. 8.

XXIV. THE RUSTED CALDRON SET UPON THE COALS.

The passage, of date Jan. 587, is the prophet's last oracle against
Jerusalem. It consists of two parts:
First, *vv.* 1—14. A parable of a rusted caldron set upon the fire—
the siege and capture of the city.
Second, *vv.* 15—27. On the death of his wife the prophet abstains
from all mourning—a sign of the silent stupefaction which the news of
the city's fall will occasion.

XXIV. 1—14. THE RUSTED CALDRON SET ON THE FIRE.

(1) *vv.* 1—5. A caldron is to be set on the fire, filled with water,
pieces of flesh cast into it and fuel piled under it that it may boil
furiously. The caldron is Jerusalem; the pieces of flesh the inhabitants; the fire and boiling the siege with its terrible severities. The
pieces of flesh shall be pulled out of the caldron indiscriminately,
symbol of the universal dispersion when the siege is over.
(2) *vv.* 6—8. Explanation: these sufferings are judgements for the
sins of the city, its bloodshed and uncleanness, which are public and
open. This blood and filthiness cleave to it like rust to a caldron.
(3) *vv.* 9—14. Rising anew into tones of menace the Divine voice
commands that the caldron be set empty upon the coals, that its rust and
foulness may be molten and consumed. This must signify the ruin in
which the city shall long lie, and the dispersion in which her inhabitants shall pine away, till her warfare be accomplished and her iniquity
pardoned.
1. The same date of the commencement of the siege is given
2 Kgs xxv. 1; Jer. lii. 4. In later times the day was kept as a fast,
Zech. viii. 19.

rebellious house, and say unto them, Thus saith the Lord GOD, Set on the caldron, set it on, and also pour water into it : gather the pieces thereof into it, even every good 4 piece, the thigh, and the shoulder; fill it with the choice bones. Take the choice of the flock, and pile also the 5 bones under it : make it boil well; yea, let the bones thereof be seethed in the midst of it.

Wherefore thus saith the Lord GOD : Woe to the bloody 6 city, to the caldron whose ¹rust is therein, and whose ¹rust is not gone out of it! bring it out piece by piece; no lot is fallen upon it. For her blood is in the midst of her; she 7 set it upon the bare rock; she poured it not upon the ground, to cover it with dust; that it might cause fury to 8 come up to take vengeance, I have set her blood upon the bare rock, that it should not be covered. Therefore thus 9

---

¹ Or, *scum*

---

3. *the caldron*] Cf. xi. 3.

4. *the pieces thereof*] those belonging to the caldron, which are to be boiled in it.

5. *pile also the bones*] lit. **a pile also of wood under it.** If "pile" could be read as a verb, *and pile also wood*, the construction would be easier. In spite of the versions *wood* must be substituted for "bones."

make it boil well] lit. make boil its boilings. The word "boilings" does not occur again; possibly by the omission of one consonant of the Heb. word we should read "boil *its pieces*," parallel to *its bones* in the next clause.

let the bones thereof be seethed] Naturally here and *v.* 4 "bones" include the flesh upon them. They are those of such parts as leg and shoulder.

6. Explanation: the caldron is Jerusalem, the bloody city.

whose rust] [The marg. "scum" is less good. The reference is to the pollution caused by deeds of blood.]

bring it out] i.e. the caldron as having contents; empty it.

no lot is fallen] The contents (the inhabitants) shall be pulled out indiscriminately. The dispersion is alluded to.

7. *the bare rock*] Cf. Job xvi. 18, "O earth, cover not thou my blood." Blood uncovered cries for vengeance. Cf. Lev. xvii. 13; Deut. xii. 16. On the idea of the openness of Jerusalem's sin cf. Is. iii. 9, "They declare their sin as Sodom, they hide it not."

8. *I have set her blood*] In *v.* 7 it was Jerusalem herself who left her bloodshed uncovered; here, as usual in the prophet, this is an appointment of God, that He may bring up judgement because of it.

saith the Lord God : Woe to the bloody city ! I also will
10 make the pile great. Heap on the wood, make the fire hot,
boil well the flesh, and make thick the broth, and let the
11 bones be burned. Then set it empty upon the coals
thereof, that it may be hot, and the brass thereof may burn,
and that the filthiness of it may be molten in it, that the
12 rust of it may be consumed. She hath wearied ¹*herself*
with toil : yet her great rust goeth not forth out of her ;
13 her rust ²*goeth not forth* by fire. ³In thy filthiness is lewdness :
because I have purged thee and thou wast not purged, thou
shalt not be purged from thy filthiness any more, till I have
14 ⁴satisfied my fury ⁵upon thee. I the Lord have spoken it :
it shall come to pass, and I will do it*; I will not go back,

---

¹ Or, *me*   ² Or, is *in the fire*   ³ Or, *For thy filthy lewdness*
⁴ Heb. *brought to rest.*   ⁵ Or, *toward*

9—14.   Rising anew into tones of threatening the Divine voice commands fuel to be heaped under the caldron, and to set it empty upon
the coals, that its brass may glow in the fire and its rust be consumed.

9.   LXX. omits the clause "Woe...city !" cf. *v.* 6.

10.   *bones be burned*] Either "burned" is used inexactly of the
powerful action of the heat in boiling, or, less naturally, the contents of
the pot are supposed to suffer directly from the fire. [Kr. conjectures,
ascribing the Heb. word to a different root, "empty out the broth";
thus causing the bones to be burnt in the pot. Or, perhaps the meaning
is that they are to be cast on the fire.] LXX. omits.

11.   *rust of it*] When the contents of the caldron have been seethed
and emptied out of it—the siege and dispersion—the caldron itself
shall be set empty upon the coals that its filth and rust may be molten
and consumed—a figure for the purifying judgements continued long
after the destruction of the city.

12.   As the words stand they seem to read : *she hath wearied* my
*labours, and her great rust goeth not out from her ; let her rust be in the
fire!* Previous efforts to purify Jerusalem have been in vain, her
uncleanness will go out only by fire (*v.* 13); cf. Is. xliii. 24. LXX.
omits first clause, which might be a duplicate of words immediately
preceding. [The marginal renderings are superior to those of the text.]

13.   *In thy...lewdness*] Or, because of thy lewd filthiness, cf. xvi. 27,
"thy lewd way."

thou shalt not be purged...more] i.e. thou shalt never be purged,
till, &c., or, shalt never be purged so as to be again clean, till, &c.

satisfied] **appeased**, lit. as marg. *brought to rest*, cf. v. 13, viii. 18,
xvi. 42.

neither will I spare, neither will I repent; according to thy ways, and according to thy doings, shall they judge thee, saith the Lord GOD.

Also the word of the LORD came unto me, saying, Son of ¹⁵₁₆ man, behold, I take away from thee the desire of thine eyes with a stroke: yet neither shalt thou mourn nor weep, neither shall thy tears run down. Sigh, ¹but not aloud; 17 make no mourning for the dead, bind thy headtire upon thee, and put thy shoes upon thy feet, and cover not thy lips, and eat not the bread of men. So I spake unto the 18 people in the morning; and at even my wife died: and

¹ Heb. *be silent.*

14. *shall they judge*] Cf. xxiii. 49. LXX. and the versions, "*I will judge*," which LXX. then amplified into an additional verse, somewhat in terms of xxii. 5. The words, though doubtless found by the translator in his MS., are hardly original.

XXIV. **15—27.** THE PROPHET'S ABSTENTION FROM MOURNING ON THE DEATH OF HIS WIFE—A SYMBOL OF THE STUPEFACTION OF THE PEOPLE AT THE NEWS OF THE FALL OF THE CITY.

16. *with a stroke*] The word need not be pressed to mean a sudden unexpected death, apart from all previous sickness.

neither shall thy tears run down] wanting in LXX.

17. *but not aloud*] lit. groan, *be silent.*

make no mourning for the dead] Two words in the Heb. must be transposed or an anomalous construction be assumed¹.

thy headtire] The "headtire" is not necessarily the priestly tiara, but the ordinary headdress (*v.* 23), which would probably be white. Putting off the shoes was a sign of calamity, 2 Sam. xv. 30; Is. xx. 2, and also covering the lower part of the face up to the upper lip. Mic. iii. 7; Lev. xiii. 45.

the bread of men] Jer. xvi. 7, "Neither shall men break *bread* for them in mourning, to comfort them for the dead; neither shall men give them the cup of consolation to drink for their father or for their mother." It may have been the custom to visit mourners and press them to eat, or, perhaps, with Kr. we should read "bread of mourners." Cf. Hos. ix. 4; Jer. xvi. 5—7, and *HDB*, Art. **Mourning.**

18. The death of the prophet's wife was no doubt an actual occurrence. And there is nothing improbable in his demeanour after it, with the view of attracting the attention of his fellow-captives. At the same time his tendency to idealise occurrences precludes absolute certainty.

¹ [The Heb. is literally "Dead men mourning thou shalt not make." Kr. with Smend and Toy transpose the two substantives, "mourning of (or for) dead men," so as to remove the harshness of the M.T.]

19 I did in the morning as I was commanded.   And the
people said unto me, Wilt thou not tell us what these things
20 are to us, that thou doest so?   Then I said unto them, The
21 word of the LORD came unto me, saying, Speak unto the
house of Israel, Thus saith the Lord GOD: Behold, I will
profane my sanctuary, the pride of your power, the desire
of your eyes, and ¹that which your soul pitieth; and your
sons and your daughters whom ye have left behind shall fall
22 by the sword.   And ye shall do as I have done: ye shall
23 not cover your lips, nor eat the bread of men.   And your
tires shall be upon your heads, and your shoes upon your
feet: ye shall not mourn nor weep; but ye shall pine away
24 in your iniquities, and moan one toward another.   Thus
shall Ezekiel be unto you a sign; according to all that he
hath done shall ye do: when this cometh, then shall ye
know that I am the Lord GOD.
25   And thou, son of man, shall it not be in the day when
I take from them their ²strength, the joy of their ³glory, the
desire of their eyes, and ⁴that whereupon they set their

---

¹ Heb. *the pity of your soul.*   ² Or, *strong hold*
³ Or, *beauty*   ⁴ Heb. *the lifting up of their soul.*

---

21.   *pride of your power*] i.e. your proud boast, or, your boasted
strong hold (*v.* 25).   The temple is referred to.
    that which...pitieth] i.e. holds dear, xxxvi. 21; Job xx. 13 [marg.
gives literal rendering of Heb.].
    23.   *pine away in your iniquities*] cf. xxxiii. 10; Lev. xxvi. 39.
    moan one toward another] The unparalleled severity of the stroke
will paralyse grief and prevent it from expressing itself by loud cries and
tears.   The only expression of their grief will be the low moaning of
distress.
    25—27.   When tidings come of the city's fall, verifying the prophet's
predictions and giving confirmation to all the principles which he had
long declared, his mouth will be opened, he will have confidence to
speak and more willing listeners before him.
    25.   *their strength*] i.e. as marg. *strong hold*; the thing in which
they placed confidence.
    joy of their glory] the glorious (or beautiful, see marg.) thing in
which they delighted.   Both expressions allude to the temple, &c.
    that whereupon they set their heart] that which is the object of their
desire, Ps. xxiv. 4.

heart, their sons and their daughters, that in that day he 26
that escapeth shall come unto thee, to cause thee to hear it
with thine ears? In that day shall thy mouth be opened 27
¹to him which is escaped, and thou shalt speak, and be no
more dumb: so shalt thou be a sign unto them; and they
shall know that I am the LORD.

And the word of the LORD came unto me, saying, Son **25**
                                                      2

¹ Or, *together with*

26. *in that day he that escapeth*] The phrase "in that day" is
used with considerable latitude, to indicate the period marked by any
great event and following it.

cause thee...thine ears] Perhaps more general: to cause it to be
heard with the ears—not the prophet's only but also those of the exiles

27. *opened to him*] Or, as marg., **together with** him, i.e. when he
comes. Cf. iii. 26, 27, xxxiii. 22. The last words of this verse refer
to the prophet's demeanour *vv.* 16—18.

SECOND DIVISION. CH. XXV.—XLVIII. PROPHECIES OF THE
RESTITUTION OF THE KINGDOM.

FIRST SECTION. CH. XXV.—XXXII. PROPHECIES AGAINST THE
NATIONS.

The prophecies of Ezekiel against the nations form a single collection
in the Book precisely as the similar oracles of Jeremiah (ch. xlvi.—li.)
and of Isaiah (ch. xiii.—xxvii.). In the Book of Ezekiel they occupy
the proper place, being an introduction to the positive prophecies
of Israel's restoration (ch. xxiii.—xxxix.). Israel occupies a place of
universal significance in the history of the world, for it is the people of
Jehovah, who is God alone. He who is God alone has become God
of Israel, and it is through Israel that He is known to the nations, and
through Israel and her history that He will fully reveal Himself to the
peoples of the world. This perfect manifestation of Himself will be
seen in Israel's restoration, when His glory shall be revealed and all
flesh shall see it together (Is. xl. 5). But this restoration of Israel
cannot be without great judgements on the nations who have hitherto
harassed her or seduced her. These judgements will awaken the nations
to the knowledge who the God of Israel is—they shall know that He
is Jehovah; and they will ensure that in the future His people shall
not be troubled or led astray. All the prophets have the presentiment
of a general judgement upon the world immediately preceding the incoming of the perfect kingdom of the Lord. The idea is shared by
Ezekiel, though, as usual, he develops it into much further details than
his predecessors had occasion to do.

The *place* of these prophecies in the Book of Ezekiel is important,
because it suggests the place which the judgements on the nations had

in his scheme of thought, and his construction of the history of redemption. So far as the prophecies themselves are concerned they
belong either to the last years of Israel's existence as a nation, or to
the period immediately following the downfall of the state. The
prophecies are seven in number, being against (1) Ammon, (2) Moab,
(3) Edom, (4) the Philistines (ch. xxv.), (5) Tyre (ch. xxvi.—xxviii.),
(6) Zidon (xxviii. 20—26), (7) Egypt (xxix.—xxxii.). Those against
the first six countries seem immediately posterior to the destruction
of Jerusalem; those against Egypt belong to the time from the 10th
to the 12th year of Jehoiachin's captivity, that is, the year before
the capture of the city, the year in which it was taken, and the year
after, with the exception of the passage ch. xxix. 17—21, belonging
to the 27th year of Jehoiachin's captivity, which is probably a later
insertion.

Chastisement overtakes the nations for two sins. First, because of
their demeanour towards Israel, the people of Jehovah. Either they
had taken part in Jerusalem's destruction (Edom, xxv. 12; the Philistines, xxv. 15), or had rejoiced over it, whether out of malice (Ammon,
xxv. 3), jealousy (Moab, xxv. 8), or for selfish reasons (Tyre, xxvi. 2);
or else they had been a snare to Israel, inspiring false trust and seducing
her from the true God (Egypt, xxix. 6). And secondly, because of
their ungodly pride and self-deification (Tyre, ch. xxviii.; Egypt, xxix.
3). This conduct of the nations and these feelings bring them into
relation with Jehovah, either mediately through Israel the people
of the true God, whom they injured or despised or seduced; or
immediately and in a wider way in their not recognising Him as
God,—Him who was God alone. Hence in all cases His judgements
upon them have this purpose and result—they shall know that I am
Jehovah[1].

The prophet has a very lofty consciousness of God, which he expresses by the word "Jehovah." To be Jehovah is to be God alone,
and all which He who is God alone is. It is from this conception
of the God of Israel that the prophet speaks. But he estimates the
conduct and feelings of the nations as if they also had or should have
the same consciousness of Jehovah, as if they knew Him as the prophet
himself does. Other prophets speak in the same way, e.g. Is. x. 6, 7.
His way of thinking arises from the fact that the one true God was
God of Israel. He whom the nations knew as Jehovah, the God of
Israel, was the one living God. And when they did despite to His
people, it was not a nationality among other nationalities that they
injured, nor a mere tribal god whom they scorned; they were moving
in a far higher plane than this, they were doing despite to the people
of Him who was God alone, and were injurious to the one living God.
Again, Jehovah being God over all, pride of heart in the nations or

---

[1] [Redp. suggests that the noteworthy omission of Babylon from the list may be
accounted for partly by the reception, on the whole kindly, experienced by the exiles
in the country where Ezekiel wrote the prophecies, and partly by the fact that he
considered Babylon as the instrument employed by God in carrying out His plans.]

their rulers, and self-deification, as when the prince of Tyre said, "I am God" (xxviii. 2), or when the Pharaoh said, "My river is mine own, and I have made it" (xxix. 3), was blasphemy against Him. This self-exaltation detracted from Him who is alone exalted (Is. ii. 11)[1]. This is the prophet's conception. In a certain way his manner of thinking may do an injustice to the nations, who might not know that Jehovah, God of Israel, was God alone. The question is not quite simple. For this pride and self-deification of rulers and nations was a sin against God, it was on the part of man a lifting-up of himself against what the human mind feels to be above it. And it is not quite clear that Israel's neighbours were altogether guiltless in not knowing Jehovah to be God alone. He was in the world, though the world knew Him not. The Light had appeared. How far men everywhere are responsible for not coming to the Light when it has anywhere appeared is a question not to be settled offhand (John xviii. 37, 38). The prophet appears to intimate that the neighbouring nations were not unaware of Israel's pretensions to be different from themselves (xxv. 8). The superiority claimed by Israel was a religious one (Deut. xxxii. 31), and when the prophet represents the nations as aware of it, he is not to be thought of as speaking merely from his own point of view (Numb. xxiii. 21—23; Lam. iv. 12).

Ch. xxv. contains prophecies directed against four peoples: *vv.* 1—7, Ammon; *vv.* 8—11, Moab; *vv.* 12—14, Edom; and *vv.* 15—17, the Philistines.

XXV. 1—7. PROPHECY AGAINST AMMON.

The name of this people is usually "the children of Ammon" (*Běnē Ammôn*). This is the name both of the people and the country (in the latter case construed as *fem. vv.* 3, 10). Ammon was recognised by Israel as a distant member of the same family with themselves (Gen. xix. 38). At an early period the people was settled on the E. of the Jordan, between the Arnon and the Jabbok (Jud. xi. 13), but before the Exodus they had been dispossessed of this territory by Amorites from the W. of the Jordan, and pushed eastward towards the desert (Numb. xxi. 21), though they could not forget their ancient claims to their former seat, even when Israel had wrested it from the Amorites (Jud. xi. 19; cf. Josh. xiii. 25). The relations of Ammon to Israel were for the most part unfriendly. In the times of the Judges they harassed the tribes E. of the Jordan, and were crushed by Jephthah (Jud. x.—xi.). Saul signalised his early reign by defeating their king, who had laid siege to Jabesh in Gilead (1 Sam. xi.). Owing to the affront offered to his ambassadors David invaded the country and took cruel vengeance on the inhabitants (2 Sam. x. 1, xi. 14, xii. 29). The Ammonites continued when opportunity offered to carry on a savage warfare with the tribes across the Jordan (Am. i. 13); and

---

[1] [To this attitude on the part of the nations Lofth. compares the reprobation directed in the choruses of Æschylus against insolent pride (ὕβρις).]

of man, set thy face toward the children of Ammon, and
3 prophesy ¹against them: and say unto the children of
Ammon, Hear the word of the Lord GOD; Thus saith the
Lord GOD: Because thou saidst, Aha, against my sanctuary,
when it was profaned; and against the land of Israel, when
it was made desolate; and against the house of Judah,
4 when they went into captivity: therefore behold, I will
deliver thee to the children of the east for a possession,
and they shall set their encampments in thee, and make
their dwellings in thee; they shall eat thy fruit, and they
5 shall drink thy milk. And I will make Rabbah a stable
for camels, and the children of Ammon a couching place
6 for flocks: and ye shall know that I am the LORD.   For

¹ Or, *concerning*

when these were carried away by the Assyrians they naturally in
company with Moab seized the depopulated country (Jer. xlix. 1;
Zeph. ii. 8).   During the struggle of Judah with Babylon they shewed
the old mischievous animosity (2 Kgs xxiv. 2), and after the fall of
the city the treacherous murder of Gedaliah the Babylonian governor
by Ishmael was instigated by their king (Jer. xl. 14).   After the Return
Ammonites are again found obstructing the pious aspirations of the
restored community (Neh. iv. 3; cf. ii. 10, 19), and true to their old
instincts they appear on the side of the Syrians in the Maccabean war
of independence (1 Macc. v. 6).

3.   *when it was made desolate*]   For the demeanour of the nations on
the destruction of Jerusalem, cf. Ezek. xxi. 28, xxxv. 13, xxxvi. 20;
Obad. 12; Lam. ii. 15, 16.

4.   *children of the east*]   the nomad tribes of the Arabian desert,
Jud. vi. 3.

set their encampments]   Cf. Jud. vi. 1—6¹.

drink thy milk]   Ammon, lying towards the desert, was a pastoral
country.

5.   *make Rabbah a stable*]   Rabbah, "great city," was the capital
(Am. i. 14); in later times it bore the name of Philadelphia, and its site
is probably marked by the ruins called Ammân.   The word "stable"
is usually rendered *habitation*, but "sheepcote" in 2 Sam. vii. 8.   It may
mean a place where animals are housed or where they pasture, cf. Is.
v. 17, xxxii. 14; Jer. xxxiii. 12; Zeph. ii. 14, 15.

¹ [This threat may have had at least a partial fulfilment when Nebuchadrezzar "in
the fifth year after the destruction of Jerusalem" made war against the Ammonites
and Moabites (Jos. *Ant.* x. 9, 7).]

thus saith the Lord God: Because thou hast clapped thine
hands, and stamped with the feet, and rejoiced with all the
despite of thy soul against the land of Israel; therefore 7
behold, I have stretched out mine hand upon thee, and
will deliver thee for a spoil to the nations; and I will cut
thee off from the peoples, and I will cause thee to perish
out of the countries: I will destroy thee; and thou shalt
know that I am the Lord.

Thus saith the Lord God: Because that Moab and Seir 8
do say, Behold, the house of Judah is like unto all the

6. *clapped thine hands*] A gesture of malicious delight, Lam. ii. 15.

7. *a spoil*] the reading *baz* must be adopted[1], cf. xxvi. 5, vii. 21,
xxiii. 46.

cause thee to perish out of the countries] [Contrast Jer. xlix. 6, if the
latter be genuine.]

know that I am the Lord] The statement is hardly to the effect that
the Ammonites shall be converted to the worship of the true God.
They shall recognise that there is one Most High, ruling in the kingdom
of men (Dan. iv. 17), and that it is He who is shaping their history;
possibly also that this God is Jehovah, God of Israel. The prophet
does not pursue the destinies of the nations beyond this recognition,
nor state what it implies. It is to be observed, however, that Israel
restored, though occupying only the land west of the Jordan, enjoys
profound peace on all sides. The nations that swell the army of Gog
(ch. xxxviii.) are not Israel's historical neighbours, but peoples from
the uttermost parts of the earth.

XXV. 8—11. Prophecy against Moab.

The Moabites, like the Ammonites, were recognised by Israel as a
kindred people (Gen. xix. 30). Technically the border of Moab on the
N. was the Arnon, but they had pretensions to the district lying beyond
this stream at least as far as the head of the Dead Sea, and these pretensions they often asserted. Practically the tribes of Reuben and Gad
seem to have been unable to make good their claim to this territory by
dispossessing the Moabites. The peoples appear to have mixed together,
and frequently Moab is found in possession of the fertile district and the
numerous cities which covered it (Mesha's Inscription). The country was
subdued by David, and on the division of the kingdom fell as a depen-
dency to northern Israel, to which it paid a yearly tribute of 200,000
fleeces of wool (2 Kgs iii. 4), though making frequent struggles for
independence (2 Kgs i. 1, iii. 5, xiii. 20). Unlike the Ammonites,
who continued a half-nomad people, the Moabites became more a
settled nation, and appear to have attained to a considerable degree of

---

[1] [So the marg. (*Ḳĕrî*) of M.T. Its text (*Kĕthîb*) has *bag*, a scribal error.]

9 nations; therefore behold, I will open the side of Moab
from the cities, from his cities which are ¹on his frontiers,
the glory of the country, Beth-jeshimoth, Baal-meon, and
10 Kiriathaim, ²unto the children of the east, *to go* against the
children of Ammon, and I will give them for a possession,
that the children of Ammon may not be remembered among

¹ Or, *in every quarter*   ² Or, *together with the children of Ammon,
unto the children of the east*

civilisation.   Their language was closely allied to Hebrew, and the art
of writing appears familiar as early as the beginning of the 9th century
(Mesha's Inscription.   See *HDB* III. 406).   After the intervention of the
Assyrians in western Asia Moab with the neighbouring peoples became
tributary to that power.   Hostilities between Israel and Moab were
frequent, and along with Ammon they helped towards the downfall of
Judah at the hands of the Chaldeans (2 Kgs xxiv. 2; Zeph. ii. 8).   Their
warfare was characterised by inhuman excesses (Am. ii. 1), and the people
are stigmatised as proud and boastful (Is. xv., xvi.; Zeph. ii. 8—10).
Moab is referred to after the Return (Ezr. ix. 1; Neh. xiii. 1; the ref.
Is. xxv. 10 is of uncertain date and meaning), and as late as Dan. xi. 41.

8.   *Moab and Seir*]   LXX. omits *and Seir*.   Ezek. elsewhere always
says "mount Seir" (xxxv. 2, 3, 7, 15), and Edom (with which mount
Seir is joined xxxv. 15) has a special prophecy directed against it
(*vv.* 12—14).   The phrase "like unto all the nations" implies knowledge
of some claim to pre-eminence on the part of Judah.   Moab rejoices
that these pretensions have received a signal refutation.

9.   *open the side*]   lit. *the shoulder* of Moab, i.e. the border or territory
of Moab conceived as looking towards other countries, as "shoulder"
has hardly reference to the shape of the Moabite territory (Is. xi. 14).
To open the side is to give invaders access to the country (Nah. iii. 13).

from the cities...frontiers]   Perhaps: "*at* the cities, at his cities in
every quarter" (see marg.).   The prep. *from* seems to indicate position,
by or *on* the cities, i.e. where they are.   Others take it in a privative
sense: *stript of* the cities.   The three towns named are given as examples
of the glory of Moab.   Beth-jeshimoth lay at the N.E. of the head of
the Dead Sea, Numb. xxxiii. 49; Josh. xii. 3, xiii. 20; it is supposed
to be *Suweimeh*, at the mouth of the Jordan.   Baal-meon, Numb. xxxii.
3, 38, more fully Beth-baal-meon (Josh. xiii. 17), and in another form,
Beth-meon (Jer. xlviii. 23), lay further inland, a little S. of Heshbon;
supposed to be *Mâ'in*.   Kiriathaim lay somewhat further south (Numb.
xxxii. 37; Josh. xiii. 19; Jer. xlviii. 1, 23); supposed to be *Karêyât*.

10.   Read, with full stop at *v.* 9: **Unto the children of the East will
I give it for possession together with** the children of Ammon (*v.* 4).
Moab and Ammon alike shall become a possession of the wandering
Bedawin.   The name of Ammon shall disappear from among the nations,
and Moab shall be visited with severe judgements.

the nations: and I will execute judgements upon Moab; 11
and they shall know that I am the LORD.

Thus saith the Lord GOD: Because that Edom hath 12
dealt against the house of Judah by taking vengeance,
and hath greatly offended, and revenged himself upon
them; therefore thus saith the Lord GOD, I* will stretch 13
out mine hand upon Edom, and will cut off man and beast
from it: and I will make it desolate from Teman; even
unto Dedan shall they fall by the sword. And I will lay 14
my vengeance upon Edom by the hand of my people
Israel; and they shall do in Edom according to mine
anger and according to my fury: and they shall know my
vengeance, saith the Lord GOD.

XXV. 12—14. PROPHECY AGAINST EDOM.

The relations of Edom to Israel were changeful. Subdued by David
it shook off the yoke under Jehoram (2 Kgs viii. 20). Reconquered
by Amaziah and Uzziah (2 Kgs xiv. 7, 22), it rebelled under Ahaz
(2 Kgs xvi. 6; 2 Chron. xxviii. 17), and from this time was probably
independent. Edomites seem to have taken part in the capture of Jerusalem by the Chaldeans, or at least to have been active in cutting off the
fugitives (Obad. vv. 10—14), and for their part in this they incurred the
lasting hatred of Israel (Obad.; Lam. iv. 21; Is. xxxiv. 5 seq., lxiii. 1—6;
Joel iii. 19; Ps. cxxxvii. 7; Mal. i. 2. Cf. Jer. xlix. 7 seq.). During
the exile the Edomites took possession of part of the land of Israel
(xxxv. 10); and in the time of the Maccabean war of independence,
like the Ammonites, they shewed their hereditary enmity to Israel (1
Macc. v. 3, 35). John Hyrcanus finally subdued them and incorporated
them in the state of Israel. Ultimately, like Moab and Ammon, the
name of Edom disappears from history, all the three peoples being
known by the general name of Arabs,—Children of the East—as Ezek.
had prophesied.

12. *hath greatly offended*] Israel as the people of the true God was
inviolable (Jer. ii. 3), except when Jehovah employed the nations to
chastise it. Too often the nations exceeded their commission, cherishing
purposes of their own (Is. x. 6 seq.), and themselves incurred guilt by
their excess (Is. xlvii. 6; Zech. i. 15).

13. Teman was in the N. of Edom (Gen. xxxvi. 11; Am. i. 11;
Jer. xlix. 7; Obad. 9), and Dedan to the south; the latter probably only
bordered on Edom (Gen. x. 7; Is. xxi. 13; Jer. xxv. 23).

14. *by the hand of my people*] Cf. Obad. 18, "the house of Jacob shall
be a fire...and the house of Esau for stubble, and they shall burn among
them, and devour them." Is. xi. 14; Zeph. ii. 9.

know my vengeance] that it is I who take vengeance upon them (v. 4);
Is. xxxiv. 8.

15   Thus saith the Lord GOD: Because the Philistines have
      dealt by revenge, and have taken vengeance with despite
16 of soul to destroy it with perpetual enmity; therefore thus
      saith the Lord GOD, Behold, I will stretch out mine hand
      upon the Philistines, and I will cut off the Cherethites, and
17 destroy the remnant of the sea coast.   And I will execute
      great vengeance upon them with furious rebukes; and they
      shall know that I am the LORD, when I shall lay my
      vengeance upon them.
26   And it came to pass in the eleventh year, in the first

XXV. 15—17. PROPHECY AGAINST THE PHILISTINES.

15. *with despite of soul*] as *v.* 6, i.e. the deepest despite of heart,
ch. xvi. 57, xxxvi. 5.
      destroy it with perpetual enmity] Cf. xxxv. 5; Am. i. 11. The
power of the Philistines was conclusively broken by David, but references
to their rancour and injuriousness when opportunity occurred run through
all the literature of Israel, Am. i. 6 *seq.* ; Is. ix. 12; Zeph. ii. 5; Obad. 19;
Joel iii. 4; Zech. ix. 5.
      16. *I will cut off the Cherethites*] [There seems to be a play on the
name in the original, *hikratti Kĕrēthîm*.] The name was given to the
inhabitants of the Philistine coast, Zeph. ii. 5, "Woe unto the inhabitants of the sea coast, the nation of the Cherethites...the land of the
Philistines." Cf. 1 Sam. xxx. 14; 2 Sam. viii. 18; Jer. xlvii. 4.
      the remnant] Cf. Am. i. 8; Is. xiv. 30; Zeph. i. 4.
      17. *with furious rebukes*] wanting in LXX. No agents are men-
tioned as the destroyers of the Philistines.

XXVI.—XXVIII. PROPHECY AGAINST TYRE.

      The three chapters xxvi.—xxviii. are occupied with Tyre, containing
threats of her destruction in various forms.
      First, ch. xxvi. Literal prophecy of Tyre's destruction at the hands
of Nebuchadrezzar.
      Secondly, ch. xxvii. Dirge over the downfall of Tyre under the
figure of a gallant ship steered into dangerous waters and suffering shipwreck.
      Thirdly, ch. xxviii. The pride and fall of the prince of Tyre.

XXVI. PROPHECY OF TYRE'S DESTRUCTION.

      The prophecy has these divisions :
      (1) *vv.* 1—6. The sin of Tyre, and therefore her downfall.
      (2) *vv.* 7—14. The instrument of her destruction, Nebuchadrezzar.
      (3) *vv.* 15—18. Dismay of the princes at the news of her ruin.
Their sorrow and lament over her.

day of the month, that the word of the LORD came unto
me, saying, Son of man, because that Tyre hath said against 2
Jerusalem, Aha, she is broken *that was* the gate of the
peoples; she is turned unto me: I shall be replenished,
now that she is laid waste: therefore thus saith the Lord 3
GOD: Behold, I am against thee, O Tyre, and will cause
many nations to come up against thee, as the sea causeth
his waves to come up.   And they shall destroy the walls of 4
Tyre, and break down her towers: I will also scrape her

(4) *vv.* 19—21. Repetition and confirmation of the threat against
her. She shall be plunged into eternal darkness, with those dead of
old, never more to rise among the living.

1. *first day of the month*] The 11th year of Jehoiachin's captivity
(i.e. B.C. 586) was that in which Jerusalem was taken. On the 9th day
of the 4th month of this year the city was stormed, and on the 10th day
of the 5th month it was destroyed (Jer. lii. 6, 12). The present prophecy
assumes the destruction of the city (*v.* 2). The month is not stated.
If the 11th year be read in xxxiii. 21 (see there), fugitives announcing
the fall of the city reached the prophet on the 5th of the 10th month of
that year. The prophecy is probably later than this date, and the
month may be the 11th or 12th.

2. The sin of Tyre: her rejoicing over the calamity of Judah, in the
hope that it will further her interests.

Aha, she is broken &c.] Rather: **Aha! the gate** (door) **of the peoples
is broken, it is turned unto me.** [So Cor. Ber. Kr.] ("Door" is
plur. as having leaves, or by attraction to the plural peoples.) The idea
appears to be that Jerusalem or Judah was a door barring the entrance
to Tyre. This door being broken and turned or opened towards Tyre,
the nations would stream with their commerce towards her. The
kingdom of Judah, situated across the great commercial routes from
the south, no doubt intercepted much of the merchandise that otherwise
would have reached Tyre, and probably exacted custom on that which
was allowed to pass. But the natural sense of "gate of the peoples"
would be door *into* the nations (Nah. iii. 13; Zech. xi. 1), and the idea
would be that the door was now opened for Tyre to enter. The sense
remains the same; the barrier which stood between Tyre and the nations
is removed.

3—6. The punishment of Tyre. Many nations shall be brought up
against her (*v.* 3); her dust shall be scraped from her into the sea, leaving
her a naked rock, a place for drying nets (*vv.* 4, 5), and her dependent
cities on the mainland shall be laid waste (*v.* 6).

3. *as the sea causeth his waves*] The comparison is powerful. It is
not the succession, but the multitude and overwhelming power of the
waves that is referred to.

4. *her dust*] her ruins, reduced to dust.

5 dust from her, and make her a bare rock. She shall be
  a place for the spreading of nets in the midst of the sea;
  for I have spoken it, saith the Lord GOD: and she shall
6 become a spoil to the nations. And her daughters which
  are in the field shall be slain with the sword: and they
7 shall know that I am the LORD. For thus saith the Lord
  GOD: Behold, I will bring upon Tyre Nebuchadrezzar king
  of Babylon, king of kings, from the north, with horses, and
  with chariots, and with horsemen, and a company, and
8 much people. He shall slay with the sword thy daughters
  in the field: and he shall make forts against thee, and cast
  up a mount against thee, and raise up the buckler against

a bare rock] Cf. ch. xxiv. 7. Tyre stood upon a small island of rock
separated from the mainland by a narrow strait. She shall be swept
from her place, and her dust scraped into the sea, leaving her island site
a bare rock, cf. *v.* 12.

5. The threat is repeated *v.* 14.

6. *her daughters…in the field*] i.e. her dependent towns on the mainland, ch. xvi. 46, xxx. 18. Tyre at this time was at the head of the
Phœnician confederation of cities, cf. xxvii. 8—11.

XXVI. **7—14.** JEHOVAH'S INSTRUMENT IN TYRE'S DESTRUCTION,
NEBUCHADREZZAR.

The description is graphic: the advance of the assailant with his
great army (*v.* 7); the siege with the powerful train of engines (8, 9);
the assault, capture, and sack of the city (10—12), which is left a
joyless ruin, a naked rock in the midst of the sea, never again to be
built (13, 14).

7. Nebuchadrezzar is the correct spelling (xxix. 18, xxx. 10), the
name being Nabû-kudurri-usur, "Nebo protect my boundary!"
Schrader, *KAT*.[3] p. 407.

king of kings] **the** king. Ezr. vii. 12; Dan. ii. 37. Already the
king of Assyria had said, "Are not my princes all of them kings?"
Is. x. 8, cf. xxxvi. 4.

from the north] more strictly north-east.

and a company, and much people] LXX. reads: "company *of* much
people" (very many nations), which may be the meaning of the Heb.

8. The cities and villages, dependencies of Tyre on the mainland,
naturally are the first to suffer. Then the siege of the insular city itself
is taken in hand. The order is precise: first the "forts," or moveable
towers[1], from which the archers shot so as to counteract the defensive

___
[1] [Lit. a bulwark, siege-wall.]

thee. And he shall set his battering engines against thy 9
walls, and with his ¹axes he shall break down thy towers.
By reason of the abundance of his horses their dust shall 10
cover thee : thy walls shall shake at the noise of the horsemen, and of the ²wagons, and of the chariots, when he shall
enter into thy gates, as men enter into a city wherein is
made a breach. With the hoofs of his horses shall he 11
tread down all thy streets : he shall slay thy people with
the sword, and the ³pillars of thy strength shall go down
to the ground. And they shall make a spoil of thy riches, 12
and make a prey of thy merchandise : and they shall break
down thy walls, and destroy thy pleasant houses : and they
shall lay thy stones and thy timber and thy dust in the
midst of the waters. And I will cause the noise of thy 13
songs to cease ; and the sound of thy harps shall be no
more heard. And I will make thee a bare rock : thou shalt 14
be a place for the spreading of nets ; thou shalt be built
no more : for I the LORD have spoken it, saith the Lord
GOD.

¹ Heb. *swords*.   ² Or, *wheels*   ³ Or, *obelisks*

efforts of the besieged (cf. iv. 2) ; then the "mount" or embankment,
which in this case was a dam thrown across the narrow strait, in order to
gain access to the walls ; then the "buckler" or shield, i.e. probably the
testudo or roof of shields under cover of which the besiegers operated,
and finally (*v.* 9) the "battering engines."

9. *axes*] [lit. as marg., *swords*, and so possibly meant here as the
instruments most ready to hand (Oxf. Dict.). But cf. Exod. xx. 25,
where the word means a tool. Moreover swords would not be of much
use against stone.]

10 *seq.* The assault, capture, and sack of the city. The description is graphic in the extreme. Cf. generally Nah. ii. When the
conqueror enters, the dust following the march of his cavalry
shall cover the city ; the walls shall shake at the rushing of his
chariots in the streets ; and the city shall be given up to slaughter and
plunder.

11. *the pillars* (marg. *obelisks*) *of thy strength*] The word is almost
always used of a pillar having religious meaning, particularly the obelisk
dedicated to Baal (2 Kgs x. 26). [According to Herod. (II. 44) Tyre
contained two such pillars dedicated to that god under his Tyrian name,
Melkart.] The meaning is "thy proud or majestic pillars," the
emblems of her worship, cf. xxiv. 21, 25. See further on xl. 48.

15 Thus saith the Lord GOD to Tyre: Shall not the isles shake at the sound of thy fall, when the wounded groan,
16 when the slaughter is made in the midst of thee? Then all the princes of the sea shall come down from their thrones, and lay aside their robes, and strip off their broidered garments: they shall clothe themselves with [1]trembling; they shall sit upon the ground, and shall tremble
17 every moment, and be astonished at thee. And they shall take up a lamentation for thee, and say to thee, How art thou destroyed, that wast inhabited [2]of seafaring men, the renowned city, which wast strong in the sea, she and her inhabitants, which caused their terror to be on all that
18 [3]haunt it! Now shall the isles tremble in the day of thy

[1] Heb. *tremblings*.   [2] Or, *being won from the seas*
          [3] Or, *inhabited her*

XXVI. **15—18.** COMMOTION AMONG THE PRINCES OF THE SEA CAUSED BY HER FALL; THEY MOURN AND TAKE UP A LAMENT OVER TYRE (17, 18).

15. *the isles shake*] the coast-lands, the island-like countries on the seaboard.
at the sound of thy fall] might mean *at the report of thy fall* but here by a strong hyperbole the prophet appears to represent the crash of the city's fall and the cries of the wounded as being heard on the neighbouring coasts, ch. xxvii. 28, xxxi. 16; cf. Jer. xlix. 21.
16. In token of mourning the princes of the sea, the rulers of the principalities and cities on all sea-coasts, shall descend from their thrones, lay aside their royal robes, and sit on the ground (Lam. ii. 10).
clothe themselves] or, *be clothed*, i.e. be enveloped in, "tremblings" (see marg.), cf. vii. 27.
17, 18. Lament of the princes over Tyre.
17. *that wast...men*] lit. inhabited *from the seas*. But the Heb. consonants should probably be read with different vowels; "made to cease from the seas."
all that haunt it] This rendering makes the ref. to be to the sea, though the present text is literally *all her inhabitants*, referring to the city. To say, however, that Tyre and her inhabitants made their terror felt by all her inhabitants is very unnatural. If the text is sound, the pronoun must refer to the "seas."
18. *the isles tremble*] See on *v.* 15. The Aramaic form of plur. appears to be adopted in order to make a variation from "isles" (ordinary form) in the next clause. The phrase "at thy departure," lit. *outgoing*, is strange; but might have a parallel in Ps. cxliv. 14.

fall; yea, the isles that are in the sea shall be dismayed at
thy departure. For thus saith the Lord GOD: When I shall 19
make thee a desolate city, like the cities that are not
inhabited; when I shall bring up the deep upon thee,
and the great waters shall cover thee; then will I bring 20
thee down with them that descend into the pit, to the
people of old time, and will make thee to dwell in the
nether parts of the earth, ¹in the places that are desolate
of old, with them that go down to the pit, that thou be not

---

¹ Another reading is, *like*.

The elegy seems confined to *v.* 17, but probably through explanatory
amplifications that have crept into the text, *v.* 18 has also been drawn
into it. LXX. reads in a shorter form:

17.   How art thou destroyed from the sea—the renowned city!
       She that brought her terror—on all its inhabitants.
18.   And the isles shall be terrified—at the day of thy fall.

V. 18 can hardly refer to the *memory* of Tyre's fall, but to the fall
itself, xxvii. 27 (xxxii. 10), which being represented as future is unsuitable to the dirge in the mouth of the princes. The verse hardly
belongs to the dirge but forms the transition to the next strophe,
vv. 19—21.

XXVI. 19—21. REPETITION AND CONFIRMATION OF THE THREAT.

19.   Tyre shall be overwhelmed in the great waters, and brought
down to the pit, with those who are dead from of old; she shall
never be inhabited nor found any more.

20.   *then will I bring*] The prophet regards Tyre's sinking beneath
the waters as her entrance upon the descent into the pit, the place of
the dead, just as frequently elsewhere (ch. xxxii.) he makes the grave the
entrance into the underworld of the dead. Cf. Is. xiv. 11, 19.

that descend into the pit] Rather: **them that are gone down into
the pit, unto the people** &c. The common phrase "they that go down to
the pit" should be rendered: *that are gone down* (past). Ezek. always
says "*with* them that are gone down," xxviii. 8, xxxi. 14: cf. Is. xiv.
19, xxxviii. 18.

The "people of old time" are those dead from of old, xxxii. 27;
Lam. iii. 6; Ps. cxliii. 3; hardly with more definite ref. to the Flood,
Job xxii. 15.

nether parts of the earth] i.e. in the underworld of the dead (xxxi. 14,
xxxii. 18—24; Lam. iii. 55; Ps. lxiii. 9), which was held to be situated
in the bowels of the earth or under the earth.

in the places that are desolate of old] According to the textual tradition (Baer, *Ezech.*) the true reading is (as marg.) "*like* places...," so
LXX., Vulg. The prophet gives Tyre a personality; when buried
under the sea she goes down into the abode of the dead, and possibly
he regards "the places that are desolate of old" as also gone down

inhabited; [1]and I will set glory in the land of the living:
21 I will make thee [2]a terror, and thou shalt be no more:
though thou be sought for, yet shalt thou never be found
again, saith the Lord GOD.

[1] Or, as otherwise read, *nor set* thy *glory &c.*
[2] Or, *a destruction* Heb. *terrors*.

and gathered in the underworld. For "that go down," render *that
are gone down.*

and I will set glory] Such an antithesis is entirely unnatural:
something further must be said of Tyre in continuation of "that thou
be not inhabited." Either render as marg.: *nor set* (thy) *glory* (reading
2 fem., with final *y* otiose), a phrase, however, nowhere else occurring;
or else the reading presumably before LXX. must be accepted: **nor
continue** (*tithyazzebi*) **in the land of the living.**

21. *make thee a terror*] lit. as marg., meaning, "I will utterly destroy
thee," xxvii. 35, xxviii. 19; cf. Ps. lxxiii. 19[1]. On "make" cf. xvi. 38.

The passage xxix. 17—21 states that Nebuchadrezzar received no
adequate reward for the service against Tyre which he served for
Jehovah. History records his thirteen years' siege of Tyre, but is silent
as to the issue of it. It is not known (1) whether he took the city, or
(2) whether it capitulated, or (3) whether he retired from it. On the
whole the second supposition may be most probable. At any rate
neither the king nor his army received wages for his service.

The prophecy was not literally fulfilled [in the sense that the city was
utterly to perish. Tyre, we know clearly, survived the results of the
siege, whatever they were. Gautier (*Ezéchiel*, p. 290) points out the
parallel afforded by Jeremiah's denunciations of Jerusalem, as destined
for utter destruction (e.g. vii. 12—15, 32—34), as compared with his
bright forecasts in ch. xxx.—xxxiii.]. Now

1. All prophecy is moral, is based on moral considerations. What
the prophet aims his threats against is not the prosperity of Tyre, but
its pride of heart, which was rebellion against Jehovah, God over all.
The humiliation of Tyre was morally as good as its ruin, in so far as it
shewed that there were higher forces in the world than itself.

2. Prophecy is always ideal in its delineations. Its threats and
promises are alike hyperbolical whether they concern Israel or the
nations. And in regard to fulfilment the same general principles must
be applied to all prophecies, those of redemption and those of calamity alike. The former are not fulfilled at once, nor at all literally,
neither need we expect immediate or literal fulfilment of the latter.
At the same time in regard to both it must be maintained that the
prophets *imagined* the fulfilment as they describe it. This, however, is
part of their idealism; the moral element is always the main thing in
their prophecies. What they predict is the exhibition of Jehovah's
moral rule of the world; the *form* in which they clothe this exhibition
may not be quite that given in history.

[1] [If we render "a terror," it can only mean, a warning to other nations.]

The word of the LORD came again unto me, saying, And 2
thou, son of man, take up a lamentation for Tyre; and say 3
unto Tyre, O thou that dwellest at the ¹entry of the sea,
which art the merchant of the peoples unto many isles,
thus saith the Lord GOD: Thou, O Tyre, hast said, I am
perfect in beauty. Thy borders are in the heart of the seas, 4
thy builders have perfected thy beauty. They have ²made 5

¹ Heb. *entrances*.   ² Heb. *built*.

XXVII. DIRGE OVER THE DOWNFALL OF TYRE.

The lament represents Tyre under the figure of a gallant, richly-
laden ship, steered by her pilots into dangerous waters and suffering
shipwreck. The passage has three main divisions:
(1) *vv.* 1—11. The ship, her timbers, furnishings, and manning.
(2) *vv.* 12—25. The wares and merchandise with which the nations
lade her.
(3) *vv.* 26—36. Her shipwreck: consternation of seafaring men
(*vv.* 26—31); their lament over her (*vv.* 32—36).

XXVII. 1—11. TYRE AS A GALLANT SHIP.

2. For the phrase "take up a lamentation" cf. xix. 1, xxvi. 17,
xxviii. 12, xxxii. 2. The word is a technical one for the dirge.
3. *entry of the sea*] lit. as marg. *entrances*, reference possibly being
to the two harbours of Tyre, one of which was to the N.E. of the
island, called the Zidonian harbour, because looking towards Zidon;
and the other on the S. or S.E. of the island, the exact position of which
is uncertain owing to the silting which has taken place. See plate in
Rawlinson, *Phœnicia*, p. 71.
of the peoples unto many isles] Cf. *vv.* 6, 15. Her traffic with the
peoples extended to many and distant coastlands.
4. *Thy borders...heart of the seas*] The phrase appears to mean not
"far out at sea," but, in the deep waters of the sea, ch. xxviii. 2, 8;
Exod. xv. 8; Jon. ii. 3; Ps. xlvi. 2. The term "borders" seems to mean
station, moorings (*v.* 25)¹. The proud ship was conscious of her beauty.
The ship is a figure for the maritime city, the mistress of trade, built
upon an ocean rock, as if moored in the sea. The city was without
doubt beautiful (ch. xxviii. 12); a similar phrase is used of Jerusalem,
Ps. l. 2, Ps. xlviii. 2; Lam. ii. 15.

¹ [But the city was not in the depths of the sea, nor can "borders" mean stations.
Rather, the figure is dropped, or there is a momentary confusion between the city
and the ship. Kr. with a slight change in the Heb. for "thy borders" renders "Thy
builders have made thee great in the heart of the seas."]

all thy planks of fir trees from Senir: they have taken
6 cedars from Lebanon to make a mast for thee. Of the oaks
of Bashan have they made thine oars; they have made thy
¹benches of ivory inlaid in boxwood, from the isles of Kittim.
7 Of fine linen with broidered work from Egypt was thy sail,
that it might be to thee for an ensign; blue and purple
8 from the isles of Elishah was thine awning.   The inhabitants

¹ Or, *deck*

5, 6.   The ship's timbers.

5.   *planks*]   The word is *dual*, referring to the two ribs of the
ship, corresponding to one another.

fir trees from Senir]   Or, *cypresses*.   The tree is mentioned as furnishing,
along with the cedar, the principal material for building the Temple,
1 Kgs v. 8.   Senir was the Amorite name of Hermon, which the
Zidonians called Sirion (Deut. iii. 9).   According to Schrader (*KAT.*³
p. 190) the name Senir was used by the Assyrians.   Hermon possibly
signifies "sacred" mountain, from its ancient sanctuary.   Senir (and so
Sirion) was supposed to mean "coat of mail."

On "mast" cf. Is. xxxiii. 23.   Whether an actual cedar was ever
used to be the mast of "some great ammiral¹" may be uncertain; the
prophet, though more exact than most prophets, is also a poet.

6.   The oars of the great ship were made of oaks of Bashan; cf.
Is. ii. 13; Zech. xi. 2.   The term "oars" occurs in another form,
v. 27, but probably with no difference of meaning.   The rest of *v.* 6
should read: **thy deck** (so marg.) **they made of ivory** (inlaid) **in
sherbin wood from the isles of Kittim** (the words *bath asshŭrim* should
no doubt be read *bithĕasshūr*).   The tree called *tĕasshūr* is mentioned as
growing in Lebanon, Is. xli. 19, lx. 13; it is usually considered to be
the tree called in Arabic *sherbîn*, a species of cedar.   Others contend
for box or larch.   The term "deck" is literally "board," e.g. of the
boards of the sanctuary, Exod. xxvi. 15 *seq.*   Kittim is Cyprus, called
after the town Kition (Larnaka), but probably the name embraced the
coasts of Asia Minor and Greece or perhaps even of Italy (Dan. xi. 30;
1 Macc. i. 1, viii. 5).

7.   The rigging and furnishing of the ship.   Her sail (ancient ships
usually had but one sail) was embroidered byssus, fine linen, out of
Egypt (xvi. 10).

The flag proper seems not to have been used in ancient navigation;
its purpose was served by the sail, as for example at the battle of
Actium, the ship of Antony was distinguished by its purple sail.   On
"broidered" cf. ch. xvi. 10, 13, 18.

the isles of Elishah]   In Gen. x. 4 Elishah is one of the sons of Javan,
i.e. Ionia or Grecian Asia.   The Targ. renders "country of Italy."
Ges. connects the name with Elis, and understands the Peloponnesus in
general, which was certainly noted for the dyes referred to in the verse.

thine awning]   lit. *thy covering* (in Is. xiv. 11 a coverlet, cf. Is. xxiii.

¹ [Milton, *Par. Lost*, i. 294.]

of Zidon and Arvad were thy rowers : thy wise men, O Tyre, were in thee, they were thy pilots. The [1]ancients of 9 Gebal and the wise men thereof were in thee thy calkers: all the ships of the sea with their mariners were in thee to [2]occupy thy merchandise. Persia and Lud and Put were in 10

---

[1] Or, *elders*   [2] Or, *exchange*

---

18), either an awning, or more probably a cabin, the sides and roof of which were of the fine stuffs named.

8 *seq.* The manning of the ship. The inhabitants of Zidon and Arvad were her rowers, and her own wise men her steersmen.

Zidon and Arvad] Zidon lay to the N. of Tyre, about half-way between it and Beirut, and was probably the oldest Phœnician town, Tyre being a colony. Zidon is the firstborn of Canaan (Gen. x. 15), and is called Great Zidon in Josh. xix. 28. It is frequently referred to in Homer (e.g. *Il.* 7. 290), who does not mention Tyre. At a later time Tyre eclipsed her mother in power and wealth. Arvad (Aradus) lay considerably more to the N. It was built on a small island, over two miles from the mainland, and, being without natural harbours, piers were laboriously constructed of huge blocks of stone, 16 feet long by 7 broad, quarried on the island. It was dependent for water upon the mainland, but when its supply was cut off recourse was had to a powerful spring of fresh water which was known to rise under the sea in the channel between the town and the mainland. This spring was isolated and the water brought by a tube to the surface. The spring is said still to exist. Arvad, now *Ruwād*, or *Ruweideh*, is often mentioned in the Assyrian annals. Tiglath-pileser I (*c.* 1100) embarked on ships of Arvad and sailed out into "the great sea," Frd. Delitzsch, *Paradies*, p. 281. See chart of Arvad, Rawlinson, *Phœn.* p. 74.

9. *ancients of Gebal*] The elders, a title of honour or office, the magistrates. Probably also the "wise men thereof" is a semi-official title (cf. *v.* 8). The power of Tyre was exerted over all her dependencies (xxvi. 17), in which men of the highest position entered all ranks of her service. Gebal (the classical Byblos, now *Jebâl*) is situated not far from the river Adonis (Ibrahim) somewhat over 20 miles N. of Beirut (Josh. xiii. 5; 1 Kgs v. 18, R.V.). The town was devoted to the worship of Beltis (Astarte) and Adonis, cf. on ch. viii. 14. The name appears in the Assyrian inscriptions, Del. *Parad.* p. 283.

thy calkers] Stoppers of chinks, carpenters [from Lat. *calcare*, to tread, press].

to occupy thy merchandise] **to handle thy wares** [lit. to exchange thy articles of exchange. Cf. marg. For "occupy"=employ cf. Luke xix. 13 in A.V.]. The representation is that the great ship was attended on by all the ships of the sea with their sailors, who trade with her and delivered her wares to her, or were busied about them (*v.* 27).

thine army, thy men of war: they hanged the shield and
11 helmet in thee; they set forth thy comeliness. The men of
Arvad with thine army were upon thy walls round about,
and [1]the Gammadim were in thy towers: they hanged their
shields upon thy walls round about; they have perfected

[1] Or, *valorous men*

10. Her army.

Her mercenaries were drawn from all quarters of the world. The
people called here "Persia" appears along with Cush and Put, African
peoples, in the army of Gog, ch. xxxviii. 5, in which, however, northern
nations as Gomer and Togarmah are also mustered. The host of Gog
includes the nations lying on the outskirts of the known world, and
Persia might be named among them, though the first certain mention of
that country is in Ezr. iv. 5, ix. 9, &c. Others have [needlessly] thought
here of some African people [such as Cush (Ethiopia), so Toy, or the
Pharusii, in N. Africa; so Dillm.]. Lud is named, ch. xxx. 5, along
with Cush and Put, as allies of Egypt (Jer. xlvi. 9 [where see note in
C.B.]); and in Gen. x. 13 Ludim is the firstborn of Mizraim (Egypt).
In Is. lxvi. 19 Lud is named after Tarshish, and probably some people
lying on the African coast, W. of Egypt, is referred to. Put (Gen. x. 6)
is son of Ham, and brother of Cush (Ethiopia), Mizraim (Egypt) and
Canaan (Phœnicia). In Ezek. xxx. 5 (Jer. xlvi. 9; Nah. iii. 9) the people
is an ally of Egypt. LXX. renders Libyans. The inhabitants of
western Egypt, or those on its western border, may be referred to.

they hanged the shield] The great ship is still spoken of. A figure of
a ship so adorned and dressed with weapons hung on its sides is given
in Layard, *Nineveh*, II. p. 388. The practice of hanging weapons on
buildings was not unknown in Israel, Song of Sol. iv. 4; 1 Macc. iv. 57.

11. *with thine army*] It is scarcely possible to render: *men of
Arvad, they were thine army*. Some proper name seems required: "the
men of Arvad and of..." Cor. conjectures Hethlon (xlvii. 15, xlviii. 1),
others, Cilicia.

the Gammadim] A proper name is certainly to be expected, but no
place, Gammad, is known. Some have suggested "they of Gomer,"
but an adj. is not formed from Gomer; Cor., Zemarites, Gen. x. 18
[Redpath identifies with the modern *Kamid-el-Lôz*, about half-way
between Beirut and Damascus]. Others, as marg., take the word as an
appellative: "valorous men." [The Vulg. following Aquila's rendering,
has *Pygmaei*.]

XXVII. 12—25. THE MARKET OF TYRE.

[The various nations bring their products in exchange for the manufactures or merchandise of Tyre.] Two words are employed for "to
trade," "to be a merchant." The words have little difference of sense
and are generally used alternately. Two words also are used in the

thy beauty.   Tarshish was thy merchant by reason of the 12
multitude of all kinds of riches ; with silver, iron, tin, and
lead, they traded for thy wares.   Javan, Tubal, and Meshech, 13

sense of *wares* or goods, though hardly differing in meaning.   Gesen.
attributed various senses to these words, as: 1, traffic, trading; 2, fair,
market-place; and 3, gain, wealth.   The words do not appear to differ
in meaning, and neither of the two probably has any other sense than
the general one of wares.   [The general sense of exchange, traffic,
adopted by the R.V. in accordance with the view of most commentators is doubtless the right one.   Davidson, however, maintains
that the passage speaks of *tribute* brought to Tyre by the other
nations in token of inferiority.   This view seems hardly defensible,
and it has accordingly been necessary to modify or omit some of
Davidson's subsequent notes so far as their language was dependent
on Davidson's interpretation.]

There is much uncertainty in the text, e.g. for "sons of Dedan," *v.* 15,
LXX. reads "sons of the Rhodians," and for Aram (Syria) *v.* 16, Syriac
reads " Edom," cf. LXX.   "man," in both cases by interchange of the
similar letters *d* and *r*.   *V.* 19 is certainly out of order, and *v.* 24 exceedingly obscure.   Owing to these obscurities the precise order followed
in the enumeration of the nations is involved in some uncertainty.
1. *vv.* 12—24, the prophet names the nations lying in the widest circle
around Tyre, beginning with the furthest west, Tarshish (Spain), and
pursuing a line along the north, Javan (Ionia), Tubal (N. of Asia Minor),
and Togarmah (Armenia).   2. If Rhodians be read in *v.* 15, a narrower
circle of the Mediterranean islands and coasts would be described.
3. *vv.* 16—19, if Edom be read for Aram, the line traced is from S. to N.,
along the eastern trade route, Edom, Judah, Damascus.   4. In *v.* 19 Uzal
(R.V. " with yarn ") seems certainly to be the name of a place in the S.
of Arabia, the other names are Arabian, Dedan, Kedar, Sheba and
Raamah.   5. The names in *v.* 23 *seq.* are more obscure, and it is not
certain whether this is the previous line carried further N. or a new line.

12.   The name Tarshish (Tartessus) was given to the district of
country lying outside the Straits of Gibraltar on the lower Baetis, the
Guadalquivir (*Wadi el Kebīr*, great river).

with silver...for thy wares] There is no evidence that the word "wares"
means "fairs," as A.V.; in *vv.* 27, 34 the things so named fall into the
waters of the sea.   Spain was famous for the metals mentioned; cf. for
silver, Jer. x. 9.   Probably Tarshish served as an entrepôt for such
products found further north, as in the Cassiterides (Scilly Islands) and
Cornwall.

13.   These three countries, Javan, Tubal, and Meshech, are usually
named together, Gen. x. 2; Ezek. xxxii. 26, xxxviii. 2, xxxix. 1; Is. lxvi.
19.   The first is the Ionians, the Greeks of Asia Minor, and the two
last have usually been identified with the Moschi and Tibareni, lying to
the S. and S.E. of the Black Sea.   Copper and "souls of men," i.e.

they were thy traffickers: they traded the persons of men
14 and vessels of brass for thy merchandise. They of the house
of Togarmah traded for thy wares with horses and war-
15 horses and mules. The men of Dedan were thy traffickers:
many isles were the mart of thine hand: they brought thee
16 ¹in exchange horns of ivory and ebony. Syria was thy
merchant by reason of the multitude of thy handyworks:
they traded for thy wares with ²emeralds, purple, and

---

¹ Or, *for a present*   ² Or, *carbuncles*

---

slaves, form the contribution of these countries. That Javan traded in
slaves appears from Joel iii. [Heb. iv.] 6; cf. Am. i. 6, 9.

14. *house of Togarmah*] Usually supposed to be Armenia or part
of it. Togarmah lay in the extreme N. of the world known to the
prophet, and the people appears in the army of Gog with other nations
from the ends of the earth (ch. xxxviii. 6; cf. Gen. x. 2). Others think
of Phrygia or Cappadocia. All these countries were noted [for Togarmah
see Herod. I. 194] for breeding horses.

horses] [Redp. wishes to retain the "horsemen" of A.V., referring
the word to mercenaries, and comparing, among other passages,
Jer. xlvi. 4 and Joel ii. 4, which, however, are not decisive.]
The ancients did not use the horse for labour. LXX. omits *mules*,
a somewhat similar word, and possibly (as Cor. conjectures) only two
words should be read: horses and mules.

15. *men of Dedan*] lit. sons of Dedan: LXX. sons of *the Rhodians*
(*r* and *d* resembling each other in Heb.). [This is probably the right
reading.] Dedan occurs again *v.* 20 [in its proper place] in connexion
with Arabian tribes, and in xxv. 13 it appears to be placed S. of
Edom, being either part of that country or bordering on it (cf. Jer.
xlix. 8, xxv. 23; Is. xxi. 13). If the reading Dedan is retained,
then, as being connected with coast lands, it has been usually placed
on the Persian Gulf. Ivory and ebony, the articles in which it
traded, might be Indian products. On the other hand the Phœnicians
certainly had colonies in Rhodes; and if Rhodians were the true reading
the "isles" would be the coasts of the Mediterranean.

mart of thine hand] The phrase "of thine hand" means *under thee*,
doing thy service, cf. *v.* 21.

horns of ivory] Tusks of elephants, so called from their resemblance
to horns. Ebony, the other article referred to, was brought from India
and Ethiopia. The African ebony was most esteemed.

16. For Syria (Aram) the Syr. reads "Edom," and so in effect
LXX. (interchange of *d* and *r* as *v.* 15). If Edom be read the line
pursued would be from S. to N., Edom, *v.* 16, Judah, *v.* 17, Damascus,
v. 18. The verse is otherwise peculiar in beginning with a precious
stone, then passing on to stuffs, and ending with precious stones.

broidered work, and fine linen, and coral, and rubies. Judah, and the land of Israel, they were thy traffickers: 17 they traded for thy merchandise wheat of Minnith, and ¹pannag, and honey, and oil, and balm.   Damascus was thy 18 merchant for the multitude of thy handyworks, by reason of the multitude of all kinds of riches; with the wine of Helbon, and white wool.   Vedan and Javan traded with 19 ²yarn for thy wares: ³bright iron, cassia, and calamus, were

---

¹ Perhaps, a kind of confection.   ² According to some ancient versions, *from Uzal.*   ³ Or, *wrought*

---

coral]   The word may mean "pearls."   The two things were perhaps confused: both were fished for in the Persian Gulf.   The precious stones might seem in favour of Edom, but the fine linen is more naturally the Syrian byssus.   LXX. simply transliterates the words for "coral" and "rubies."

17.   Judah and the land of Israel furnished Tyre with wheat, honey, oil, and balsam.

traded for thy merchandise wheat]   Minnith is supposed to be the Ammonitish place of that name (Jud. xi. 33).   LXX. renders "ointments"; and Cor. conjectures "spices" (Gen. xliii. 11; Is. xxxix. 2; 2 Kgs xx. 13).   The term "pannag" is otherwise unknown; marg. "confection" is supported by the Targ., while Cor. conjectures "wax" (*donag*).   [Redp. suggests "millet," one of the Latin names for that grain, viz. *panicum*, occurring in Cæsar, *B.G.* II. 22.]   The "honey" referred to is no doubt that of wild bees, not grape honey.   The "balm" mentioned, a product of Gilead (Jer. viii. 22), and of Palestine (Gen. xliii. 11), was not the genuine balm, which was peculiar to Arabia, but an odoriferous resin (LXX. Vulg.) exuding from the mastic tree (Pistacia lentiscus).

18.   *for the multitude of thy handyworks*]   [The LXX. omit, probably rightly.]

wine of Helbon]   This is repeatedly mentioned as a choice wine in the Assyrian inscriptions.   The Persian kings also preferred it on their table.   Cf. Hos. xiv. 7; Song of Sol. viii. 11.   The place is identified with *Chalbûn*, N.E. of Damascus.

white wool]   Possibly, wool of *Zachar*, though a place of this name is unknown.

19.   *Vedan*]   a place unknown.   Hardly Weddân, between Mecca and Medina.   Dedan has been conjectured, but that occurs in *v.* 20.   LXX. omits the word, and renders "Javan" by "wine," the two substantives having a close resemblance.

with yarn]   rather, as marg., *from Uzal.*   Uzal (Gen. x. 27; 1 Chron. i. 21) is supposed to be identical with San'āa, the capital of Yemen in S. Arabia.   The text is probably in disorder.   Possibly the

20 among thy merchandise.   Dedan was thy trafficker in
21 precious cloths for riding.   Arabia, and all the princes of
Kedar, they were the merchants of thy hand; in lambs,
and rams, and goats, in these were they thy merchants.
22 The traffickers of Sheba and Raamah, they were thy
traffickers: they traded for thy wares with chief of all
23 spices, and with all precious stones, and gold.   Haran

first words of *v.* 19 should be attached to *v.* 18. So LXX. which
reads *v.* 19, "from Uzal (Azel) came wrought-iron" &c. Cor. follows
LXX., supplying all the words after Helbon out of the Assyrian wine
lists: "wine of Helbon and Zimin and Arnaban they brought to thy
market. From Uzal came wrought iron" &c. The "bright iron"
may refer to the sword blades, for which Yemen was famous. The
calamus or sweet cane (Jer. vi. 20; Is. xliii. 24) supplied one of the
ingredients of the holy oil for anointing the priests (Exod. xxx. 23, 24),
and so did the cassia.

bright] [marg. *wrought*, lit. apparently, "smooth."]

cassia] [Cf. Exod. xxx. 24; probably the dried inner bark of a kind
of cinnamon tree found in S. India.]

calamus] [A sweet-smelling cane from India.]

20. On Dedan cf. *v.* 15; xxv. 13; Gen. xxv. 3.

21. *were the merchants of thy hand*] i.e. serving thee. Cf. Is. lx. 7,
"all the flocks of Kedar shall be gathered together unto thee." The
Arab nomads were rich in flocks. Kedar (Gen. xxv. 13, second son of
Ishmael) was the name of an important people toward the N. of Arabia.
In Is. lx. 7 they are named along with the Nabateans; in Jer. xlix. 28
they are threatened with destruction by Nebuchadrezzar, as they were
threatened at an earlier time with an attack from the Assyrians (Is. xxi.
26). Outside of Scripture they are mentioned first in the inscriptions of Assurbanipal (667—626 B.C.), where they are represented as
dwelling between the Gulf of Akaba and Babylon. Cf. the ref. in
Jer. ii. 10.

22. *traffickers of Sheba*] The abode of this people was in the S.W.
of Arabia, the ruins of their capital Marib still remain, six days' journey
E. of San'āa, the capital of Yemen. Their caravans (Job vi. 19) traded
to Syria and other countries with gold, precious stones, and aromatics
(1 Kgs x. 2, 10; Is. lx. 6; Jer. vi. 20; Ps. lxxii. 10, 15).

Raamah] Raamah was son of Cush and father of Sheba and Dedan
(Gen. x. 7). Raamah probably lay on the Persian Gulf.

23. The places named may be regarded as an extension of the line
from S. to N. in *vv.* 19—22, though the names are given rather in the
order W. to E. Haran in Mesopotamia, two days' journey S.E. of
Edessa, on a branch of the Euphrates, was a sacred city and place of
pilgrimage, and also an emporium of trade. The defeat of Crassus by
the Parthians [B.C. 53] took place there [Latin, Carrhae]. Canneh

and Canneh and Eden, the traffickers of Sheba, Asshur *and* Chilmad, were thy traffickers. These were thy traffickers 24 in choice wares, in ¹wrappings of blue and broidered work, and in chests of rich apparel, bound with cords and made

¹ Or, *bales*

may be Calneh (Gen. x. 10; Am. vi. 2), otherwise Calno (Is. x. 9), a city in Babylonia. Its site has not been identified. Von Gutschmidt (*Encycl. Brit.*, art. Phœnicia) identifies Canneh with Cænæ. Eden, spelled somewhat differently from the Eden of Paradise, is elsewhere named in connexion with Haran, Is. xxxvii. 12 (2 Kgs xix. 12), and said to be in Telassar (Tel Asshur).

the traffickers of Sheba] It is strange that these should be mentioned again (*v.* 22). For "Eden...Sheba" LXX. reads: *these were thy traffickers*, i.e. Haran and Canneh. It has been supposed that the merchants of Sheba frequented the fairs of Haran and thence made their way westward along the trade route to Phœnicia.

Asshur and *Chilmad*] LXX. reads *and* between the words. Asshur if taken in its usual sense would be Assyria. Others think of Sura, or Essureieh, on the Euphrates. G. Smith conjectured that Chilmad was *Kalwâdha* near Bagdad. LXX. reads *Charman*, which suggests Caramania¹.

24. The first half of the verse may read: **These were thy merchants with splendid apparel, cloaks of purple and broidered work.** The second half is obscure owing to the occurrence of some words not found elsewhere.

in chests of rich apparel] The term rendered "chests" occurs Esth. iii. 9, iv. 7 in the sense of "treasures," from root meaning to hide, lay up, a sense common to all the dialects. In Eth. it means to wind in grave-clothes for purposes of burial, but has no special reference to clothing or textile fabrics. The sense "chests" is without evidence. A term virtually the same as that rendered "rich apparel" occurs in Assyrian of stuffs for clothing; and a similar word is used of the night heavens, according to Jensen (*Babylonian Cosmol.* p. 6 *seq.*) from the mixed colour, blue-gray. It appears to be used of fabrics woven of differently coloured materials ["rope or fabrics of two strands or colours," *Oxf. Lex.*].

bound with cords] This should refer to the "chests," but this is not probable. More likely: **with cords twined and durable**, the "cords" themselves being the article of commerce. "Cords" can hardly be thread. The rendering "made of cedar" is altogether unlikely, some sense like strong, firm, or durable is more probable [so *Oxf. Lex.*]. The cords were probably of wool as well as of flax, of divers colours, and

¹ [But we should probably read, by the addition of a Heb. consonant and different vocalisation, *and all the Medes.* So Kr., Ba., Ber.]

25 of cedar, among thy merchandise. The ships of Tarshish
were thy caravans for thy merchandise: and thou wast
replenished, and made very glorious in the heart of the seas.
26 Thy rowers have brought thee into great waters: the east
27 wind hath broken thee in the heart of the seas. Thy riches,
and thy wares, thy merchandise, thy mariners, and thy
pilots, thy calkers, and the [1]occupiers of thy merchandise,
and all thy men of war, that are in thee, [2]with all thy
company which is in the midst of thee, shall fall into the
28 heart of the seas in the day of thy ruin. At the sound
29 of the cry of thy pilots the [3]suburbs shall shake. And all

[1] Or, *exchangers*   [2] Or, *and in*   [3] Or, *waves*

used for fastening hangings or other purposes, Esth. i. 6. The Babylonian weaving was very celebrated, cf. xvi. 10, xxiii. 6, also the
"Babylonish mantle," Josh. vii. 21.

25. The "ships of Tarshish" here are deep-sea ships, great ships
trading to the most distant coasts, Is. ii. 16; Ps. xlviii. 7.

were thy caravans] The camel has been called the ship of the desert,
but conversely to call an "east indiaman" a caravan is too brilliant for
the prophet[1]. Probably by a slight change of reading: "the ships of
Tarshish *did serve thee with* (in) thy wares" (*vv.* 13, 17, &c.), cf. Is. lx.
9, 10, and above *v.* 9. So [Cor. following] Aquila (Field).

XXVII. **26—31.** THE VESSEL STEERED BY HER PILOTS INTO
DANGEROUS WATERS, IS SHIPWRECKED AND HER CARGO AND
CREW CAST INTO THE SEA (*vv.* 26, 27). DISMAY AND LAMEN-
TATION OF ALL SEAFARING MEN (*vv.* 28—31).

26. The allegory does not need interpretation. How far her states-
men precipitated the fall of Tyre is unknown; it was the east wind
that broke her in the heart of the sea—a force above that of men (Ps.
xlviii. 7).

27. *and thy wares*] The verse is interesting for the enumeration
which it gives both of the crew and of the cargo. The cargo is
described in three words: riches, wares, and merchandise—the last
two words meaning the same thing virtually, though differing in shade
of idea. The crew consists of (1) sailors, (2) pilots, (3) calkers (carpenters), (4) handlers of the wares, and (5) men of war.

with all thy company] Supported by LXX. against marg.

28. *the suburbs*] According to tradition (Baer, *Ezech.* p. 93) the term
here is differently pointed from that rendered "suburbs," e.g. ch. xlv. 2.

[1] [But the Heb. verb simply means *to travel* (Is. lvii. 9), and this sense is accepted
by Kr. and Ber. That of A.V. "did sing of thee," taken from a root identical in
consonants, is quite unsuitable.]

that handle the oar, the mariners, *and* all the pilots of the sea, shall come down from their ships, they shall stand upon the land, and shall cause their voice to be heard over thee, 30 and shall cry bitterly, and shall cast up dust upon their heads, they shall wallow themselves in the ashes: and they 31 shall make themselves bald for thee, and gird them with sackcloth, and they shall weep for thee in bitterness of soul with bitter mourning.   And in their wailing they shall take 32 up a lamentation for thee, and lament over thee, *saying*, Who is there like Tyre, like her that is brought to silence in the midst of the sea?   When thy wares went forth out 33 of the seas, thou filledst many peoples; thou didst enrich the kings of the earth with the multitude of thy riches and of thy merchandise.   [1]In the time that thou wast broken by 34 the seas in the depths of the waters, thy merchandise and all thy company did fall in the midst of thee.   All the 35

[1] According to some ancient versions, *Now thou art broken...are fallen &c.*

The latter term means the free space surrounding a city or building. If the sense of the present word were the same, reference would be to the lands or coasts in the vicinity of Tyre, a sense far from natural. Jerome conjectured "fleets" (Ew.).   In Is. lvii. 20 the verb describes the violent action of the waters of the sea (Am. viii. 8), and R.V. marg. suggests *waves* here—the waves shall quake at the cry of thy pilots.

29.   All seafaring men raise a lamentation over the shipwreck of the gallant vessel.

30.   On the first sign of sorrow cf. Job ii. 12, and on the second Jer. vi. 26; Mic. i. 10; Esth. iv. 1.

31.   For these signs of grief cf. ch. vii. 18; Is. xv. 2, xxii. 12; Jer. xvi. 16, xlvii. 5; Mic. i. 16.

XXVII. 32—36.   LAMENT OVER TYRE.

The lament appears to be in elegiac metre.   The word "wailing" is a contracted form (*ni = nehi*).

33.   *thy wares went forth*] i.e. when they were landed from the sea on many shores, many people were filled, satisfied, enriched, cf. Is. xxiii. 3 (R.V.).

34.   *In the time that thou wast broken*] or, as marg., with change of points: *Now thou art broken...are fallen.*   The reading "time" is difficult, though cf. Jer. ii. 17[1].

[1] [The Heb., as it stands, is scarcely translatable.]

inhabitants of the isles are astonished at thee, and their
kings are horribly afraid, they are troubled in their counte-
36 nance.   The merchants among the peoples hiss at thee;
thou art become ¹a terror, and thou shalt never be any
more.

28   The word of the LORD came again unto me, saying, Son
2 of man, say unto the prince of Tyre, Thus saith the Lord
GOD: Because thine heart is lifted up, and thou hast said,

---

¹ Or, *a destruction*   Heb. *terrors*.

---

36. "Hiss" here is hardly the expression of malicious joy, rather of
astonishment and dismay, or other vivid emotion, 1 Kgs ix. 8.

art become a terror]   Cf. marg.   The sense is, thou shalt be utterly
destroyed, cf. xxvi. 21.

XXVIII.   THE FALL OF THE PRINCE OF TYRE.

The chapter has three parts :

(1) *vv.* 1—10. The sinful pride of the prince of Tyre and his
destruction.

(2) *vv.* 11—19. Lament over his fall and expulsion from the
garden of God.

(3) *vv.* 20—26. To this is added a prophecy against Zidon.

XXVIII. **1**—10.   THE SIN OF THE PRINCE OF TYRE (*vv.* 1—5),
AND HIS DESTRUCTION (*vv.* 6—10).

The prince of Tyre of the time was probably Ithobaal II.   It is not,
however, any individual prince that the prophet threatens, but the ruler
of Tyre, who is the embodiment of the spirit of the proud commercial
city.   The sin with which the prophet charges the prince is pride of
heart and self-deification.   The prince—who is but the impersonation
of the spirit of the community—was very wise, wiser than Daniel
(*v.* 3).   His wisdom expressed itself and found scope in his commerce
and manufactures and in his arts.   These produced wealth and splendour, which led to ungodly arrogance (*vv.* 4, 5) : the prince said, "I am
God, I dwell in the abode of God" (*v.* 2).   For this deifying of himself
in his own mind he shall be brought down.   Strangers, the most
terrible of the nations, shall assail him, and he shall die the death of
the uncircumcised—those whose bodies are unburied or unhonoured in
their burial.

2. *I am a god*] or, **I am God**. Ezekiel speaks from his own point of
view, which recognises but one God, not from that of polytheism.   The
prince set his heart as the heart of God; he felt and acted as if divine¹.

---

¹ [But the R.V. seems a more probable rendering than that of Davidson. The
prince naturally speaks from his own polytheistic point of view.]

I am a god, I sit in the seat of God, in the ¹midst of the
seas; yet thou art man, and not God, though thou didst set
thine heart as the heart of God: behold, thou art wiser than 3
Daniel; there is no secret that they can hide from thee:
by thy wisdom and by thine understanding thou hast gotten 4
thee ²riches, and hast gotten gold and silver into thy
treasures: by thy great wisdom *and* by thy traffic hast 5
thou increased thy ²riches, and thine heart is lifted up
because of thy ²riches: therefore thus saith the Lord GOD: 6
Because thou hast set thine heart as the heart of God;
therefore behold, I will bring strangers upon thee, the 7

---

¹ Heb. *heart*.   ² Or, *power*

There is not the slightest allusion, of course, to actual worship being
paid to the prince; it is his own feeling alone, his pride and self-
exaltation, that is referred to.

I sit in the seat of God] Naturally the prince speaks of his own
abode, Tyre; but he regards it as divine. He is God, and it is the seat
of God. There is no doubt allusion to the idea that there was a seat of
God or the gods; the prince identified Tyre with it. The beauty and
splendour of the place, its richness and renown, possibly also its
isolation, make it something not of the earth. In Is. xiv. the king of
Babylon affects to seat himself beside the Most High; here the prince
of Tyre identifies himself with God.

3. *wiser than Daniel*] Cf. on ch. xiv. 14. The language appears
ironical. It does not follow from the allusion that the story of Daniel
was known in Tyre.

no secret...hide] or, no secret *is hidden*. In xxxi. 8 the word seems
to mean "be equal to," "come up to." This sense would require a
personal subject, which might be got if for "secret," lit. *closed*,
we understand the meaning to be as Numb. xxiv. 3, 15, viz. a person
closed of eyes, i.e. inspired. The versions differ widely from one another.

4 *seq.* The wisdom of the prince, who is but the incarnation of
the spirit of the city, displayed itself in his commercial enterprise, in
his skill in arts and manufactures, for which the Tyrians were famous,
and thus he amassed such riches and surrounded himself with such
splendour that he deemed himself God (*v.* 6). Already Homer calls
the Zidonians *poludaidaloi* (*Il.* 23. 743), "working with great skill."

7 *seq.* His chastisement because of his self-deification. As Nebuchadrezzar affected to set himself in the sides of the North but was
brought down to the sides of the pit (Is. xiv. 13—15), the prince of
Tyre shall die an ignominious death. The "terrible," i.e. most terrible,
of the nations are the Chaldeans, cf. the prophet's contemporary Hab.
i. 6—10. See ch. vii. 21, xxx. 11, xxxi. 12, xxxii. 12.

terrible of the nations : and they shall draw their swords against the beauty of thy wisdom, and they shall ¹defile thy
8 brightness.   They shall bring thee down to the pit ; and thou shalt die the deaths of them that are slain, in the heart
9 of the seas.   Wilt thou yet say before him that slayeth thee, I am God? but thou art man, and not God, in the
10 hand of him that ²woundeth thee.   Thou shalt die the deaths of the uncircumcised by the hand of strangers : for I have spoken it, saith the Lord GOD.
11   Moreover the word of the LORD came unto me, saying,

----

¹ Or, *profane*   ² Or, *profaneth*

the beauty of thy wisdom] The beauty is not regarded as the product of his wisdom, but rather as the expression of it, that in which it clothes itself.   Cf. *v*. 12.

defile thy brightness] **profane**, as marg., cf. *v*. 17.   The term "profane " is used on account of the prince's assumption of divinity.

8. *deaths*] the **death**.   [The plural in the Heb. is intensive, meaning violent death.]

9. *but thou art*] Rather : **whilst thou art man, and not God**.   The last clause "in the hand," &c. is wanting in LXX.

10. *deaths of the uncircumcised*] the **death**.   The term "uncircumcised" is employed by the prophet not in its usual sense but in reference to the dead, who suffer death from the sword, and whose bodies either lie unburied and dishonoured or are flung indiscriminately into the earth with no funeral honours. Cf. xxxi. 18.   Deprivation of burial did not hinder the dead persons from descending into Sheol, the place of the dead, but the dishonour done them here followed them there, and they were subject to reproach.   Cf. the same representation Is. xiv. 19, 20, where it is an entire misconception to consider "stones of the pit" to refer to a paved mausoleum, and thus a sumptuous burial.   The stones of the pit are the lowest pit.

strangers] Nebuchadrezzar's hosts.   Cf. xxxi. 12.

XXVIII.   11—19. LAMENT OVER THE FALL OF THE PRINCE OF TYRE.

The passage is of extreme difficulty partly from the obscurity of several expressions in it, which do not occur again, and partly from allusions not now intelligible.   The general drift of the passage is, however, plain.
(1) *vv*. 12—15.   The prince of Tyre is represented as a glorious being placed in Eden the garden of God.   He was the perfection of beauty, was set on the mountain of God, and was perfect in his ways from the day he was created till iniquity was found in him[1].   (2) *vv*. 16—19.

----

[1] [Prof. A. A. Bevan (*J. Th. St.* IV. 500 ff.) discusses the reason for Ezekiel's placing the king of Tyre far above the rest of mankind.   The following is a summary of his argument.   The oldest sanctuaries of the Semites were natural gardens, i.e.

He fell from his high place through pride because of the multitude of his riches, and was therefore expelled from the garden of God.—Towards the end of the passage the allegory of a being in paradise is departed from and the actual circumstances of the prince and his city are more literally referred to. The text of LXX. diverges in important particulars from the Heb.

Particular difficulties, however, are numerous. 1. The expression "sealest up the sum," *v.* 12, is very obscure. For the participle "sealest" the ancient versions read signet or *ring*. That there is reference to a ring seems plain from *v.* 13. 2. Again the cherub is referred to. There can be no doubt that the prophet has in his mind the story of Paradise (Gen. ii. iii.). The cherub naturally belongs to the Paradise of God. In the Heb. text, as at present pointed (though the pointing is very anomalous), the prince is compared to the cherub, or said to be or to have been the cherub. The text, however, permits the reading *with* or *beside* the cherub (*v.* 14, so LXX.). The prince sinned and was expelled from the garden of God where he was placed. The idea of the prophet is that pride and self-deification were the sin of the prince and caused his expulsion. This, however, in Ezek. is the sin of all the foreign princes or nations, Egypt no less than Tyre, and cannot be held part of a tradition of the Fall, or of Paradise. That the prophet does refer to a Fall and expulsion from Paradise or destruction of the transgressor seems plain (*vv.* 16, 17). But any fall of the cherub is not hinted at anywhere in the Old Test.; on the contrary the cherubs are represented as watchers and protectors of the garden of God against men (Gen. iii. 24). There are references in the Old Test. to the sin of higher beings (e.g. Gen. vi. 1; Is. xxiv. 21), but the prophet's allusions to the cherubs in other places make it very improbable that he should think of them as sinning. 3. It is probable, therefore, that it is the history of the first man that floats before his mind. The term "created" applied to the prince would hardly be used of the cherub. It is not unlikely, however, that Ezek. was in possession of traditions regarding Paradise more ample than those in Gen. or different from them. At the same time the divergences may be due to his own tendency to idealise. The prince of Tyre is represented as wiser than all men, even than Daniel; and in Job xv. 7, 8 the first man born is spoken of as possessing supernatural wisdom. The prophet might have before his mind that Wisdom which was the first of God's works of old

oases (Rob. Smith, *Rel. Sem.* 2nd ed. pp. 102 ff.). Hence artificial sanctuaries were decorated to represent gardens. Solomon's Temple, familiar to Ezekiel, had cherubim, palm trees, and flowers (1 Kgs vi. 28, 32). We may reasonably suppose (1 Kgs v. 2 ff.) that the style and decorations of that temple were taken from Tyrian models as prototypes. Hence the prophet's attitude to the sanctuary at Tyre and the king as its chief minister. This throws light on details, such as the precious stones (*v.* 13), all of which appear in the high-priest's breastplate (Exod. xxviii. 17 ff., xxxix. 10 ff.). The king of Tyre was upon "the holy mountain of God" (*v.* 14, cf. 16). In most places the local sanctuary stood, as in Jerusalem, upon an eminence overlooking the city (Rob. Smith, *op. cit.* p. 172). So, according to Renan's careful investigation of the site, the great temple of Melkart at Tyre stood upon the highest part of the larger island.]

12 Son of man, take up a lamentation for the king of Tyre, and
   say unto him, Thus saith the Lord GOD: Thou sealest up
13 the ¹sum, full of wisdom, and perfect in beauty. Thou wast
   in Eden the garden of God; every precious stone was thy
   covering, the ²sardius, the topaz, and the diamond, the
   beryl, the onyx, and the jasper, the sapphire, the ³emerald,
   and the ⁴carbuncle, and gold: the workmanship of thy
   tabrets and of thy pipes was in thee; in the day that thou

---

¹ Or, *measure* Or, *pattern*   ² Or, *ruby*   ³ Or, *carbuncle*
              ⁴ Or, *emerald*

(Prov. viii.), and His architect in creation, and who realised herself in
the symmetry of the universe.

   12.   *king of Tyre*]   The prophet appears to use the terms " king "
and " prince " (*nagîd*, or *nasî*) indifferently.   LXX. of Ezek. reserves
the term " king " for the rulers of Babylon and Egypt, except in general
expressions like " kings of the earth," or, " of the nations " (xxvii. 33,
35, xxxii. 10).

   sealest up the sum]   The term " sum " is found only again ch. xliii. 10
of the construction or idea of the temple, there rendered " pattern "; see
marg. there and here.   The verb is used of the work of God in ordering
creation by weight and measure, Job xxviii. 25; Is. xl. 12, 13.   The
phrase " thou sealest " is pointed as ptcp. *art the sealer of*, but some
MSS. and the ancient Versions read *art the seal-ring of*.   [Kr., changing
one consonant, explains as " the wise one (who is perfected in wisdom)."]
To " seal " has always the natural sense, or means to close up, fasten
up; it seems nowhere to mean to round off, complete, or consummate.
LXX. omits " full of wisdom,"¹ and the first words are in parallelism
to " the perfection of beauty."   This would suggest that the first words
describe what the prince is or was, not what he did.   The term rendered
" sum " may mean *symmetry* (perfection), and the whole: *thou wast the
seal-ring of symmetry* (perfection), *and the perfection of beauty*.   In this
case the prince is compared to a seal-ring of exquisite workmanship.
On the other hand if ptcp. be read, " thou wast the sealer of symmetry,"
the conception of something impressing symmetry (upon all things)
seems expressed.   There might then be an allusion to the Wisdom;
cf. the comparison of light to a seal, Job xxxviii. 14.

   13.   The term rendered " covering " does not occur again.   Possibly
" emerald " and " carbuncle " should be transposed.   These precious
stones are mentioned in sets of three, being nine in number, to which
LXX. adds three more, the ligure, the agate, and the amethyst, as in
the high-priest's breastplate (Exod. xxviii. 19), while Syr. reduces the
number to eight.   Possibly the original number may have been very
much smaller.   Kr. omits on metrical grounds.

   of thy tabrets and of thy pipes]   It is obvious that timbrels and pipes

---

¹ [So Kr. makes the words a gloss.]

wast created they were prepared. Thou wast the anointed 14
cherub that covereth: and I set thee, *so that* thou wast
upon the holy mountain of God; thou hast walked up and
down in the midst of the stones of fire. Thou wast perfect 15

are out of place here. It is also probable that the preceding words
and gold should be disjoined from the list of precious stones. Render:
and of gold was the workmanship of thy sockets and grooves.
Reference is unmistakably to the setting of precious stones [*Oxf. Lex.*
"settings and sockets"], and while possibly a person might be supposed
to be covered or clothed with the jewels mentioned, the phrase "thy
sockets" seems to recall the figure of the ring. The phrase "they were
prepared" is wanting in LXX. and the last words "in the day that thou
wast created" should probably go to the next verse.

14. *Thou wast the anointed*] The word "Thou" is pointed here
anomalously as Numb. xi. 15; Deut. v. 24. It may more naturally be
read *with* [so LXX.] or *beside*. The terms rendered "anointed"
and "that covereth" are wanting in LXX. (also in *v.* 16). No
meaning can be attached to anointed cherub, probably render cherub
with spreading wings [so Vulg. *cherub extentus*]. The other
phrase "that covereth" is used to describe the cherubim over the
mercy-seat, whose wings covered it, and (at least in the temple of
Solomon) extended from wall to wall of the most holy place (Exod.
xxv. 20, xxxviii. 9; 1 Chron. xxviii. 18). The whole clause may be
read thus: *In the day that thou wast created with the outspread cherub
that overshadoweth I set thee; thou wast* &c.

holy mountain of God] [See introductory note to *vv.* 12—19.]
Different representations of the abode of God were current; it was
sometimes spoken of as a mountain and sometimes as a garden. The
mountain here is the same as the garden of *v.* 13, cf. *v.* 16. It is the
abode of God, where the cherub was and where the prince was placed
on the day when he was created. The allusion to the mount of assembly
in Is. xiv. 13 is obscure. The combinations of Frd. Delitzsch (*Paradies*)
and Jeremias (*Bab. Assyr. Vorstellungen vom Leben nach dem Tode*)
are controverted by Jensen, who makes it probable that Arâlu, the
"mountain of the countries," is not a special mountain *on* the earth,
but the earth itself conceived as a mountain, under which lay the
primary ocean. Neither is there the slightest foundation for the
supposition that the prophet compares the prince of Tyre to a Gryph
guarding treasure upon the mountain of God.

hast walked up and down] **didst walk** in the midst of (the) stones of
fire. The "stones of fire" might be flashing precious stones (Assyr.
aban ishâti, precious stone, Frd. Del., *ibid.* p. 118); more probably
there is some reference to the phenomena attending the divine presence
and manifestation, ch. i. 13, x. 6, cf. Exod. xix. 18; Is. vi. 6; Ps.
xviii. 14. [Kr. here and *v.* 16 for "stones of fire" substitutes "sons of
God."] Among the Mohammedans the shooting stars are held to be

in thy ways from the day that thou wast created, till un-
16 righteousness was found in thee.   By the multitude of thy
traffic they filled the midst of thee with violence, and thou
hast sinned: therefore have I cast thee as profane out of
the mountain of God; and I have destroyed thee, O cover-
17 ing cherub, from the midst of the stones of fire.   Thine

thunderbolts hurled at the eavesdropping demons who pry into the
divine secrets. ["According to Herod. II. 44 the temple at Tyre
contained...a column of emerald *which shone by night*." Bevan,
in loco cit.]

15.   The sin and fall of the prince.   The term "the day that thou
wast created" is very unsuitable if applied to the cherub.   The sons of
God existed before creation, Job xxxviii. 7.

16.   *By the multitude*] or, "in the multitude." [Here the figure
gives place for a moment to the underlying reality; the idea of the
prince merges in that of the city.]

they filled] or [with slight change in the Heb. verb], **thy midst**
(heart) **was filled with wrong, and thou didst sin.**   LXX., "thou
didst fill."

therefore have I cast] lit. *therefore have I profaned thee* (casting thee)
out of the mountain.

and I have destroyed thee]   Perhaps, with a slight change of text, *and
the* (covering) *cherub hath destroyed thee* (driving thee) *from the midst of
the stones of fire.*   But the construction in 1st pers. *I have destroyed* is
more probable.

With the words wanting in LXX. put in brackets the verses would
read: "Thou art the (or, a) seal of symmetry, (full of wisdom,) and
the perfection of beauty.   13 Thou wast in Eden the garden of God;
every precious stone was thy covering, the sardius, the topaz, and the
diamond, the beryl, the onyx and the jasper, the sapphire, the carbuncle
and the emerald; and gold was the workmanship of thy sockets and
grooves in thee in the day that thou wast created" (they were prepared).
Or, drawing the last words to the beginning of *v.* 14.— 14 "In the day
that thou wast created I set thee with the (outspread, the covering)
cherub, thou wast in the holy mountain of God, in the midst of the
stones of fire (thou didst walk).   15 Thou wast perfect in thy ways
from the day that thou wast created, till iniquity was found in thee.
16 In the multitude of thy traffic thy midst was filled with wrong
(LXX. thou didst fill), and thou didst sin: therefore I have profaned
thee (and cast thee) from the mountain of God; and I have destroyed
thee, O covering cherub, (driving thee) from the midst of the stones
of fire."

17.   The prince's sin was self-exaltation because of his beauty and
wisdom.   The prince is but the representative of the city and its
inhabitants; the beauty of the one (xxvii. 3) and the wisdom of the
other (xxvii. 8, 9) are attributed to him.   The prophet's own deep

heart was lifted up because of thy beauty, thou hast corrupted thy wisdom by reason of thy brightness: I have cast thee to the ground, I have laid thee before kings, that they may behold thee. By the multitude of thine iniquities, in 18 the unrighteousness of thy traffic, thou hast profaned thy sanctuaries; therefore have I brought forth a fire from the midst of thee, it hath devoured thee, and I have turned thee to ashes upon the earth in the sight of all them that behold thee. All they that know thee among the peoples 19 shall be astonished at thee: thou art become a ¹terror, and thou shalt never be any more.

And the word of the LORD came unto me, saying, Son 20 21

---

¹ Or, *a destruction* Heb. *terrors.*

humility before Jehovah makes him recoil from the self-exaltation of men elsewhere.

corrupted thy wisdom] i.e. lost thy wisdom over, or amidst, thy splendour.

that they may behold thee] i.e. as a spectacle to feast their eyes upon.

18. *profaned thy sanctuaries*] The phrase occurs ch. vii. 24 ; here, however, where the prince is spoken of, "sanctity" or personal sacredness rather than "sanctuary" seems the sense required. It is doubtful if the word can bear this meaning. LXX. reads: "because of the multitude of thine iniquities and the wrong of thy traffic *I have profaned* thy sanctuaries, and I will bring forth a fire." The tenses in M.T. are all in the perfect of threatening, and the threats here pass away from the prince and apply more to the city. On "fire" cf. ch. xix. 14.

have turned thee to ashes] Any reference to the Phœnix, consumed in a self-kindled fire, has little probability. The idea of the city, of the spirit and activity of which the king is the embodiment, tends more and more to take the place of the idea of the king. This is evident from the closing words in *v.* 19, which are identical with those referring to the city, ch. xxvii. 36.

19. *art become a terror*] Cf. xxvi. 21, xxvii. 36.

shalt never be any more] [See on xxvi. 21.]

XXVIII. 20—26. PROPHECY AGAINST ZIDON.

The passage has three parts :

(1) *vv.* 20—23. The Lord shall send great judgements on Zidon, by which means He shall get His greatness and holiness recognised, and they shall know that He is God. (2) *v.* 24. Thus shall all that vex Israel round about come to an end and cease. (3) *vv.* 25, 26. Israel when restored shall thus dwell securely, all that were hostile to her

of man, set thy face toward Zidon, and prophesy against it,
22 and say, Thus saith the Lord GOD: Behold, I am against
thee, O Zidon; and I will be glorified in the midst of thee:
and they shall know that I am the LORD, when I shall have
executed judgements in her, and shall be sanctified in her.
23 For I will send into her pestilence and blood in her streets;
and the wounded shall ¹fall in the midst of her, with the
sword upon her on every side; and they shall know that
24 I am the LORD. And there shall be no more a pricking
brier unto the house of Israel, nor a grieving thorn of any
that are round about them, that did despite unto them;
and they shall know that I am the Lord GOD.
25   Thus saith the Lord GOD: When I shall have gathered
the house of Israel from the peoples among whom they
are scattered, and shall be sanctified in them in the sight of
the nations, then shall they dwell in their own land which

---

¹ Or, *be iudged*

---

having been removed; and she shall know Jehovah her God to be
God alone. These words suggest the explanation both of the judgements upon the nations and of the position which they occupy in the
prophet's Book. See introd. to ch. xxv. and *v.* 1 there.

21. In Gen. x. 15 Zidon is the firstborn of Canaan, and it was pro-
bably the parent city of Tyre, which lies twenty miles further south.
The modern town bears the name *Saida*. See chart of Zidon in Rawl.
Phœnic. p. 66.

22. *be glorified*] Or, *get me glory* (honour). So for "be sanctified"
get me sanctifying, or "shew myself holy." To get sanctifying for
himself is to get recognition as God alone, and that which God alone is.
To "get glory" is included in to "get sanctifying."

23. *wounded shall fall*] Or, "fall thick," if the word be read as
an intensive. [Marg. *be judged*, as in A.V. text, is improbable.] The
judgements on Zidon shall bring home to her that there is a great God
and that He has sent them. This God is Jehovah, God of Israel, God
alone. The prophet speaks from his own belief.

24. "Brier" is a slightly different form of the word translated
"thorn" in ch. ii. 6. The term "pricking" is used of the leprosy
(Lev. xiii. 51, "fretting").

25. *sanctified in them*] i.e. *through them*, in their restoration. Jehovah
is sanctified through the chastisement of the nations who distress His
people, and He is sanctified through His people's restoration. On
"sanctify" cf. *v.* 22.

I gave to my servant Jacob. And they shall dwell securely 26
therein; yea, they shall build houses, and plant vineyards,
and shall dwell securely; when I have executed judgements
upon all those that do them despite round about them;
and they shall know that I am the LORD their God.

my servant Jacob] Cf. ch. xxxvii. 25; the phrase already in Jer.
xxx. 10, and frequently in Is. xl.—lxvi.

26. *dwell securely*] Or, with confidence, *feeling* secure, Jer. xxiii. 6;
Am. ix. 14; Is. lxv. 21; Ezek. xxxiv. 27, xxxviii. 8, xxxix. 26. An
illustration of the promise is seen in ch. xxxviii., xxxix.

know that I am JEHOVAH their God] This oft-repeated phrase is
not a mere formula. The prophet's idea is that Jehovah does all,
brings all calamities, causes all catastrophes and revolutions in states,
and guides the fortunes of Israel in the sight of the nations, with one
great design in view—to make Himself, the true and only God, known
to all mankind.

XXIX.—XXXII. PROPHECY AGAINST EGYPT.

With the exception of the passage ch. xxix. 17—21 the prophecies
against Egypt belong to a time shortly anterior to the fall of Jerusalem
or shortly after it. Ch. xxix. is dated about seven months before the
capture of the city; ch. xxx. 20 *seq.* about four months, and ch. xxxi.
about two months before that event, while ch. xxxii. falls somewhat
more than a year and a half later than the destruction. The active
participation of Egypt in the affairs of Israel all this time, the hopes
reposed in her by the people (Lam. iv. 17), and the disappointments
caused by her, explain the large space devoted by the prophet to her
character and her destinies in the purposes of Jehovah.

The general thought prevailing in the prophecy is the same as that
in other parts of Ezekiel's book, viz. that Jehovah, God of Israel, is
the one true God, and that all the movements among the nations, the
overthrow of some and the triumphs of others, are His operations, and
that they are but parts of a general rule and direction of the world, the
design of which is to make Himself known to all the nations as the one
living and true God. The two sins for which Egypt, represented by
Pharaoh, is chastised are, first, pride of heart which recognises no God
above it, which says, "My river is mine own, and I have made it"
(xxix. 3); and second, the deceptive fascination which the imposing
and pretentious power of the Nile valley exerted on the people of God,
seducing them away from trust in Jehovah alone (cf. Is. xxx. 1—5,
xxxi. 1—3), and proving always a delusive support (xxix. 6, 7). This
reed which, so far from supporting, pierced the hand that leant on it,
must be broken for ever, that in the future (the new age about to dawn)
the people of Jehovah may no more be tempted to trust in it.

Egypt, however, is a different kind of power both from the petty

29   In the tenth year, in the tenth *month*, in the twelfth *day*
of the month, the word of the LORD came unto me, say-
2 ing, Son of man, set thy face against Pharaoh king of
Egypt, and prophesy against him, and against all Egypt:

peoples like Edom and Moab, and from Tyre the great commercial
mart of the nations. The smaller nations suffer because of their
despite against Israel, and in suffering they learn what Jehovah is.
Tyre did not affect to be a conqueror. She was the lady to whom the
nations brought their merchandise of precious ores and jewels, rich cloths
and sweet perfumes. The prince of Tyre prided himself upon his
wisdom, his skill in seamanship and commerce, his brilliant ingenuity
in the arts, and on his beauty and splendour. The sin of Tyre was
this ungodly pride of mind, and this wholly secular devotion to trade.
But Egypt is a world power. It rules nations (xxix. 15). It is a
great cedar, envied by the trees in the garden of God (xxxi. 9), in the
branches of which all the fowls of heaven nest, and under the shadow
of which all the beasts of the field bring forth (xxxi. 6). It aspires
to universal dominion. Hence in treating of it the prophet's mind
takes a wider sweep. He thinks of Jehovah as God over all, and of
His operations as embracing the world. The judgement of Egypt is
the day of the Lord (xxx. 3); it is the time of the Gentiles. Hence
its overthrow is felt over the world (xxxii. 10). Creation shudders;
the waters stand motionless (xxxi. 15). Jehovah is known to the ends
of the earth (xxx. 19, 26).

Each of the four chapters is formed in the main upon the same
model, containing first, a general threat of destruction upon Egypt,
represented by the Pharaoh, under some allegorical designation (e.g.
the crocodile); secondly, a more particular detail of the instrument
whom Jehovah shall use (the king of Babylon), the destruction of
the country and the dispersion of its inhabitants; to which, thirdly,
in several of the chapters a description is added of the effect on the
nations and all creation which these terrible convulsions shall produce.
These events shall take place on the stage of the world, with mankind
as spectators; Jehovah shall brandish His sword in the eyes of the
nations, and nature and men will shudder (xxxii. 10). Ch. xxxii. ends
with a dirge chanted over the interment of Pharaoh, which is one
of the most weird passages in literature.

XXIX. GENERAL THREAT OF JUDGEMENT ON PHARAOH AND HIS PEOPLE.

(1) *vv.* 1—7. Pharaoh is presented under the allegory of a great
crocodile inhabiting the waters of Egypt, and the population as
fishes. Jehovah with His hook shall draw him out of his waters, with
his fishes cleaving to his scales, and shall cast his carcase upon the
desert, where the fowls and the beasts shall batten on him. The causes

speak, and say, Thus saith the Lord GOD: Behold, I am 3
against thee, Pharaoh king of Egypt, the great dragon
that lieth in the midst of his rivers, which hath said, My
river is mine own, and I have made it for myself. And I 4
will put hooks in thy jaws, and I will cause the fish of thy

of this judgement on Pharaoh and his people are, his ungodly pride
(v. 3), and the fact that he has always proved a delusive confidence to
Israel, seducing them from their single trust in Jehovah (vv. 6, 7).

(2) vv. 8—12. Explanation of the allegory. A great conqueror,
stirred up by Jehovah, will overthrow Pharaoh, destroy his people, and
desolate his land. The inhabitants shall be scattered into all countries,
and Egypt shall remain utterly desolate, trodden by the foot neither of
man nor of beast, for the space of forty years.

(3) vv. 13—16. At the end of forty years Egypt shall be restored,
but only to attain the rank of a mean power, meaner than all the
kingdoms of the earth. It shall no more rule over nations, and no
more from its imposing greatness be a temptation to the people of
Jehovah to put their trust in it. The term of forty years is considered
by the prophet to be the time of Chaldean supremacy. At the end of this
period the world shall be revolutionised. [See sub-note on v. 13.]

(4) vv. 17—21. A passage of date 570 B.C., probably inserted after
the prophecies against Egypt had been reduced to writing—hardly
after the book had been published—and suggested by the termination
of Nebuchadrezzar's thirteen years' siege of Tyre. It consists of a
promise to Nebuchadrezzar that Egypt shall be given him as a recompense for the service which he served in Jehovah's behalf against Tyre,
for which service he failed at Tyre to obtain the adequate reward.

1—7. Pharaoh under the allegory of the crocodile, and the population as fishes. Jehovah draws him out of the waters with His hook
and flings him on the land.

3. *the great dragon*] i.e. the crocodile. Conversely the present
Arabs with some humour name the crocodile *Far'un* (Pharaoh).

midst of his rivers] the arms of the Nile and canals.

My river is mine own] The Nile. The prophet is well aware what
the Nile is to Egypt, and he represents Pharaoh, who, just like the
prince of Tyre, is the impersonation of the spirit and disposition of the
people of Egypt, as equally well aware. The Nile is the life and the
wealth of the land. And Pharaoh in his pride claims to be the creator,
the author of it. To the prophet's profoundly religious mind this is
blasphemous arrogance.

have made it for myself] A peculiar construction, but not impossible,
cf. Zech. vii. 5. But probably we should read simply, *I have made it.*

4. *hooks*] This is suggested by the monster inhabiting the waters.
Possibly the crocodile was occasionally caught with hooks, as Herodotus
[II. 70] affirms (cf. ch. xxxii. 3), although Job xli. 1 seems to doubt the
practicability of it. On "hooks," ch. xxxviii. 4; Is. xxxvii. 29.

rivers to stick unto thy scales; and I will bring thee up out of the midst of thy rivers, with all the fish of thy rivers
5 which stick unto thy scales. And I will leave thee *thrown* into the wilderness, thee and all the fish of thy rivers: thou shalt fall upon the ¹open field; thou shalt not be brought together, nor gathered: I have given thee for meat to the
6 beasts of the earth and to the fowls of the heaven. And all the inhabitants of Egypt shall know that I am the LORD, because they have been a staff of reed to the house of
7 Israel. When they took hold of thee ²by thy hand, thou didst break, and didst rend all their shoulders: and when they leaned upon thee, thou brakest, and madest all their
8 loins to ³be at a stand. Therefore thus saith the Lord GOD: Behold, I will bring a sword upon thee, and will cut off from
9 thee man and beast. And the land of Egypt shall be a

¹ Heb. *face of the field.*   ² Or, *by the handle* Another reading is, *with the hand.*   ³ Or, as some read, *shake* See Ps. lxix. 23.

fish of thy rivers] A figure for the population of the country of rivers; hardly merely for the army of Pharaoh.

5. *will leave thee* thrown] I will **throw thee down upon.**

brought together] does not differ from "gathered," meaning "buried," cf. Jer. viii. 2, xvi. 4, xxv. 33. The great dragon's carcase shall be flung upon the fields, which means death to the water monster; and the fowls and beasts shall feed on it. It is not necessary to give a special meaning to the fowls and beasts, they belong to the figure of the carcase, ch. xxxix. 17 *seq.*; Is. xviii. 6; Jer. vii. 33, xxxiv. 20.

6. The people of Egypt shall learn as of old (Exod. vii. 5, &c.) who it is that sends such judgements upon them.

staff of reed] A staff or stay which was but a reed, and broke when leant upon (*v.* 7). Cf. Is. xxxvi. 6; 2 Kgs xviii. 21. The figure of the reed was natural when speaking of Egypt.

7. *took hold...by thy hand*] Rather: **take hold of thee with the hand,** as in marg. And all the verbs are better put in the present: **take hold...dost break...dost rend,** &c.

madest...to be at a stand] Rather: **makest** all loins **to shake,** as marg. (reading *him'adta* for *ha'amadta,* Ps. lxix. 24).

8—12. For this irreligious self-exaltation Egypt shall be made a desolation from Migdol to Syene, even to the border of Ethiopia.

8. The name of the conqueror of Egypt is not indicated in this preliminary threatening. The sword that comes on Egypt is the sword of the Lord, cf. xiv. 17, xxxii. 11, 12, 13. The land shall be utterly desolated, man and beast swept away. It need scarcely be said that these prophetic threatenings have always an element of the ideal in them.

desolation and a waste; and they shall know that I am the
LORD: because he hath said, The river is mine, and I have
made it.   Therefore behold, I am against thee, and against 10
thy rivers, and I will make the land of Egypt an utter waste
and desolation, ¹from the tower of Seveneh even unto the
border of Ethiopia.   No foot of man shall pass through it, 11
nor foot of beast shall pass through it, neither shall it be
inhabited forty years.   And I will make the land of Egypt 12
a desolation in the midst of the countries that are desolate,
and her cities among the cities that are laid waste shall be
a desolation forty years: and I will scatter the Egyptians
among the nations, and will disperse them through the
countries.   For thus saith the Lord GOD: At the end of 13

---

¹ Or, *from Migdol to Syene and even &c.*

9.   The ungodly overweening pride of Egypt is chiefly mentioned
as the cause of its humiliation.   It is a common idea that pride draws
forth the judgement of Jehovah, who is alone exalted (Is. ii., iii.).   The
prophet assumes that this pride is irreligious and an offence against
Jehovah.   However sedulously devoted the Egyptians might be in
serving their own gods, their religion did not prevent this self-deification, which was an offence against Him who was God alone.

10.   *the tower of Seveneh*]   Rather, as marg., **from Migdol to
Syene and even** &c.—from Lower Egypt to the southern border of
Upper Egypt.   Migdol is said to have been situated 12 miles S. of
Pelusium, upon the N. border of Lower Egypt (Exod. xiv. 2; Jer. xliv.
1, xlvi. 14; Numb. xxxiii. 7).   Syene (ch. xxx. 6), the modern Assouan,
was on the S. border of Upper Egypt.   Cush or Ethiopia lay to the
south of Pathros or Upper Egypt; its capital lay near the 4th Cataract,
between *Abu Hamed* and old Dongola.

11.   *No foot of man*]   See xxxii. 13, cf. xxxiii. 28, xxxv. 7; Jer.
ii. 6.   The desolation of Egypt shall continue forty years, the period
of Chaldean supremacy (cf. iv. 6).

12.   Cf. xii. 15, xxvi. 19, xxx. 7.

13—16.   After forty years of desolation Egypt shall be restored,
though only to the rank of a humble kingdom.   It shall no more rule
over the nations (*v.* 15); and no more be a confidence to the house
of Israel, seducing them away from trust in Jehovah alone.

13.   *At the end of forty years*]   Ezekiel considers forty years—a
general expression like Jeremiah's seventy years—to be the period
of Babylonian supremacy in the world.   At the end of this period
a change in the aspect of the world shall supervene under Jehovah's
guidance; Israel shall be restored (ch. iv. 6), and the other nations
subject to Babylon shall be reinstated.   Egypt, however, shall

forty years will I gather the Egyptians from the peoples
14 whither they were scattered: and I will bring again the
captivity of Egypt, and will cause them to return into the
land of Pathros, into the land of their ¹birth; and they shall
15 be there a ²base kingdom.   It shall be the basest of the
kingdoms; neither shall it any more lift itself up above
the nations: and I will diminish them, that they shall no
16 more rule over the nations.   And it shall be no more
the confidence of the house of Israel, bringing iniquity to
remembrance, when they turn to look after them: and they
shall know that I am the Lord GOD.

¹ Or, *origin*   ² Heb. *low.*

be restored only to be a humble state in comparison of her former
greatness¹.

14.   *land of Pathros*] i.e. Upper Egypt or the Thebaid, ch. xxx. 14;
Is. xi. 11; Jer. xliv. 15.   The name is said to mean "south land."

their birth] or, as marg., *their origin*, cf. xvi. 3². For the phrase
"bring again the captivity," i.e. probably, *turn the fortunes*, cf. xvi. 33.

a base kingdom] i.e. a low or humble state, ch. xvii. 6, 14³.

16.   *the confidence of the house of Israel*]   Cf. Is. xxx. 2, 3, xxxvi. 4, 6.

bringing iniquity to remembrance]   The phrase occurs again ch.
xxi. 23, 24; Numb. v. 15; 1 Kgs xvii. 18, and appears to mean *to
accuse* before God.   The phrase here is scarcely in apposition to "confidence," but is rather parallel to that word and a further description
of Egypt—*no more a confidence* and *a reminder of iniquity*.   Egypt was
a seduction to Israel, leading them to trust in it and distrust Jehovah;
it was an accuser of Israel before Jehovah, calling Israel's iniquity to
His mind.   The iniquity lay primarily in trusting in Egypt, but it might
be wider and more general (1 Kgs xvii. 18).

when they turn to look] in Israel's turning to the Egyptians for help.
Cf. xxiii. 27, and on x. 11.   In the happy time of Israel's restoration
not only shall attack and enmity on the part of the surrounding nations
be removed, but all temptation also to look to any for their salvation
but their God alone.

they shall know] seems to be said of Israel.   See last note.

To all the prophets the day of the Lord is near (Joel ii. 1; Zeph. i. 1;
Is. vii.).   In Is. xxiii. 15 seventy years are named as the period

¹ [Gautier (*op. cit.* pp. 295 f.) by the aid of two inscriptions fixes as dates of Nebuchadrezzar's invasions of Egypt B.C. 572 and 568; while the overthrow of his
Empire by that of Persia took place B.C. 538.]

² [Menes, the first historical king of the country, came from This near Abydos in
Upper Egypt, and the earliest dynasties lived in Memphis on the borders of Upper
and Lower Egypt.   The South was thus the aboriginal country.   Cf. Herod. II.
4, 15.]

³ [It was reduced to complete subjection by Cambyses, B.C. 525.]

And it came to pass in the seven and twentieth year, in 17
the first *month*, in the first *day* of the month, the word
of the LORD came unto me, saying, Son of man, Nebu- 18
chadrezzar king of Babylon caused his army to serve a
great service against Tyre: every head was made bald, and
every shoulder was peeled: yet had he no wages, nor his

of Tyre's humiliation, at the end of which time (*vv.* 17, 18) she shall
be remembered and dedicate her hire to the Lord. In Jeremiah this
period is the duration of the captivity of Judah. Such numbers as
forty, seventy, are general. They imply however that the prophets
conceived of the time as comparatively short. It is less easy to suggest
an explanation of this mode of conception. What has been named
"perspective" in prophecy offers no explanation, for this so-called
perspective is but another name for the thing to be explained. The
explanation is to be sought rather on these lines : 1. The prophets
deal with principles, with what might be called absolute conceptions.
Such conceptions are good and evil, Jehovah and the false gods, true
religion and idolatry, the kingdom of Jehovah and the power of the
heathen world. What the prophets depict is usually a conflict of these
principles, and every conflict which they perceive seems to them the
absolute and final one, because it is a conflict of principles. True
religion comes out of the struggle victorious—the Kingdom is the
Lord's. 2. Moving thus among principles the mind of the prophets
either took no note of time, or else, as they deal in general with great
movements of their own day, these present or imminent movements
assume an absolute moral and religious meaning. They appear the
embodiment of the principles which fill the prophetic mind. Consequently their issue is the final decision, which therefore appears at
hand. When the prophets embody their general conception of the
nearness of the final crisis in numbers, these numbers are usually round,
and express merely a powerful religious presentiment.

17—21. A later passage of date 570, sixteen years after the
fall of Jerusalem, written probably after Nebuchadrezzar's thirteen
years' siege of Tyre had come to an end, and inserted among the
prophecies relating to Egypt already collected. Nebuchadrezzar had
served a great service for Jehovah against Tyre, for which neither he
nor his army had received wages. Jehovah will recompense him for
his service against Tyre by giving him the land of Egypt.

18. On spelling of Nebuchadrezzar cf. xxvi. 7.

every head was made bald] Not by the *length* of time but by the
hard service, the rubbing of the armour or the burdens borne on head
and shoulder. Arabic poets refer to the baldness caused by the head-
pieces. The siege of Tyre lasted thirteen years, but, while this is well
attested, history is silent as to the issue of the siege. Whatever the
issue was Nebuchadrezzar and his army did not reap adequate reward
from it—he had no wages for his service done for Jehovah.

army, from Tyre, for the service that he had served against
19 it: therefore thus saith the Lord GOD: Behold, I will give
the land of Egypt unto Nebuchadrezzar king of Babylon;
and he shall carry off her multitude, and take her spoil,
and take her prey; and it shall be the wages for his army.
20 I have given him the land of Egypt ¹as his recompence
for which he served, because they wrought for me, saith the
Lord GOD.
21   In that day will I cause an horn to bud forth unto the
house of Israel, and I will give thee the opening of the
mouth in the midst of them; and they shall know that I am
the LORD.

¹ Or, for *his labour wherewith he served*

19. *multitude*] [The Heb. word generally means a confused noise,
as of a crowd, but Cor. and Kr. make it mean here and in xxx. 10
pomp, ostentatious display. Cf. the sense of "abundance," "wealth,"
which the word has in Ps. xxxvii. 16; Eccles. v. 9 (Heb. 11); Is. lx. 5.]
20. *because they wrought*] or, *for that which* they wrought for me.
The subject is still Nebuchadrezzar and his army; it was Jehovah's
work in which they served against Tyre.
21.   The passage concludes with a promise to Israel.
In that day]   An indefinite term common in the prophets generally.
The ref. is to the period when Nebuchadrezzar shall have humbled Egypt.
After that shall the time of Israel's prosperity come in. Cf. Is. iv. 2,
xi. 10, xix. 18, 19.
an horn]   The "horn" is the symbol of power (Lam. iv. 3); with the
budding of the horn power waxes or is exhibited. The reference is
general, to the restoration of Israel to prosperity and influence, hardly
particularly to the raising up of the personal Messiah (Ps. cxxxii. 17).
On the figure cf. 1 Kgs xxii. 11; Am. vi. 13; Jer. xlviii. 25;
1 Sam. ii. 1.
the opening of the mouth]   The prophet felt his mouth closed by the
incredulity of the people, and the improbability, as it seemed to them,
of his predictions. His mouth was opened and he had boldness of
speech when his anticipations were verified. It is the causing of a
horn to bud to Israel that will give the prophet opening of the mouth.
All his prophecies since the exile had been prophecies of Israel's
restoration, and Israel's restored felicity will fulfil them. The phrase
"give thee the opening of the mouth" means little more than "give
verification to thy words." The idea of the prophet's own presence
when this occurs is hardly to be pressed¹.

¹ [Kr. inclines to the view that the phrase denotes an utterance of praise and
thanksgiving, as opposed to predictions of punishment.]

The word of the LORD came again unto me, saying, 30
Son of man, prophesy, and say, Thus saith the Lord GOD: 2
Howl ye, Woe worth the day! For the day is near, even 3

XXX. FURTHER PROPHECIES AGAINST EGYPT.

Ch. xxx. consists of two prophecies, the first of which, *vv.* 1—19, in all probability belongs to the same date as xxix. 1—16, that is, about seven months before the fall of Jerusalem; and the second, *vv.* 20—26, is dated four months before the capture of the city. The second prophecy seems to have been suggested by some actual reverse inflicted on Pharaoh, called "breaking his arm" (*vv.* 21, 22), and further disaster is threatened against him.

Unlike the petty nations lying around Israel Egypt is a world power. Its influence is felt over all nations, and its history and destinies interest and affect the world. When Jehovah interposes to deal with it mankind and nature feel His presence. His interposition is the day of the Lord, a day of darkness and terror over all. When Egypt is judged creation wraps herself in a pall.—Like the other prophecies in Ezekiel the chapter is filled up with details within its general frame. The main ideas, however, are these: 1. Egypt with her many allied nations, whose troops compose her vast and many-coloured army, shall be overthrown. 2. Her great cities, the centres of her life and restless activity, shall be cast to the ground, and her teeming population scattered among all the nations. 3. Her idols and all her idolatries shall cease, and her native princes (closely connected with her priesthood and worship) shall be cut off. And Jehovah shall be known.

2. *Howl ye*] The day of the Lord is one of terror and lamentation, Am. v. 20; Is. xiii. 6; Zeph. i. 7, 14; Joel ii. 1 *seq.*

3. *the day is near*] The "day" of the Lord is never in the prophets a mere calamity or judgement from God. It is the time of Jehovah's final interposition in the world to do judgement, to chastise evil, and give the crowning victory to His own cause. This day has a universal bearing: particularly, it falls in terror and calamity upon the heathen, the foes of Jehovah's kingdom, but also upon the sinners in Zion, those who are at ease and settled on their lees (Zeph. i. 12), the proud and the oppressors of the poor (Is. ii. 12). The presentiment of this day is common to all the prophets, and the knowledge of it exists among the people (Am. v. 18). The feeling of its nearness, however, was awakened in various ways: either by great convulsions among the nations or calamities, in which Jehovah was so visibly operating that His final interposition seemed at hand (Is. xiii.; Zeph. i. 7; Joel ii. 1); or by a moral condition of the world which it was felt He must intervene to chastise and put an end to (Is. ii., iii.). Naturally the convulsions or calamities which awakened the presentiment of the nearness of the day passed over and the day was deferred, but this does not justify the supposition that the prophets mean by the expression merely a great calamity or judgement.

the day of the LORD is near, a day of clouds; it shall
4 be the time of the heathen.   And a sword shall come
upon Egypt, and anguish shall be in ¹Ethiopia, when the
slain shall fall in Egypt; and they shall take away her
multitude, and her foundations shall be broken down.
5 ¹Ethiopia, and Put, and Lud, and all the mingled people,
and Cub, and the children of the ²land that is in league,
shall fall with them by the sword.
6   Thus saith the LORD: They also that uphold Egypt shall
fall, and the pride of her power shall come down: ³from

¹ Heb. *Cush*.   ² Or, *the land of the covenant*
³ Or, *from Migdol to Syene*

the time of the heathen] the **nations**, the foes of Jehovah's kingdom
and people, when Jehovah shall be revealed to them and they shall be
judged. Is. ii., iii., xiii. 22; Jer. xxvii. 7; Ezek. vii. 7, xxii. 3.

4.   *her multitude*] See ch. xxix. 19; cf. *vv.* 10, 15, ch. xxxi. 2.
The term "foundations" is suggested by the idea of a building overthrown.   Reference is hardly to the allies and mercenaries on whom
Egypt relied in war, rather to the classes and institutions in which
the strength of the state lay.

5.   See on xxvii. 10; Heb. is **Cush** and **Put** and **Lud**.   For Cush
LXX. reads Persians as xxvii. 10, for Put Cretans, and for Lud
Lydians.

the mingled people] perhaps **foreigners**.   In Jer. xxv. 24 these so
named ('*ereb*) are represented as having kings and dwelling in the
desert (cf. 1 Kgs x. 15), and in *v.* 20 they are named next to the
kings of Uz.   On the other hand in Jer. l. 37 they are spoken of as
being in the midst of Babylon.   Hence the sense of "mercenaries"
has been suggested.   In the present passage some distinct people seems
intended.   [Kr., following Aq., Symm., reads "Arabians."]

Cub]   [The name does not occur again.   LXX. (apparently)
"Libyans," and in Nah. iii. 9 the Lubim appear beside Cush, Egypt,
and Put.   Possibly we should read N for C, Nubians.]

the land that is in league] Cf. marg., *the land of the covenant*.
Reference can hardly be to the land of Israel, or to refugees from
Israel in Egypt.   Either some definite country is meant, the name of
which would be suggested by the prophet's description, or "land" is
used collectively—all allied lands¹.

6.   *uphold*] [lit. *lean upon* (so as to prop up).   Cf. this same verb
in a different application ("leaned upon") in xxiv. 2 marg.]

¹ [Probably, by a slight change in M.T. we should for "covenant" read Cherethites,
i.e. Philistines.   See on xxv. 16.   Lofth. points out that Jer. xxv. 20 has "the
mingled people," Uz (?="Cub") and then the Philistines.]

the tower of Seveneh shall they fall in it by the sword, saith the Lord GOD. And they shall be desolate in the 7 midst of the countries that are desolate, and her cities shall be in the midst of the cities that are wasted. And they 8 shall know that I am the LORD, when I have set a fire in Egypt, and all her helpers are ¹destroyed. In that day shall 9 messengers go forth from before me in ships to make the careless Ethiopians afraid; and there shall be anguish upon them, as in the day of Egypt; for, lo, it cometh.

Thus saith the Lord GOD: I will also make the multitude 10 of Egypt to cease, by the hand of Nebuchadrezzar king of Babylon. He and his people with him, the terrible of the 11 nations, shall be brought in to destroy the land; and they shall draw their swords against Egypt, and fill the land with the slain. And I will make the rivers dry, and will sell the 12 land into the hand of evil men; and I will make the land

¹ Heb. *broken*.

from the tower of Seveneh] rather **from Migdol to Syene**; cf. xxix. 10.

7. A frequently recurring expression; cf. xxix. 12.

8. "Fire" is a frequent figure for war and its desolations, *vv.* 14, 16, ch. xv. 5, xx. 47, xxxix. 6.

9. *messengers...in ships*] Cf. Is. xviii. 2. The Heb. word for "ships" occurs again Numb. xxiv. 24; Is. xxxiii. 21. [LXX., reading one consonant differently, has *hastening*. This is accepted by Cor. and Ber., but in support of "ships" see the similar passage in Is. xviii. 1, 2.]

go forth from before me] This means more than that messengers go in ships from Egypt, where Jehovah is present. He sends them; His intervention in Egypt is designed to alarm the world, and bring Himself to its knowledge.

as in the day] Read with LXX. **in the day** (om. *as*), Is. xxiii. 5.

10. The instrument whom Jehovah uses is here named for the first time, except in the later passage, ch. xxix. 17—21.

multitude] See note on xxix. 19.

11. *terrible of the nations*] Cf. ch. xxviii. 7, xxxi. 12, xxxii. 12.

12. *make the rivers dry*] Cf. Is. xix. 5, 6. The expression is scarcely figurative (Is. xliv. 27); the drying up of her rivers would be the severest calamity that could befall Egypt, as indeed in all her history, whenever her canal system has been allowed to fall into disrepair, the country has sunk into wretchedness.

hand of evil men] See ch. vii. 24; Jer. xv. 21; cf. Is. xix. 4, "a cruel lord."

desolate, and [1]all that is therein, by the hand of strangers:
I the LORD have spoken it.

13 Thus saith the Lord GOD: I will also destroy the idols,
and I will cause the [2]images to cease from Noph; and there
shall be no more a prince out of the land of Egypt: and I
14 will put a fear in the land of Egypt. And I will make
Pathros desolate, and will set a fire in Zoan, and will exe-
15 cute judgements in No. And I will pour my fury upon Sin,
the strong hold of Egypt; and I will cut off the multitude
16 of No. And I will set a fire in Egypt; Sin shall be in
great anguish, and No shall be broken up: and Noph *shall
17 have* adversaries [3]in the day-time. The young men of Aven

---

[1] Heb. *the fulness thereof.*   [2] Or, *things of nought*   See Ps.
xcvi. 5.   [3] Or, *all the day*

---

13. *destroy the idols*] On "idols" ch. vi. 5. The clause is
wanting in LXX.

the images to cease] lit. "the not-gods," a favourite term of Isaiah's,
e.g. xix. 1, 3, though found only here in Ezek. For "not-gods"
(*'ĕlîlîm*) LXX. has "magnates" (*'ēlîm*), which no doubt gives a good
parallelism to the next clause, and is supported by Cor., Ber.; cf. Is.
xxxiv. 12.

put a fear] Cf. Is. xix. 16, Egypt "shall fear because of the shaking
of the hand of the LORD of hosts, which he shaketh over it." Noph (in
Hos. ix. 6 Heb. *Moph*) is Memphis, the most important city of Lower
Egypt, lying on the left bank of the Nile, somewhat south of the modern
Cairo. Is. xix. 13; Jer. ii. 16, xliv. 1, xlvi. 14.

14. Pathros is Upper Egypt, or its capital, xxix. 14. Zoan, or
Tanis, the modern *San*, on the south shore of lake *Menzaleh*, according to Numb. xiii. 22 built seven years after Hebron, cf. Ps. lxxviii.
12, 43.

15. Sin, called here the "strong hold of Egypt," is usually identified
with Pelusium, which lying on the N.E. frontier of the country might
be considered the key to it.

multitude of No] i.e. No-Amon (Nah. iii. 8) or Thebes [now Luxor],
the capital of Upper Egypt, Jer. xlvi. 25.

16. *Sin*] [In this *v.* LXX. reads Syene.]

broken up] i.e. broken through by armed assault, cf. xxvi. 10 (last
words).

adversaries in the day-time] Cf. Zeph. ii. 4, "they shall drive
out Ashdod at the noonday" (Jer. xv. 8). The construction is unnatural, and the text may be in some confusion. LXX. reads differently.
[Kr., altering "adversaries" to a verb which gives a play on the
proper noun, renders "and Memphis—its day becomes as night."]

17. *young men of Aven*] i.e. On or Heliopolis, "city of the sun," and of Pi-beseth shall fall by the sword: and these *cities* shall go into captivity.   At Tehaphnehes also the day shall 18 ¹withdraw itself, when I shall break there the yokes of Egypt, and the pride of her power shall cease in her: as for her, a cloud shall cover her, and her daughters shall go into captivity.   Thus will I execute judgements in Egypt: and 19 they shall know that I am the Lord.

And it came to pass in the eleventh year, in the first 20 *month*, in the seventh *day* of the month, that the word of

¹ Another reading is, *be dark.*

Jer. xliii. 13; cf. Gen. xli. 45.   The obelisk known as Cleopatra's Needle belonged to the sun temple in On; and in the vicinity of the ruins near the village *Matariyeh* stands the sycomore under which tradition affirms that the Holy Family rested in their flight to Egypt. The modern name is *Ain Shems* (sun-fountain), a few miles N.E. of Cairo.

Pi-beseth] i.e. Bubastos or Bubastis, Egyptian Pa Bast, house of Bast or Pasht, the goddess to whom the cat was sacred, and who herself was represented under the aspect of the cat.   The cat mummies were here preserved.   The place lay on the Pelusiac arm of the Nile; the ruins, bearing the name *Tell Basta*, are not far from the modern *Zagazig.*   Herod. [II. 60] mentions that at a yearly festival held here as many as 700,000 people would assemble.

18.   *Tehaphnehes*] spelled somewhat differently Jer. ii. 16.   Jer. xliii. 8 speaks of a royal palace there, and in xlvi. 14 it is named along with Memphis as a chief city in Egypt.   Its site is probably the modern *Tell Defneh* (Daphnae), near the Pelusiac arm of the Nile, south of lake *Menzaleh*, about 30 miles S.W. of the ancient Pelusium.

the yokes of Egypt] must here be those imposed by Egypt, a sense not very suitable to the connexion.   A different pointing would give *sceptres* (so LXX. and modern commentators generally) or *staves*—but "staves" in the sense of supports is more than doubtful (cf. Is. xiv. 5).

her daughters] this may be literal (cf. *v.* 17, young men of On) or mean, "her cities."

19.   The purpose of these convulsions among the nations is that Jehovah the true God may be known; and this purpose will not fail.

XXX. **20—26.**   A new prophecy against Egypt, four months before the fall of Jerusalem.

Pharaoh seems to have quite recently suffered a defeat (*v.* 21), and a complete disaster to his power is threatened (*v.* 22).   This idea is expressed in a figure: one of his arms has been irremediably broken, it cannot be healed so as again to grasp the sword (*v.* 21).   But both arms shall be broken, the strong one as well as the disabled one, and

21 the LORD came unto me, saying, Son of man, I have
broken the arm of Pharaoh king of Egypt; and, lo, it
hath not been bound up to apply *healing* medicines, to put
a roller to bind it, that it be strong to hold the sword.

22 Therefore thus saith the Lord GOD: Behold, I am against
Pharaoh king of Egypt, and will break his arms, the strong,
and that which was broken; and I will cause the sword to

23 fall out of his hand. And I will scatter the Egyptians
among the nations, and will disperse them through the

24 countries. And I will strengthen the arms of the king of
Babylon, and put my sword in his hand: but I will break
the arms of Pharaoh, and he shall groan before him with

25 the groanings of a deadly wounded man. And I will hold
up the arms of the king of Babylon, and the arms of
Pharaoh shall fall down; and they shall know that I am the

the sword shall fall out of his hand (*v.* 22). But Jehovah will make
strong the arms of Nebuchadrezzar, and put His own sword into his
hand, which he shall stretch out over Egypt. It is Jehovah's sword
that Nebuchadrezzar wields, and Egypt shall be scattered among the
nations.

21. *broken the arm*] While the Chaldeans were besieging Jerusalem the army of Pharaoh Hophra (Apries) advanced and compelled
them to raise the siege, Jer. xxxvii. 5; cf. xxxiv. 21. The Egyptians
were repulsed and the siege renewed. It is possible that breaking the
arm of Pharaoh refers to this circumstance. At all events the distinction between the two arms, and the threat that both the sound and
the fractured one shall be altogether broken, suggest that an actual
past occurrence is referred to in the figure of *v.* 21.

a roller to bind it] i.e. a bandage. For the word cf. xvi. 4, Job
xxxviii. 9.

23. The consequence of breaking Pharaoh's arms will be the utter
defencelessness of the people of Egypt, which shall be scattered into
all lands. In *v.* 26 their dispersion is looked at from the other side,
and said to follow from Jehovah's strengthening the arms of the king
of Babylon.

24. *groan before him*] Pharaoh shall groan before Nebuchadrezzar
as a wounded man groans. The figure is well pursued. The "arm"
sometimes means the "helper," but here the two champions appear as
if engaged in a personal combat. Jehovah strikes down the arms of
Pharaoh, and the sword falls from his grasp; He strengthens the arms
of Nebuchadrezzar, putting His own sword into his hand. And thus
the king of Egypt, mortally wounded, groans before his adversary from
his death-stroke. Cf. xxviii. 9.

LORD, when I shall put my sword into the hand of the king of Babylon, and he shall stretch it out upon the land of Egypt. And I will scatter the Egyptians among the nations, 26 and disperse them through the countries; and they shall know that I am the LORD.

26. See on *v.* 23.

XXXI. PHARAOH UNDER THE FIGURE OF A GREAT CEDAR CUT DOWN AND FLUNG UPON THE GROUND.

The passage has three parts:

(1) *vv.* 1—9. Pharaoh, the impersonation of the spirit and might of Egypt, was a lofty cedar, with spreading branches, and its top in the clouds. All the fowls lodged in the branches, and all the beasts brought forth their young under it. Its waters nourished it and made it great. The trees in the garden of God did not equal it; all the trees of Eden envied it.

(2) *vv.* 10—14. The great tree shall be cut down by the mighty one of the nations, and thrown upon the ground. Its bulk shall fill the mountains and valleys of the land. All the nations shall depart from under the shadow of it; and the fowls and beasts of the field shall feed on it. Its heart was lifted up because of its great height, therefore it shall be cut down, that none of the trees lift themselves up and put their heads among the clouds.

(3) *vv.* 15—18. Nature shall shudder and put on blackness over the fall of Pharaoh. And the great trees of the garden of God that are gone down to the pit shall be comforted when Pharaoh and his auxiliaries descend among them.

The allegory is easily read. The mighty cedar, burying its head in the clouds, is the proud king and his powerful state, aspiring to a greatness that belongs to heaven. The fowls and beasts lodging under the shadow of the tree are the nations of the earth seeking his protection and subject to him (Dan. iv. 12). The trees in the garden of God are other mighty states impersonated in their rulers. The universal meaning which was given to the judgement on Egypt by representing it as the day of the Lord in ch. xxx. is suggested here in other ways, by the imposing height of the cedar, unapproachable by other trees in the garden of God; by the fowls and beasts of the field lodging in the tree—all nations seeking the protection of the Pharaoh; by the shock which all nature receives when the great tree is cut down and flung upon the ground; and finally by the commotion occasioned in Sheol when Pharaoh descends among the dead (ch. xxxii.; Is. xiv.). In some points the allegory has incongruities, as was natural. Pharaoh is a great cedar, but it is his waters—the Nile—that nourish him, and give him an altitude to which the trees of Eden cannot aspire. The cedar is in Lebanon, the home of cedars, but also by the great deep,

31   And it came to pass in the eleventh year, in the third
month, in the first *day* of the month, that the word of the
2 LORD came unto me, saying, Son of man, say unto Pharaoh
king of Egypt, and to his multitude; Whom art thou like
3 in thy greatness? Behold, the Assyrian was a cedar in
Lebanon with fair branches, and with a shadowing shroud,
and of an high stature; and his top was among the ¹thick
4 boughs.   The waters nourished him, the deep made him to
grow: her rivers ran round about her plantation; and she sent
5 out her channels unto all the trees of the field.   Therefore

¹ Or, *clouds*

and probably too in Eden (*v.* 11).   The trees, once in Eden, descend
into Sheol with those that are gone down to the pit.

1.   The date is about two months before Jerusalem fell.

2.   *his multitude*] the population of Egypt; hardly merely his
army.

Whom art thou like]   The question seems to imply that none can
be compared to him; he is unapproached in his greatness; cf. *v.* 18.

3.   *the Assyrian was a cedar*]   It is evident that the Assyrian has
nothing to do here; any comparison of Egypt to Assyria is without
motive.   Besides *v.* 3 is repeated in *v.* 10, and spoken of Egypt (cf.
v. 18).   The word "asshur" here is the name of a tree.   It is either the
same as *tĕasshûr* (ch. xxvii. 6), or this form should be read here.   Render:
Behold a stately cedar in Lebanon (lit. a *tĕasshûr* of a cedar); or, "behold
a *sherbin*, a cedar in Lebanon"—the more general "cedar" being added
after the species; or omit one of the words as a gloss.

a shadowing shroud]   The word for "shroud," usually rendered
"forest," must refer to the closely interwoven branches, hardly to the
underwood.   The phrase is wanting in LXX.

the thick boughs] better, as marg., the **clouds**, so *vv.* 10, 14; cf.
xix. 11.

4.   *made him to grow*] i.e. made him lofty.   There is probably,
however, the figure of a parent nourishing his offspring.   The word
"made to grow" is rendered "brought up" (children), Is. i. 2; cf.
xxiii. 4.   The waters rear the tree as their child.   The waters are those
of Egypt.   "The deep" seems to refer to the store of waters supposed
to be contained within the earth.

her rivers ran]   The construction is anomalous.   It is easiest to read
(with LXX.): *she* (the deep) *made her rivers to run round...and sent
out.*   Or possibly: "as for her rivers, they ran," &c.

her plantation] "her" refers to the "deep," which nourished the
plantation, though this is not quite natural.

her channels] the small canals for irrigation.   The plenteous waters
nourished the great tree and the other trees alike.

his stature was exalted above all the trees of the field; and his boughs were multiplied, and his branches became long by reason of ¹many waters, when he shot *them* forth. All the fowls of heaven made their nests in his boughs, and 6 under his branches did all the beasts of the field bring forth their young, and under his shadow dwelt all great nations. Thus was he fair in his greatness, in the length of his 7 branches: for his root was by ¹many waters. The cedars in 8 the garden of God could not hide him: the fir trees were not like his boughs, and the plane trees were not as his branches; nor was any tree in the garden of God like unto him in his beauty. I made him fair by the multitude of his 9 branches: so that all the trees of Eden, that were in the garden of God, envied him.

Therefore thus ²said the Lord GOD: Because thou art 10 exalted in stature, and he hath set his top among the

---

¹ Or, *great*   ² Or, *saith*

---

5. *his boughs were multiplied*] Wanting in LXX.
when he shot them *forth*] i.e. his branches, cf. xvii. 6, 7. Others: "when it (the deep) sent them (the waters) forth"; cf. *v.* 4.

6. The "fowls" and "beasts" are as much figurative as the tree; they are probably interpreted by "nations" in the end of the verse; cf. xvii. 23; Dan. iv. 12, 14. But see Jer. xxvii. 6.

8. *could not hide him*] Probably: **equal him**, compare with him. (The verb seems related to the common particle "over against" or "alongside of," i. 20, xlviii. 13, &c.)
plane trees] See Gen. xxx. 37; cf. Ps. civ. 16; Numb. xxiv. 6. The trees in the garden of God are naturally the most lofty.

9. *I made him fair*] But the idea of his beauty being conferred by God is foreign to the connexion¹. His stateliness was due to his great waters, beside which he was planted; it was the fruit of *nature*, which in this passage is rather contrasted with God. The words are wanting in LXX., and may be a marginal gloss on "beauty," which a reader attributed to God. [Cor. and Ber. omit, but Kr. retains the words as necessary for the rhythm.] If the words be omitted, the last clause of *v.* 8 should probably be closely connected with *v.* 9: "and no tree in the garden of God was like unto him, because of (in) the multitude of his branches."

---

¹ [Nevertheless the idea seems not unnatural, whether the thought is (as Kr.) that the Maker can destroy that which He has made, or that his greatness was due to Jehovah, though (*v.* 10) he attributed it to himself (Is. xxxvii. 24).]

11 ¹thick boughs, and his heart is lifted up in his height; I will even deliver him into the hand of the mighty one of the nations; he shall surely deal with him: I have driven him out

12 for his wickedness. And strangers, the terrible of the nations, have cut him off, and have left him: upon the mountains and in all the valleys his branches are fallen, and his boughs are broken by all the watercourses of the land; and all the peoples of the earth are gone down from his shadow,

13 and have left him. Upon his ruin all the fowls of the heaven shall dwell, and all the beasts of the field shall be

14 upon his branches: to the end that none of all the trees by the waters exalt themselves in their stature, neither set their top among the thick boughs, nor that their mighty ones

¹ Or, *clouds*

XXXI. 10—14. BECAUSE OF HIS PRIDE IN HIS HEIGHT HE SHALL BE CUT DOWN. NEBUCHADREZZAR, THE MIGHTY ONE OF THE NATIONS, SHALL HEW HIM TO THE GROUND, AND THE BEASTS SHALL FEED ON HIM. SUCH JUDGEMENT MUST OVERTAKE ANY GREAT TREE THAT EXALTS ITSELF INTO THE HEAVENS.

10. *the thick boughs*] the **clouds**, as marg.

11. *the mighty one of the nations*] Nebuchadrezzar.

for his wickedness] The alternative (Heb.) reading is: *according to* his wickedness. On "driven out" cf. Gen. iii. 24. The whole clause, "I have...wickedness," appears to have been absent from LXX.

12. The tenses in *vv.* 11 *b*, 12, 13 are perfects of threatening: the fut. would be plainer, "shall drive out," "shall cut off," &c. On "terrible" cf. xxviii. 7.

left him 1°] **cast him down**, ch. xxxii. 4; Am. v. 2. His great trunk covers the land and fills the watercourses. The nations who dwelt under his shadow, seeking his protection, have fled away from him (Dan. iv. 11).

left him 2°] The LXX., reading a verb differing by one consonant from the M.T., have "and (or, for) they have cast him down." The words [if they be not a gloss; so Kr.] seem an emphatic repetition from the beginning of the verse.

13. *his ruin*] i.e. his fallen trunk and branches, ch. xxxii. 4, xxxix. 17; Is. xviii. 6.

14. The downfall of Pharaoh is a chastisement for his pride and a warning.

trees by the waters] i.e. other nations.

in their stature] It is not merely pride of heart because of the stature, it is the stature itself, the shooting up of their top among the clouds— aspiring to a greatness belonging only to heaven—that is the sin.

thick boughs] **clouds**, as *v.* 10.

nor that their mighty ones stand up] i.e. display themselves in their

stand up in their height, *even* all that drink water: for they are all delivered unto death, to the nether parts of the earth, in the midst of the children of men, with them that go down to the pit.

Thus saith the Lord GOD: In the day when he went 15 down to ¹hell I caused a mourning: I covered the deep for him, and I restrained the rivers thereof, and the great waters were stayed: and I caused Lebanon ²to mourn for him, and all the trees of the field fainted for him.   I made 16 the nations to shake at the sound of his fall, when I cast

----

¹ Heb. *Sheol*.   ² Heb. *to be black*.

----

height. The phrase "all that drink water" is a circumlocution for "trees" fed by water.

nether parts of the earth] i.e. Sheol, the place of the dead, deep down in the earth, or under it.

the children of men] i.e. men in general, common men. The meaning is hardly that expressed in Ps. xlix. 10, that all die, the wise as well as the fool and the brutish, and that the "mighty ones" have no privilege over common men in this respect; the death referred to here is rather the violent death, the death of those slain with the sword, attended with no funeral honours. Cf. ch. xxxii. 17 *seq.*

them that go down] them that **are gone down** to the pit. So everywhere.   The allegory of the tree here passes over into the reality.

15. Creation puts on mourning and is paralysed at Pharaoh's fall. Lebanon is covered with blackness, and all the trees faint.

down to hell] to **Sheol**, the place of the dead.

I caused a mourning] Rather: **I caused to mourn, I covered** the deep for him.   The term "covered" (wanting in LXX.) is used as in xxxii. 7, "cover the heaven, and make the stars thereof dark," having the same meaning as "caused to mourn." The "deep" and the "rivers" are those mentioned in *v.* 4, but though the ref. is to the Nile and the waters of Egypt, a universal magnitude is given to these, they are the "deep" absolutely.   This deep which had nourished the great cedar is covered with mourning and paralysed by his fall, she is motionless, her waters are checked.

caused Lebanon to mourn] lit., as marg., *made* Lebanon *black*, in mourning. The prophet's representation naturally is not quite consistent. The home of Pharaoh, as a cedar, is Lebanon, but it is the waters of Egypt, magnified here into the "deep" absolutely, that nourish him.   Hence both the deep and Lebanon, with all the trees thereon, mourn and faint (Is. li. 20) over his fall.   What the language primarily expresses is the idea of the world-wide importance of the Egyptian power, so that, as the greatest forces of nature minister to its growth, all creation is affected by its fall. Cf. xxxii. 9, 10.

16. *at the sound of his fall*] See on xxvi. 15 ; cf. xxxii. 10.

him down to ¹hell with them that descend into the pit:
and all the trees of Eden, the choice and best of Lebanon,
all that drink water, were comforted in the nether parts
17 of the earth. They also went down into ¹hell with him unto
them that be slain by the sword; yea, they that were his
arm, *that* dwelt under his shadow in the midst of the
nations.

18 To whom art thou thus like in glory and in greatness
among the trees of Eden? yet shalt thou be brought down
with the trees of Eden unto the nether parts of the earth:
thou shalt lie in the midst of the uncircumcised, with them

¹ Heb. *Sheol.*

to hell...into the pit] to **Sheol** with them that **are gone down** to the
pit, ch. xxxii. 18; Is. xiv. 15. The nations living on the earth shake
with terror (ch. xxvi. 15) at the noise of his fall; while those already
gone down to the pit are "comforted" that one so mighty has fallen as
well as themselves, xxxii. 19, 31; Is. xiv. 10. The language does not
imply that those comforted were hostile to Pharaoh.

the trees of Eden] The figure of "trees" for states, or for the representatives of states like Pharaoh, is continued. The term Eden is used
generally to suggest great trees or the place where trees are found, for
the next words describe the trees as the "choice and best of Lebanon."

the choice and best] An anomalous construction, which is obviated
in LXX. by the omission of "best."

drink water] i.e. trees nourished by water, *v.* 14.

17. *They also...into hell*] **These also are gone down into Sheol**, ref.
being to the "trees of Eden," *v.* 16.

they that were his arm, that dwelt] **and his arm, that dwelt.** His
"arm" means his helpers (xvii. 9). The construction is difficult (read
probably constr. plur. of ptcp. for "that dwelt"; an omission of the
relative is improbable); cf. xxxii. 15. LXX. points "his seed" for
"his arm," but that "seed" could mean underwood (Cor.) has no
probability.

18. The question implies that Pharaoh had no peers. Yet though
incomparably greater than the other trees his fate shall be the same as
theirs—he shall be brought down with them to the nether parts of the
earth. LXX. reads the first half of the verse thus: "To whom art thou
like? Go down, and be brought down with the trees of Eden [lit.
luxury, pleasantness] to the nether parts of the earth," cf. xxxii. 19.

the uncircumcised] The term is applied to those slain with the
sword, and buried indiscriminately with no funeral rites, ch. xxviii.
10; cf. xxxii. 19, 21, 24, &c. [In these chs. it seems equivalent to outcast, uncivilised. The Egyptians in point of fact practised circumcision
(Josh. v. 9).]

that be slain by the sword. This is Pharaoh and all his
multitude, saith the Lord GOD.

And it came to pass in the twelfth year, in the twelfth **32**
month, in the first *day* of the month, that the word of the
LORD came unto me, saying, Son of man, take up a lament- 2
ation for Pharaoh king of Egypt, and say unto him, Thou wast
likened unto a young lion of the nations: yet art thou as
a dragon in the seas; and thou brakest forth ¹with thy

---

¹ Or, *in*

XXXII. FINAL PROPHECY AGAINST PHARAOH.

The chapter contains two parts:
First, *vv.* 1—16. A lament over Pharaoh.
Second, *vv.* 17—32. A funeral dirge over the interment of him and
his multitude.
The line of thought in *vv.* 1—16 resembles that in the other chapters:
(1) *vv.* 1—6. Pharaoh, represented as a dragon in the waters, is
dragged out by the net of Jehovah, and flung upon the land, where all
fowls and beasts feed on him. His carcase fills the land and his blood
the watercourses.
(2) *vv.* 7—10. Shock of nature and commotion among the nations,
even the most distant and unknown to Egypt, over his fall.
(3) *vv.* 11—16. The instrument of his destruction is the king of
Babylon. The overthrow of Pharaoh and his people shall be complete.
The land shall be desolate and life shall cease in it; no foot of living
creature, man or beast, shall trouble its waters, which shall run smooth
and dead.

1.   The prophecy is dated the first of the twelfth month of the twelfth
year, nearly a year and seven months after the fall of Jerusalem. Syr.
reads *eleventh* year.

2.   *wast likened unto a young lion*]   The construction is exceedingly
hard (cf. xxxi. 18).   So far as the form of words goes we might rather
translate, "O lion of the nations, *thou art undone*" (Is. vi. 5; Hos. x.
15), thus rendering another root identical in consonants.   The prophet
has a fondness, however, for using the Niph. (Cf. xiv. 4, 7, xix. 5,
xxxiii. 30, xxxvi. 3.)   The words can hardly mean: "thou thoughtest
thyself a young lion."   Cf. xxxviii. 13.

yet art thou]   Cf. Is. xix. 5, xxvii. 1; Job xli. 23.   The construction
seems to imply an antithesis between this clause and the previous one.

brakest forth with (marg., *in*) *thy rivers*]   The term "break
forth" is used of coming forth out of the womb (Ps. xxii. 9; cf. Job
xxxviii. 8), and also of those in ambush breaking out of their hiding-
place (Jud. xx. 33).   The term describes not the origin of the monster but
his activity; cf. "fouledst."   Ew. [with whom agree Cor., Ber., Kr. and
others] conjectured for "in thy rivers," *with thy nostrils*—"thou didst

rivers, and troubledst the waters with thy feet, and fouledst
3 their rivers.   Thus saith the Lord GOD: I will spread out
my net over thee with a company of many peoples; and
4 they shall bring thee up in my net.   And I will leave thee
upon the land, I will cast thee forth upon the open field,
and will cause all the fowls of the heaven to settle upon
thee, and I will satisfy the beasts of the whole earth with
5 thee.   And I will lay thy flesh upon the mountains, and fill
6 the valleys with thy ¹height.   I will also water with thy blood
the land wherein thou swimmest, even to the mountains,
7 and the watercourses shall be full of thee.   And when I
shall extinguish thee, I will cover the heaven, and make
the stars thereof ²dark; I will cover the sun with a cloud,
8 and the moon shall not give her light.   All the bright lights

---

¹ Or, as otherwise read, *worms*   ² Or, *to mourn*

---

spout (cause spray) with thy nostrils"; cf. Job xli. 18—20.   The object
of the verb is wanting here, however, and the verb is employed intransitively.   Cf. however, Mic. iv. 10.

their rivers]   Or, streams—those of the waters.   The vitality of the
monster and his violent activity are suggested by his troubling the waters
and fouling the streams.   Cf. the opposite idea, *vv.* 13, 14.

3.   Jehovah shall drag him out with His net by means of many peoples
(*vv.* 11, 12).   On the figure, cf. xii. 13, xvii. 20; Hos. vii. 12.

4.   *will leave thee*]   *will* **cast thee down**; cf. xxix. 5.   See xxxi. 13,
xxxix. 17 *seq.*

5.   Cf. xxxi. 12.   Other suggestions for "height," such as marg.,
"worms," have little probability.   Kr. renders by "carcase."

6.   *I will also water with thy blood the land wherein thou swimmest*]
Probably : **I will also water the earth with the outflow of thy blood,**
lit. "with thy outflow from thy blood." · It is possible that "from thy
blood" is an explanatory gloss to "with thy outflow."   Cf. Is. xxxiv. 3.

7.   *extinguish thee*]   Pharaoh is regarded as a brilliant luminary; cf.
Is. xiv. 12, "How art thou fallen from heaven, O day star, son of the
morning !"   It is doubtful if there is any ref. to the constellation of
the dragon.   The dragon (Job iii. 8, ix. 13, xxvi. 12) is not a constellation but a purely ideal representation of the eclipse or the storm-cloud
which swallows up the lights of heaven.   The phenomena in the verse
are those usually characteristic of the dissolution of nature on the day
of the Lord (Is. xiii. 10; Joel ii. 31, iii. 15; Am. viii. 9); but here
they express rather the shock which creation receives when one so great
meets with destruction.

8.   *bright lights*]   lit. luminaries of light.

of heaven will I make ¹dark over thee, and set darkness upon thy land, saith the Lord God. I will also vex the hearts of 9 many peoples, when I shall bring thy destruction among the nations, into the countries which thou hast not known. Yea, 10 I will make many peoples amazed at thee, and their kings shall be horribly afraid for thee, when I shall brandish my sword before them; and they shall tremble at every moment, every man for his own life, in the day of thy fall. For thus 11 saith the Lord God: The sword of the king of Babylon shall come upon thee. By the swords of the mighty will 12 I cause thy multitude to fall; the terrible of the nations are they all: and they shall spoil the pride of Egypt, and all the multitude thereof shall be destroyed. I will destroy 13 also all the beasts thereof from beside ²many waters; neither shall the foot of man trouble them any more, nor the hoofs of beasts trouble them. Then will I ³make their waters 14 clear, and cause their rivers to run like oil, saith the Lord God. When I shall make the land of Egypt desolate and 15

¹ Or, *to mourn*   ² Or, *great*   ³ Heb. *cause their waters to settle.*

upon thy land] possibly with LXX.: upon *the earth*. The extinction of the lights in heaven referred to in the previous clause suggests a more general darkness than one over Pharaoh's own land.

9. *vex the hearts*] or, **trouble**. The precise feeling is not grief, and certainly not anger (A.V. marg.); in *v.* 10 it is dismay, and then terror for themselves.

bring thy destruction among] hardly means "bring the news" of thy destruction; the destruction itself occurs among the nations, they observe it; cf. "brandish my sword before them," *v.* 10. But perhaps we should read with the LXX. "thy captivity," i.e. "thy captives."

into the countries] **unto countries**. The effect of Pharaoh's fall shall be felt by nations lying beyond the horizon of his knowledge; cf. Is. lv. 5.

11. It is the king of Babylon who shall execute the Lord's judgement upon Egypt.

12. *terrible of the nations*] Cf. on xxviii. 7, xxix. 19.

13. The desolation of Egypt shall be complete, man and beast swept away; cf. Zeph. i. 3. These pictures both of desolation and felicity are always ideal; cf. xxix. 11.

14. The waters of Egypt, no more troubled by the foot of man or beast, shall run smooth like oil.

make their waters clear] Cf. the noun, xxxiv. 18. No more trampled, they shall settle and run smooth.

15. The end of this desolating judgement shall be that Jehovah shall

waste, a land destitute of ¹that whereof it was full, when I shall smite all them that dwell therein, then shall they know
16 that I am the LORD. This is the lamentation wherewith they shall lament; the daughters of the nations shall lament therewith: for Egypt, and for all her multitude, shall they lament therewith, saith the Lord GOD.

¹ Heb. *the fulness thereof.*

be known. This is the purpose and the effect of all His interpositions among the nations. Exod. vii. 5, xiv. 4, 18.

16. Lit. *It is a lamentation and they shall chant it* (LXX. "thou shalt chant it"); *the daughters of the nations shall chant it; over Egypt and over all her multitude shall they chant it.* The daughters of the nations, in *v.* 18 the daughters of the famous nations, chant the dirge because professional wailers were chiefly women; cf. Jer. ix. 17, "call for the mourning women...and let them...take up a wailing for us."

XXXII. 17—32. DIRGE SUNG AT THE INTERMENT OF EGYPT AND ITS MULTITUDE.

Several things are observable in this remarkable passage:
1. It is a funeral dirge primarily over the multitude or nation of Egypt; and so in the case of the other nations referred to, Asshur, Elam, and the rest. These peoples are all gone down to Sheol, uncircumcised, slain with the sword. There in the world of the dead each people has an abode to itself. Around one chief grave the graves of the general mass are gathered. The chief grave is probably that of the prince, he being considered the genius, the embodiment of the spirit and being of the nation. The prophet regards the nations, even when no more existing on earth, as still having a subsistence in the world of the dead (cf. on Sodom, ch. xvi.). They are beings, who, having once lived, continue throughout all time. Though passed from the stage of history they still subsist in Sheol.
2. The prophet uses two words for the world of the dead, "the pit" and Sheol. The former name seems suggested by the grave, which is regarded as the entrance to Sheol, and indicates what kind of place Sheol is. It is a vast burying-place, deep in the earth, and full of graves. The nationalities spoken of have, like Egypt, all fallen by the sword, and the scene on earth is transferred to the world below. The nation and its prince are represented as slain on the battle-field, and the graves that crowd the field, the prince or genius of the nation in the midst, and those of the multitude around, are let down so to speak into Sheol beneath, where they abide. This scene of overthrow, the final experience of the nation on earth, expresses the meaning of the nation's history and the verdict of God upon it, and it is consequently transferred to the world of the dead and made eternal. In this respect the idea of the prophet in regard to nations coincides with the general view of

the Old Testament regarding individuals; the judgement of God regarding a man's life becomes manifest at the close of it on earth, and the state of death but perpetuates the manner of the end of life.

3. For, of course, the prophet desires to express by his representation a moral truth. The nations which he mentions are those that have come into conflict with Israel, although their sin is regarded as more general than this. They are chiefly the contemporary peoples whom Nebuchadrezzar, under commission from Jehovah, was to destroy, though Asshur belongs to an earlier time. Although, therefore, the nations can hardly be supposed to fall under a common judgement, the day of the Lord, the effect is the same. Their fate is the judgement of Jehovah upon them, His verdict in regard to their life as nations. Their common sin is violence : they put their terror in the land of the living. And their fate is but the nemesis of their conduct : taking the sword they perish by it. The history of nations is the judgement of nations. But the nations like individuals continue to subsist, they bear their shame in Sheol for ever.

4. The text of the passage is in considerable disorder. The LXX. offers a briefer and smoother text, though it is also marked by singular blunders (cf. *vv.* 29, 30). It can hardly be doubted that the Hebrew is to some extent overgrown with glosses. The meaning too is in some parts obscure. The passage has affinities with Is. xiv., but the representations there are in some respects different, and care must be taken to allow each passage to speak for itself. It is doubtful if any ideas to be called specially Babylonian be found in either of the prophets. There are two points of some difficulty in the interpretation: 1. There are two names for the world of the dead, "the pit" and Sheol; are they different in meaning? or, do they indicate, if not strictly a different locality in the underworld, a different condition? The usage of other passages appears decidedly against any distinction[1]. The term "pit" is used of what we so call, e.g. of the pit into which Joseph was cast (Gen. xxxvii. 24), of the "dungeon" into which Jeremiah was thrown (Jer. xxxviii. 6 *seq.*), and the like (Jer. xli. 7). The ideas of the people regarding the world of the dead were formed by looking into the grave and from the condition of the body in death. The world of the dead was created by the shuddering imagination out of these things. Apparently the name "pit" was given to the underworld because the grave was the mouth of it. The "pit" is used in parallelism with Sheol, and in the same sense, e.g. Ps. xxx. 3, lxxxviii. 3, 4. 2. Another question closely connected is this. Certain persons called the mighty (*vv.* 21, 27) are referred to and spoken of as being in Sheol (R.V. "hell"), and the question is, are these persons, though in Sheol, in a condition in some measure different from those like Pharaoh and his

---

[1] [Others, however, e.g. Ber. and Kr., see a division of the underworld into two parts, viz. "the pit," as the destination of the general multitude, and Sheol, as receiving the mighty ones. See *v.* 21. Kr., following Smend, comments on this as the first indication of distinct destinies after death, although as yet having no reference to moral deserts.]

17　It came to pass also in the twelfth year, in the fifteenth
　　day of the month, that the word of the LORD came unto
18　me, saying, Son of man, wail for the multitude of Egypt,
　　and cast them down, even her, and the daughters of the
　　famous nations, unto the nether parts of the earth, with
19　them that go down into the pit. Whom dost thou pass
　　in beauty? go down, and be thou laid with the uncircum-
20　cised. They shall fall in the midst of them that are slain
　　by the sword: ¹she is delivered to the sword: draw her away

¹ Or, *the sword is appointed*

multitude, slain by the sword? Unfortunately in both verses the Heb.
and Greek disagree. In *v.* 27 Heb. reads: "they (Meshech and Tubal)
shall not lie with the mighty ones," while LXX. omits the *not*, making
their destiny the same. See sub-note.

17. The month is not specified, but presumably the same month as
that named in *v. 1* is intended, the twelfth. The present passage
would in that case date a fortnight later than *vv.* 1—16. LXX.
reads *first* month of twelfth year; if this reading were followed the year in
v. 1 must be read eleventh (with Syr.).

18. The lament is primarily over the multitude or nationality of
Egypt.

cast them down, even her] Probably: **cause them to go down, thou
and the daughters of famous nations.** In *v.* 16 the daughters of the
nations were spoken of as chanting the dirge over Pharaoh and his
multitude. The prophet (LXX. *v.* 16) and these daughters together
chant the lament. They are said to "cause the multitude to go down"
because in their lament they describe their going down. The reading
"thou" for "her" implies only a slight change in the consonantal text
(אתה–אותה), and the "daughters of famous nations" cannot be those
that are interred, but those who inter. It is Pharaoh and his multitude
who are plunged into the pit (cf. *v.* 31).

them that go down] that **are gone down**, xxvi. 20, xxxi. 16.

19. *Whom...pass in beauty*] i.e. surpass; Ew., pass in fortune.
Probably the meaning is simply, To whom art (wast) thou superior?
The multitude of Egypt or the Pharaoh as the genius of the nation is
addressed.

go down] i.e. to the grave, or pit. "Uncircumcised" has in all the
passage the sense of dishonoured, profaned in death, and differs little
from slain with the sword, *vv.* 21, 24, cf. xxxi. 18. The pass. imper.
"be thou laid" is very rare. It is perhaps found in Jer. xlix. 8.

20. *she is delivered to the sword*] Rather, as marg.: **the sword is
appointed**, lit. *given*, a peculiar phrase and wanting in LXX.

draw her away] i.e. Egypt down into the pit. LXX. reads the
clause differently: "and all his multitude shall lie" still, or, "sleep"
(the sleep of death).

and all her multitudes. The strong among the mighty shall 21
speak to him out of the midst of ¹hell with them that
help him: they are gone down, they lie still, even the
uncircumcised, slain by the sword. Asshur is there and 22
all her company; his graves are round about him: all of
them slain, fallen by the sword: whose graves are set in the 23

¹ Heb. *Sheol*.

21. The Pharaoh and his multitude are supposed here to have
descended into Sheol, and the "mighty ones" already there address
them (cf. Is. xiv. 8, 10) or speak of them.

The strong among the mighty] lit. *the strong of the mighty*, where
"strong" is not a class among the mighty, but identical with them—
the strong mighty ones (gen. of appos.). In LXX. "strong" is wanting
as in *v.* 27. The word "strong" is that rendered *mighty one* of the
nations, xxxi. 11. It is probably distinct (though the same in spelling)
from the word *God*, xxviii. 2.

speak to him] Or, *of* him. The words that follow seem spoken in
regard to Pharaoh—though such a meaning is rather flat.

that help him] **his helpers**, auxiliary nations. The meaning must
be that the mighty speak to (of) Pharaoh and his helpers, hardly that
Pharaoh's helpers already gone down join the mighty in mocking
Pharaoh¹.

In LXX. these three verses stand in a different order, viz. *vv.* 20 *a*,
20 *b* (read differently), 21 *a*, 19, and the first three words of *v.* 20
again,—"In the midst of them that are slain with the sword shall they
fall with him, and all his multitude (strength) shall lie still. And the
mighty (lit. giants, *v.* 27) shall say unto thee: Be thou in the depth
of the pit; to whom art thou superior? go down, and lie still with
the uncircumcised, in the midst of them that are slain with the sword."
Probably neither text presents the original, though the general meaning of both is the same. It is in favour of Heb. that it begins with
the interrogation, and rather against the LXX. that it makes the
address rather prolix. The "mighty" who speak are in any case
those already in Sheol, and not persons upon the earth such as the
Babylonians (Hitz.).

22, 23. ASSHUR. [The Assyrian empire had for its original capital
the city of Asshur, now *Kal'at Sherkāt*, on the W. bank of the Tigris,
about 60 miles S. of Nineveh.]

22. *her company*] In ref. to the other peoples "multitude" is used.
The term "company" may be used of the many nationalities in the
Assyrian empire, cf. xxiii. 24.

his graves...him] The gender varies as the country (fem.), or king,
as representative of the people, is thought of. The ref. here is to the

¹ [Kr.'s rendering, though involving somewhat violent change in M.T., seems
good and is supported by the LXX. "Thou and thy helpers come down, lie still,
among the uncircumcised, slain by the sword."]

uttermost parts of the pit, and her company is round about
her grave: all of them slain, fallen by the sword, which
24 caused terror in the land of the living.   There is Elam and
all her multitude round about her grave: all of them slain,
fallen by the sword, which are gone down uncircumcised
into the nether parts of the earth, which caused their terror
in the land of the living, and have borne their shame with
25 them that go down to the pit.   They have set her a bed
in the midst of the slain with all her multitude; her graves
are round about her: all of them uncircumcised, slain by
the sword; for their terror was caused in the land of the
living, and they have borne their shame with them that
go down to the pit: he is put in the midst of them that

king.   LXX. uses the *masc.* pron. throughout.   The text here is shorter
in LXX., but no difference of sense arises.

23.   *uttermost parts of the pit*] i.e. the depths or bottom of the pit.

caused terror] Cf. xxvi. 17, 20.   This phrase must mean that Asshur
inspired terror into the nations by his might; to suppose that the
meaning is that the *fate* of Asshur by the judgement of God caused terror
(Hitz.) is altogether false, cf. *vv.* 24, 25, 26, 27, 32.

24, 25.   ELAM.

Elam, said to mean Highlands, lay E. of the Tigris, and touched
Assyria and Media on the N., Media and Persia on the E., and on the
S. the Persian Gulf.   An early expedition of Elam into the land of the
Jordan is referred to Gen. xiv. 1 *seq.*   The country was incorporated
into the Assyrian empire, in the armies of which it served (Is. xxii. 6,
cf. xi. 11), and on the fall of this empire it probably asserted its independence.   It appears independent in the time of Jeremiah, who
threatens it with destruction at the hands of Nebuchadrezzar (Jer. xlix.
34, 39).

24.   *and have borne their shame*] Their shame is that which adheres
to them as slain with the sword and unhonoured[1].   The consequences
of their life shewed themselves in the manner of their death, and abode
upon them.   Cf. xxxvi. 6, 7.

them that go down] that **are gone down**.

25.   The verse is greatly a repetition of *v.* 24, and is wanting in
LXX., except the words "in the midst of *them that be* slain," which
are attached to *v.* 24.   The words "that are gone down to the pit"
usually close the verse, *vv.* 18, 24, 29, 30; and if the verse be retained
the last clause should probably be omitted as an accidental repetition
of the first clause, due to the copyist's eye straying from "pit" in 25
to "pit" in 24.   The three words retained in LXX. cannot stand by
themselves.

[1] [Or (see sub-note on *vv.* 17 ff.) as having been assigned to the ignominious
division of the underworld.]

be slain. There is Meshech, Tubal, and all her multitude; 26 her graves are round about her: all of them uncircumcised, slain by the sword; for they caused their terror in the land of the living. ¹And they shall not lie with the 27 mighty that are fallen of the uncircumcised, which are gone down to ²hell with their weapons of war, and have laid their swords under their heads, and their iniquities are upon their bones; for *they were* the terror of the mighty in

---

¹ Or, *And shall they not lie &c.?*   ² Heb. *Sheol.*

---

26. MESHECH AND TUBAL. See on xxvii. 13; cf. xxxviii. 2.

her graves...her] On genders cf. *v.* 22.

27. *they shall not lie*] LXX., Syr. omit the neg.: *and they are laid* with the giants. Ew. would retain the neg., reading as an interrogation with an affirmative sense [see R.V. marg.]: "And shall they not lie with...?," which is not very natural.

that are fallen of the uncircumcised] LXX. fallen *of old* [so Cor., Ber., Kr.]. This reading has considerable probability, although the other reading might stand. Some scholars would also alter "fallen" (*nophĕlim*) into Nephilim (cf. Gen. vi. 4); an unnecessary change. For "hell" read **Sheol.**

have laid their swords] **they laid** (indeterminate subject)—equivalent to the passive: and their *swords were laid.*

their iniquities] The reference is still to the "mighty"; to change the subject spoken of, making the clause refer to Meshech and Tubal, is most unnatural.

for they were *the terror*] **because the terror of the mighty was in the land.** The clause explains the preceding, as e.g. why their iniquities were upon their bones, and would certainly be easier if the reading had been: "because the terror *of their might*" (*gĕbūrām*, which possibly should be read with the Syr.), precisely as in *vv.* 29, 30. So Hitz., Corn.

Verse 27 is difficult. The reading "they shall not lie with the mighty" suggests the idea that the mighty who fell of old, and went down to Sheol in full armour, and had their swords laid under their heads, occupy a more honourable place in Sheol than such a rout as Meshech and Tubal, who are counted unworthy to lie beside them. This idea is not probable in itself, and cannot be reconciled with other parts of the verse. The last clause "because the terror of the mighty (or, of their might) was in the land of the living" ascribes the same sin to these mighty as is charged against Asshur and the rest (*vv.* 23, 24, &c.), and for which they bear their shame. Again, the phrase "their iniquities are upon their bones" can have no other meaning than that their evil and violence were interred with their bones, and continued to cleave to them—that they went down unhouseled, disappointed, unaneled, cut off in the blossom of their sin. The conjecture of Cor. "their *shields* were upon

---

EZEKIEL   17

28 the land of the living. But thou shalt be broken in the
   midst of the uncircumcised, and shalt lie with them that are
29 slain by the sword.   There is Edom, her kings and all her
   princes, which [1]in their might are laid with them that are
   slain by the sword: they shall lie with the uncircumcised,
30 and with them that go down to the pit.   There be the
   princes of the north, all of them, and all the Zidonians,
   which are gone down with the slain; [2]in the terror which
   they caused by their might they are ashamed; and they lie
   uncircumcised with them that are slain by the sword, and
   bear their shame with them that go down to the pit.
31 Pharaoh shall see them, and shall be comforted over all
   his multitude: [3]even Pharaoh and all his army, slain by

---

[1] Or, *for all their might*   [2] Or, *for all the terror*
[3] Or, *Pharaoh and all his army are slain &c.*

---

their bones" is altogether destitute of probability[1]. LXX. renders
"giants," as it does Gen. vi. 4, and possibly it thought of the antedilu-
vian race (see note above). The prophet may have had this race in his
mind, but more probably his reference is a wider one (cf. xxxii. 12,
xxxix. 18, 20). Even if he referred to the giants before the Flood, it is
anything but likely, with Gen. vi. before him and with his moral
temper, that he would assign an honourable place in Sheol to those
violent desperadoes. The weird touch "went down to Sheol in their
weapons of war, and had their swords laid under their heads," probably
means that the manner of their death and burial was in keeping with
the violence and bloodshed which was the occupation of their life.
The usages and sentiments of chivalry were not yet known to Ezekiel.
The clause should, therefore, probably be read as in M.T.

28.   *But thou shalt*] **Thou also shalt**. The Pharaoh is addressed.
The phrase "shalt be broken" is wanting in LXX. which reads "Thou
also shalt lie in the midst of the uncircumcised, with them that have
been slain with the sword."

29.   EDOM. Cf. xxv. 12.

in their might] Better (as marg.) *for all their might*, i.e. notwithstanding their might.

are laid] The term "laid," lit. *given*, means rather *put, consigned.*

them that go down] that **are gone down**.

30.   The princes of the North and the Zidonians. The former are
probably those of the Syrian states, and the Zidonians represent the
Phœnician principalities in general.

in the terror] Rather, as marg., **for all the terror**.

31.   *comforted over all his multitude*] The Heb. order is : over all

---

[1] [This reading, however, is adopted also by Ber. and Kr., and gives a good sense,
as a reference to primitive methods of burying warriors.]

the sword, saith the Lord GOD.   For I have put ¹his terror 32
in the land of the living: and he shall be laid in the midst
of the uncircumcised, with them that are slain by the sword,
even Pharaoh and all his multitude; saith the Lord GOD.

¹ Another reading is, *my*.

his multitude, slain with the sword, even Pharaoh and all his army,
saith, &c.   The words "slain with...his army" are wanting in LXX.
On "comforted," cf. xiv. 22, xxxi. 16.   Pharaoh will be "comforted"
by the sight of all these nations in the pit, suffering the same humiliation
as himself and his multitude.

32. *I have put his terror*] Marg., *my* terror, as all the versions.
[The Heb. text reads "his," but the Heb. marg. (*Kĕrī*) "my."]
Throughout the passage "to put terror" is uniformly employed of
the conduct of the various nations when on the stage of history.   If
used of Jehovah here it would be intended to express a vivid contrast—it is *He* who ultimately puts His terror on the world when He
interposes to overthrow these tyrannical and violent nations; cf. Is.
viii. 13.   This somewhat sensational antithesis is not natural, and does
not harmonise with the next clause.   If *his* terror be read, the power
of Pharaoh and the terror he caused would be attributed to Jehovah.
But this is an idea out of harmony with the whole representation, which
ascribes the supremacy of the peoples named to their own violence or
to the gifts of nature.   It is just the point insisted on in all these chapters
on the nations that their power was a self-exaltation and rebellion against
Jehovah, and for this they perish by the sword and are doomed to eternal
dishonour.   It seems almost imperative to retain *his* terror, and alter
the verb to the 3rd pers.—*for he caused his terror*...therefore he shall be
laid, &c.   So probably Targ., which paraphrases as in *vv.* 23, 24, 25,
26.   Similarly Jer. in his Comm. on Ezek.   [This change is also supported by good modern commentators, e.g. Kautzsch, Cor., Kr.]

SECOND SECTION.   CH. XXXIII.—XXXIX.   PROPHECIES OF
ISRAEL'S RESTORATION AND ETERNAL PEACE.

Only one date appears in connexion with these prophecies, that in
xxxiii. 21.   Though this date does not stand at the beginning of ch.
xxxiii. *seq.*, it may be held to indicate generally the time to which the
whole seven chapters are to be assigned.   There is something suspicious,
however, in the date of the arrival of the fugitives—fifth day of tenth
month of twelfth year—nearly a year and a half after the fall of the
city.   The Syr. read or conjectured eleventh year, which would leave
about six months for the news of the city's fall to be carried by messengers
to the exiles in Babylon, and this date is now very generally accepted.
The various chapters may not all belong to the same period.   The
dates throughout the book are little else than rubrics of a very general
kind, under which, in default of more precise details, a number of

discourses, extending over considerable periods, have been grouped. The occupation of part of the country by Edom (xxxv. 36) would not take place just close upon the fall of the kingdom; and perhaps the state of despondency of the people and their sense of sinfulness (xxxiii. 10) was one which the fall of the country and the confirmation of the predictions of the prophet took some time to create in their minds. The precise dates are of little consequence, it is the general situation alone that is important. The fall of the city is presupposed (xxxiii. 21), the overthrow of the royal house (xxxiv.), the extinction of the nationality (xxxvii.), the dispersion of the people among all nations (xxxvi. 16 *seq.*), the occupation of part of the country by Edom and the neighbouring tribes (xxxv.; cf. Jer. xli.), and the complete prostration of men's minds under their calamities and the unbearable burden of the sin that had occasioned judgements so unparalleled (Lam. i. 12, ii. 13, 20, &c.). Only the prophet stood erect, while all others were overwhelmed in despair. The greatness of the blow had stunned them, and, as the prophet had foreshewn (xxiv. 23), a stupor had fallen on them. Yet the Lord had not made a full end of Israel. The old era was closed, but a new era was about to open, and a new Israel about to arise. It is of this new era that the prophet has now to speak, and of the hopes of the new Israel and of the conditions of being embraced in it. It is in these chapters that the prophet's contributions to Old Testament theology are chiefly to be found. The passage contains these general conceptions:

First, ch. xxxiii. The function of the prophet in preparation for the new age. It is to awaken the moral mind, to create the sense of individual worth and responsibility, and to shew that the conditions of belonging to the new Israel are moral only. This chapter defines the place of the individual human mind, and its duties; the following chapters describe rather the Divine operations in bringing in the new and perfect kingdom of the Lord.

Second, ch. xxxiv. The royal house, the shepherds of the people, had destroyed alike themselves and the flock (xvii., xix. 14). The Lord Himself will take in hand the gathering of His scattered sheep together, and the feeding of them henceforth; He will appoint His servant David to lead them.

Third, ch. xxxv.—xxxvi. The land, the mountains of Israel, usurped by aliens, shall be rescued from their grasp and given again to the people as of old. The reproach of barrenness shall no longer cleave to it; the mountains of Israel shall shoot forth their branches and yield their fruit to the people, and man and beast shall be multiplied.

Fourth, ch. xxxvii. The nation is dead and its bones bleached, but there shall be a resurrection of the dead people and a restoration of them to their own land. Two kingdoms shall no more exist there, but the Lord's people shall be one, and His servant David shall be prince over them for ever.

Fifth, ch. xxxvii.—xxxix. The peace of His people shall be perpetual. The Lord shall be their everlasting defence. When the armies of Gog come up from the uttermost regions of the earth, with all the nations which have not heard Jehovah's fame nor seen His glory, to assail His people, drawn by the hope of boundless plunder, they shall be destroyed by fire out of heaven.

XXXIII. THE FUNCTION OF THE PROPHET.

Though the prophet seems the chief figure in the chapter, he is really but the medium through whom the principles of the new kingdom of God and the conditions of entering it are enunciated. These principles are: (1) that God desires that men should live. (2) The new Israel shall be composed of members who enter it individually. (3) The condition of entering on man's part is repentance. (4) Man is free to repent—to do good or do evil. The righteous may fall from his righteousness and sin; and the sinner may turn from his evil and do righteousness. He that doeth righteousness shall live; and the soul that sinneth shall die. These principles of the worth and freedom of the individual man, though latent in many parts of the Old Testament, had never been stated so explicitly before. They are no more than what all men will now allow. If pressed indeed and regarded as exhaustive they might seem to ascribe more power to man than he possesses. But in subsequent chapters the prophet lays sufficient emphasis upon the operation of God in regenerating the individual mind and in founding the new kingdom. It would be a novelty indeed if an Old Testament writer were found ascribing too much to man and too little to God. There is a certain vagueness in the prophet's delineation. It is evident that he is moving among religious principles, and that the enunciation of them is his chief interest; the time and circumstances in which they shall operate are left indefinite. When he says that the righteous shall live and the sinner die, the question, When? naturally occurs. No precise answer is given. But there floats before his view an approaching crisis. The advent of the new era presents itself as a moment of trial and decision; it is like the approach of war upon a people (*vv.* 1—6). The remarkable passage ch. xx. 33—44 may be compared in supplement of the present chapter.

The chapter contains these parts:

(1) *vv.* 1—6. Illustration taken from life—the part of the watchman in war. It is his duty to blow the trumpet when danger is coming. If he does so, the fate of those who hear will lie at their own door. If he fails, the blood of those that perish will be on his head.

(2) *vv.* 7—9. Such is the place of the prophet: the same are his duties and responsibilities.

(3) *vv.* 10—20. This is the place of the prophet, but the state of the people's mind is such that his warnings may be addressed to deaf ears. Their calamities have stunned and paralysed the people; they feel lying under an irrevocable doom, entailed upon them by their past history— our sins be upon us, we pine away in them; how, then, shall we live? Nothing is reserved for them but to bear the inexhaustible penalty of their past evil, until, like those in the wilderness, they fall prostrated beneath it. In answer to this stupor of despair comes the voice from heaven with two consoling words: first, that Jehovah has no pleasure

33

2 And the word of the LORD came unto me, saying, Son of man, speak to the children of thy people, and say unto them, When I bring the sword upon a land, if the people of the land take a man from among them, and set him for 3 their watchman: if, when he seeth the sword come upon 4 the land, he blow the trumpet, and warn the people; then whosoever heareth the sound of the trumpet, and taketh not warning, if the sword come, and take him away, his 5 blood shall be upon his own head. He heard the sound of the trumpet, and took not warning; his blood shall be upon him: whereas if he had taken warning he should have 6 delivered his soul. But if the watchman see the sword come, and blow not the trumpet, and the people be not warned, and the sword come, and take any person from among them; he is taken away [1]in his iniquity, but his blood 7 will I require at the watchman's hand. So thou, son of man, I have set thee a watchman unto the house of Israel;

[1] Or, *for*

in the death of the sinner, but desires that all men should turn and live; and secondly, it is not by that which men have been that they shall be judged, but by that which they shall become. The past writes no irrevocable doom over men.

(4) *vv.* 21—29. Fugitives from Judaea arrive among the exiles saying that the city is smitten. This confirmation of all the prophet's past predictions opens his mouth and gives him boldness to address his countrymen. He proceeds to pass judgement on those left in the land, and to state anew that the conditions of inheriting the land are only moral.

(5) *vv.* 30—33. The confirmation which the fall of the city gave to the prophet's past predictions awakened the interest of his fellow exiles in him and his words.

1—6. The illustration—duty of the watchman in war.

3. The trumpet was the signal of danger, Hos. viii. 1; Am. iii. 6; Jer. vi. 1.

4, 5. He that heareth the trumpet and taketh not warning, his blood shall be on his own head; he is responsible for his own death, which shall not be laid at the door of the watchman.

6. Although in *v.* 2 Jehovah is said to bring the sword upon the people (xiv. 17), and presumably for their sin, the language of the present verse leads over from the illustration to the thing meant to be illustrated.

7—9. Similar to the part of the watchman is that of the prophet. Cf. ch. iii. 17 *seq.* The evil, corresponding to the sword in the

therefore hear the word at my mouth, and give them warning from me.   When I say unto the wicked, O wicked man, 8
thou shalt surely die, and thou dost not speak to warn the
wicked from his way; that wicked man shall die [1]in his
iniquity, but his blood will I require at thine hand.   Never- 9
theless, if thou warn the wicked of his way to turn from it,
and he turn not from his way; he shall die [1]in his iniquity,
but thou hast delivered thy soul.

And thou, son of man, say unto the house of Israel: 10
Thus ye speak, saying, [2]Our transgressions and our sins are
upon us, and we pine away [1]in them; how then should we
live?   Say unto them, As I live, saith the Lord GOD, I have 11
no pleasure in the death of the wicked; but that the wicked
turn from his way and live: turn ye, turn ye from your evil

---

[1] Or, *for*   [2] Or, *Truly our transgressions &c.*

---

illustration, in regard to which the prophet is to warn the people, is left
undefined.   As in the case of all the prophets, however, the turning point
in the fortunes of the exiles appeared to Ezek. to be of the nature of a
Divine interposition and judgement, and it is this general idea that colours
his language.   Except in the two or three passages, xiii. 5, xxx. 3, cf.
xxxviii. 19, the day of the Lord is not referred to in Ezek.

10—20.   Despondency of the people, making the prophet's appeals
to them of none effect.   Removal of the despair by two gracious words
from the Lord.

10.   The people had come to regard their calamities as due to their
sins and as evidence of them.   They had come round to the prophet's
view of their history, for they saw his predictions fulfilled.   But the
new view came with a crushing weight upon them.   The calamities of
their country were unparalleled (Lam. i. 12, ii. 13, 20, iii. 1, iv. 6, 9),
and equally unparalleled must have been their guilt (Lam. i. 9, 14, ii. 14,
iv. 13, v. 7).   And their calamities seemed final, their sin was expiable
only by their complete destruction.

we pine away]   Or, waste away.   The word expresses not mental
but physical wasting away, ending in complete dissolution.   See the
very similar figures, Is. x. 18, xvii. 4; cf. Ezek. iv. 17, xxiv. 23;
Lev. xxvi. 39.

11 *seq.*   Jehovah's answer to the people's despondency and despair of
"life."   These verses must be estimated from that point of view to
which they are an answer.   The passage is not directly an affirmation
of the rectitude of God, although this is indirectly affirmed in answer to
the people's objection, founded on traditional ways of thinking, that the
Lord's ways are not equal.   The Divine rectitude is not the point of
view from which the prophet looks; he speaks in answer to the people's

12 ways; for why will ye die, O house of Israel?　And thou,
son of man, say unto the children of thy people, The
righteousness of the righteous shall not deliver him in the
day of his transgression; and as for the wickedness of the
wicked, he shall not fall thereby in the day that he turneth
from his wickedness: neither shall he that is righteous be

despondency.　And his answer is twofold: first, God's desire is that
men should live; and secondly, the past is not irrevocable.　Not
according to what men have been but according to what they shall be or
become, will God judge them.

12.　It would have been enough to illustrate the earnest exhortation,
Turn ye, why will ye die? (v. 11) by the assurance that, if the wicked
turns, his past sins will not be remembered against him (v. 16).　But
the prophet states the truth in a more general form.　His purpose is
to teach also the general truth that the past of one's life does not of
necessity determine the future either in itself or in the judgement of
God.　This, next to the assurance of God's gracious will regarding
men (v. 11), was the truth most needed to comfort the people and
awaken them out of the stupor which lay on them into a moral life and
activity again.

It is merely to distort the prophet's words to say that he teaches
that a man's past life goes for nothing, and that he will be judged
merely according to what he is found doing "at the moment" of the
judgement.　The prophet is not speaking of moments.　He speaks to
men overwhelmed by a judgement of God which seemed to leave no
hope for the future, and he lays down the principle needful for the
moral awakening of the people that the past is not irrevocable, that a
future of possibility lies before them.　It is too true that the evil of a
man's past life prolongs itself into the future and that sin cannot at
once be done with.　Yet we "believe in the forgiveness of sins"; and
this is the truth which the prophet desires to teach his countrymen,
overwhelmed with the thought of their own evil past.　When he says
the righteous shall "live" he means by "living" the complex thing,
having the favour of God, and having an external felicity corresponding
to this.

Old Testament prophets and saints were hardly able to conceive
the first of these two things existing apart from the second.　And
the prophet probably still considers them inseparably connected.
And hence, when teaching that the son shall not suffer for the sins of
the father, and that the righteous shall "live" and the wicked "die,"
he has been charged with inculcating a doctrine more false to reality
than the old one which it was designed to supersede.　But here again
a certain injustice is done to the prophet.　No doubt when he uses the
word "live" he employs it in the pregnant sense, viz. to enjoy the
favour of God and to have this favour reflected in outward felicity.
But Ezekiel agrees with Jeremiah in relegating the principle that the

able to live thereby in the day that he sinneth. When I 13
say to the righteous, that he shall surely live; if he trust to
his righteousness, and commit iniquity, none of his righteous
deeds shall be remembered; but [1]in his iniquity that he
hath committed, [2]therein shall he die. Again, when I say 14
unto the wicked, Thou shalt surely die; if he turn from
his sin, and do [3]that which is lawful and right; if the wicked 15
restore the pledge, give again that he had taken by robbery,
walk in the statutes of life, committing no iniquity; he shall
surely live, he shall not die. None of his sins that he hath 16
committed shall be remembered against him: he hath done
that which is lawful and right; he shall surely live. Yet the 17
children of thy people say, The way of the Lord is not
equal: but as for them, their way is not equal. When the 18
righteous turneth from his righteousness, and committeth
iniquity, he shall even die [4]therein. And when the wicked 19
turneth from his wickedness, and doeth that which is lawful
and right, he shall live thereby. Yet ye say, The way of 20
the Lord is not equal. O house of Israel, I will judge you
every one after his ways.

[1] Or, *for*   [2] Or, *for it*   [3] Heb. *judgement and righteousness.*
                    [4] Or, *for them*

children shall not suffer for the sins of the father to the new era
about to dawn. Neither prophet is laying down a new principle
which is to obtain in the world, the world going on as it had done
before. Ezek. feels himself, as all the prophets do, on the threshold of
a new Epoch, the era of the perfect kingdom of God, and it is in
this new era that the principle which he enunciates shall prevail. See
at the end of ch. xviii.

13.   Cf. iii. 20, xviii. 24.

14.   Cf. iii. 18, xviii. 27.

that which is lawful] lit., cf. marg., (just) *judgement and justice.*

15.   Instances of a return to righteousness on the part of the wicked,
cf. xviii. 7; Ex. xxii. 1, 4; Num. v. 6, 7.

the statutes of life] Statutes by walking in which a man shall live,
ch. xiii. 21, xx. 11; Lev. xviii. 5. As elsewhere, "life" is used in the
pregnant sense of enjoyment of the favour of God and the external
prosperity which is the reflexion and seal of it.

16.   Cf. xviii. 22.

17.   Cf. xviii. 25, 29.

18, 19.   These verses sum up the whole principles of the passage,
cf. xviii. 26, 27. On *v.* 20 cf. xviii. 25, 29.

21 And it came to pass in the twelfth year of our captivity,
in the tenth *month*, in the fifth *day* of the month, that one
that had escaped out of Jerusalem came unto me, saying,
22 The city is smitten. Now the hand of the LORD had been
upon me in the evening, afore he that was escaped came;
and he had opened my mouth, until he came to me in the
morning; and my mouth was opened, and I was no more
23 dumb. And the word of the LORD came unto me, saying,

21, 22. Fugitives from Judaea arrive among the exiles announcing
that the city had fallen. This confirmation of all the prophet's anticipations, which the exiles had received with so much incredulity,
opened his mouth, gave him confidence to speak before his fellow
exiles. And he announces what shall be the fate of those left in the
land (*vv.* 23—29).

21. The date here given is about a year and a half after the city's
fall. Considering the constant intercourse between the mother country
and the exiles this period is very long. Some Heb. MSS. as well as the
Syr. read *eleventh* year, leaving about six months for the news to travel
by messenger. (Eleven and twelve are easily confused in Heb.)

our captivity] that of Jehoiachin, ch. i. 2. "One that had escaped,"
lit. *the escaped*, may refer to one or be collective and denote the body of
fugitives, cf. xxiv. 26.

22. Though the date is inserted here, it is probably to be understood
as applicable to the whole chapter, for *vv.* 1, 2 the prophet is commanded to speak publicly to the children of his people. In the evening
he felt the hand of the Lord upon him, he fell into an excited condition.
Thoughts such as those in *vv.* 1—20 of the new Israel that God would
create and of the conditions of belonging to it filled his mind. He was
well aware that the city's fall was inevitable, to him it was as good as
fallen. And full of the new thoughts of the future he felt himself
standing before his fellow exiles with an impulse strong upon him to
speak to them of this future in the name of the Lord. In the morning
the fugitives arrived with the confirmation of all his past predictions.

until he came to me] **should come**: against his coming, Ex. vii. 15.
[Kr., with a change of one consonant, would read *at the time when*,
instead of "until."]

no more dumb] i.e. silent, Ps. xxxix. 2; Is. liii. 7.

23—29. The confirmation by the fugitives of all his previous predictions gave the prophet boldness to speak anew, and what he says
is but a continuation of what he had said before, and what had been
so literally confirmed. He had predicted the city's fall because of its
sins, and his prophecy had been verified; those remaining in the
land continue in the sins for which the city fell, and its fate shall
certainly overtake them. The judgement must be carried out till
the offences cease. But the teaching of these verses is the natural

Son of man, they that inhabit those waste places in the 24
land of Israel speak, saying, Abraham was one, and he
inherited the land: but we are many; the land is given us
for inheritance.   Wherefore say unto them, Thus saith the 25
Lord God: Ye eat with the blood, and lift up your eyes
unto your idols, and shed blood: and shall ye possess the
land?   Ye stand upon your sword, ye work abomination, 26

supplement also to that in *vv.* 1—20.   Those remaining in the land
presume that they shall inherit the land because they are in it, notwithstanding their evil conduct : the inheritance of the land will
be given on different conditions (*vv.* 1—20, cf. xxxvi. 25—38,
xxxvii. 23).

24.   For those remaining in the land even before the fall of the city
cf. xi. 5—12, 14—21; Jer. xxiv.   Those remaining in the land after its
capture (2 Kings xxv. 22) express their confident hopes.   Though
reduced in numbers they are still many in comparison of the single
individual Abraham.   Yet he was multiplied in such a way as to take
possession of the land ; much more may they hope yet to assert their
claims to it.   They perhaps hardly argued on mere natural probabilities ;
they felt themselves the heirs of the promises made to Abraham, and in
spite of disasters hoped that Jehovah would fulfil them to them. [Cf. Matt.
iii. 9; Luke iii. 8; John viii. 39.]   They display the same temper as the
people had always shewn ; they have a faith in Jehovah but no knowledge of what Jehovah is (Am. v. 14; Hos. iv. 1; Jer. iv. 22, v. 2, 4).
Another prophet of this age applies the wonderful history of Abraham and
his multiplication to comfort the few men of Israel who followed after
righteousness, Is. li. 2.

inhabit those waste places]   the ruined cities chiefly, *v.* 27; but cf.
xxxvi. 4.

the land is given us]   Words of confident anticipation.

25.   The claim of the remnant is repudiated by Ezek. with indignation.
They persist in the sins for which their country fell, and the same
judgement shall overtake them.

Ye eat with the blood]   i.e. eat flesh slaughtered in such a way that
the blood remains in it.   According to the law animals had to be
killed in such a manner as to drain away the blood, which was poured
into the ground, when not dashed upon the altar.   An example of a
prohibited way of slaughtering was breaking the neck, Is. lxvi. 3.
Cf. Lev. xvii. 10, xix. 26; Deut. xii. 16; 1 Sam. xiv. 32.   See on
xviii. 6, 11, 15, xxii. 9.

lift up your eyes]   See xviii. 6.   On "shed blood," xxii. 6, 9.

26.   *stand upon your sword*]   The sense hardly is, "the footing on
which ye deal with men is the sword"; but probably, "ye occupy
yourselves with the sword," cf. xliv. 24.   [Kr. Ye rely upon your sword.
Gen. xxvii. 40.]

work abomination]   The term is mostly applied to religious practices

and ye defile every one his neighbour's wife: and shall ye
27 possess the land? Thus shalt thou say unto them, Thus
saith the Lord GOD: As I live, surely they that are in the
waste places shall fall by the sword, and him that is in the
open field will I give to the beasts to be devoured, and they
that be in the strong holds and in the caves shall die of the
28 pestilence. And I will make the land a desolation and
an astonishment, and the pride of her power shall cease;
and the mountains of Israel shall be desolate, that none
29 shall pass through. Then shall they know that I am the
LORD, when I have made the land a desolation and an
astonishment, because of all their abominations which they

contrary to the pure religion of Jehovah. On the other sin named
cf. xviii. 6, xxii. 11. Verses 25, 26 are wanting in LXX. The passage
is vigorous and apart from the anomalous form [1] of the word for "ye
work" altogether unsuspicious. The omission in LXX. may have
arisen from the eye of the translator straying from the words "Lord
GOD" *v.* 25 to the same words *v.* 27.

27. The "waste places" are the desolate cities; those that still hover
about these ruins shall be slain by the enemy. The "open field" is
the country, now depopulated and the possession of wild beasts; and
the "strong holds," coupled with caves, are the natural fastnesses of
the land. Those taking refuge there shall die of the pestilence, due to
crowding and famine. The remnant shall be exterminated from the land.

28. Cf. vii. 24, xxiv. 21, xxx. 6, 7. The "mountains of Israel" are
the mountain land of Israel.

XXXIII. 30—33. DEMEANOUR OF THE PEOPLE TOWARDS THE PROPHET.

The confirmation which the fall of the city gave to the prophet's
past predictions awakened the interest of his fellow exiles in him and
his words. They congregated together in knots under the shadow of
the walls and in the doors of the houses discussing his sayings. Recent
events had given him a more prominent place in their thoughts. There
was something also in the new truths he was uttering, in his outlook
into the future and in his appeals to the individual mind, causing each
to turn his eyes inward upon himself, that touched them and awakened
a certain reality of concern. Still it was in the main curiosity rather
than genuine seriousness that led them to listen to him. There was
a certain charm, more perhaps in the kind of future presented by the
prophet than in his manner of presenting it, which was like sweet
music; but though they listened the drift of their minds was too
steadily set in another direction to be changed.

---

[1] [According to Cor., Ber., Kr. merely a scribal error.]

have committed. And as for thee, son of man, the children 30 of thy people talk of thee by the walls and in the doors of the houses, and speak one to another, every one to his brother, saying, Come, I pray you, and hear what is the word that cometh forth from the LORD. And they come 31 unto thee as the people cometh, and they sit before thee as my people, and they hear thy words, but do them not: for with their mouth they shew much love, but their heart goeth after their gain. And, lo, thou art unto them as [1]a 32 very lovely song of one that hath a pleasant voice, and can play well on an instrument: for they hear thy words, but they do them not. And when this cometh to pass, 33 (behold, it cometh,) then shall they know that a prophet hath been among them.

And the word of the LORD came unto me, saying, Son 34 2

[1] Or, *a love song*

30. *talk of thee*] **the children of thy people who talk together of thee...they speak.** The construction has a certain inconsequence in it. For "talk together" cf. Mal. iii. 16. The "walls". afforded a shade, under which men gathered for conversation.

one to another] The form "one" is Aramaic rather than Heb. The clause says the same thing as next clause and is wanting in LXX.

31. On "come unto thee" cf. viii. 1, xiv. 1, xx. 1.

as my people] The construction is very hard. LXX. omits.

with their mouth...love] The language is peculiar, but can hardly have any other sense. LXX., Syr. read: *for falsehood is in their mouth, and their heart goeth after their defilements, &c.* The term "gain" has, especially in later books, the general sense of advantage, self-advancement, Is. lvi. 11.

32. *a very lovely song of one*] rather, as marg., *a love song*, lit. "thou art to them a love song; as one that hath." The comparison "as a love song" is as usual inexact; "as" merely indicates the circumstances—as when there is a love song. The prophet is compared to the singer.

33. *And when this cometh to pass*] **but when it cometh to pass.** The general *it* (fem. as usual in general references) is the judgement or crisis, the idea of which underlies all the prophet's words and is presupposed in them. Cf. ii. 5.

XXXIV. THE FORMER SELFISH SHEPHERDS OF THE FLOCK, AND THE FUTURE GOOD SHEPHERD.

The past history of the people and their future are presented under the common allegory of a flock. The shepherds are the rulers.

of man, prophesy against the shepherds of Israel, prophesy,
and say unto them, even to the shepherds, Thus saith the
Lord GOD: Woe unto the shepherds of Israel that do
feed themselves! should not the shepherds feed the sheep?
3 Ye eat the fat, and ye clothe you with the wool, ye kill
4 the fatlings; but ye feed not the sheep.   The diseased have
ye not strengthened, neither have ye healed that which
was sick, neither have ye bound up that which was broken,
neither have ye brought again that which was driven away,
neither have ye sought that which was lost; but with force

(1) *vv.* 1—10.   The evil shepherds of Israel fed themselves and not
the flock.   And thus the sheep were scattered over all the earth.   The
Lord will rid His sheep out of the hand of these shepherds.

(2) *vv.* 11—16.   Jehovah Himself will undertake the care of His
sheep.   He will seek them out and gather them from all the nations,
and will bring them again to the mountains of Israel, where they shall
feed in plentiful pasture.

(3) *vv.* 17—22.   He will judge also between sheep and sheep,
between the strong and the weak.   The strong shall no more push
with the horn and thrust with the shoulder; neither shall they alone
eat the good pasture and drink the clear water.   These pushing rams
and he-goats are the magnates, whose oppression of the common people
is so common a theme in the early prophets.

(4) *vv.* 23—31.   The Lord will raise up a good shepherd to rule
His flock, even His servant David.   And in those days to come the
earth shall be transfigured: showers shall bless the land and the earth
shall yield her increase.   And the peace of the people shall be perpetual: they shall no more fear the heathen abroad, and no more
suffer from scarcity at home.   [Our Lord as the Good Shepherd (John
x. 11) is one of the earliest representations found in the catacombs at
Rome.   See *Dict. Chr. Ant.* II. p. 1892.]

2. *the shepherds*] i.e. the rulers[1].   The term is chiefly used in later
writings (Jer. ii. 8, iii. 15); it occurs, however, in Zech. ix.—xi., the
date of which is disputed [now accepted as post-exilic].   On Zedekiah
cf. ch. xvii., and on his immediate predecessors, Jer. xxii. 10—30.   In
general, Jer. xxiii., xxv. 32 *seq.*   [For the metaphor cf. the Homeric
ποιμὴν λαῶν.]

even to the shepherds] Possibly this is a marginal heading which has
crept into the text, cf. Jer. xxiii. 9, and the reading may be, *Thus saith
the Lord GOD: Woe unto....*

3. *Ye eat the fat*] LXX. [probably rightly] the *milk* (the consonants
are the same).   Cf. Is. vii. 22; Zech. xi. 16.

4. Five classes are here mentioned, in *v.* 16 only four, the "diseased"

---

[1] [Not, as in Milton's application of the language in *Lycidas*, "The hungry sheep
look up and are not fed," a corrupt and grasping priesthood.]

and with rigour have ye ruled over them.   And they were 5
scattered, because there was no shepherd: and they became
meat to all the beasts of the field, and were scattered.
My sheep wandered through all the mountains, and upon 6
every high hill: yea, my sheep were scattered upon all the
face of the earth; and there was none that did search or
seek *after them*.   Therefore, ye shepherds, hear the word 7
of the LORD: As I live, saith the Lord GOD, surely for- 8
asmuch as my sheep became a prey, and my sheep became
meat to all the beasts of the field, because there was no
shepherd, neither did my shepherds search for my sheep,
but the shepherds fed themselves, and fed not my sheep;
therefore, ye shepherds, hear the word of the LORD; Thus 10
saith the Lord GOD: Behold, I am against the shepherds;
and I will require my sheep at their hand, and cause them
to cease from feeding the sheep; neither shall the shepherds feed themselves any more; and I will deliver my sheep
from their mouth, that they may not be meat for them.
For thus saith the Lord GOD: Behold, I myself, even I, 11
will search for my sheep, and will seek them out.   As a 12
shepherd seeketh out his flock in the day that he is among
his sheep that are scattered abroad, so will I seek out my
sheep; and I will deliver them out of all places whither
they have been scattered in ¹the cloudy and dark day.
And I will bring them out from the peoples, and gather 13
them from the countries, and will bring them into their
own land; and I will feed them upon the mountains of
Israel, by the watercourses, and in all the inhabited places of
the country.   I will feed them with good pasture, and upon 14

¹ Heb. *the day of clouds and thick darkness.*

being wanting, and " strengthen" used here of the diseased is said there
of the sick.   The "broken" is the hurt or bruised; the "lost" that
which has wandered away of itself, in distinction from that "driven
away" by violence.
   5. The allegory is simple enough.   Owing to the evil and selfish
government of the rulers the people became the prey of all the nations
round about them.   The figure of the flock indicates, however, the
affection of Jehovah for His people and His compassion over their
sufferings.

the mountains of the height of Israel shall their fold be:
there shall they lie down in a good fold, and on fat pasture
15 shall they feed upon the mountains of Israel. I myself
will feed my sheep, and I will cause them to lie down,
16 saith the Lord GOD. I will seek that which was lost, and
will bring again that which was driven away, and will bind
up that which was broken, and will strengthen that which
was sick: and the fat and the strong I will destroy; I will
17 feed them in judgement. And as for you, O my flock,
thus saith the Lord GOD: Behold, I judge between cattle
18 and cattle, as well the rams as the he-goats. Seemeth it a
small thing unto you to have fed upon the good pasture,
but ye must tread down with your feet the residue of your
pasture? and to have drunk of the clear waters, but ye must
19 foul the residue with your feet? And as for my sheep,

XXXIV. **11—22.** JEHOVAH HIMSELF WILL UNDERTAKE THE CARE OF HIS FLOCK.

11—16. Jehovah first seeks out His sheep (*v.* 11), then He delivers
them out of the places where they are scattered (*v.* 12), then He leads
them into their own land (*v.* 13), where He feeds them upon the
mountain heights of Israel (*vv.* 14, 15).

16. The Lord's treatment of His flock will be in all things the
reverse of the treatment given them by the evil shepherds.

the fat and the strong I will destroy] [referring to the sheep, i.e. the
people who acquire unlawful gain and oppress their fellows. "Guard"
for "destroy," adopted by Cor., Ber. and others, by a very slight
change in one consonant, is scarcely probable].

in judgement] i.e. just judgement; *in rectitude and justice.* Cf. such
demands as those in Is. i. 17, iii. 15, v. 8; Mic. ii. 1, 2, iii. 1—4.

17—22. Not only shall the cruel shepherds be removed and the flock
delivered out of their hands and fed by the Lord Himself; the injuries
inflicted by members of the flock on each other shall no more prevail.
The strong shall no more push the weak or drive them from the good
pasture.

17. *between cattle and cattle*] between **sheep and sheep**, even **the
rams and the he-goats.** The "rams" and "he-goats" explain the
second word "sheep." Jehovah will judge between one class (the poor
and weak) and another (the strong and tyrannous). Cf. xxii. 27, 29;
Am. ii. 7, iii. 9, iv. 1.

18. The words are addressed to the rams and he-goats—the magnates
[who oppress the poor. The sheep are divided into two classes, the
oppressed and the oppressors.]

clear waters] lit. **settled waters**, cf. xxxii. 14.

they eat that which ye have trodden with your feet, and they drink that which ye have fouled with your feet.

Therefore thus saith the Lord GOD unto them: Behold, I, 20 even I, will judge between the fat cattle and the lean cattle. Because ye thrust with side and with shoulder, and push all 21 the diseased with your horns, till ye have scattered them abroad; therefore will I save my flock, and they shall no more 22 be a prey; and I will judge between cattle and cattle. And 23 I will set up one shepherd over them, and he shall feed them, even my servant David; he shall feed them, and he shall be their shepherd. And I the LORD will be their 24

23—28. Instead of the many worthless shepherds of old there shall in the future be one good shepherd, even David, and Jehovah shall in truth be God of Israel.

23. *my servant David*] The meaning cannot be that David would in person revive and reappear. It is more doubtful whether the prophet means that the line or family of David would again occupy the throne or that a single person would be king. It is possible that this question was not strictly before his mind; it is the character of the ruler that he thinks of. The oriental mind hardly distinguishes between an ancient personage and one who appears in his power and spirit; when it compares it identifies. The new prince over the people will be David, the servant of the Lord. Both the person and the reign of David were idealised. He was not in general terms but in truth the man after God's own heart. His rule was not merely extensive, it was universal. He gave the people victory and secured them peace—he was a leader and commander of the peoples (Is. lv. 4; Ps. xviii. 43). Such shall be the king of the restored community when Jehovah is indeed the God of Israel. For it is to be noted that in Messianic prophecy it is Jehovah who *saves* the people (*v.* 22 and preceding verses); then He appoints a shepherd over the restored community, who feeds them in righteousness and peace. The Messiah is the king of the saved community, which he rules in the fear of the Lord with all royal and godly qualities; and the virtues of his character, fruit of the spirit of the Lord, communicate themselves to those whom he rules (Is. xi.). It is possible that the phrase "one shepherd" is to be interpreted as in xxxvii. 24, with the meaning that the two kingdoms shall be one, and that this is part of the meaning of the term "David," cf. Hos. i. 11, iii. 5; Am. ix. 11. See more fully on ch. xxxvii.

24. *I the LORD will be their God*] This is the goal towards which all movements strive; when this is reached perfection is attained and the covenant with its aims fully realised, cf. xxxvii. 27; Jer. xxxi. 31; Ex. xxix. 45. The meaning of the words is very profound, implying closer fellowship and deeper feelings accompanying it than can well be expressed.

God, and my servant David prince among them; I the
25 LORD have spoken it.   And I will make with them a
covenant of peace, and will cause evil beasts to cease out
of the land: and they shall dwell securely in the wilderness,
26 and sleep in the woods.   And I will make them and the
places round about my hill a blessing; and I will cause
the shower to come down in its season; there shall be
27 showers of blessing.   And the tree of the field shall yield
its fruit, and the earth shall yield her increase, and they
shall be secure in their land; and they shall know that
I am the LORD, when I have broken the bars of their yoke,
and have delivered them out of the hand of those that
28 ¹served themselves of them.   And they shall no more be
a prey to the heathen, neither shall the beast of the earth

¹ Or, *made bondmen*

my servant David prince]   David is here called "prince"; in xxxvii.
22, 24 he is named "king" (though LXX. avoids the term).   The term
"prince" is common in Ezek., and does not imply a dignity inferior to
that of royalty.   [Ezekiel's picture of the future ruler in this ch. is much
more glowing than that suggested of his position in the theocratic
State (ch. xl.—xlviii.).   See e.g. xlv. 9, xlvi. 2.]

25.   *a covenant of peace*]   a covenant securing everlasting peace and
therefore implying the removal of all that would injure or disturb
them.   In Hos. ii. 20 the sense is somewhat different: Jehovah makes
a covenant for them with the beasts of the field, that they shall not
hurt.   In Hos. "beasts" is used literally (cf. Is. xi. 6), here figuratively,
meaning foes, heathen assailants, though the figure of the flock is still
maintained.   Cf. Lev. xxvi. 6.   The "wilderness" is the uncultivated
pasture land as distinguished from that under tillage, covered with
crops or fruit-trees (Carmel).   Even in the "woods," the parts covered
with bush, the haunts of wild beasts, the flock shall sleep safely.

26.   *make them...a blessing*]   i.e. altogether blessed (Gen. xii. 2;
Is. xix. 24), as the last words of the verse imply.   Cf. for the construction
xvi. 38, xxvii. 36, xxviii. 19, xxxiii. 28.   The language of the clause is,
however, not very natural; LXX. reads: "and I will set them round
about my hill" (the word "blessing" wanting).   [Kr. reads "And I
will give them rain in its season."]

showers of blessing]   i.e. bringing blessing, not, composed of blessing,
v. 27, Joel ii. 23—27; Lev. xxvi. 4.

27.   *bars of their yoke*]   i.e. the yoke bound upon them, Lev. xxvi. 13;
Jer. ii. 20, where read "thou hast broken."   [The yoke rested on the
neck of the beasts, and was fixed on by forked pieces of wood joined
under the neck by a fork or chain.   See Art. *Yoke*, in *HDB*.]

devour them; but they shall dwell securely, and none shall make them afraid. And I will raise up unto them a ¹planta- 29 tion for renown, and they shall be no more ²consumed with famine in the land, neither bear the shame of the heathen any more. And they shall know that I the LORD their 30 God am with them, and that they, the house of Israel, are my people, saith the Lord GOD. And ye my sheep, the 31 sheep of my pasture, are men, and I am your God, saith the Lord GOD.

¹ Or, *plant*   ² Heb. *taken away*.

29. *a plantation for renown*] lit. for a name, i.e. a plantation which shall be (or, so as to be) renowned ; cf. for the phrase xxxix. 13 ; Is. lv. 13. The ref. is not to the person of the Messiah, but to the luxuriant fertility and vegetation of the earth in the Messianic age. Comp. Ps. lxvii., lxxii. 16 ; Am. ix. 13 ; Hos. ii. 21 ; Joel ii. 23 *seq.* The land of Israel was subject to droughts and famine (xxxvi. 15, 30 ; 1 Kings xvii. *seq.* ; Jer. xiv. 1—6, 18 ; Joel i.). In the regeneration this reproach shall no more fall on it, ch. xxxvi. 3, 6, 15.

30. *am with them*] The people's consciousness of salvation shall be, so to speak, a double one, that Jehovah is their God and that they are His people. The two things might seem identical, but the second suggests a feeling regarding themselves which belongs to the perfect enjoyment of salvation.

31. *ye my sheep...are men*] Omit "are men" with LXX. and read : *and ye are my sheep, the sheep of my pasture, and I am your God.*

XXXV.—XXXVI. THE LAND.

After the review of the dark history of the "shepherds" of the people in the past and the promise of the good shepherd who shall rule the restored community, securing protection and peace to them for ever, there follows a similar oracle in regard to the Land of Israel. The passage has three divisions :

First, ch. xxxv. Negatively, a threat against Edom. Edom had shewn despite to the people all through their history : particularly, first, it had expressed malicious joy over the desolation of the country at the time of its great calamity, which it had helped forward (*vv.* 5, 11—15) ; and secondly, it had arrogated to itself the right to take possession of the country, though it was Jehovah's abode (*vv.* 10, 12). Therefore desolation shall overtake the mountain of Seir ; it shall be made desolate when all the earth rejoices (*vv.* 14, 15).

Secondly, ch. xxxvi. 1—15. Positively, an oracle in behalf of the mountain land of Israel. It shall be delivered out of the hand of the

35   Moreover the word of the LORD came unto me, saying,
2 Son of man, set thy face against mount Seir, and prophesy
3 against it, and say unto it, Thus saith the Lord GOD:
Behold, I am against thee, O mount Seir, and I will stretch
out mine hand against thee, and I will make thee a desolation
4 and an astonishment.   I will lay thy cities waste, and thou
shalt be desolate ; and thou shalt know that I am the LORD.
5 Because thou hast had a perpetual enmity, and hast given
over the children of Israel to the power of the sword in the
time of their calamity, in the time of the ¹iniquity of the end :
6 therefore, as I live, saith the Lord GOD, I will prepare
thee unto blood, and blood shall pursue thee : sith thou

¹ Or, *punishment*

heathen who are round about, and they shall bear their shame (*vv.*
1—7).
Thirdly, *vv.* 16—38.   The redemptive principles illustrated in all
this—not for Israel's sake but for His own name's sake it is that Jehovah
doeth all these things for His people.

XXXV.   THREAT AGAINST EDOM.

1.   On Edom cf. xxv. 12 *seq.*
2.   *set thy face against*]   Cf. ch. vi. 2.
mount Seir]   Virtually synonymous with Edom.   Cf. Gen. xxxii. 3.
3.   *stretch out mine hand*]   Cf. vi. 14.   Edom shall be made a complete desolation, and it shall realise whose hand it is that falls so heavily
upon it (*v.* 4).
5.   The causes of the judgement on Mount Seir.   These causes are
three : first, its perpetual hatred of Israel, xxv. 15 ; Am. i. 11 ; second,
its malicious joy over the downfall of Israel and the part it took in the
destruction of the people in the day of their calamity, when the consequences of their guilt fell upon them, Obad. *vv.* 10—14 ; and third,
Edom's invasion of the land and seizure of it as their own, though the
Lord dwelt in it (*v.* 10).
hast given &c.]   Cf. Jer. xviii. 21 ; Ps. lxiii. 10.
iniquity of the end]   either, the final punishment of iniquity, or, the
iniquity whose punishment was seen in the end (of the state).   Cf.
ch. vii.   The phrase is found also in xxi. 30.   The ref. is to the
destruction of Jerusalem ; so the "calamity" referred to is the downfall
of the city and state, as Obad. *v.* 13 ; cf. Ps. cxxxvii. 7, "the day of
Jerusalem."
6.   *prepare thee unto blood*]   lit. **make thee blood** (cf. xvi. 38, and on
xxxiv. 26), i.e. all blood—give thee over to universal slaughter.   The
clause " I will...pursue thee " is wanting in LXX.

hast not hated blood, therefore blood shall pursue thee.
Thus will I make mount Seir an astonishment and a 7
desolation; and I will cut off from it him that passeth
through and him that returneth.   And I will fill his moun- 8
tains with his slain: in thy hills and in thy valleys and in
all thy watercourses shall they fall that are slain with the
sword.   I will make thee perpetual desolations, and thy 9
cities shall not ¹be inhabited: and ye shall know that I am
the LORD.   Because thou hast said, These two nations and 10
these two countries shall be mine, and we will possess it;
²whereas the LORD was there: therefore, as I live, saith 11
the Lord GOD, I will do according to thine anger, and
according to thine envy which thou hast shewed out of thy
hatred against them; and I will make myself known among
them, ³when I shall judge thee.   And thou shalt know 12

¹ Another reading is, *return.*   ² Or, *though*   ³ Or, *according as*

sith thou hast not hated]   The words might mean: *surely thou hast
hated* (hatest) blood, and blood shall..., a sense not very clear, but
probably similar to xi. 8, "Ye fear the sword, and I will bring the
sword."   [For "sith"=since, see W. Aldis Wright, *Bible Word-Book.*]

7.   *passeth through...returneth*]   A phrase like "shut up and free,"
used to denote all classes, cf. "the shod and the barefoot" in Arab.
LXX. has altered into "man and beast," the usual phrase after "cut
off," e.g. xxv. 13.

9.   *cities shall not be inhabited*]   So Heb. text *teshabnah.*   The Heb.
marg. (*Ķĕrî*) reads the word so as to give the sense *return* (so A.V.),
an inferior reading which possibly reposes on xvi. 55.

10.   In aggravation of its historical bearing towards Israel and
its participation in her overthrow, Edom has proceeded to lay hands
upon the territory of the two houses of Israel, although it is the place
of the Lord's abode and consecrated by His presence.

These two nations]   Judah and Israel.

whereas the LORD]   Or, *although* the Lord was there; cf. xlviii. 35.
The ref. appears to be to the time when the people were in the land,
and the Lord dwelt in it in the midst of them, consecrating it by His
presence.   This relation of His to the land was unalterable; and Edom
had "profaned" His holy abode.

11.   Amos i. 11 also uses the word "anger" of Edom's demeanour.
LXX. reads the verse in a shorter form.   "Therefore, as I live, saith
the Lord, I will do unto thee according to thine enmity, and I will
make myself known unto thee, when I shall judge thee."

among them]   i.e. Israel, or, those who behold it.   Or (cf. LXX.)
in thee (Edom, changing one letter), which is more pointed, cf. *v.* 12.

¹that I the LORD have heard all thy blasphemies which thou
hast spoken against the mountains of Israel, saying, ²They
13 are laid desolate, they are given us to devour. And ye
have magnified yourselves against me with your mouth, and
have multiplied your words against me: I have heard it.
14 Thus saith the Lord GOD: When the whole earth rejoiceth,
15 I will make thee desolate. As thou didst rejoice over the
inheritance of the house of Israel, because it was desolate,
so will I do unto thee: thou shalt be desolate, O mount
Seir, and all Edom, even all of it: and they shall know that
I am the LORD.

¹ Or, *that I am the LORD; I have heard &c.*   ² Or, *It is*

12. *all thy blasphemies*] Or, **contumelies**, 2 Kings xix. 3.

14. *When* &c.] Probably: "*To the rejoicing of* the whole
earth will I make thee desolate." This gives the requisite antithesis to
v. 15: as Edom rejoiced over the destruction of Judah, the whole earth
will be overjoyed at her desolation.

15. The clause "As thou didst...do unto thee" is wanting in LXX.
As Edom had been active in the destruction of Judah, their own
desolation must follow. The author of the Lamentations has a presentiment that the next great act of Divine judgement will be on Edom
(Lam. iv. 22; cf. Is. xxxiv., lxiii. 1—6). The great empires which
brought destruction upon Jerusalem were acting under commission
from Jehovah and the work was according to His will. But in the
first place there is a difference between the work itself and the spirit in
which it is done. Jehu received commendation for his act in cutting off
the seed of Ahab, but later his house was extirpated for the guilt of this
same "blood of Jezreel" (Hos. i. 4). The Assyrian was entrusted with
a commission against the ungodly nation; but he meant not so, it was
in his heart to cut off nations not a few (Is. x. 7), and the decree that
he should be broken upon the mountains of Israel went out against him
(Is. xiv. 25). Nebuchadrezzar was the "servant" of the Lord, but
because Babylon laid her yoke heavily on the aged of the people, not
considering the issue of such things, bereavement and widowhood shall
come upon her in one day (Is. xlvii. 6—8). Here the prophet reprobates both the actions and the spirit of Edom, and threatens that
Jehovah will recompense them into their bosom. In ancient modes of
thought the people and their god were one. The people were but the
reflexion of the god, they were the people of Chemosh or Milcom or
Jehovah. All wars were religious wars, wars against a god who
animated and gave strength to his people (Ex. xii. 12). Edom's
despite was to some extent in the strict sense directed against Jehovah.
In truth they knew Jehovah only as the God of Israel, but it was He
whom they knew, though they might not have such knowledge of Him

And thou, son of man, prophesy unto the mountains of **36**
Israel, and say, Ye mountains of Israel, hear the word of
the LORD.   Thus saith the Lord GOD: Because the enemy **2**

as Ezek. had attained to.   But it is possible to be guilty of great sins
against God, even though they are done unwittingly and without full
knowledge of that which He is.

And in the second place, Edom received no commission from Jehovah
against His people.   Their place in history and among the nations of
the earth gave them no significance in relation to Israel, or in Jehovah's
providence embracing all the world.   The contact of Israel with the
nations exercising universal empire over the earth, if it did not suggest
conceptions of Jehovah's universal power and dominion to the prophets,
at least gave them occasion for expressing to the people and to all time
such conceptions ; and this period of Israel's history lent a breadth and
elevation to prophecy to which in political conditions such as existed in
earlier times it could never have attained.   The transportation of
colonies of Israelites also into the Assyrian and Babylonian empires,
besides purifying the religion of the people from its dependence on
ritual observance and making it more inward among those who continued to adhere to it, leavened the populations of these heathen nations
with truer conceptions of Deity and religion.   The writers of this age
often refer to the strangers joining themselves to the covenant of the
Lord (Is. xiv. 1, 2, lvi. 1—8), and no doubt the same influence was
exerted by Israel, if not to the same extent, in Babylon and the countries of the East, as that with which we are familiar in later times in
Rome and the empire of the West.   In such respects Edom had no
importance, and hardly entered into the larger designs of Jehovah with
regard to His people and mankind.

XXXVI. POSITIVE PROPHECY IN BEHALF OF THE LAND.

(1) *vv.* 1—7. The mountain land of Israel shall be delivered out of
the hand of the heathen round about, who have usurped it.   These
nations shall bear their shame.

(2) *vv.* 8—15. The land shall in the age to come be luxuriantly
fruitful.   The reproach that it ate up its inhabitants shall no more
fall upon it.

(3) *vv.* 16—38. The redemptive principles illustrated in these
blessings of the future, and in all Israel's history.   Not for Israel's
sake but for His own name's sake it is that Jehovah will accomplish
these things.

1 *seq.* Deliverance of the mountains of Israel from the nations who
have usurped them.   The passage is the reversal of all that which was
threatened in ch. vi.

mountains of Israel] i.e. mountain land of Israel, vi. 2, xvii. 22,
xxxiii. 28, &c.

2. Cf. xxv. 3, xxvi. 2.

hath said against you, Aha! and, The ancient high places
3 are ours in possession: therefore prophesy, and say, Thus
saith the Lord GOD: Because, even because they have made
you desolate, and swallowed you up on every side, that ye
might be a possession unto the residue of the nations, and
ye are taken up in the lips of talkers, and the evil report of
4 the people: therefore, ye mountains of Israel, hear the word
of the Lord GOD; Thus saith the Lord GOD to the mountains and to the hills, to the watercourses and to the valleys,
to the desolate wastes and to the cities that are forsaken,
which are become a prey and derision to the residue of the
5 nations that are round about: therefore thus saith the Lord
GOD: Surely in the fire of my jealousy have I spoken against
the residue of the nations, and against all Edom, which have
appointed my land unto themselves for a possession with the
joy of all their heart, with despite of soul, to cast it out for

ancient high places] "High places" is not used here in the usual
religious sense of rural sanctuaries, but said of the mountain land of
Israel, cf. Deut. xxxii. 13; 2 Sam. i. 19, 25. For ancient or "eternal" as
an epithet of mountains cf. Gen. xlix. 26; Deut. xxxiii. 15; Ps. xxiv.
7. [But here they are rather called "ancient" as having a long history
attached to them.] For "high places" LXX. reads "wastes," cf. perpetual desolations, xxxv. 9.

3. *Because, even because*] Cf. xiii. 10. The passage throughout
betrays passionate feeling on the part of the prophet. His patriotism
is aglow as the loved mountains of his native land rise before his
mind; cf. the pathetic words in reference to the exiled king, xix. 9.
Hence the excitation and solemnity displayed in introducing the prophecy, which itself is expressed (*vv.* 7 *seq.*) only after four or five commands to utter it (*vv.* 3, 4, 5, 6). For "made desolate" [by an
alteration of the Heb. consonants] *gaped for* might be read, Is. xlii. 14.

and ye are taken up] Or, and **are come up upon the lips**, Deut.
xxviii. 37; Lam. ii. 15; Dan. ix. 16 (Niph. not unusual in this verb,
Jer. xxxvii. 5).

5. *fire of my jealousy*] "Jealousy" is injured self-consciousness;
it is the reaction of Jehovah's sense of Himself against the injurious
conduct of Edom and the nations in relation to Him or that which is
His, cf. *my* land.

to cast it out] The expression is difficult both in grammar (as xvii.
9) and meaning. To take "cast it (the land) out" in the sense of
cast out the inhabitants is not quite natural, though cf. xxiv. 6. The
reading may be faulty. [We should rather transpose two words and
render *to despoil its pastures.*]

a prey: therefore prophesy concerning the land of Israel, 6
and say unto the mountains and to the hills, to the watercourses and to the valleys, Thus saith the Lord GOD:
Behold, I have spoken in my jealousy and in my fury,
because ye have borne the shame of the heathen: therefore 7
thus saith the Lord GOD: I have lifted up mine hand,
saying, Surely the heathen that are round about you, they
shall bear their shame. But ye, O mountains of Israel, ye 8
shall shoot forth your branches, and yield your fruit to my
people Israel; for they are at hand to come. For, behold, 9
I am for you, and I will turn unto you, and ye shall be tilled
and sown: and I will multiply men upon you, all the house 10
of Israel, even all of it: and the cities shall be inhabited,
and the waste places shall be builded: and I will multiply 11
upon you man and beast; and they shall increase and be
fruitful: and I will cause you to be inhabited after your
former estate, and will do better *unto you* than at your
beginnings: and ye shall know that I am the LORD. Yea, 12
I will cause men to walk upon you, even my people Israel;
and they shall possess thee, and thou shalt be their inheritance, and thou shalt no more henceforth bereave them of

6. *borne the shame of the heathen*] the shame cast on them by the
heathen, cf. *v.* 15, xxxiv. 29.

7. *lifted up mine hand*] The gesture of taking an oath, xx. 5.
Render *I lift up*, and so *I speak, vv.* 5, 6.

bear their shame] As Israel has borne the shame of the reproaches
and taunts of the heathen, so they, when their destruction cometh (as
it is near), shall bear the shame of it.

8—15. Positive promise to the mountain land of Israel. In the age
of the regeneration, which is at hand, it shall be luxuriantly fruitful
(*vv.* 8, 9), and populous (*vv.* 10—12); it shall no more kill its inhabitants with scarcity (*vv.* 13, 14), nor any more be subject to the reproach
of the nations on this account (*v.* 15).

8. *at hand to come*] The presentiment of the prophet is that the
restoration of the people and the age to which all these promises which
he gives (ch. xxxiii.—xxxvii.) belong is close at hand.

10. Cf. *v.* 33; Is. lviii. 12, lxi. 4; Zech. viii. 12.

11. Jer. xxxi. 27, xxxiii. 12, 13; Hos. ii. 23; Zech. viii. 4, 5. For
"former estate," i.e. former condition, cf. xvi. 55.

your beginnings] i.e. early or former estate, Job viii. 7, xlii. 12.
The phrase "increase and be fruitful (multiply)," common in some
parts of Pent. (Priests' Code), is wanting in LXX.

12. *bereave them of children*] Properly the term has this meaning,

13 children. Thus saith the Lord GOD: Because they say unto
    you, Thou *land* art a devourer of men, and hast been a
14 bereaver of thy [1]nation; therefore thou shalt devour men no
    more, neither [2]bereave thy [1]nation any more, saith the Lord
15 GOD; neither will I [3]let thee hear any more the shame of
    the heathen, neither shalt thou bear the reproach of the
    peoples any more, neither shalt thou cause thy [1]nation to
    stumble any more, saith the Lord GOD.

16   Moreover the word of the LORD came unto me, saying,

---

[1] Another reading is, *nations*.　　　[2] Another reading is, *cause to
stumble.*　　　[3] Or, *proclaim against thee*

but here it is used generally, to bereave the people, i.e. destroy its
members, Jer. xv. 7.

13. Comp. the report of the spies, Numb. xiii. 32, the land "is
a land that eateth up the inhabitants thereof." The land whose population perishes of scarcity is regarded as itself devouring them. It is
doubtful if there is any reference to such things as the unhealthy
situation of the land (2 Kgs ii. 19), or even to the wars by which
the country had been decimated. The true meaning is given *v.* 30.

a bereaver of thy nation] i.e. population, and so *vv.* 14, 15. The
Heb. text rightly reads the sing. The pl. "nations" (*Kĕrî*, which the A.V.
follows) could hardly refer to the two nations, Israel and Judah (xxxv.
10), although it might possibly be used like "peoples" of the nation considered as made up of a number of portions (Hos. x. 14). The land of
Israel was subject to droughts (Jer. xiv. 1; 1 Kgs xvii. *seq.*; Am. iv. 7),
to blasting and mildew (Am. iv. 9), as well as to the scourge of locusts
(Joel i.). Comp. the struggles with famine which the returned exiles
had, Hag. i. 10, 11, ii. 17.

15. *cause thy nation to stumble*] Rather: **bereave thy nation** any
more. The word "stumble" is read in the Heb. text in *v.* 14, but corrected in Heb. marg., and the same correction should be made here
(*shakal* = bereave, *kashal* = fall). The clause is wanting in LXX.

XXXVI. 16—38. NOT FOR ISRAEL'S SAKE BUT FOR HIS OWN
    NAME'S SAKE DOES JEHOVAH DO ALL THIS IN BEHALF OF
    HIS PEOPLE.

The passage is remarkable and deserves to be studied almost more
than any other part of Ezek. when one is seeking to understand his
general conceptions. It exhibits his philosophy of history (cf. ch. xx.),
and also describes with great beauty the principles of Jehovah's redemption of His people, and how step by step this shall be accomplished.
The prophet reviews the history of the people from the beginning,
running it out till it is lost in its eternal issues, and shewing how it will
read to all the nations of the earth the true lesson of that which Jehovah,

Son of man, when the house of Israel dwelt in their own 17
land, they defiled it by their way and by their doings: their

the God of Israel, is, and leave ineffaceable impressions on the mind of
His own people.

First, *vv.* 16—23. The history with its significance up to Israel's
final restoration.—The people defiled the land with their idolatries and
bloodshed (*v.* 17); therefore the fury of Jehovah was kindled and He
poured it out upon them, scattering them among the nations (*vv.* 18,
19). By these disasters which the people brought upon themselves
they "profaned" Jehovah's name among the heathen. The nations,
ignorant of the nature of Jehovah, and incapable of divining the moral
principles of His rule of the world and of His people, attributed the
calamities of Israel to the feebleness of their God, who was unable to
defend them, saying, These are the people of Jehovah, and they are
gone forth out of His land. Thus the greatness and power of Jehovah,
who is God alone, was detracted from, and the knowledge of Him by
the nations—which He wills in all that He does to convey to them—was
delayed or frustrated (*v.* 20). Therefore for the sake of His holy name
He will interpose and turn the fortunes of His people, that He may be
sanctified in the eyes of the nations and known by them to be God
omnipotent (*vv.* 21—23, cf. *vv.* 35, 36).

Secondly, *vv.* 24—38. The history of Jehovah's restoration of His
people and their full redemption in its successive steps, with the
eternal impressions which this history will engrave upon the people's
minds.—In the prophet's view Jehovah must vindicate Himself in the
eyes of the nations by the restoration of Israel, not because He is a
mere tribal god who will do something for His people, but because He
is God alone, and His manifestation of Himself to the nations of the
world is the goal towards which all history runs.

Jehovah "sanctifies" Himself in the sight of the nations not only by
convincing them of His power, but even more if possible by displaying
His moral rule of His people (cf. xxxix. 23, 24), and by the spiritual
regeneration which He works among them (*vv.* 25 *seq.*). But though
this great thought of Jehovah's revelation of Himself in the sight of
the nations be attractive to the prophet, having touched upon the redemption of Israel he becomes absorbed in these internal operations of
Jehovah among his own people, which he pursues in all their details,
and the wider thought of their influence on the heathen is not reverted
to till *vv.* 35, 36. (1) Jehovah will take His people from the nations
and bring them again to their own land (*v.* 24). (2) Then He will
sprinkle clean water upon them and wash them from all their past
impurities (*v.* 25). (3) He will also regenerate them, giving them a
new heart and a new spirit, putting indeed His own spirit within
them (*vv.* 26, 27). (4) In this spirit they shall walk in His statutes and
judgements, and thus shall inherit the land for ever, which the Lord
will greatly bless (*vv.* 27—30). (5) Surrounded thus on all sides by the
tokens of Jehovah's goodness, and looking at themselves and at their

way before me was as the uncleanness of a woman in her
18 separation. Wherefore I poured out my fury upon them for
the blood which they had poured out upon the land, and
19 because they had defiled it with their idols: and I scattered
them among the nations, and they were dispersed through
the countries: according to their way and according to their
20 doings I judged them.   And when they came unto the

past doings with the new mind which the Lord will give them (*v.* 26),
they shall loathe themselves because of all their former impurity and
evil, for it is not for what they have been that Jehovah does this to
them (*vv.* 31, 32). (6) Thus when Israel's captivity is brought back
the nations shall learn the true meaning of their dispersion, and the
nature of Jehovah their God, who disperses and restores (*vv.* 33—36).

XXXVI. 16—23. ISRAEL'S PAST HISTORY AND THE PRINCIPLES WHICH IT ILLUSTRATES.

17. When in their own land the people defiled it with their doings.
The land was "holy," being sanctified by Jehovah's presence in it. The
sins of the people, idolatry and bloodshed, desecrated it and made
it unclean.   Holy embraces "clean" under it, as the general does
a particular, Jer. ii. 7; Lev. xviii. 25.   Ezek., however, seems to
call all sins "uncleanness." This way of speaking and thinking could
hardly have arisen except under the influence of a law of ceremonial
defilements (which were *real* defilements) and purifications.

uncleanness of a woman in her separation] the **uncleanness of a
woman's impurity.** Lev. xv. 19. The comparison expresses the
extreme of loathing, ch. vii. 20.

18. The effect of these sins was to awaken the fury of Jehovah.
The "blood" may be murder from violence or judicial murder, so
often reprobated in the earlier prophets, or it may be the sacrifice of
children, xvi. 36, xxiii. 37.

19. The consequences of Jehovah's wrath—the people were scattered
by Him among all the nations, vii. 3, xviii. 30.

20. These disasters which the people of Jehovah brought on themselves led to the desecration of His name among the heathen. The
nations judged Him weak and unable to protect His people. In the
eyes of the nations the interests of the god and his people were one;
if a people was subdued by another it was because its god was too
feeble to protect it. Naturally the idea of a god exercising a moral
rule over His own people would not yet occur to them. That Jehovah
so rules is the lesson which the history of Israel, its dispersion and
restoration, is intended to read to the nations of the earth. This
lesson was one which Israel itself was slow to learn, and when Amos
(iii. 2) read it to them, it was perhaps as strange to some as it might be
to the heathen.

nations, whither they went, they profaned my holy name;
in that men said of them, These are the people of the LORD,
and are gone forth out of his land.   But I had pity for 21
mine holy name, which the house of Israel had profaned
among the nations, whither they went.   Therefore say unto 22
the house of Israel, Thus saith the Lord GOD: ¹I do not
this for your sake, O house of Israel, but for mine holy
name, which ye have profaned among the nations, whither
ye went.   And I will sanctify my great name, which hath 23
been profaned among the nations, which ye have profaned
in the midst of them; and the nations shall know that I am
the LORD, saith the Lord GOD, when I shall be sanctified in
you before ²their eyes.   For I will take you from among the 24

¹ Or, *I work not for &c.*   ² Or, according to another reading, *your*

they profaned] i.e. Israel.   Israel by bringing their dispersion upon
themselves led to the desecration of Jehovah's name by the nations, and
hence they are said directly to have profaned His name (*v.* 21).
   in that men said of them, &c.] i.e. though the people of Jehovah, they
have been driven into exile out of the land.   He has not been able to
protect them.
   21.   Cf. xx. 9, 14.
   22.   *I do not* this *for your sake*] better, as marg., *I work not for &c.*,
not for what Israel has been or deserved.   The ref. is to Israel's past
history ; such a meaning as that it is not for any interest which He has
in Israel or in order to benefit them that Jehovah delivers them, but
only to magnify His own name, is entirely extraneous to the passage and
a distortion of its sense.   Cf. Is. xliii. 22—28, xlviii. 9—11.   "Name"
is not equivalent to person, but is a reflexion or expression of the person ;
hence all that is due to, or can be said of, the person is due to the name
and can be employed of it.
   23.   *sanctify my great name*]   To sanctify is the opposite of to profane.   As the latter term means to detract from the power, majesty,
or purity of Jehovah, or from any of those attributes which belong to
His Godhead, to sanctify is to manifest or make these attributes conspicuous.   Hence the effect of Jehovah's sanctifying His name is that
the heathen know Him to be Jehovah—God alone and all that which
He is who is God alone.   In *v.* 22 "holy name," here "great name";
"greatness" is an element in "holiness."
   be sanctified in you]   Or reflexive: *shew myself holy* ; where "holy"
embraces the attributes of Deity as a whole.   Israel is the subject
through which Jehovah shews Himself to be God, i.e. by His operations
in Israel in the sight of the nations.
   24 *seq.*   These operations are His restoration and regeneration of

nations, and gather you out of all the countries, and will
25 bring you into your own land. And I will sprinkle clean
water upon you, and ye shall be clean: from all your filthi-
26 ness, and from all your idols, will I cleanse you. A new
heart also will I give you, and a new spirit will I put within
you: and I will take away the stony heart out of your flesh,
27 and I will give you an heart of flesh. And I will put my

Israel. It is certainly possible that the more internal operations of
Jehovah on Israel (*vv.* 25 *seq.*)—His washing them with clean water and
putting a new spirit within them that they shall walk in His statutes,
are considered part of Jehovah's sanctifying what Himself in the sight of
the nations. They do express better what Jehovah is than a mere
exhibition of power, cf. xxxix. 23, 24; Is. lxi. 3, lxii. 2. At the
same time this more general idea seems to pass from the prophet's
mind in the delight with which he dwells on Israel's religious regeneration. The wider idea is at any rate returned to in *vv.* 33 *seq.*

25. Dogmatically, sprinkling with clean water might seem merely
to express the idea of the forgiveness of past sins. The figure is taken
from the washings by which ceremonial defilement was removed, and
the figure is part of the idea. By their relation to the idols and service
of them the people contracted uncleanness. And when the kind of
service which this was is considered, the debasing forms which it took,
and the immoralities which accompanied it or formed part of it (Hos.
iv. 13, 14), the depth of defilement will be understood and the strong
figure *v.* 17 will not appear too strong.

26. *A new heart*] The "heart" is used here generally of the
nature. Formerly their heart was strong, obdurate, unimpressible and
rebellious (ii. 4, iii. 7); now they shall receive a "heart of flesh,"
impressible and soft, sensitive to the Divine admonitions and will. The
phrase shews that in the Old Testament no idea of corrupt inclination
attaches to the term "flesh" (xi. 19). According to usage "spirit"
expresses the ruling principle in the mind, the force that gives direction
and motion to the current of thought and conduct, or that prevailing
current itself. The heart is more passive and receptive and but re-
sponds to influences, the spirit is active and regulative. Jer. xxxii.
37—39.

27. *put my spirit*] This great promise is one which does not appear
prominently in the prophets till the exile. In Is. xi. the Messianic
king has the spirit of Jehovah in all the manifoldness of his operation,
and in xxxii. 15 the hope is expressed that "the spirit shall be poured
on us from on high" (though the passage is held by some to be later
than Is.); but it is in exile and post-exile times that the idea is first
expressed with great certainty, e.g. Ezek. xxxvi. 27, xxxvii. 14; Joel
ii. 28; Zech. iv. 6 (xii. 10). Jeremiah does not use the expression,
though his promise that Jehovah will write His law on men's hearts
(xxxi. 33) seems to have much the same sense, or at least it expresses

spirit within you, and cause you to walk in my statutes, and
ye shall keep my judgements, and do them.   And ye shall 28
dwell in the land that I gave to your fathers; and ye shall
be my people, and I will be your God.   And I will save you 29
from all your uncleannesses: and I will call for the corn,
and will multiply it, and lay no famine upon you.   And I 30
will multiply the fruit of the tree, and the increase of the
field, that ye shall receive no more the reproach of famine
among the nations.   Then shall ye remember your evil 31
ways, and your doings that were not good; and ye shall

the "new spirit" of Ezek., and in the New Testament this new spirit is
the spirit of God.   There always attaches to "spirit" the idea of power
in operation, the spirit of God is God exerting power.

to walk in my statutes]   Being endowed with the spirit of God they
will walk in His statutes, for these are expressions of His spirit.   The
spirit of God will appear both as an inward impulse to fulfil God's
will, and as a power to do it.   In the Old Testament the spirit of God,
even the prophetic spirit, is usually a dynamic influence, an elevation
of the natural human faculties.   The "statutes and judgements" are
not the mere external enactments of the law; they embrace all the
moral laws to which Ezek. so often refers (e.g. ch. xviii., xxii., xxxiii.),
and it is doubtful if the prophet refers specially to written laws at all.

28.   Again, the consequence of walking in Jehovah's statutes will
be that they shall inherit the land for ever, cf. xxviii. 25, xxxvii. 25.
The promise attached to the fifth commandment—the first commandment with promise—belongs to the commandments given to Israel as
a whole.   The keeping of them was the condition of remaining in the
land.   When the people disregarded them they were driven out, and
only when their former sins were forgiven could they be restored
(Is. xl. 2).   It may be a question whether there be now any connexion between Israel and the land of Canaan.   If there be, the
condition of restoration to it is faith and obedience on the part of
the people.   A restoration of Jews still in unbelief to Canaan, even
if it should occur, could have no meaning so far as the redemptive
providence of God is concerned, and would not enter into any relation
with the Old Testament scriptures.   Comp. the order stated *v.* 33.

29.   *save you from...uncleannesses*]   Or, **I will save** (deliver) **you out
of your**...   The phrase "save out of" is pregnant, meaning "save you
by purifying you from"..., hardly, save you from the consequences of...
Cf. xxxvii. 23, and reading there.

call for the corn]   Cf. xxxiv. 27, 29; Hos. ii. 21; Jer. xxxi. 12
(cf. 2 Kgs viii. 1).

30.   Cf. xxxiv. 27 *seq.*

31.   Cf. vi. 9, xvi. 61, 63, xx. 43.

loathe yourselves in your own sight for your iniquities and
32 for your abominations. Not for your sake ¹do I *this*, saith
the Lord GOD, be it known unto you: be ashamed and
33 confounded for your ways, O house of Israel. Thus saith
the Lord GOD: In the day that I cleanse you from all your
iniquities, I will cause the cities to be inhabited, and the
34 waste places shall be builded. And the land that was
desolate shall be tilled, whereas it was a desolation in the
35 sight of all that passed by. And they shall say, This land
that was desolate is become like the garden of Eden; and
the waste and desolate and ruined cities are fenced and
36 inhabited. Then the nations that are left round about you
shall know that I the LORD have builded the ruined places,
and planted that which was desolate: I the LORD have
spoken it, and I will do it.

¹ Or, *do I work*

32. The verse is closely connected with the preceding : ye shall
remember your former evil, for not for your sakes do I this—not
because of your good deserving (*v.* 22) ; on the contrary their own
ways when thought upon could only cause them shame. In Lev. xxvi.
45 "for their sakes" means "to their benefit," on their behalf.

33—36. The prophet returns to the lessons which Israel's history,
the author of which is their God, will read to the nations of the world.
When they behold the desolated land of Israel become like the garden
of Eden they shall form another judgement regarding Jehovah, and
know that which He is, and the meaning of the history of His people.

33. The order stated here is of course a necessity : as the sins of the
people caused them to be cast out of their land, their forgiveness must
precede their restoration to it. In the prophets events are not events
merely, they are exhibitions of moral principles. So in Is. xl.—lxvi.
the restoration of Israel to Canaan is preceded by the atonement for
their sins by the servant of the Lord (Is. xl. 2).

35. *garden of Eden*] Cf. xxviii. 13, xxxi. 8, 9.

36. *I...have builded...planted*] The words hardly express a general
characteristic of Jehovah, but refer to the fact that it is He who has restored
Israel—comp. last words of the verse. Reflecting on Jehovah's restoration of the people the nations will recognise not merely His power, but
also the deeper principles which underlie His government of His people.

37, 38. A single point in the Lord's restoration of Israel is made
prominent, the multiplication of the people. The terrible threats of the
diminution of their numbers (*v.* 12), and of the destruction both of
those remaining in the land and those going into exile, were no
doubt to a great extent fulfilled (Lam. v.). The scanty population of

Thus saith the Lord GOD: For this moreover will I be 37
inquired of by the house of Israel, to do it for them; I will
increase them with men like a flock. As the ¹flock for 38
sacrifice, as the flock of Jerusalem in her appointed feasts;
so shall the waste cities be filled with flocks of men: and
they shall know that I am the LORD.

¹ Heb. *flock of holy things.*

Jerusalem is referred to by Nehemiah nearly a century after the first exiles
returned (vii. 4). The old promise that they should be as the sand of
the sea is here repeated, cf. *vv.* 10, 11, 33 ; Jer. xxxi. 27 ; Hos. i. 10 ;
Zech. ii. 4.

37. *will I be inquired of*] Almost: *I will let myself be inquired of,*
which embraces not merely the inquiry or request on the part of the
people, but the response to it on the part of the Lord. Cf. xiv. 3,
xx. 3, 31. As usual "this" refers to what follows—the multiplication
of the people.

38. *the flock for sacrifice*] The appointed feasts may be the three
great yearly festivals, though in point of fact Ezek. does not refer to
Pentecost, or the feast of Weeks, in his concluding chapters. The
comparison shews that already in pre-exile times enormous numbers of
sacrificial animals were brought to Jerusalem for offerings at the feasts.

Probably no passage in the Old Testament of the same extent offers
so complete a parallel to New Testament doctrine, particularly to that
of St Paul. It is doubtful if the Apostle quotes Ezek. anywhere, but
his line of thought entirely coincides with his. The same conceptions
and in the same order belong to both—forgiveness (*v.* 25) ; regeneration,
a new heart and spirit (*v.* 26) ; the spirit of God as the ruling power in
the new life (*v.* 27) ; the issue of this, the keeping of the requirements
of God's law (*v.* 27 ; Rom. viii. 4) ; the effect of being "under grace"
in softening the human heart and leading to obedience (*v.* 31 ; Rom. vi.,
vii.) ; and the organic connexion of Israel's history with Jehovah's revelation of Himself to the nations (*vv.* 33—36 ; Rom. xi.). The prophet's
idea of the Divine pedagogic is not precisely the same as that of the
Apostle, and the present passage has in some particulars to be supplemented from ch. xvi. As put here it is Israel's historical experiences,
their dispersion and restoration, with the thoughts which these suggest,
that impress the nations and teach them what Jehovah is.

XXXVII. THE PEOPLE.

The last step in the reconstruction of the new Israel is the resurrection of the people. The nation is dead, and its bones scattered and
dry. But it shall rise from the dead ; the bones shall come together
and the spirit of life from Jehovah shall enter into them and they shall
live. The passage has two parts :

37   The hand of the LORD was upon me, and he carried me
out in the spirit of the LORD, and set me down in the midst
2 of the valley; and it was full of bones; and he caused me
to pass by them round about: and behold, there were very
3 many ¹in the open valley; and lo, they were very dry. And

              ¹ Heb. *upon the face of the valley.*

First, *vv.* 1—14, the resurrection of the people of Israel from death,
and their restoration to their own land.

    Second, *vv.* 15—28, the union of the two houses of Israel, Judah and
Ephraim, when restored, under one head, even David.

XXXVII. 1—14. THE VISION OF ISRAEL'S RESURRECTION FROM THE DEAD.

    The vision seems suggested by the saying current among the people,
"Our bones are dried up, and our hope is lost; we are clean cut off."
This idea and feeling of the people takes form in the vision which the
prophet saw in the valley. The language of the people is figurative:
they speak of the nationality, which is no more,—it is dead and its
bones scattered and dry¹. And this idea regarding the nationality,
figuratively expressed by the people, is embodied to the prophet in a
vision. Hence the passage is not a literal prophecy of the resurrection
of individual persons of the nation, dead or slain; it is a prophecy of
the resurrection of the nation, whose condition is figuratively expressed
by the people when they represent its bones as long scattered and dry.
Perfect consistency is not maintained by the prophet: in *vv.* 1, 2 the
dry bones are represented as lying on the face of the valley, very many
and very dry; in *v.* 12 the people are represented as buried and brought
up out of their graves. Hosea had already used the figure of resurrection
for the resuscitation of the nation (vi. 2, xiii. 14); but, though the
language used both here and by Hosea shews familiarity with the idea
of the raising again of individuals, this is not what is prophesied. In
Is. xxvi. 19; Dan. xii. the actual resurrection of individual members of
Israel is predicted, cf. Job xiv. 13 *seq.*

    1. *The hand of the LORD*] The prophetic ecstasy from the Lord,
ch. i. 3. On "spirit" of the Lord cf. iii. 14, viii. 3, xi. 24. The
"valley" is probably that mentioned early in the Book, iii. 22.

    2. *the open valley*] lit., as marg., *upon the face of the valley.* The
bones were strewed over the valley in vast numbers, and they appeared
bleached and dry. Their great number no doubt was suggested by the
actual fact that vast multitudes of the people had been slain with the
sword or had otherwise perished; and their "dryness" expresses at

    ¹ [We may still say, however, with Skinner (*Ezekiel*, p. 342) that it was no mere
figure of speech which these exiles employed when they thought of their nation as
dead....Not only were the outward symbols of national unity destroyed, but the
national spirit was extinct.]

he said unto me, Son of man, can these bones live? And I
answered, O Lord GOD, thou knowest.   Again he said unto 4
me, Prophesy over these bones, and say unto them, O ye
dry bones, hear the word of the LORD.   Thus saith the 5
Lord GOD unto these bones: Behold, I will cause ¹breath
to enter into you, and ye shall live.   And I will lay sinews 6
upon you, and will bring up flesh upon you, and cover you
with skin, and put breath in you, and ye shall live; and ye
shall know that I am the LORD.   So I prophesied as I was 7
commanded: and as I prophesied, there was a ²noise, and
behold an earthquake, and the bones came together, bone
to his bone.   And I beheld, and lo, there were sinews upon 8
them, and flesh came up, and skin covered them above:
but there was no breath in them.   Then said he unto me, 9
Prophesy unto the ³wind, prophesy, son of man, and say to

---

¹ Or, *spirit*   ² Or, *thundering*   ³ Or, *breath*

least the utter deadness of the nation and the apparent hopelessness of
its revival, if not that it had been long dead (*v.* 11).

3.   To the question, Can these bones live? the prophet, looking at
them, could not answer Yea (even to the Apostle attainment unto the
resurrection of the dead was something ineffably lofty, Phil. iii. 11),
and yet in the presence of Him who put the question he could not
answer No (Rom. iv. 17—21; Heb. xi. 19).   With reverence he
answers, Thou knowest (Rev. vii. 14).

4—6.   The prophet is bidden prophesy to the bones and promise
them life from Jehovah.

5.   The act of putting breath within them, being the main and final
step of giving them life, is mentioned first as if it embraced all.

6.   Then follow the details of their becoming actual men of flesh
and blood.

7—10.   As the prophet spoke there was a great sound and the bones
came together, bone to his bone, and they became clothed with flesh;
but as yet there was no breath of life in them.

7.   *a noise*] marg. *thundering*.   The Heb. is lit. *voice*, but it is used
in the sense of thunder in Ps. xxix. 3 ff.

behold an earthquake]   An accompaniment or symbol of the mar-
vellous phenomenon (cp. Matt. xxvii. 51); or "a rushing" as the word
is rendered in iii. 12, 13.   The noise is that occasioned by the rising
and rushing of the bones together.

9.   The order described in the creation of man (Gen. ii.) is observed here: first the body was formed and then the breath of life was
breathed into it.

Prophesy unto the wind]   Or, *breath*.   [See marg. readings.]   In

the ¹wind, Thus saith the Lord GOD: Come from the four
winds, O ²breath, and breathe upon these slain, that they
10 may live.   So I prophesied as he commanded me, and the
breath came into them, and they lived, and stood up upon
11 their feet, an exceeding great army.   Then he said unto me,
Son of man, these bones are the whole house of Israel:
behold, they say, Our bones are dried up, and our hope is
12 lost; we are clean cut off.   Therefore prophesy, and say
unto them, Thus saith the Lord GOD: Behold, I will open
your graves, and cause you to come up out of your graves,
O my people; and I will bring you into the land of Israel.

¹ Or, *breath*   ² Or, *wind*   Or, *spirit*

Heb. the same word means wind, breath, and spirit.   The sign of
life, the breath, is seen to be identical with the wind or air, and by an
intensification of meaning common to many languages the "breath"
becomes the principle of life, or the living principle itself, the spirit.
Tennyson makes Nature say (etymologically) "The spirit does but
mean the breath"; but though the words be identical the ideas are
different.   The breath needful to be life in the vast multitude now
created must be furnished by wind coming from all quarters of the
heavens.

upon these slain] Or, **into** the slain.   What is needful to make
living men of them is breath in their nostrils.   That which God did
Himself to the individual man when created, even breathe into his
nostrils the breath of life, is here accomplished by the wind from the
four quarters of the heavens at His command breathing into the innumerable multitude.   The wind from the four corners of the heavens is
but a symbol of the universal life-giving spirit of God (*v.* 14).

11—14.   Explanation of the vision.

11.   *the whole house of Israel*] viz. Judah and Ephraim.

our hope is lost]   Those who speak are the living members of the
nation, and it is of the nationality that they speak.   The destruction
and dissolution of the nation appeared to them final.   It could no
more be revived than the dry bones could be made to live.   This
feeling often appears in exile writings, e.g. Is. xl.—lxvi. (xlix. 14, &c.);
cf. the singular struggling against the idea, Lam. iii. 20 *seq.*

clean] i.e. wholly; lit. *for ourselves*, a rendering of the ethical dat.,
which merely gives vividness to the words "we are cut off," or expresses
the feeling of those who speak by reflecting the action back upon
the subject.   The term "cut off" (otherwise uncommon) is used also
of the Servant of the Lord, Is. liii. 8.

12.   The figure is varied here, the people are regarded as dead and
buried and their revival is an opening of their graves.   The phrase

And ye shall know that I am the LORD, when I have opened 13
your graves, and caused you to come up out of your graves,
O my people. And I will put my ¹spirit in you, and ye 14
shall live, and I will place you in your own land: and ye
shall know that I the LORD have spoken it, and performed
it, saith the LORD.

¹ Or, *breath*

"bring you into the land of Israel" shews, however, that the language is still used figuratively of the resuscitation of the dead nation and not literally of the resurrection of deceased individuals.

14. The symbol of the wind breathing into the slain is here explained: it is the spirit of Jehovah that gives life, Ps. civ. 30. The connexion shews that the spirit of the Lord here is merely the life-giving spirit, and not the regenerating spirit, as in xxxvi. 27—though the distinction is merely part of the figure. The resuscitation of the dead nation could come about only through their moral regeneration, and hence in Is. xl.—lxvi. this is part of the work of the Servant of the Lord (Is. xlix. 8—12, lxi. 1).

The passage is of great interest, apart from its own beauty, as casting light upon the condition of the people's mind. The prophet is fond of quoting expressions from the mouth of the people (e.g. xi. 3, xii. 22, 27, xvi. 44, xviii. 2, 25, 29, cf. xxxiii. 17, 20, xx. 49, xxxvi. 20, &c.), and probably the words here used were actually heard. They shew a state of despondency quite natural and one no doubt greatly prevalent. Indeed in all the prophets of this age the hope that exists is hope only in Jehovah, which believes that in spite of past disasters their God will yet save the people. It is only by giving moral significance to Israel's calamities on the one hand, and on the other by animating the revolutions and commotions among the nations with Jehovah's purpose, that the faith of the prophets themselves is sustained. The prophetic hopes of this period are based on dogmatic presuppositions, e.g. that Jehovah is the true and living God and that there is none else; that Israel is His people and has His true revelation among them, which is imperishable and which must accomplish the purpose for which it was given and become effectual in making a true people of the Lord (Is. lv.); and that the purpose of the one God must embrace all the nations of the earth, between whom and Jehovah Israel is the link of communication. The prophetic views as to how Jehovah shall use Israel to give the nations the knowledge of Himself differ. In Is. xl. *seq.* Israel becomes the light of the nations—having the true knowledge of God it imparts it to the heathen. In Ezekiel it is their own observation and reflexion on Israel's history that reveals to the nations Jehovah's true nature. In all, however, the work of redemption is the work of Jehovah. Here His restoration of Israel is reanimation of the dead through His life-giving spirit.

¹⁵₁₆   The word of the LORD came again unto me, saying, And
thou, son of man, take thee one stick, and write upon it,
For Judah, and for the children of Israel his companions:
then take another stick, and write upon it, For Joseph, the
stick of Ephraim, and ¹*for* all the house of Israel his com-
17 panions: and join them for thee one to another into one
18 stick, that they may become one in thine hand.   And when
the children of thy people shall speak unto thee, saying,
19 Wilt thou not shew us what thou meanest by these? say
unto them, Thus saith the Lord GOD: Behold, I will take
the stick of Joseph, which is in the hand of Ephraim, and
the tribes of Israel his companions; and I will put them
²with it, *even* with the stick of Judah, and make them one
20 stick, and they shall be one in mine hand.   And the sticks

¹ Or, of   ² Or, *together with him unto* (or *to be*) *the stick of Judah*

XXXVII. 15—28.   PROPHECY OF THE REUNION OF THE RESTORED
ISRAEL INTO ONE KINGDOM, RULED BY ONE KING, EVEN DAVID.

(1) *vv.* 15—23. Symbol of the union of Judah and Israel into one
kingdom, with its explanation.
(2) *vv.* 24, 25. There shall be one king over the new nation,
even David.
(3) *vv.* 26—28. Jehovah's covenant with the people shall be everlasting, and His presence will sanctify them.
16. *one stick*] i.e. staff, or rod, equivalent to sceptre, Numb. xvii. 2;
so *vv.* 17, 19, 20.
children of Israel] After the fall of the Northern Kingdom the name
Israel was often used of Judah, the only remaining part of it[1].   Here
Israel of the north is called Joseph or Ephraim.
the stick of Ephraim] probably either the words are a gloss (so Cor.,
Ber., Toy) or we should read *with Ephraim,* &c. (so Kr.).
19.   Explanation of the symbolical action.
put them with it, &c.] better, as marg.   The construction is rather
unnatural (for *eth*, cf. xiv. 22, xliii. 17, others would read *el*).   [The
converse action is to be found in Zech. xi. 14.]
in mine hand] Vulg. reads *in his hand* (so Ew.), i.e. Judah's, and
LXX. actually *in the hand of Judah.*   LXX. either read *his* hand and
interpreted it of Judah, or took the final *y* of *my* hand as an abbrevia-
tion for Yehudah.   On the one hand the united staff or sceptre might
be given into the hand of Judah, as the ruler of the one kingdom was

[1] [But the expression here may well include a reference to the permanent dwelling
or temporary sojourn of members of the northern tribes in Judah.   See 2 Chr. xi. 12,
13, 16, xv. 9, xxx. 11. So Redp.]

whereon thou writest shall be in thine hand before their
eyes.   And say unto them, Thus saith the Lord GOD: 21
Behold, I will take the children of Israel from among the
nations, whither they be gone, and will gather them on
every side, and bring them into their own land: and I will 22
make them one nation in the land, upon the mountains of
Israel; and one king shall be king to them all: and they
shall be no more two nations, neither shall they be divided
into two kingdoms any more at all: neither shall they defile 23
themselves any more with their idols, nor with their detestable things, nor with any of their transgressions: but I will
save them ¹out of all their dwelling places, wherein they
have sinned, and will cleanse them: so shall they be my
people, and I will be their God.   And my servant David 24
shall be king over them; and they all shall have one
shepherd: they shall also walk in my judgements, and
observe my statutes, and do them.   And they shall dwell 25
in the land that I have given unto Jacob my servant,

¹ Or, according to some ancient versions, *from all their backslidings*

to be David (Am. ix. 11; Hos. iii. 5).   On the other hand there is no
trace in the passage of any pre-eminence of Judah over Israel of the
north.

20.   This symbolical action may have been actually performed,
though the supposition is scarcely necessary, cf. xii. 3.

22.   This promise runs throughout all prophecy.   The disruption of
the state was felt even by Hosea, a native of the north, to have introduced a schism into the one kingdom of Jehovah, and to have broken
the unity of the consciousness of the community, to which the consciousness of the one God corresponded.   Hos. i. 11, viii. 3, 4; Is.
xi. 13; Jer. iii. 18.   The one God, the husband of the community,
required that the community should also be one, with a single affection
and service.   Cf. xxxiv. 23, 24.

23.   Cf. xxxvi. 25.

out of all their dwelling places] better, as marg. [transposing the
letters in the Heb.].   So LXX., cf. xxxvi. 29.

24.   *my servant David*]   Cf. xxxiv. 23, 24.   Here the term "king"
is applied to the ruler of the future (*v.* 22); in other places "prince."
The words seem used indifferently, cf. xix. 1, xxii. 25.   Cf. xxxvi. 27.

25.   Cf. xxxvi. 28.

Jacob my servant]   Jacob is here the patriarch himself, not as in
Is. xl. *seq.* a name for the people.   He is referred to as the ancestor of
Israel in Hos. xii. 12.   Cf. ch. xxxiii. 24; Is. xli. 8, li. 2, lxiii. 16.

wherein your fathers dwelt; and they shall dwell therein,
they, and their children, and their children's children, for
ever: and David my servant shall be their prince for ever.
26 Moreover I will make a covenant of peace with them: it
shall be an everlasting covenant with them: and I will
¹place them, and multiply them, and will set my sanctuary
27 in the midst of them for evermore. My tabernacle also
shall be ²with them; and I will be their God, and they shall
28 be my people. And the nations shall know that ³I am the
LORD that sanctify Israel, when my sanctuary shall be in the
midst of them for evermore.

¹ Or, *give* it *them*   ² Or, *over*   ³ Or, *I the* LORD *do sanctify*
Israel

their prince for ever] It is not at all probable that " David my
servant" means either the Davidic house or a line of kings. But
possibly the point whether the king would be one person living for
ever is not before the prophet's mind. It is the quality of the new
people and the new ruler that he specially refers to; the point whether
generation after generation of the people shall dwell in the land and
prince succeed prince is hardly in his mind. The unity of the people
and the unity of the ruler, one such as David; the character of the
people (*v.* 24) and their perpetual possession of the land—these are
the elements of the prophet's idea, and further questions are not
touched. In xliii. 7, xlv. 8, a succession of princes appears presupposed, but the idea hardly belongs to the present passage.

26. *a covenant of peace*] Cf. xxxiv. 25; Is. lv. 3; Jer. xxxii. 40.

my sanctuary] The name given by the prophet to the temple as
the dwelling place of Jehovah (*v.* 27) and specially sanctified or made
holy by His presence.

27. *My tabernacle also*] **And my dwelling place.** The words
repeat the idea in *v.* 26. The last words of the Book are, " The LORD
is there." The phrase *with* them, i.e. by or beside them (cf. ii. 6),
might mean (as marg.) *over* them, reference being to the situation of
the temple, high above the city (xl. 2), but this has little probability.
It would be more natural to take *over* in the ideal sense of a protection
to them. The sanctuary, however, does not protect, it sanctifies, although they being sanctified will be protected by Jehovah (ch. xxxviii.,
xxxix.). The expression " I will be their God " varies the idea of
His dwelling place being with them, xi. 20, xiv. 11, xxxvi. 28.

28. The presence of Jehovah makes the house wherein He dwells
a sanctuary (holy place), and the presence of His sanctuary (He being
there, xlviii. 35) among the people sanctifies them or makes them
" holy "—a term which expresses two things: being the possession
of Jehovah, and being in disposition and life all that the people of

Jehovah must be. The idea that Jehovah's presence "sanctifies" the people is common. Jehovah's dwelling place being among the people for ever the nations shall know that He "sanctifies" them. To sanctify is not to protect, it is to make the people His own and worthy of Him, but this implies protection. Jer. ii. 3, "Israel was holiness unto the LORD, the firstfruits of his increase: all that devour him shall be held guilty." The ideas in this verse lead naturally over to the episode of Gog's invasion, the issues of which so remarkably illustrate them.

The restoration of Israel includes the tribes of the north as well as Judah. All the prophets of this age regard the northern exiles as still existing, cf. Jer. iii. 12—15; Is. xlix. 5, 6, and the strong passage Is. xliii. 5—7, "every one that is called by my name," i.e. every member of the people of the Lord. Cf. the present prophet's disposition of all the tribes in the holy land, ch. xlviii.

XXXVIII., XXXIX. INVASION OF THE RESTORED ISRAEL IN THE LATTER DAYS BY GOG AND ALL THE NATIONS LYING IN THE OUTSKIRTS OF THE WORLD, AND ISRAEL'S PROTECTION BY JEHOVAH.

These two chapters are closely connected with ch. xxxvii. 28, "the nations shall know that I am the LORD that sanctify Israel." This recalls to the prophet's mind the invasion of Gog, a great and final attack on Israel by the nations, and he introduces the description of it here, as it illustrates so conspicuously what is said in xxxvii. 21—28. For the invasion of Gog is an episode out of connexion with the restoration of the people, which has formed the theme of the preceding chapters (xxxiii.—xxxvii.). It lies far in the future (vv. 8, 16), long after Israel has been restored, and when it has dwelt long in peace in its own land (vv. 8, 11). The sedulous care with which the land is purified from the carcases of Gog's host, every bone being carefully collected and the whole buried beyond the Jordan, is sufficient evidence of the holiness of Israel and the land at the time of Gog's attack (xxxix. 11—16).

The prophet is not the author of the idea of this invasion. It had been predicted of old by the prophets of Israel, prophesying over long periods (xxxviii. 17, xxxix. 8). Neither is it probable that the idea was one read out of certain prophecies merely by Ezekiel. More likely it was an idea widely entertained. The former prophecies on which the belief was founded are not to be supposed to have contained the name of Gog, any more than the prophecies applied by the author of Is. xl. seq. to the career of Cyrus need have referred to him by name.

The conception is rather shadowy and vague. The time is indefinite, —it is far into the years to come; the nations who cluster around the standard of Gog, himself a somewhat nebulous personage, are those lying in the uttermost regions of the world, which had been heard of but never seen. The most distant north and the most distant south send their contingents to swell the innumerable host, and the far-off commercial peoples Sheba and Dedan and Tarshish follow his camp (*vv.* 3, 5, 6, 13). The description seems almost a creation, the embodiment of an idea[1]—the idea of the irreconcilable hostility of the nations of the world to the religion of Jehovah, and the presentiment that this must yet be manifested on a grander scale than has ever yet been. Hence the supernatural magnitude of the outlines of the picture (*vv.* 9, 16, 20). The main idea of the prophet, however, is quite perspicuous. With the exception of Ethiopia, a somewhat general name for the most distant south, none of the historical nations appears under Gog's banner. These nations that came into connexion with Israel during her history have already learned to know Jehovah (ch. xxv.—xxxii.). They have not been exterminated, but His glory has been revealed to them and they no more trouble the peace of the restored Israel (xxxvi. 36). But the nations lying in the outskirts of the earth, as another prophet expresses it, "have not heard my fame, neither have seen my glory" (Is. lxvi. 19), and He who is God alone must reveal Himself to all flesh, for He has sworn by Himself that to Him every knee shall bow (Is. xlv. 23). Such is the meaning of this last act in the drama of the world's history. As it is Jehovah's final revelation of Himself to all the nations of the earth, it is accompanied by all those terrors and convulsions in nature which in earlier prophets usually signalise the day of the Lord (xxxviii. 19—23). This indeed is peculiar in Ezek. that he places Jehovah's great and last revelation of Himself *after* the restoration of His people to peace and felicity, while in the earlier prophets it precedes or accompanies their restoration; as it does even in prophets after him (Is. xl. 5; Ps. cii. 16). In this order he is followed by the Apocalypse (Rev. xix. 11, xx. 7). Besides the display of Jehovah's might in the overthrow of Gog and in the terrible convulsions of nature, His moral being and rule is also revealed through His people, for His protection of them now that they are holy and true casts light to the nations on His former dispersion of them (xxxix. 23).

Gog is styled prince of Rosh, Meshech, and Tubal, nations lying in the extremities of the north (*v.* 15). Other nations are joined to these, lying in the furthest south (*v.* 5). And in the train of these warriors come the hosts of far-off commercial peoples, camp followers intent on gain (*v.* 13). It is, therefore, self-evident that the Chaldeans are not represented under the name of Gog. The Chaldeans are Jehovah's mandatories, commissioned to chastise His people, and humble the ungodly pride of such nations as Egypt and Phœnicia, and Ezekiel's prophecies contain no threats against Babylon. He intimates indeed that the supremacy of that power is but temporary, naming 40 years as the term when a new condition of the world will arise, which presupposes her decline and fall. But the invasion of Gog appears to him to be far away in the indefinite future, long after the promises

---

[1] ["Il nous apparaît comme l'incarnation typique de la puissance terrestre dans tout ce qu'elle a de plus redoutable." Gautier, *op. cit.* p. 313.]

And the word of the LORD came unto me, saying, Son of **38**
man, set thy face toward Gog, of the land of Magog, the ²

of the Lord to His people have been fulfilled, and this fulfilment must
be preceded by the overthrow of the Chaldean power.

The passage extends to ch. xxxix. 24, where the prophet resumes
the point of view occupied in ch. xxxiii.—xxxvii. prior to the Restoration of Israel.

XXXVIII. THE INVASION OF GOG, AND HIS DESTRUCTION.

(1) *vv.* 1—9. Gog's enterprise regarded as the purpose and operation of Jehovah. The Lord will bring Gog forth with all his allies.
He is commanded to hold himself in readiness to go up against Israel.

(2) *vv.* 10—13. Gog's enterprise regarded as due to his own evil
purposes. Evil thoughts shall come into his mind, and he will resolve
to invade Israel, to spoil a spoil and to get him much prey. The
merchant nations shall follow his camp intent on gain.

(3) *vv.* 14—16. Gog's coming up and his bringing up have the
same result or purpose eventually: Jehovah shall be "sanctified" in
(through) him, and the nations shall know that He is God.

(4) *vv.* 17—23. Gog's attack had long been predicted by former
prophets. On that day Jehovah will reveal Himself in all His majesty
and shake terribly the earth. All creation shall be terror-stricken before
Him, and all that is lofty on the earth shall be thrown down (Is. ii., iii.).
He will bring destruction on Gog, causing a supernatural panic in his
host and turning the sword of the confederates against one another,
and overwhelming them in tempests of hail and fire from heaven.
Thus will the nations fear His holy name.

XXXVIII. 1—6. THE GREAT ARRAY OF GOG WHICH JEHOVAH SHALL LEAD FORTH.

2. *set thy face toward Gog*] Cf. xxxv. 2, 3. The meaning of the
word *Gog* is obscure. Schrader (*KAT.* on the passage) refers to the
name of the Lydian king Gyges, given as Gu-gu in the Assyr. inscriptions, on the one hand, and on the other to Gagi, name of the ruler of
a country in the East, the situation of which is uncertain. This land
apparently lay north of Assyria (Frd. Del. *Par.* pp. 246–7)[1].

Gog, of the land of Magog] Gog is the prince and Magog his country
(xxxix. 6). (In construction "land of Magog" is *acc.* of direction or
in loose apposition to Gog[2].)

---

[1] [Kr. inclines to identifying the name with Gagâia, which appears in the Tel-el-
Amarna tablets (*KB.* v. 5) as a barbarian designation connected with some northern
region.]
[2] [Its situation is quite uncertain. Lagarde (see *Oxf. Lex.*) places it in a
mountainous region between Cappadocia and Media. The name occurs as a son
of Japheth, Gen. x. 2.]

¹prince of Rosh, Meshech, and Tubal, and prophesy against
3 him, and say, Thus saith the Lord GOD: Behold, I am
   against thee, O Gog, ¹prince of Rosh, Meshech, and Tubal:
4 and I will turn thee about, and put hooks into thy jaws, and
   I will bring thee forth, and all thine army, horses and horsemen, all of them clothed in full armour, a great company
   with buckler and shield, all of them handling swords:
5 Persia, Cush, and Put with them; all of them with shield
6 and helmet: Gomer, and all his hordes; the house of
   Togarmah in the uttermost parts of the north, and all his

---

¹ Or, *chief prince of Meshech*

---

prince of Rosh] [better than A.V. and marg. *chief prince of Meshech*.
Gautier, however (*Ezéchiel*, p. 311 note), prefers the latter.] Rosh is
impossible to identify. Of course any connexion between the name and
Russia is to be rejected. Frd. Del. (*Par.* p. 322) refers to the land of
Râsh (mât Ra a-shi) of the inscriptions, situated on the borders of Elam
on the Tigris. [As connected here with Put (*v.* 5), it may be the same as
the Rasses of Judith ii. 23. So Redpath.] The geography of the prophet
is no doubt vague and general, but this position as well as that of
Gagi referred to above appears to lie too far east. The rendering
"chief prince" would imply an unusual construction (chief-priest is
different), and it is difficult to guess what chief prince or overlord could
mean. On Meshech, Tubal, cf. xxvii. 13, xxxii. 26¹.

4. *I will turn thee about*] or, I will *lead thee*. The sense entice or
"decoy" (Ew.) has scarcely evidence (Is. xlvii. 10). The clause "and
I will turn...jaws" is wanting in LXX. Putting hooks into the jaws
suggests unwillingness and compulsion (ch. xxix. 4; 2 Kgs xix. 28),
whereas Gog comes up of his own accord. This, however, is not
quite conclusive, as Jehovah is leading him on to his destruction.

in full armour] Rather: **clothed gorgeously** (cf. xxiii. 12). The
host of Gog is probably not exclusively cavalry, though these are
specially mentioned; and besides their vast numbers their splendid
uniforms and heavy armour are vividly pictured.

5. Cf. on xxvii. 10, xxx. 5.

6. Cf. xxvii. 14; Gen. x. 2.

the uttermost parts of the north] lit. *recesses of the north*, Is. xiv. 13.
Gomer, Assyr. *Gimir*, is usually identified etymologically with the
Kimmerians. Schrader (*KAT. in loc.*) and others understand Cappa-
docia.

---

¹ [The expedition "is no doubt modelled upon the great irruption of the Scythians
into Asia (Herod. I. 104—6), which took place *c.* 630 B.C., and which is in all
probability alluded to in Jer. iv. 3—vi. 30," Driver, *Genesis*, p. 115. Magog has been
commonly understood as denoting the Scythians since the time of Josephus (*Ant.*
I. 6. 7).]

hordes: even many peoples with thee. Be thou prepared, 7
yea, prepare thyself, thou, and all thy companies that are
assembled unto thee, and be thou a ¹guard unto them.
After many days thou shalt be visited: in the latter years 8
thou shalt come into the land that is ²brought back from
the sword, that is gathered out of many peoples, upon the
mountains of Israel, which have been a continual waste:
but it is brought forth out of the peoples, and they shall
dwell securely, all of them. And thou shalt ascend, thou 9
shalt come like a storm, thou shalt be like a cloud to cover
the land, thou, and all thy hordes, and many peoples with
thee. Thus saith the Lord GOD: It shall come to pass in 10
that day, that things shall come into thy mind, and thou

¹ Or, *commander*   ² Or, *restored*

XXXVIII. 7—9. INJUNCTION TO GOG TO BE IN READINESS FOR THE LATTER DAYS WHEN JEHOVAH SHALL LEAD HIM FORTH.

7. *a guard unto them*] The term means something to be kept or observed, a rallying point; Gog shall be the leader of the peoples. For "unto them" LXX. reads "unto me," giving the meaning that Gog shall be kept "in reserve" by Jehovah for His future operations (*v.* 8). [R.V. marg. *commander* implies a needless alteration of M.T.]

8. *thou shalt be visited*] Not in the frequent sense of visited with punishment, but in the sense of recalled to mind in order to be employed (cf. usage xxiii. 21). Others: *mustered*, which is not very natural; and the meaning "thou shalt receive orders" (from Jehovah) can hardly be supported from usage. From the position of the prophet the invasion of Gog seems to belong to the far distant future, to a time after the people have been restored and have enjoyed long peace and great felicity.

the land] here used as equivalent to the people of Israel.

continual] A natural exaggeration for the exile period, which seemed endless, see xxxvi. 2, cf. xxxv. 9.

dwell securely] Or, in confidence. The term always expresses the feeling of safety.

9. *like a storm*] Cf. on the figure Is. xxi. 1, xxviii. 2; Jer. iv. 13. The rapidity of the movements of Gog (cf. Hos. viii. 1), and their destructiveness, as well as the infinite masses of his host (Num. xxii. 5; Jud. vi. 5), are expressed by the comparison with the storm and cloud.

XXXVIII. 10—13. GOG'S INVASION PROMPTED BY HIS OWN EVIL PURPOSES.

10. *things*] lit., words, i.e. purposes. Is. viii. 10, "speak the word, and it shall not stand." Cf. xiv. 3.

11 shalt devise an evil device : and thou shalt say, I will go up
to ¹the land of unwalled villages ; I will go to them that are
at quiet, that dwell securely, all of them dwelling without
12 walls, and having neither bars nor gates : to take the spoil
and to take the prey ; to turn thine hand against the waste
places that are *now* inhabited, and against the people that
are gathered out of the nations, which have gotten cattle
13 and goods, that dwell in the ²middle of the earth. Sheba,
and Dedan, and the merchants of Tarshish, with all the
young lions thereof, shall say unto thee, Art thou come to
take the spoil? hast thou assembled thy company to take
the prey? to carry away silver and gold, to take away cattle
and goods, to take great spoil?

¹ Or, *an open country*   ² Heb. *navel.* See Judg. ix. 37.

11. Cf. Deut. iii. 5; 1 Sam. vi. 18; Jud. xviii. 27. "Securely,"
i.e. in confidence, *v.* 8.

12. On "take the spoil" cf. xxix. 19; Is. x. 6. The phrase "turn
the hand upon" is always used in a hostile sense (Is. i. 25). Verses 11,
12 give the prophet's idea of the condition of the restored community
and of the state of the world in those days which permits it. He does
not furnish details, but previous prophecies (ch. xxv.—xxxii.) describe
how all the nations formerly hostile to Israel are humbled or taken out
of the way. The period of Israel's restoration is a time of universal
peace. Only distant nations on the outskirts of the world, that have
never entered upon the stage of history, remain unaware of the fame
and glory of the God of Israel (Is. lxvi. 19). The same circle of ideas
appears in the passage relating to the period of a thousand years in the
Apocalypse: outside the historical world there remain distant nations
unaffected by the kingdom of Christ.

middle of the earth] lit., as marg., the *navel* of the earth, i.e. the
mountain land of Israel, the centre of the earth, cf. *v.* 5. The prophet
speaks of the world as known in his day.

13. The merchant peoples are roused to excitement by the enterprise of Gog; probably it is the hope of gain by trafficking with him
for his spoil that excites them—hardly envy at the rich harvest lying
before him. On Sheba xxvii. 22; Dedan xxvii. 15; Tarshish xxvii. 12.

all the young lions thereof] Cf. xix. 3, 5, xxxii. 2. The term might
be thought not very suitable to a troop of camp followers intent merely
on traffic. It is probably used generally to describe the eminence of
these merchant people—hardly to represent them as *thirsting* for gain,
as lions for prey! [We should probably, by a slight change in M.T.,
read *all the Cyprians*, omitting "thereof"; or, *all the merchants
thereof.*]

Therefore, son of man, prophesy, and say unto Gog, 14
Thus saith the Lord GOD: In that day when my people
Israel dwelleth securely, shalt thou not know it? And thou 15
shalt come from thy place out of the uttermost parts of the
north, thou, and many peoples with thee, all of them riding
upon horses, a great company and a mighty army: and thou 16
shalt come up against my people Israel, as a cloud to cover
the land; it shall come to pass in the latter days, that I will
bring thee against my land, that the nations may know me,
when I shall be sanctified in thee, O Gog, before their eyes.

XXXVIII. **14—16.** THE PURPOSE AND ISSUE OF GOG'S INVASION:
THAT THE NATIONS MAY KNOW JEHOVAH, WHEN HE IS
SANCTIFIED IN GOG.

14. *shalt thou not know it*] It is the peaceful and unprotected
condition of the people, along with their wealth, that tempts Gog to
invade them. LXX., however, reads: shalt thou not *stir thyself up*,
or, *arise*, which gives a more vigorous sense (Is. xli. 25; Jer. vi. 22)
[so Cor., Kr. and others], though the Heb. is quite good. "Securely,"
in confidence.

15. Cf. *vv*. 4, 6, xxxix. 2.

16. Cf. *v*. 9.

when I shall be sanctified] Or, get me sanctifying, i.e. recognition as
"holy"—"holy" having the meaning of all that which God alone is.
The rendering "shew myself holy" is less natural, though the meaning
is virtually the same. Jehovah shews His great deeds in the sight of
the nations, and thus they recognise His Godhead, cf. *v*. 23. He gets
Him sanctifying "in" or through Gog, as the object on whom His
great operations of power are manifested.

In these verses Jehovah is represented on the one hand as bringing
up Gog in order that He may be sanctified in him in the sight of the
nations; and on the other hand Gog is represented as coming up of
his own will, prompted by evil purposes, by the hope of an easy conquest and by lust of spoil. The first representation must not be
pressed as if this case of Gog were something special, as if Jehovah
for no object but to shew His power brought up against His people a
leader and nation from the ends of the earth, who otherwise would
have remained in peace in their distant abodes. Such a view
of the episode of Gog forgets in the first place the other side of the
representation, viz. that Gog comes up of his own will, and with evil
intent. It is the hope of any easy conquest and lust of spoil that animates him as well as the merchant peoples who follow in his train.
This spirit of irreligious traffic on the part of these peoples is reprobated by the prophet and represented as antagonistic to the religion of
Jehovah, just as it is in the case of Tyre (xxvi.—xxviii.). And secondly

17 Thus saith the Lord God : Art thou he of whom I spake in
old time by my servants the prophets of Israel, which
prophesied in those days for *many* years that I would bring
18 thee against them ?　And it shall come to pass in that day,
when Gog shall come against the land of Israel, saith the
Lord God, that my fury shall come up into my nostrils.
19 For in my jealousy and in the fire of my wrath have I

this view forgets the general teaching of the prophet, to the effect that
Jehovah is in truth the author of all the great movements in the world,
and that His operations have one great end in view, to reveal Himself
as that which He is to the nations of the world.　His raising up Gog
with this view is not a special thing, but one among many other
similar things.　To signalise it as something distinct and lift it out
of the general current of the prophet's conceptions creates an untrue
impression of his teaching.

17—23.　This invasion of Gog has been long predicted.　It shall be
the occasion of a final manifestation of Himself by Jehovah to creation
and the nations, which shall inspire universal awe, and leave in the
minds of all mankind the knowledge of Jehovah, and that which He is.

17.　The question gives vividness to the fact of Gog's invasion
having been long predicted, and identifies him with the subject of
these predictions.　These former prophecies had not named Gog ; the
identification is matter of inference.

in those days for many *years*]　The construction is peculiar, but this
is probably the sense.　Gog, though not by name, had formed the
subject of repeated predictions by many prophets.　The prophecies
referred to are probably such as Zeph. i. (iii. 8), which agrees with
Ezek. *v.* 20 in mentioning the fishes of the sea (again only Hos. iv. 3),
and Jer. iii.—vi. (Is. xvii. 12 *seq.*).　The age of Joel may be later
than Ezek., and passages like Joel iii., Zech. xiv., possibly repose
rather on him, or at all events shew the continued prevalence of the
same ideas, which indeed passed as current conceptions into the Apo-
calyptic prophecy dating from this age.　The passage Mic. iv. 11 *seq.*
is also of uncertain date.　It is possible that the invasion of the
Scythians may have suggested the prophecies of Zeph. and Jer.,
though the supposition is less necessary in the case of the latter
prophet[1].　It is not likely, however, that Ezekiel's renewal of the
prophecy was occasioned by any fresh movements among these northern
nations occurring in his time (Sm., Kuen.), because he regards the
inroad of Gog as an event to happen in the far distant future.

18.　*come up into my nostrils*]　The idea is that of a fiery breath
appearing in the nostrils.　Deut. xxxii. 22 ; Ps. xviii. 8.

19.　*have I spoken*]　i.e. *do I speak* ; cf. xxi. 36, xxxvi. 5, xxxix. 25.

[1] [There can scarcely be a doubt, however, that some of Jeremiah's prophecies
as originally uttered referred to a Scythian invasion.]

spoken, Surely in that day there shall be a great shaking in
the land of Israel; so that the fishes of the sea, and the 20
fowls of the heaven, and the beasts of the field, and all
creeping things that creep upon the earth, and all the men
that are upon the face of the earth, shall shake at my
presence, and the mountains shall be thrown down, and the
steep places shall fall, and every wall shall fall to the
ground. And I will call for a sword against him unto all 21
my mountains, saith the Lord GOD: every man's sword
shall be against his brother. And I will plead against him 22
with pestilence and with blood; and I will rain upon him,
and upon his hordes, and upon the many peoples that are
with him, an overflowing shower, and great hailstones, fire,
and brimstone. And I will magnify myself, and sanctify 23
myself, and I will make myself known in the eyes of many
nations; and they shall know that I am the LORD.

The word "shaking" is the usual one for earthquake, e.g. in xxxvii. 7,
but the general term is better here. Cf. the cognate verb "shall shake"
in *v.* 20, and cf. Hag. ii. 6, 7; Matt. xxiv. 7.

20. The terror of creation before the majesty of Jehovah shall be
universal, and all that is high shall be brought down. The passage
agrees with the usual prophetic descriptions of the day of the Lord,
cf. Zeph. i. 1 *seq.*; Is. ii., iii.; Jer. iv. 23—26. It describes Jehovah's
final manifestation of Himself in His fury and jealousy. In the earlier
prophets this manifestation of His majesty by Jehovah usually precedes
or accompanies the final restoration of His people, here it is postponed
until long after they have entered upon the rest of God in their own
land. In other words that which earlier writers view as one scene,
comprising Jehovah's revelation of Himself and the final restoration
of His people, is resolved into two, one of which takes place long after
the other. The same difference is observable in the New Test. between
the representation of the Apocalyptist and that of the other writers.

21. *every man's sword*] sign of a supernatural panic caused by
Jehovah, Jud. vii. 22; 1 Sam. xiv. 20. LXX. read the first clause:
"I will summon against him also all terrors" (i.e. a panic) [and this,
which can be justified as a very possible original form of the Heb. text,
receives support from Cor., Ber. and Kr. For internecine strife among
invaders cf. Judg. vii. 22].

22. *I will plead*] i.e. contend [cf. xvii. 20]. Jehovah's pleadings are
often great acts of judgement, Is. lxvi. 16; Jer. xxv. 31. Cf. Ezek. v. 17,
xiv. 19; Is. xxix. 6, xxx. 30; Ps. xi. 6, for similar judgements.

23. Thus will Jehovah magnify Himself—manifest His greatness
and power; and sanctify Himself—shew Himself to be "holy," i.e.

39 And thou, son of man, prophesy against Gog, and say,
Thus saith the Lord GOD : Behold, I am against thee, O
2 Gog, ¹prince of Rosh, Meshech, and Tubal : and I will turn
thee about, and will lead thee on, and will cause thee to
come up from the uttermost parts of the north ; and I will
3 bring thee upon the mountains of Israel : and I will smite
thy bow out of thy left hand, and will cause thine arrows
4 to fall out of thy right hand. Thou shalt fall upon the
mountains of Israel, thou, and all thy hordes, and the
peoples that are with thee: I will give thee unto the ravenous
birds of every sort, and to the beasts of the field to be

---

¹ Or, *chief prince of Meshech*

---

one who is God, xxxvi. 23. Then shall He be known as that which
He is by all the nations of the earth. [Redpath points out that the
language of Ecclus. xxxvi. 4 ("As thou wast sanctified in us before
them, so be thou magnified in them before us") seems to have been
suggested by this *v.* See the whole passage.]

XXXIX. RESUMPTION OF THE PROPHECY AGAINST GOG.

(1) *vv.* 1—7. Renewal of the prophecy: Gog shall be broken on
the mountains of Israel by a divine interposition.

(2) *vv.* 8—16. For seven years the wood of his weapons shall suffice
the people for fuel. It will take seven months to bury his dead. His
burial-place shall be beyond the Jordan, east of the Dead Sea; and
the land shall be carefully purified of every bone of his host.

(3) *vv.* 17—24. Jehovah invites the fowls of the heaven and the
beasts of the earth to a great feast, a sacrificial meal which He shall
slay for them. They shall eat the flesh of princes and mighty men,
be sated with fat and drunk with blood. And this interposition of
Jehovah to protect His restored and now righteous people shall teach
the nations that Israel's former expulsion from the land was due to
their iniquity.

(4) *vv.* 25—29. The prophet, abandoning the point of view of
Gog's invasion in the future, occupied by him in these two chapters,
returns to the position he occupied in predicting Israel's restoration
(ch. xxxiii.—xxxvii.), which he prophesies anew.

1. Cf. xxxviii. 2, 3.

prince of Rosh, &c.] Cf. xxxviii. 2.

2. *will lead thee on*] The word "lead" does not elsewhere occur.
A.V. ("leave but the sixth part of thee") derives (erroneously) from
the numeral "six."

3. The northern warriors were bowmen.

4. Cf. *v.* 17, xxxviii. 21.

devoured.   Thou shalt fall upon the open field: for I have 5
spoken it, saith the Lord GOD.   And I will send a fire on 6
Magog, and on them that dwell securely in the ¹isles: and
they shall know that I am the LORD.   And my holy name 7
will I make known in the midst of my people Israel ;
neither will I suffer my holy name to be profaned any more:
and the nations shall know that I am the LORD, the Holy
One in Israel.   Behold, it cometh, and it shall be done, 8
saith the Lord GOD ; this is the day whereof I have spoken.
And they that dwell in the cities of Israel shall go forth, 9
and shall make fires of the weapons and burn them, both
the shields and the bucklers, the bows and the arrows, and
the handstaves, and the spears, and they shall make fires of
them seven years: so that they shall take no wood out of 10
the field, neither cut down any out of the forests ; for they

¹ Or, *coastlands*

6.   For Magog see xxxviii. 2.

in the isles] the **countries**, i.e. the coastlands and adjacent islands
of the Mediterranean.   The armies of Gog and his allies are annihilated
on the mountains of Israel, but the judgement extends simultaneously
to their distant abodes, that the ends of the earth may know and fear
the Lord.

7.   *neither will I suffer*, &c.]   Jehovah's holy or divine name was
profaned,—His majesty and power were detracted from—when Israel
His people were subjected by the heathen and dispersed abroad from
their own land (xxxvi. 20).   Israel's sins constrained Jehovah to cast
them out of His land, and thus to profane His holy name.   Now they
are another people, a new heart has been given them, and His signal
protection of them in their defenceless condition (xxxviii. 11) from so
extreme a danger (xxxviii. 4—6) will reveal both to Israel and to the
nations what Jehovah is, and what are the principles on which He
rules His people (*v.* 23).   Thus shall His name be sanctified—He
shall be known to be God alone, all powerful and righteous.

8.   The words vividly bring into the presence of the speaker the
great catastrophe.   Rev. xvi. 17, xxi. 6.

9.   The wood of the weapons of Gog's warriors shall serve the
people of Israel as fuel for seven years, they shall go neither to gather
faggots for fire in the fields nor to cut down any wood out of the
forests (*v.* 10).   [The number seven (cf. *v.* 12) expresses completeness.
Cf. Rev. i. 4, 12, 16, &c.]

handstaves] probably those with which the animals ridden upon or
others were driven¹.

¹ [Cf. Numb. xxii. 27.   But as occurring between arrows and spears some kind of
weapon must be meant.   So *Oxf. Lex.*   Cf. Kr. "clubs."]

shall make fires of the weapons: and they shall spoil those
that spoiled them, and rob those that robbed them, saith the
Lord GOD.

11 And it shall come to pass in that day, that I will give
unto Gog a place for burial in Israel, the valley of them that
pass through ¹on the east of the sea: and it shall stop them
that pass through: and there shall they bury Gog and all
his multitude: and they shall call it The valley of ²Hamon-
12 gog. And seven months shall the house of Israel be
13 burying of them, that they may cleanse the land. Yea, all
the people of the land shall bury them; and it shall be to
them a renown, in the day that I shall be glorified, saith the

¹ Or, *in front of*   ² That is, *the multitude of Gog*.

11. Gog's burial-place shall be east of the Dead Sea.

a place for burial] lit. *a place there a grave*. But the construction
in the Heb. is an impossible one. No doubt the Heb. word for "there"
(*shām*) should have been read with a different vocalisation (*shēm*), as it
was read by the LXX.,—a place of renown (name), a grave in Israel
[and so Cor., Ber., Toy, Kr.].

valley of them that pass through] In *vv.* 14, 15 the word is used of
those appointed to go through the land in search of the scattered bones.
The term cannot have that sense here. Ew. conjectured that it was
a term applied to the hosts of Gog, *the invaders*, from their overflowing the country (Is. viii. 8). The reading of *v.* 14, however, which
would be the strongest support of this view, is doubtful. The expression is probably a proper name; the "valley of the passers through"
may have been so named as the usual route of communication between
the east and west of the sea. Others by altering the points read "the
(or, a) valley of Abarim" (Hitz., Cor.) [so also Ber., Kr. Abarim
was a mountain or mountain range (Numb. xxvii. 12, xxxiii. 47;
Deut. xxxii. 49) E. of the Dead Sea].

it shall stop them that pass through] i.e. the passengers. The valley
shall be filled up with the graves of the innumerable hosts of Gog, so
that the way of passers through shall be barred. A.V. "shall stop the
noses of the passengers" has no probability. Neither LXX. nor Syr.
read the words "those that pass through"; the former renders: "and
they shall build up the mouth of the valley round about."

Hamon-gog] i.e. Gog's multitude.

12. It shall take all Israel (*v.* 13) seven months to bury Gog's dead.
The bones scattered over the land defiled it, for it was holy to the Lord,
and they must be gathered and interred, cf. *vv.* 14, 16.

13. *a renown*] Or, *a glory* (lit. a name), viz. that they have seen
their last enemy destroyed by their God. The triumph is theirs, being
His, Ps. cxlix. 9.

Lord GOD. And they shall sever out men of continual 14
employment, that shall pass through the land to bury [1] them
[2] that pass through, that remain upon the face of the land,
to cleanse it: after the end of seven months shall they
search. And they that pass through the land shall pass 15
through; and when any seeth a man's bone, then shall he
[3] set up a sign by it, till the buriers have buried it in the
valley of Hamon-gog. And [4] Hamonah shall also be the 16
name of a city. Thus shall they cleanse the land. And 17

---

[1] Or, *with them that pass through those that remain &c.*   [2] Some
ancient versions omit the word rendered *that pass through*.   [3] Heb.
build.   [4] That is, *Multitude.*

in the day that I shall be glorified] i.e. *on* the day (at the time) when
I shall be glorified (or, glorify myself).

14. When the remains that are visible shall all have been buried,
men shall be appointed whose continual task it shall be to go through
the land to search for any bones that may have been overlooked. When
they find a bone they shall set up a sign beside it that the buriers may
come and inter it (*v.* 15).

of continual employment] lit. continual men (same phrase as "continual" burnt offering),—men constantly occupied.

to bury them that pass through] The words "that pass through"
should probably be omitted (as in marg.) with LXX., and we should
read **to search for** (so Cor., Ber., Kr.) **those that remain**, &c. After
seven months have been consumed in burying the masses of the
dead everywhere visible, occasional bodies or bones may still be left,
having escaped notice. These shall be diligently searched for by the
"continual men." Those who would retain the words "them that
pass through" ("passengers" of A.V.) here read, *to bury them that
pass through* (i.e. the invaders), even *those that remain* (cf. the other
marg. reading in R.V.). The construction is unnatural, and any play
of words between two classes of "passers through," viz. invaders and
searchers, has no probability. In *v.* 15 "they that pass through," i.e.
the searchers, are distinguished from the buriers, and a reader finding
"buriers" in the present verse assumed that they were different from
the searchers, and added "with those that pass through" (the searchers)
on the margin.

15. *set up*] lit. build.

a sign] lit. a mark, or signpost. On Hamon-gog, cf. *v.* 11.

16. Hamonah is *fem.* of Hamon, *multitude*, and presumably of the
same meaning. The words, however, are enigmatical and alien to the
connexion[1]. The last clause, "Thus shall they cleanse the land," suggests

---

[1] [Perhaps "Hamonah…city" should be omitted as a gloss; the clause that follows
fits on well to *v.* 15.]

thou, son of man, thus saith the Lord GOD : Speak unto the
birds of every sort, and to every beast of the field, Assemble
yourselves, and come ; gather yourselves on every side to
my sacrifice that I do sacrifice for you, even a great sacrifice
upon the mountains of Israel, that ye may eat flesh and
18 drink blood. Ye shall eat the flesh of the mighty, and
drink the blood of the princes of the earth, of rams, of
lambs, and of goats, of bullocks, all of them fatlings of
19 Bashan. And ye shall eat fat till ye be full, and drink blood
till ye be drunken, of my sacrifice which I have sacrificed
20 for you. And ye shall be filled at my table with horses and
chariots, with mighty men, and with all men of war, saith

the previous mention of some action which has this result. The Versions,
however, are in agreement with Heb. text. If the text be correct, the
prophet's meaning is that a city shall also be built in commemoration
of Gog's overthrow ; naturally this city must be supposed situated near
the valley of Hamon-gog, because its name Hamonah (multitude), if the
city were situated elsewhere, would not of itself suggest any connexion
with Gog.

17 *seq.* The great sacrificial feast provided by Jehovah for the
fowls of heaven and the beasts of the field. [Cf. Rev. xix. 17, 18.]
They shall eat the flesh of the mighty and drink the blood of princes
of the earth (17—20). And thus shall that which Jehovah is be made
known both to Israel and the heathen ; and the nations shall understand, from Jehovah's defence of His godly people now, why it was that
aforetime He inflicted such evils upon them and cast them out of His
land (21—24).

17. *to my sacrifice*] The eating of flesh was of rarer occurrence in
ancient times than it is now. All slaughtering of animals was a sacrificial
act. The blood and some parts of the victim were given to Jehovah ;
and the rest eaten before Him by the company. Hence the terminology
here ; Jehovah's slaughter of His enemies is to afford a sacrificial feast.
Cf. Zeph. i. 8 ; Is. xxxiv. 6.

18. The actual victims sacrificed were princes and mighty men ;
here they are described as rams and goats—the usual animals sacrificed.
Jer. li. 40.

fatlings of Bashan] Bashan was a pastoral country, producing the
fattest and greatest beasts. Cf. Deut. xxxii. 14 ; Am. iv. 1 ; Is. xxxiv.
6, 7 ; Ps. xxii. 12.

20. *my table*] It is the Lord that holds the sacrificial feast here (*v.* 19),
and it is His table to which He invites the fowls and beasts.

horses and chariots] It is scarcely necessary to point with LXX.
horse *and rider* ; " chariot " suggests that those borne in the chariot
are intended. The term rendered " chariot " seems used, however, of

the Lord GOD. And I will set my glory among the nations, 21
and all the nations shall see my judgement that I have
executed, and my hand that I have laid upon them. So 22
the house of Israel shall know that I am the LORD their
God, from that day and forward. And the nations shall 23
know that the house of Israel went into captivity for their
iniquity; because they trespassed against me, and I hid my
face from them: so I gave them into the hand of their
adversaries, and they fell all of them by the sword.
According to their uncleanness and according to their 24
transgressions did I unto them; and I hid my face from
them.

Therefore thus saith the Lord GOD: Now will I bring 25
again the captivity of Jacob, and have mercy upon the
whole house of Israel; and I will be jealous for my holy

"riding-beasts," e.g. the ass and the camel, Is. xxi. 7, 9; and there is
no intimation elsewhere that Gog's army rode in chariots: they were
horsemen and bowmen.

21. The great discomfiture of Gog will reveal Jehovah's power to the
nations. None but God alone could deal so wonderfully. Cf. xxxviii.
16, 23.

22. And Israel from that day will feel secure in the protection of
Jehovah their God; all misgivings which the past might create will disappear, and they shall know that now Jehovah is indeed their God.

23. Jehovah's dealing with His people Israel is the great lesson
which He reads to the heathen; it is the history of Israel in the hand of
Jehovah their God that reveals to the nations what Jehovah is. For the
nations knew Jehovah only as God of Israel, and it was thus only
through Israel that He could reveal Himself to them. This last great
event in the history of Israel, Jehovah's signal defence of them now that
they are His people in truth, casts light on His former hiding of His face
from them. Deeper elements than mere power enter into His rule of His
people; a conception of God is suggested to the nations unlike any they
had hitherto entertained—there is a God who is omnipotent and who
rules the nations in righteousness, the God of Israel.

25 *seq.* The prophet returns to the point of view occupied in
ch. xxxiii.—xxxvii., before the restoration of Israel. The transition is
suggested by the words "I hid my face from them" (*v.* 24). This shall
no more be (*v.* 29); they shall be restored, and dwell safely in their land
(*v.* 26), and Jehovah shall be their God in truth.

25. *bring again the captivity*] or, *restore the fortunes of.* Cf. xvi. 53,
xxi. 14. The word is in any case a different one from that in *v.* 23,
which means "went into exile."

jealous for my holy name] little different from "my divine name."

26 name.   And they shall bear their shame, and all their
   trespasses whereby they have trespassed against me, when
   they shall dwell securely in their land, and none shall make
27 them afraid ; when I have brought them again from the
   peoples, and gathered them out of their enemies' lands, and
28 am sanctified in them in the sight of many nations.   And
   they shall know that I am the LORD their God, in that I
   caused them to go into captivity among the nations, and
   have gathered them unto their own land ; and I will leave
29 none of them any more there ; neither will I hide my face
   any more from them : for I have poured out my spirit upon
   the house of Israel, saith the Lord GOD.

The prophet represents Jehovah as acting from the sense of that which
He is.   The representation is to be explained from the profound sense
which the prophet, and other prophets, had of the Godhead of Jehovah,
with all that Godhead meant.   Cf. xx. 9, 14, 22, 44.

26. *And they shall bear their shame*]   The phrase "bear shame" is
not used in the sense of bearing the outward disgrace (xxxii. 24, 25, 30,
xxxiv. 29, xxxvi. 7), but in the sense of bearing the inward feeling of
unworthiness, which the undeserved goodness of Jehovah creates (xvi.
52, 54, xxxvi. 31).   The word "bear" is written defectively and by a
change of a point might mean "forget."   While "forget their shame"
however might well be said, shame meaning reproach (Is. liv. 4), "forget
their trespasses," implying complete obliteration of the unhappy past, is
so powerful an idea that it causes surprise[1].   Either idea is beautiful;
whether the idea be that the redeemed people sit in abashed gladness,
the memory of former evil adding depth to the gladness, or whether it
be that the assurance that Jehovah is their God (*v.* 22) is so exalted that
the memory of former sad days is wholly wiped out by it.

29. *for I have poured out my spirit*]   This states in brief all the
regenerating influences more fully dwelt upon in xxxvi. 25—31[2].   Cf.
Joel ii. 28 ; Zech. xii. 10.   On first clause, Is. liv. 8—10 ; Jer. xxxi.
3 *seq.*

THIRD SECTION. CH. XL.—XLVIII. FINAL CONDITION OF THE
                    REDEEMED PEOPLE.

This concluding section of Ezekiel's prophecy is in many ways
remarkable, and the main idea expressed by it needs to be carefully
attended to.

----

[1] [Yet why, if God does not remember His people's sin (Jer. xxxi. 35 and
elsewhere), should not they forget it ?]

[2] [The Heb. perfect is used in a future perfect sense, "When I shall have
&c."]

The passage is separated by an interval of twelve or thirteen years from the latest of the other prophecies (except the brief intercalation, xxix. 17 *seq.*). It stands therefore apart from the rest of the Book, with the ideas of which it is not easy in some parts to reconcile it. Some scholars indeed (Stade, *Hist.* II. 37) consider that in the interval Ezekiel had broken with his former conceptions. There does seem to be a discrepancy between the place assigned to the "Prince" in this passage and the more elevated part which the Lord's "servant David" plays in earlier chapters.

On the whole, however, the passage can be only understood if we keep before our minds all the teaching of the earlier part of the Book, and also suppose that the prophet had it vividly before his own mind. This passage contains no teaching. All that the prophet wished his people to learn regarding the nature of Jehovah and the principles of His rule, His holiness, His wrath against evil and His righteous judgements, has been exhausted (iv.—xxiv.). All that he desired to say about the revelation of Jehovah's glory to the nations, that they may know that "He is Jehovah," and may no more exalt themselves against Him in self-deification, and no more disturb or seduce His people, has been said (xxv.—xxxii.). And the great operations of Jehovah's grace in regenerating His people, and in restoring them to their own land, have been fully described (xxxiii.—xxxvii.). All this forms the background of the present section. The last words of i.—xxxix. are: "Neither will I hide my face any more from them: for I [shall] have poured out my spirit upon the house of Israel, saith the Lord GOD." The people are washed with pure water, a new heart and spirit is given to them, the spirit of Jehovah rules their life, and they know that Jehovah is their God.

Therefore the present section gives a picture of the people in their final condition of redemption and felicity. It does not describe how salvation is to be attained, for the salvation is realised and enjoyed; it describes the people and their condition and their life now that their redemption has come. This accounts for the strange mixture of elements in the picture—for the fact that there is "so much of earth, so much of heaven" in it. To us who have clearer light the natural and the supernatural seem oddly commingled. But this confusion is common to all the prophetic pictures of the final condition of Israel redeemed, and must not be allowed to lead us astray. We should go very far astray if on the one hand fastening our attention on the natural elements in the picture such as that men still exist in natural bodies, that they live by the fruits of the earth, that death is not abolished, that the "Prince" has descendants, and much else, we should conclude that the supernatural elements in the picture such as the elevation of Zion above the mountains (cf. Is. ii.), the change in the physical condition of the region of the holy city (cf. Jer. xxxi. 38; Zech. xiv. 10), and the issue of the river from the Temple spreading fertility around it and sweetening the waters of the Dead Sea (Zech. xiv. 8; Joel iii. 18), were mere figures or symbols, meaning nothing but a higher spiritual condition after the restoration, and that the restoration described by Ezekiel is no more than that restoration which might be called natural, and which took place under Zerubbabel and later. Ezekiel of course expects a restoration in the true sense, but it is a restoration which is complete, embracing all the scattered members of Israel, and final, being the entrance of Israel upon its eternal felicity and perfection, and the enjoyment of the full presence of Jehovah in the midst of it. The restoration expected and described by the prophet is no more the restoration that historically took place than the restoration in Is. lx. is the historical one. Both are religious ideals and ideal constructions of the final state of the people and the world. Among other things which gave rise to what appears to us an incompatible union of natural and supernatural were two fundamental conceptions of the Hebrew writers. They could not conceive of a life of man except such a life as we now lead in the body. This bodily life could be lived nowhere but upon the earth, and it could be supported only by the sustenance natural to man. Ezekiel considers death still to prevail in the final state. In this he is followed by some prophets after him (Is. lxv. 20), who do not expect immortality but only patriarchal longevity, a life like the "days of a tree" (v. 22), while others assume that death will be destroyed (Is. xxv. 7, 8). The other conception was that true religious perfection was realised only through Jehovah's personal presence among His people, when the tabernacle of God was with men. The words with which Ezekiel closes his Book are: "And the name of the city from that day shall be, *Jehovah is there*." To us a bodily life of man upon the earth such as we now live, and a personal presence of Jehovah in the most real sense in the midst of men, appear things incompatible. To the Hebrew mind they were not so, or perhaps in their lofty religious idealism the prophets did not reflect on the possibility of their ideals being realised in fact. The temptation, however, to allegorise the prophetic pictures of the final state, and to evaporate from them either the natural or the supernatural elements, must be resisted at all hazards.

Consequently we should go equally far astray on the other hand if, fastening our attention only on the supernatural parts of Ezekiel's picture, such as the personal presence of Jehovah, the stream that issues from the Temple, and other things, we should conclude that the whole is nothing but a gigantic allegory; that the Temple with its measurements, the courts with their chambers, the priests and Levites with their ministrations—that all this to the prophet's mind was nothing but a lofty symbolism representing a spiritual perfection to be eventually reached in the Church of God of the Christian age. To put such a meaning on the Temple and its measurements and all the details enumerated by the prophet is to contradict all reason. The Temple is real, for it is the place of Jehovah's presence upon the earth; the ministers and the ministrations are equally real, for His servants serve Him in His Temple. The service of Jehovah by sacrifice and offering is considered to continue when Israel is perfect and the kingdom the

Lord's even by the greatest prophets (Is. xix. 19, 21, lx. 7, lxvi. 20; Jer. xxxiii. 18).

There can be no question of the literalness and reality of the things in the prophetic programme, whether they be things natural or supernatural, the only question is, What is the main conception expressed by them? It would probably be a mistake to suppose that the picture given by the prophet in this section is a picture of the life in all its breadth of Israel redeemed. Many sides of the people's life do not come into consideration here. For the prophet's view regarding these his previous chapters must be consulted. The Temple, the ministrants and their ministrations, and also the Prince and people are all here spoken of from one point of view. As already said the section is not a description of the way by which salvation is to be attained, it is a picture of salvation already realised and a people saved. The sacrifices and ministrations are not performed in order to obtain redemption, but at the most to conserve it. They have two aspects: first, they are worship, service of Jehovah; and secondly, they have a prophylactic, conservative purpose, to secure that the condition of salvation be in no way forfeited. The salvation and blessedness of the people consists in the presence of Jehovah in His Temple, among men. His people, though all righteous and led by His spirit, are not free from the infirmities and inadvertencies incidental to human nature. But as on the one hand, the presence of Jehovah sanctifies the Temple in which He dwells, the land which is His, and the people whose God He is, so on the other hand any uncleanness in the people, the land or the Temple, disturbs His Being and must be sedulously guarded against or removed. It was former uncleannesses that caused the Lord to withdraw from His House (viii.—xi.); and it is only when it is sanctified that He returns to it (xliii.). Hence the care taken to guard against all "profaning" of Jehovah, and to keep far from Him anything common or unclean. First, the sacred "oblation [1]," the domain of the priests, Levites, prince, and city is placed in the centre of the restored tribes, Judah on one side of it and Benjamin on the other (xlv. 1—8, xlviii. 8 seq.). In the midst of this "oblation" is the portion of the priests, that of the Levites lying on one side, and that of the city on the other. In the middle of the priests' portion stands the Temple. This is a great complex of buildings, around which on all sides lies a free space or suburbs. Then comes a great wall surrounding the whole buildings, forming a square of five hundred cubits. Within this wall is an outer court; and within this an inner court, accessible only to the priests, even the prince being debarred from setting his foot in it. In this inner court stands the altar, and to the back of it the Temple House. The House has also a graduated series of compartments increasing in sanctity inwards—an outer apartment or porch, an inner or holy place, and an innermost, where the presence of Jehovah abides. Only the priests can serve at Jehovah's table, the altar, and enter the house, and only the Levites can handle the sacred offerings of the people, whether to

---

[1] [See note on ch. xx. 40.]

slay them or boil them for the sacrificial meal. All these arrangements have one object in view, to guard against disturbance to the holiness of Jehovah, who dwells among His people.

This, however, suggests another point. It has been remarked in disparagement of the prophet that he makes little reference to moral law in this section, occupying himself with mere "ceremonial." The objection forgets two things: first, that this final picture of the people's condition is formed by the whole great passage, ch. xxxiii.—xxxvii. It is a people forgiven and sanctified and led by the spirit of God which the prophet contemplates in ch. xl. *seq.* He does not inculcate morality, because he feels that morality is assured (xxxvi. 25—29). It is true that the people is not perfect, but they only err from inadvertency. But secondly, these errors of inadvertency disturb the Divine holiness equally with offences which we call moral. The distinction of moral and ceremonial is unknown to the Law, and if possible more unknown is the idea of a factitious "ceremonial" which has a moral symbolical meaning. The uncleannesses and the like which we now call "ceremonial" were held to be real uncleannesses and offensive to God, and the purifications were not symbolical but real purifications. These things which we name ceremonial belong rather to the aesthetic in our view than to the moral, but in Israel they were drawn in under the *religious* idea equally with what was moral.

[See *HDB*, Article *Temple*, for a reconstruction of Ezekiel's Temple. Representations of its elevations are necessarily conjectural, the prophet giving no hint of its style of architecture in that respect. Symmetry, as a symbol of perfect holiness, is Ezekiel's ruling principle in the whole vision. The Temple itself seems closely modelled on that of Solomon; not so the courts, which the prophet accordingly describes in detail. The returned exiles in the days of Ezra and Nehemiah were in no condition to attempt any such construction as Ezekiel sketched, and had to content themselves with much humbler things. For any indications of the influence of Ezekiel's vision upon the arrangements of the second Temple see Rob. Smith, *O.T. in the Jewish Church*, 2nd ed., pp. 442 ff. Flinders Petrie (*Egypt and Israel*, pp. 102—110) considers that the remains of the Temple of Jewish settlers in Egypt at Tel-el-Yehudiyeh, thirty miles N. of Cairo, are an exact copy of Zerubbabel's Temple. They do not resemble Ezekiel's design.

The details of Ezekiel's Temple "shed a light nowhere else vouchsafed to us upon the ideals of Hebrew art, influenced, perhaps, by Babylonian masterpieces, yet entirely national and puritan." Lofthouse, Introd. note to ch. xl.]

XL.—XLIII. THE NEW TEMPLE.

The passage contains these divisions:

First, xl. 1—27. Preface (*vv.* 1—4); description of the gateway into the outer court with its various chambers (5—16), and of the outer court itself with its buildings (17—27).

In the five and twentieth year of our captivity, in the 40
beginning of the year, in the tenth *day* of the month, in the
fourteenth year after that the city was smitten, in the selfsame day, the hand of the LORD was upon me, and he
brought me thither.   In the visions of God brought he me 2

Second, xl. 28—47. Description of the gateway into the inner court
with its chambers, and of the inner court itself.

Third, xl. 48—xli. 26. Description of the House or Temple itself
with the annexed buildings.

Fourth, ch. xlii. Description of the other buildings in the inner court,
with the dimensions of the whole.

Fifth, xliii. 1—12. Entry of Jehovah into the House thus prepared
for Him, to dwell there for ever.

Sixth, xliii. 13—27. Description of the altar of burnt offering in the
inner court, and of the rites to be performed in order to consecrate the
whole edifice.

XL. 1—27. THE OUTER GATEWAY AND COURT.

In the 25th year of Jehoiachin's captivity, which was the 14th year
after the fall of the city (B.C. 572), the prophet fell into a prophetic
trance (*v.* 1); he seemed transported to the land of Israel and set
down upon a high mountain, on which was a great building (*v.* 2).
At the gate of the building there stood a man with a line of flax in his
hand and a measuring reed (*v.* 3). The prophet is commanded closely
to observe all that is shewn him, and to declare it to the house of Israel.

1. *our captivity*] that of Jehoiachin, in which the prophet himself
had been carried away (B.C. 597). With the exception of ch. xxix.
17—21, dating from the 27th year (B.C. 570), these chapters are the
latest part of the Book.

the beginning of the year] In post-biblical Heb., the words mean
the first day of the year, and so possibly here. The phrase does not
otherwise occur. The ecclesiastical year or old style began with the
month Abib (March—April), and is that referred to here[1].

selfsame day] ch. xxiv. 2.   On "hand of the LORD," cf. i. 3.

brought me thither] The word "thither" must refer to the "city"
which "was smitten." LXX. omits, connecting *vv.* 1 and 2 and leaving
out "brought he me," *v.* 2: "he brought me in the visions of God to
the land of Israel."

2. *visions of God*] ch. i. 1, viii. 3, xi. 24.

[1] [This seems by no means certain. The old Heb. year began in the autumn, as
the Jewish civil year does now. The Babylonian calendar on the other hand made it
begin in the spring. The festival of the Blowing of Trumpets, prescribed in Lev.
xxiii. 23 ff., and occurring on the first day of the seventh month, seems to be there
associated with the commencement of a year (cf. Lev. xxv. 9), while the relation
which holds between Lev. xvii.—xxvi. ("Law of Holiness") and Ezekiel (see *Introd.
to Pent.* in this series, pp. 240—255) lends a probability to identity in the mode of
dating. See further in *HDB*, Art. *Time*.]

into the land of Israel, and set me down upon a very high
mountain, whereon was as it were the frame of a city on the
3 south.   And he brought me thither, and behold, there was
a man, whose appearance was like the appearance of brass,
with a line of flax in his hand, and a measuring reed; and
4 he stood in the gate.   And the man said unto me, Son of
man, behold with thine eyes, and hear with thine ears, and
set thine heart upon all that I shall shew thee; for to the
intent that I might shew them unto thee art thou brought
hither: declare all that thou seest to the house of Israel.
5   And behold, a wall on the outside of the house round
about, and in the man's hand a measuring reed of six

a very high mountain]   The site is the ancient hill of Zion, but it is
now ideally exalted above the hills, Is. ii. 2; Zech. xiv. 10; cf. Ezek.
xvii. 22, xx. 40. [Cf. Rev. xxi. 10.]

whereon...the frame of a city] i.e. a city-like, or, citadel-like building.
The ref. is to the Temple, with its complex of buildings (*v.* 3).

on the south] The pre-exile Temple at any rate occupied the southern
slope of the hill, and possibly Ezek. recalls this.   For "on the south"
LXX. [perhaps rightly] read *fronting* me (*neged* for *negeb*).

3.   *there was a man*] The "man" is not to be identified with Jehovah
Himself, who brought the prophet to him.   It is scarcely necessary to
inquire who the man is.   He is a creation of the prophet's own mind,
a living symbol of the revelation of God.   This revelation personified
has the attributes of Jehovah Himself; hence the man is like burnished
brass (i. 7), and speaks with authority (*v.* 4). Cf. xliv. 2, 5. [For "brass"
see on xxii. 20.]

a line of flax] For measuring greater dimensions (xlvii. 3, cf. Jer.
xxxi. 39), as the reed usually for smaller. [Cf. Rev. xi. 1.]

in the gate] Or, *at*. The east gateway is meant, *v.* 6.

4.   The man, like the Lord Jesus, addresses the prophet as "Son
of man," see on ii. 1 and cf. xliv. 5. The prophet is commanded to see
and hear and lay to heart all that is revealed to him, for he has to declare
it to the house of Israel, xliii. 10.

5.   A wall surrounded the whole temple buildings (xlii. 20) [here
called "the house"].   This wall ("the building") was a reed thick
and a reed high. The reed was six cubits, each cubit being a cubit
and a handbreadth, i.e. a handbreadth larger than the lesser cubit in
use. [Probably the ordinary cubit was approximately 18 inches and
the longer one 21 [1].]

---

[1] [In Egypt two cubits were in use from the earliest times, the "short" of 6 and
the "royal" of 7 handbreadths, the ratio thus corresponding respectively to the
Heb. one in ordinary use and that employed in Ezekiel's measurements, adopted
apparently in order to correspond exactly to that of Solomon's Temple (1 Kings vi. 2;

cubits long, of a cubit and an handbreadth each: so
he measured the thickness of the building, one reed;
and the height, one reed. Then came he unto the gate 6
which looketh toward the east, and went up the steps
thereof; and he measured the threshold of the gate,
one reed broad: ¹and the other threshold, one reed broad.

¹ Or, *even one threshold*

XL. 6—16. THE OUTER GATEWAY ON THE EAST SIDE.

As the Temple lay east and west, the eastern gateway was the
natural entrance. Through it Jehovah entered to take up His abode
in the new House (xliii. 4); it was therefore to be kept shut (xliv. 1, 2).
The measurements of this gate are given in detail, *vv.* 6—16; those of
the N. and S. gateways are said to be similar.

6. The threshold. After measuring the surrounding wall the man
entered the gateway. On the outside of the entrance, ascending to it,
were steps, seven in number, as is stated in connexion with the N. and
S. gateways (xl. 22, 26). Thus the gateway was elevated above the
ground outside, and on the same level with it was the outer court.
Again, from the outer court an ascent of eight steps went up to the
gateway leading into the inner court (xl. 31), and the inner court was
on the same level as the gateway. Finally, an ascent of ten steps led
up to the entrance to the house itself (xl. 49 marg.), which thus stood
on a raised platform above the inner court which surrounded it. According to xli. 8 the ten steps to the house were equal to six cubits
of elevation; if the steps leading up to the gateways were of the same
dimensions they would together amount to nine cubits, so that the
elevation of the house above the level outside the surrounding wall
(*v.* 5) would be 15 cubits. The whole structure formed three terraces,
each rising above the other inwards.

the threshold] The space between the steps and the guardrooms
is called threshold, being just the breadth of the wall, 6 cubits.
Fig. 1, *a.*

and the other threshold] This is no translation of the original, which
syntactically is scarcely translatable. The words "and the other
threshold, one reed broad" are probably a gloss suggested by the fact
that there was a second threshold (*v.* 7). The definition "broad" is
suspicious, because, though in general the smaller dimension might
be named breadth, and the larger one length, the prophet going from
E. to W. calls measurements in that direction "length" (*v.* 7), and
the direction N. to S. "breadth," even should it be the larger dimension
(*v.* 11). The words are wanting in LXX.

---

2 Chron. iii. 3). The exact length or lengths of the O.T. cubit remain uncertain,
but actual cubit-rods surviving in Egypt make it possible to determine the length of
the "royal" cubit as 20·63 inches. See Petrie, *Encycl. Brit.*⁹ XXIV. 483 *a.*]

[In each of the Figures the points of the compass are as follows :

and the measurements as given in Figures 1, 2, are in cubits. See on
xl. 5.]

FIG. I. OUTER GATEWAY.

a	Threshold at the top of the seven entrance steps, xl. 6.
bb	Guardrooms, xl. 7.
c	Threshold leading to porch, xl. 7.
d	Porch, xl. 8.
ee *ff* }	Breadth of the threshold (*a*), xl. 11.
gh *ik* }	Wall spaces between the guardrooms, xl. 7, 10.
lm	Wall space between third guardroom and porch (*d*), xl. 7.
no	Wall-front or jambs on either side of the exit from the porch into the outer court, xl. 9, 16.
fg *hi* *kl* }	Barriers before the guardrooms, xl. 12.
mn mn	Length of the porch from E. to W., xl. 14.

FIG. 2. TEMPLE HOUSE.

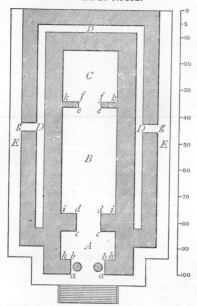

A	Porch, xl. 48.
ab	Front or jamb of the advancing wall on each side of the entrance to the porch, xl. 48.
bc	Smaller dimension (E. and W.) of the porch (*A*), xl. 49.
bh, *hb*	Jambs of the entrance, xl. 48.
hh	Larger dimension (N. and S.) of the porch (*A*), xl. 49.
B	Holy place, xli. 1, 2.
C	Most holy place, xli. 3, 4.
cc	Space between the two shoulders (*di*, *id*) giving entrance from the porch (*A*) to the holy place (*B*), xli. 2.
cd cd	Jambs of the entrance from the porch (*A*) to the holy place (*B*), xli. 1.
di, *id*	Shoulders, i.e. pieces of wall running N. and S. of the entrance, xli. 2.
DDD	Side-chambers in three stories, xli. 5.
EE	Margin remaining free outside the side-chambers N. and S., xli. 11.
ee ff	Entrance to the most holy place, xli. 3.
fk, *kf*	Walls projecting (N. and S.) on either side of the entrance, xli. 3.
gg	Doors into the side-chambers from the free margin (*E*), xli. 11.

7 And every ¹lodge was one reed long, and one reed broad; and *the space* between the lodges was five cubits; and the threshold of the gate by the porch of the gate toward the
8 house was one reed. ²He measured also the porch of the gate
9 toward the house, one reed. Then measured he the porch of the gate, eight cubits; and the ³posts thereof, two cubits; and
10 the porch of the gate was toward the house. And the lodges

---

¹ Or, *guard chamber*
² This verse is omitted in several ancient versions and Hebrew MSS.
³ Or, *jambs* and so throughout this chapter, and in ch. xli. 1, 3.

---

7. The guardrooms. Fig. 1, *bb*, p. 320.

every lodge was] **the guardrooms were**—the Heb. sing. is used collectively. These chambers were used as sentry-boxes or guardrooms (1 Kings xiv. 28), where the temple officers were stationed to preserve order and keep the house. Of these guardrooms there were three on each side of the gateway (*v.* 10). They were without doors towards the gateway inside, being merely protected on that side by a barrier or fence (*v.* 12), this allowing the keepers full view of the gateway. They were provided with windows (*v.* 16), and possibly at the back with doors leading into the outer court (cf. *v.* 13). The measurements 6 cubits long and broad refer to the inner area.

between the lodges] lit. between **the guardrooms was five cubits**. Between two guardrooms a wall-front of five cubits faced the gateway. Of these wall-fronts there were only two, because the guardrooms were but three. Fig. 1, *gh*, *ik* (p. 320).

threshold of the gate] Beyond the three guardrooms and the two intervening wall-fronts there was another space called a threshold, of the same dimensions as the first (*v.* 6), leading into the large apartment called the porch (*v.* 9). Fig. 1, *c*.

8. *porch of the gate toward the house*] Or, *toward the inside.* The sense is the same in either case: the porch, Fig. 1, *d*, of the outer gate lay at the inner end of the building, looking into the court, while the porch of the inner gate lay at the outer end of the gate-building.

We should (with marg.) omit this *v.* The copyist's eye when he came to the word *gate v.* 8 went back to the same word *v.* 7, the clause following which he repeated. Some MSS. and all the ancient versions, except Targ., omit.

9. *the posts thereof*] The posts are the projecting wall-fronts or jambs (as marg.) on either side of the exit or door from the porch into the outer court, Fig. 1, *no*. The thickness of this jamb was two cubits.

was toward the house] i.e. on the end of the gateway building toward the interior, and looking into the outer court. This is specially mentioned

of the gate eastward were three on this side, and three on that side; they three were of one measure: and the posts had one measure on this side and on that side. And he 11 measured the breadth of the opening of the gate, ten cubits; and the length of the gate, thirteen cubits; and a border 12 before the lodges, one cubit *on this side*, and a border, one

because in the inner gateway buildings the porch was on the side away from the house.

10. The measurer, having passed through the whole length of the gateway E. to W., and named each particular thing on one side of it, viz. threshold (*v.* 6), guardrooms (*v.* 7), wall space between guardrooms (*v.* 7), inner threshold to porch (*v.* 7), porch and its posts (*vv.* 8, 9), with their dimensions, now states that there were three guardrooms on each side, all of the same size, and mentions some other points.

the posts had one measure] Probably the "posts" here are not the jambs of the door of the porch (*v.* 9), but the wall-fronts or spaces between the guardrooms (*v.* 7), Fig. 1, *gh, ik*. There were two of these on each side of the passage, each measuring five cubits.

11. *breadth of the opening*] The "breadth"—the measure from N. to S.—of the outside entrance was 10 cubits, Fig. 1, *ee, ff*; and this was the breadth of the passage all along, except perhaps before the guardrooms, the barrier in front of which on both sides contracted it from 10 to 8 cubits (*v.* 12).

length of the gate] i.e. the **gateway**. This statement that the length of the gateway was 13 cubits is very obscure. The length of the gateway was 50 cubits (*v.* 15). "Length" is a measurement from E. to W., and cannot be taken in the sense of "height." It has been suggested that possibly the whole gateway of 50 cubits was not covered; that it consisted of a covered portion at each end, with an unroofed space in the middle, and that this covered portion is here referred to. But no ground appears for calling one part of the passage the gateway; and further the guardrooms and intermediate spaces were provided with windows, a fact which suggests that the whole was roofed over. LXX. read or perhaps interpreted "breadth," which is equally obscure[1].

12. *border before the lodges*] A **barrier before the guardrooms, one cubit**, Fig. 1, *fg, hi, kl*. The meaning appears to be that the barrier took away a cubit on each side from the passage, reducing it from 10 to 8 cubits opposite the guardchambers. The height of the barrier would probably not be very great. The measure of "a cubit" can hardly be the height, as all the measurements refer here to breadth.

[1] [But, if we adopt the LXX. reading, may not "breadth" mean breadth of the whole gateway, as distinguished from the gate itself (opening of the gate), i.e. while *ff* was 10, *gg* was 13 cubits?]

cubit on that side; and the lodges, six cubits on this side,
13 and six cubits on that side. And he measured the gate
from the roof of the one lodge to the roof of the other, a
14 breadth of five and twenty cubits; door against door. He
made also posts, threescore cubits; and the court *reached*
15 unto the post, the gate *being* round about. And *from* the

13. The gate-building was 25 cubits across, i.e. from the outside N. to the outside S. [If so, we can still make the space *gg* 13 (see on *v.* 11) by omitting in our measurement the thickness of the walls.] The measurement is made from roof to roof of the guardrooms. LXX. read (more naturally) "wall." [Kr. changing one Heb. consonant reads "back" for roof.] The meaning is clear. The measurement inside was three cubits less, viz. passage 10, a guardroom on each side 6+6, in all 22, leaving for each back wall 1½ cubits, *vv.* 21, 25, 29.

door against door] Or, *opposite to* door. Possibly each guardroom on both sides of the gateway had a door in the back wall opening into the outer court. Others less naturally suggest three doors of the gate lengthways, viz. that before first threshold, that before inner threshold, and the exit out of the porch.

14. Verse 14 is obscure. In the first place "he made" is suspicious, everywhere else it is "he measured." In the second place the number 60 cubits is incomprehensible. The idea that the "posts" were prolonged into pillars of such a height is altogether improbable. Besides, the "posts" are accurately distinguished from pillars, for which another word is employed (*v.* 49). It is to be observed that the measurer first passes in from E. to W. along one side of the gateway, mentioning the different things with their dimensions of which it was composed. Having reached the porch at the inner end he returns, noting that the two sides of the gateway were in all respects alike. Then from *v.* 11 onwards he gives measurements of the *breadth* of various parts of the gateway, the entrance (*v.* 11), the contraction opposite the guardrooms (*v.* 12), and finally the breadth of the whole gate-building (*v.* 13). While, however, the breadth of all other parts of the gateway has been given, that of the "porch" at the inner end has not been mentioned, though its length from E. to W., Fig. 1, *mn*, was stated to be 8 cubits (*vv.* 8, 9). It is probable, therefore, that *v.* 14 supplies this measurement. Render: **and he measured the porch, twenty cubits**—reading *porch* (*ailam*), for *posts* (*ailim*), and 20 for 60, in both cases with LXX. The 20 are inside measurement, N. to S.; 22 might have been expected, for the back wall of the guardrooms was 1½ cubits, but a chamber like the porch used for assemblies and feasts (xliv. 3) might well have a wall of 2½ cubits thick, as in point of fact the wall to the W. was two cubits (*v.* 9).

reached unto the post, the gate being *round about*] At any rate with present pointing: *and unto* (touching on) *the post was the court, the gate*

forefront of the gate at the entrance unto the forefront of
the ¹inner porch of the gate were fifty cubits. And there 16
were closed windows to the lodges, and to their posts
within the gate round about, and likewise to the ²arches:

¹ Or, *porch of the inner gate*   ² Or, *colonnade* The meaning of
the Hebrew word is uncertain.

being &c. It is probable, however, that "post" is either a repetition of
unto, and should be struck out, or else that it is a consequence of the
false reading "posts" in first clause, and should be read "porch" as
there (so in *v.* 37). The latter is more probable : *and unto* (adjoining)
the porch was the court, round about the gate. The omission of prep.
before "gate" is difficult, but cf. acc. 1 Kgs vi. 5, and the more
remarkable case Ezek. xliii. 17. Thus we should read the whole *v.*,
"And he measured the porch, twenty cubits, and adjoining the porch
was the court round about the gate." LXX. read differently, and Syr.
wants the clause¹.

15. Measurement of the whole length of the gate-building, 50
cubits.

the forefront of the gate] i.e. the outside front.

forefront of the inner porch of the gate] i.e. the front of the porch at
the inner end of the gate. From the outside front of the gate to the
inner front, lying on the court, was 50 cubits. The sense is clear though
the text may need slight emendation.

16. The description of the gateway building concludes with a ref. to
the way in which it was lighted.

closed windows] i.e. fastened, not capable of being opened like
ordinary windows (2 Kgs xiii. 17). Windows were usually openings
with fixed lattice-work. But here the meaning may be loopholed
or splayed, widening out toward the inside. [So *Oxf. Lex.* Cf.
1 Kgs vi. 4 with Burney's note.]

to their posts] i.e. those of the guardrooms (see Figure 1, *gh, ik*). The
ref. is to the 5 cubit thick wall-fronts between the guardrooms. Cf.
v. 10.

to the arches] Probably : and **to the porch thereof**, i.e. of the gate.
There are three words in this chapter which need to be distinguished :
(1) "post" (*'ail*), the meaning of which is certain from *v.* 9. It means
the front face (thickness) of a wall that projects forward (*v.* 9), especially
the jamb (on each side) of an entrance, e.g. xl. 48, of the entrance to
the porch of the house, and xli. 3 of the entrance to the house itself,
cf. 1 Kgs vi. 31. It seems also certainly used of the front (thickness)
of any wall that springs forward, the side of which bounds a space, and

¹ [It must have been the court, not (as in R.V.) the gate, that is described as
"round about." To obtain this meaning, however, a slight emendation of the M.T.
is necessary.]

and windows were round about inward: and upon *each* post
were palm trees.

17 Then brought he me into the outer court, and, lo, there
were chambers and a pavement, made for the court round
18 about: thirty chambers were upon the pavement. And the
pavement was by the ¹side of the gates, answerable unto the

¹ Heb. *shoulder.*

so of the fronts of the walls which bounded the guardrooms (previous
note and *v.* 10). (2) The second is "porch" (*'ûlām*), the meaning of
which is also clear. It refers to the large apartment which lay at the
inner end of the outer gate (*vv.* 8, 9), and at the outer end of the inner
gate, and also to the apartment which formed the outmost of the three
divisions of the house (*v.* 48). (3) The third word is that rendered
"arch" (*'ailām*), marg. *colonnade*. The term occurs only in this chapter.
The punctuators always make it plur. (*'ailīm*), though the text appears
to make it sing.: except xl. 16, 30 (fem. plur.; in xli. 15 mas. pl. of
'ûlām). These plurals are of doubtful authenticity. In regard to the
word it appears (1), that it is clearly distinguished from "post" (*'ail*),
xl. 21, 24, 29, 33, 36. (2) The LXX. does not know the pronunciation
ulam, uniformly transliterating *ailam*. (3) Even Heb. uses *'ailam* in the
sense of *'ûlām* (porch), e.g. certainly xl. 31, 34, 37 (and probably xl. 23,
26), where it is said that the "porch" (*'ailam*) was toward the outer
court. There is no evidence that the word has any other sense than
"porch." The pronunciation *ailam* (*'êlam*) is Assyr. also, the word
meaning "anything in front" (Frd. Del., in Baer's *Ezech.*).

and windows] Probably: and *the windows*.

upon each post were palm trees] The "post" here is that of *v.* 9,
viz. the wall-front or jamb on each side of the egress from the porch
into the outer court, Fig. 1, *no*. This alone was decorated with
palm trees.

XL. **17—27.** MEASUREMENTS OF THE OUTER COURT AND
REMAINING GATES.

17. *outer court*] The prophet passed into the outer court. Round
about on the inside of the surrounding wall of this court (*v.* 5) was
a pavement, probably of stone, Fig. 3, B (p. 327), and on the pavement
chambers, thirty in number, Fig. 3, C. The chambers ran round the
wall on three sides, the W. being occupied with other buildings (xli. 12).
The chambers were probably used for meetings and feasts; the ancient
high places had such a feast chamber (1 Sam. ix. 22), cf. Jer. xxxv. 4,
xxxvi. 10. It is not stated how the chambers were disposed, whether
singly or in blocks. They were apparently of several stories (xlii. 6),
but did not occupy the corners of the wall, in which kitchens were
situated (xlvi. 21—24).

FIG. 3. TEMPLE COURTS.

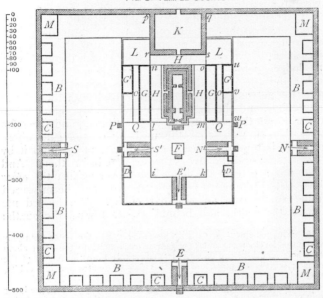

B	Pavement, probably of stone, round about the inside of the wall surrounding the outer court, xl. 17.
C	Thirty chambers on this pavement, running round the walls on three sides, viz. N. E. S., xl. 17.
D	Chambers for the priests who serve, xl. 44.
F	Altar, xliii. 13—17.
GG	Longer range of chambers, xlii. 1.
G'G'	Shorter range of chambers, xlii. 7.
H	Court or passage between the chambers and the temple platform, xli. 12.
iklm	Square of 100 cubits, forming the inner court, xli. 13.
K	Building in the inner court behind the temple on the W., xli. 12.
LL	Priests' kitchens, xlvi. 19.
MM	People's kitchens, xlvi. 21.
O	Walk between the blocks of chambers, xlii. 4.
Q	See on xlii. 2.
rpsq	Large building W. of the temple and divided from it by H, xli. 12.
uvw	Length of the space allotted to chambers (GG), xlii. 7, 8.

19 length of the gates, even the lower pavement. Then he measured the breadth from the forefront of the lower gate unto the forefront of the inner court without, an hundred 20 cubits, *both* on the east and on the north. And the gate of the outer court whose prospect is toward the north, he 21 measured the length thereof and the breadth thereof. And the lodges thereof were three on this side and three on that side; and the posts thereof and the arches thereof were after the measure of the first gate: the length thereof was 22 fifty cubits, and the breadth five and twenty cubits. And the windows thereof, and the arches thereof, and the palm trees thereof, were after the measure of the gate whose prospect is toward the east; and they went up unto it by 23 seven steps; and the arches thereof were before them. And there was a gate to the inner court over against the *other* gate, *both* on the north and on the east; and he measured 24 from gate to gate an hundred cubits. And he led me toward the south, and behold a gate toward the south:

18. The pavement is called "lower" because the outer court lay below the level of the inner (*v.* 34); it extended into the court along the whole length of the gateway ["answerable unto the length of the gates"; see Figure 3, B], and was therefore (the outer wall of 6 cubits, *v.* 5, being subtracted) 44 cubits broad.

19. The "lower" gate is the outer gate (on *v.* 18). From the inner front of this gate to the outer front of the gate of the inner court facing it was 100 cubits.

both *on the east and on the north*] The words are loosely appended, the points being stated from which the measurements were taken, viz. E. and N. [They are very possibly a gloss, suggested by their occurrence in *v.* 23.]

20. The dimensions of the N. gate were as those of the E. gate.

21. *the lodges*] **guardrooms**.

the arches thereof] **the porch thereof**. See on *v.* 16. Probably all the words, guardroom, post, porch, should be read in the sing. as collectives in the Heb. The difference is unimportant except in regard to "porch."

22. The outer gate was elevated above the ground outside, and reached by a flight of seven steps.

and the arches thereof were before them] Probably: **and the porch thereof was to the inside**, i.e. at the inner end of the gate, looking toward the interior of the whole temple-buildings, cf. *vv.* 31, 34, 37.

23. For "and on the east" LXX. reads rightly: "just as the gate looking toward the east" (*v.* 19).

and he measured the posts thereof and the arches thereof according to these measures.   And there were windows in 25 it and in the arches thereof round about, like those windows: the length was fifty cubits, and the breadth five and twenty cubits.   And there were seven steps to go up to it, and the 26 arches thereof were before them: and it had palm trees, one on this side, and another on that side, upon the posts thereof.   And there was a gate to the inner court toward 27 the south: and he measured from gate to gate toward the south an hundred cubits.

Then he brought me to the inner court by the south 28 gate: and he measured the south gate according to these measures ; and the lodges thereof, and the posts thereof, 29 and the arches thereof, according to these measures: and there were windows in it and in the arches thereof round about: it was fifty cubits long, and five and twenty cubits broad.   And there were arches round about, five and twenty 30 cubits long, and five cubits broad.   And the arches thereof 31

24.   *the arches*] the **porch.**   LXX. more fully : "he measured the guardrooms thereof and the posts &c.," as *vv.* 29, 33, 36.

25.   *in the arches thereof*] **in the porch** thereof.

26.   *the arches...before them*] **the porch thereof was to the inside,** cf. *v.* 22.   The palm trees belong exclusively to the "posts," i.e. the jambs of the egress from the porch into the court.

XL. 28—37.   THE INNER COURT AND ITS GATEWAYS.

The measurement of the outer court was finished at the S. gate. Opposite to this was the S. gate of the inner court at a distance of 100 cubits (*v.* 27), and the measurement of the inner court naturally begins with the S. gate.   The gates of the inner court were similar in all respects to those of the outer court, except that in the former the " porch " lay at the outer end of the gateway, looking into the outer court (*vv.* 31, 34, 37).

29.   *arches thereof*] better, **porch** thereof.

30.   The verse is wanting in LXX. [B, though it is found in AQ] and some MSS., and in others is deleted.   No object belonging to the gateways has hitherto been mentioned to which the measurements can apply.   The verse may have arisen from an inaccurate repetition of the measurements given in *v.* 29.

31.   Render : **And the porch thereof was toward the outer court,** cf. *vv.* 34, 37.

were toward the outer court; and palm trees were upon the
32 posts thereof: and the going up to it had eight steps.   And
he brought me into the inner court toward the east: and he
33 measured the gate according to these measures; and the
lodges thereof, and the posts thereof, and the arches thereof,
according to these measures: and there were windows
therein and in the arches thereof round about: it was fifty
34 cubits long, and five and twenty cubits broad.   And the
arches thereof were toward the outer court; and palm trees
were upon the posts thereof, on this side, and on that side:
35 and the going up to it had eight steps.   And he brought me
to the north gate: and he measured *it* according to these
36 measures; the lodges thereof, the posts thereof, and the
arches thereof; and there were windows therein round
about: the length was fifty cubits, and the breadth five and
37 twenty cubits.   And the posts thereof were toward the
outer court; and palm trees were upon the posts thereof,
on this side, and on that side: and the going up to it had
eight steps.
38   And a chamber with the door thereof was by the posts at

palm trees...posts] Cf. *vv.* 16, 26.
   33. *lodges...arches*] **guardrooms...porch.**
   34. *arches thereof*] **porch thereof.**
   36. As before for *lodges...arches* read **guardrooms...porch.**
   37. *the posts...outer court*] Probably: **And the porch thereof was
toward the outer court,** cf. *vv.* 31, 34. So LXX. The "posts" are
mentioned immediately after, and said to be decorated with palm trees,
vv. 16, 26, 31.

XL. 38—43.   Sacrificial appointments connected with the
                          inner gate.

   The verses are in some respects obscure. The text of LXX. differs
in some points, but is hardly consistent with itself. The arrangements
for slaughtering spoken of are of course connected with the inner gateway, but points not clear are: (1) which gateway, the N. or the E.?
and (2) the position of the tables, *v.* 40; were they situated in the inner
court at the long sides of the gateway, or in the outer court in front of
the gateway, on either side of the steps leading up to it?
   38. *by the posts at the gates*] **by the porch of the gate.** The plur.
gates can hardly be right. It is not probable that slaughtering took
place at more than one gate. LXX. reads *gate* (sing.) and also *porch*,

the gates; there they washed the burnt offering. And [1]in 39
the porch of the gate were two tables on this side, and two
tables on that side, to slay thereon the burnt offering and
the sin offering and the guilt offering. And on the *one* side 40
without, [2]as one goeth up to the entry of the gate toward
the north, were two tables; and on the other side, which
belonged to the porch of the gate, were two tables. Four 41
tables were on this side, and four tables on that side, by
the side of the gate; eight tables, whereupon they slew *the*
sacrifices. And there were four tables for the burnt offering, 42

---

[1] Or, *by*   [2] Or, *at the stairs of the entry*

---

cf. *v.* 37. The chamber whose entry was from the porch must have
been contiguous to the porch, but is not further described.

there they washed] not the usual word Lev. i. 9. Both words occur
in Is. iv. 4; 2 Chr. iv. 6. LXX. thinks here of a drain or runnel for
carrying off the sacrificial blood.

39. The verse states what was *in* the porch, in antithesis to *v.* 38.
Possibly the words "to slay thereon" are used generally, not of the
actual slaughtering, but of the manipulation of the flesh of the victims.
In *v.* 41 it is said that there were eight tables on which they slew, four of
which were certainly outside the porch. If the burnt, sin, and trespass
offerings (LXX. omits burnt offerings here) were slain *in* the porch, there
would remain only the peace offerings to slay outside.

40. *on the* one *side without*] Side, lit. *shoulder*, is used generally of
the side of the gate projecting lengthways into the court (*v.* 18), or of
the side lengthways of a wall (xli. 2). According to this interpretation
the tables would be at the sides of the gate *in* the inner court. Others
think that the "shoulders" might be the front parts of the gate-building
on either side of the steps leading up to it, and that thus the tables
would stand in the outer court, two at each angle formed by the steps
and the front of the gate. This use of "shoulder" is less natural, but
cf. xlvii. 1, 2; 1 Kings vii. 39.

as one goeth up...the gate toward the north] For *as one goeth up*
(*ôleh*) might be read *at the stairs* (*ôlah*, as marg.). The difficulty lies in
the word "north" or "northwards." The rendering of the R.V. is the
most natural. Others think of the E. gate and render: *and on the*
side without, on the N. as one goeth up to the entry of the gate.
Another possible rendering would be : "by the stair, at the entry to
the gate northwards," i.e. on the N. side of the entry (Lev. i. 11). On
the whole the rendering of R.V. is most probable, but the language
hardly decides which gate is meant. See after *v.* 43.

42. The phrase "for the burnt offering" is very indefinite. These
stone tables seem too small to slay the offerings upon, and the end of the

of hewn stone, a cubit and an half long, and a cubit and
an half broad, and one cubit high: whereupon they laid
the instruments wherewith they slew the burnt offering and
43 the sacrifice.   And the ¹hooks, an handbreadth long, were
fastened ²within round about: and upon the tables was the

---

¹ According to some ancient versions, *ledges*.   ² Or, *in the building*

---

verse intimates that instruments for slaughtering were laid on the stone
tables.

43.   *hooks*] The word rendered *hooks* occurs in the sense of cattle-pens
(Ps. lxviii. 13 [Heb. 14]), a meaning precluded here by the dimension,
a handbreadth. Such hooks fitted up "within," i.e. in the porch, might
be used for hanging the carcases upon in order to flay them (Targ.).
The meaning "hooks" is, however, not certain. LXX. assumes
that the stone tables are still referred to and points differently,
reading "lip" or "border" for "hooks": "and they shall have a
border of hewn stone inwards round about of a span broad." Cf.
xliii. 13, 17.

flesh of the oblation] Except in a clause of xx. 28 (wanting in LXX.)
the word for "oblation," *korban*, is not used by Ezek., though it is
common in Lev. and Numb. The present clause seems to say little.
The reading of the LXX. is preferable, "and over the tables above
(they shall have) coverings, to protect them from the wet and from the
heat."

The verses 38—43 are no doubt in some disorder. They suggest
several questions not easily settled. Upon the whole it is improbable
that slaughtering took place at more than one gate. The expression
"toward the north" indeed (*v.* 40) seems decisive on this point.
Either the N. gate is intended, or the N. side of the E. gate, no other
gate having a N. side. There are several things in favour of the N.
gate:

(1) In *vv.* 35—37 the prophet was at the N. inner gate, and no
intimation is given that he was transported to another gate in *v.* 38.
(2) In the Law slaughtering is ordered to be performed on the N. side
of the altar in the case of the burnt, sin, and trespass offerings (Lev. i. 11,
iv. 24, 29, 33, vi. 25, vii. 2, xiv. 13); no injunction is given in the case
of the peace offering (iii. 2, 8, 13). (3) In ch. viii. 5 the "gate of the
altar" is certainly the N. gate. (4) The E. gate, both inner and outer,
was to be kept shut except on sabbaths and new moons (xlvi. 1), or
on other occasions when the prince wished to offer a freewill offering
(xlvi. 12). In favour of the E. gate there is the supposed meaning
of *v.* 40; but the rendering, "on the north as one goeth up to the
entry," is hardly tenable (*v.* 40). Ew. indeed for "gates" *v.* 38 would
read "east gate"—a purely arbitrary amendment. And altogether
unhappy is his proposal to read for *without* (*miḥûzah*), *v.* 40, "runnel"

flesh of the oblation. ¹And without the inner gate were 44
chambers for the singers in the inner court, which was at
the side of the north gate; and their prospect was toward
the south: one at the side of the east gate having the
prospect toward the north.   And he said unto me, This 45
chamber, whose prospect is toward the south, is for the
priests, the keepers of the charge of the house.   And the 46
chamber whose prospect is toward the north is for the
priests, the keepers of the charge of the altar: these are
the sons of Zadok, which from among the sons of Levi
come near to the LORD to minister unto him.   And he 47
measured the court, an hundred cubits long, and an hundred
cubits broad, foursquare; and the altar was before the
house.

¹ The Sept. has, *And he led me into the inner court, and, behold,*
two chambers in the inner court, one at the side of the gate that looketh
toward the north, having its prospect toward the south, and one at the
side of the gate toward the south, but looking toward the north.

(*mĕrûzah*)—the verb " to run " being never used of the running of water
or fluids.

XL. 44—46.   CHAMBERS FOR THE PRIESTS WHO KEEP THE
HOUSE AND SERVE THE ALTAR.   Fig. 3, D (p. 327).

44.   This *v.* must be corrected according to *vv.* 45, 46 as follows,
with the help of the LXX. (cf. R.V. marg.): **And he brought me into**
the inner court, and behold, two chambers in the inner court, one
at the side of the N. gate, and its prospect was toward the S.;
and one at the side of the S. gate, having its prospect toward the N.
The chambers were for priests.   The words for "two" and "singers"
could easily be confused in MSS.

45.   *charge of the house*]   " House " is used generally of the whole
temple-buildings.   Here those having the charge of the house are called
" priests," elsewhere the charge of the house is assigned to the Levites,
cf. ch. xliv. 15—31.   This charge embraced several duties: e.g. that of
keeping the gates (xliv. 11), and that of slaying the sacrifices (xliv. 11)
and preparing the sacrificial meal for the people (xlvi. 24).

46.   The other chamber was for the ministrants at the altar; these
were the sons of Zadok, xliv. 15—31.

XL. 47.   MEASUREMENTS OF THE INNER COURT.

Lines drawn along the inner fronts of the inner gates, and along the
front of the house, gave a square of 100 cubits.   Fig. 3, *iklm*.   In this

48   Then he brought me to the porch of the house, and measured each post of the porch, five cubits on this side, and five cubits on that side: and the breadth of the gate was three cubits on this side, and three cubits on that side.

49 The length of the porch was twenty cubits, and the breadth eleven cubits; [1]even by the steps whereby they went up to it: and there were pillars by the posts, one on this side, and another on that side.

---

[1] The Sept. has, *and by ten steps they went &c.*

---

space stood the altar in front of the house, Fig. 3, F, and being high it could be seen through the gates. The place between the temple and the altar was specially sacred. On altar cf. xliii. 13—17.

XL. 48—XLI. 4. MEASUREMENTS OF THE TEMPLE HOUSE, IN ITS THREE PARTS, PORCH, HOLY PLACE, AND MOST HOLY PLACE.

48, 49. The porch. Fig. 2, A (p. 321).

48. *post of the porch*] The "post" is as before the front or jamb of the advancing wall on each side of the entrance. Fig. 2, *ab*. This wall was 5 cubits thick.

breadth of the gate was three cubits] This is supposed to mean the two bits of wall (N. to S.) on either side, the fronts of which formed the posts or jambs of the entrance, Fig. 2, *bh*. But *gate* cannot have this sense. We must read with the LXX.: *and the breadth of the entrance was fourteen cubits, and the side pieces of the entrance of the porch were three cubits on one side and three cubits on the other side.* These measures are correct and probably original, for 14 (entrance, Fig. 2, *aa, bb*) + 6 (3 + 3) = 20, the extent of the porch N. to S. (*v.* 49).

49. Here "length" is the larger dimension N. to S. (1 Kings vi. 3), Fig. 2, *hh*; and breadth the smaller E. to W.; Fig. 2, *bc*.

breadth eleven cubits] **twelve** cubits, as LXX. The number eleven cannot be reconciled with the other measurements. The length of the house E. to W. was 100 cubits, viz. 5 (wall, *v.* 48) + 12 (porch, here) + 6 (wall of holy place, xli. 1) + 40 (holy place) + 2 (wall of holiest, xli. 3) + 20 (holiest, *v.* 4) + 6 (wall, *v.* 5) + 4 (annexe, *v.* 5) + 5 (outer wall of annexe, *v.* 9) = 100.

even by the steps whereby] Read as marg. with LXX., and **by ten steps they went up** &c.; involving the alteration of one Heb. consonant. For the number "ten" see on *v.* 6. Beside the posts stood two pillars, one on either side of the entrance. These would narrow in some measure the entrance of 14 cubits. These pillars correspond to the Jachin and Boaz of Solomon's temple (1 Kings vii. 21).

And he brought me to the temple, and measured the **41**
posts, six cubits broad on the one side, and six cubits broad
on the other side, which was the breadth of the [1]tabernacle.
And the breadth of the entrance was ten cubits; and the 2
[2]sides of the entrance were five cubits on the one side, and
five cubits on the other side: and he measured the length
thereof, forty cubits, and the breadth, twenty cubits.   Then 3
went he inward, and measured each post of the entrance,
two cubits: and the entrance, six cubits; and the breadth
of the entrance, seven cubits.   And he measured the length 4
thereof, twenty cubits, and the breadth, twenty cubits,

---

[1] Heb. *tent*. See Ex. xxvi. 22—25.   [2] Heb. *shoulders*.

XLI. 1, 2.   MEASUREMENT OF THE "TEMPLE," THE HOLY PLACE,
Fig. 2, B, p. 321.

1.   The "posts" or jambs of the entrance wall were 6 cubits thick,
Fig. 2, *cd*.
breadth of the tabernacle] Heb. *tent*. The word does not occur in
the prophet except in the compounds Oholah and Oholibah. Read:
"on the other side: **the breadth of the posts**[1]."
2.   The entrance way between the posts N. to S. was 10 cubits.
Fig. 2, *cc*, *dd*.
sides of the entrance] lit. shoulders, i.e. the pieces of wall running N.
to S. on each side of the entrance, Fig. 2, *di*, that is, 10+5+5=20
cubits, breadth of the house. The length (E. to W.) of the "temple"
or holy place was 40 cubits.

XLI. 3, 4.   THE MOST HOLY PLACE, Fig. 2, C.

3.   The wall was 2 cubits thick, Fig. 2, *ef*.
breadth of the entrance, seven cubits]   The actual door or entrance,
Fig. 2, *ee*, *ff*, was 6 cubits (preceding clause); the present statement,
therefore, refers to the walls on either side of the entrance (N. to S.).
We must read with LXX.: *and the entrance six cubits; and the
side pieces of the entrance seven cubits on one side and seven cubits on the
other*. Fig. 2, *fk*. That is 6+7+7=20, breadth of the house as before
(*v.* 4). It is to be observed that while Ezek., being a priest, enters the
holy place along with the guide he refrains from entering the most holy
place, which the angel alone enters. [Cf. Heb. ix. 7.]
4.   The most holy place was a square of 20 cubits.

---

[1] [But we should rather (with Cor. and Kr. following LXX.) consider the
words a gloss. "Tabernacle" does not occur elsewhere in Ezekiel. Toy, Ber. and
others substitute for it (by a change of one consonant) "posts," but then the remark
is a meaningless repetition.]

before the temple : and he said unto me, This is the most
5 holy place.   Then he measured the wall of the house, six

before the temple] *in front of.* The "temple" is the holy place,
1 Kings vi. 3, 5.

XLI. 5—11. THE SIDE CHAMBERS OR ANNEXE TO THE HOUSE.

The text in some places is confused, but the general meaning is clear.
Round about the wall of the house on three sides (N., W., and S.) were
built side-chambers in three stories, thirty chambers in each story, in the
space marked DDD, Fig. 2 (p. 321). The chambers on the ground
floor were 4 cubits wide (N. to S.), but in the second story the width was
greater than in the first, and in the third story greater than in the second.
The reason of this greater wideness of the upper stories was that the wall
of the house on which the chambers were built diminished in thickness
as it ascended. This wall was 6 cubits thick at the base (*v.* 5), but it was
reduced at two points as it ascended. The same arrangement had place
in Solomon's temple—"on the outside he made rebatements in the wall
of the house round about" (1 Kings vi. 6). The effect of this decrease
in the thickness of the wall (in Solomon's temple a cubit each time) was
that the chambers in the second and third stories became so much broader.
In consequence of this narrowing of the wall of the house at two points
two ledges ran round the wall on three sides, and on these ledges the
beams that supported the second and third stories of the side-chambers
rested, without being let into the wall (*v.* 6). The wall of the side-
chambers was thus on one side the wall of the house; on the other side
they had a wall of their own, 5 cubits thick (*v.* 9). The whole structure,
house and side chambers, was built upon a raised platform, 6 cubits
higher than the level of the inner court (*v.* 8). The buildings, however
(temple and side-chambers), did not quite cover the platform: a margin
of 5 cubits ("that which was left," *vv.* 9, 11) remained free outside the
side-chambers, on two sides (N. and S.), Fig. 2, EE; and from this free
space the doors into the side-chambers opened, one on the N. and
another on the S., Fig. 2, *gg* (*v.* 11). Further, on the walls of the inner
court, N. and S., were chambers for the priests, Fig. 3, GG', and
between the temple-platform and these cells ran a passage or court of
20 cubits ("the separate place," *v.* 12). This court ran round the temple-
platform on three sides (N., W., S.), Fig. 3, HHH (p. 327). The way in
which one story of the side-chambers communicated with another is
described only generally (*v.* 7); in Solomon's temple the communication
is supposed to have been by a spiral staircase, or more probably by a
ladder and trap-doors[1]. It is evident that the prophet reproduces in the
main the arrangements of the temple, hence he refers to the several things,
even when first mentioning them, as *the* so and so, assuming that they
are well known.

5.   The wall of the house at its base was 6 cubits thick, and the

[1] [See Burney on 1 Kings vi. 8, where the EVV. following the LXX. render the
Heb. "winding stairs."]

cubits; and the breadth of every side-chamber, four cubits, round about the house on every side. And the side-6 chambers were in three stories, one over another, and thirty in order; and they entered into the wall which belonged to the house for the side-chambers round about, that they might have hold *therein*, and not have hold in the wall of the house. And ¹the side-chambers were broader as they 7

¹ Or, *there was an enlarging, and a winding about still upward to the side-chambers: for the winding about of the house went still upward round about the house*

breadth (N. to S.) of the side-chambers on the basement was 4 cubits. If the rebatements in the wall of the house were the same here as in Solomon's temple, the second story would be a cubit broader than the ground floor, and the third a cubit broader than the second (1 K. vi. 6), i.e. 4, 5 and 6 cubits. In Solomon's temple the side-chambers were larger, measuring 5, 6, and 7 cubits.

6. The Heb. would naturally read: "And the side-chambers were side-chamber against side-chamber three and thirty times"—which would give 33 chambers. But LXX. and some other versions read: "and the side-chambers, side-chamber against side-chamber, were thirty, thrice," i.e. thirty in three stories (cf. 1 K. vii. 4, 5). It is probable that the chambers were thirty in each story; those in the outer court were also thirty (xl. 17), and Josephus is cited as witness for this number (Cor.).

the wall which belonged to the house for the side-chambers] It must not of course be supposed that the house had two walls,—a separate one for the chambers. The word "entered into" must either be taken as a noun: *and there were intakes in the wall of the house for the side-chambers*; or it must be altered into some other word having this sense (1 K. vi. 6, LXX. uses the same word here as there)—*and there were rebatements* &c.; or some word of this meaning has fallen out before "entered into."

might have hold] It is self-evident that the second and third stories must have been supported in some way by the wall of the house, which was their own wall on one side, and mere contact with a perpendicular wall could be no support. The beams had support on the wall, but were not let *into* the wall in holes.

7. What the verse is meant to say is that the side-chambers widened in the second and third stories through the rebatement of the wall of the house. The present text being assumed, it might read: "And there was a widening of the side-chambers and an encompassing (by them) ever upwards; for the encompassing of the house was (the more) ever upwards, round about the house"—the meaning being that the higher the three-story building rose the broader it grew and the closer it encompassed the house, i.e. appeared to encroach upon the house owing to

encompassed *the house* higher and higher; for the encompassing of the house went higher and higher round about
the house: therefore the breadth of the house *continued*
upward; and so one went up *from* the lowest *chamber* to
8 the highest by the middle *chamber.* I saw also ¹that the

---

¹ Or, *that the house was high round about*

---

the retreat of the wall. LXX. omits "encompassing" after "widening"
and reads: *And the breadth of the upper story of the chambers was
according to the addition from the wall,* i.e. enlarged by the rebate in
the wall—giving the same general meaning.

the breadth of the house] The words mean: the house became broader
upwards—an impossible sense. Either "house" must be omitted with
LXX., or the clause read: "and it broadened toward the house (or,
inwards) ever upward." The subject is the side building.

and so one went up] The words state how the various stories communicated with one another, according to the clear statement, 1 K. vi. 8.
Read: **and from¹ the lowest one went up to the middle story, and
from the middle to the highest**; or possibly with R.V., *by* the
middle chamber. Cf. LXX.: "that they might go up from the
chambers below to the upper chambers, and from the middle chambers
[but the reading is dubious] to the third story." Syr. is equally
distinct.

XLI. 8—11.   THE RAISED PLATFORM UPON WHICH THE HOUSE
AND THE SIDE-CHAMBERS STOOD.

The house and the annexe stood on a platform raised a full reed, i.e.
6 cubits above the level of the inner court (*v.* 8). The platform was
reached in front of the house by a flight of 10 steps (xl. 49, see note
there) from the court. The outside wall of the annexe was 5 cubits thick
(*v.* 9). A space of 5 cubits of the platform remained unoccupied by the
buildings (*v.* 11), Fig. 2, EE. Then came a free space of 20 cubits
running round the platform (*v.* 10), Fig. 3, HHH. Finally came other
buildings in the inner court, one behind the house on the W. (*v.* 15),
Fig. 3, K; and others on both sides of it, N. and S. (xlii. 1 *seq.*),
Fig. 3, GG, G′G′.

8. *I saw also*] An uncommon form of expression; usually it is said,
and there appeared, which LXX. probably read here². For (marg.)
"height" (*gobah*) probably "raised pavement" (*gabbah*, cf. Gabbatha,

---

¹ [Emending וְכֵן, "and so," to וּמִן].

² The curious word in LXX. καὶ τὸ θραελ appears to be a transliteration of this
reading with following prep. *l* attached, וְתרא ל (fem. apoc. impf. niph.).

house had [1] a raised basement round about: the foundations of the side-chambers were a full reed [2]of six great cubits. The thickness of the wall, which was for the side-chambers, 9 on the outside, was five cubits: [3]and that which was left was the place of the side-chambers that belonged to the house. And between the chambers was a breadth of twenty cubits 10

---

[1] Heb. *height*.   [2] Or, *of six cubits to the joining*   [3] The Sept. has, *and that which was left between the side-chambers that belonged to the house and between the chambers was &c.*

John xix. 13) should be read—**and the house appeared as having a raised pavement round about,** lit. there appeared (belonging) to the house &c., cf. ch. x. 8. All that was seen of the platform was the passage of 5 cubits round about the building (*v.* 11). "House" includes both the temple proper and the side-chambers. This is supplemented by saying that the foundations of the side-chambers were 6 cubits high [1]—of course house and side-chambers were on the same level.

six great cubits] rather as marg., **six cubits to the joining,** or angle. [*Oxf. Lex.* suggests that the word is an architectural term.] The words cannot be a description of the kind of cubit, nor, since the foundations are being described, can there be any reference to the height within of the side-chambers or to the point of junction of one story with another.

9. The outside wall of the side-chambers was 5 cubits; and there was left a part of the raised platform not covered by buildings (*v.* 11).

that which was left was] This clause is in some disorder; and must be connected with *v.* 10. The text clearly distinguishes between "that which was left" (*munnach*), i.e. the outer margin of the raised platform left free of buildings, which was 5 cubits broad (*v.* 11), Fig. 2, EE (p. 321), and the "enclosed space" or "close" (*gizrah*), Fig. 3, HHH (p. 327). In *v.* 9, "that which was left" cannot differ from the same in *v.* 11, where it is undoubtedly the remainder of the raised platform. Some words have fallen out in *v.* 9. It is easiest perhaps to supply the words "five cubits" from Syr. and read : *and that which was left was* 5 *cubits ; and between* (reading *bēn* for *bēth*) *the side-chambers of* (belonging to) *the house, and the cells,* was a breadth of 20 cubits, &c. All the versions agree as to *v.* 10, but "between the cells (chambers)" cannot mean between something else and the cells. The "cells" or chambers here are undoubtedly those on the N. and S. walls of the inner court (xlii. 1 *seq.*), which were separated from the house buildings by the court of 20 cubits, Fig. 3, GG, G'G'.

---

[1] [Corresponding to the height attained by the ten steps (see on xl. 6), by which the level of the temple-platform and the side-chambers was reached.]

11 round about the house on every side. And the doors of the side-chambers were toward *the place* that was left, one door toward the north, and another door toward the south: and the breadth of the place that was left was five cubits round 12 about. And the building that was before the separate place at the side toward the west was seventy cubits broad; and the wall of the building was five cubits thick round about, 13 and the length thereof ninety cubits. So he measured the house, an hundred cubits long; and the separate place, and

11. The verse states plainly that the place that was left, i.e. the margin of platform unoccupied by buildings (Fig. 2, EE), was 5 cubits broad, and that the doors of the side-chambers opened upon it, one on the N. and another on the S. side, Fig. 2, *gg*. It is evident that the side-chambers could have doors nowhere else, for their wall on one side was the wall of the house, in which doors could not be permitted; and the measurements seem to shew that the margin of raised basement did not go round the house on the west. In Solomon's temple there was probably only one door, on the S. side, 1 Kings vi. 8.

XLI. 12. THE BUILDING BEHIND THE HOUSE ON THE WEST, Fig. 3, K.

To the west of the house proper, but divided from it by the 20 cubits of the "separate place" (Fig. 3, H), was a large building, 70 cubits broad (E. to W. Fig. 3, *rp*, *sq*), and 90 long (N. to S. Fig. 3, *rs*, *pq*)—breadth being the smaller and length the larger dimension here. The wall of the building all round was 5 cubits thick. The measurements 70 and 90 are inside. The uses which this building served are not specified, they were probably general. [Kr. suggests identity with the "Parbar," open summer-house, of 1 Chron. xxvi. 18.]

before the separate place] i.e. the court of 20 cubits broad (Fig. 3, H), which ran round the house. "Before" is opposite to or facing.

XLI. 13—15 a. GENERAL MEASUREMENTS OF LENGTH AND BREADTH OF BUILDINGS.

These measurements form three squares of 100 cubits. First, the inner court forms a square of 100 cubits when lines are drawn along the front of the house and in front of the inner ends of the gates, Fig. 3, *iklm*. Secondly, the house buildings form a square of 100 cubits, when the 20 cubits of "separate place" N. and S. of them are included, Fig. 3, *lmno*. And thirdly, the building W. of the house buildings forms a square of 100 cubits when the twenty cubits of "separate place" are added to its dimensions from E. to W., Fig. 3, *nopq*.

13. Two measurements of 100 cubits E. to W.

the house, an hundred cubits long] namely, 5 (wall of porch, xl. 48) + 12 (porch, xl. 49) + 6 (wall of holy place, xli. 1) + 40 (length of holy place,

the building, with the walls thereof, an hundred cubits long; also the breadth of the face of the house, and of the separate 14 place toward the east, an hundred cubits.

And he measured the length of the building before the 15 separate place which was at the back thereof, and the galleries thereof on the one side and on the other side, an hundred cubits ; and the inner temple, and the porches

xli. 2)+2 (wall of holiest, xli. 3)+20 (length of holiest, xli. 4)+6 (wall of house, xli. 5)+4 (side-chambers, *v.* 5)+5 (wall of side-chambers, xli. 9)=100. Here it is evident that on the W. of the house the margin or "that which was left" of the raised basement does not appear. It existed only on two sides N. and S., where the doors of the side-chambers opened from it ; on the W. the "separate place" skirted the wall of the side-chambers.

separate place, and the building] The "building" here (though spelt differently) can be no other than that mentioned *v.* 12, Fig. 3, K. The "separate place" or court of 20 cubits, Fig. 3, H, being added to this building formed a length of 100 cubits, viz. 20 (separate place)+5+5 (two walls of building)+70 (interior of building)=100, Fig. 3, *np.*

14. Two measurements of 100 cubits from N. to S.

The front of the house buildings, the "separate place" on each side of them being included, gives 100 cubits, namely, 20 (breadth of house) +6+6 (side walls)+4+4 (side-chambers)+5+5 (walls of side-chambers)+5+5 (remainder of raised basement)+20+20 (separate place) =100, Fig. 3, *lm.*

15. The "length" here is reckoned from N. to S.

which was at the back thereof] Rather : **behind which it was.** The building, while lying "over against" the "separate place," was behind it, i.e. to the W. of it. If this construction be not adopted the meaning is, which (building) was behind it (the separate place)—an independent clause. The length of the building as it lay along the "separate place" N. to S. was 100 cubits, i.e. 90 (interior, *v.* 12)+5+5 (side walls, *v.* 12) =100. Fig. 3, *rs.* The term rendered "galleries" is of uncertain meaning. It occurs only xli. 15, 16 and xlii. 3, 5. If the reading be right here it can mean nothing else but walls, or something equivalent to walls and occupying the same space, according to *v.* 12. Syriac uses a term by which it also renders the "walls" of the altar, *v.* 22.— The verse should end at the word *cubits.*

XLI. **15** *b seq.* DESCRIPTION OF THE INSIDE OF THE HOUSE, WITH ITS ORNAMENTATION.

The details of measurement were exhausted in *v.* 15 *a.* The prophet proceeds now to describe the interior of the house in two particular points: (1) the woodwork with which the house in its walls, &c., was covered, 15 *b*—16 *a*; and (2) the ornamentation of this woodwork, 16 *b seq.* The text is in some disorder, and the unknown term rendered

16 of the court; the thresholds, and the closed windows, and the galleries round about on their three stories, over against the threshold, cieled with wood round about, and *from* the ground up to the windows; now the windows were covered;

"galleries" causes perplexity, though two general statements are plainly made, viz. that the whole interior of the house was covered with wood, and that this woodwork from floor to roof was ornamented in the holy place and in the holiest with cherubs and palms (in the porch perhaps with palms only). With no more changes than are absolutely necessary *vv.* 15 *b*—16 *a* might read: "and the temple (i.e. holy place), and the inner house (holiest), and the porch of the court (more probably, and its outer porch), 16 and the thresholds, and the closed windows and the galleries round about the three of them, opposite the threshold (i.e. towards the interior) were panelled (wainscotted) with wood (or, were polished wood) round about." This would state generally that the whole interior was wainscotted. But the jump from "thresholds" (A.V. "door posts") to "closed windows" in *v.* 16 is unnatural. It is probable that for "thresholds" should be read with LXX. *cieled* (or, wainscotted). It is certainly probable that the roofing is described; the verb read by LXX. (*sāphan*) is always used of the roof-work in the description of Solomon's temple (1 Kgs vi. vii., unless vii. 7 be an exception, a clause wanting in LXX.); and LXX. understood it so here (*v.* 20). Further the fact that the closed windows, which must have been toward the roof, are mentioned in immediate connexion, is in favour of the roof-work. What the "galleries" were is obscure. LXX. either did not read the word or rendered it "narrow openings" (slit windows). "On their three stories" (*v.* 16) should be **to the three of them** (the holy place, the holiest, and the porch, *v.* 15) [so Kr.]. Pointed thus the reading is: *and the temple and the inner house* (holiest) *and the porch of the court* (or, and its outer porch) *were covered with a roof-work, and they three had their closed windows and their galleries round about.*

16. *over against the threshold*] It looks as if some words had fallen out of the text here. LXX. reads: *and the house and the adjoining parts were wainscotted with wood round about, and the floor* &c. The present Heb. text, even if read, *and over against the threshold was a wainscotting of wood,* is too short to give the necessary sense—"over against the threshold" would be rather obscure as an expression for the whole interior of the house. The words "over against the threshold" can hardly be regarded as a definition of the locality of the "galleries," as if these were borders or dados going round the foot of the walls (Sm.).

16 *b seq.* The ornamentation of the interior. Here also there is some obscurity: *and from the floor unto the windows* (*and the windows were covered*), 17 *and unto the space above the door, and unto the inner house and without, and on all the walls round about in the inner* (house) *and the outer* [were measures and], 18 *there were made cherubs and palm*

to *the space* above the door, even unto the inner house, 17
and without, and by all the wall round about within and
without, [1] by measure. And it was made with cherubim 18
and palm trees ; and a palm tree was between cherub and
cherub, and every cherub had two faces ; so that there was 19
the face of a man toward the palm tree on the one side,
and the face of a young lion toward the palm tree on the
other side : *thus was it* made through all the house round
about.   From the ground unto above the door were 20
cherubim and palm trees made : [2] thus was the wall of the
temple.   As for the temple, the door posts were squared ; 21

---

[1] Heb. *measures.*   [2] Another reading is, *And as for the wall of
the temple, the door posts were squared.*

---

trees, so that, &c.   The words in parenthesis "and the windows," &c.,
may not be original.   The phrase "and without" hardly refers to the
porch, but rather to the outer house or holy place ; as it does not appear
that cherubs were carved on the wall of the porch.   The word "measures"
is wanting in LXX.   If genuine the term "measures" might possibly
imply that the wall was panelled into compartments, and that in each
of these was carved a cherub and a palm.   The term *middoth*, from a root
meaning to measure or spread out, is common enough, but could hardly
be used of a casing or wainscotting of wood.   Boettcher suggested
"carvings," a sense which would add nothing to the general meaning.
V. 20 is rather in favour of the omission of the word[1].

18, 19.   Only the two chief faces of the cherub were represented,
that of a man and of a lion.

20.   The prophet is to be conceived as standing in the holy place,
and when he speaks of the "door" he evidently refers to the end walls
and not to the side walls.   It remains obscure whether it be the "door"
of the holiest or that of the holy place to which he refers.

thus was the wall of the temple]   The word for "the temple" is marked
as suspicious by dots over it, and is omitted in some MSS. and in the
ancient versions.   The clause is to be connected with *v.* 21 [and rendered
as in marg.].

21.   *As for the temple, the door posts were squared*]   The text is very
uncertain, the versions deviating from Heb. and from one another.
Syriac read : "And the wall of the temple was four-square"—omitting
"door posts."   LXX.: "And the holy place (holiest) and the temple
opened (spread out) four-square"—reading "holy place" for wall, and

---

[1] [Kr., joining the Heb. rendered "measures" with the first word (slightly
altered) in M.T. of *v.* 18 ("And it was made") renders : "within and without were
gigantic figures, cherubim, &c."; cf. for the sense "gigantic," Numb. xiii. 32;
Jer. xxii. 14.]

and as for the face of the sanctuary, the appearance *thereof*
22 was [1] as the appearance *of the temple*. The altar was of
wood, three cubits high, and the length thereof two cubits;
and [2] the corners thereof, and the [3] length thereof, and the
walls thereof, were of wood: and he said unto me, This is
23 the table that is before the LORD. And the temple and

---

[1] Or, *as the* former *appearance*   [2] Or, *it had its corners; and &c.*
[3] The Sept. has, *base*

"opened" for door-posts. It is probable that something is said of the
holiest, because the next clause refers to an article that stood in front
of it. It is also probable that the "door" referred to *v.* 20 is that
from the holy place into the holiest. But the witnesses leave us uncertain whether something be said about the wall or about the door-
posts. If about the first, the reading may be: *and the wall of the holiest
was four-square* (Hitz., Cor.). Reference, however, might be to the
door-posts. In Solomon's temple those of the holy place appear to
have been four-cornered, and those of the holiest five-cornered (1 Kgs
vi. 31, 33).

the face of the sanctuary…of the temple] This and the marg. are purely
conjectural. Something seems to have fallen out of the text or possibly
the clause is to be connected with *v.* 22. Perhaps: **and in front of
the sanctuary** (the holiest) **was the appearance as the appearance
22 of an altar of wood three cubits the height thereof**, &c. So
LXX. and partly Syr. "In front of the holiest (lit. the holies = holy
places) there stood an object having the appearance of an altar of
wood," and so Kr. The present text might read: "and (as for) the
front of the sanctuary, the appearance was as the appearance," i.e. it
had the appearance which is well known and does not need further
description—a form of speech common enough in Shemitic, but quite
improbable here.

22. The altar was 3 cubits high and 2 long. LXX. adds that it was
2 broad.

the length thereof, and the walls thereof, were of wood] Read, **the base**
thereof, after LXX.; so Cor., Kr. and others; cf. Ex. xxvi. 19 *seq.*
The altar had corners, probably somewhat raised, but not horns. It was
wholly of wood, and is called the table which is before the Lord. The
term "table" is applied to the altar of burnt-offering xliv. 16 (cf. Mal.
i. 7, 12). This is quite natural, as the flesh was the bread of Jehovah
(xliv. 7). Ezek. does not name any other object in the holy place
besides this table, and it is probable that he refers here to the altar-like
table of shewbread, the cakes on which would also be considered an
offering of bread for the Lord.

23—26. The doors of the holy place and the holiest.

The temple or holy place and the holiest had each a two-leaved door;
and each of the leaves was again divided into two leaves.

the sanctuary had two doors. And the doors had two 24
leaves *apiece*, two turning leaves; two *leaves* for the one
door, and two leaves for the other. And there were made 25
on them, on the doors of the temple, cherubim and palm
trees, like as were made upon the walls; and there were
thick beams of wood [1] upon the face of the porch without.
And there were closed windows and palm trees on the 26
one side and on the other side, on the sides of the porch:
thus were the side-chambers of the house, and the thick
beams.

[1] Or, *before the porch*

23. *two doors*] i.e. each had a double or two-leaved door.

24. *And the doors*] i.e. the leaves of the door had again two leaves,
so that the doors of the holy place and of the holiest were folding doors,
each composed of four small leaves, like a screen.

25. The doors of the holy place were carved with cherubs and palm
trees just as the walls (*vv.* 17 *seq.*).

thick beams...upon the face] The word rendered "thick beams" (*'ab*)
occurs again 1 Kgs vii. 6 in connexion with a porch, but is of uncertain
meaning. Here it is said to lie outside the porch and in front of it, and
might be the "landing" at the top of the flight of steps. Others think
of an overhanging on the front of the roof, to protect the entrance.
But in 1 Kgs vii. 7 the *'ab* fronts the pillars, as here it faces the porch.
Therefore perhaps: "and a landing of wood in front of the porch on
the outside" [or, more probably, a veranda of some kind]. No doubt
"without" might describe the lie of the porch in reference to the house
and not the lie of the *'ab* in reference to the porch; in which case the
'ab would be something between the holy place and the porch, and in
fact the description in *v.* 26 refers to the *inside* of the porch. Still this
is less probable.

26. The "sides" (lit. shoulders) are the side walls of the porch, but
whether the walls on both sides of the entrance be meant, or the end-
walls (N. and S.), cannot be decided. There should be a full-stop at
porch. The next statement is incomplete: And the side-chambers of
the house and the landings....

XLII. OTHER BUILDINGS OF THE INNER COURT.

The chapter has three divisions:

First, *vv.* 1—12. The chambers in the inner court.

Secondly, *vv.* 13, 14. The uses of these chambers for the priests.

Thirdly, *vv.* 15—20. Measurements of the outer wall and area of
the whole temple-buildings.

1—12. The chambers in the inner court.

In the inner court on the two sides N. and S. of the house or temple
proper were erected blocks of cells for the use of the priests, where they

42　　Then he brought me forth into the outer court, the way
toward the north : and he brought me into the chamber

ate the holy things and deposited their sacred garments. They are
those referred to xli. 9 *seq.* The block on the N. side is fully described
(*vv.* 1—9), and that on the S. of the house is said to be similar in all
respects (*vv.* 10—12). The block on the N. extended from the "separate place" to the N. wall of the inner court, a breadth of 50 cubits, all
the space available. The block of cells had two wings, one 100 cubits
long running along the "separate place," Fig. 3, G, the other 50 cubits
long, Fig. 3, G', running along the N. wall of the inner court—both
measurements E. to W. Between the two wings of the block ran a
walk of 10 cubits broad and 100 cubits long, i.e. the whole length of
the longer wing, Fig. 3, O, and on this walk the doors into the chambers
opened, i.e. looking to the N. (at least in the longer wing). The chambers
were built in three stories, but those of the third story were narrower
than those of the other two, because a "gallery" in the uppermost story
took up some space. The chambers had no pillars like those in the
outer court. There was an entrance-way leading to the chambers from
the outer court, through the wall of the inner court, but its precise
situation is not indicated.

1—3. These verses may read consecutively: "And he brought me
forth into the inner court, the way toward the north ; and he brought
me unto the chambers that were over against the separate place, and
that were over against the (wall-) building toward the north, 2 (even)
in front of the length of 100 cubits with the doors toward the north ;
and the breadth was 50 cubits, 3 over against the 20 cubits belonging
to the inner court, and over against the pavement belonging to the
outer court, gallery (being) over against gallery in the third story."

1. *the outer court*] LXX. the *inner* court. Something may be said
for both readings. On the one hand the entrance-way to the chambers
was from the outer court, and the prophet might have been first brought
to the outer court and then by this way to the chambers in the inner
court. This, however, is rather a complicated movement, and is not
indicated ; and perhaps the "inner" of LXX. has most probability.
The position of the prophet is pretty clear, it was on the E. of the
chambers, to the N. of the longer wing and facing it, Fig. 3, Q.
LXX. reads "over against the gate toward the N."

into the chamber] **unto the chambers.** The word is sing. as collective.
The "separate place" is the 20 cubits broad court running round the
house on its three sides, Fig. 3, H. The longer wing of the block of
cells ran along this "separate" place its whole length of 100 cubits,
Fig. 3, G. The "building toward the N." is the wall of the outer
court with its blocks of cells (xl. 5), Fig. 3, B, C. As there was nothing
between the wing of chambers on the N. wall of the inner court and
this "building" or wall of the outer court with its cells, except the
mere level of the court, the one is said to be over against the other.

that was over against the separate place, and which was over against the building toward the north. Before the 2 length of an hundred cubits was the north door, and the breadth was fifty cubits. Over against the twenty *cubits* 3 which belonged to the inner court, and over against the pavement which belonged to the outer court, was gallery against gallery [1] in the third story. And before the 4 chambers was a walk of ten cubits breadth inward, a way

[1] Or, *in three stories*

---

2. *V.* 2 states the precise place which the prophet was brought to—it was in front of, or so as to face, the longer wing of chambers, or the walk of 100 cubits before them, i.e. he was slightly to the N. of this longer wing, and to the E. of the whole block. This seems more natural than to suppose the "length of 100 cubits" to be the separate place. Probably, Fig. 3, Q.

was the north door] As above: **with the doors toward the north** (*v.* 4). This is rather hard in construction, and for "with the doors" might be read: *on the side* toward the N. (*peath* for *pethah*). So LXX. The breadth N. to S. of the whole block of chambers was 50 cubits (cf. *v.* 4).

3. The breadth of the block having been mentioned in *v.* 2, *v.* 3 adds in what directions this breadth extended or lay on either hand (N. and S.), viz. towards the 20 cubits of the separate place (Fig. 3, H) on the S., and toward the pavement running round the wall of the outer court (xl. 17) on the N. (cf. *v.* 1), Fig. 3, B. The term "gallery" is obscure, but here it seems to mean a passage running round the chambers, in front of them, and so taking away from their area.

in the third story] lit. in *the thirds*, i.e. third chambers (Gen. vi. 16). What is meant by "gallery over against gallery" is rather obscure. Most naturally the galleries or gangways round the highest story would be supposed to lie towards the interior of both wings, i.e. on the "walk" of 10 cubits running between the wings (Fig. 3, O), because if they lay toward the outside of the wings respectively it is difficult to see how they could be said to lie "over against" or to face one another, for in that case both wings of the chambers in the third story would lie between them. It is altogether unnatural to suppose that by the second "gallery" any galleries in the chambers of the outer court on the one side, or any galleries in the structure of the house proper on the other, are referred to.

4 may be read: "And before the chambers was a walk of 10 cubits breadth inward, with a length of 100 cubits; and their doors were toward the north."

4. *inward*] i.e. between the two wings (Fig. 3, O). Or possibly: (leading) *into the inner court.*

of ¹ one cubit; and their doors were toward the north.
5 Now the upper chambers were shorter: for the galleries
took away from these, more than from the lower and the
6 middlemost, in the building.   For they were in three
stories, and they had not pillars as the pillars of the courts:
therefore *the uppermost* was straitened more than the lowest
7 and the middlemost from the ground.   And the ²wall that
was without by the side of the chambers, toward the outer
court before the chambers, the length thereof was fifty
8 cubits.   For the length of the chambers that were in the
outer court was fifty cubits: and, lo, before the temple

    ¹ According to some ancient versions, *a hundred cubits.*
    ² Or, *fence*

    a way of one cubit]   A mere error of transcription for: *a length of*
100 *cubits.*   So LXX., Syr.   In *v.* 16 the words "cubit" and "hundred"
(spelt with the same three letters in different order) have again been
confused in the Heb. text.   The doors of the chambers were to the N.,
i.e. opened upon this passage of 10 cubits, between the wings.

    5.   The uppermost story was contracted by the gallery, so that its
area was smaller than that of the other two stories.

    6.   *the pillars of the courts*]   Read with LXX.: pillars of *the outer
ones*, i.e. the chambers in the outer court.   Probably there is a transcrip-
tional error here in the Heb., cf. xli. 15.

    7—9.   The shorter wing of chambers.   Read together the verses run:
"And the wall that was without, beside the chambers which were
toward the outer court, facing the (other?) chambers, the length thereof
was 50 cubits.   8 For the length of the chambers that were toward the
outer court was 50 cubits; but those toward the temple were 100 cubits.
9 And below these chambers was the entrance-way on the east when
one goeth to them from the outer court, at the beginning of the wall of
the court"—-the first words of *v.* 10 being connected with *v.* 9.

    7.   *wall...without*]   i.e. not forming part of the block of cells, but ex-
tending eastward from the end of the shorter wing, and therefore said
to be beside the cells that lay towards the outer court.   Fig. 3, *vw.*

    before]   *in front of* or *facing*—-still said of the wall (Fig. 3, *vw*).
The "chambers" seem to be those of the longer wing.   The piece of
wall would face them; but the words might be (though less likely) a
second specification of the position of the piece of wall referred to in
regard to the shorter wing (cf. *v.* 2).   The length of this piece of wall
was 50 cubits.   The reason is stated in *v.* 8.

    8.   The shorter wing of chambers lying toward the outer court was
50 cubits long.   Fig. 3, *uv.*

    and, lo,...the temple]   The exclamation *and lo!* is rather unnatural, a
slight change of punctuation gives, *but those.*   The expression "before

were an hundred cubits. And from under these chambers 9
was the entry on the east side, as one goeth into them
from the outer court. In the thickness of the [1]wall of the 10
court toward the east, before the separate place, and before

---

[1] Or, *fence*

---

the temple" is difficult, for usually "temple" means merely the holy
place. The word "before" makes no difficulty. It means merely
"facing," and does not imply the "front" of the temple in the
technical sense. The LXX. (so Ew., Cor.) reads differently: *and
these* (the shorter wing, Fig. 3, G') *faced the others* (the longer,
Fig. 3, G), *together 100 cubits*—"together" referring to the shorter
wing and wall (Fig. 3, *uv + vw*).

   9.   *under these chambers*] i.e. the shorter wing.

   10 *a*.   *thickness of the wall*] Probably : *at the beginning* (or, head) *of
the wall* (cf. *v.* 12)[1] *of the court*, to be connected with *v.* 9. The "wall"
is that piece of wall referred to *v.* 7, and the "beginning of it" is the
point where the way enters from the outer court, Fig. 3, P.   In xlvi. 19
this is stated to have been at the shoulder (the long side) of the
N. gate.   It is said that the doors into the chambers were from the
"walk" of 100 cubits long fronting the longer wing (Fig. 3, O), and
possibly also that this walk led into the inner court (*v.* 4), consequently
the entrance-way from the outer court must have lain as far east as the
end of this "walk," which it led to and so reached the chambers.   The
area of 100 × 50 on which the cells stood, though not wholly covered by
the cells, must have been in some way marked off from the general
level of the court, and the entrance-way from the outer court was on
the east front of it ; and it was probably in this entrance-way that
the prophet had his position (*vv.* 1—9), Fig. 3, Q.

   10 *b*—**12.**   The corresponding chambers on the south side of the
temple-house.   The text is undoubtedly in great confusion, and has been
amended in various ways.   Taken as nearly as possible as it stands it
reads : "Toward the south, over against the separate place and over
against the (wall-) building, there were chambers, 11 with a way before
them, like the appearance of the chambers which were toward the
north, as long as they and as broad as they, and according to all their
goings out, and according to their fashions.   And according to their
doors, 12 so were the doors of the chambers that were toward the south ;
there was a door at the beginning of the way, to wit the way before
the corresponding (?) wall, on the east as one entereth into them."

   10.   For "east" must be read **south**, according to *vv.* 12, 13 and
the whole scope ; cf. xliv. 44.   The "building" as in *v.* 1 is the wall of
the outer court with its stories of cells, Fig. 3, B, C.   On the one side
the chambers faced the separate place, and on the other side the shorter
wing looked towards the buildings in the outer court.

   [1] [So Ber., Kr., but Cor. would omit "in the...court."]

11 the building, there were chambers. And the way before
them was like the appearance of *the way of* the chambers
which were toward the north; [1]according to their length
so was their breadth: and all their goings out were both
according to their fashions, and according to their doors.
12 And according to the doors of the chambers that were
toward the south was a door in the head of the way, even
the way directly before the [2]wall toward the east, as one
13 entereth into them. Then said he unto me, The north
chambers and the south chambers, which are before the
separate place, they be the holy chambers, where the priests
that are near unto the LORD shall eat the most holy things:
there shall they lay the most holy things, and the meal

---

[1] Or, *they were as long as they, and as broad as they*   [2] Or, *fence*

11. *way before them*] The term "way" here seems used of the
10 cubits broad walk running between the two wings of the block of
chambers (*v.* 4), Fig. 3, O. LXX. renders "walk" as there. For
"appearance" LXX. reads *measures*. The "their" refers to the
chambers on the north side of the court (*vv.* 1—9); those on the south
side were like them in all particulars.

12. As the text reads it is easiest to attach the last words of *v.* 11 to
v. 12. The sense resulting from this change is not very natural. Possibly
v. 11 should end as R.V., in which case *v.* 12 must be amended : *and
the doors of the chambers were toward the south. There was* &c. In
this point they differed from the other chambers, the doors of which
were toward the north (*v.* 4).

The term rendered "corresponding" in note on *vv.* 10—12 (R.V.
directly) is quite unknown. In the Targ. and post-biblical Heb. a
similar word appears to mean *suitable, excellent*—the appropriate wall.
The word is no doubt corrupt.

13, 14. Uses to which the chambers were put.

These cells serve two purposes : the priests shall eat in them the most
holy things; and they shall deposit there the sacred garments when they
put them off to go into the outer court among the people. The "most
holy things" were the portion of the meal-offering not consumed on the
altar (Lev. ii. 3, 10, vii. 9—11, x. 12), and the flesh of the sin and
trespass offerings, except the flesh of the sin-offering for the high-priest
and congregation, which was burnt outside the sacred buildings (Lev.
vi. 30, vii. 6).

13. *before the separate place*] *over against*, as *vv.* 1, 10, i.e. the longer
wing on the N. and on the S. Nothing specially is said as to the
uses of the shorter wing.

lay the most holy things] Naturally the meal-offering had to be baked

offering, and the sin offering, and the guilt offering; for the place is holy. When the priests enter in, then shall they 14 not go out of the holy place into the outer court, but there they shall lay their garments wherein they minister; for they are holy: and they shall put on other garments, and shall approach to that which pertaineth to the people.

Now when he had made an end of measuring the inner 15 house, he brought me forth by the way of the gate whose prospect is toward the east, and measured it round about. He measured on the east ¹side with the measuring reed, 16 five hundred reeds, with the measuring reed round about.

¹ Heb. *wind*.

before being eaten, and the flesh of the sacrifices boiled. Being most holy things they must be kept in a holy place.

14. *the priests enter in*] The ref. is not to the holy cells, but to the house or more probably the inner court, in which the altar stood.

go out of the holy place] probably the whole inner court is meant, with its contents, house and chambers, seeing it is contrasted with the outer court.

that which pertaineth to the people] i.e. the outer court.

XLII. 15—20. MEASUREMENTS OF THE WHOLE COMPLEX OF THE TEMPLE-BUILDINGS ON THE OUTSIDE.

The measuring angel began by measuring the height and thickness of the outside surrounding wall (xl. 5); then he entered the outer gate, passing into the outer court, the measurements of which were made (xl. 6—27); then he entered the inner court, containing the house and cells, all of which he measured (xl. 28—xlii. 14). These measures being completed, the angel now returns to the outside by the way he entered, the eastern gate, and finishes by measuring the compass of the whole temple-buildings outside. These buildings, the surrounding wall being measured, form a square of 500 cubits.

15. *measured it*] i.e. whole building, along the outer wall.

16. *five hundred reeds*] Read **cubits**, and see note on *v.* 4. Five hundred reeds, the reed being 6 cubits, would give a measurement of 3000 cubits. No allusion is made to such a space surrounding the house buildings anywhere else. On the contrary in xlv. 2 the area of the temple-buildings is said to be 500 cubits square, and the free space about it 50 cubits. LXX. omits the word "reeds" everywhere in these verses, expressly giving "cubits" in *v.* 17. In *v.* 20 (Heb.) allusion is made to the *wall*, and "reeds" is omitted. That the outer wall of the temple-buildings formed a square of 500 cubits appears from measurements given elsewhere. Taking the direction N. to S.

17 He measured on the north ¹ side, five hundred reeds, with
18 the measuring reed round about. He measured on the
   south ¹side, five hundred reeds, with the measuring reed.
19 He turned about to the west ¹ side, and measured five
20 hundred reeds with the measuring reed. He measured it
   ² on the four sides: it had a wall round about, the length
   five hundred, and the breadth five hundred, to make a
   separation between that which was holy and that which
   was common.

43   Afterward he brought me to the gate, even the gate that

---

¹ Heb. *wind*.   ² Heb. *toward the four winds*.

we have 50 (outer gate, xl. 21) + 100 (gate to gate, xl. 23) + 50 (inner
gate, xl. 36) + 100 (inner court, xl. 47) + 50 (inner gate) + 100 (gate to
gate) + 50 (outer gate) = 500. Or going from E. to W. the result is the
same : 50 (outer gate) + 100 (gate to gate) + 50 (inner gate) + 100 (inner
court) + 100 (house, xli. 13) + 100 (building behind house, xli. 13) = 500.
    17. *round about*] The word is wanting in *v.* 18, and *v.* 19 reads :
he turned about and measured. LXX. reads in the latter way in all the
verses 16, 17, 18, "and he turned to...and measured," attaching the
word to the beginning of the following verse, no doubt rightly, cf. a
similar case 1 S. xiv. 21. In LXX. also *vv.* 18 and 19 are transposed,
the natural order round the wall being followed.
    20. Holy and common are used here relatively, just as *v.* 13 the
inner court is relatively holy in contrast with the outer to which the
people had access. Cf. xliii. 12, where the limits of the house are said
to be "most holy." In xlv. 4 the priests' land surrounding the temple
is called "holy," "It is an holy portion of the land ; it shall be for the
priests &c.," and in xlviii. 12 "most holy," "It shall be unto them (the
sons of Zadok) a thing most holy."

XLIII. ENTRY OF JEHOVAH INTO THE HOUSE.

    The measurements of the whole temple-buildings being completed,
the prophet sees Jehovah return to it by the E. gate, by which he had
seen Him leave the old Temple (ch. xi. 23). The vision of the glory of
the Lord was like that seen on former occasions (ch. i. and x.). The
chapter has three divisions :
    (1) *vv.* 1—12. Entry of Jehovah into His house.
    (2) *vv.* 13—17. Measurements of the altar of burnt-offering.
    (3) *vv.* 18—27. Sacrifices and ceremonies to be employed in dedi-
cating the altar.
    1—12. The glory of Jehovah enters the house by the E. gate. The
sound of His chariot was as the sound of many waters, and His glory
lightened the earth (*vv.* 1—4). The prophet hears one speaking to him

looketh toward the east: and behold, the glory of the God 2
of Israel came from the way of the east: and his voice was
like the sound of many waters: and the earth shined with
his glory. And it was according to the appearance of the 3
vision which I saw, even according to the vision that I saw
when I came to destroy the city; and the visions were like
the vision that I saw by the river Chebar: and I fell upon
my face. And the glory of the LORD came into the house 4
by the way of the gate whose prospect is toward the east.
And the spirit took me up, and brought me into the inner 5
court; and behold, the glory of the LORD filled the house.

from the house and saying that the defilements to which the house had
been exposed through idolatries and the burial of kings near it shall
henceforth cease (*vv.* 6—9). The prophet is commanded to make
known to the people the fashion and ordinances of the house (*vv.* 10—12).

2. *and his voice*] and **the sound of him was like the sound.**
Reference is to the sound made by the cherubim in their flight. Cf.
St John's vision[1] Rev. i. 15, xviii. 1.

3. *And it was according to*] Read: **And the appearance which I
saw was like the appearance which I saw when I came**—the word
"appearance" at the beginning of the verse being omitted in
the Heb.

I came to destroy] Reference is to ch. viii.—xi. and the destruction
of the city there seen in vision by the prophet. He was carried to
Jerusalem to witness the destruction, and he calls this his coming to
destroy it.

and the visions were like the vision] like the **appearance.** The words
"and the visions" are rather unnatural; LXX. reads: "and the vision
of the chariot which I saw was like &c." The "chariot," i.e. the
whole theophany of cherubim and wheels, is often spoken of in later
times (e.g. Ecclus. xlix. 8), but is nowhere named in the Bible
(but cf. 1 Chr. xxviii. 18). The reading of LXX. is probably a gloss
in explanation of the Heb., which is awkward. Possibly the word
"visions" should be omitted:…the city, *and like the appearance that
I saw by the river Chebar.* Cf. iii. 23, where LXX. interpolates
"according to the vision."

4. The glory of the Lord enters the house by the E. gate, by which
He had departed from the old Temple, x. 19, xi. 22, 23.

5. The prophet, who hitherto was at the E. gate outside (*v.* 1), is

[1] [For the influence of Ezekiel upon the writer of the Apocalypse we may also
compare the vision of Ezek. ch. i. with that of Rev. iv., specially the description of
the living creatures; Ezek.'s utterances against Tyre xxvi.—xxviii. with the denunciation of Babylon, Rev. xviii.; Gog and Magog, as represented in Ezek. xxxviii., xxxix.
with Rev. xx. 7—10; the measurement of sacred places, Ezek. xl.—xliii. with Rev.
xi. 1 ff., cf. xxi. 15—17, besides numerous other passages.]

6 And I heard one speaking unto me out of the house; and
7 a man stood by me. And he said unto me, Son of man,
this is the place of my throne, and the place of the soles
of my feet, where I will dwell in the midst of the children
of Israel for ever: and the house of Israel shall no more
defile my holy name, neither they, nor their kings, by their
whoredom, and by the carcases of their kings [1]*in* their high
8 places; in their setting of their threshold by my threshold,
and their door post beside my door post, and there was *but*
the wall between me and them; and they have defiled my

---

[1] Or, according to another reading, *in their death*

---

brought by the spirit into the inner court, from which he perceived the
house to be filled with the glory of the Lord.

6. *and a man*] No doubt the same man is meant as before. The
prophet was transported into the inner court by the spirit, not led as in
other instances by the man, who, however, reappears at his side. The
man is merely the Divine voice and word personified and interposed
between the Lord and the prophet, hence though Ezekiel appears to
hear one speaking from the house, the voice immediately takes the
shape of a man beside him.

7. this is *the place of my throne*] **this is the place of my throne...
for ever**. No change of reading is implied but the emphatic position
of "the place" &c. requires to be expressed by some such word as
"this is," or, "Behold." On "soles of my feet" cf. Is. lx. 13, lxvi. 1;
Lam. ii. 1; Ps. cxxxii. 7; 1 Chr. xxviii. 2.

by their whoredom] Their idolatries, cf. ch. viii.

in *their high places*] Probably, as marg.: **in their death**, i.e. when
dead, Lev. xi. 31, 32. So some MSS., and Targ., by change of one vowel.
The ref. is to the burial of the kings in the vicinity of the temple. The
passages Lev. xxvi. 30; Jer. xvi. 18, to which appeal is made, do not
sustain the idea that "carcase" could be used as a mere name of
opprobrium for idols (Ps. cvi. 28 is of doubtful meaning). In the
former passage the hewn down idol is a carcase just as the slain man is;
and in Jer. xvi. 18 the use of the word "dead body" is not figurative[1].
It is true that there is no record of kings being buried close to the
temple, but their sepulchres were in such vicinity that in comparison
with the new ideal of holiness[2] they could not but be held to bring
defilement to the dwelling-place of Jehovah, the living God. *V.* 9
seems conclusive for this reading.

8. Ref. is to the fact that the royal palace and the first temple stood
virtually within the same enclosure and presented the appearance of one
edifice. See the sketch in W. R. Smith's Art. Temple, *Encyc. Brit.*

---

[1] [This, however, cannot be considered certain.]
[2] [Lofth. points out that, as shewn by 1 Sam. xxv. 1; 1 Kings ii. 34, in older
times dead bodies did not carry the idea of pollution.]

holy name by their abominations which they have committed: wherefore I have consumed them in mine anger.
Now let them put away their whoredom, and the carcases 9
of their kings, far from me, and I will dwell in the midst of
them for ever.

Thou, son of man, shew the house to the house of Israel, 10
that they may be ashamed of their iniquities: and let them
measure the ¹pattern.   And if they be ashamed of all that 11
they have done, make known unto them the form of the
house, and the fashion thereof, and the goings out thereof,
and the comings in thereof, and all the forms thereof, and
all the ordinances thereof, and all the forms thereof, and all
the laws thereof, and write it in their sight: that they may
keep the whole form thereof, and all the ordinances thereof,
and do them.   This is the law of the house: upon the top 12
of the mountain the whole limit thereof round about shall
be most holy.   Behold, this is the law of the house.

¹ Or, *sum*

10—12.   The prophet is commanded to shew to Israel the fashion
and ordinances of the house that they may observe them.

10.   *ashamed of their iniquities*] i.e. in disregarding the ordinances of
the Lord's house, in defiling it (*vv.* 7, 8), and in committing its services
to the hands of uncircumcised aliens (xliv. 7), and the like.

measure the pattern] [marg. *sum*.   For the word see on xxviii. 12.]
LXX. has, "and its appearance and its pattern."   Cf. xlii. 11, where
"measures" and "appearance" were also interchanged.

11.   The verse seems overgrown with amplifications or repetitions.
LXX. omits: "and the comings in thereof and all the forms thereof."
The second "and all the forms thereof" seems an accidental misreading
and consequent duplication of the following "and all the laws thereof."
Cf. xliv. 5, where the "ordinances" and "laws" of the house again
come together.

XLIII. **13—17.**   THE ALTAR OF BURNT-OFFERING IN
THE INNER COURT.

The altar was a large structure, built of stone, and rose in terraces,
contracting by means of two rebatements towards the top.   It consisted:
(1) of a basement [the "bottom" of *vv.* 13, &c.], with a border or
moulding on the top or edge of it.   (2) Two cubits above this basement
in which the altar proper stood, was the first rebatement, a cubit broad,
so that there ran a ledge (R.V. "settle") of a cubit round about the altar
on its four sides (*vv.* 13, 14).   (3) Four cubits above this first rebatement

13   And these are the measures of the altar by cubits: (the
cubit is a cubit and an handbreadth:) the [1]bottom shall
be a cubit, and the breadth a cubit, and the border thereof
by the edge thereof round about a span: and this shall be
14 the [2]base of the altar.   And from the bottom [3]upon the
ground to the lower [4]settle shall be two cubits, and the

[1] Or, *hollow* Heb. *bosom*.   [2] Heb. *back*.   [3] Or, *at*   [4] Or, *ledge*

came the second rebatement, also a cubit broad, so as to form in
like manner a ledge ["settle"] of a cubit round about the altar (v. 14).
(4) Then four cubits upwards from this ledge was the altar area or
platform proper, the "hearth of God," having horns rising up at the
four corners (v. 15).   The area of this altar-hearth was a square of
12 cubits (v. 16).   At the higher rebatement or ledge ("settle") the
area was 14 cubits square (v. 17).   Probably, therefore, at the lower
rebatement the area was 16 cubits square and the basement 18 cubits.
Thus the structure had the appearance of four square blocks, each
narrower in area than the one below it, and each thus appearing set into
the one under it.   Such structures built in stages were common in the
architecture of the East; see examples in Rawlinson, *Phœnicia*,
pp. 166 *seq.*

XLIII. 13.   The basement of the altar.

13.   *the bottom shall be a cubit*] lit. "its bottom a cubit," i.e. in depth
or height, and so in breadth.   [For the cubit as a measure see on xl. 5.]
The bottom, lit. *bosom*, appears to be the basement in which the altar
proper was set; it was a cubit high and extended a cubit in breadth
beyond the first block or stage of the altar proper.   The idea that the
"bosom" means a drain or gutter running round the foot of the altar
to carry away the blood seems without any support.   This basement
extended a cubit all round beyond the lowest stage of the altar proper,
and on the outer edge of this space of a cubit there was a border of a
span [half a cubit], probably, in height.   This border may have been
a moulding, or possibly a very low parapet or close screen, running
round the outer edge of the ledge of one cubit.   Either would suggest
the idea of a bosom in which the altar proper was placed.

   the base of the altar] the **elevation**.   The word is that rendered
"eminent place" xvi. 24, 31, 39 (see notes), and refers to the basement
on which the altar proper stood.   Cf. xli. 8.   LXX. divides the letters
differently and better, reading, *this is the height of the altar*, and
attaching the clause to the following verse.

14.   Two cubits up from the basement the fabric underwent the first
contraction, being let in a cubit.   Thus a ledge [so marg. supported by
Oxf. Lex.] of a cubit broad was formed running all round the altar.
R.V. calls this a "settle," i.e. a bench.   The altar narrowed in dimension

breadth one cubit; and from the lesser settle to the greater
settle shall be four cubits, and the breadth a cubit. And 15
the ¹upper altar shall be four cubits; and from the ²altar
hearth and upward there shall be four horns. And the 16
altar hearth shall be twelve *cubits* long by twelve broad,
square in the four sides thereof. And the settle shall be 17
fourteen *cubits* long by fourteen broad in the four sides
thereof; and the border about it shall be half a cubit;

---

¹ Heb. *Harel.*   ² Heb. *Ariel.* See Is. xxix. 1.

---

not gradually like an obelisk, but at two places. Cf. the similar way
in which the wall of the house retreated, xli. 6.

At a height of four cubits above the first rebatement came another,
of the same breadth of a cubit, so that a second ledge of a cubit broad
was formed round the altar on its four sides.

15. *the upper altar*] lit. the hearth of God (Is. xxix. 1). The word
here is spelt *har'ēl* (mount of God?), and in the next clause *'ări'ēl*
(hearth of God). LXX. spells both alike, and probably they do not
differ. The form *'ări'ēl* is also Moabite (Mesha inscr. ll. 12, 17). From
the second ledge up to the altar-hearth or platform was a distance of
four cubits, and from the altar area rose four horns, one at each corner.
LXX. for "four" reads "a cubit"—as the height of the horns.

16. The preceding measurements have referred to height. Those
referring to breadth or area are now given. The altar-hearth or platform was 12 cubits square.

17. The "settle" referred to here is the higher or greater one (*v.* 14).
Its area was a square of 14 cubits. The verse appears to say that this
uppermost ledge had a border and an "enclosure" or setting just as the
basement had. If so, the "setting" or bosom was that for the Harel
arising out of the block, and its size, a cubit, is simply the ledge itself.
There is no ground at least to suppose that the "border" and setting
refer to the altar-hearth—from which the measurer has descended and
come down at any rate as far as the uppermost ledge. It may be made
a question whether in the last half of *v.* 17 he has not descended to the
foot of the edifice, and whether the "border" and "bosom" be not those
already referred to in connexion with the basement (*v.* 13). For (1) the
measurements are the same—a span (*v.* 13) being equivalent to half a
cubit (*v.* 17). (2) Immediately after mention of the "border" and bosom
or setting the "steps" are referred to by which the altar as a whole was
ascended, which seems to imply that the speaker conceived himself
upon the ground (*v.* 17). (3) Further in *v.* 20 blood is to be put upon
the horns of the altar-hearth, upon the four corners of the upper ledge
(settle), and upon the "border" round about; and it is certainly natural
that the blood should be put on all the stages of the altar, the top, the
middle, and the basement.

and the bottom thereof shall be a cubit about; and the
steps thereof shall look toward the east.

18   And he said unto me, Son of man, thus saith the Lord
God : These are the ordinances of the altar in the day
when they shall make it, to offer burnt offerings thereon,
19 and to sprinkle blood thereon.   Thou shalt give to the
priests the Levites that be of the seed of Zadok, which are
near unto me, to minister unto me, saith the Lord God,
20 a young bullock for a sin offering.   And thou shalt take of
the blood thereof, and put it on the four horns of it, and on
the four corners of the settle, and upon the border round
about : thus shalt thou cleanse it and make atonement for

For "bottom" read **basement**. The whole height of the altar was
probably 12 cubits and the basement a square of 18. Thus height of
basement 1 (*v.* 13) + 2 (lowest block) + 4 (higher block) + 4 (block of
altar-hearth) + 1 (horn) = 12. On breadth see preliminary remark to
vv. 13—17.

XLIII. 18—27. SACRIFICES AND CEREMONIES BY WHICH THE ALTAR WAS CONSECRATED AND INAUGURATED.

The general purpose of the altar is to offer burnt-offerings upon and
to sprinkle blood thereon. The statement in *vv.* 19, 20 is somewhat
elliptical, the writer's object being to advert specially to the difference
between the sin-offering on the first day and that on the following days.
Hence he describes the ritual of the sin-offering on the first day fully,
omitting to refer to the burnt-offering, which he mentions only in connexion with the second and following days. And when in *v.* 25 it is
said that a goat for sin-offering and a young bullock and a ram were
offered for seven days, the difference between the sin-offering on the
first day (a bullock) and that for the following six days (a goat) is not
adverted to, the burnt-offering being the same all the seven days.

18.   The general purpose of the altar. The burnt-offering was wholly
consumed on the altar, of the other offerings only the fat.

19.   *the priests the Levites*]   [A Deuteronomic expression (Deut.
xvii. 9, xviii. 1 ; cf. xxi. 5, xxiv. 8, xxvii. 9) found elsewhere in Ezek.
only in xliv. 15.]

Zadok] [who displaced Abiathar, when the latter was involved in the
rebellion of Adonijah (1 Kings i. 7).   Zadok anointed Solomon (*v.* 45)
and so is naturally named here in the restoration of the ideal "David."
See further on xliv. 15.]

The phrase "saith the Lord Jehovah" adds solemnity to the statement
that only the sons of Zadok shall minister at the altar (xliv. 15 *seq.*).
[The sin-offering now for the first time comes into prominence.]

20.   Blood was to be put on the four horns of the altar-hearth, on

it. Thou shalt also take the bullock of the sin offering, 21
and he shall burn it in the appointed place of the house,
without the sanctuary. And on the second day thou shalt 22
offer a he-goat without blemish for a sin offering; and they
shall cleanse the altar, as they did cleanse it with the
bullock. When thou hast made an end of cleansing it, 23
thou shalt offer a young bullock without blemish, and a
ram out of the flock without blemish. And thou shalt 24
bring them near before the LORD, and the priests shall cast
salt upon them, and they shall offer them up for a burnt
offering unto the LORD. Seven days shalt thou prepare 25
every day a goat for a sin offering: they shall also prepare
a young bullock, and a ram out of the flock, without
blemish. Seven days shall they make atonement for the 26
altar and purify it; so shall they ¹consecrate it. And when 27

¹ Heb. *fill the hands thereof*. See Ex. xxix. 24.

the four corners of the (upper) settle, and on the border; see on *v.* 17.
To "cleanse" is to purify from sin, to "un-sin," if such a word could
be formed.

21. The sin-offering was burnt wholly in a place outside the whole
temple area, i.e. outside the space enclosed by the 500 cubits square
wall (xlii. 16 *seq.*), possibly in the space of 50 cubits (xlv. 2) lying
round the outer wall. Cf. Ex. xxix. 14; Lev. iv. 11, vi. 23, xvi. 27;
Heb. xiii. 11.

he] [rather *one* indefinitely].

22. On "cleanse" cf. *v.* 20. The ceremonies with the blood and
the burning outside were no doubt the same as those on the first day,
vv. 20, 21.

23. The burnt-offering, following the sin-offering, was a young
bullock and a ram.

24. The burnt-offering was wholly consumed on the altar, salt being
sprinkled on the flesh. [In connexion with sacrifices according to the
Priestly Code salt was used only to season meal-offerings, Lev. ii. 13.]

25. The statement is somewhat general; strictly the he-goat was
offered only on six days (*v.* 19), but the burnt-offering was the same
on all the seven.

26. The ceremonial of consecrating the altar lasts seven days.

consecrate it] i.e. the altar, lit. fill its hand (or, hands). The
phrase is properly said of the priests, to install; here of the altar,
to inaugurate it. Originally the expression had probably a literal
meaning, to put the things to be offered into the hands of the priests
(Lev. viii. 25 *seq.*), but later it came to be used generally in the sense

they have accomplished the days, it shall be that upon the eighth day, and forward, the priests shall make your burnt offerings upon the altar, and your peace offerings ; and I will accept you, saith the Lord GOD.

44   Then he brought me back the way of the outer gate of the sanctuary, which looketh toward the east ; and it 2 was shut.   And the LORD said unto me, This gate shall be shut, it shall not be opened, neither shall any man enter in by it, for the LORD, the God of Israel, hath entered in by

---

of initiate, consecrate (Ex. xxviii. 41, xxix. 9, 29, 33, 35 ; Lev. vii. 37 ; Numb. iii. 3 ; Judg. xvii. 5, 12), cf. Ex. xxxii. 29. Wellh. *Hist.* p. 152, argues that the priest's hand was originally "filled" with money (Jud. xvii.).   The phrase "fill the hand" of one appears also in the general meaning "to invest with office" in Assyrian ; Frd. Del. *Heb. Lang.* p. 20 ; *Prolegomena*, p. 48.

In all the above passage it is the altar that is consecrated, not the priests.   The consecration of the altar appears to carry with it that of the whole sanctuary.   The altar needs atonement not because it is a work of human hands, but because it belongs to the things of the world. The sin of the world has defiled all things, penetrating even to the precincts of the place where Jehovah abides as He is in Himself (Heb. ix. 23).   The passage can scarcely be compared with Ex. xxix. and Lev. viii. because there the ceremonies refer to the consecration of the priests chiefly and little to the altar.   Cf. Ex. xxix. 36 ; Lev. viii. 11, 15, 33.   In these passages the altar is said to have been anointed with oil, a ceremony wanting in Ezek. ; the sin-offering was a young bullock *each* day and the burnt-offering simply a ram each day.

XLIV.—XLVI.   ORDINANCES REGARDING THE TEMPLE.

These ordinances define who shall minister in it, priests and Levites (ch. xliv.) ; the revenue of the priests, the Levites, and the prince, with the duties devolving on the prince in upholding the ritual (xlv. 1—17); the special and daily services in the temple, and the special offerings of the prince (xlv. 18—xlvi.).

XLIV.   THOSE WHO SHALL MINISTER IN THE TEMPLE.

The passage contains these parts :
(1) *vv.* 1—3.   An ordinance regarding the eastern gate : it shall be kept shut because by it the Lord entered into the house.
(2) *vv.* 4—14.   Precepts regarding the subordinate ministrants, who keep the gates of the house and perform such offices as slaughtering the victims.   These subordinate services shall no more be performed, as they have been to the desecration of them, by uncircumcised

it; therefore it shall be shut. As for the prince, he shall 3
sit therein as prince to eat bread before the LORD; he shall
enter by the way of the porch of the gate, and shall go out
by the way of the same. Then he brought me the way of 4
the north gate before the house; and I looked, and behold,
the glory of the LORD filled the house of the LORD: and
I fell upon my face. And the LORD said unto me, Son of 5
man, ¹mark well, and behold with thine eyes, and hear with
thine ears all that I say unto thee concerning all the ordinances of the house of the LORD, and all the laws thereof;

¹ Heb. *set thine heart upon.*

foreigners (*vv.* 4—9). But the Levites, who ministered as priests at
the high-places when Israel went astray from Jehovah, shall perform
such services. For their former sin they shall bear their iniquity and
be excluded from the holy functions of the priesthood proper, though
permitted to take part in the service of the house in a subordinate
place (*vv.* 10—14).

(3) *vv.* 15—31. Precepts regarding the priests (i.e. those who
minister at the altar), e.g. that they shall be the sons of Zadok alone
(*vv.* 15, 16); regarding their garments in their ministrations (*vv.* 17 *seq.*);
their marriage (*v.* 22); their functions as teachers of the people and
judges (*vv.* 23, 24); their preservation from defilement by contact with
the dead (*vv.* 25—27), and their maintenance (*vv.* 28 *seq.*).

1—3. The prophet is brought to the outside of the outer gate,
which he observes to be shut. It must be kept shut because the glory
of the Lord entered by it into the house. None shall enter by it.

3. The only exception is in favour of the prince. He shall "eat
bread before Jehovah" in this gate, i.e. partake of the sacrificial meal
there. Though not expressly stated it is implied that the meal shall be
partaken of in the porch of the gate, which looked into the outer court
(see xl. 8). The statements in ch. xlvi. make it probable that even the
prince did not enter through the E. gate from the outside, but passed
into the outer court through some other gate, and entered the porch
from the court.

to eat bread] [i.e. to partake of the sacrificial meal. Cf. Jethro in
Exod. xviii. 12.]

4—9. The former practice of employing uncircumcised foreigners to
minister and to keep the charge of the house shall absolutely cease.

4. The prophet is brought by way of the N. gate into the inner
court before the house. From his position in front of the house he
beholds the glory of the Lord filling the house, and falls on his face.

5. He is commanded to give heed to all the ordinances and laws
regulating the future service of the house.

and ¹ mark well the entering in of the house, with every
6 going forth of the sanctuary. And thou shalt say to the
rebellious, even to the house of Israel, Thus saith the Lord
GOD : O ye house of Israel, let it suffice you of all your
7 abominations, in that ye have brought in aliens, uncircumcised in heart and uncircumcised in flesh, to be in my
sanctuary, to profane it, even my house, when ye offer my
bread, the fat and the blood, and ²they have broken my
8 covenant, ³*to add* unto all your abominations. And ye
have not kept the charge of mine holy things : but ye have
set keepers of my charge in my sanctuary for yourselves.

¹ Heb. *set thine heart upon.*   ² Most ancient versions have, *ye.*
³ Or, *in all*

entering in of the house] The phrase to the end of the verse is a
general designation for all the functions of the house, those who shall be
permitted to enter it (*vv.* 10—14), with the manner of their going in
and coming out (*vv.* 17—21).

6. The "rebellious," lit. rebellion, a term frequently used in ch.
i.—xxiv. (e.g. ii. 5, iii. 9, xii. 2, xvii. 12, xxiv. 3), but dropped since
the fall of the city. Recollection of the former abominations practised
in the sanctuary again brings it to the prophet's lips.

7. *aliens*] i.e. foreigners. What is reprobated is not of course
allowing foreigners to present sacrifices to Jehovah, which they might
do (Lev. xvii. 10, 12 ; Numb. xv. 14), but allowing them to *officiate* in
the offering, and in general in the ministry of the sanctuary. It is not
ascertainable to what extent these uncircumcised heathen were permitted
to fill the subordinate offices about the temple, such as those of keepers
of the gates and assistants to the priests, but just as the kings employed
foreign mercenaries as guards (who were employed even in the temple,
2 Kgs xi. 7), it appears that persons not Israelites and not incorporated in Israel by the necessary rites, were employed in the temple.
They were probably captives taken in war and the like (Josh. ix. 27 ;
1 Sam. ii. 13 ; Zech. xiv. 21 ; cf. Ezr. viii. 20, ii. 58). This is regarded
by the prophet as a profanation of the temple and an infraction of the
covenant between Jehovah and Israel. It is the latter from the nature
of the case. Israel was the people of the Lord and His service must
be performed by Israel. These heathen were uncircumcised both in
flesh and heart, their service was purely mercenary, and without
religious reality. For "and they have broken" read with LXX. "and
ye have broken."

the fat and the blood] [the portions of the peace-offering which were
given to the Lord, the rest being eaten.]

8. *ye have set keepers*] Read : ye have *set them* as keepers, [and

Thus saith the Lord GOD, No alien, uncircumcised in heart 9
and uncircumcised in flesh, shall enter into my sanctuary,
of any alien that is among the children of Israel. But the 10
Levites that went far from me, when Israel went astray,
which went astray from me after their idols; they shall
bear their iniquity. Yet they shall be ministers in my 11
sanctuary, having oversight at the gates of the house, and
ministering in the house : they shall slay the burnt offering
and the sacrifice for the people, and they shall stand before
them to minister unto them. Because they ministered 12
unto them before their idols, and became a stumblingblock
of iniquity unto the house of Israel; therefore have I lifted
up mine hand against them, saith the Lord GOD, and they
shall bear their iniquity. And they shall not come near 13
unto me, to execute the office of priest unto me, nor to
come near to any of my holy things, unto the things that
are most holy : but they shall bear their shame, and their
abominations which they have committed. Yet will I make 14

instead of "for yourselves" read *therefore* at the beginning of *v.* 9.
Cf. the LXX. See Zech. xiv. 21].

9—14. Such services shall not be performed by foreigners any
more, but by the Levites who formerly ministered at the high-places.
Because of their sin in leading the house of Israel astray they shall bear
their iniquity and be excluded from the priesthood.

10. *which went astray*] Most naturally refers to Israel, cf. *v.* 15 ;
though it might refer to the Levites, cf. xlviii. 11. To "bear iniquity"
is to bear the penalty of it, ch. iv. 4. On "idols," ch. vi. 4.

11. *Yet they shall be ministers*] Rather, **And** *they* &c. The clause
explains how these Levites shall bear their iniquity—they shall be de-
graded from the priestly office and reduced to the place of subordinate
servants.

The verse is closely connected with *v.* 10. The services which
the Levites shall be allowed to perform are such as having charge
of the gates, slaying the burnt-offering and the peace-offering for the
people and in general ministering to them, e.g. cooking the sacrificial
flesh for their meals (xlvi. 24). To "stand before" is to serve,
Numb. xvi. 9.

12. Cf. ch. vii. 19, xiv. 3, 4, xviii. 30. On "idols," see *v.* 10.
lifted up mine hand] i.e. sworn, ch. xx. 5.

13. *V.* 13 is closely connected with *v.* 12 ..."bear their iniquity, and
they shall not come near unto me."

14. *Yet will I make*] **And** I will make. The prophet, as was
natural to him, takes a severe view of the conduct of the priests of the

them keepers of the charge of the house, for all the service thereof, and for all that shall be done therein.

15 But the priests the Levites, the sons of Zadok, that kept the charge of my sanctuary when the children of Israel went astray from me, they shall come near to me to minister unto me; and they shall stand before me to offer unto me 16 the fat and the blood, saith the Lord GOD: they shall enter into my sanctuary, and they shall come near to my table, to 17 minister unto me, and they shall keep my charge. And it shall be that when they enter in at the gates of the inner court, they shall be clothed with linen garments; and no wool shall come upon them, whiles they minister in the 18 gates of the inner court, and ¹within. They shall have linen tires upon their heads, and shall have linen breeches upon their loins; they shall not gird themselves with *any*

¹ Or, *in the house*

high-places, laying much of the blame of Israel's defection upon them (*v.* 12).

15, 16. The priests of the family of Zadok alone shall be priests in the new Temple. These continued faithful to Jehovah when the provincial priests went far from Him. The judgement of the prophet may be to some extent a comparative one. The worship at Jerusalem never sank to the level of the licentiousness and corruption prevailing at the rural sanctuaries, though undoubtedly the record of the reform of Josiah reveals great corruptions at Jerusalem also (2 Kgs xxiii.). How far these were introduced by the kings, such as Manasseh, despite the opposition of the priests, cannot be ascertained. The reforms of Hezekiah most probably, and certainly those of Josiah, were promoted by the priests (2 Kgs xxii.). For Zadok see on xliii. 19. Since remote times the Zadokites had served in the temple, and upon the whole the prophet's favourable judgement of them is no doubt justified (cf. 2 Kgs xi.; Is. viii. 2).

16. *my table*] The altar of burnt-offering is no doubt meant, cf. on xl. 46, xli. 22.

17—19. The garments of the priests.—In the service of the sanctuary they shall wear only linen clothing, drawers and head-dresses. In Ex. xxviii. 39, 42, xxxix. 27; Lev. xvi. 4, the coats and bonnets of the priests are byssus (possibly cotton)¹.

17. *no wool*] [Perhaps referring to the legislation against wearing garments of mixed stuffs (Lev. xix. 19; Deut. xxii. 11), or to avoid sweat, *v.* 18 *b*.]

¹ [Rather, fine linen.]

thing that causeth sweat. And when they go forth into the 19
outer court, even into the outer court to the people, they
shall put off their garments wherein they minister, and lay
them in the holy chambers, and they shall put on other
garments, that they sanctify not the people with their
garments. Neither shall they shave their heads, nor suffer 20
their locks to grow long; they shall only poll their heads.
Neither shall any priest drink wine, when they enter into 21
the inner court. Neither shall they take for their wives 22
a widow, nor her that is put away : but they shall take

18. Sweat is regarded as uncleanness.

19. The sacred garments shall be worn only in the inner court, and
in ministration. Before going out into the outer court the priests shall
put them off and deposit them in the sacred cells, xlii. 13, 14.

that they sanctify not the people] i.e. by bringing that which is holy
in contact with them [and thus making them unintentionally to be in a
special manner dedicated to God]. The enactment is not a precaution
against defilement of the holy garments, at least in form, though it may
be a precaution against confusion of the sacred and the common. Cf.
xlvi. 20; Ex. xxix. 37, xxx. 29; Lev. vi. 27 [1]. The words "even
into the outer court" are probably an accidental repetition. LXX.
omits.

20. The priests shall poll or cut the hair of their heads, and neither
shave their heads bald nor let the hair flow loose. Shaving the head
bald was a sign of mourning (Lev. xxi. 5, 10, cf. Ezek. xxiv. 17), and
forbidden both to priests and people as a practice of the heathen (Deut.
xiv. 1) ; though the prophets frequently refer to it as a token of disaster
and mourning (Is. iii. 24, xxii. 12 ; Jer. xvi. 6; Am. viii. 10; Mic. i.
16). Lev. x. 6 indicates that letting the hair flow loose and dishevelled
was also a sign of grief. The phrase appears used both of this practice
and of the Nazirite custom of allowing the hair to remain uncut (Numb.
vi. 5, cf. Numb. v. 18). [The belief that the hair was specially fitted
to mark union with the Divine Being seems to have arisen from its
continuing to grow as long as life lasts. See Rob. Smith, *op. cit.*
pp. 323 *seq.*, 481 *seq.*]

21. On this prohibition cf. the narrative Lev. x. 1—9.

22. The marriage of the priests. They shall marry only virgins, or
the widows of former priests. In Lev. xxi. 14 marrying a widow of
any kind is forbidden to the high-priest, but no restriction is imposed
on the priests (*v.* 7). Ezek. makes no allusion anywhere to a high-
priest. [The restriction imposed in this verse is one of the instances
of apparent discrepancies between Ezekiel and the Law adduced

---

[1] [For instances of this "contagiousness of holiness" among other nations see
Rob. Smith, *Religion of the Semites*, p. 451, ed. 1907.]

virgins of the seed of the house of Israel, or a widow that is
23 the widow of a priest.   And they shall teach my people
the difference between the holy and the common, and cause
24 them to discern between the unclean and the clean.   And
in a controversy they shall stand to judge; according to my
judgements shall they judge it: and they shall keep my
laws and my statutes in all my appointed feasts; and they
25 shall hallow my sabbaths.   And they shall come at no dead
person to defile themselves: but for father, or for mother,
or for son, or for daughter, for brother, or for sister that
26 hath had no husband, they may defile themselves.   And
after he is cleansed, they shall reckon unto him seven days.

by the Jewish writer Rashi in his commentary on the Talmudic
treatise *Chagigah* (13 *a* Tal. Bab.).   See on Lev. xxi. 14 in this
Series.]

23, 24.   General duties of the priests towards the people.   They
shall teach the people to distinguish between the holy and the common,
between the clean and the unclean, cf. xxii. 26; Lev. x. 10; Hag. ii.
11; Mal. ii. 7.

24.   They shall also act as judges in causes that arise among the
people.   It is not certain that Ezek. commits the office of judge to the
priests exclusively, cf. xlv. 9.   In Deut. xvii. 8 *seq*., xix. 17, xxi. 5, the
priests sit in difficult cases along with the judges who shall be in those
days (cf. Deut. xxi. 19, xxii. 15; Ex. xviii. 21, 22; 2 Chr. xix. 8—10).
In Ezekiel's final state of the kingdom of the Lord, however, only cases
of misunderstanding, not of wrong, would arise.   Finally it is the duty
of the priests to see that the laws and statutes of the Lord be observed
at all the appointed feasts, or sacred occasions (xlv. 17 *seq*.), and that
the sabbath be sanctified, cf. xxii. 26.

25—27.   Regulations for their necessary contact with the dead.
They shall approach the dead bodies only of their nearest relatives,
father, mother, son, daughter, brother, and unmarried sister.   From
the defilement caused by this contact they must purify themselves
before resuming their service in the inner court.   It is curious that no
reference is made to the priest's wife among the relatives with whose
dead bodies they may defile themselves.   The same omission occurs
Lev. xxi. 1—3.   In Ezek. xxiv. 15 *seq*. it is understood that he would
naturally shew tokens of mourning for his wife.   The two things, however, are not identical, and Ezek. was not an acting priest.   According to
Lev. xxi. 11 the high-priest was not to defile himself by going near any
dead body whatever.   How defilement was contracted is explained
Numb. xix. 14.

26.   *after he is cleansed*] i.e. the priest.   The length of time during
which he shall remain unclean is not stated.   In ordinary cases he who

And in the day that he goeth into the sanctuary, into the 27
inner court, to minister in the sanctuary, he shall offer his
sin offering, saith the Lord GOD. And they shall have an 28
inheritance; I am their inheritance: and ye shall give
them no possession in Israel; I am their possession. They 29
shall eat the meal offering, and the sin offering, and the
guilt offering; and every devoted thing in Israel shall be
theirs. And the first of all the firstfruits of every thing, 30
and every ¹oblation of every thing, of all your oblations,
shall be for the priests: ye shall also give unto the priest

¹ Or, *heave offering*

touched a dead body was unclean seven days (Numb. xix. 11). After
his cleansing the priest must count seven days, which would imply
exclusion from his official duties for 14 days.

27. Before resuming his functions the priest presents a sin-offering.

28—31. The maintenance of the priest. He shall have no inheritance among the people: the Lord is his inheritance. [Redp. compares
our word clergy, derived from *clerus*, κλῆρος, allotment.] He shall eat
the meal-offering, the sin- and guilt-offerings; everything put to the
ban shall be his, and the best of all the firstfruits and of all the dues.

28. *they shall have an inheritance*] The clause cannot (as in A.V.) refer
to the sin-offering (*v.* 27), which was burnt entire outside the sanctuary.
To translate: *This shall be their inheritance* (viz.) *I am their inheritance,* making the words "I am" &c. subject, is too artificial. The
balance of sentence seems to require, *they shall have no inheritance;
I am* &c., corresponding to the second half of the verse. So Vulg.
[followed by Cor., Ber, Toy, Kr. and others], cf. Numb. xviii. 20;
Deut. x. 9, xviii. 1, 2; Josh. xiii. 14, &c.

29. Cf. Lev. ii. 3, vii. 9—11, for the meal-offering; Lev. vi. 18, vii.
6, 7; Numb. xviii. 9, 10, for the sin- and guilt-offerings; and for that
which was put to the ban or "devoted" to Jehovah, Lev. xxvii. 28;
Numb. xviii. 14.

They] The pronoun is emphatic, as though the point had hitherto
been doubtful.

devoted] [lit. set apart. See Exod. xxii. 20 for examples of its
application, and for the different species of separation *HDB.* Art.
Ban.]

30. *And the first*] Or, *the best.* Cf. Ex. xxiii. 19, xxxiv. 26;
Deut. xviii. 4. [Numb. xviii. 13 extends the permission to others than
priests.]

and every oblation] Or, as marg., *heave offering.* [Rather, contribution. See Driver, *Exod.* p. 263.] Numb. xv. 19, xviii. 19. It means
a part taken from a larger whole, cf. xlv. 1, &c., where the portion of
land dedicated to the use of the priests and Levites is so called.

the first of your [1]dough, to cause a blessing to rest on thine
31 house.	The priests shall not eat of any thing that dieth of
itself, or is torn, whether it be fowl or beast.

45	Moreover, when ye shall divide by lot the land for

[1] Or, *coarse meal*

of your dough]	The term occurs again only Numb. xv. 20, 21 ; Neh.
x. 37, and is of doubtful meaning. LXX., *dough* ; Targ., Syr., *baking
trough* ; others, *coarse meal*. On the "blessing," Mal. iii. 10 ; Prov.
iii. 9, 10.

31.	On this prohibition Ex. xxii. 31 ; Lev. xxii. 8. Cf. Lev. xvii. 15.
The injunctions in *v.* 30 are very general. The prophet presupposes
former customs familiar to the people, which he desires to continue.
Everywhere in these chapters his directions are in the main a reproduc-
tion of a past customary and understood practice.

XLV. **1—17.** THE PORTIONS OF LAND ASSIGNED FOR MAINTENANCE
TO THE PRIESTS, LEVITES, AND PRINCE RESPECTIVELY ; WITH
THE DUES WHICH THE PEOPLE SHALL PAY THE PRINCE, IN
RETURN FOR WHICH HE SHALL PROVIDE MATERIALS FOR
THE RITUAL.

(1) *vv.* 1—8. The oblation (*terumah*) of land for maintenance of
priests, Levites, and prince, and for the city.
(2) *vv.* 9—12. Regulations as to just standards of weight, measure,
and coinage.
(3) *vv.* 13—17. Dues to be paid the prince in respect of his being at
the charge of providing the materials of ritual.
In the centre of the country a portion of land shall be measured off
25,000 long and 20,000 broad. The measure is no doubt cubits, not
reeds, though this is stated only in regard to the free space around the
sanctuary (*v.* 2). Length is the measure E. to W., and breadth that
from N. to S. This region is to be divided into two parallel strips
E. to W., one of 25,000 long and 10,000 broad, which shall be for the
priests (*v.* 4), and another N. of this, of the same length and breadth,
which shall be for the Levites (*v.* 5). Parallel to this on the S. side of
the priests' domain, of the same length (25,000) with it and 5000 broad,
there shall be a portion of land for the possession of the city. In the
midst of it the city shall be situated (*v.* 6). These three portions thus
form a square of 25,000 [each side of which will measure about 8½ miles].
Finally the land from the E. side of this square to Jordan, and from
the W. side of it to the sea shall be for a possession to the prince
(*vv.* 7, 8).

1.	*divide by lot*] So the phrase originally signified, but probably it
came to mean merely "divide" or assign portions to. Ezek. definitely
fixes the position of the tribes, and each tribe appears to have the same
extent of territory assigned to it.

inheritance, ye shall offer an oblation unto the LORD,
[1]an holy portion of the land: the length shall be the
length of five and twenty thousand *reeds*, and the breadth
shall be [2]ten thousand: it shall be holy in all the border
thereof round about. Of this there shall be for the holy 2
place five hundred *in length* by five hundred *in breadth*,
square round about; and fifty cubits for the [3]suburbs
thereof round about. And of this measure shalt thou 3
measure, a length of five and twenty thousand, and a
breadth of ten thousand: and in it shall be the sanctuary,
which is most holy. It is an holy portion of the land; 4
it shall be for the priests, the ministers of the sanctuary,
which come near to minister unto the LORD; and it shall
be a place for their houses, and an holy place for the
sanctuary. And five and twenty thousand in length, and 5

---

[1] Heb. *holiness*.   [2] The Sept. has, *twenty*.
[3] Or, *open space*

offer an oblation] Cf. xliv. 30, note.
holy portion of the land] i.e. *out of*, or *from* the land.
breadth...ten thousand] Grammar as well as context require **twenty
thousand**, cf. *vv.* 3, 5, xlviii. 10, 18. In *v.* 3 this "measure" is
divided into two portions each 10,000 broad. So LXX. For "reeds,"
no doubt, **cubits**.

2.   In this sacred territory, more particularly in the half of it assigned
to the priests (*vv.* 3, 4), shall the sanctuary be situated, a square of 500,
surrounded by a free space of 50 cubits on all sides. The 500 are certainly cubits, cf. xlii. 20.

the suburbs thereof] What the "suburbs" are appears from Numb.
xxxv. 4; viz. an open space around the walls of an enclosure, a city,
or building, held to belong to the building or city, but not occupied
by it. It is the liberties of a city or the precincts of an edifice, xlviii.
15, 17.

3.   The portion of the sacred land assigned to the priests shall
consist of a tract 25,000 long by 10,000 broad.

the sanctuary, which is most holy] **sanctuary**, (even) **the most holy
thing**.   The area of land is holy, the sanctuary most holy.

4.   *an holy place for the sanctuary*] lit. *a sanctuary for the sanctuary*.
The use of "sanctuary" in the sense of sacred territory can hardly be
supported by evidence, though the idea of a sacred territory around
a sacred house or locality is a common one in the East. LXX.
reads: "a place for houses set apart for their sanctity" [adopted
by Cor., Toy, and Kr.], i.e. possibly: houses set apart for them

ten thousand in breadth, shall be unto the Levites, the
ministers of the house, for a possession unto themselves,
6 *for* [1] twenty chambers. And ye shall appoint the possession
of the city five thousand broad, and five and twenty
thousand long, side by side with the oblation of the holy
7 portion : it shall be for the whole house of Israel. And
whatsoever is for the prince *shall be* on the one side and on
the other side of the holy oblation and of the possession of
the city, in front of the holy oblation and in front of the
possession of the city, on the west side westward, and on
the east side eastward : and in length answerable unto one
of the portions, from the west border unto the east border.
8 [2] In the land it shall be to him for a possession in Israel :
and my princes shall no more oppress my people ; but they

---

[1] The Sept. has, *cities to dwell in.*   [2] Or, *As touching*

(the priests), they being holy. No satisfactory emendation has been
proposed.

5.   for *twenty chambers*] Probably, as marg., with LXX.: **for cities
to dwell in.**   Cf. the same words Numb. xxxv. 2 ; Josh. xiv. 4.   In *v.* 6
Jerusalem, with its suburbs, is assigned a tract of land only half as
much as that given to the Levites.

6.   The city possesses a strip of land 5000 cubits broad and 25,000
long, running parallel to the portion of the priests, cf. xlviii. 15.   The
city shall stand in the midst of this tract, which it entirely covers N. to
S., cf. xlviii. 16, 17.

7.   The domain of the prince.   A portion of land shall fall to the
prince equal in breadth (N. to S.) to the whole square assigned to the
priests, Levites, and city (viz. 25,000), and extending on both sides of
this square to the borders of the country, to the Jordan on the E., and
the sea on the W.   The "portions" here are the tracts of land
assigned to the tribes respectively (ch. xlviii.).   These stretched across
the country from the Jordan to the sea.   The portion of the prince in
like manner stretches across the whole country, only it is interrupted in
the middle by the 25,000 square tract assigned to priests, Levites, and city.
Cf. xlviii. 21.

8.   *In the land*] lit. in respect of the land.   Others: *for a domain* it
shall be..., for a possession.   The article must then be omitted, and the
use of "land" in this sense is unnatural.

my princes] The language *my* is unusual.   In *v.* 9, "princes of Israel,"
and so LXX. here.   It is possible that Israel was represented in Heb.
MSS. merely by the initial letter, which is the same as the last letter of
"princes" (in the 'construct state'), and that one of the letters fell out.
On the oppressions of the princes, cf. xxii. 25, xxxiv. ; Jer. xxii. 17.

shall give the land to the house of Israel according to their tribes.

Thus saith the Lord GOD : Let it suffice you, O princes 9 of Israel : remove violence and spoil, and execute judgement and justice; take away your ¹exactions from my people, saith the Lord GOD. Ye shall have just balances, and a 10 just ephah, and a just bath. The ephah and the bath shall 11 be of one measure, that the bath may contain the tenth part of an homer, and the ephah the tenth part of an homer : the measure thereof shall be after the homer. And the 12 shekel shall be twenty gerahs : twenty shekels, five and twenty shekels, fifteen shekels, shall be your maneh. This 13

¹ Heb. *expulsions.*

9—17. The dues to be given the prince, and his obligations to provide the materials for the ritual.

9 *seq.* The former unjust and irregular exactions of the princes shall cease. These exactions had not only been oppressive in their nature, but unjust and arbitrary from want of a fixed standard in weights, measures, and currency.

9. *take away your exactions*] lit. *remove your expulsions* (so marg.) from my people. The reference is probably to unjust extrusion of persons from their possessions, of which the early prophets often complain, Is. v. 8; Mic. ii. 9, iii. 2, 3, and the story of Naboth, 1 Kgs xxi. [Cf. 1 Sam. viii. 1, &c.]

10. Cf. Lev. xix. 35, 36 ; Deut. xxv. 13—15 ; Mic. vi. 10, 11 (the accursed scanty ephah) ; Prov. xi. 1, xvi. 11, xx. 10. From this it appears that the words of Am. viii. 5, "making the ephah small and the shekel great and dealing falsely with balances of deceit," are more than a figure.

11. The homer is assumed as the standard both for liquid and dry measures. [It was equivalent approximately to 11 bushels or to 90 gallons.] The ephah was a tenth of the homer, dry measure ; and the bath a tenth of the homer, liquid measure, Is. v. 10.

12. Cf. Ex. xxx. 13 ; Lev. xxvii. 25 ; Numb. iii. 47, xviii. 16. The verse at present is without meaning. The text is grammatically suspicious, and the way in which " fifteen " is supposed to be expressed, viz. " ten and five," is without parallel. Read after LXX. (cod. Alex.) : **And the shekel shall be twenty gerahs ; five** (shekels) **shall be five, and ten shekels ten, and fifty shekels shall be your maneh** (mina). The statement that " five shekels shall be five," &c., does not imply that there were five and ten shekel pieces, but means that just weighing of money shall prevail, and five go for five, no more and no less. The

is the oblation that ye shall offer; the sixth part of an ephah from an homer of wheat, and ye shall give the sixth 14 part of an ephah from an homer of barley: and the set portion of oil, of the bath of oil, shall be the tenth part of a bath out of the cor, *which is* ten baths, even an homer; 15 for ten baths are an homer: and one lamb of the flock, out of two hundred, from the [1]fat pastures of Israel; for a meal offering, and for a burnt offering, and for peace offerings, 16 to make atonement for them, saith the Lord God. All the people of the land [2]shall give unto this oblation for the 17 prince in Israel. And it shall be the prince's part to give the burnt offerings, and the meal offerings, and the drink offerings, in the feasts, and in the new moons, and in the sabbaths, in all the appointed feasts of the house of Israel:

[1] Heb. *well watered.*   [2] Heb. *shall be for.*

passage has been fully discussed by Bertheau (*Zur Gesch. der Israeliten*, pp. 8—14), whose table of money weights may be given (p. 14):

Talent	1				
Maneh	60	1			
Shekel	3,000	50	1		
Beka	6,000	100	2	1	
Gera	60,000	1000	20	10	1

Cf. Ex. xxxviii. 25; Lev. xxvii. 3, 16; Josh. vii. 21; 1 Kgs x. 17; Ezr. ii. 69; Neh. vii. 71[1].

13. *oblation...offer*] The people are addressed. The due which they shall pay the prince is one-sixtieth in grain.

14. The cor was another name for the homer, 1 Kgs iv. 22 [Heb. v. 2], v. 11 [Heb. v. 25]; 2 Chr. ii. 10 [Heb. 9], xxvii. 5.

ten...homer] The words are wanting in LXX. The due in oil was one-hundredth part.

15. The due out of the flock was one in two hundred.

from the fat pastures] lit. *the watered* land of Israel (Gen. xiii. 10). LXX. reads, *out of all the families* of Israel [and so Cor., Ber., Toy, Kr.]. These dues from the flock and from the soil were for purposes of sacrifice and offering (*v.* 17).

16. The words "All the people of the land" are anomalous grammatically; LXX. omits "of the land."

17. In return for these dues paid him by the people the prince shall be charged with providing the sacrifices for public worship.

[1] [A. R. S. Kennedy, *Lev.* in *Cent. Bible*, p. 58, or in *HDB.* Art. *Money* (III. 422) makes the shekel to be "the so-called Phœnician silver shekel of 224 grains, and its value about 2s. 9d." It would thus weigh just a little more than the Jewish shekels now extant.]

he shall prepare the sin offering, and the meal offering, and the burnt offering, and the peace offerings, to make atonement for the house of Israel.

Thus saith the Lord GOD : In the first *month*, in the first 18 *day* of the month, thou shalt take a young bullock without blemish ; and thou shalt cleanse the sanctuary. And the 19 priest shall take of the blood of the sin offering, and put it upon the door posts of the house, and upon the four corners of the [1] settle of the altar, and upon the posts of the gate of

[1] Or, *ledge*

he shall prepare] or, **provide**.

The "feasts" were the three great festivals, Passover or unleavened bread (Easter), the feast of Weeks, or Pentecost, and the feast of ingathering or Tabernacles at the end of the vintage. Ezekiel, however, seems to give no place to Pentecost.

to make atonement] A reconciling or "atoning" efficacy appears attributed by the prophet to all the various kinds of sacrifices.

XLV. 18—XLVI. 24. THE OFFERINGS TO BE MADE AT THE FEASTS AND OTHER APPOINTED SEASONS.

(1) xlv. 18—25. Offerings at the feasts.
(2) xlvi. 1—11. Offerings for the sabbaths and new moons.
(3) *v.* 12. Voluntary offerings of the prince.
(4) *vv.* 13—15. The daily burnt-offering.
(5) *vv.* 16—18. Case of the prince alienating any part of his landed estate to his children.
(6) *vv.* 19—24. Kitchens for boiling the offerings eaten by the priests, and those partaken of by the people.

XLV. 18—25. OFFERINGS AT THE FEASTS.

18—20. The stated atonement for the sanctuary twice in the year— on the first day of the first month (*v.* 18) ; and on the first day of the seventh month (*v.* 20). [Contrast with this the *one* annual day of atonement on the tenth day of the seventh month (Lev. xvi. 29), prescribed by the Priestly Code.] The sin-offering on both occasions shall be a young bullock *to cleanse*, better : **to make atonement for** the sanctuary (xliii. 20).

19. Ceremonial with the blood. The blood shall be put on the door-posts of the house (xli. 21), on the four corners of the great "settle" of the altar (xliii. 20), and upon the door-posts of the gateway of the inner court—which gateway is not specified, probably that at which the victims were slaughtered. Gateway, however, might be used collectively.

20 the inner court. And so thou shalt do ¹on the seventh *day* of the month for every one that erreth, and for him that is
21 simple : so shall ye make atonement for the house. In the first *month*, in the fourteenth day of the month, ye shall have the passover, a feast of seven days ; unleavened bread
22 shall be eaten. And upon that day shall the prince prepare for himself and for all the people of the land a bullock for
23 a sin offering. And the seven days of the feast he shall prepare a burnt offering to the LORD, seven bullocks and seven rams without blemish daily the seven days ; and a
24 he-goat daily for a sin offering. And he shall prepare a meal offering, an ephah for a bullock, and an ephah
25 for a ram, and an hin of oil to an ephah. In the seventh *month*, in the fifteenth day of the month, in the feast, shall

---

¹ The Sept. reads, *in the seventh month, on the first day of the month.*

20. *seventh* day *of the month*] The text can hardly be so rendered. Probably : **in the seventh month, on the new moon** (i.e. the first day). LXX. (as marg.) fully : "in the seventh month, on the first day of the month." An atonement was made for the sanctuary, purifying it from the defilements of the people, at the beginning of each half-year. No mention is made of burnt-offerings, but cf. xlvi. 6, 7.

every one that erreth] i.e. not for any particular person had in view, but for the people on account of there being among them persons who have erred unwittingly or through simplicity, i.e. natural slowness which may not have apprehended the exact requirements of duty. Ezekiel is speaking of the people in their perfect condition, when, of course, only such mistakes will be committed as are due to inadvertence and the limitations to which the mind of man is subject.

make atonement for the house] Cf. Lev. xvi. 16, 18.

XLV. 21—25. THE FEASTS. THE PASSOVER ON THE FOURTEENTH OF THE FIRST MONTH.

21. *feast of seven days*] So no doubt Heb. should be read, with the ancient versions. At present it reads : "a feast of weeks of days." Ezekiel omits all ref. to the so-called feast of Weeks, i.e. Pentecost, seven weeks after the unleavened bread, when the sickle was put into the grain [although it appears in Exod. xxiii. 16; Lev. xxiii. 15; Deut. xvi. 10. Neither does he mention the feast of Trumpets (Lev. xxiii. 24)].

22. *prepare for himself*] **provide**, *v.* 17, and so in *vv.* 23, 24.

23. *seven bullocks* &c.] [a much greater burnt-offering than that pre-scribed in Numb. xxviii. 16, 25.]

25. Feast of Tabernacles on the fifteenth day of the seventh month.

he do the like the seven days; according to the sin offering, according to the burnt offering, and according to the meal offering, and according to the oil.

Thus saith the Lord GOD: The gate of the inner court **46** that looketh toward the east shall be shut the six working days; but on the sabbath day it shall be opened, and in the day of the new moon it shall be opened. And the prince 2 shall enter by the way of the porch of the gate without, and

The "feast" is that of Tabernacles, the feast *par excellence* of the year, concluding the yearly round of festivals (Is. xxix. 1). [In the "Law of Holiness" (Lev. xxiii. 36), and in the Priests' Code (Numb. xxix. 35) an eighth day is added.] For this feast the prince makes the same provision as for the feast of unleavened bread (*v.* 23).

XLVI. 1—7. OFFERINGS FOR THE SABBATH AND NEW MOON.

The prince was to be under obligation, besides providing for the great festivals of unleavened bread or Passover and Tabernacles (xlv. 21, 25), and for the special new moons in the first and seventh months (xlv. 18, 20), to furnish offerings also for the sabbaths and the ordinary new moons. The east gate of the inner court was to be kept shut six days of the week (the outer being always shut), but opened on the sabbaths and also on the new moons (*v.* 1). On these days the prince was to come by way of the porch and advance as far as the door-posts of the inner gate, there worshipping while the priests were offering the burnt- and peace-offerings (*v.* 2). The gate was to remain open till the evening. While the prince could come as far as the threshold of the inner gate[1], the people were to stand without before the inner east gate to worship (*v.* 3).

2. *porch of the gate without*] It is difficult to decide whether "without" describes porch or gate. If porch, then the porch of the inner gate is meant, which lay "without," i.e. towards the outer court (xl. 31, 34; 37). If "without" refers to gate, then the porch of the outer gate is meant. In the latter case the prince would cross the outer court from the porch of the outer gate and enter the inner gate, cf. xliv. 3. Neither is it certain whether the "posts" and "threshold" are those at the outer end of the inner gate, or those at the end opening into the inner court. The technical "threshold" lay at the inner end, inasmuch as the inner gate was the outer gate reversed (xl. 6). It is possible that the prince .was allowed to enter the inner gateway and advance to the inner end of it so as to have a full view of the operations of the priests at the altar, without, however, being permitted

1 [These restrictions may be contrasted with the freedom granted in the Monarchical period, as shewn in 1 Kgs viii. 22: 2 Kgs xvi. 12. The ceremonial is more like that when Joash was presented to the people, 2 Kgs xi. 14; 2 Chr. xxiii. 13.]

shall stand by the post of the gate, and the priests shall
prepare his burnt offering and his peace offerings, and he
shall worship at the threshold of the gate ; then he shall go
forth : but the gate shall not be shut until the evening.
3 And the people of the land shall worship at the door of that
gate before the LORD in the sabbaths and in the new moons.
4 And the burnt offering that the prince shall offer unto the
LORD shall be in the sabbath day six lambs without blemish
5 and a ram without blemish ; and the meal offering shall be
an ephah for the ram, and the meal offering for the lambs
6 as he is able to give, and an hin of oil to an ephah.   And
in the day of the new moon it shall be a young bullock
without blemish ; and six lambs, and a ram ; they shall be
7 without blemish : and he shall prepare a meal offering,
an ephah for the bullock, and an ephah for the ram, and for
the lambs according as ¹ he is able, and an hin of oil to an
8 ephah.   And when the prince shall enter, he shall go in by
the way of the porch of the gate, and he shall go forth by
9 the way thereof.   But when the people of the land shall
come before the LORD in the appointed feasts, he that
entereth by the way of the north gate to worship shall
go forth by the way of the south gate ; and he that entereth
by the way of the south gate shall go forth by the way of
the north gate : he shall not return by the way of the gate
whereby he came in, but shall go forth straight before him.

¹ Heb. *his hand shall attain unto.*

to set his foot in the inner court.   In this case " porch " would be that of
the inner gate.
   4, 5.   On the sabbath the burnt-offering shall be six lambs and a ram,
and the meal-offering an ephah of flour for the ram and what the prince
thinks good for the lambs; and the libation a hin of oil.
   6, 7.   For the new moons the burnt-offering, in addition to that of
the sabbath, shall be a young bullock, and a correspondingly increased
meal-offering with a libation as for the sabbath.
   8, 9.   The gates by which prince and people shall come in and go out.
The prince shall come in by way of the porch of the gate, and shall go
out the same way, i.e. probably the porch of the inner east gate, and
he shall go back as he entered, without passing into the inner court.
The people shall not go out by the gate at which they came in, but by
the opposite gate—those entering by the N. gate shall leave by the S.
and conversely.

And the prince, when they go in, shall go in in the midst of 10
them ; and when they go forth, ¹ they shall go forth *together*.
And in the feasts and in the ²solemnities the meal offering 11
shall be an ephah for a bullock, and an ephah for a ram,
and for the lambs as he is able to give, and an hin of oil to
an ephah. And when the prince shall prepare a freewill 12
offering, a burnt offering or peace offerings as a freewill
offering unto the LORD, one shall open for him the gate that
looketh toward the east, and he shall prepare his burnt
offering and his peace offerings, as he doth on the sabbath
day : then he shall go forth ; and after his going forth one
shall shut the gate. And thou shalt prepare a lamb of the 13

¹ Some ancient authorities have, *he shall go forth*.
² Or, *appointed feasts*

10. *they shall go forth* together] marg. *he shall go forth*. So we must
read with LXX., the prince being subject. Read in either way the words
mean that the prince and people come in and go out simultaneously.
This would suggest that the worshipping of the prince and people was
contemporaneous with the act of the priests in offering, and that when
this act was over the people dispersed and the prince departed. The
Syr. followed by Cor. reads : *but the prince in their midst, by the gate
at which he came in shall he go out*—finding a repetition of *v.* 8, giving
a freedom to the prince denied to the people (*v.* 9).

11. General regulation in regard to the meal-offering ; it shall be the
same both at the feasts proper (xlv. 21, 25), and at the solemnities or
stated seasons, such as new moons, &c.

12. Regulation when the prince presents a freewill offering. [For
these see Lev. vii. 16 *seq*.] The east (inner) gate shall be opened for him
on such occasions as on the sabbaths and new moons. Cf. Lev. vii. 16,
xxxiii. 28 ; Numb. xv. 3, xxix. 39 ; Deut. xii. 6 ; Am. iv. 5.

XLVI. 13—15. THE DAILY OFFERING.

There shall be a daily offering, a lamb for a burnt-offering, with one-
sixth of an ephah of flour and the third part of a hin of oil for a meal-
offering. This shall be presented every morning. In earlier times
the daily offering in practice appears to have been a burnt-offering in
the morning and a meal-offering in the evening (2 Kgs xvi. 15, cf.
1 Kgs xviii. 29, 36). In Numb. xxviii. 3, 8 the daily offering is
a lamb morning and evening, with one-tenth of an ephah of flour
and one-fourth of a hin of oil morning and evening for meal-offering ;
to which is to be added one-fourth of a hin of wine for drink-offering.
Ezek. nowhere refers to wine in the offerings.

13. *thou shalt prepare*] LXX. *he shall prepare* ; so *v.* 14 [i.e. either
the prince or, indefinitely, one, a priest]. Cf. xlv. 17.

first year without blemish for a burnt offering unto the
LORD daily: morning by morning shalt thou prepare it.
14 And thou shalt prepare a meal offering with it morning by
morning, the sixth part of an ephah, and the third part
of an hin of oil, to ¹moisten the fine flour; a meal offering
unto the LORD continually by a perpetual ordinance.
15 Thus shall they prepare the lamb, and the meal offering,
and the oil, morning by morning, for a continual burnt
offering.

16   Thus saith the Lord GOD: If the prince give a gift unto
any of his sons, it is his inheritance, it shall belong to his
17 sons; it is their possession by inheritance. But if he give
of his inheritance a gift to one of his servants, it shall be his
to the year of liberty; then it shall return to the prince;
18 but as for his inheritance, it shall be for his sons. Moreover the prince shall not take of the people's inheritance,
to ²thrust them out of their possession; he shall give
inheritance to his sons out of his own possession: that my
people be not scattered every man from his possession.

¹ Or, *mix with*   ² Heb. *oppress.*

14. *to moisten*] or, besprinkle. Cf. the corresponding substantive to
the Heb. verb used here, Song v. 2, "*drops* of the night."

XLVI. **16—18.** CASE OF THE PRINCE ALIENATING ANY PART OF
HIS LANDED PROPERTY TO HIS SONS OR SERVANTS.

17. *year of liberty*] In Jer. xxxiv. 14 the year of liberty is that
of the freeing of the bondservant in the seventh year; and this year
may be meant here. Cf. Is. lxi. 1. Otherwise the year of Jubilee,
the fiftieth year, is referred to, when all landed property that had been
alienated reverted to its original owner, Lev. xxv. 10, xxvii. 24.

but as for his inheritance...sons] i.e. the portion of his inheritance
which the prince may bestow on his sons shall remain theirs, without
reverting to the prince (*v.* 16). LXX., Syr. more clearly: *the inheritance of his sons, it shall be theirs.*

XLVI. **19—24.** THE KITCHENS FOR THE PRIESTS (*vv.* 19, 20),
AND PEOPLE (*vv.* 21—24).

The kitchens for cooking the sin- and guilt-offerings and baking the
meal-offering, the holy things to be consumed by the priests (xliv. 29),
were situated in the inner court at the furthest part of the court westward, to the west of the holy cells (xlii. 1—14), and on both sides of the
erection called the "building" (xli. 12, 13, Fig. 3, K) which lay behind

Then he brought me through the entry, which was at the 19 side of the gate, into the holy chambers for the priests, which looked toward the north: and behold, there was a place on the hinder part westward. And he said unto 20 me, This is the place where the priests shall boil the guilt offering and the sin offering, where they shall bake the meal offering; that they bring them not forth into the outer court, to sanctify the people. Then he brought me forth into the 21 outer court, and caused me to pass by the four corners of the court; and behold, in every corner of the court there was a court. In the four corners of the court there were 22 courts [1] inclosed, forty *cubits* long and thirty broad: these four in the corners were of one measure. And there was 23 a row *of building* round about in them, round about the

[1] Or, *joined on*

the house. Thus they were within the spaces marked LL. The inner court on the west reached back to the boundary wall of the outer court, which on that side was the wall of the inner court, and in the two corners, N. and S., the priests' kitchens were placed. The prophet is brought to those on the N. side; those on the S. were similar.

19. *through the entry*] the *entrance-way*, viz. that mentioned xlii. 9. Since xliv. 4 the prophet had been before the house. The holy chambers are those described, xlii. 1—14.

a place on the hinder part westward] i.e. at the western extremity of the court. In Fig. 3 the kitchens, LL, should probably be extended back to the wall.

20. *to sanctify the people*] Cf. note on xliv. 19.

21—24. The kitchens for cooking the sacrificial meals of the people. These were situated in the four corners of the outer court. In each of the four corners was a small enclosure or court 40 cubits long and 30 broad (*vv.* 21, 22); and in these were situated the kitchens, where the "ministers of the house," the subordinate officials (xliv. 10—14), boiled the people's offering for their sacrificial meal (*vv.* 23, 24), Fig. 3, M.

22. *courts inclosed*] The term "inclosed" is obscure, not occurring elsewhere. LXX. appears to have read: *small* (the Heb. words differ in one letter only).

these four in the corners] lit. *the four of them had one measure*, they being *in the corners*. The word *in the corners*, or, *cornered*, is deleted in the traditional Heb. text by points over it, and not rendered in LXX. and Vulg.

23. The description is brief. The "row" is probably not a series of separate buildings running round the court, but a continuous course

four, and it was made with boiling places under the rows
24 round about. Then said he unto me, These are the boiling
houses, where the ministers of the house shall boil the
sacrifice of the people.

47   And he brought me back unto the door of the house;
and behold, waters issued out from under the threshold
of the house eastward, for the forefront of the house was
toward the east: and the waters came down from under,
from the right side of the house, on the south of the altar.
2 Then brought he me out by the way of the gate northward,
and led me round by the way without unto the outer gate,
by the way of *the gate* that looketh toward the east; and
3 behold, there ¹ ran out waters on the right side. When the

¹ Or, *trickled forth*

of building, in which at the bottom ("under" the row) were recesses
in which were the hearths where the pots were set in which the
sacrifices were cooked. The hearth usually consisted of some stones
within which the fire was put and upon which the pot was set.
    24. The "ministers" are the subordinate officials—the Levites.

XLVII. THE STREAM THAT ISSUED FROM THE TEMPLE.

The chapter contains two parts:
    (1) *vv.* 1—12. The stream issuing from the temple, that fertilised
the desert and sweetened the waters of the Dead Sea.
    (2) *vv.* 13—23. The boundaries of the holy land; and the privileges
of strangers attaching themselves to the tribes.
    1—12. The river issuing from the temple. A thousand cubits
from the gate the waters were ankle deep, but speedily they became a
river so deep that it could be crossed only by swimming (*vv.* 3—5). A
luxuriant nature attended the course of the stream; trees grew on every
side, ever green and with unfailing fruit, the leaves of which possessed
a healing virtue (*vv.* 7, 12). The desert place to the east became trans-
formed, and the bitter waters of the Dead Sea into which the river
flowed were made sweet, and swarmed with life like the great sea on
the west. Fishermen peopled the shores from En-gedi to En-eglaim;
only the marshes by the seaside remained salt (*vv.* 6—12).
    1. From the outer court (xlvi. 23) the prophet was brought again to
the door of the house. There he saw waters issuing from beneath the
threshold on the right, that is the south side, which flowed east, passing the altar on the south side.
    2. The eastern gates being shut (xliv. 2, xlvi. 1) the prophet is led
out by the N. gate, round to the outer E. gate, at which he beheld the
stream emerge into the open at the S. side of the gate.

man went forth eastward with the line in his hand, he measured a thousand cubits, and he caused me to pass through the waters, waters that were to the ankles. Again 4 he measured a thousand, and caused me to pass through the waters, waters that were to the knees. Again he measured a thousand, and caused me to pass through *the waters*, waters that were to the loins. Afterward he measured 5 a thousand; *and it was* a river that I could not pass through: for the waters were risen, waters to swim in, a river that could not be passed through. And he said 6 unto me, Son of man, hast thou seen *this*? Then he brought me, and caused me to return to the bank of the river. Now when I had returned, behold, upon the bank 7 of the river were very many trees on the one side and on the other. Then said he unto me, These waters issue 8 forth toward the eastern region, and shall go down into the Arabah: and they shall go toward the sea; into the sea *shall the waters go* which were made to issue forth; and the waters shall be healed. And it shall come to pass, that 9

3. A thousand cubits from the place of emergence the waters were ankle deep.

4, 5. Successive measurements shewed a depth to the knees, the loins, and finally an impassable river. The word rendered "river" is the usual one for "brook" or wady, viz. a stream with its valley or gorge.

6. *to the bank*] Perhaps: **along** the bank. *River* is brook or wady as *v.* 5.

7. Both banks of the wady, as is everywhere seen, were covered with trees.

8. The direction of the stream was eastward into the Dead Sea. *the eastern region*] lit. circle, or, *district*, the same word as Galilee (Is. ix. 1). Cf. Joshua xxii. 10, 11, "the circuits of the Jordan."

into the Arabah] what is now also called the Ghor, the depression of the Jordan valley, the Dead Sea, and southward as far as the Gulf of Akaba; Deut. i. 1, iii. 17; Josh. xviii. 18. [The northernmost point of the Dead Sea is 16 miles E. of Jerusalem.]

toward the sea...issue forth] The construction is difficult. For "into the sea" LXX. read "the waters." [The insertion by R.V. of "shall the waters go" is scarcely justifiable. Kr. and others amend to, "and when it comes to the sea, the bitter waters, then the waters, &c." A simpler emendation would give, "and the waters that were made to issue forth shall go into the sea, and the waters (thereof) shall be healed."]

every living creature which swarmeth, in every place whither
the [1] rivers come, shall live; and there shall be a very great
multitude of fish: for these waters are come thither, [2]and
the waters of the sea shall be healed, and every thing shall
10 live whithersoever the river cometh.   And it shall come to
pass, that fishers shall stand by it: from En-gedi even unto
En-eglaim shall be a place for the spreading of nets; their
fish shall be after their kinds, as the fish of the great sea,
11 exceeding many.   But the miry places thereof, and the
marishes thereof, shall not be healed; they shall be [3]given
12 up to salt.   And by the river upon the bank thereof, on
this side and on that side, shall grow every tree for meat,
whose leaf shall not wither, neither shall the fruit thereof
fail: it shall bring forth [4]new fruit every month, because

---

[1] Heb. *two rivers.*   [2] Or, *that all things may be healed and live*
[3] Or, *given for salt*   [4] Heb. *firstfruits.*

---

9.   *every living creature*]   The word is used of the smaller animals,
particularly the smaller aquatic creatures—these shall come to life and
swarm in the waters of the Dead Sea.   This sea is entirely destitute
of life.

the rivers come] lit. the *two rivers.*   The dual (LXX. have sing.) may
have arisen from a misunderstanding of Zech. xiv. 8, where one stream
goes to the Dead Sea and another to the western sea.

10.   En-gedi, the modern *'Ain Jidi,* "kid's well," situated about the
middle of the west shore of the Dead Sea.   En-eglaim has not been
identified; it probably lay N. toward the mouth of the Jordan.   It has
been supposed to be *'Ain-el-feshhah,* Robinson II. 489 [(so Kr., Lofth.),
a village at the N.W. end.   Tristram, *Bible Places,* p. 93 (see *Encycl.
Bibl.*) suggests *'Ain Hajleh* in the same neighbourhood].   The word
differs in spelling from Eglaim, Is. xv. 8, which probably lay to the
south of the sea.

11.   The marshes around the sea shall not be sweetened, but left as
beds for digging salt.   The saltness of the Dead Sea is due to the strata
of salt rocks which surround it.

12.   Cf. Ps. i. 3; Jer. xvii. 8; Rev. xxii. 2.

meat] food.

This beautiful representation of the healing stream, issuing from the
temple and fertilising the desert as well as changing the bitter waters
of the Dead Sea into sweet, so that they yield abundant sustenance to
men, rests on some natural and some spiritual conceptions common in
Ezekiel's day.   One natural fact was this, that there was a fountain
connected with the temple-hill, the waters of which fell into the valley
east of the city and made their way towards the sea. [The pool of

the waters thereof issue out of the sanctuary: and the
fruit thereof shall be for meat, and the leaf thereof for
healing.

Siloam was "situated at the S.W. side of the Temple mount, at the
lower end of the Tyropoeon valley. From a very ancient time it has
been connected, by a rock-hewn tunnel, with an intermittent spring
(St Mary's Well) on the opposite (eastern) side of the hill, outside the
city wall." Skinner, note on Is. viii. 6.] Long ere this time the gentle
waters of this brook, that flowed fast by the oracle of God, had furnished
symbols to the prophets [Is. *loc. cit.*; Joel iii. 18; Zech. xiv. 8]. Such
waters in the East are the source of every blessing to men. The religious conceptions are such as these: that Jehovah Himself is the giver
of all blessings to men, and from His presence all blessings flow. He
was now present in His fulness and for ever in His temple. Hence the
prophet sees the life-giving stream issue from the sanctuary. Another
current idea was that in the regeneration of men, when the tabernacle
of God was with them, external nature would also be transfigured.
Then every good would be enjoyed and there would be no more evil
nor curse. The desert would bloom like the rose, and the field that
aforetime was thought fruitful should be accounted no better than bush.
The barren land toward the east and the bitter waters of the sea were a
contradiction to the ideal of an external nature subservient in all her
parts to man in the fellowship of God. Therefore the desert shall be
fertilised and the waters of the sea healed, and all things minister to
man's good. But "good" to the Israelite was not exclusively spiritual,
it was also material. It would be an error to regard this fertilising,
healing stream in the light of a mere symbol for blessings which we call
"spiritual." It is well fitted in other connexions to be such a symbol;
but to take it so here would be to overstep the limits of the Old Testament and anticipate a later revelation. As yet the Israelite had no
conception of a transcendent sphere of existence for men in the fellowship of God, such as we name heaven. Man's final abode even in his
perfect state was considered to be still on the earth. God came down
and dwelt with men; men were not translated to abide with God. But
God's presence with men on earth gave to earth the attributes of heaven.
Yet man's needs remained, and God's presence was the source of all
things necessary to supply them. When he had the needful blessings
the Israelite saw in them the tokens and the sacraments of God's favour
and presence with him; and conversely when God was near him he was
assured that he should want no good thing (Ps. xxxiv. 10).

XLVII. 13—21. The boundaries of the new holy land.

On the east the boundary shall be the Jordan from Hazar-enon on
the north to the salt sea on the south, for in the time of restitution the
promised land shall be confined to Palestine west of the Jordan, according to the oath sworn by God unto the fathers (Gen. xii. 7, xiii. 15,

13   Thus saith the Lord GOD : This shall be the border,
     whereby ye shall divide the land for inheritance according
     to the twelve tribes of Israel : Joseph *shall have* ¹portions.
14 And ye shall inherit it, one as well as another ; ²concerning
     the which I lifted up mine hand to give it unto your
     fathers : and this land shall fall unto you for inheritance.
15 And this shall be the border of the land : on the north side,
     from the great sea, by the way of Hethlon, unto the enter-
16 ing in of Zedad ; Hamath, Berothah, Sibraim, which is

     ¹ Some ancient versions have, *two portions.*
     ² Or, *for that I lifted up*

xvii. 8, xxviii. 13).   On the west the boundary shall be the Mediterranean sea.   The boundaries on the N. and S. are particularly defined,
the towns being mentioned by which they run, but the places named
are mostly unknown.   The boundaries are in the main the same as
those laid down in Numb. xxxiv. [except that here no territory E. of
Jordan is included].

13.   The tribe of Joseph, being composed of two great families, shall
have "portions," i.e. two lots (perhaps *dual* should be read)¹.   There
still remained twelve tribes, therefore, even when Levi was provided for
by the sacred Terumah or oblation.

15.   The northern border.   The two ends of the line of delimitation
on the N. are the great sea on the west and Hazar-enon on the east.
The line passes from west to east, bending, towards its termination at
least, towards S.E.   In its way it skirts the territory of Hamath and
that of Damascus.

unto the entering in of Zedad]   Cf. *v.* 20 and xlviii. 1, a frequent
phrase, as in Numb. xxxiv. 8 ; Josh. xiii. 5 ; Jud. iii. 3 ; 1 Kgs viii.
65.   In the last place it seems to mean the southern boundary of
Hamath.   Unfortunately the point on the western sea from which the
line starts is not specified, as the situation of Hethlon is unknown.
The entrance to Hamath must be either the mouth of the Bukāʿ, the
great plain between the Libanus on the W. and the Anti-Libanus on the
E., by which one goes N. to Hamath, or it must be the plain between
the North end of the Libanus and the Nusairīyeh mountains, opening
from the sea and running east.   This would throw the boundary-line
north of Tripoli, and south of Arvad.   In Josh. xiii. 5, the land of the
Gebalites, i.e. Gebal (Byblus) to the N. of Beirut, is regarded as part of
Israel's possession.   Except here in 1 Chr. v. 9 the phrase is only used
of Hamath.   Following xlviii. 1, and Numb. xxxiv. 8, the places of
Zedad and Hamath may be changed, as LXX. also seems to have read
Hamath before Zedad.—15 "And this shall be the boundary of the land :

     ¹ [Probably, however, the clause is a copyist's gloss.   The remark would have
been superfluous in Ezekiel's time, the fact that Ephraim and Manasseh were reckoned
separately being long established and familiar.]

between the border of Damascus and the border of Hamath ;
¹Hazer-hatticon, which is by the border of Hauran. And 17
the border from the sea shall be Hazar-enon at the border
of Damascus, and on the north northward is the border of
Hamath.   This is the north side.   And the east side, be- 18
tween Hauran and Damascus and Gilead, and the land

¹ Or, *the middle Hazer*

on the N. side, from the great sea by the way of Hethlon, where the
way goeth unto Hamath, by Zedad, 16 Berothah, Sibraim, which is
between the border of Damascus and the border of Hamath, even unto
Hazer-hatticon, which is by the border of Hauran." If we could suppose the entry to Hamath not the southern one by the plain of Cœle
Syria, but the western one from the sea to the N. of Tripoli, Hethlon
might be the modern *Heitela* (Robinson's Map, 1852). Zedad has been
supposed to be *Sadad*, S. of Emesa (*Homs*) and not far from Riblah.
With Berothah, cf. Berothai, 2 Sam. viii. 8. In Numb. xxxiv. 9 Ziphron
seems to occupy the place of Sibraim here. In Numb. the line appears
to run E. as far as Zedad, and then to change its direction to the S. till
it ends at Hazar-enan.

17. The verse repeats and sums up *vv.* 15, 16, with special reference
to the countries lying on the N. of the northern border of Israel. In
v. 17 Hazar-enon is named as the extremity of the northern boundary,
in *v.* 16 Hazer-hatticon (i.e. as marg., the middle Hazer). The places
must be identical, whether *hatticon* be a misreading or not. LXX. reads
Saunan, Cod. Alex. Eunan, and in xlviii. 1, Numb. xxxiv. 9, Enon here
is spelt Enan. In *v.* 16 the place is said to be on the border of Hauran.
The boundary is first stated generally as going from the sea to Hazar-
enon, and then in the contrary direction north, Hamath being the country
to the N. It is not certain that Hauran is the district now so called, but
it is probable. Wetzstein (Del. *Psalms* III. 439, Eaton's Trans.), identifies the village of Hadar at the eastern foot of Hermon with Hazar-enon.
In all likelihood the end of the boundary line is hereabouts; in Deut.
iii. 8 Hermon is the northernmost point of conquest, and Ezek. would
probably follow this. The northern boundary followed an easterly
course from the sea, Hamath lying on the N., then a southerly course
having Damascus on the E., till it terminated at Hazar-enon between
Damascus and Hauran. But at what point of the sea it started, and in
what latitude the line to the east ran is obscure. The identifications
of Hethlon with *Heitela* and of Zedad with *Sadad* would give the latitude of Emesa (*Homs*), which is very far north; see Porter, *Five Years
in Damascus*, II. 354 *seq.* and map. More likely the prophet fancied
the starting-point on the W. to be about Tyre.

18. The eastern border.

In *v.* 16 the easternmost point of the north border was said to be
Hazar-enon on the border of Hauran. The E. boundary will therefore

of Israel, shall be Jordan ; from the *north* border unto the
19 east sea shall ye measure.   This is the east side.   And the
south side southward shall be from Tamar as far as the
waters of Meriboth-kadesh, to the brook *of Egypt*, unto the
20 great sea.   This is the south side southward.   And the
west side shall be the great sea, from the *south* border as
far as over against the entering in of Hamath.   This is the
21 west side.   So shall ye divide this land unto you according
22 to the tribes of Israel.   And it shall come to pass, that ye
shall divide it by lot for an inheritance unto you and to the
strangers that sojourn among you, which shall beget children
among you ; and they shall be unto you as the homeborn
among the children of Israel ; they shall have inheritance
23 with you among the tribes of Israel.   And it shall come to

start from this point. The verse may read: "and the east side: from
between Hauran and Damascus, between Gilead and the land of Israel
shall be the Jordan, from the (north) boundary to the eastern sea, even
unto Tamar; this is the east side."   The line starts from Hazar-enon,
a place lying where Damascus and Hauran adjoin one another (*v.* 16).
Instead of Hazar-enon, however, the point of contact between Damascus and Hauran is named as the starting-point (for the last two *umibben*
read *ben* and *uben*).   From this point the line runs south; its course is
the Jordan between Gilead and the land of Israel.   The order Hauran,
Damascus, Gilead is entirely incomprehensible (for Hauran lay S. of
Damascus) if R.V. be followed.   The phrase "shall ye measure" is no
doubt a misspelling for "unto Tamar" (LXX. Syr., *d* for *r*), from which
the southern border starts in *v.* 19.   Tamar probably lay S. or S.W. of
the Dead Sea.   The Onomasticon (Ed. *Lagarde*, p. 85) says: "one
day's journey from Mampsis as you go to Aelia (? Elath) from Hebron."
Robinson identifies Mampsis with Malatha, in his view *el Milh.*

19.   The southern boundary.   The delimitation on the S. is more
fully described Numb. xxxiv. 3—5 ; Josh. xv. 1—4.   There Kadesh is
called Kadesh-barnea, here Meriboth-kadesh (elsewhere Meribah),
i.e. waters *of strife* of Kadesh, Numb. xxvii. 14.   The brook of Egypt
is the Wady el Arish [which starts from about the middle of the Sinaitic
peninsula, and reaches the sea *c.* 80 miles E. of the Pelusiac mouth of
the Nile].

21—23.   The land so bounded shall be divided equally among the
tribes ; and strangers sojourning in Israel shall inherit just as those born
in the land.   The stranger shall have his inheritance among the members
of the tribe in which he sojourns[1].

[1] ["A scanty population would often need thus to increase its numbers." Lofth.,
who refers also to Maine, *Ancient Law, chap. ii.*   Cf. provision for "strangers"
in the "Law of Holiness" (Lev. xvii.—xxvi.), see Lev. xvii. 13, xix. 10, xxiv. 16.]

pass, that in what tribe the stranger sojourneth, there shall
ye give him his inheritance, saith the Lord GOD.

Now these are the names of the tribes: from the north **48**
end, beside the way of Hethlon to the entering in of
Hamath, Hazar-enan at the border of Damascus, northward
beside Hamath; and they shall have their sides east *and*

XLVIII. THE DISPOSITION OF THE TRIBES IN THE LAND.

(1)   *vv.* 1—7.   The tribes north of the sacred oblation of land.
(2)   *vv.* 8—22.   The oblation in its various divisions: for the priests,
the Levites, the city, and the prince.
(3)   *vv.* 23—29.   The tribes situated south of the oblation.
(4)   *vv.* 30—35.   The gates of the city.

All the tribes are now settled on the West of the Jordan.   The land
is divided into zones running from E. to W. of the country, one of which
falls to the lot of each tribe.   The dimensions of the zone are not mentioned, neither is there any indication whether the greater or less breadth
of the country from the Jordan to the sea was taken into account.   The
oblation of land given to the priests and Levites lay not strictly in the
middle of the country, but in the neighbourhood of Jerusalem, and therefore more toward the south; hence seven tribes are located to the north
of the oblation and five to the south of it.   Of the tribes beyond Jordan
the half of Manasseh is now united with the other half, forming one
tribe, and receiving one portion; while Gad and Reuben are provided
with new settlements, the former in the extreme south, and the latter in
the northern half of the country.   Judah and Benjamin change places,
the former lying to the north of the oblation and the city, and the latter
to the south.   In other respects the position of the tribes remains
nearly what it was, except that Issachar and Zebulun have to be provided for in the south.   It is perhaps accidental that the children of
Leah and Rachel occupy the centre, while the sons of the handmaids
are placed at the extremities.

1—7.   The tribes to the north of the sacred oblation.

1.   Dan on the furthest north.   The verse as it stands has probably
some confusion of text.   It may read: "Now these are the names of the
tribes: on the furthest north, alongside of the way to Hethlon, as one
goeth to Hamath, as far as Hazar-enan on the border of Damascus,
even on the north alongside of (the land of) Hamath—he shall have
the east side (and) the west side: Dan one (portion)."   First the
boundary line W. to E. is specified from the sea to Hazar-enan (xlvii.
16, 17), and then is mentioned the country bounding the portion on the
north, viz. Hamath.   The *he* in "he shall have" is Dan, already in the
writer's mind.   We might have expected "he shall have the east side
even unto the west side," or from the east side, &c., as in the following
verses.   The former sense is supported in LXX.

2 west; Dan, one *portion*. And by the border of Dan, from
3 the east side unto the west side; Asher, one *portion*. And
by the border of Asher, from the east side even unto the
4 west side; Naphtali, one *portion*. And by the border of
Naphtali, from the east side unto the west side; Manasseh,
5 one *portion*. And by the border of Manasseh, from the
6 east side unto the west side; Ephraim, one *portion*. And
by the border of Ephraim, from the east side even unto the
7 west side; Reuben, one *portion*. And by the border of
Reuben, from the east side unto the west side; Judah, one
portion.
8   And by the border of Judah, from the east side unto the
west side, shall be the oblation which ye shall offer, five
and twenty thousand *reeds* in breadth, and in length as one
of the portions, from the east side unto the west side: and
9 the sanctuary shall be in the midst of it. The oblation
that ye shall offer unto the LORD shall be five and twenty
thousand *reeds* in length, and ten thousand in breadth.

2—7. After Dan in the furthest north bordering on the land of
Hamath comes Asher (*v.* 2), Naphtali (*v.* 3), the whole reunited tribe
of Manasseh (*v.* 4), Ephraim (*v.* 5), Reuben transferred from the other
side of the Jordan (*v.* 6), and finally Judah (*v.* 7).

8—22. The oblation or Terumah in the centre of the country. This
oblation is a tract of 25,000 cubits broad, N. to S., and in length equal
to the portions of the tribes E. to W. This oblation is first specified in
its whole extent (*v.* 8); then the portion of it to be assigned to the
priests is described (*vv.* 9—12); then the portion of the Levites (*vv.* 13,
14); then the part of the oblation belonging to the city (*vv.* 15—20);
and finally the portion of the oblation which shall constitute the inheritance of the prince (*vv.* 21, 22).

8. reeds *in breadth*] **cubits in breadth**, i.e. N. to S. This is the
breadth of the whole part subtracted from the territory of the country,
and devoted to the priests, the Levites, the city, and the prince. In
length it goes from the Jordan to the sea, just "as one of the portions,"
i.e. the portions of the tribes. The sanctuary shall be situated in the
centre of this oblation, viz. in the portion assigned to the priests—that
assigned to the Levites being on the north and that assigned to the city
on the south.

9—12. The domain assigned to the priests. This is mentioned first,
not because it actually borders on Judah—the Levites border on Judah—
but because it is the most important.

9. *ten thousand in breadth*] LXX. **twenty** thousand. This reading
assumes that *v.* 9 refers to the portion assigned to priests and Levites

Dan

Asher

Naphtali

Manasseh

Ephraim

Reuben

Judah

Prince's portion	Domain of Levites	Prince's portion
	Priests' domain □ Sanctuary	
	City land | City | City land	

Benjamin

Simeon

Issachar

Zebulun

Gad

10 And for these, even for the priests, shall be the holy oblation ; toward the north five and• twenty thousand *in length,*
and toward the west ten thousand in breadth, and toward
the east ten thousand in breadth, and toward the south five
and twenty thousand in length : and the sanctuary of the
11 LORD shall be in the midst thereof. [1]*It shall be* for the
priests that are sanctified of the sons of Zadok, which have
kept my charge ; which went not astray when the children
12 of Israel went astray, as the Levites went astray.   And
it shall be unto them an oblation from the oblation of the
13 land, a thing most holy, by the border of the Levites.   And
answerable unto the border of the priests, the Levites shall
have five and twenty thousand in length, and ten thousand
in breadth : all the length shall be five and twenty thousand,
14 and the breadth [2] ten thousand.   And they shall not sell of
it, neither exchange it, nor shall the firstfruits of the land be
15 alienated : for it is holy unto the LORD.   And the five
thousand that are left in the breadth, in front of the five

---

[1] Or, *The sanctified* portion shall be *for the priests of the sons &c.*
[2] The Sept. has, *twenty.*

---

together. So *v.* 13 end. The length E. to W. is 25,000, because the
prince's domain lies between it and the Jordan on the one side, and
between it and the sea on the other.

10.   *toward*] **on.**

11.   *that are sanctified of the sons*] The Heb. words should be
divided differently with the LXX.: *It shall be for the priests that are
sanctified, the sons* of Zadok.   On the erring of the Levites, cf. xliv. 10.

12.   Cf. xlv. 3 *seq.*

13.   The portion of the oblation of land assigned to the Levites.—
The portion of the Levites is of the same extent as that of the priests,—
25,000 long (E. to W.) by 10,000 broad (N. to S.).   It runs "over
against," i.e. alongside of the priests' domain, and lies to the north
of it.

14.   Seems to apply to the united domain of priests and Levites.
the firstfruits] Possibly : this *firstfruits,* or, *best*—the term being
applied to the holy oblation in distinction from the rest of the land.

15—20.   The portion of the oblation assignable to the city.—The
remaining 5000 in breadth (N. to S.) shall belong to the city, with the
same length as the portions of the priests and Levites, viz. 25,000, as it
is said "in front of (i.e. in length) the 25,000."   On "suburbs," cf.
xlv. 2—they are the free space round the city.

and twenty thousand, shall be for common use, for the city,
for dwelling and for suburbs: and the city shall be in the
midst thereof. And these shall be the measures thereof; 16
the north side four thousand and five hundred, and the
south side four thousand and five hundred, and on the east
side four thousand and five hundred, and the west side
four thousand and five hundred. And the city shall have 17
suburbs; toward the north two hundred and fifty, and
toward the south two hundred and fifty, and toward the
east two hundred and fifty, and toward the west two hundred
and fifty. And the residue in the length, answerable unto 18
the holy oblation, shall be ten thousand eastward, and ten
thousand westward: and it shall be answerable unto the
holy oblation; and the increase thereof shall be for food
unto them that labour in the city. And they that labour in 19
the city, out of all the tribes of Israel, shall till it. All the 20

16. The city shall be a square of 4500 cubits [i.e. about one and a
half miles each way].
17. The "suburbs" or free space round the city shall be 250 cubits
on all the four sides. Adding the 250 on the N. and on the S. of the
city to the 4500 it appears that the whole *breadth* of the 5000 assigned
to the city was occupied by it and its suburbs from N. to S.
18. As the city with its suburbs was a square of 5000 cubits, there
remained of the 25,000 in length assigned to it a portion 10,000 long on
the E. and another equally long on the W. In their length these portions lay "over against," i.e. along, the holy portion of the priests.
that labour in the city] The words are very difficult. It is plain
that the 10,000 cubits of land E. and W. of the city serve to supply
the inhabitants of the city with food. The restored land is a land of
husbandmen, and those who dwell in the city live from the city's domain.
Either "serve" or "cultivate" must be taken in the sense of inhabit
and the words be read: "for food to them that *inhabit the city*, 19 and
they *that inhabit the* city" &c.; though such a usage has no parallel.
[Kr. takes this to be the sense, and suggests the Latin *colere urbem* as a
justification.] Or, the word "city" must be taken in a general sense of
the city and its domain of land: "for food *to the tillers of the city*, 19 *and
they that till the city*" &c.
19. *that labour in the city*] Those who render *inhabit* (Hitz.) consider that the verse states directly who the inhabitants of the city shall
be: "and as for the inhabitants of the city, they shall inhabit it (reading
fem.) out of all the tribes of Israel." On the other supposition: "and
they that till the city shall till it (the domain of land) out of all the
tribes of Israel." This rendering also states, though indirectly, that

oblation shall be five and twenty thousand by five and twenty thousand: ye shall offer the holy oblation four-square, with the possession of the city.

21   And the residue shall be for the prince, on the one side and on the other of the holy oblation and of the possession of the city, in front of the five and twenty thousand of the oblation toward the east border, and westward in front of the five and twenty thousand toward the west border, answerable unto the portions, it shall be for the prince: and the holy oblation and the sanctuary of the house shall

22 be in the midst thereof.   Moreover from the possession of the Levites, and from the possession of the city, being in the midst of that which is the prince's, between the border of Judah and the border of Benjamin, shall be for the prince.

the city shall be common to all the tribes of Israel, and that whoever comes to sojourn there shall live by the land belonging to the city. However the words be translated, there is no ref. to *two* classes of persons—citizens and labourers.

20. The verse means that the holy oblation when the possession of the city is included forms a square of 25,000 by 25,000.

21, 22. The domain of the prince. The domain of the Levites, priests and city formed a square of 25,000 cubits in the heart of the country. The portion of the prince shall be the land from the E. of this square to the Jordan, and from the W. of it to the sea. The "five and twenty thousand" here is the breadth N. to S.; the prince's domain shall be of the same breadth and be in front of the square on the E. and W.

21.   *answerable unto the portions*] Or, **by the side of the portions.** The "portions" here are those of the tribes, which run from the Jordan to the sea; the prince's domain shall run alongside of them, i.e. Judah's on the N. and Benjamin's on the S. And the holy oblation lies between the two halves of the prince's domain.

22.   *Moreover from the possession*] **And** from. The verse gives again the breadth of the prince's possession, by stating the two limits N. (the Levites) and S. (the city) of the central oblation. All the land lying between these limits, in other words between the tribes of Judah and Benjamin, shall belong to the prince.

being in the midst] i.e. lying between the two halves of the prince's portion.

XLVIII. **23—29.** THE TRIBES LYING SOUTH OF THE OBLATION.

First, Benjamin, which changes places with Judah, and bounds the oblation on the south (*v.* 23). The two tribes that formed the ancient

And as for the rest of the tribes : from the east side unto 23
the west side ; Benjamin, one *portion*.   And by the border 24
of Benjamin, from the east side unto the west side ; Simeon,
one *portion*.   And by the border of Simeon, from the east 25
side unto the west side ; Issachar, one *portion*.   And by 26
the border of Issachar, from the east side unto the west
side ; Zebulun, one *portion*.   And by the border of Zebulun, 27
from the east side unto the west side ; Gad, one *portion*.
And by the border of Gad, at the south side southward, 28
the border shall be even from Tamar unto the waters of
Meribath-kadesh, to the brook *of Egypt*, unto the great sea.
This is the land which ye shall divide by lot unto the tribes 29
of Israel for inheritance, and these are their several portions,
saith the Lord GOD.

And these are the goings out of the city ; on the north 30
side four thousand and five hundred *reeds* by measure :
and the gates of the city shall be after the names of the 31
tribes of Israel ; three gates northward : the gate of Reuben,
one ; the gate of Judah, one ; the gate of Levi, one : and 32
at the east side four thousand and five hundred *reeds* ; and

kingdom of Judah still have the prerogative of lying nearest the sanctuary.   Then Simeon, formerly located in the south (*v.* 24).   Then
successively Issachar (*v.* 25), Zebulun (*v.* 26), and finally Gad (*v.* 27).
The two former are brought down from the north, and Gad from
beyond the Jordan.

28.   The southern border is again given as stated in xlvii. 19.
· *the brook...sea*]   Cf. xlvii. 19.

XLVIII. **30—35.**   THE CITY WITH ITS TWELVE GATES, NAMED
AFTER THE TRIBES.   Cf. Rev. xxi. 12 *seq*.

30.   *goings out of the city*] i.e. the extensions on all sides.
cubits *by measure*] i.e. in extent.   The 4500 are naturally *cubits*, not
"reeds."   The city proper lies foursquare, each side being 4500.   But
on each side is a free space of 250 cubits, so that, when these are included,
the city forms a square of 5000 cubits.
31.   The measurement proceeds from W. to E.   The gate of Reuben
was thus the westernmost on the north of the city ; Judah's in the
centre, and Levi's toward the east.
32.   Of the three gates on the east side Benjamin's was in the centre,
Joseph's[1] to the north, and Dan's to the south.

[1] [Now reckoned as one, in order to admit Levi, when restricting the total to
twelve.   See on xlvii. 13.]

three gates : even the gate of Joseph, one ; the gate of
33 Benjamin, one ; the gate of Dan, one : and at the south side
four thousand and five hundred *reeds* by measure ; and
three gates : the gate of Simeon, one ; the gate of Issachar
34 one ; the gate of Zebulun, one : at the west side four
thousand and five hundred *reeds*, with their three gates :
the gate of Gad, one ; the gate of Asher, one ; the gate of
35 Naphtali, one.   It shall be eighteen thousand *reeds* round
about : and the name of the city from that day shall be,
[1] The LORD is there.

---

[1] Heb. *Jehovah-shammah.*   See Ex. xvii. 15.

33.   Those on the south were Simeon, Issachar, and Zebulun, tribes
now all located in the south of the country.
34.   The gates on the west were those of Gad, Asher, and Naphtali.
35.   The whole circumference of the city was 18,000 cubits, or somewhat under six miles.   Josephus (*Bell. Jud.* v. 4, 3) reckoned the
bounds of Jerusalem in his day at 33 stadia, or about four miles.   For
" reeds," **cubits.**
The LORD *is there*]   Cf. Rev. xxi. 3, "And I heard a great voice out
of the throne saying, Behold, the tabernacle of God is with men, and
he shall dwell with them, and they shall be his peoples, and God himself shall be with them, and be their God."   The prophet beheld
Jehovah forsake His temple (xi.), and he beheld Him again enter it (xliii.);
now He abides in it among His people for ever.   The covenant ran that
He should be their God and they His people; this is perfectly fulfilled
in His presence among them.   The end in view from the beginning has
been reached.

INDEX